W9-APY-179

NEW WORLDS

NEW WORLDS

A RELIGIOUS HISTORY OF LATIN AMERICA

JOHN LYNCH

YALE UNIVERSITY PRESS
NEW HAVEN AND LONDON

For information about this and other Yale University Press publications, please contact:
U.S. Office: sales.press@yale.edu   www.yalebooks.com
Europe Office: sales @yaleup.co.uk   www.yalebooks.co.uk

Set in Minion Pro by IDSUK (DataConnection) Ltd
Printed in Great Britain by MPG Books Group Ltd, Bodmin, Cornwall

Library of Congress Cataloging-in-Publication Data

Lynch, John, 1927–
    New worlds: a religious history of Latin America / John Lynch.
      p. cm.
    ISBN 978-0-300-16680-4 (cl: alk. paper)
    1. Latin America—Church history. 2. Latin America—Religion—History. I. Title.
    BR600.L96 2012
    278—dc23

                                                                              2011041757

A catalogue record for this book is available from the British Library.

10 9 8 7 6 5 4 3 2 1

For my wife and my family

Parce Domine, parce populo tuo:
Ne in aeternum irascaris nobis
Liber Usualis

Contents

Preface   *xii*
List of Abbreviations   *xvi*
Glossary   *xvii*

1 RELIGION AND EMPIRE
The Spanish Church on the Eve of the Conquest   1
Amerindian Religions: Mayan, Aztec, and Inca   6
Mexico: A Mendicant Mission   11
Peru: A Conqueror's Religion   18
Culture and Religion   22
The Struggle for Justice   24
The Portuguese Version   28

2 CHRISTIANITY IN A NEW WORLD
Justice and Peace for the Indians   32
Idolatry Campaigns   38
Inquisition   45
The Jesuit Way   48
Brazil: Between Europe and Africa   52
The Church and Slavery   56

3 RELIGION IN THE AGE OF ENLIGHTENMENT
The Enlightenment in the Hispanic World   64
The Church Subservient   67
Expulsion of the Jesuits   72
Priests and People   81
Enlightenment and the Indian World   86
Indian Resistance   90
Missionary Expansion   94
The Church in the Eighteenth Century   98

4 INDEPENDENCE: A SINFUL REVOLUTION
The Crisis of the Colonial Church 106
The Ideological Roots of Independence 110
The Church Responds to Independence 114
Papal Hostility 121
The Religion of the Liberators 124
The Post-Colonial Church 126

5 CREATING A LATIN AMERICAN CHURCH
Continuity and Change 129
Priests and Prelates 132
Laity and Elites 141
The Romanization of the Latin American Church 147
Reform and Renewal 153
New Evangelists 154
Religion in Brazil through Monarchy and Slavery 157

6 THE RELIGION OF THE PEOPLE
Traditions of Belief 161
Popular Religion, Formal Religion 168
Search for the Millennium 174
Millenarian Signals: Argentina 176
Messiahs in Brazil 179
Millenarian Rebels in Mexico 182

7 CHURCH AND STATE IN A LIBERAL WORLD
Protestantism, Positivism, and Catholic Responses 185
The Church and the Secular State 190
Brazil 191
Argentina and the Southern Cone 194
Andean America 201
Central America 220
Mexico 222
Gains from Losses 227

8 NEW CENTURY, NEW CHALLENGES
Social Messages 229
Argentine Responses 231
Echoes from Andean America 238
Raising Consciences in Mexico 242
Martyr of the Mexican Revolution 248

Warriors for Christ 250
The Church in 1930: Inheritance and Legacy 252

9 The Church and the Dictators
Brazil: Hard-line Model 254
Populist Dictator: Perón and the Church 259
The Argentine Church and the Military Dictators 266
Complicity 269
Christian Democracy, a Chilean Option 273
Allende: Fateful Interlude 280
Pinochet 282

10 Religion and Revolution
Cuba: A Silent Church 287
Promise and Prejudice in Nicaragua 295
El Salvador: Sanctity in a Time of Killing 306
Guatemala: War in the Land of Peace 315

11 Difference and Diversity
The Jews in Latin America 324
Afro-Latin American Religions 331
Protestants and Pentecostals 335

12 Between Liberation and Tradition
Liberation Theology 344
Base Communities 351
Council and Conference 354
The Voice of Rome 360

Notes 367
Bibliography 390
Index 399

Preface

THERE ARE MANY faces to religion. The present book focuses on religious history and historical development rather than theological issues and forms of spirituality, though these are not ignored. Within this framework it studies the life of the Church and the reception of Christianity by the peoples of Latin America and has a social as well as a religious dimension. The works of modern theologians, historians, evangelists, and catechists have enriched the subject in recent years and there is now enough material to make a modern history of religion in Latin America possible, though not enough to make it superfluous. The historian has space to take a new look at old issues, aiming to strike a balance between the long colonial period and the shorter but more eventful modern age.

The narrative follows the course of the subject from the Spanish conquest to recent times. It avoids the concept of the 'spiritual conquest' of the New World, an approach no longer favoured by modern perceptions. Spanish evangelists encountered traces of ancient American religions. In the subsequent fusion each side strove to impose or preserve the maximum possible amount of their own culture. The result was a certain continuity of Indian religion and survival of ancestral ways within a new Christian structure. In the conquest and colonization of America the Church played a crucial role, and the evangelization of the diverse regions of the subcontinent was regarded as a Christian duty by priests and friars and a vital means of control by colonial officials. To preach a religion free from political pressures, some missionaries devised an alternative evangelization, such as the peaceful preaching of the Gospel by Bartolomé de Las Casas, the hospital villages of Vasco de Quiroga in Mexico modelled on More's *Utopia*, and the reductions of the Jesuits in Paraguay.

Roman in faith and morals, the colonial Church was Spanish in organization and discipline. This model, transmitted through the agencies of bishops, priests, and religious, was implanted in the sixteenth and seventeenth centuries. In the eighteenth century, however, under pressure from Bourbon monarchs, the colonial Church became unmistakably a state Church. The task of the historian is to trace this process and to identify the two features, wealth and privilege, which made the Church vulnerable to Bourbon policy. The narrative will record not only the religion of clerical elites but also the faith of the people. Priests throughout the Americas made a distinction between morality and piety: their people were believers but sinners. The faith was sound but behaviour imperfect, and adultery, concubinage, drunkenness, murder, and theft were widespread. The gap between faith and morals was an enduring though not exclusive feature of Latin American Catholicism and a source of scorn to outside observers.

The trauma of political independence divided the Church but eventually forced it to disavow the colonial state and to collaborate with national governments. Spain was replaced by Rome as the fountainhead of doctrine and discipline. At the First Vatican Council Latin American prelates adopted conservative positions on matters of faith and morals, and supported the definition of papal infallibility. The Romanization of the Latin American Church coincided with the liberalization of Latin American states. In the second half of the nineteenth century the Church had to accept the loss of temporal power and privilege and the triumph of the secular state. The book will seek to explain the wide variations of Church–state relations in the different countries of Latin America, and will suggest that where the Church was large, in clergy and resources, as in Mexico, it was more likely to provoke anti-clericalism and envy, but was also in a stronger position to defend itself. The ensuing conflict would probably be bitter and lead to wars of religion.

The twentieth century brought further problems for religion. It required the dramatic impact of social conditions and urgent prompting from Rome to alert the Church to the need for change. Mass immigration and incipient industrialization seriously tested the institutions of the Church. Gradually the great cities of Latin America were transformed and often de-christianized. The papal encyclical *Rerum Novarum* (1891) proclaimed the rights of labour and the injustices of economic liberalism, and advocated a degree of state intervention in favour of workers. It was a cry of alarm as well as a call for justice, and in Latin America the message met with a varied response: in some countries prompt and serious, in others slow and timid; among the lower clergy with some enthusiasm, among the hierarchies less so.

The reaction of the Church to populist dictators, such as Perón in Argentina, is a phase which the book will seek to clarify. More serious challenges to religion were presented by the military dictators of the second half of the twentieth century. Divisions between traditionalists and progressives became more pronounced as the Church had to define its policies towards repressive regimes, speak out for social justice, and make clear its defence of human rights. The historian has to make distinctions not only between traditionalists and reformists but also between younger clergy influenced by their seminary experience outside Latin America who sought to add a social dimension to the Church's message, and some of their more radical colleagues who advocated a socialist and Marxist version of Christianity.

Further impetus to modernization was given by the Second Vatican Council. The assertion in favour of religious toleration went against many ingrained prejudices of an older Catholicism, while the promise of greater collegiality raised hopes, some of them false, for a more inclusive Church. Liberal Catholics in Latin America were disillusioned by the response of the hierarchies to Vatican II and by the pace of change in its aftermath. While the present narrative does not aim to give equal treatment to every single country, it seeks to include all major issues, and it studies regional differences in religious experience, between the southern cone, Andean America, and the Caribbean; the position of the Church following the Cuban and Nicaraguan revolutions and its response to the Pinochet regime in Chile are also examined. Ideology was changing. In Brazil, in particular, liberation theology inspired new thinking about social conflict and social change, and *basismo* (grassroots religion) was regarded by some as a model for future religious development and by others as a deviation from orthodoxy.

In addition to the main narrative the book also studies a number of special subjects which stand out for their singularity and general interest. (1) The Spanish struggle for justice in the conquest of America and the defence of the Indians by Las Casas and others in the face of conquerors and colonists has generated a spirited debate among historians. (2) The case of slavery and the slave trade was an issue from which the Church did not emerge with its reputation intact, and in the case of Brazil drew the rebuke that 'our clergy's desertion of the role of the Gospel assigned to it was as shameful as could possibly be'. (3) The Jesuit reductions and so-called 'Jesuit state' in Paraguay are more than a curiosity; they illustrate some of the basic problems of religion in conditions of colonialism. (4) The concept of popular religion distinct from official religion is frequently invoked by historians and sociologists, But the word 'popular' has many connotations. Religion too is notorious for its diversity. Together the terms can cause confusion. (5) Liberation theology, its development, controversies and implications, is a story worth telling, and in the religious history of countries such as Brazil and Nicaragua it cannot be ignored. It may emerge in the course of the book that some of these themes form a thread of continuity in concern for justice and peace running from the Church of the early conquest to that of later times.

Some historians now speak of 'Latin American religions' rather than 'religion', and it is true that native American, African, and Protestant traditions have all been part of the Latin American experience, while modern evangelical churches have also taken root. These tendencies will not be neglected, nor will the presence of the Jewish community be forgotten. But the evidence suggests that for five centuries the defining religion of Latin America has been Catholic and this is the assumption on which the book has been written.

I am grateful for the support of Robert Baldock in the preparation of this book and for the collaboration of his team at Yale University Press in its production. I am grateful to Beth Humphries for her careful copy-editing and greatly improving my manuscript. I am also indebted to Leslie Bethell for first directing my attention to the history of Latin American religion, which had not previously been a research interest of mine. He persuaded me to write a chapter on the Church for his distinguished work, *The Cambridge History of Latin America*, 1995, and this began my engagement with the subject. I thank my son Jonathan for contributing computer skills when they were needed. I am grateful to Guadalupe Jiménez for her collaboration in Mexico. In London the British Library has been indispensable in the search for material. And as always, my wife Wendy has been there to give support for work in progress and to keep me going.

Abbreviations

ANH	Academia Nacional de Historia, Caracas
BAE	Biblioteca de Autores Españoles
CEHILA	Comisión de Historia de la Iglesia en América Latina
HAHR	*Hispanic American Historical Review*
HGIAL	*Historia General de la Iglesia en América Latina*
HIHF	*Historia de la Iglesia en Hispanoamérica y Filipinas*
JLAS	*Journal of Latin American Studies*

Glossary

alcalde	district magistrate
audiencia	high court of justice with administrative functions
cabildo	town council
cabildo abierto	*cabildo* enlarged for extraordinary meeting
cacique	Indian chieftain
capellanía	chantry, private ecclesiastical benefice
caudillo	leader, whose rule is based on personal power
chapetón	South American nickname for peninsular Spaniard
comunero	popular rebel
corregidor	district officer
cordobazo	urban riot in Córdoba, Argentina, in May 1969
curaca	see *kuraka*
curandero	folk healer, medicine man
cura	priest
doctrina	curacy or parish of Indians
encomendero	possessor of an *encomienda*
encomienda	grant of Indians
fuero	right, privilege, pertaining to profession or community
golpe	coup
hacendado	owner of hacienda
hacienda	large landed estate, plantation
huaca	sacred place, shrine, relic venerated in the Inca religion
ilustrado	enlightened
kuraka	Andean ethnic chief
ladino	mestizo, non-Indian
mestizo	of mixed white and Indian descent
mita	forced labour recruitment of Indians in rotation for mining
montonero	guerrilla fighter

palenque	community of runaway slaves
pardo	mulatto, of mixed white and black descent
Porfiriato	regime of Porfirio Díaz in Mexico
porteño	of Buenos Aires, inhabitant of Buenos Aires
sertanejos	inhabitant of Sertão
vicariato	assumption by Spanish crown of papal authority over the colonial Church
zambo	of mixed black and Indian decent

CHAPTER 1

❦

Religion and Empire

The Spanish Church on the Eve of the Conquest

ON THE EVE of the conquest of America the Spanish Church had little sense of mission, and the destined source of evangelization for the next three centuries was itself a dry well. According to the Catholic Monarchs, Ferdinand and Isabella, writing in 1488, 'the Church has never been in such ruin and so badly ruled and governed as it is now; all the income that it should be spending on the poor and on charitable works is being wasted by the clergy on material matters, while the service of God and the good of the Church are totally neglected.'[1] During the great grain shortage and hunger of the years 1503–6 many of the clergy preferred to profit from its production and even to export grain rather than relieve the starving people. In Spain the interests of religion, society, and the state were entwined, and the Church was a leading actor in the life of the nation. But it had lost prestige and property in the civil wars of the mid-fifteenth century, in which its most powerful members had participated on one side or the other for reasons that had little to do with religion; and like other groups, it reacted vehemently to any attack on its privileges.

The see of Toledo, one of the greatest concentrations of religious, secular, and economic power in Europe, was ruled by prelates who were more interested in status than evangelization. The behaviour of many of the higher clergy was indistinguishable from that of the aristocracy, whence they usually came; and a warrior-bishop, like Archbishop Alfonso Carrillo, was not an exceptional figure, nor were those who openly lived with women. Against these, however, should be set the example of Hernando de Talavera, whose academic qualifications from the University of Salamanca were placed at the service of the queen and the state but also of his order, the Jeronymites, and the wider care of souls. In 1492 he became the first archbishop of Granada and undertook the evangelization of this former

Muslim territory, using Arabic and adapting prayers to accommodate the newly converted, a mission that was never completed.

The monastic orders, with few exceptions – notably the Carthusians and Franciscan Observants – had abandoned their original discipline, and their monasteries were often little more than places of diversion. When the Catholic Monarchs undertook to reform the religious orders many of their members had to be forcibly expelled from their houses, and the Dominicans of Salamanca defended themselves with arms. The secular clergy were no better. Products of existing norms, which made virtually no provision for the training of priests, they were often completely unprepared for the performance of their duties; in 1473 the Council of Aranda had to order the clergy to celebrate mass at least four times a year. In periods of decline, of course, it is usually the vices of the clergy, not their virtues, that receive publicity. The Spanish Church was not devoid of piety and purpose, and standards were preserved among the middle ranks of bishops, abbots, and canons.

The Catholic Monarchs, who were conscious of their power over the Church, had material on which to work, and with the collaboration of Cardinal Francisco Jiménez de Cisneros they were able to begin the long-needed task of reform, an essential feature of which was careful selection of candidates for preferment. For this reason, as well as in the interests of their own sovereignty, they were anxious to reduce the jurisdiction of Rome. They were determined to control as well as to reform, and it was in their reign that the independence of the Spanish Church was undermined and its relationship with Rome curtailed, an essential feature of Spanish religion soon to be exported to America. In order to control the Spanish clergy they sought to establish the rule that nominations to important benefices be made by the crown and not by the papacy. After a struggle they obtained from Sixtus IV the right to petition in favour of their candidates for all the major ecclesiastical benefices in Spain, with an understanding that the candidates presented by the crown would in fact be the ones appointed by Rome. And even this right was gradually extended to more and more benefices and eventually to those in the New World. The concern of the Catholic Monarchs for religion can be exaggerated. They had little appreciation of the wider problems of the Church. The papacy earned little prestige from the pontificate of Alexander VI, a Spanish Borgia elected with the active support of Ferdinand and Isabella, and henceforth a firm ally of their political and colonial interests, and the sponsor of their title *Reyes Católicos*. Even within Spain reasons of state sometimes took precedence over the needs of the Church; Ferdinand, who had to find sinecures for the brood of illegitimate children with whom he encumbered the country, made one of them, Alonso de Aragón, archbishop of Zaragoza; Alonso's own illegitimate son succeeded him in the see.

The Catholic reform in Spain predated the Reformation and was accompanied by an intellectual and spiritual revival which went beyond a negative correction of faults. Apart from Queen Isabella, acting as she did from personal faith and reasons of state, the principal agent of reform was Francisco Jiménez de Cisneros, provincial of the Franciscans in Castile, archbishop of Toledo and primate of Spain from 1495, Inquisitor General from 1507, and twice regent of the kingdom, a man of power and influence, ruthless with his opponents and inflexible in his various objectives, which included financing conquests in North Africa, regulating the secular clergy, and publishing a missal in the Mozarabic rite. His attempt to reform the diocesan clergy, exhorting them to chastity, cure of souls, and preaching the Gospel, met with limited success. Immoral and worldly priests continued to be found in Spain as in other parts of Christendom, and among the episcopacy dignity was often more highly regarded than austerity. But Spaniards were tolerant of their priests. The young Saint Teresa was sympathetic towards her confessor, an errant priest with a mistress, and she blamed not the man but the woman 'who would hesitate at nothing to gain her desires'.[2]

In general, the secular clergy were not equal to their mission. This was one of the reasons for the progress of the religious orders, especially the mendicants, who came to form a spiritual elite to whom laymen looked as the true representatives of the Christian ideal. Jiménez himself undertook the reform of his own order, installing Observants in place of Conventuals. The Dominicans had already undertaken a programme of reform based on stricter observance of the rules of the order and accompanied by an educational and theological revival. Thanks to these efforts the standards of monasticism in Spain and the numbers of its adherents, with almost 200 Franciscan friaries, were superior to those found elsewhere in Europe, and it was no coincidence that in the reigns of Charles V and Philip II it was Spain's missionaries who carried the Christian faith to new frontiers.

Jiménez strengthened theological studies and gave them a new status. The University of Alcalá, his own creation, joined the University of Salamanca as a leading centre of learning in Europe, distinguished not only for its theological, canonical, and biblical studies but also for its promotion of the humanities, languages, and medicine, and recognized for its publication of the Polyglot Bible. The religious renaissance begun by Jiménez was exemplified by the Dominican theologians of the Salamanca school and later by the newly formed Society of Jesus, and enabled Spanish theologians both to expound Catholic doctrine in the great contemporary debate with Protestantism and to make significant contributions to the problems of empire, race relations, and international law, which were posed by Spain's unique position in the Atlantic world. On the other hand, the Spanish reform was initiated under royal auspices and independently of Rome, whose own religious revival it anticipated by many years. This helped to increase the power of the crown in ecclesiastical affairs and its influence in the evangelization of the Americas.

How did the mass of the people respond to the efforts of bishops and priests?[3] What effect did the reforms of Isabella and Cisneros have on those less instructed in Catholic faith and morals? The Spanish people were inspired by a traditional religiosity accumulated from the past, as they flocked to mass, processions, shrines, and other popular devotions, unperturbed by the glaring abuses, dysfunctional clergy, and their own sinfulness.* This was the *religiosidad popular* in which the conquerors of Mexico and Peru were also formed and which stirred their sense of mission. It expressed a religiosity which priests and missionaries encouraged, as they struggled to respond to other pressures.

In a Church troubled by the spectres of Judaism and Islamization a surge of preaching and catechizing was to be expected. Sermons on traditional Catholic themes such as devotions to Our Lady became common, and the production of catechisms of Christian doctrine multiplied, some targeted at converting Jews, some at the Moriscos of Granada after their baptism in 1500. Although there was no Spanish version of the Bible, passages from the Old and New Testaments were translated into Spanish and circulated to those who could read. The events of Christ's Passion and death were enacted at Eastertime, while the adoration of the Eucharist and elaborate processions during the feast of Corpus Christi gave visible expression to sacred truths. The cult of the Immaculate Conception was popular in Spain long before it was proclaimed as a dogma of faith, while pilgrimages to Marian shrines, especially to Guadalupe, were popular social as well as religious occasions.

Pressure to conform was a potent impulse to religion, as was evident during the war of Granada, when a preaching operation on behalf of the bull of crusade was authorized in which teams of campaigners consisting of preachers, sellers of bulls, and treasurers with their scale of tariffs traversed the towns and villages of the peninsula. From these it was difficult to escape without losing face. Recourse to popular practices of this kind was probably more common than reception of the sacraments, which was in general neglected. Some of the popular expressions of Catholicism verged on the superstitious, while others were the work of the confraternities which proliferated at the end of the fifteenth century.

Evangelical fervour, soon to be projected overseas, began nearer home. There were two targets: Jews, who had gained an enviable role in finance, commerce, and the bureaucracy, and Moors, whose presence in Africa and the Mediterranean was regarded as a threat to the religious and economic interests of Spain. After the frightening experience of religious terror in the period 1391–1415 many Jews decided that conversion was preferable to persecution and then, having taken that step, eased their way back into public life, in finance, the bureaucracy, and even the Church. Against the Jews a twin-track policy was adopted. In 1492 the Jews were expelled. For many, already suffering from envy and intolerance, this was a further inducement to conversion. The crown balanced the demands of religion to expel with the needs of the economy to retain, expelling a minority and forcibly converting the rest. The decree of expulsion was a scourge but not a final solution. How could convert Jews be watched and controlled? The Catholic Monarchs, propelled by a wave of popular prejudice and clerical fanaticism, and sympathetic to anything which reinforced their own central power, responded positively to the idea of an Inquisition, one which would be a national not a papal institution and would involve strong state control.

The jurisdiction of the Inquisition was confined to Christians and it was not a means of converting unbelievers by force. It punished heresy and apostasy, but not the profession of a different faith, baptism being a precondition of heresy. For this reason, Jews, Muslims, and American Indians were excluded from its authority. The Inquisition never persecuted a Jew for being a Jew, or a Muslim for being a Muslim. It pursued converts from each faith who were suspected, rightly or wrongly, of being secret apostates. The Inquisition was established, in 1480, primarily to investigate *conversos*, who for the next three centuries were universally suspected of being crypto-Jews.[4] The truth of the matter became a problem for the Inquisition and for later historians. Were the *conversos* secret Jews and therefore legitimate targets, or were they true Catholics persecuted for other reasons – race, greed, politics? Historians are not sure and there are various opinions on the sincerity or otherwise of the *conversos*. Inquisitors had few doubts. The expulsion of 1492 is sometimes seen as an invitation to convert and stay. The interpretation is not entirely convincing, for, as the Jews well knew, to stay was to encounter another form of expulsion: an expulsion from Spanish society. This took place when those alleged to lack purity of blood were barred from holding public office, carrying arms, exercising certain professions, and wearing particular styles of clothing. The statutes of purity of blood represented a mixture of religious fanaticism, race prejudice, social ambition, and political exclusivism. These efforts to protect orthodoxy from the remnants of Judaism were exported to America and became part of the religious baggage of Spain in the New World.

The fusion of religious and political ideals in the Spain of the Catholic Monarchs revived the spirit of crusade against Islam which had been dead for over a century. Without Granada the reconquest was incomplete and Spain itself dismembered; and with the joint forces of Castile and Aragon ready for action the time had come to reduce the last remnants of Islam on Iberian soil. The war for Granada was long and bitter and it was ten years before the Moorish kingdom was overcome. A settlement followed, deceptively generous: the Moors were allowed to remain in the country with their own religion, laws, and magistrates. On these terms the Catholic Monarchs entered the Alhambra in triumph on 2 January 1492. But Isabella and her advisers found it impossible to tolerate Muslims. For the acquisition of Granada added a new dimension to the problem by increasing the number of Moors in Spain to some 500,000 out of a population of 7 million. And there was no perfect solution. The Moors left in Castile in the wake of the reconquest, the *mudéjares*, were subject to ever harder pressure to conform. From 1502 Isabella initiated in Castile the policy of forced conversion, giving the Moors the alternative of baptism or expulsion. Conversions, however, were nominal and the Moriscos, unlike the convert Jews, did not integrate into Spanish society; they remained immune to the preaching and the missions of the Church.

The logical process of crusade against Islam was to take the war across the narrow sea separating Spain from North Africa; this would also serve Spanish strategic interests by giving additional protection to the southern flank of the peninsula. With its forces freed from the war of Granada, Castile was ready to turn reconquest into expansion and challenge Islam in the Mediterranean. But almost before the challenge was made Spain turned away from North Africa. In 1492 Columbus discovered America; crusading and imperial ideals began to focus on the New World, which was soon recognized as a far more fruitful field of empire. Expansion in Africa and in America were not irreconcilable; the search for a way to outflank Islam was one of the impulses behind the early voyages of discovery. Ferdinand promoted a policy of expansion in North Africa and in the early years of the sixteenth century launched a series of expeditions across the Mediterranean. But the economic prospects were meagre compared with those in America; the expansion southwards was not sustained and its achievements were not sufficient to contain the combined power of the Ottoman Turk and the Barbary states. America was a new world to conquer, a world of silver as well as souls. And a rapacious metropolis could still preach the Gospel.

Amerindian Religions: Mayan, Aztec, and Inca

Many Spaniards found it difficult to believe that Christianity had never reached the New World, and they expected to find peoples amenable to their faith. Legends that the apostles Thomas and Bartholomew had preached in the Americas were readily believed. It was conceded that with the lapse of time the apostolic teaching had been engulfed by the ancient religions of the New World. Nevertheless, certain aspects of American religious practices were thought to resemble the Christian. Crosses found in Yucatán were conceivably left there by Spaniards who had fled beyond the seas at the time of the Muslim invasion of the peninsula. Bartolomé de Las Casas, the pro-Indian campaigner, gave credence to such ideas, when he wrote in the *Apologética historia* that in Yucatán and elsewhere the Christian Trinity was not unfamiliar.[5]

Soon they learnt of other myths compatible with the religion they knew. Topiltzin, the great Toltec priest-king and holy man, was brought up in Tepoztlan, the centre of the cult of Quetzalcoatl, the Plumed Serpent, of which he became high priest. But he was corrupted, sinned, and was banished from Tula. Eventually he went eastwards towards Veracruz and the Aztecs saw him in Cortés. The Spanish chronicler, Diego Durán, was impressed by his life, which 'has led me and others to believe that, since the natives were also God's creatures, rational and capable of salvation, He cannot have left them without a preacher of the Gospel. And if this is true, that preacher is Topiltzin, who came to this land.' Like St Thomas the Apostle he was a sculptor, and we know that 'this apostle was a preacher to the Indians'.[6] Everything Duran saw convinced him that 'these people knew something of the Divine Law, the Holy Gospel, and of the Beatitudes', and that there had been an evangelist in Mexico.

But native Americans already had a religious history and this was built on their indigenous cosmologies and rituals, in which the worlds of the spirit and the flesh were closely merged, and ancient ceremonies expressed the meaning of the heavens, the earth, and the life they knew.

Maya religion, practised in the region of southern Mexico, Guatemala, and Honduras, was closely integrated with human activity and daily life. Evidence from native pictographs, Spanish chronicles, and surviving archaeology reveals gods and goddesses, creators of rain and winds, and the sources of agriculture, commerce, medicine, war, and death. Religion was a complex body of myth and legend, of knowledge derived from calendars, and was a ritual preserved and presented by priests and holy men. The practice of religion took the form of a series of rituals expressing the annual recurrence of work and production. The Maya had a cyclical and unchanging notion of time and believed that history was repetitive, that the events in one cycle would be repeated in all successive cycles. Therefore the calendar could be used not only to record the past but also to predict the future as it unfolded in succeeding cycles, while people were left without control over their fate. In this view of the world, history and prophecy were indivisible, as in the Christian Book of Revelation. Christianity had much to answer for in the ordeal of the Maya, but on the positive side it promised to release them from their cyclical prison and make them free to accept time and progress and to live as individuals contributing to history and change.

Mayan civilization had already passed its great days, weakened by the forces of nature and the advance of its northern neighbours. But greater shocks were to come. The Mayan sacred text, the *Book of Chilam Balam*, 'foretells' the Spanish invasion, the conquest of the Maya, and future sufferings of the oppressed people. 'Those white people, we wept at their coming. They came from the east. Then they arrived here, the bearded men, The *guayaba* people, And manifested the white God Standing on the tall pole.'⁷ The secret Quiché text, *Popol Vuh*, discovered and translated by a Spanish priest at the beginning of the eighteenth century, tells the story of creation by the Maker gods who create first the earth, then the animals, and after some delay while they experimented with clay and wood, made men from the yellow and white ears of corn, a vital material at the core of Mayan culture; finally they made women, beautiful creatures and looking like princesses.⁸ The spiritual world of the Maya rests on a universal creation myth, comparable to the Christian story and beginning like the Gospel of St John with 'the Word'; but it was a different word. Here there are many deities, some of them heroes with human traits; and the Mayan underworld is peopled by deities placated by human sacrifice.

Central Mexico was an urban civilization composed of city states in alliance or at war. Tribes from the north migrated into the area, bringing with them the Nahuatl language and an origin myth about a place called Aztlan, source of the term Aztec. Finally, in the twelfth century BC, came the Mexica, who established their island city about 1325. They were a warrior people, integrating their tribal cult with the Mesoamerican solar cult and the ancient practice of human sacrifice, and living by a military code which inspired them to dominate most of Mesoamerica. Among the spoils of war brought back by their armies two were particularly valued – prisoners for sacrifice, and tribute for profit – and so their capital grew in wealth and power. The Aztecs, to use the term traditionally favoured by historians, thus ruled a tributary empire, its subject peoples and their leaders restless in their allegiance. Its capital was Tenochtitlán, which became the religious centre of the Aztec world, headed by hereditary nobles and serviced by virtual slaves.

Human sacrifice to appease the gods was inherent in Aztec ritual. Victims for all the sacrifices, men and women, were either taken in war or bought in slave markets, and could number over a thousand throughout Mexico on major feast days. At the temple of Huitzilopochtli on the feast of the god, victims, totally naked, were made to ascend the steps of the pyramid and thrown on their backs. The priests opened the victims' chests and ripped out their hearts with their own hands and held them up to the sun, while the bodies were sent rolling down the steps of the temple; the skulls were then delivered to the priests of the temple who strung them on a rack for exhibition, and the flesh was distributed for eating.

Among the variations of ritual sacrifice, on the feast of the goddess Xochiquetzal two young maidens were brought forth, noblewomen of the royal lineage, who were dressed up and jewelled and made to scatter maize. Then, 'when the hour came, the two girls were slain. Their breasts were opened and their hearts taken out. Four ministers held them down by the hands and feet. When the priests killed these two noblewomen, to indicate that they died virgins their legs were crossed one upon the other and their hands extended. They were sent rolling down the steps.'[9]

Aztec religion has been reconstructed from archaeological sources revealed in temples and plaques, but also from native chroniclers and Spanish texts such as Bernardino de Sahagún's *General History of the Things of New Spain*, also known as the Florentine Codex, whose author made himself fluent in Nahuatl, the language of the Mexica. Sahagún recorded many of the stories about the god Quetzalcoatl, the Plumed Serpent, the god of wind and ally of the rain gods, a symbolic figure in Mesoamerican culture, a hero who moved across time and space and was due to return from the east to Mexico in 1519, the year in which Hernán Cortés invaded the lands of the Mexica, an invasion described by the Codex in graphic detail.[10] There were other gods of fire and water and pulque, associated with particular regions, peoples, and products.

Diego Durán, reporting in the 1570s, had a different take on Mexican ritual. He began by deploring the ignorant destruction of ancient pictographic documents and historical chronicles by the early conquerors and evangelists. 'Ignorant men ordered them burned, believing them idols, while actually they were history books worthy of being preserved instead of being buried in oblivion, as was to occur. Even for the ministry we profess, that of the salvation of souls and aid to the natives, they left us in darkness.'[11] 'The most solemn and celebrated feast in all the land was that of the god called Huitzilopochtli. Much is remarkable about this feast and its rites since it was a mixture of divine ceremonies. Some resemble those of our Christian religion; others, things of the Old Testament; and still others, diabolical and satanical were invented by the Indians.'

The commandments of the Aztecs were similar to the Ten Commandments, and included orders to honour their gods, their fathers and their mothers, not to kill, not to commit adultery and not to steal, the main difference being that the Aztec commandments carried greater punishments in this life, and not in the afterlife, 'since they disclaimed knowledge of the perils of the afterlife. So it was that these people faced death without sorrow or fear.'[12] The Indians believed in the power of water to wash away sin: 'In this the Indians were not too far from the truth, since in the substance of the water God placed the Sacrament of Baptism with which we are cleansed of original sin.' Aztec ritual also contained a form of communion. After their ceremonies, dances, sacrifices, and games had ended, the actors, dignitaries, and priests of the temple took the image of the idol, made of dough, and stripped it of its ornaments; they then broke it into small fragments [tzoalli] which everyone received with great awe and reverence, believing they were eating the flesh of the gods.[13] Parallel feast days were celebrated on more or less the same day, the old hiding behind the new, or, as Durán would have it, the devil tricking the Indians into serving him. Durán was impressed by the fine order in which these people lived, the high level of Indian social organization, their laws, commandments and discipline, their insistence on hierarchy and soil stratification. In spite of their paganism they kept their laws, rites, and ceremonies admirably. Older Indians lamented the loss of the old order under the new Spanish dispensation, 'when they see the young people today, eighteen and twenty years old, utterly shameless, drunkards, thieves, murderers, bandits, gluttons, loaded with girls'.[14]

The Inca empire, centred on Cuzco, was relatively young at the time of the conquest and consisted of a number of Andean groups conquered and ruled by the Inca, who relied upon a large military establishment and an efficient bureaucracy to hold the union. The sources for the study of Andean culture and religion, apart from excavations, consist of Indian oral narratives transcribed by Spaniards, such as the Huarochiri Manuscript, and the Royal Commentaries of the mestizo chronicler Garcilaso de la Vega, the Inca, described by the historian John Hemming as unreliable but regarded by others as distinguished. Society was highly structured to maintain an elaborate road system and an agriculture nurtured by irrigation and terracing. Religion too was organized and hierarchical. A spontaneous belief among the people in the power of the sun developed into the cult of the sun, but the Inca elite went further, believing in a single Supreme Being, Pachacamac, abstract and unknowable. 'If I were asked,' wrote Garcilaso, 'I, who by the infinite mercy of God, am a Catholic Christian, what God is called in my language, I should reply, Pachacamac, because in the current speech of Peru there is no other name than that to denote God.'[15] There were gods of the earth, the moon, the sea and, highest of all, the sun god, Inti. Inti was represented on earth by the Inca emperor, while his wife, the Coya, represented the moon. In Cuzco, Garcilaso tells us, all the priests of the house of the sun were Incas of royal blood, and in the provinces too the highest priests were Incas. There were numerous 'convents' for nuns, some of whom remained virgins all their lives without leaving the convent, while others became concubines of the king.

Mexico: a Mendicant Mission

There were no clergy on the first voyage of Columbus, though the enterprise was inspired by evangelization and Columbus himself was convinced of his providential mission: he was a servant chosen by God to take the faith to new peoples. Las Casas recorded that in matters of the Christian religion he was a devout Catholic and prefaced everything he said and did with the words 'in the name of the most Holy Trinity'. Confident in his own knowledge and experience, which drove him to reach the Orient by sailing west, Columbus twice visited the Franciscan monastery of La Rábida and received decisive support from Fray Antonio de Marchena and Fray Juan Pérez, who spoke for him to Queen Isabella. The Dominican Fray Diego de Deza, a professor of theology at Salamanca, was another decisive influence at the court. But in the end, as he confessed, it was the inspiration of the Holy Spirit and the conviction born of divine assistance that sealed his confidence.

There were missionaries on the seond voyage but they contributed nothing. Ignorant of the language, they had no idea how to adapt to the land or the people. It was not until the arrival of the Franciscans and Dominicans that any progress was made. In the large colonizing expedition of 1502 there were seventeen Franciscans. By 1535 they were well established throughout the Caribbean, in Santo Domingo, Cuba, Puerto Rico, and Jamaica, and in Panama; but the Caribbean Indians were killed or remained hostile, so these were staging posts to greater fields in Mexico and Peru. In 1514 the Dominican Pedro de Córdova with the help of the crown organized from Spain a peaceful expedition of some twenty religious 'to those parts of the Tierra Firme that were not disturbed and scandalized by Christians, to teach and preach to the Indians without the presence of other people and the use of any force whatever, following the example of the apostles'. This was the Chiribichí settlement on the eastern coast of Venezuela. Meanwhile the Franciscans in Hispaniola organized their own expedition to Cumaná, reinforced in 1516–19, by which time they had built two churches, two monasteries, established a school for Indian children, introduced new plants such as oranges and melons, and brought in metal tools. But in 1520 the Indians rose, attacking first the Dominicans and then the Franciscans, and in the face of continued hostility the mission was ended early in 1522.[16]

The cause of failure was not far to seek. Mission territories suffered from the incursions of Spaniards, and even the Las Casas mission to Cumaná was not entirely 'pacific' for it included settlers who erected fortresses and possessed arms. Venezuela would prove a challenge to evangelization. During the fierce Indian wars in Venezuela Spanish behaviour appalled the chroniclers. In the expedition against Tamanaco in the territory of the Mariches in 1572–73, a soldier named Tapia, walking with the advance guard along the Guaire River, saw a baby girl lying in the sand, abandoned by her fleeing mother.

> Forgetting the morality of a human being and his obligation as a Catholic, Tapia seized the infant by one foot, and shouting 'I baptize you in the name of the Father, the Son, and the Holy Spirit', he threw her into the river where she was submerged in its waters. Pedro Alonso [the commander], to punish this iniquity, ordered Tapia's hand cut off, but several soldiers intervened and the sentence was suspended.

Tapia met retribution the next day when he was shot through the heart by an Indian arrow.[17]

In the early decades the friars were given great space and power. In addition to preaching the Gospel they were permitted to act as parish priests, and to be bishops and archbishops. The first official mission to Mexico began on 13 May 1524 with the arrival of twelve Franciscans, the so-called 'twelve apostles', who made their way inland from the coast, bare-foot, ill-clad, and exuding humility, through crowds of natives who five years earlier had encountered a different column, armed and mounted. 'Motolinia', they exclaimed, and learning that this meant 'the poor one', Fray Toribio de Benavente took the name as his own. In Mexico City they were met by Cortés and his soldiers, who in a scene carefully staged to impress the natives knelt before the friars and made to kiss the hands of their disconcerted countrymen. 'On seeing Cortés whom they regarded as an idol or god kneeling before the friars', the soldier-chronicler Bernal Díaz recorded, 'all the Indians followed his example and from then onwards they received them with similar marks of respect'.[18] Cortés took over from Columbus as God's messenger. Bernardino de Sahagún argues that conquest was necessary to open the way for the Catholic faith and that Cortés was an instrument of God's plan for the Indians.

The next fifty years was the great age of the friars, Franciscans, Dominicans, and Augustinians. Motolinia and his companions made a sustained effort to learn the language and to preach without books. It was normal to teach the Indians the whole of Christian doctrine, holding back on nothing, including such difficult mysteries as the Eucharist and the Trinity, and moral hurdles such as the condemnation of drunkenness and polygamy. First they had to define who God was and to explain that Holy

Mary was not God. Then having explained the immortality of the soul and the evil of the devil, they taught them, in Nahuatl, the Our Father, Hail Mary, the Creed and the Ten Commandments, the seven mortal sins and works of mercy, all of which they were expected to know by heart. And they urged them to come to baptism, to weekly mass and yearly confession. 'And so they began to come to baptism and to seek the kingdom of God.'[19] The friars were concerned to teach the Indians not only Christian theology but also Christian moral behaviour and to convey the Christian concept of sin, expecting the Indians to live a Christian moral life.

Appearances could often deceive, and just when the friars thought they had made a breakthrough and achieved outward conformity they discovered that 'at night the Indians continued to meet and call upon the devil and celebrate his feasts with many and diverse ancient rites'. The going was hard, a struggle against the inherent strength of Indian religion, against the exploitation of the Indians by the colonists for tribute and labour, and the ravages of epidemic disease. Motolinia listed ten great 'plagues' that befell the Indians with the conquest, including: epidemics, death in battle, famine, brutal overseers on estates, taxes and tributes, death in gold mines and in the rebuilding of Mexico City, and enslavement, all this caused by the greed of Spaniards. The Indians in Central Mexico, where Church and state were more firmly established and Spaniards more numerous, found it difficult to evade Christianity. But in remoter areas they passively resisted and clung to ancient cults, as Durán admitted.[20] As the Indian gods and their view of the world were declared false and the new doctrine proclaimed, Indian lords and priests abandoned their sanctuaries in the cities and retreated to remote areas, and to hiding places in caves and mountains. They became in effect an underground Church, capable of thwarting pursuit by Spanish religious authorities and their allies among neophytes. Christianization was now associated with exploitation and disease, and the friars themselves made these points, as they preached the Gospel by example as well as instruction.

The friars persisted, and could see the first signs of popular religiosity among the Indians, who were transferring their old religious enthusiasm to the new rites. They especially favoured devotions and processions of the Blessed Sacrament, Our Lady, and the saints, and they responded to enactments of the Christmas story and the celebration of the Epiphany, Palm Sunday, Holy Thursday, Corpus Christi, and All Souls Day. Motolinia tells us that during Lent 'many of the men abstain from intercourse with their wives'. 'The Indian lords and principal men, adorned and dressed in their white tunics and shawls embroidered with feathers, and with bouquets of roses in their hands, dance and sing in their own tongues hymns of the feast that they are celebrating, to their own music.'[21] The friars left their imprint on Mexico. The Franciscans established a college of theology and liberal arts for Indian youth at Tlatelolco. Motolinia, Andrés de Olmos, and Bernardino de Sahagún conducted their ethnographic researches, and great manuscripts of cultural contact were produced. These friars and their like were the elite of Spain's clergy, possessing higher educational and ethical standards than were normal; they were accepted by the natives and learnt the languages, they built churches and monasteries, and they undertook a struggle for justice for the Indians.

The Franciscans dominated the central area of Mexico, followed by Dominicans in 1526 and Augustinians in 1533. The twelve apostles and their provincial, Fray Martín de Valencia, performed extraordinary feats of mass baptism and conversion. They were idealists coming from an austere reform tradition and seeking to recreate the purity of St Francis's original movement. They believed that among 'new' people, unencumbered by the heresies and excesses of the European Church they could fashion a huge Christian following and start a movement that would lead to the second coming of Christ. They dreamed of a Mexico where they and the Indians alone would together lay the foundations of a new Christianity, imposing themselves between the subject populations and the conquerors.

Belief in the millennium was at the heart of this Franciscan message, drawing on the prophecies of the Cistercian monk, Joachim of Fiore (1135–1202). Joachim saw history as three great periods: the age of the Father under the dispensation of the Old Testament; the age of the Son under the New Testament; and the approaching age of the spirit, when new religious orders would convert the whole world and usher in the Church of the spirit. Driven by their apocalyptic vision and missionary zeal, the Franciscans interpreted events in Mexico as living proof of the advent of a new age and the creation of a new society. They were willing to dispense with lengthy catechesis in favour of rapid mass baptism. Motolinia tells how he was called to an Indian town to confess the sick and to baptize. When he arrived he found thirty-two sick people to confess, 200 couples to marry, many to baptize, and one dead man to bury. On that day the friars baptized 1,500 children and adults and heard fifteen confessions.

The friars Motolinia and Mendieta proclaimed that the Indians would be freed from their tribulations through baptism; secure in the expectation of the second coming of Christ and the Last Judgement, they would vindi-cate the policy of mass conversion and give Mexico a leading place in Christian history before it climaxed in the end of the world. From about 1540, however, missionary policy became more severe and a number of dissidents were persecuted and arraigned before the Inquisition, just as epidemics and population decline were weakening Indian society. As times grew harder, the Indian nobility took care to preserve their status and power, while the friars set Christianized children against their 'idolatrous' parents. Although retaining some power and privilege the religious orders had to learn to deal with other competing powers: the administration, the *audiencias* (high courts), bishops, and secular priests. They had to look anew at colonial society, where the number of Spanish mestizos, blacks, and mulattos was growing; they had to be accommodated in the Church, while the Indian population was diminishing. Independent actors in the conquest, the friars now became partners and servants of the colonial state.

As the heroic days of evangelization passed they were succeeded by a time of division and conflict, first between the conquerors and their successors, then within the Church. In the first generation of Spanish rule the conquerors and the early mendicants, Franciscans, Dominicans, and Augustinians, established the initial power structure of the colony. Many conquerors became *encomenderos* (holders of grants of Indians) taking labour and tribute from their Indians, while the mendicants garnered conversions. As the colony grew, however, more Spaniards arrived seeking wealth and power, and the crown was forced to exert its sovereignty. It also eventually moved to restrain the power of the regular clergy in favour of the seculars. The two were uneasy allies. The regulars wanted evangelization to remain in their hands, to be conducted in native languages, and to keep their converts separate from Spanish society. The seculars were more integrated into that society; they sought to decrease the power of the regular clergy, to control the Indians, and to tax them for their own salaries. By the mid-sixteenth century the face of the mendicants was changing. Later arrivals together with creole friars born in the colony became more closely absorbed into local society and, distracted by disputes with other orders and among themselves, they no longer displayed the pioneering spirit of the early Franciscans. The growth in the number of secular clergy and the decline of the Indian population made it possible for the Indians to be served by seculars rather than the friars; this was what the crown and the hierarchy preferred.

As was to be expected, Christianized Indians divided up more or less as Europeans did, between the devout, the routine, and the indifferent. Some understood the Christian faith and morals and were scrupulous in their practice. In Mexico they found a kind of continuity between their old and new beliefs, especially in the purifying effects of water, in the moral value of purity, in the sacraments of baptism and confession as outward signs of inward grace, and in the exaltation of Mary for her virginity. 'Thus Nahuan ideas about pollution and cleansing were used by the friars as a rhetorical aid in their preaching, creating a strong continuity between native and Christian thought.'[22] The control of passions in pursuit of moral behaviour was a virtue in Indian religion as well as in Christianity. In both religions the faithful were exhorted to overcome temptation and avoid occasions of sin. Sahagún advises girls on how they should guard their virginity: 'You will look at no man's face, you will smile at no man. Protect your body and protect your heart so that you do nothing that is an offence to our lord God.'[23] The friars noticed that penitential exercises such as fasting and sexual abstinence were a major component of Nahua rituals. Whether attributed to previous evangelization, diabolic imitation, or expression of natural virtue, these practices were thought to be in harmony with Christian ideas and could be adapted to the new religion and to the Christian calendar. Although the Nahuas observed moderation in sex, and condemned adultery, abortion, and homosexuality, attitudes which the friars could approve, they had no concept of virginity or celibacy as virtues, and they allowed pre-marital sex. So the friars had to struggle to impose a new moral code, and in addition promote the virtue of temperance. Marriage posed a problem. How could they persuade Indians to give up a multitude of wives and select only one for Christian marriage, when many of the wives were held for their value in alliances and earning capacity as well as for sexual love? The friars managed to introduce a marriage contract, but in some places they had to overlook subsequent concubines and mistresses.

Evangelization was demanding on catechist and convert. The sacrament of confession caused particular problems for the Mexican Indians.

> Today the natives continue with their fear of admitting or revealing their sins, even in confession. They are afraid that if they admit the truth they will receive some earthly harm or punishment, ignoring the afterlife as if it did not exist. Therefore our priests do wrong when they become rough or angry at the weak Indians in confession, threatening them and menacing them with gestures. They well know the weakness of these people; they should know that it is imperative to show kindness, patience, and love in the act of confession, so as to avoid sacrileges resulting from an exhibition of severity.

It was also necessary to have a better knowledge of the Indian languages 'to examine the tangled consciences of penitents'.[24] Durán was convinced that priests who behaved in this way should be suspended in perpetuity.

In the second half of the sixteenth century the numbers going to confession decreased. Towards 1566 over 80 per cent of the adult population died without confession in the archbishopric of Mexico. In Mexico City the number confessing was less than 10 per cent in 1556. Many Indians failed to distinguish between venial and mortal sins or to count the number of times sins had been committed. Some confessors advocated accommodation, others better instruction. Some regarded the Indians as ignorant and rustic; others saw that they could assimilate Christianity and genuinely attend mass and the sacraments. In Peru the Jesuit José de Acosta recorded in 1589 that in spite of deficiencies many thousands of Indians were good Christians, and apart from lust and drunkenness there were no other reasons to reproach them on religious grounds; and he declared that he heard with greater satisfaction 'the rough confessions of the poor Indians than the refined and and grief-stricken confessions of the Spaniards'.

By the end of the sixteenth century Mexico was politically and religiously stable. Superficially at least the Indians were good Catholics, and Indo-Christian churches and chapels graced the countryside. A number of dioceses had been established, each with its cathedral and bishop. Religious orders had settled and expanded, though they were now less dynamic. The secular clergy were increasing and coexisting with religious. The Indians were submissive, paid tribute, and were loyal subjects of the crown. But the great population loss was a shock to Indian society and placed a greater burden on the rest, for which the Church could offer no relief. As the Indians diminished, new social groups had come into being – creoles, mestizos, Negroes, mulattos, and other ethnic groups, to all of whom the Church administered mass and the sacraments in chapels and parishes.

Meanwhile the faith was spreading southwards. Pedro de Alvarado led the military conquest of Guatemala in 1524, penetrating from Socomoco to Iximché, Escuintla and beyond. By means of alliance with the Cakchiquel group against the Quiché group and by use of implacable violence, 'killing, ravaging, burning, robbing and destroying all the country wherever they came', according to Las Casas, the Spaniards managed by 1527 to establish a permanent settlement among the highland Maya in the valley of Almolonga and called it Santiago de los Caballeros. Chaplains became priests to the settlers, if they could pay them, and settlers competed for the services of the few secular clergy who were there. These early clergy constituted a diocese under a bishop, Francisco Marroquín, appointed in 1534, but the bishop had only a few priests and the diocese nominal boundaries. Antonio de Remesal, the biographer of Las Casas, described such priests as 'poor idiots and ignorant', who, 'understanding that within their dioceses in Spain they could not achieve any office or ecclesiastical benefice', crossed the Atlantic in the hope of improving their lot. Remesal thus implied that American dioceses received the failures and have-nots from Spain, more or less like military and civilian emigrants. In the second half of the sixteenth century, however, 'a republic of friars and Indians' took shape in highland Guatemala. It only vaguely resembled the millennial kingdom inspired by the early friar missionaries. But the friars succeeded in their peaceful conquest and founded towns and communities.

Elsewhere in Maya territory, in Yucatán, Christianity was also making progress. Modern research has identified three levels of religion among the Maya. As a result of conquest the Mayas essentially lost access to universal religion which explains the whole of life and the universe, and instead were reduced to a secondary level of local cults of the saints, supplemented by a tertiary or lower sphere of private superstition and shamanistic folk-healing.[25] The Indian social structure adapted to this. The Maya elite dominated both the organization of processions, rituals, and feast days, and funded the expenses through the income derived from communal lands set aside for that purpose. The same men, descendants of pre-conquest rulers and priests, led their people in the new religion as *mayordomos* of confraternities and caciques of their villages.

The records of the Maya jaguar priests in Yucatán, the *Book of Chilam Balam*, written down later in the Latin-based alphabet developed by Franciscan friars, express a sense of loss and suffering introduced with Christianity, yet accept the temporal inevitability of these events: on the one hand the calamities of conquest and colonization, the land seizures, labour service, and tribute exactions, and on the other hand the advent of the true God. According to the *Chilam Balam*, 'And there was great theft of tribute: there was the great theft of Christendom. There was the establishment of the seven sacraments: the word of God is great. Take it and welcome it ... Then came the burden of tribute, then came Christianity. Then descended the rope coming from the sky.'[26]

Misery, yet resignation, and some survival of ancient beliefs. But it was not hopeless. A strong element of Christian millenarianism which they received either from the Franciscan missionaries or from their own reading of the Book of Revelation enabled them to think of a second coming of Christ and deliverance from earthly misery. In 1696 the priests of Itza, a community unconquered deep in the jungles of Petén, advised their people to accept Christianity and Spanish rule precisely because their readings of the time sequence indicated the inevitability of this infliction.[27]

Peru: A Conqueror's Religion

Christianity came to Peru as a conquest. When Atahualpa entered the plaza where Francisco Pizarro and his companions were awaiting him, the Dominican Vicente Valverde approached with a breviary in his hand and immediately spoke to him 'of the things of God', inviting him to embrace the true religion.[28] The Inca was irritated and complained of Spanish depredations. He took the breviary, examined it, and threw it to the ground. They should have explained things to him differently, reported Pedro de Cieza de León, conquistador and chronicler, 'but the friars never preach around here except where there is no danger of raised lances'.[29] Thereupon Valverde, 'the skirts of his habit flying high, rushed back to Pizarro, telling him that this tyrant Atahualpa was like a wounded dog and that they should attack him', and so raised the alarm which unleashed the Spanish attack, a vicious attack in which over 2,000 Indians were slaughtered without loss of a single Spaniard.

The conquest, therefore, was made in the name of evangelization, but among the conquerors themselves religion was a formal and ritual element, their religiosity not in doubt but their prime objective treasure and Indian labour. This does not make them entirely insincere. Pizarro is supposed to have admonished the captive Atahualpa 'that all their idols were vanity ... there is only one God, creator of heaven and earth and of all things visible and invisible'. During discussions on the execution of Atahualpa Valverde threatened to have him burned, 'the words of a soldier not of a priest', another Spaniard said.[30] On his way to execution Atahualpa was accompanied by Valverde, who urged him to convert to Christianity and abandon his beliefs; Atahualpa asked to be baptized, and the friar baptized him. Then they strangled him. So Valverde was an accomplice, but in the end a kind of justice was done, for those guilty of his death died brutally themselves. Valverde was not a bad man, and in Cuzco he worked hard for the Indians and was promoted to be bishop of Panama. On his way there his ship had to put into the island of Puná for repairs; there he fell into the hands of cannibal Indians who killed him, cooked him in chilli and ate him.

Evangelization in Peru was slower than in Mexico and met greater Indian resistance. Cieza observed that the Indians were well disposed to receive the Gospel in spite of the defects of evangelization, which during Pizarro's time lacked a strong clerical presence; and the conquest of Peru was tarnished with cruelty and corruption. 'There were few friars and no bishop, which was the reason there was little progress in what was most important – the conversion of these peoples. And if there were any friars, they were just as avaricious as the seculars, surreptitiously trying to stuff their purses.'[31] During the civil wars between Spaniards in Peru in 1537–51 there was no respite for the Indians. On the contrary they paid for the consequences: both sides used them as shock troops, for service and transport duties, and forced labour, and they also suffered from malnutrition and disease. The clergy too, regulars and seculars, were involved on one side or the other of the conflict, to the neglect of the Indians. One observer denounced, with a few honourable exceptions, the behaviour of the Christians, including prelates and priests, who accepted that 'the Indians may be robbed, deprived of their liberty, ill-treated by many lords, tortured and killed, because they don't provide gold, deprived of their women who are debauched, and of their children, who are corrupted and enslaved, and all of them banished from their own houses, lands, and properties', and, he adds, 'all these people rightly say, "Who is the god of the Christians, who serve him in this way?"'[32] Fray Domingo de Santo Tomás, who witnessed the harsh treatment and heavy mortality of the Indians in Peru, denounced the iniquity of the *encomenderos* and their demands on native labour which left the Indians no time for religion, and he criticized the complicity of their allies among the *curas*.

Inca Peru was a conquest waiting to happen. An empire and a state religion with firm structures and warring rulers, these were ready made for a takeover. The Andean Indians believed in God, in the saints, in interme- diaries such as Pachacamac, and in the devil. According to many Spanish theologians, the Indians had no difficulty in making a synthesis of a supreme God and their own image of a creator-god, for both had the same basic content, despite the different local gods. Missionaries wondered whether there was foreknowledge of the Christian faith, and some preached to encourage passage from Viracocha, the creator-god, to the true God, from local *huacas* to Christian 'huacas', that is the Virgin Mary and the saints. Missionaries blamed the devil for evil in the world, and Indians accepted the devil into their pantheon.[33] Sun worship was the official religion, but Viracocha had also been adored and invoked, as the Christians prayed to their God. The Indians were acquainted with rites which seemed to foreshadow the sacraments of baptism, confession, and even the Eucharist, and they had institutions such as Virgins of the Sun which curiously resembled Catholic convents. Yet the Andean content of these beliefs was not forgotten as the Indians reinterpreted Christian teaching within their own religious framework, creating a form of synthesis. The missionaries accepted this, ignoring the influence of the *curacas* and native ministers, who encouraged their people not to confess idolatry at their Easter duty, for it would reveal too much information about Inca religion and its survival.

The mestizo Garcilaso de la Vega, while defending the validity of Inca theology and the religious practice of his mother's people, also maintained that these simply prefigured Christian truth, the religion of his father. But Christian truth, he argued, could never have taken root in the Andes had its way not been prepared by the Incas. Yet within Peru Andeans and Spaniards disagreed with each other and among themselves as to whether Andean religious expression had any legitimate place within Christianity and, if so, how it should be accommodated. Garcisalo recalled that when he was growing up in Cuzco Spaniards were objecting to Andeans using the name of Pachacamac to refer to the Christian God. Another Christian doctrine that Garcilaso, like Cieza, found to have been foreshadowed in

Andean and Inca religion was the resurrection of the body, in which Andeans sought not so much a vision of God as a 'tranquillity of soul'. Garcilaso gave several examples of what he regarded as legitimate continuities of thought between Inca and Christian festivals, especially the rituals of the festival of Inti Raimi and its attendant agricultural celebration, which the Andeans continued to celebrate as Corpus Christi. Extirpators pounced, but other Spaniards took a more tolerant view.[34]

José de Acosta, distinguished Jesuit missionary, viewed the sacred maize bread the Incas consumed at Inti Raimi as the work of the devil, a false imitation of the Catholic Eucharist. Garcilaso sought to discredit this view. He also regarded demonized Andean versions of the Trinity, such as Acosta, scorned as fictions of the Spanish imagination, because knowledge of the Trinity came from revelation, to which the Indian had access only after the Spanish invasion. Moreover, to suppose that Andean people had succumbed to these temptations of the devil amounted to exaggerating the power of Satan. In divine revelation the devil was only a subordinate figure and a secondary cause of experiences and events. The sacraments of the Catholic Church silenced all the demons in Peru. The providential explanation of the fall of the Inca empire saw it as God's reward for the faith and missionary zeal of the Spaniards. Garcilaso did not accept this. He argued that the previous religious knowledge of the Andeans enabled them to understand the Gospel without great explanations, and they did not deserve the extirpation campaigns against Andean religion that were now taking place.[35] On the other hand, some priests and missionaries living in Andean villages and observing their ritual and beliefs were convinced that conversions still left much from the past in Andean cults that must be extirpated.

The Inca state cult imposed on Andean peoples in the century before the arrival of the Spaniards was displaced by the Spanish conquest and supplanted by the Catholic Church. Yet regional beliefs and cults survived in one form or another and proved more difficult to replace.[36] The Andean protest movement of the 1560s known as *Taki Onqoy*, Dance of Disease, was a powerful, though localized, assertion of Inca religion, confined mainly to Huamanga, where it could be described as 'a violent response to the European colonization of Peru, based on native tradition'.[37] In the words of a Spanish observer, Canon Cristóbal de Albornoz, its adherents, most of them Indian Christians, would 'dance and tremble while moving in a circle, and in the dance they would call on the devil and on their *huacas* and idols, at the same time abjuring the true faith of Jesus Christ and all the teachings they had received from Christians and priests'.[38] They sought to liberate themselves from the Christian God, who favoured only the Spaniards and had assisted them in conquering the Inca Atahualpa;

now the defeat of the Christians was at hand and the *huacas* would send all of them diseases and kill them. At a time when the outward manifestations of Inca religion seemed to have gone, when Inca sites and temples were derelict or destroyed, this frightened the Spaniards and brought into question the success of evangelization and the validity of conversions. It showed that the regional deities who predated the Inca empire were not so easily discarded, and it was these more than the deities of the Inca state that re-emerged in Taki Onqoy.

The leaders of Taki Onqoy described themselves as messengers of Titicaca and the other *huacas*, deities who, unlike the Christian God, cared for Indians. The Andeans must separate themselves from the invaders: they must avoid Spanish food and clothing, refuse to attend church and catechism classes, and never enter Spanish dwellings. The suppression of Taki Onqoy took several years, but it was never a real danger to the colonial state, being absent from Spanish towns and confined to *encomiendas*. It was followed in 1571 by the invasion and destruction of the last enclave of the Inca state, Vilcabamba, though there is no evidence of collusion between the two centres of resistance. Overt rebellion was now over, and conversions could go ahead, accompanied by extirpation. But missionaries still had much to learn. They were still mistaking the symbol for the substance. They failed to distinguish between culture and religion, and did not learn to separate survival of Andean religion within Christian practice from mere local custom. Therefore they had the unfinished task of accurately recognizing signs of an underground practice of Andean rituals.

Culture and Religion

Culture and religion are not the same thing. A society can acquire a new religion without abandoning its previous behaviour, language, customs, works of art, and traditions. To Fray Diego Durán, a perceptive observer and chronicler of post-conquest Mexico, the Indian practice of eating dogs, moles, weasels, and other unclean things at fiestas, weddings, and baptisms was not only abominable but idolatrous, recalling the sacrifice of these creatures to the gods in heathen times: 'Even today, though they are Christians, the awe and fear of their ancient law is still strong.'[39] Yet the use of indigenous customs or liturgy in Christian worship was not necessarily a sign of continued belief in the native religions. The mixture of the remnants of the indigenous liturgy with Christian rites did not always mean 'mixed religion' or syncretism. Historian and anthropologist Nancy Farriss has moved beyond the syncretic model to view religious change in terms of dialogue and creative synthesis and a continual process of interaction.[40] No doubt some paganism survived even among Christianized

Indians. The rituals of sweeping, use of fires, self-flagellation, offerings and incense, all were pre-conversion practices now put to Christian use. Durán concedes that some survivals of pagan customs had been turned into offerings to the true God, but insists that others were pure idolatry. 'God help us to understand this salad, this mixture which they have made of their ancient superstitions and of our Divine Law and ritual.'[41] Other Spanish observers were less sensitive and often misunderstood native religiosity. Some missionaries were intransigent and in cultivating the flowering faith sought to uproot noxious weeds, especially alleged devil worship; in the process they destroyed numerous artefacts that were pictorial and not religious. The Jesuit José de Acosta, no friend of Andean religion, complained that this was happening in Peru in the 1580s; some missionaries destroyed purely pictorial representations in the mistaken belief that these were idolatrous. In the following century campaigns to extirpate idolatry became the scourge of Indian culture.

Was the confusion of Indian cultural traits and pure religion by Spaniards a genuine mistake or deliberate policy? It has been argued that it was not done out of ignorance or ineptitude, that the Church knew what it was doing. To preserve one, you removed the other, and this meant everything 'other' – that is cultural as well as religious deviation. Most priests and officials were convinced that religious authority and colonial control could only be imposed by removing from Indian life every departure from Spanish cultural habits and social customs, no matter how trivial. Spanish policy sought to transform the political and material framework of native life, introducing Spanish ways and institutions: evangelization meant hispanicization. The friars in their letters, sermons, doctrinal works, and guides for confessors insisted that every thought and deed, from those associated with domestic routine to procedures employed in agriculture, crafts, and social relations, had to be restrained and reformed.[42]

But how far were these practices religious? Were they not simply cultural? Were family statues, bracelets, and toys, truly idols or merely keepsakes? In any case domestic rituals did not basically challenge Christian beliefs. The struggle against sickness and death tempts sufferers to reach for any remedy, and if Indians had recourse to sacred objects, rites, sorcerers, plants, songs, and invocations, these might be classified as superstitions, which have always accompanied Christianity without being treated as idolatrous. Even a perceptive and benevolent observer such as Durán insisted that innocent-looking things such as girls' earrings and traditional songs and music were harmful signs of enduring superstition and magic, though he attributed them to confusion and poor instruction.[43] If the distinction between idolatry and superstition was not always observed by the religious authorities, by the eighteenth century many previous manifestations of 'idolatry' had been demoted to relatively harmless superstitions; the real idolaters were a minority and not wholly representative of indigenous culture.[44]

While cultural relativism was rejected by colonial churchmen, religious syncretism could not be entirely avoided.[45] A certain convergence between Christianity and older beliefs was almost inevitable, if the hope of achieving universal conversion by peaceful means was to be achieved. Otherwise in regions such as Yucatán, the prospect was one of endless conflict and resistance.[46] There were also possible approaches between aspects of Catholicism and pre-Hispanic religions of America which eased the transition to Christianity. So the minor figures of the Quiché gods were assimilated to Christian saints, which helps to explain the popularity that saints' cults came to enjoy during the colonial period and the role they played in popular religion. In Mexico, Indians came to identify Santiago's horse as an autonomous agent of divine power, the successor of jaguars and serpents.

Peaceful conversion, through preservation of certain beliefs and practices from the past, was also seen in the use of Indian assistants by the Church. By employing traditional Indian leaders, missionaries ensured that the persons who played an active role in the establishment of the new religion, such as sacristans, acolytes, and catechists, would be exactly the same individuals who had occupied similar positions before the conversion. This obviously had an effect on the kind of Christian observance that took root.[47] It also meant that, while the Indian elites were targeted successfully, some of the popular sectors escaped the Spanish net. Even so, Indian Christianity was fundamentally authentic, though often imperfect. Popular religion in Mexico and in Central and Andean America emerged from the colonial regime practising orthodox rites, embellished with local variants, and could be defined as a mode of faith among Catholic communities which conformed to the catechism in matters of doctrine but expressed itself primarily in external ritual and devotion to the Blessed Virgin and the saints.

The Struggle for Justice

Spain had received confirmation of its discoveries from the papacy, the only international authority of the time. None of the missionaries questioned the validity of the papal grant as the title of Spain's dominion in America. What they did dispute was the extent of the grant, what type of rule it authorized, and what methods of conquest were legitimate. The model of Christ himself, contrasted with the unacceptable behaviour of many conquistadors, especially the abuses in the Caribbean and Mexico, led some missionaries to seek another way, which they described as apostolic and peaceful evangelization. The conversion and protection of the Indians made the friars objects of suspicion to Spanish settlers, and people began to say 'these friars are destroying us and preventing us being rich and making slaves of the Indians ... They are a set of old bastards.'[48]

Should conversions be forced or free? Surely they must be a free act of the will. The first missionaries were aware of the tradition of the Church, which from the Fathers onwards veered between freedom and coercion. Heathens must be free; but errant Christians had to be forced back into the fold. St Thomas Aquinas distinguished between unbelievers, who have never received the faith and should in no way be coerced into accepting it, and heretics who are rebels against faith and Church and can be compelled to obey or be punished. Not all theologians agreed with this argument but it was the dominant line. It followed that the Inquisition could be used against the Indians, partly to enforce uniformity but also as a means of colonial control; and in the 1520s Indians were already being prosecuted for various sins and lapses into 'idolatry', as Inquisitors believed that they could prosecute 'anything that appeared to be sinful'.[49] But the Inquisition was too crude an agency to deal with masses of unenculturated Indians or to distinguish between cultural and religious differences. Confession was found to be a more appropriate religious response and a more effective means of control than an institution using torture, punishment, and confiscation of property. From the 1540s the use of the Inquisition against Indians was discontinued and in 1571 the Indians in the Spanish colonies were formally removed from the jurisdiction of the Holy Office.[50]

Church opinion, as expressed in the First Mexican Provincial Council in 1555, decided that Indians needed protection to prevent exploitation by Spaniards. But it was an ambivalent gesture: the Indians had basic human rights and were in many ways equal to Spaniards; but in other ways they were regarded as intellectually and morally inferior, and so their weakness needed a paternalistic response. In general, though ecclesiastics might deplore the treatment of the Indians, they could not stop it without changing the whole system of conquest and colonization, and they did not have the will or the power to do that. The early religious were supportive yet critical of Columbus, but beyond getting information back to Spain to alert the Spanish authorities they could not prevent destructive expeditions. The Laws of Burgos (1512) regulated *encomiendas* (grants of Indians who paid tribute in labour and/or money), but also legitimized them. Deliberations in Valladolid produced the *Requerimiento* (1514) which, read out to Indians as a legal text, required them to submit peacefully to Spanish rule or face war and its painful consequences. This made the conquest lawful in Spanish eyes and the Church did not at that point demur. The first ecclesiastics to oppose armed conquests under any circumstances were Bartolomé de Las Casas, still a secular priest, and the

Franciscan Remigio de Faulx, both in 1518. The conquest of the Aztec empire by Cortés in 1519–21 did not provoke any immediate debate, perhaps because of his own propaganda and the support of the Franciscans for a messianic mission. Denunciation of armed expeditions surfaced again in 1531: first by Las Casas, then by various religious in New Spain (Mexico). Las Casas stated categorically in 1531 that 'there has not been any just war up to now on the part of the Christians'. He complained of 'violent and unjust wars' that were contrary to 'all divine and natural law' and justified defensive action of the Indians against the Spaniards. A priest, *encomendero*, and participant in the conquest of Cuba in 1512–14, Las Casas now saw the light, publicly renounced his *encomiendas* and began a campaign against the whole system. He was supported by four Dominicans who arrived in Cuba in 1515. Various Church-inspired projects in Hispaniola, Puerto Rico, and Cuba to settle free Indians as peasants outside the *encomienda* system all failed. Las Casas now took up the challenge of peaceful evangelization and colonization and constructed his whole agenda around these principles.[51]

In contrast to the admiration evoked by Cortés, Pizarro received a bad press for his behaviour in Peru. The emperor was disgusted by the execution of Atahualpa, and Fray Valverde was criticized for his participation in the death of the Inca. Francisco de Vitoria, theologian and political philosopher of the Salamanca school, stated in 1534 that he did not understand the justification of the war in Peru, and a number of religious who arrived in Peru after the conquest criticized the conduct of the war and the behaviour of Pizarro. Las Casas, now a Dominican, wondered if the Council of the Indies, the supreme authority under the crown for all colonial affairs, had considered 'whether the death of Atahualpa and the seizure of his kingdom and treasure were justified'. Events in Peru constituted a shock to the conscience and provoked a wave of anti-war feeling. Las Casas returned to the theme in 1534, 1535, and 1542, insisting on the intrinsic evil of actions which had caused so much suffering to the Indians, an attitude shared by a number of bishops and religious in Mexico. The New Laws of 1542 spoke of 'discoveries', not conquests, but introduced nothing new on the subject. Las Casas complained that they did not prohibit 'any war or conquest', whatever they did about *encomiendas*. His reply was elaborated in his work *The Destruction of the Indies* (1542), in his demand for an end to armed expeditions in Yucatán (1545), and in his insistence that conquerers had a duty to restore what they had seized (1546). In 1547 he declared that 'the Spaniards have not up to now waged any just war in any part of the Indies', and his pressure was seconded by the anti-war statements from the Dominicans in Mexico in 1544 and the Junta Eclesiástica of Mexico in 1546.

The Spanish crown took note and in 1549 suspended armed expeditions pending the conclusions reached by the Junta of Valladolid in 1550–51. From these the crown and its advisers seem to have concluded that the harm caused by wars of conquest challenged the Christian conscience. In 1556 it prohibited war if there were other means of political annexation available, of which the local *audiencia* was to be the judge. In 1573 the crown forbade conquest as a system of political annexation of a territory, but still permitted a defensive war. Nevertheless, many churchmen defended war as a legitimate strategy in the Indies. Among them was Vasco de Quiroga, humanist and humanitarian.

Vasco de Quiroga, judge and bishop, was in his late fifties when he first went to Mexico. He was already influenced by humanist ideas and in particular by the *Utopia* of the English humanist Thomas More (1516) before his arrival in the New World in 1531. His ideal was to persuade the Spanish authorities to build an Indian commonwealth which would be a model of primitive Christianity and humanist tolerance. Failing in this, he worked ceaselessly at his own expense to apply his ideals to two native communities, *pueblos hospitales* or 'benéficos' for poor Indians, both called Santa Fe, one on the outskirts of Mexico City, the other on the shores of Lake Pátzcuaro in Michoacán, working models of his master plan. He sought to create in these pueblos a primitive Christianity, a Utopia in the New World, an alternative to the modern renaissance state, a life free of soldiers and violence. Quiroga's legacy can be seen in the shrine and in rich local traditions which have preserved his memory among the Indians, proof of his sympathy with native cultures and his preference for a minimal role for Spaniards and Spanish rule; and they reveal his intellectual kinship with Thomas More.

Already in his *Información en derecho* he expressed the conviction that Indians would respond peacefully when they saw the good works and words of Christians, 'and they would be pacified without the sword or the lance or the arrow'. 'We have to approach them as Christ approached us'.[52] He advanced the idea of empire as a means of expansion of faith, and this by peaceful means. Though he never abandoned the apostolic method, he later seemed to favour war followed by evangelization, a position different from that of Las Casas. First as a judge then from 1538 as bishop of Michoacán, Quiroga argued for the segregation of the Indians. In 1531 he projected the *pueblos hospitales*, which in his plan of 1535 would have more than 60,000 inhabitants each and two friars, the viable ratio of religious to Indians in the conditions then prevailing in Mexcio. There would be no Spaniards.

The use of Indian labour was regarded by many reformers as an abuse and an obstacle to evangelization. But not by all. In general ecclesiastical opinion was divided between those who opposed it as illicit and harmful to the religious and physical welfare of the Indians, and those who believed that it was impossible to suppress. These included bishops, secular clergy, and monasteries, who often had title to *encomiendas*. Among the opponents were the allies and supporters of Las Casas, whose pressure influenced the enactment of the New Laws in 1542. These prohibited the granting of *encomiendas* to royal officials, bishops, and religious houses, and forbade the application of *encomienda* to any more Indians; existing ones were to pass to the crown on the death of the present holder. This caused an uproar in Peru and opposition among a sector of religious until the law was annulled in 1556.

There was still the question of *repartimientos* (forced wage labour). Church opinion was divided over the morality and legitimacy of forced labour, whether *repartimiento* or *mita*. Both in Mexico and in Peru, the balance tipped in favour of allowing it, under strict conditions. These inevitably tended not to be followed. In Peru Viceroy Toledo, accepting the advice of a junta consisting of the archbishop of Lima, three Dominicans, and one Jesuit, considered the use of force in *repartimientos* as legitimate. Religious opinion continued to be divided.

The Portuguese Version

Portugal, preoccupied with its African possessions, was later than Spain in colonizing and evangelizing in America. Bulls of crusade had already been issued by the papacy authorizing the Portuguese to occupy discovered lands. Their discoveries in Africa and round the Cape of Good Hope towards the east were regarded as a crusade against Islam, attacking the Muslims in a pincer movement. Portugal and Spain did not see themselves as conceding any temporal power to the papacy. They were simply looking for legitimacy, the opportunity to avow a religious mission, to pre-empt the claims of rival powers, and to confirm the existing facts of discovery and occupation, in a judgement from the highest international authority of the time. From 1493 a series of papal bulls were issued, granting absolute power and jurisdiction over new territories in return for their submission to the Church. Since the bulls effectively transferred ultimate control of the American Church from the papacy to the crown, Spain found these terms congenial. It foreshadowed the complete fusion of Church and state in colonial Spanish America. The original bulls of donation and demarcation were modified by the Treaty of Tordesillas (1494) which adopted a new line of demarcation running from north to south 370 leagues to the west of Cape Verde. In due course this would assign Brazil to Portugal.

The discovery and exploration of Brazil in the early sixteenth century and the exploitation of its resources by a system of trading factories at strategic points along the coast established an empire different from that of Spain. Brazil began as a trading empire, rather than an empire of settlement, similar to and indeed part of Portuguese expansion in Africa and the Atlantic islands.[53] By 1530, however, Portugal was forced to initiate colonization and settlement or risk losing Brazil to foreign rivals. At the same time hopes of exploiting Brazil's potential as Spain was exploiting its American colonies led to greater political control, with authority devolved to proprietary captaincies with absolute powers. But the Portuguese crown retained the right of patronage, whereby the monarchs or their agents appointed priests to parishes and bishops to dioceses, built churches and convents, and exercised ecclesiastical jurisdiction, in an arrangement which characterized the Brazilian Church from then onwards.

This transitional stage was overtaken by real colonial control in the second half of the century when a governor general, officials, soldiers, and approved colonists placed Brazil under centralized royal power, based on a more productive economy. A growing sugar industry in the tropical coastal zone of the north-east now emerged. Once Brazil's economic potential became more evident the importance of the colony as a source of royal revenue was also appreciated and it could no longer be left to hereditary fiefdoms and private enterprise. Labour too had to be mobilized and a policy developed for the Indians. Those who were peaceful were given royal protection and subjected to evangelization. Rebellious Indians and those who resisted Christianity could be legally enslaved and made available for use by the colonists.[54] The Church sought new souls. The sugar industry demanded slave labour. What was it to be? Religion or resources?

Whereas in Spanish America the mendicant orders were the chief agents of evangelization, in Brazil the king chose the Jesuits, whose order had been founded in 1540 and whose members were mobile and talented enough to become modern missionaries, bringing primitive peoples into civilized communities and associating conversion with acculturation. The first governor general, Tomé de Souza, was accompanied by six Jesuits led by Manoel da Nóbrega who was followed by José de Anchieta, a native of the Canary Islands and author of a rudimentary grammar in Tupí-Guaraní. Initial responses by the neophytes were unfavourable, ranging from defection to outright hostility.

The Jesuits also had to contend with the intransigence of Bishop Pedro Fernández Sardinha, whose ignorance of conditions on the ground led him to forbid them from catechizing in native languages and ordered them to preach the Gospel in Portuguese. He was also hostile to the establishment of reductions, the preferred Jesuit method of evangelization. They sought to remove Indians from their villages and concentrate them in *aldeias* where they would be more open to Christian teaching. This would also seclude the Indians from the labour demands of the Portuguese settlers. But religion was always overshadowed by the question, universal in the Americas: could the Indians be justly enslaved? Whatever the method of evangelization, there was no escape from the dilemma and missions were accompanied where necessary by military support.

The Jesuits were needed both as missionaries and as officials. The crown and its agents did not have the intellectual and administrative resources to run the colony on their own. They needed the Jesuit order. Father Nóbrega and his secretary Anchieta became an integral part of the colonial state, not only converting and pacifying Indians and rebuffing colonists but supplementing the work of royal officials and, with the development of Jesuit schools, laying the foundation of Brazilian education. The Jesuits assumed that they had to start from nothing. Nóbrega wrote in 1549 that the Indians of Brazil had no knowledge of God, they worshipped nothing, and did not even have idols:[55] a stimulus to his order perhaps but not entirely true. The Jesuit colleges provided missionaries for their village missions, especially in the area around Salvador da Bahia. Although the Jesuits learnt to locate the missions away from the sugar plantations to protect their Indians from labour demands, they did not abandon the coast; here they continued to minister to the white population and their black slaves.

The Jesuits themselves became owners of slaves and dependent on their labour in their colleges, landed estates, and mission settlements. Soon they were an economic power in Brazil, developing arable and pastoral agriculture rivalling that of the colonists, whom they also deprived of easy access to Indian labour. With the creation of the Jesuit Province of Brazil they effectively removed themselves from the jurisdiction of the bishop. Other religious orders such as the Franciscans also divided their activity according to the structure of the colonial state and operated in coastal friaries, landed estates, and mission settlements in the interior. Their diversity gave them a certain independence and ability to carry out their mission. This was also the experience of the Carmelites and Benedictines, and they too held African slaves.

The early decades of the Christian religion in Brazil left traces which endured for the whole of the colonial period and beyond. In the first place, heavy dependence on the crown made a deep imprint on the Brazilian Church and created a model of state control which would be difficult to change. Second, the slave economy from which the Church emerged and from which it indirectly drew its resources made the Brazilian

Church party to a historic injustice, for which it only repented in the nineteenth century.

Spanish America too was formed in the image of its colonial past. More thoroughly evangelized than Brazil, it nurtured a Church shadowed by a hovering state, a model of Catholicism strictly orthodox in doctrine but with some concession to Indian culture, a readiness to experiment in the life of the spirit and to tolerate voices of dissent when the welfare of the people was at stake, and a popular base of traditional pieties. These would be enduring marks of Spanish American religion. But the new world proclaimed by the friars was still far away and duties of justice, reconciliation, and welfare had still to be resolved.

CHAPTER 2

Christianity in a New World

Justice and Peace for the Indians

THE ARRIVAL IN Spain of Indian slaves brought by Columbus in 1495 caused moral confusion at court but eventually right reason prevailed and they were returned to their homeland in 1500. From then on royal policy insisted that the natives of the Indies, as vassals of the crown, could not be enslaved. But there were three exceptions. The Caribs were regarded as cannibals and propitious for slavery. Indian prisoners taken in a just war also qualified for slavery. And Indians already slaves of Indians and now bought or 'rescued' by Spaniards, *indios de rescate* as they were called, were also lawfully enslaved. Arguments among churchmen raged over the subject and although they attacked abuses and most of the exceptions in general they accepted the policy. Finally the Dominicans went to Rome for judgement and Paul III declared in the bull *Sublimis Deus* (2 June 1537) that Indians were human and could not be deprived of liberty or reduced to slavery, even if they were not Christians. In 1542 the Spanish crown prohibited slavery and ordered the liberation of those who had been enslaved. But realistically this was not the end of the matter, for *encomenderos* treated their Indians as their property and behaved as though they were slaves.

There were further questions. Were Indians genuinely converted? Did they make good Christians? Results were mixed. In Chile conversions were regarded as good. A Jesuit reported in the sixteenth century that he had rarely met such good Christians as those on his mission to the island of Santa María; they 'appeared to be Christians like those of the early Church, and in confession many show no signs of mortal sin, and I was astonished to see the fidelity observed by married men who had previously had many wives'. Chilean Indians were assiduous in attendance at church and hymn-singing: 'It was lovely to hear them in their houses and fields singing the prayers and hymns taught to them by the priests.'[1]

There were alternative voices of evangelization, some campaigning for a peaceful approach, without recourse to violence or military columns. On 20 December 1511 the Dominican Antonio de Montesinos, preaching in Hispaniola against the maltreatment of the Indians, asked officials and settlers, 'Are these Indians not men? Do they not have rational souls? Are you not obliged to love them as you love yourselves?'[2] Following the fiasco of Cumaná and with possible feelings of guilt for mixing profit and piety, there was a strong current among the Dominicans in America against coercion of any kind; the only weapons were the power of the Gospel and the doctrine of peaceful evangelization espoused by St Thomas Aquinas and other theologians. The Indians would not truly convert or abandon their idols except by conviction; faith by force would be suspect. The Franciscan Bishop Juan de Zumárraga opposed armed expeditions and argued for carrying the Gospel to the Indians peacefully and gradually, following the example of Christ and the apostles.

On the face of it, the Dominicans did not seem to be leaders among the humanitarians. They expanded robustly from the mid-sixteenth century and were active in establishing monasteries and churches, supported by money from land and tributes, all of which were characterized by large-scale magnificence and wealth. These extended from Mexico City southwards to Oaxaca and Chiapas, while in the east the order gloried in the elaborate Santo Domingo de Puebla de los Angeles (1534) which became one of the most celebrated of all Mexican churches; and from Mexico onwards to Guatemala and further to Peru. Their ostentation drew criticism from some observers, but Diego Durán defended them on the grounds that they could not afford to appear inferior to the lavishness and craftsmanship of Mexican temples; 'yet in our time there are those who say that a small, squat adobe church is enough for our God!'[3] But it was the struggle of one man on behalf of the Indians that brought the Dominicans to the fore and raised their profile in the battle for justice.

Born in Seville, the son of a merchant, Bartolomé de Las Casas migrated to the New World to make his way first in the Caribbean where he joined the conquerors as a planter and *encomendero*; and although he was already an ordained priest he paid more attention to working the Indians than converting them. But Spanish colonizing methods, resulting in hunger, exhaustion, and death for the Indians, began to prick his conscience and convince him, as it had already convinced other Dominicans and reformers, that the *encomienda* was harmful and sinful. Against the strictures of Las Casas and Montesinos the colonists fought back and both sides lobbied at court. A junta deliberated, and declared that the Indians were free but could be obliged to work. This was translated into the Laws of Burgos, the first royal confirmation of the *encomienda* system. In Cuba in 1514 Las Casas reached a decision to champion reform. He gave up his Indians and denounced the *encomiendas* in his sermons. Policy, however, was made in Spain, so he returned there in 1515. Energetic, sharp minded, physically strong, and an eloquent lobbyist, he was fit for the task he gave himself. But so far he was unknown.

In his *Historia de las Indias* Las Casas declared his belief that God had chosen him for his service and freed him from worldly ambition in order to pursue his providential mission.[4] But his early efforts, to abolish the *encomienda* and promote an alternative method of colonization through peasant emigration from Spain all ended in failure. Casting around for the relief of Indian slavery, he proposed in 1518 that Negro slaves be imported. He did not 'introduce' the slave trade, as is sometimes alleged; slaves were already in demand by many interests, especially for sugar plantations. But it took some time for him to realize that Negro slavery was just as evil as Indian slavery. In 1531 he repeated his original advice and took a Negro slave with him to Chiapas. By the time he returned to Spain in 1552 he had come to realize the total injustice of Negro slavery and in a spirit of contrition he rejected his former views, making a form of repentance in his *Historia*, where he inserted a long account of the injustice of the African slave trade and apologized for his original suggestion.

Las Casas joined the Dominican order in 1522 and lay low for the next decade, beginning his *Historia* in 1527, and in 1539 *De unico vocationis modo* (The Only Way of Attracting All People to the True Religion), a scholarly book showing great biblical, patristic, and theological learning. The work was designed to establish the theory and law of missions for all time and in many respects it anticipates the criteria of Vatican II in its decree *Ad Gentes Divinitus*, which exhorts Christians to adapt to other cultures and includes justice and peace as essential goals of the missionary process. Las Casas intended his work to be the theoretical infrastructure of all his projects of evangelization and protection of peoples. He makes two basic propositions. First, teach the Gospel to all men, and do not treat the Indians in an unjust or tyrannical way; moreover, they were owed restitution for the robberies they had suffered. Second, it was not merely illegal to employ force to convert them, but an unnecessary evil, and counter-productive. 'One and one only is the method', he concludes, 'that Divine Providence instituted in all the world and at all time to teach men the true religion, namely that which persuades the understanding with reason and gently attracts the will; and this is common to all men without any differences because of errors, sects, or corrupt customs.'[5] And the proof he offers comes from Scripture, the Church Fathers, and papal decrees. According to theologian Juan Ginés de Sepúlveda, if persuasion did not work, war and conquest were justified. Las Casas denied this, arguing that the faith can attract only by free will, unconstrained by violence, for Christ sent his apostles as sheep among wolves.

As a lobbyist for his causes in Spain, Las Casas was at the mercy of a conjunction of factors. Success depended on particular churchmen and politicians who happened to be in charge. It depended too on the financial situation and indirectly on foreign policy and war; if the crown was seriously short of money then revenue from the Indies was more important than justice. Finally it depended on an ongoing debate on the theory and practice of empire. So Las Casas had to judge the best time to move.[6] Even then a favourable order, such as that of 17 October 1540, 'no one shall enter to make war or disturb these Indians', might not be acceptable to colonial authorities and their settler supporters, and might never be applied. In the years 1541–43 he worked for the Indians on three fronts: he denounced the 'destruction' of the natives in sensational detail; he charged members of the Council of the Indies with venality; and he presented fundamental proposals for reformist legislation. He advised the emperor Charles V that all the Indians should be immediately withdrawn from *encomiendas* and be placed under the crown, leading to the entire and instant abolition of Indian slavery. His campaign against mistreatment of the Indians inspired the New Laws of 1542, which would eventually have abolished *encomiendas*, but while these caused rebellion in America and split the Church on reform and its consequences for colonists, they did not satisfy Las Casas, for he was advocating abolition there and then.

A key message of Las Casas was to insist on conversion without armed force. He did not stop at theory but put his plan into action in Tuzulutlán, an unconquered region of Guatemala not under Spanish control, having little to offer in resources and labour and whose Indians were hostile.[7] He accepted the bishopric of Chiapas in the hope of at least enforcing the New Laws, though reluctantly, for he was convinced that he could best advance the cause of the Indians at court. From the governor of Guatemala he secured a contract to bring the Indians to the faith and the royal service through the ministration of friars alone, on condition that *encomiendas* would not be granted and no Spaniard would be allowed to enter the territory for five years. His personal direction of the project lasted only a year but in that time promising preparations were made for future evangelization. The friars composed verses in the Quiché tongue telling of the creation, the fall, and redemption by Christ. Agreement was reached with the Indian chiefs, to whom protection and honours were promised in return for allowing the religious to preach the Gospel. The results were modest but positive, and were gained despite the opposition of the Spanish settlers and reluctance of officials. By 1547 the peaceful conquest was recognized as a fact; a region of Guatemala had been brought under Spanish control by missionary friars and not by soldiers. The Dominicans founded towns and preached their message, and

Charles V renamed Tuzulutlán ('the land of war') Vera Paz ('the land of peace').

Yet Vera Paz did not remain an unblemished idyll. Attempts to spread the mission drew resistance from hostile Indians. In 1555 two missionaries who refused escorts were killed along with their Christian followers. Antonio de Remesal, admirer and biographer of Las Casas, had no hesitation in calling them martyrs.[8] But Christian Indians retaliated and to the dismay of the Dominicans their vengeance left some 300 Indians dead.[9] So twelve years into peaceful evangelization the Dominicans were seeking to modify the principles of Las Casas, though not without debate and disagreement within their own ranks. Among the Indians too there was doubt and a feeling of vulnerability, as they lacked confidence in the capacity of the Dominicans to continue the mission or to provide enough friars to complete the task. There were never more than five or six in Cobán in northern Guatemala, and no sign of successors. 'The fathers were bound to fail,' thought the Indians, 'because they had no children, they did not marry, they did not want women ... they would leave no descendants.'[10] But in spite of some failures, these were the exception, and Vera Paz remained a land of peace, closed to soldiers and to any incomers other than the Dominicans. Later the record of the mission was mixed, though the spirit of peace was never wholly extinguished and Vera Paz remained under Dominican jusrisdiction for almost 300 years, a unique tribute to Las Casas and the struggle for justice.

The combination of an able leader and favourable political circumstances did not occur again. Among officials and settlers Las Casas became a hate figure, identified as the author of the New Laws. He was especially detested in Guatemala and Chiapas, slave territories and *encomienda* strongholds par excellence that had few other resources for settlers than their Indian populations. He became 'one of the most hated men who had ever been in the Indies, great or small, ecclesiastic or layman, and there were some who would never mention his name without a thousand execrations.'[11] In Chiapas at Easter 1545 he linked the Easter duty to freeing Indian slaves. Aware that clergy and even friars did not agree with him, he restricted the right to hear confession to two cathedral clergy, with instructions to withhold absolution to slaveholders and slave traders, and refer them to himself; and he arrested a recalcitrant dean of the cathedral who defied his orders. In Easter week a crowd rioted, freed the dean, blockaded the Dominican monastery, and stormed into the bishop's house to argue with Las Casas himself.[12]

In spite of these efforts and experiments, conqests and abuses continued, and so did the great dispute on the nature of the Indian and the waging of a just war. The controversy reached its peak in Valladolid in 1550–51, when a debate authorized by Charles V took place between the distinguished theologian Juan Ginés de Sepúlveda and Bartolomé de Las Casas. Sepúlveda, appealing to Aristotle, maintained that the Indians were all natural slaves, culturally inferior to Spaniards, and their need of 'tuition' justified war against them; furthermore, their 'unnatural' crimes such as cannibalism deprived them of their rights of dominion and freedom; finally, he argued, the papal donation was a valid charter for Spanish conquests.[13]

Las Casas appealed to Scripture to deny the justice of war against the Indians, who could be converted by peaceful means. Although war was commanded by God against certain nations, this was not against idolaters in general but only against the Canaanites and other tribes; he denied the rudeness of the Indians' nature and produced abundant evidence to prove his statement. Peaceful conversion was the best approach, as proved by the Dominican success in Vera Paz. Of two evils it was always better to choose the lesser: human sacrifice was a lesser evil than indiscriminate warfare. Las Casas and his allies, however, were lone voices. Franciscan opinion tended towards peaceful evangelization devoid of conquerors but protected by escorts and *presidios* (garrisons), and once missionaries were admitted they could be accompanied by colonists. Royal policy still admitted the possibility of force and conquest, and missionaries were authorized to enter 'with armed force ready to overcome those who resist them'.[14]

As for Las Casas, he resigned the bishopric of Chiapas in 1550 and in 1551 took up residence in the Dominican College of San Gregorio, Valladolid, where he continued to be the spokesman for Indian interests and Dominican missions in Mexico and Guatemala, acting as defender and historian and exhorting his fellow Dominicans to stand firm at a time when their solidarity on justice for the Indians seemed to be weakening. In Seville in 1552–53 he assembled and published eight tracts from his previous works, and in 1554–63, now in his eighties, he completed research on two major works, *Historia de las Indias*, written in the conviction that God might punish Spain for misdeeds in America, and *Apologética Historia*, a vast compilation of data designed to prove that the Indians were rational; they compared favourably with the peoples of ancient history and were hardly inferior to Spaniards.[15] And he undertook yet another cause, lobbying, with some success, Prince Philip, who was then in England, against the Peruvian *encomenderos* who were campaigning hard for perpetuity. In his *Twelve Doubts*, written at the age of 90, he opened with a scathing review of the Spanish conquest and exploitation of Peru, and posed a series of questions on the restitution of wealth thus obtained.[16] He resolved all these doubts by insisting on restitution, even by the crown.

Indian converts were not the only Christians in Spanish America. As mestization increased and other variations of race mixture made their appearance, so Christian society became more complex. Spanish America was being transformed by social change. By 1600 the first generation of American-born Spaniards had taken root and occupied dominant positions as landowners, manufacturers, merchants, and capitalists. Spanish American whites now called themselves *criollos* and were conscious of a difference between themselves and *peninsulares*; they displayed some aversion to Spanish immigrants and began to demand access to office. These attitudes were mirrored in the ranks of the clergy and religious orders, and there was sometimes resentment when it was thought that priests and friars from Spain were being promoted ahead of creole clergy to cathedral chapters and offices in the religious orders.

Yet the American Church was now a multiracial Church, and as bishops looked out from their palaces and priests from their pulpits they saw a faithful composed not even mainly of pure whites, but of mestizos, mulattos, zambos (black-Indian mixture), and other racial groups. These were treated not as people of the mission but as parishioners who were expected to conform to the normal doctrines, rituals, and liturgies of the universal Church, attend Sunday mass, obey the commandments, receive the sacraments, and pay their dues. This did not prevent the development of a *criollo* religiosity or American styles of worship. Popular devotions could be seen at many local shrines and images, sometimes situated at the site of a vision, sometimes the favourites of particular social groups; such was the Lord of the Miracles in Lima, carried in procession and favoured by the blacks and the poor. In Mexico devotion to Our Lady of Guadalupe, founded on the tradition that in 1531 Mary appeared to a poor Indian named Juan Diego, whose cape received an imprint of her image, outgrew a local cult to become a great national symbol and focus of Mexican identity.[17]

Idolatry Campaigns

Churchmen differed on the sincerity of Indian conversion. In Mexico chroniclers, priests, and other observers were impressed by the Catholic devotion of the Mexican Indians, their respect for the sacraments, and their love of processions, oratories, shrines, and pious objects. The legacy of the early missionaries and subsequent parish priests bore fruit in the numerous confraternities and religious feasts of the Indians. In the late seventeenth century Fray Agustín de Vetancourt, a parish priest of the Indians for forty years, spoke of long and pious processions of his Indians with their crosses and images, vivid enactments of Holy Week and the resurrection.

Yet indigenous religious beliefs and practices lived on. To what extent? Hernando Ruiz de Alarcón, a rural priest who knew Nahuatl, investigated idolatry in the Taxco-Cuernavaca area in the early seventeenth century and wrote a treatise on the subject, *Tratado de las supersticiones . . . que oy viven entre los Indios naturales* (1629), citing incantations and specific cases of idolatry.[18] Alarcón does not claim that he uncovered any disbelief in Christianity, suggesting that this was a cultural, not a religious, phenomenon. Pre-conquest ritual and vocabulary were simply used in non-religious aspects of daily life, concerned with production and health, reinforcing Christian forms rather than replacing them. And he does not claim that the practices were universal, but rather that they predominated in the hills and thinly populated areas remote from the main centres of Hispanic population.

Reports from other parts of Spanish America were not so promising. Among the apparently converted Indians in Maní in Yucatán, the heartland of the Franciscan missions, idols were discovered in a cave in May 1562. Some forty local Indians freely confessed to ownership of the objects, which were regarded as propitious for rain and crops, and claimed that others too worshipped idols. So the Franciscans rounded them up, tortured them by *garrucha* (hoist), and collected more idols. The use of torture by unauthorized religious was illegal, as were lashing, fining, and jailing without proper trial. Then Diego de Landa intervened and his name became a byword for cruelty and repression. He increased the rate of mass arrests and indiscriminate torture. After sentence the Indian penitents were tied to the whipping post for the prescribed number of lashes, and it was reported that their bodies were so torn by the preliminary tortures that 'there was no sound part on which they could be flogged'.[19]

More than 4,500 Indians were tortured during three months of this inquisition, a veritable reign of terror, and an official inquiry later established that 158 died during or as a direct result of the interrogation. At least thirteen committed suicide to escape torture and many were left crippled. The idols and the jewelled skulls of their ancestors were burned at the command of the Spanish friars. This signalled the end of the old rites and the definite beginning of the new religion. Landa claimed that it was an episcopal inquisition and therefore legitimate, but legal norms and procedures were not followed, simply invented. 'The unashamed violence of the Franciscan inquisition', concludes a modern historian, 'is at once the best evidence for the political domination they [the Franciscans] had achieved in the peninsula, their anger at Indian betrayal, and their sense of the desperate urgency of the situation.'[20] Landa later justified the emergency measures, stating that 'meanwhile they would all become idolaters and go to hell'.

Yucatán was not well evangelized. The Franciscan friars monopolized power and there was no competition from other orders. This was the real problem, not idolatry. Very few friars were proficient in Mayan, or moved outside the main centres of Spanish population. Landa went for powerful statements; he built a magnificent monastery at Izamal, which Bishop Toral describes as 'a splendid thing to see and a scandal to permit, and that certainly St Francis would condemn', especially as it would house at the most one or two friars.[21]

As for the Mayas, they had mixed views of Christianity: 'the descendants of the former rulers are brought to misery; we are christianised, while they treat us like animals'.[22] The prevailing mood was one of passivity and acceptance of fate. The Spaniards saw the Mayas as recalcitrant. A seventeenth-century cleric lamented the sullen unwillingness of the Yucatán Maya to learn the basic doctrines of Christianity. Despite being flogged into church for weekly instruction, examined in doctrine at marriage, and attending at yearly confession for generations, 'they have little affection for the Church, or for mass and the holy sacrifice'. In Yucatán there was virtually no sign of the usual accompaniments of popular piety – the rosaries, shrines, and images so abundant in Mexico. Yet they lavished care on their village churches, keeping them filled with flowers, and sang the hymns in their own tongues.[23]

The highlight of the campaign in Maní, 12 July 1562, was a living theatre of processing friars, Indian penitents, Spanish officials, and piles of idols and skulls for burning. Sentences were pronounced and immediately executed: up to 200 lashes, even for one who had simply failed to denounce his father. The Indians became terrified of Landa, and of other Franciscans, for Landa was not alone in the persecution. Villages fled before the arrival of the friars and looked to the *encomenderos*, who now, in an ironic reversal of roles, were seen as protectors, forced to intervene by the very violence of the tortures they witnessed: the hoist, worsened by weights, water torture, and other cruelties, some of them abhorrent even to hardened colonists. Many Indians hastily confessed to non-existent idolatry to stop the torture, though they were then forced to find and produce the evidence, and further tortured if they failed.

Secular officials from Mérida town council urged Landa to desist, but he was utterly intransigent and declared that idolatry would continue to be dealt with rigorously. Landa's final triumph came when he 'discovered' that some Indians of Sotuta province with the authority of their chiefs had returned to the Maya practice of human sacrifice and ritual killing of victims inside the village church. These were usually children stolen from other villages; and some victims were subject to crucifixion before having their hearts cut out.[24] Such was Landa's proud justification of his campaign, atrocities to punish atrocities. At this point a new bishop, Francisco de Toral, himself a Franciscan, arrived to establish reason and order.

Toral reached Mérida in August 1562; he promptly forbade any further use of torture and began to free imprisoned Indians. He was sceptical of the campaign and suspicious of Landa and his friars. He ordered new investigations, free of torture, and these convinced him that the Indians had been guilty of no more than trivial idolatries, the result of poor teaching, and had been victims of Landa's cruelties and anger. Landa's friars were also blamed, though less than their leader. They too were intransigent; they rallied round Landa and refused to collaborate with Toral. Friars who believed in mass baptism and saw conversion as a collective action could easily believe in mass defection and reversion to Maya rites. But the charge of human sacrifice had not been proved, and even the idolatry was exaggerated. Gradually the balance moved in the bishop's favour.

Landa was forced to retreat and return to Spain to protect his position and defend himself before the Council of the Indies. There followed a long battle of wits, as well as lobbies, though a group of Maya Indian chiefs – 'we who are the chiefs of the land who did not have to write lies' – regarded Landa as the main author of their miseries: 'may he and his companions suffer penance for the evil they have done us'.[25] But Landa was exonerated and his actions justified by a committee weighted in his favour. It was Bishop Toral who was blamed, while Landa returned to Yucatán as a bishop in 1573 with thirty hand-picked friars to restore the shattered mission. Spanish justice on display. He no longer received the same deference there, and when he attempted to start a punitive process against alleged backsliding of Indians in Campeche he was stopped in his tracks by the combined action of Indian and secular authorities.

Landa came to believe that the Indians had systematically deceived him and the friars; outwardly Christians, taught by friars who had learnt their languages, they remained secretly attached to their ancient beliefs and rites. He had finally come to realize, he said, that only through punishment could such a people be improved. He still believed in his campaign and its success in stopping idolatry and inducing repentance. It was a brief respite. In 1603 a Yucatán-born secular cleric claimed to see evidence of organized, deliberate idolatry. Second-generation Christians, he said, pursued their old rituals under cover of night, or even vanished into the bush for 'three or four weeks at a time', drinking *balche*, feasting, adoring their idols, chanting their histories, often in hidden caves.[26] The so-called 'idolatry' confessions, with accounts of ritual killing of animals, and the offering of food and drink to old idols often in Christian churches, were freely confessed by Indians before they were even threatened with torture. Care was taken to conceal these ceremonies from Spaniards, but the offenders felt secure with other Indians.

The dilemma of persuasion or extirpation was also an issue in Peru. Evangelization had followed an orthodox pattern: friars and Jesuits preached, dioceses were founded, archbishops appointed, and Indian parishes, or *doctrinas*, established. So the Indians embraced the faith, learning the catechism (soon published in Quechua and Aymara as well as Spanish), attending mass, and incorporating too some of their ancient beliefs. The Spaniards were not immediately aware of the depth of Indian religion and they mistook the conversions they saw among the aristocracy for the whole of Andean religion, overlooking the endurance of popular beliefs. They observed idolatry as nothing more than worship of the sun, the cult of the *huacas*, and respect for sacred mummies. But these were survivals of the aristocratic and official rites of the Incas, not the popular manifestations of indigenous religions. Successive church councils in Lima, in 1537, 1551, and 1567, sought to establish the norms of the Council of Trent in faith and morals and Church organization. The Council held in Lima in 1551 in effect passed a retrospective sentence of collective damnation on all Indians who had inhabited Peru prior to the Spaniards, based on the teaching frequently invoked in contemporary sermons that the practice of idolatry inevitably entailed hellfire. The Third Council of Lima convoked by the saintly Archbishop Toribio Alfonso de Mogrovejo in 1582, whose sensitive approach to Indian culture contrasted with the harder line of the Jesuit Acosta, was more persuasive in facilitating Indian practice of religion, including reception of the sacraments, and took steps to publish religious material in Quechua and Aymara.

A different take on Inca history was presented by the Indian chronicler, Felipe Guaman Poma de Ayala. His *Nueva Crónica* describes the Spanish age as a world *al revés*, a world turned upside down, in contrast to the pure religion of Inca times which, apart from idolatry, expressed a kind of natural Christianity in which the Indians observed God's commandments and practised works of mercy. 'Oh what good people!' he sighs. 'Notice this, Christian readers, the goodness of these new people, and learn from them about the true faith and service of God and the Holy Trinity.' Conquest was followed by exploitation at the hands of priests as well as officials. Guaman described the poor Indian devoured by six animals representing his oppressors: a serpent (the *corregidor*), a jaguar (the Spaniard), a lion (the *encomendero*), a fox (the priest), a cat (the lawyer), and a rat (the cacique), a united ruling class seeking to exploit him, to demand his labour, seize his women, rob him of the little he had. Many Indians, it is true, have been corrupted by the conquest, Guaman wrote. Guaman acknowledges this as he sees men abandoning their family and lands, dressing like Spaniards to serve the new rulers, the women seduced by Spaniards and Africans, breeding a new race of mestizos, all sectors losing their former deference to law and order. 'God sends his punishment to every man and house in the world . . . And there is no remedy.'[27]

In a letter to Philip III Guaman advocates a return to the laws and practices of the past, restricting Spaniards to towns and leaving Indians to the government of their lords. The Indian elite would have a role as mediators between Spaniards and natives. From the Indians too priests should be recruited, so that they could teach Christianity in a form understandable by the common people. The restitution of ancestral hierarchy would enable Indians to recover former virtues of obedience and social cooperation. In Guaman's new history Christian revelation is seen to supplement a natural morality known to the Indians but now corrupted by the Spaniards. There is a further conclusion to draw from this thesis: culture and religion can be separate, and a convert does not have to abandon Andean tradition.

The approach to evangelization differed between different clergy. Secular officials were also interested, because Indian resistance to Christianity implied resistance to the colonial state. Juan Polo de Ondegardo, *corregidor* of Cuzco, an expert in locating and destroying *huacas* and holy places, was the author of a treatise *Los errores y supersticiones de los indios* (1559), used by the bishops in the Second and Third Councils of Lima to formulate decrees dealing with Indian parishes. In 1566 Polo clashed with Domingo de Santo Tomás, bishop of Cuzco. A number of baptized Indians had gathered to listen to Polo speaking on the subject of idolatrous worship, in the presence of Fray Domingo: 'Polo spoke to the Indians in the presence of their bishop and made them confess that they possessed the *huacas* he named to them and told them how bad it was . . . And they answered that no one had ever informed them that it was bad.'[28] Fray Domingo did not address the Indians in the absolutist terms Polo used; he had a more lenient approach to idolatry, not out of negligence, but from a conviction similar to that of Las Casas, that conversion to Christianity was a gradual and voluntary process.[29] And the new archbishop of Lima, Toribio de Mogrovejo, a hands-on evangelist eventually canonized by the Church, urged the use of Indian languages in the *doctrinas* and greater respect for Indian cultures.

Extirpation of idolatry came in waves, usually dependent on the enthusiasm of the religious and civil authorities and sometimes of individual priests. There was a division within ecclesiastical opinion in Peru on the extent of idolatry and its treatment.[30] The majority argued for a more restricted interpretation of idolatry and against heresy hunts, and imputed self-interest and power-seeking to the extirpators. The latter followed a Spanish tradition in treating witchcraft – in Peru sorcery – as a fraud, not as heresy. This was another form of attack, for it greatly devalued the role and power of the Indian religious specialist. In Peru there were campaigns of extirpation from 1607 when Francisco de Avila began investigating cults, myths, and *huacas* in his parish of San Damián in Huarochiri. In December 1609 he displayed his discoveries in Lima and began an

Inquisition-like procedure. The confiscated *huacas*, along with a large collection of ancestral mummies taken from their burial places, were piled up in the Plaza de Armas. In the presence of the viceroy, city dignitaries, and a crowd of people, Avila preached in Quechua against idolatry, and then the mummies, *huacas* and other confiscated objects were put to the flames. As a bonus the Andean religious enthusiast, Hernando Paucar, 'a great teacher of idolatry' according to Avila, was tied to a stake, whipped, and exiled to Chile. In the course of the seventeenth century similar rituals of destruction and punishment, sponsored by the archbishop, were enacted not only in Lima but in many Andean towns and villages, evidence not of serious idolatry but of cultural survival of an Inca past.

Guaman Poma witnessed the early age of evangelization, when the Gospel was preached to all peoples, succeeded by the age of extirpation, which sought to destroy all traces of non-Christian culture and when true preachers were succeeded by professional destroyers. He had been tolerant of the first extirpations, for he viewed the Spanish invasion of Peru as a restoration of true religion preached long before the advent of the apostle Bartholomew and distorted by Inca impositions. But as an old man forty years later he had nothing but contempt for the new wave of extirpation conducted by Avila who used this as an opportunity to confiscate Indian property, enrich corrupt officials, and displace the Andean aristocracy. And it was impossible to prove innocence, for 'the good doctor Avila' would confiscate as evidence of idolatry articles of adornment Andeans customarily wore and ceremonial vessels they used when celebrating traditional Quechua festivals. The pastors had abandoned their sheep when they were most needed, protested Guaman. 'Where are you now, God of heaven? Where is your servant his holiness the pope? Where are you, Our Lord?'[31] The interpretation of Guaman Poma was not so bizarre, for it maintained in effect that extirpation did not distinguish between culture and religion, a valid distinction which Church and state failed to understand. Extirpation, moreover, moved the Church closer to secular authority, for it would have been impossible to apply without the support of the colonial state.

There were rival factions within Indian communities: those gathered round the Catholic priest, the nativist group looking to the shaman, and the *kuraka* and his allies. Each of these used the idolatry trials to advance their own intrests.[32] Indians learnt how to manipulate the trials to settle community disputes, or to remove an unpopular *kuraka*. So Indian religion adapted itself and survived the anti-idolatry campaigns, preserving its popular manifestations of processions, reverence for Christ, the Virgin, and the saints, accompanied by drinking and exuberance, and pilgrimages to favourite shines such as that of Our Lady of Copacabana at Lake

Titicaca. As against those historians who argue for a distinct survival of Andean religion, there is another interpretation:

> A simple and strict adhesion to traditional Andean practices and worship – however transformed – was impossible for most Indian people, even if it had been the desired option. Some small groups and isolated individuals seem to have fled to the pumas and remote ravines in an effort to live virtually undisturbed by Spanish demands, but for the vast majority of Indians in the mid-colonial Lima region membership and participation in a Catholic parish was both presumed and accepted. No matter what hesitation they felt, no matter what reconciliations they had made between the Andean and Christian belief systems, most people heard mass, attended doctrine classes, and observed at least the basic sacraments.[33]

Inquisition

In 1509 a royal decree issued to Diego Colón, governor of Hispaniola, ordered that to preserve the Catholic faith 'Moors, heretics, Jews, and *conversos*' would not be admitted to the Indies. The policy was frequently renewed, and among the qualifications for emigration to the Indies was proof of being 'old Christian'. At first orthodoxy and heresy were in the hands of the provincials of religious orders and later those of the bishop. These 'apostolic inquisitors' heard cases arising from infringements of public morality, such as blasphemy, bigamy, and concubinage. The Inquisition in Spain targeted *conversos*, that is Jews who had converted to Christianity and were suspect as Judaizers, but not Jews as such. Similarly, in America, Christianized Indians who lapsed were regarded as guilty. A number of trials of Indian converts who had lapsed into idolatry were held, the most notorious being that ordered by Juan de Zumárraga, bishop of Mexico; this was the trial of the cacique Carlos de Texaco, who was condemned for heresy, 'relaxed' to the secular arm and burned at the stake in 1539. The severity of the punishment earned Zumárraga a rebuke from the crown and later influenced the decision of the Spanish government to exclude recently converted Indians from the jurisdiction of the Inquisition.

A primitive inquisition operated in Mexico in the period 1522–71, first under friar inquisitors then under episcopal jurisdiction. A number of heresy cases were heard: two alleged Judaizers were burned at the stake in Mexico in 1528 and in the 1560s there were cases against English, French, and Dutch Protestants. In Yucatán the monastic inquisition continued to operate outside the jurisdiction of Mexico City in the 1560s. Following the decree of Philip II in 1569, the Tribunal of the Holy Office of the

Inquisition began to function in Lima in 1570 and in Mexico in 1571, and a third tribunal was established in Cartagena in 1610. So the direction and pursuit of heresy and deviant behaviour was taken out of the hands of the bishops and diocesan inquisitors and given to the new Office of the Inquisition in 1570. This represented a shift of ecclesiastical authority towards the crown, taking from bishops one of the powers traditionally identified with their office; it represented too the centralization and consolidation of civil and religious authority. Indians were specifically excluded from this jurisdiction; it was only to be used against old Christians and their descendants. The tribunals heard evidence and deliberated in secret, the accused was unable to confront his accusers, and sentences varied in severity.

Portuguese *conversos*, whose commercial activities in Spanish America were more or less tolerated by the authorities, though not by the Spanish monopolists, drew the hostility of the Inquisition of Lima, which was served by *familiares*, spies and agents of the tribunal in the Spanish *consulado* (merchant guild). The Inquisition began to strike at the Portuguese and prosecuted them ever more severely from 1600, culminating in a campaign comparable to that against the *conversos* in Spain. In 1634, to break up an alleged crypto-Jewish conspiracy, it rounded up numerous Portuguese Jews in Lima and Cartagena who were involved in the slave trade and in the mining, Atlantic and Pacific trades, and subjected them to trial, resulting in large confiscations of silver and money. From then until 1640 the Portuguese were harassed on all sides, burned at the stake, imprisoned, fined, and stripped of their property. Meanwhile in Mexico too the Inquisition had been pressing on the Portuguese since the 1620s. From 1642 the Mexican Inquisition carried out a series of autos-da-fé culminating in the large ceremony of 11 April 1649 at which there were 109 penitents, all but one of whom were convicted of Judaizing, and thirteen of whom were executed. 'Relaxation' to the secular arm usually meant the death penalty by burning at the stake. Under the Lima tribunal 28 out of 650 cases in the period 1600–1700 resulted in execution.

Francisco de la Cruz, a Dominican in Peru, claimed to have received communications direct from God through the medium of a mestiza, María Pizarro, who believed herself to be an angel. Cruz had a large following. His vision of a new Church, including marriage for priests and polygamy for the laity, seemed to raise the spectre of the *alumbrados* (Spanish illuminists) as well as threatening the critical relations between the Church, the colonists, and the crown. For Cruz not only taught that his New World Church was to replace the old and corrupt Church in Europe, but advocated that the Indians, who were to be the instruments of the coming metropolis, should be kept in perpetual *encomienda*. This support for an institution that both the crown and the Church regarded as a threat to their authority was of course welcomed by the colonists themselves. So Cruz was both a heretic and a political menace. After a lengthy and public trial he was condemned together with a number of his associates and burned at the stake in 1578.[34]

Indians were exempt from the jurisdiction of the Inquisition but not from religious investigation. There was an office of *provisor*, a diocesan official under the bishop who investigated crimes against the faith by Indians throughout the colonial regime. The procedure was not unlike that of the Inquisition on which it was based and worked in parallel, giving rise to some conflicts of jurisdiction. So the faith and the morals of Indians were kept under scrutiny, though application of its rules was patchy. In fact the great majority of colonial Mexicans never had any contact with the Inquisition. The small minority charged never came to trial, because of insufficient evidence, and there were few convictions and even fewer executions.[35] The *procesos* reveal recourse to idolatry, sorcery, and sacrifice within a political context of native resistance to Spanish power. In general the Indians sought to manipulate inquisitorial procedures by denouncing Spanish-appointed caciques as idolaters in order to deprive them of office. There were also denunciations for idolatry and human sacrifice by Indians who wanted to attack their own rivals for power, hoping to replace them in the new political hierarchy. There were further issues. Indian sorcerers, curers, witches, and seers, who tried to perpetuate the old beliefs, some of whom established schools among the young and openly attacked Spanish religion and culture, were regarded as subversive of Church and state. Moreover, they supported concubinage and bigamy as symbols of resistance to the new religion. So intolerance was a product of many factors and not only or even mainly of religion.

The Indian concept of the devil caught the attention of Spanish Inquisitors,[36] who tended to use the devil as a convenient explanation for everything negative in Indian religion. The Indians, however, at first used their own idea of the devil to resist the new religion, to counteract Christianity, and to propitiate their own deities, and it was only gradually used to resist evil by orthodox Christian means. Among the non-Indian popular sectors, the mestizos, mulattos, and poor Spaniards of colonial society, the devil was also well known, and the use of demonic pacts and invocations by peasants, artisans, and slaves was always of interest to Inquisitors, though the motivation of these groups appears to have been one of protest against injustice and oppression at the hands of Christians. It was only gradually, in the eighteenth century, that the Mexican Inquisition became sceptical about demoniacs and their spiritual advisers.

The Jesuit Way

Jesuit colonization in Paraguay and Moxos stood aside from the Spanish colonial state and its Church ally, and this was deliberate. Yet the Jesuits could never totally isolate their missions from the corruption of the secular world and the perils of outside pressure, particularly the demands of the Spanish settlers for Indian territory and labour, and the advancing Portuguese presence from Brazil. Their mission system signified the inter-action of two imperatives: the conversion of the Indians and the creation of a new socio-economic environment based on Iberian models. As the Indians saw it, these missions gave them specific benefits, mainly regular deliveries of tools and hardware and the opportunities offered by new social and political structures; these inducements encouraged the Indians to abandon their tropical forest culture and enter mission territory.

The Jesuits followed the other missionary orders into Spanish America. Lima received its first Jesuits in 1568, thirty years after the arrival of the Dominicans, the Franciscans, and the Augustinians. As a latecomer, the Society sought areas abandoned or unclaimed by the other orders, and followed a route southwards from Lima, establishing colleges in Cuzco (1571), Potosí (1576), La Paz (1580), and eventually a residence in Santa Cruz de la Sierra (1587) on the south-eastern frontier of Peru. They expanded rapidly, and from the end of the sixteenth century until the expulsion of the Society in 1767 they had between 450 and 520 members in Peru.[37] From Peru the Jesuits accompanied conquest bands into Moxos from the 1590s and by the mid-seventeenth century they had independent contact with the Moxo Indians.[38]

The Jesuits were resourceful. They entered Moxos, as they reported, 'without arms or soldiers, accompanied only by some Christian Indians (our guides and interpeters)'.[39] A missionary would approach an Indian village and leave useful goods at strategic points or capture a stray Indian, treat him well, and send him back. They then moved into a Moxo village themselves, learning the language, trading goods, and demonstrating through a non-violent European presence that they were the only alterna-tive to slavers. If the Indians responded peacefully, the next stage was to group them into reductions, the ideal Jesuit solution, providing for their material needs by introducing more plants and cattle, educating them in European arts and crafts, and forming a unit that could be controlled and protected. After the initial evangelization mission stations settled into a parish-style existence, with a church and school, which combined religious instruction (in catechism form) with reading, writing, and arithmetic. Teaching was in the native vernacular, though some of the Indian elite learnt Spanish. Under Jesuit tutelage Indian neophytes developed the ability to deal with the world outside the missions. A Jesuit correspondent reported his astonishment, 'that in the space of but one year a savage race of men, who had scarce anything human about them but the name and shape, should yet have imbibed sentiments of good nature and piety ... with the grace of God, we shall make of this people not only a Church of true Christians but likewise a city and perhaps a kingdom of men, who may live together agreeably to the most perfect laws of society'.[40]

An essential condition was to preserve their villages from outside intervention. But the Jesuits had to modify this model in response to Indian reactions and in the course of the eighteenth century to incorporate Indian culture into their system. It was also a struggle to preserve the missions from the corrupting influences of the secular world. The expansion of the Portuguese empire posed a particular threat to the Jesuit missions, which were in fact the frontiers of the Spanish empire. The traditional slave-hunting expeditions of the *bandeirantes* from São Paulo intensified in the eighteenth century when Brazilian gold mines raised the demand for slave labour. This was in addition to the Spanish pressure on land and labour, though the Jesuits obtained a royal decree expressly forbidding all Spaniards from coming into the missions or having the least correspondence with the Indians belonging to it. 'This is the New World,' commented a Jesuit from eastern Europe: 'the Indians who had previously stagnated as imbeciles, were converting into human beings and Christians; while, what is even more novel, white men, often of European descent, have become wild beasts and imbeciles.'[41]

Meanwhile, from 1607 the Jesuits founded missionary villages in the territory of Misiones along the rivers Paraguay, Paraná and Upper Uruguay, and by 1739 there were thirty of these – the famous Jesuit reductions of Paraguay, among them Santa María, San Ignacio, and the magnificent Trinidad, the ruins of its church and the beauty of its carvings still fascinating. In little more than 150 years the Jesuits, negotiating their way through tribal rivalries and warrior suspicions, and moving away from areas vulnerable to the infamous *bandeirantes*, gradually extended their sphere of influence over the tribes of the Upper Amazon, eastern Bolivia, Chiquitos, the Chaco, Paraguay, and the Pampas. The most favourable subjects of Jesuit government were the Guaraní Indians of the middle and upper Paraguay and Uruguay rivers.[42]

The thirty missions established in this area were characterized by a high degree of collectivism and a unique political position, based on exchange of benefits. The Guaraní wanted protection from the *paulistas*, the Portuguese slave hunters from Brazil, and from the labour demands of the Spanish settlers. The Jesuits were able to reject the colonists' demands for Indian labour, and the communities comprised a kind of frontier garrison at the disposal of the Spanish authorities as laid down in the regulations of 1649, in return for which their freedom from *encomienda* was confirmed and a decrease in tribute conceded.[43] A basic condition of the whole system was isolation of the Indians from contact with any whites except the Jesuit fathers themselves, who as well as protectors were providers, distributing gifts of tools, cutlery, and clothes. The Jesuits too wanted benefits. They were driven first by their commitment to evangelization of the New World. Second, they believed in their European way of life as a superior model and expected conversion to affect behaviour and lifestyle and bring their Indians to a higher civilization. Finally, in the background was the Spanish government which saw that an important space was now occupied by new subjects and a vulnerable frontier sealed, and which came to regard the Guaranís as the 'Guardians of the Frontier'.[44] The Jesuit response to these challenges was to arm their neophytes and create a native militia. This was also the Indians' ambition. The Guaraní army thus became an integral part of the reductions. Father Bernardo Nusdorffer, the provincial, ordered in 1747 that 'every Sunday the exercise of arms will take place without exception, so that the Indians become proficient in using rifles and bow and arrow, in order that they can defend their lands, their wives, and children'.[45]

The value of the Jesuit experiment has been extensively debated. A leading historian concludes: 'It is probable that the Guaranís in the reductions at least enjoyed much better material conditions after the initial period of adaptation . . . than if they had been left to their own resources.'[46] The communism of the Guaraní reductions is a myth. The Jesuits strove to develop a sense of individual property among the Indians by encouraging them to plan a surplus trade with the Spanish towns and by giving them cattle to build up herds of their own.[47] Mission leadership was cosmopolitan. The national origins of the Jesuits in the Americas show a mixture of Spaniards, Europeans, and creoles. In Paraguay there were few local creoles among mission priests. The reason for this was that the small white population in Paraguay waged continuous battles with the Jesuits over Indian labour and political influence, making local creoles unlikely recruits for the order. In Moxos, however, in the eighteenth century, 39 per cent of the Jesuits were Spaniards, 35 per cent creoles, and 24 per cent non-Spanish Europeans, most of them Italians and Germans, but also including Hungarians, French, Flemings, Belgians, and one Irish.[48]

There was a dualism in Jesuit thought. On the one hand it reflected a utopian view of primitive man, focusing on the purity of the Indian and his environment. The eighteenth-century missionary, Alonso Messia, represented this trend in describing Indian worship in the Moxos mission stations, free of European folk accretions. To his mind, the primitive conditions in Moxos had purified Catholic religion of many of its secular additions.[49] But a second trend, based on experience and observation, can be seen in the writings of José de Acosta, distinguished theologian and missionary. His *De procuranda indorum salute* (1576) divides infidels of the world into three types: Chinese and Japanese, who had cities, laws, and books; Aztecs and Incas who manifested some facets of culture but lacked books; and people who lacked all institutions and whom he describes as 'scarcely human'.[50] The last group, which included many South American tribes, were to be treated as children and converted by the application of inducement and force in equal measure.

Francisco Javier Eder, a Jesuit from Central Europe, described the Baure mission stations in the mid-eighteenth century in a chronicle which follows the second tradition, characterizing the native people as capricious, vindictive, and only superficially converted to Christianity a century after the beginning of missions in Moxos. He concluded his answers to those who criticized the Jesuit regime as paternal by asking rhetorically, 'Who in the world could be more childish than these people? What do they most deserve: pity, anger? Or rather, an indulgent smile?'[51] He regarded the Indians as unfit for the office of judge because of their character and temperament. Spaniards were even less qualified and in any case they would not be obeyed. The Jesuits were the only possible candidates for office. The Indians were utterly addicted to drink, slaves of chichi. They were 'prone to sensuality', getting their lasciviousness from their parents, and this was why the missionaries encouraged them to marry so young; 'and even so we rarely succeed in getting the girls to their nuptials as virgins'.[52] Yet the women were superior to the men in their innocence and sincerity of spirit. The Mojos Indians found it impossible to understand celibacy and it became a daily subject of discussion among them. A man without a woman was beyond their experience and they could only assume that the Jesuit fathers were special beings, born of virgins, possessing a nature that they themselves could not attain. Eder regarded this as an important asset of the Jesuits and a valuable, if involuntary, missionary strategy. Eder himself had an asset – a sense of humour.

The Jesuits established a form of self-government in their Paraguayan and Moxos missions based on a European model. In Paraguay there was a *corregidor*, and there were councillors and traditional *cabildo* (municipal) officials, appointed, according to some chroniclers, elected according to others. These officials were drawn from the caciques and Indian elite groups, so previous leaders continued to hold political power and organized work in the fields and workshops, supervised communal services, and enforced local laws. The Jesuits were reputed to be authoritarian and to make themselves absolute. But as in any society someone had to be responsible for law and order, and their jurisdiction, in which they acted as judges as well as priests, was confined to traditional punishments: prison, whipping, and banishment.

Indian workers produced, for export throughout the region, as well as for subsistence, wax, textiles, cacao, sugar and rice. But the economic base of the reductions was yerba maté and cattle. 'Jesuit tea' was exported to the Río de la Plata, Peru, and Chile, and it became a popular drink, reported to have a calming and beneficial effect. Distribution and sale were controlled by the Jesuits and this was a source of controversy, with allegations of price-fixing and profiteering. Cattle and their products gave the Guaranís a secure supply of food and drink and an income from the sale of hides. The Indians also had a distinct capacity for artisan work, and if they were not themselves inventive they had an excellent memory, could copy any art, sculpture, woodwork, ironwork, textiles and musical instruments, which they could make in European style and play perfectly.

On this distant frontier of the Spanish empire a mission culture took shape. Churches were built, houses, ranches, farms and light industries all made their appearance in a former wilderness, and behind them was a support network of funds and personnel, Jesuit superiors, colleges, and directors in South America and Europe. The native people preserved much of their autonomy. Traditional leaders retained their positions and expanded their functions, and the introduction of Spanish models of government actually enlarged the political elite and their experience.[53] In each village a cross was erected, a symbol of the new religion and a sign that this people was under the protection of the Spanish crown.[54]

Brazil: Between Europe and Africa

Antônio Vieira, celebrated Jesuit of the seventeenth century, regarded colonization as God's way of bringing the peoples of the world to knowledge of the true faith. According to this view, evangelization was impossible without colonization and each needed the other. Vieira described religious practice as 'enforced devotion'. The enforcement began on the exit from Portugal: only Catholics were allowed to emigrate and only Portuguese priests to preach the Gospel; these were carefully vetted, though a controlled number of foreign priests were allowed to volunteer for the Brazilian mission. Apart from doctrine, religious affairs were directed not by Rome but by the Portuguese crown, on whom bishops and clerical institutions depended. Orthodoxy was maintained by inquisitorial methods, though not by a formal Inquisition. Social services were an adjunct of religion, and the Santa Casa de Misericórdia, whose resources included buildings, plantations, and mills, and which operated in the principal towns, also managed a hospital, medical school, pharmacy, hostels for girls, and banking services.

Vieira argued strongly for the abolition of slavery in many of his writings, but the slavery he was thinking of was that of the Indian rather than the Negro. He regarded Negro slavery as the only way of maintaining the sugar economy of Brazil and the interests of his own Society. 'Brazil is sugar, and sugar is the black man,' he would say, and 'Brazil has its body in America and its soul in Africa'. In the ultimate analysis, for Vieira reason of state prevailed. Brazil could not survive without Negro slaves. He knew their sufferings, but he exhorted them to accept their destiny as their own Calvary.

The population of Brazil was concentrated in the narrow coastal strip where sugar plantations flourished, and life was spread between the Great House, the slave house, and the chapel. The African slaves learnt Christianity not so much from priests and catechisms, and much less from works of theology, all of which were in short supply on the plantations, but from instant exposure to the daily prayers and devotions celebrated in the chapel of the Great House. Europe and Africa met not only in the economic and social life of Brazil but also in the religious life, where the Portuguese model imposed by the plantation owner was translated by the slaves into prayers, saints, feasts, processions, pilgrimages, and other elements of popular religion. The framework was the plantation, not the conventional parish.

In 1707 the archbishop of Bahia sought to regulate the Christianity of the plantations by reminding priests and owners of their duty to evangelize the slaves, 'since the owners are obliged to teach Christian doctrine to servants and slaves, or have it taught'. Slaves had to be taught the basic elements of the catechism and to be urged to accept baptism and other sacraments:

> Since experience has revealed to us that among the many slaves who exist in this archbishopric there are many so coarse and rude that although their masters make every possible effort to reach them, they always seem to know less. While pitying them for their coarseness and misery, we grant permission to the vicars and curates to administer to them the sacraments of baptism, penance, extreme unction, and matrimony, it being apparent to them that, although the masters have been diligent in teaching them, the slaves are too coarse to learn.

The instruction encapsulates the assumptions of Brazilian Christianity; its acceptance of slavery, the dominant role of the master in the life of the slave, and his dependence on the master for religion as well as the basics of life and work.[55]

Yet this was an idealistic view of evangelization. The Jesuit André João Antonil in his work *Cultura e opulencia do Brasil por suas drogas e minas*

(1711) characterized the work of the priest on a sugar plantation as saying mass in the plantation chapel according to Christian doctrine, hearing confessions, settling disagreements, and honouring God and the Virgin in litanies and the rosary; and without living in the owner's house, he was to teach the owner's children. This was not the work of a parish priest, answerable to a diocesan bishop for the whole of his flock, but that of a chaplain serving the plantation and its owner.

The seven Jesuits who landed in Bahia in 1549 arrived with other priorities. Priests of a newly established order intent on saving souls for Christ and the Church, they soon identified the great evil in this plantation economy: the relation between master and slave. It was a cause of anxiety and discussion among them in the following decades, and they decided to organize a 'strike of the confessionals', refusing absolution to anyone who revealed in confession that they owned slaves. Opposed by the secular clergy and the bishop, the Jesuits tried to hold their ground, in effect challenging the whole Brazilian economy. The situation was intolerable to the Brazilian authorities in Church and state and an embarrassment to their own order. The Visitor sent by the order to Brazil wasted no time in putting a stop to the movement by ordering its leaders back to Portugal.[56]

Nevertheless, the religious life of the Brazilian blacks had some expression outside the plantation. Brotherhoods, or *irmandades*, whose main focus was devotion to saints in general or to particular saints and who won the approval of the Church authorities, also had a social dimension. Members, mainly free blacks or wage slaves with the means to support themselves, organized care for the sick and the poor, and developed a leisure life of their own. The Black Brotherhood of Our Lady of the Rosary in Recife had its own church, built and supported by its members, where the mass, the rosary, and traditional Catholic devotions were accompanied by dances and other entertainments, attesting to a community spirit among Brazilian blacks and providing a further expression of popular religion. But ordination to the priesthood was closed to blacks and mulattos. The Church and religious orders insisted on purity of blood for candidates to holy orders, and when mulattos sought admission to the Jesuit College in Bahia in order 'to improve the fortunes of their colour' they were refused.

Outside traditional and popular Catholicism some Brazilians practised the religion of their African forebears.[57] Different groups – the Bakongo from Angola and Congo, the Yoruba from Ghana, Togo, and Nigeria, the Dahomans – preserved a religious memory expressed in beliefs and rituals modified by their American experience. Religious beliefs involved the worship of gods and goddesses personifying natural phenomena, and the worship of family ancestors and rulers of African dynasties; rituals included elaborate funeral rites. These are sometimes described as a new meeting of

Africa and Europe, a syncretism of African and Catholic religions, but are properly defined as a distinct development with a character of its own, offshoots of Catholicism perhaps but not part of the Church. This eclectic religion contained some traditional Catholic practices, such as the rosary, but also African animism, a belief that objects carry mystical powers, divination and even in some cases a new messianism, with claims by some African leaders to be deities. African cults in Brazil were practised in secrecy and left few records. In the event they were not recognized as forms of Catholicism by the Church authorities. Nor were they approached with discretion. It was beyond the knowledge of Christian missionaries that Africa was humanity's birthplace and that spirituality first emerged from this continent. After Christianity, Islam, and Hinduism, African spirituality was the largest spiritual tradition in the world, and its message influenced African people's view of life, death, the cosmos, and the transcendent, before they met Christianity in Brazil. The first missionaries overlooked the Africans' existing spirituality. The converts' minds were seen as a *tabula rasa*, their culture was largely ignored, and when blacks and slaves persevered with their cultural and religious practices they were viewed as deviants or heretics, while public performance of African song and dance was strictly prohibited.

Slavery posed many problems for the Church and not all the answers were exemplary. The historian can begin by asking: why were masters not preferred as baptismal godparents? One answer points to the theological incompatibility between slavery and the sacraments. The master owns the body of the slave. Baptism makes a person a Christian, cleansed of original sin, and a member of the Church. The baptismal sponsor, the godparent, undertakes to protect, instruct, and help the godchild to save his soul, which implies a degree of equality between the two, impossible between master and slave. The problem was avoided by selecting a godparent other than the slave's master, and the slaves themselves usually chose a non-master.[58]

Brazil was Europe's main source of sugar and its plantations were supplied with labour from Africa. By the early seventeenth century Brazil had become a major market for black slaves, and Angola was its main supplier. The Jesuits in Luanda, therefore, were strategically placed to observe the presence of slave ships and the departure of their human cargoes. But they did not come out against the slave trade. They argued that if the authorities in Church and state allowed it, then it could be accepted in conscience, and in any case the capture of slaves was the capture of souls. If cruelty or injustice was involved in the actual capture, that was wrong, but how do you tell? The rector of the Jesuit College in Luanda, Luis Brandão, was asked by Alonso de Sandoval in Cartagena de

Indias if the slaves he had seen in Brazil had been legally captured or not. He replied: 'to seek among the ten or twelve thousand Negroes who leave this port every year some who have been captured illegally is impossible, no matter how diligently it is done. And to lose so many souls that are saved among the many captured legally, in order to rescue an unknown number who have been taken illegally, hardly seems to be in the service of God.'[59] A devious answer, leaving a larger question unanswered. Was the Church's record on slavery one of service to God?

The Church and Slavery

There were blacks in Spain from at least the early fifteenth century, increasing through capture, trade, and the use of slaves. Some of these went to Spanish America with their masters or as auxiliaries of the conquest. They were followed by blacks taken there in the slave trade from Africa for use as manpower, first under individual licences from 1493 to 1595, then under *asientos*, or monopoly contracts, from 1595 to 1789, and finally in a free slave trade until 1812. The main ports of entry were Cartagena, Portobelo, Veracruz, and Buenos Aires, and some 10 million were taken from Africa to the Americas in the whole of this period, 4 million to Brazil.

Theologians were divided on slavery.[60] Some, such as Juan Ginés de Sepúlveda, followed the Aristotelian doctrine that certain peoples (Indians and Negroes) were slaves by nature. Others saw in Negro slavery a providential protection of American Indians. Yet others, such as Domingo de Soto and Francisco de Vitoria, following the law of nations, allowed slavery caused by purchase, just war, punishment for certain crimes, commutation of the death penalty, and sale by parents in case of extreme need. But manumission was recommended by Soto for conscience's sake. Fray Tomás de Mercado, a Dominican with American experience, argued in his *Suma de trato y contrato* (1587) that although the slave trade was allowed by the law of nations and by national laws, it was – by the evidence of the facts – illicit and the cause of mortal sin. Fray Alonso de Montufar, bishop of Mexico, wrote in 1560 to Philip II that it was a contradiction to maintain African slavery, having abolished Indian slavery, because Negroes too received baptism in good faith. Fray Bartolomé de Albornoz, a Dominican professor of the University of Mexico, went further and argued in his *Arte de los contratos* (1576) that slavery was to be condemned as without justification, and the slave trade was 'against conscience because it is an unjust war and manifest robbery'. But his book was placed on the Index and prohibited by the Inquisition. Jesuit theologians were equivocal and concerned not to rock the boat. They accepted slavery and never openly condemned it, but they condemned the iniquities of the slave trade and their members administered to slaves in the Americas. In the mid-eighteenth century a Mexican Jesuit, Francisco Javier Alegre, attacked those who under the guise of defending Indians imposed on blacks the harsh yoke of slavery. Another Mexican Jesuit, Francisco Javier Clavijero was also in favour of freedom for slaves. In short, there were occasional voices of reason but not a constant and continuous opposition in Church institutions or religious orders to slavery and the slave trade or defence of blacks.

The papal record on the slave trade was hardly less pusillanimous than that of the theologians.[61] Pope Pius II in 1462, addressing the bishop of Rubicón de las Canarias, condemned the slave trade as a great crime and censured Christians who enslaved Negroes. Pope Paul III, in his letter of 29 May 1536 to Cardinal Juan Tavera, archbishop of Toledo, ordered that the Indians should not be reduced to slavery. In his bull *Veritas ipsa* (7 October 1537), he declared 'that the said Indians and all other people who may later be discovered by Christians must not in any way be deprived of their liberty, even though they are not of the faith of Christ'. Pope Urban VIII in his bull *Commissum nobis* (22 April 1639), directed to the attention of Portugal, renewed the statements of his predecessors on slavery and defended the liberty of the Indians of Brazil, Paraguay, and the Río de la Plata. Benedict XIV, in the apostolic constitution *Inmensa pastorum* (20 December 1741) directed to the bishops of Brazil and the king of Portugal, issued a similar defence. And Pius VII stated, in a letter to the king of France (20 September 1814), 'we forbid any ecclesiastic or layman from affirming that this slave trade is for any reason lawful'. Finally, Gregory XVI in the bull *In supremo apostolatus fastigio* (3 December 1837), prohibited the trade in Africans and Indians and cited again the letters of his predecessors on slavery.

The bulls of Urban VIII and Benedict XIV were obviously directed to the Indians of America, though the second was also applied in practice to Negro slavery from Africa. But the conclusion to be drawn from papal history is that until Popes Pius VII and Gregory XVI the slave trade was not condemned in any document, though Rome was aware enough through its own bureaucracy that international opinion could not defend it. Why was this? Was it prudence and caution on a controversial subject? Was it pressure from the Spanish state, exercising its undoubted power in American affairs? Was it a reflection of the mentality of the time? Whatever the answer, it was not a good record from an institution which should have been a defender of justice and freedom. If Pius II's statement in 1462 was too early for America and had no subsequent resonance, that of Gregory XVI in 1837 arrived too late, when abolition was already a live issue sponsored by others. Statements of Pius III, Urban VIII, and Benedict XV can be invoked as evidence of the Church's stance against a slave trade, but they all refer to the Indians.

Individual cries of protest against slavery were not welcome in Church or state. Bartolomé de Las Casas, who in 1516 had suggested that slaves be imported to the Antilles, came to regret the idea and by 1560 he maintained that the enslavement of Negroes was as unjust as that of Indians. The same opinion was held by Vasco de Quiroga, and years later by Fray Alonso de Montúfar, archbishop of Mexico, who in a letter to the king wrote, 'We do not know what justification there can be for making the Negroes more prone to slavery than the Indians, since they receive the holy gospel in good faith and do not make war against Christians.' In the seventeenth century the clergy of Cartagena were aware of the prevalence and iniquity of race prejudice. In 1614, preaching in the mining district of Zaragoza, Father Luis de Frías declared, 'It is a greater sin to strike a blow at a black than to a figure of Christ [pointing to the crucifix on the altar] because to strike a blow at a black is to strike a living image of God, and to strike an image of Christ is to do it to a dead image'. These sentiments were regarded as so shocking that he was denounced to the Inquisition and his case sent to Spain, where he was described as a new Luther. Others demanded freedom for fugitive slaves, and Bishop Antonio María Cassiani, protector of the *palenque* (community of runaway slaves) of San Basilio, declared, 'I cannot understand why the Negroes have to be slaves.'[62]

Equally severe were the denunciations by Alonso de Sandoval, a Spanish Jesuit scholar and reformer, author of a work of research on the tribal structure of African slaves, and a caring evangelist working out of Cartagena.[63] Along with Pedro Claver, a Catalan Jesuit ordained in America who bound himself to be 'slave of the slaves for ever', he qualifies as a supporter of justice for blacks and slaves. Apart from his pastoral work among the Negroes Sandoval was one of the few Europeans of the time to explore the African background of the blacks brought to America, and to expose the cruelties and abuses inflicted on the 6–7,000 slaves brought to Cartagena each year. He met each slave ship to offer food, water, and medical relief, though he did not and could not break the system.

Jesuit-educated in Barcelona, pilgrim to Montserrat, student in the Society's college in Majorca, where he was deeply inspired by the humble gatekeeper, brother Alfonso who 'watched the door', as Gerard Manley Hopkins tells us, Pedro Claver long hesitated before becoming a priest, and only after two more years of theology in Bogotá did he take the final step of ordination, encouraged by his master and companion Alonso de Sandoval. In their college in Cartagena the Jesuits had slaves for agriculture and domestic labour, so paradoxically Claver had access to slaves from the start.

From these he recruited a group of interpreters who became his friends and associates, catechists too, for he allowed them to instruct new slaves while he sat among the pupils, though others in the order disapproved, reluctant to lose useful labourers. Evangelization was systematic, starting with the sign of the cross and continuing with the Our Father, Hail Mary, the Creed, and the mystery of the Trinity. Six thousand blacks a year were baptized in Cartagena. Claver spread his acts of mercy to all the dispossessed; he ministered personally to lepers and prisoners, and was a protector and helper of runaway slaves. A reluctant Negro hangman recalled, 'The execution took place in the main square. Father Claver brought wine in a glass which he gave to the condemned man, and to me too, which gave me strength to go through with it. I made up my mind to be converted through Father Claver's charity.' Social work and the mission work were indistinguishable. The mass of the slaves might be nominally Christianized but their faith was not profound, and the ritual and practices of their ancestral religions survived, especially among those who passed rapidly through Cartagena to the plantations and mines, where witchcraft and other African practices were rife. The last years before Claver's death in 1654 were ironically made worse by his treatment at the hands of the slave Joaquín assigned to look after him, and who instead neglected, bullied, and maltreated the helpless old man. But people recognized his sanctity and in his final days flocked to see him. He was canonized by Pope Leo XIII in 1888.

There was opposition to Sandoval and Claver from various interest groups. From slave owners, whose priority was slave labour and who objected to Jesuits putting ideas beyond their station into the heads of slaves and preaching a kind of equality. From clergy, who had little inclination for pastoral work among slaves. And from other Jesuits, not all of whom were sympathetic to Claver's work, which was thought to be eccentric and out of line with the general interest of the order, while his compassion for the poor, the sick, and the blacks, especially in the leprosarium, did not appeal to all of his brethren. The Jesuit order did not condemn slavery. According to Sandoval, the missionary should console the Negroes by preaching to them of 'the great mercy of the Lord in bringing them to a Christian land, where it is better to be a captive than to live as a free man in their own country; for here, though the body suffers hardship in captivity, the soul rests in liberty through baptism'. A flawed argument and a spurious contrast. From the labours of evangelization, concluded Sandoval, 'two conclusions follow: first, that these Negroes are not brute beasts, as I have heard some say, for hereabouts they try to make out that they are incapable of being Christians, nor must they be reputed childish or mentally defective, because they are grown-up men and as such should be given baptism, preceded by an act of will on their part.'[64]

The clergy and religious orders possessed the greatest number of slaves in Spanish America. Monasteries and convents had slaves in their service and on their haciendas, and often lived on the income which slave labour brought them. Bishops appointed to America took slaves in their retinue. One bishop of Cartagena was described as so poor that he possessed only two slaves. Many clerics left slaves in their will as bequests.

The Jesuits in South America used slave labour on their estates and in their colleges, especially in Tucumán, Córdoba, Asunción, and Buenos Aires. In Peru Jesuit coastal haciendas were worked by large forces of slaves, and in the eighteenth century their Peruvian colleges were among the largest slaveholders in Spanish America.[65] The Jesuits adopted the conventional criteria of the time: slaves were a preferred form of labour, because they were economical and were more suited to work in the tropics, encouraged by the lash if necessary. They believed that blacks produced more than Indians in tropical agriculture, for example in sugar-cane zones. The Jesuits attempted to create slave families, to reproduce black labour. But they were no more successful than lay owners in preserving their slaves from the climate and from overwork.

The Jesuit record in colonial slavery differed in two ways from that of their lay contemporaries. First, the Jesuits in the eighteenth century held on to slaves in enterprises where lay owners were changing to free labour. Also in the eighteenth century the Jesuits increased their slave numbers, as did lay owners, where expanding markets demanded. In Peru the Jesuits had 5,000 slaves in 1767; in Paraguay they had from 1,323 to 2,000 in the first third of the eighteenth century; and in Córdoba they had 1,043. Second, the Jesuits practised effective slave management, as is shown by the absence of slave revolts on Jesuit estates and the low rates of flight; and they needed no armed support from the colonial state. Efficient estate management was a primary objective. The Jesuit economy was integrated and self-sufficient, each sector supplying the needs of the others; their capital accumulation was effective; hierarchical values were instilled, which encouraged obedience, and the Jesuits promoted baptism and marriage. There was 'close integration of ritual, work and punishment; a kind of Christian servitude, within a context of paternalistic hierarchy'.[66] The Jesuit method was fair and benevolent, but severe, and it included physical punishment. The expulsion of the Jesuits from their estates in 1768 was followed by revolt, desertion, and decline, highlighting their previous stability.

Abolition of slavery was a remote prospect in colonial America but this did not deter two Franciscan missionaries in the Caribbean, defiant voices raised for justice in a cause that the law forgot.[67] José de Jaca (1645–89), a Spanish Capuchin in Venezuela, and Epifanio de Moirans, a French missionary in Cumaná (coastal Venezuela), met in Havana in 1681 and there they drew up indictments of slavery. Jaca had resided for a time in Cartagena, where he seems to have been affected by the slavery around him and its critics. In addition to their reports describing and condemning slavery and all those who participated in it, from king to plantation owner, the two friars preached from pulpits that slavery was contrary to justice and they refused absolution to slaveholders. Jaca's lengthy *Resolución* on freedom for Negroes was drawn from traditional Christian and Catholic principles: human rights, the natural law, the Negro as a faithful member of the Church – arguments backed by practical knowledge of the Indies and crowned by the authority of Scripture. 'So God created man in his own image, in the image of God he created him; male and female he created them' (Genesis 1: 27).[68] The conclusion was inescapable: African slavery was unjust. Justice demanded that slaves should be restored to freedom; masters who refused to liberate their slaves could not receive absolution. Moirans argued further that owners were obliged to restore to their slaves not only liberty but also the price of their work and compensation for harm.[69] The two friars inevitably aroused the anger of slave-owners and the opposition of clerical and colonial authorities. They were detained and imprisoned in Cuba, prevented from preaching and hearing confessions, excommunicated, and sent back to Spain. There they were tried and imprisoned in 1685.

The Council of the Indies advised the king, Charles II, that without Negro slaves for work on the land, in plantations, and in *obrajes* (workshops), 'it will be impossible to maintain the Indies'.[70] So the argument was effectively closed. The two friars were prohibited from returning to America, and the slave trade continued. As for Rome, its response was ambiguous and noncommittal, powerless as it was to change Spain's American policy and still reluctant to give a moral lead. Abolitionists would look in vain for support from the papacy. The lesson from on high was – keep off this subject. Courageous Capuchins had challenged the system and been promptly punished, a predictable conclusion.

The Church's treatment of Negroes was flawed in theory and practice. Church synods and councils legislated for the religious and moral welfare of slaves and blacks: they were to be baptized as soon as possible after disembarking but only after instruction, and they had a right to rest and attend mass on Sundays. Church policy insisted on the right of blacks, slave and free, to marry and stay together, often in opposition to masters who might want to separate them for different work, and the culture of the blacks themselves who often preferred the so-called *matrimonio de fuga* or *unión consensual*. And against the opposition of the colonial state the Church authorized mixed marriages between blacks and whites.

But there was not a word in condemnation of the slave trade, and the law was often ignored. There were some exceptional prelates and priests who made an effort to care for the spiritual and temporal life of the blacks in Peru, New Granada, and the Spanish Caribbean, and there were some black pueblos and parishes where they received special attention, but the clergy in general were not renowned for their dedication to blacks, nor were the religious orders, with the exception perhaps of the Jesuits. The Jesuits in America made a special effort among Negroes and sought them out at points of arrival, in the streets, workshops, and accessible haciendas. Their Negro mission was not necessarily social, but one of baptism, catechism classes, confraternities, and corporal works of mercy, and where the Jesuits had a college or residence, in Lima, Havana, Veracruz, or Cartagena, the mission made an impact. Confraternities of Negroes were organized according to tribes (nations), social criteria (free and slave), and colour (pardos or mulattos, blacks, and others). In Lima and Cartagena many Jesuits assigned to the Negro mission learnt African languages and produced catechisms in these languagaes, or else used special interpreters. Jesuit missions apart, however, Negroes in general were not as fully Christianized as mestizos, and Church authorities were not too concerned.

In spite of being regarded as neophytes, blacks, unlike Indians, were not exempt from the jurisdiction of the Inquisition. The tribunals of colonial Mexico (80 cases), Lima (100), and Cartagena (76) all pursued cases against Negroes. The most common charges were witchcraft, sorcery, blasphemy, curses, pacts with the devil, bigamy, and false doctrines on sex, and punishments included whipping, banishment, confiscation of property, and the galleys.

Indian slavery was a case apart. Theoretically it had been outlawed in all of Spain's possessions in 1542 with the publication of the New Laws, and the prohibition was reiterated in the *Recopilación* (Spanish law code) of 1680. But on the remote margins of the Spanish empire, in Chile, Amazonia, and New Mexico, Indian slavery was tolerated as a way of compensating the settlers who colonized those regions. So Indians who refused to submit to Spanish rule and resisted the word of God could be captured as slaves 'in a just war and kept in bondage' for ten to twenty years, for, as Francisco de Vitoria had stated, 'it is better for them to be slaves among Christians than free in their own lands'.[71] From this it was only another step for Spaniards to conduct raids into Indian territory, ostensibly to punish heathen rebels but in reality to capture slaves. In 1752 Governor Vélez Cachupín reminded colonists that Indian slavery was illegal, but it was tolerated in New Mexico 'so that they [captives] can be instructed in our Holy Catholic Faith ... [and] win their own salvation in honor and glory of God, our Lord'.[72] After slaving expeditions the children were taken to the priest to be baptized and given a name. By 1800 Indian slaves in New Mexico numbered as many as 7,000 out of a total Spanish population of 19,276.

Blacks and mixed groups were marginalized even in the sacraments. The Church accepted a form of racial discrimination in its baptismal records; in parish churches there were separate baptismal registers for each ethnic group and variations in fees for white, black, and Indian. Sometimes blacks shared a register with Indians, but in most cases they had their own register, called *libros de negros esclavos o de pardos y morenos*. Could blacks be ordained as priests? There was some difference of opinion among those who considered the matter:

> Whether free Negroes may be ordained, or prevented from being ordained by their colour is a matter of debate among theologians. Some regard it as unlawful and ordination not possible, because it would cause a great scandal to see a Negro ascend to the altar and say mass among white people who have few Negroes in their ranks, and these with low occupations and mostly slaves. Other authors, and very serious ones, are of the opinion that such ordinations are not unlawful and indeed very possible, and in those places where there are numerous Negroes who rise to the level of captains and other military ranks without causing scandal, we have also seen some who are priests and inspire great devotion among the people.[73]

But in practice right up to the end of the colonial regime holy orders were forbidden to Negroes, mulattos, and their immediate descendants, a reflection of contemporary prejudices, because they were classified as the descendants of infidels and slaves, and mulattos were regarded as illegitimate.[74]

The history of race in Latin America is full of paradox, not least in the case of the Jesuits, saviours in Paraguay, slave-owners elsewhere. The record of the Church on slavery is riddled with inconsistency, evasion, and prevarication, a legacy lightened only by the efforts of a few campaigners. Pressed to explain this great sin of omission, the historian is left with a stark question. Why, for so long, did the Church – the papacy, the hierarchies, the theologians, the faithful – not apply a few simple Christian principles and follow the teachings of the Gospel?

CHAPTER 3

∽

Religion in the Age of Enlightenment

The Enlightenment in the Hispanic World

THE ENLIGHTENMENT WAS not a friend of Christianity. The trend towards deism and free-thinking, the criticism of religious institutions, the growth of lay and secular culture were all signs of a new intellectual order in which reason dethroned revelation and religion became a system to defend rather than a message to proclaim. But the defence of religion, at least in the Hispanic world, was not equal to the intellectual challenge of the Enlightenment and the Church lost the argument by default. Individuals there were, in Spain and America, who sought to reconcile faith and freedom, and to expose traditional beliefs to the light of modern knowledge. But they were not encouraged. Spanish bishops struck out indiscriminately, regarding all *ilustrados*, even the most moderate, as no less enemies of Catholic truth than the *philosophes* and encyclopaedists.

In a society where there was no freedom of expression, where the civil power and the Inquisition exercised strict control over speech and writing, it became impossible to assert that religion too could be reasonable and that Catholic enlightenment should not be confused with deism. A gulf opened between Catholic intellectuals and conservative prelates.[1] Even legitimate reform suffered: the movement for Scripture in the vernacular, for which there was support in Spanish America, was denounced by traditionalists as subversive. The fact that advocates of the right to translate appealed to French example was only another ground for resistance. It was 1782 before the Inquisitor General, Felipe Bertrán, decreed freedom to publish and read the Scriptures in the vernacular, and 1790 before a Spanish translation of the Latin Vulgate appeared. Yet when all was said, the Enlightenment was a minority cause in Spain. If Spanish values were under threat and bishops fulminated from their palaces, the fact remained that the majority of Spaniards were still loyal to their traditional religion.

Spanish America was not immune to winds of change from Europe. Elites were aware that government was now said to be derived from natural rights and social contract, and that among the basic rights were liberty and equality. They understood that these rights could be discerned by reason, and reason, they heard, had no greater enemy than the Catholic Church. A new principle of government was emerging, that of the greatest happiness of the greatest number, a happiness that was measured to a large extent in terms of material advantage. Hobbes and Locke, Montesquieu and Rousseau, Paine and Raynal, all the texts of liberty had readers in Spanish America. Could these appeal to Catholics? Many Catholic laymen in Spanish America, taking a lead from Pedro Rodríguez de Campomanes and Gaspar Melchor Jovellanos in Spain, were partisans of enlightenment, welcomed the new thought, and were even disposed to apply it in the reform of the Church. Without abandoning Catholic belief, they were anti-clerical, hostile to Rome, in favour of a more primitive Christianity, and scornful of popular superstitions. The growth of scepticism in religion, however, and the specifically anti-Christian offensive of the *philosophes* not only represented intellectual positions; they also supported proposals to increase the power of the state over the Church. Many Spanish reformers shared this desire.

The literature of the French *philosophes* entered Spanish America from the middle years of the eighteenth century in the baggage of officials, military personnel, viceroys, merchants, even priests. It enjoyed relative freedom of circulation, in the course of which it became known to a number of the colonial elite among bureaucratic, academic, legal, and clerical groups, most of them linked to colonial capitals and commercial centres. Peru was the home of a group of intellectuals, many of them products of the Royal College of San Carlos, members of the Economic Society and contributors to the *Mercurio Peruano*, who were acquainted with the writings of Locke, Descartes, and Voltaire, and familiar with ideas of social contract, the primacy of reason, and the cult of freedom. But what did this mean? Ideas can be read out of curiosity as well as conviction, to dispel as well as to disseminate. The Enlightenment was a known but not a dominant philosophy in America; as in Spain, its growth was meagre, weakened by conservatism and confined by tradition, and chronologically its impact was late, concentrated in the last decades of the eighteenth century. In a sense Spanish religion was self-protecting through traditional usage and did not need the safeguard of the Inquisition. In any case, by the eighteenth century the American Inquisition was a spent force and only stirred itself when it noticed the advent of the French Revolution.

The Spanish Inquisition had always been an instrument of state as well as of Church, an extirpator of treason and heresy alike. The Bourbon

Inquisition was the same. For much of the eighteenth century, however, the Lima tribunal was inert, absorbed by its own internal problems and disputes with the colonial administration. In the period 1700–1750 it held only seven autos-da-fé and in 268 cases delivered four sentences of punishment. In 1750–1804 there were only four autos and fifty-one cases, most of them trivial. The prosecution of Manuel Lorenzo de Vidaurre in 1793 revealed the penetration of the Enlightenment but the evidence was not treated as a major issue. The Mexican Inquisition was equally inert, preoccupied with its own bureaucratic existence and more or less indifferent to the intellectual and moral affairs of the viceroyalty. Most of its attention was directed towards traditional heresies, though it condemned, ineffectually, works of Rousseau, Montesquieu, Voltaire, and D'Alembert. In the years after 1789, however, news of the French Revolution stirred it into activity. The tribunal began to react, alarmed apparently less by religious heterodoxy than by the political content of the new philosophy, which it regarded as seditious, 'contrary to the security of states', full of 'general principles of equality and liberty for all men', and in some cases a medium for news of 'the frightful and damaging revolution in France.'[2] But political subversion was also presumed to be an attack on revealed religion. Among the several hundred works prohibited in the years after 1789, older English texts did not escape and the complete works of Alexander Pope were banned, 'for showing a kind of tolerance alien to Catholicism'. Anything that questioned kings and their God-given right to rule was condemned.

In the event the Inquisition lost the battle for minds. The real danger came not from the mere penetration of foreign ideas but from the spirit of the age, which tended to undermine inherited certainties. Faced with criticisms of the colonial order by creoles, and the influx of new principles of politics and economics from abroad, the Inquisition could not keep pace with events and had to relax many former rigidities. Heterodoxy was difficult to pin down, for in general the Enlightenment inspired in its American disciples less a philosophy of liberation or a rejection of religion than an independent attitude to received ideas and institutions, a preference for reason over authority, experiment over tradition, science over speculation.

The clerical elite, provided they trod warily, could participate in modernization, publicize the value of useful knowledge and applied science, and vindicate belief in the beneficent influence of the state. As Archbishop Viceroy Caballero y Góngora explained to his successor in Bogotá, it was necessary to substitute the useful and exact sciences for pointless speculations, and in a kingdom such as New Granada, with products to exploit, roads to build, mines to drain, there was more need of people trained to observe and measure than to philosophize. Modernization of this kind was more concerned with technology than with politics. This was the limit of clerical thinking. In Spanish America the obstacles to change were greater even than in Spain and the risks to innovators more serious. Independence of thought was interpreted as a step towards political independence, and at that point the actions of the Inquisition were reinforced by those of the colonial administration. Authorities in Church and state, however, could not prevent the growing laicization of culture, evident in the Río de la Plata and elsewhere among the products of universities and colleges, who were now insisting on their right to search independently for knowledge free of the constraints of a theology and philosophy taught by priests. This trend was to grow during independence and the early republic, when the intellectual interests even of the clerical elite became more lay-orientated. A distinction now emerged between the secular and the religious: secular culture enjoyed autonomy and religion lost much of its secular power. In these circumstances any rupture in the hitherto seamless web uniting culture and religion was not with the Church but with Church control of culture.

If this were the only consequence of the Enlightenment in Latin America, the Church might be thought to have escaped relatively unscathed. But the philosophy of the eighteenth century had left two shoots waiting to flower: utilitarianism, the legitimizing idea of early republicanism; and liberalism, the later nemesis of the Church. Meanwhile, the mere threat of the Enlightenment was enough to cause the Church to reaffirm its solidarity with the old regime, in the event a losing cause.

The Church Subservient

The Church in Spanish America, Roman in faith and morals, was Spanish in organization and discipline. This was obvious from the earliest years of its foundation. But in the eighteenth century under relentless pressure from the Bourbon monarchs and their officials the colonial Church became unmistakably a state Church. Bourbon policy, in Spain and America, aimed to win power for Spain and regain its position in the world; to this end it focused on reform of the state, its agencies and its resources. In relation to the Church this involved two basic objectives: to curtail the wealth of the Church, whose income was regarded as a deficit on royal revenue, and to undermine ecclesiastical privilege, long regarded as an obstacle to political and financial control. Various subtexts accompanied these policies. The religious orders were subject to closer scrutiny by government in Madrid and viceroys in America, and the secular clergy too had their freedom circumscribed. Supporters of the Bourbon state among officials and creoles were often critical of the clergy, though this was an expression of anti-clericalism without doctrinal significance. In any case the state had to tread carefully, for the clergy still had local power and a social position, seen among other things in their influence over the popular classes. The *curas* were strategically located in town and country in a network of surveillance and control which was useful, indeed essential, to the secular arm. Parishioners would think twice before confronting this face of Spanish power. After three centuries of priestly rule, few Indians or peasants were in a position to challenge the guardians of faith and morals.

The higher clergy, royal appointees who took an oath of loyalty to the king, were disposed to accept regalism – that is the assertion of the rights of the sovereign in ecclesiastical affairs at the expense of the pope – by upbringing and mentality, as well as by self-interest. Many ecclesiastics extolled the position of the king in the sacred order of things. Some defended the doctrine of the divine right of kings, asserting that all power came directly from God to the king, bypassing the idea of the popular origin of sovereignty inferred from the neo-Thomists. Among these were the vicar general of the diocese of Buenos Aires, Juan Baltasar Maciel, Bishop Pérez Calama in Quito, Archbishop Lorenzana, Francisco Fabián y Fuero, and Manuel Abad y Queipo in Mexico. The *Catecismo real* (1786) of José Antonio de San Alberto, archbishop of La Plata, a text approved by many other prelates and recommended in their own dioceses, taught the faithful the old organic concept of authority, that the king could not be subject to the people because that would be to make the head subject to the feet. 'The origin of kings is truly divine, their power proceeds from God and their thrones are the thrones of God himself.' San Alberto rejected the idea of authority as 'opinion and consent of the people', an error directly contrary to Scripture, for as St Paul says, 'by me kings rule' and 'all power is from God'. He lists the major prerogatives of the king, starting with legislative supremacy, immunity from prosecution, right to obedience from subjects and the authority to tax, and proceeds to enumerate the minor details. He utterly defends royal patronage in America and the need to conserve it intact against any opposition, an obligation even more binding on bishops and magistrates who take an oath of fealty on assuming their appointments. Fidelity to the sovereign is an 'essential duty' of every vassal, under grave spiritual and temporal sanctions. In a pastoral letter directed against subversive propaganda in 1790 San Alberto used a flight of imagery inspired directly by recent Bourbon reforms:

> If kings reign, govern, order, reward and punish on God's account and by virtue of the authority which He has granted them, within their kingdoms they are Vice-Gods, His Vicars or visible images ... You the clergy, scattered among the twelve provinces and hundred and fifty four districts of our jurisdiction,

are like Ministers or Intendants of the Lord's Exchequer ... while we are the
Superintendent-general.[3]

The decline of Church authority in relation to the state had already
begun before the advent of the Bourbons in 1700. Originally Church and
state were viewed as equal partners in ruling the Spanish empire. But in the
seventeenth century royal bureaucrats in America had slowly chipped
away at the autonomy of the Church, and the Council of the Indies gradually brought new bishops into line. The campaign inaugurated by royal
officials was taken up by the crown itself. This was the project of Charles
III: to curtail the independence of the Catholic Church in America, by
attacking its judicial and fiscal exemptions. Beyond this, boundaries
between the two jurisdictions were increasingly defined in favour of the
crown. Under Charles III and his successors the crown curtailed the
Church's independent judicial functions. Some matters that had traditionally been handled indiscriminately by both ecclesiastical and royal courts,
such as inheritance, became the sole province of the crown. Others that
had been shared by ecclesiastical courts, the Inquisition, and royal courts,
such as the prosecution of couples living together in concubinage, also
became the sole preserve of royal courts. At the same time, despite their
protests about growing royal control, ecclesiastical judges were becoming
increasingly reluctant to press decisions that might antagonize powerful
political and economic interests.[4] Many churchmen realized that espousing
ecclesiastical causes that did not coincide with the interests of the royal
bureaucracy could damage their own careers. As a result not only did the
eighteenth-century Church become less combative, but Church officials
became increasingly solicitous of the opinion and goodwill of the royal
bureaucracy, and more careful to listen to high court judges.[5] This trend
would culminate in a major assault on ecclesiastical privilege initiated by
Charles III.

The influence of the Church, economic and moral, was something
which the state found it vital to control, by patronage and by the *vicariato*.
The Church itself had little room for manoeuvre in the face of renewed
regalism, for it owed its traditional privileges to close ties to the crown and
its acceptance of royal patronage. The holders of all ecclesiastical benefices
were appointed by the king, subject to technical and automatic approval by
the pope in the case of bishops and by the diocesan authorities in the case
of lower benefices. The crown already knew of their suitability, that is that
they were likely to cooperate, because viceroys and governors observed and
reported on them, and the clergy were prepared to be cooperative in order
to obtain promotion. So the clergy were subservient because they were
dependent. As the bishop of Durango reported to the viceroy of Mexico in

1768: 'In the Indies the secular officials and the clergy serve the same superior, which is the King, our Master. From his royal hand I have received
three curacies, two prebends, and, lastly, his generosity has raised me to the
high position of bishop ... The Dean, canons and curates all serve by his
royal will. How then could we fail to observe his adorable commands?'[6]

In addition to the prerogatives deriving from the right of presentation,
the Spanish crown had a further system of control over the Church based
on the royal *vicariato*, that is on the king's function as God's vicar general
in the American Church, an authority derived ultimately from God. This
was intended to extend royal power at the expense of papal authority and
assumed that the pope's authority in the Indies devolved upon the king.
Consequent control over ecclesiastical discipline was not only accepted but
welcomed by American prelates. Archbishop Lorenzana and Bishop Fabián
y Fuero, for example, invited the crown's intervention for reform of the
secular and regular clergy in Mexico, a reform probably necessary but also
intended, as the Provincial Council declared, 'to preserve healthy principles of love and obedience to Your Majesty among the clergy', of which
there was abundant evidence in the Council itself.[7] This type of intervention, however, could be self-defeating, for it was exercised through the
colonial bureaucracy, which allowed many opportunities for appeals and
delay.

Not content with strengthening existing controls, Bourbon government
asserted a new right against the Church, the right to nullify clerical immunity. The Spanish clergy, like the military, possessed valuable *fueros*, which
gave them immunity from civil jurisdiction, a corporate privilege long
defunct in most parts of Europe. In attacking the power, though not the
doctrine, of the Church, Bourbon reformers identified clerical immunity
as one of their prime targets and aimed to bring the clergy under the jurisdiction of the secular courts. Then, with the defences of the Church weakened, they hoped to lay hands on its property. In 1795 the crown issued a
rescript incorporating articles of a projected new code of law for the Indies
in which absolute immunity from royal courts, hitherto enjoyed by all
ecclesiastics, was abrogated in cases where members of the clergy were
judged guilty of 'grave and atrocious crimes'.

The clergy reacted vigorously. While they did not challenge Bourbon
regalism, they bitterly resented any infringement of their personal privilege. They resisted Bourbon policy and were supported in many cases by
pious laymen. In Mexico only fifteen cases were heard against the clergy in
secular courts. They argued that in attacking the clergy the crown was
attacking its essential supports in America. Once the clergy lost their
immunity and power society itself would lurch out of control and the
Indians would become ungovernable. In 1799 leading bishops and chapters

in Mexico addressed extensive memorials to the crown, protesting against
the abrogation of the absolute immunity of the clergy. In 1804 and again in
1809 the archbishop of Mexico, Francisco Javier de Lizana y Beaumont,
criticized these attacks on the clergy and the exercise of ecclesiastical jurisdiction, because, he claimed, 'it was principally through the secular and
regular clergy that the Americans have been and are loyal to God and king
. . . He who has the priests has the Indies.'[8]

The lower clergy, whose *fuero* was virtually their only asset, suffered the
more serious loss. The slightest attack on a cleric's immunity was perceived
as an attack on all clerics. The sense of outrage can be seen in the autobiography of José Miguel Guridi, priest and lawyer, who describes a case
heard in Mexico City in 1799, denouncing it as 'a terrible blow to the
immunity of the clergy, which shocked all ecclesiastics and horrified
the people'.[9] The facts were not entirely to the credit of the clergy. Manuel
Arenas, parish priest of Quimixtlan, had arrested the chief Indian official
of the village, placed him in the stocks, and given him twenty-five lashes.
The intendant of Puebla, Manuel Flon, entered the presbytery by night
with a picket of soldiers, and arrested and imprisoned the priest in the
public gaol of Puebla, an action supported by the viceroy and *audiencia*.
Guridi was shocked to see 'the ultimate outrage by the state and the arro-
gance of some officials believing they already had ecclesiastics in their grip'.
Everyone looked to the bishop to defend clerical immunity, but he did
nothing. In the event the accused was cleared in court and Guridi recorded
a successful case. But conflict between civil and ecclesiastical jurisdiction
was now common and criminous clerks appeared in various guises as
violent aggressors, adulterers, and lawbreakers, who civil officials believed
were treated too leniently by the Church courts. While he defended his
fellow priests in the civil tribunals, Father Guridi was also paying court to
two women of his acquaintance in Mexico City.

The Church was retreating even in matters of morals. One area in which
this could be seen was that of marriage policy. Traditionally the Church
had defended the freedom of couples to marry against parental or official
pressure.[10] Now marriage practice was increasingly controlled by royal
courts and officials, who did not hesitate to prohibit unions regarded as
unsuitable, a trend which the bishops accepted. As the Church yielded its
traditional independence to royal authority, so it abandoned its support for
personal choice in marriage; this enabled the state to intervene with greater
frequency, backing the views of parents and their opposition to 'unequal
marriages'. The Fourth Mexican Provincial Council confirmed this trend.
In matrimonial cases, it was decreed that marriage partners must be
equals. The equality they had in mind was social and racial. The Church in
effect accepted the secular bias of state and society and preferred wealth

and position as criteria for permission to marry; status rather than free consent. The Council also decreed that the authority of fathers in families was derived from divine, natural, and positive law, and this extended to marriage choices.

Secular control over marriage law reached a further stage in 1776 when the Spanish king issued a decree requiring parental consent to the choice of a marriage partner for all persons under the age of 25. Two years later this law was extended to America, allowing parents for the first time to apply a formal ban on their children's choice of a marriage partner.[11] The jurisdiction of the Church, the traditional defender of free will in matrimony, was reduced: royal rather than Church courts were to arbitrate disputes; bishops were ordered not to authorize marriage of under-25s without parental consent and to defer to royal courts. The state thus asserted its secular authority and its absolute power at the expense of the Church. If the Church lost some of its freedom, so did young people; they lost a significant freedom, which had previously allowed them to evade prolonged parental authority and marry the spouse of their choice. The losers, clergy and young alike, sought to recover their position, usually without success. Whatever the original intention of the new rule – deference to the interests of the royal family and the Spanish aristocracy – when applied in America it had further social results. There the great fear among white families was of racially mixed marriages, a defining mark of social status. This definition was added to the decree when it was applied to America. It did not apply to all interracial unions, only to those of whites with blacks and those of whites with slave ancestors: mestizos (from the union of Spaniards and Indians) were acceptable, mulattos and zambos not so.[12]

As the Bourbons strove to control the Church, to reduce its jurisdiction and tap its resources, the secular bishops and clergy were already too dependent on the state for their careers and their livelihoods to offer serious resistance. They accepted the principle, if not all the details, of state control in matters of religion and collaborated wholeheartedly in Bourbon rule in America. The monarch in Madrid, the bishop in his diocese, both occupied the imperial palace. And from the imperial palace came dire action against the Jesuits, which culminated in the dissolution of the order in 1773.

Expulsion of the Jesuits

The Jesuit order was a force to be reckoned with in Spanish America. In 1766 there were some 2,500 Jesuits there, living and working in missions, colleges, and estates.[13] The order had resources in property as well as people, and was one of the largest land- and slave-owners in the Americas.

In Mexico it owned forty-one rural estates, twenty-seven colleges, and numerous churches. In Chile Jesuit property, including slaves, cattle, real estate, and financial resources, amounted to 1,961,148 pesos, a sum greater than the annual budget of the colony.[14] Suddenly, in July and August 1767, all Jesuits, creoles as well as peninsular Spaniards and foreigners, were expelled from America and their properties confiscated. The expulsion was conducted with military precision and followed a similar pattern in all the major Jesuit houses. A detachment of troops would appear without warning late at night and order the residents to prepare for a long journey. Escorted to the nearest port, they embarked for Europe, most of them to Italy. A reluctant pope was persuaded to admit them to his states, some 5,000 Jesuits in all from Spain and America, there to live on a pension of 100 pesos a year, paid in effect from their own confiscated property.

Official obsession with secrecy and security was superfluous. There was no resistance. In Mexico the expulsion merged with tax and other grievances to provoke popular riots and revolts. In Guanajuato mobs atttacked government buildings. In San Luis Potosí a crowd seized the Jesuit fathers and refused to permit them to be taken into exile. Repressive measures, including eighty-five hangings, were sanctioned by the authorities. A flood of anonymous pamphlets and fly-sheets accused the government of planning to destroy the Catholic religion, while Lorenzana and Fabián y Fuero were criticized for their sycophantic pastoral letters in which they applauded the expulsion as a divine judgement on 'impious and fanatical Jesuits'.

The Río de la Plata witnessed a different spectacle. At three o'clock in the morning of 12 July 1767 Fernando Fabro, a military officer dispatched from Buenos Aires with eighty soldiers, rang the doorbell at the Jesuit College in Córdoba. The porter who opened the door found two pistols at his chest. The 133 Jesuits of the College, priests and novices, were herded into one room at bayonet point to hear the royal decree ordering their expulsion, and the expropriation of their property. They then spent ten days imprisoned in the refectory, while Fabro made an inventory of their possessions.[15] On 23 July they were all put in transports and taken to Buenos Aires where, on 19 August 1767, they were embarked for Spain, arriving at Puerto de Santa María on 6 January 1768. Meanwhile Governor Bucareli, fearing Indian opposition of the kind experienced in the Guaraní war, enforced the expulsion of the Jesuits from their missions in Paraguay with a veritable army of troops. These precautions, plus the need to find replacements for the Jesuits, prolonged the operation in Paraguay, but eventually it too was carried out peacefully and without opposition. In Chile, on receiving his secret orders in August 1767, the governor had all the Andean passes closed, shipping stopped, auxiliaries recruited, and at 3 a.m. on 26 August his troops surrounded Jesuit houses throughout the colony, arrested the astonished inmates, and sent them under escort to the port of Valparaiso. The inventory of Jesuit property was begun immediately.

Expelled by the state, the Jesuits received no lifeline from the Church. Bourbon bishops resented any claim to exemption from their jurisdiction; and their solidarity with the crown was notorious. On both counts they distrusted Jesuits. In Mexico Bishop Fabián y Fuero, encouraged by Lorenzana, justified the expulsion as a 'legitimate use of the rights which God gave the king along with his crown'.[16] Lorenzana himself enumerated his own charges against the Jesuits in a series of pastoral letters: (1) They were guilty of the pernicious doctrine of probabilism with its attendant lax moral principles, and promoted the doctrine of tyrannicide. (2) They spread false doctrines and fanaticism in convents of nuns. (3) They were greedy for wealth and power, claimed precedence over other orders and independence of the bishops, and sought to influence students in their favour. (4) In Mexico they accumulated riches, business, and property, and their well-stocked haciendas even produced fighting bulls. Lorenzana exhorted the faithful 'to obey and be silent', and to give unqualified assent to the king, who had been 'commissioned by God to guard his subjects from influences dangerous to their faith'.[17] Lorenzana went further: he persuaded the royal authorities to demand the extinction of the Society of Jesus, a statement cited by Spanish officials in their successful lobbying of the papacy for such a decision in 1773. In Mexico, therefore, the faithful observed two current manifestations of state religion: an arbitrary exercise of power and forceful repression of resistance.

In the Río de la Plata area the colonial state was faced with a dilemma. On the one hand the Jesuits were alleged to be the leaders behind the War of Paraguay (1754–56) and the king was convinced that 'members of the Society were solely responsible for the resistance of the Indians.'[18] On the other they appeared to be indispensable to the missions in a country chronically short of clergy. Manuel Antonio de la Torre, bishop of Paraguay from 1756, a Spaniard from the secular clergy, began with good relations with the Jesuits and his diocesan visitation reported favourably not only on their pastoral work but also on their care for the welfare of the Indians, whose standard of living was superior to that of many Spaniards in Paraguay.[19] Later, as bishop of Buenos Aires at the time of the expulsion, De la Torre decided on discretion and followed the official line.

Charles III treated the expulsion of the Jesuits from all his kingdoms as a secret between himself and God. In the Pragmatic of 2 April 1767 he claimed that he acted from the 'supreme executive power which the Almighty has placed in my hands' but gave only the vaguest of reasons: 'the obligation by which I am bound to maintain my peoples in subordination, tranquillity and justice, and further urgent, just and necessary reasons which I keep in my royal soul'. But this was not a lofty argument between the Enlightenment and religion, between a progressive government and a burnt-out order. Power was the spur. Charles III had an innate prejudice against Jesuits.[20] He saw an insidious and wealthy organization which had once defended regicide. They still retained their special vow of obedience to the pope and their reputation as papal agents. An order with an international organization whose headquarters were outside Spain was regarded as inherently incompatible with absolutism and they were thought to be obstacles to important government objectives. Their opposition to one of the Bourbons' favourite 'causes', the canonization of the anti-Jesuit bishop of Puebla, Juan de Palafox, and their general ubiquity in Church and state confirmed Charles III in his view that Jesuits were troublemakers and a challenge to royal power. He had the resolute support of his ministers, some of whom came from a class which resented the influence of the Jesuits in university education and their affiliation with the higher aristocracy.

The Jesuits also had enemies among a wider clerical and lay public. Their defence of good works as well as faith in the process of salvation and their more relaxed interpretation of Catholic moral theology brought them into conflict not only with Jansenists but also with other orders, and they had few friends among Augustinians and Dominicans. Memories of the time when they virtually monopolized the royal confessional and controlled ecclesiastical patronage and policy were still fresh and there were many clerics who bore a personal grudge against the Society of Jesus. Religious conflict became a code for political positions. To be a 'Jesuit' meant to belong to a group of elitist graduates and to disapprove of reforms introduced by plebeian ministers; to be a 'Jansenist' was to be a supporter of regalism, an opponent of Rome, and a friend of heterodoxy. Crisis came in 1766 when food and tax riots in Madrid directly challenged the government. Although there were obvious social and economic reasons for the disturbances the government preferred to believe that they had been instigated by the Jesuits and their allies who wished to change the government and block further reform. This version of events was assiduously promoted by Pedro Rodríguez de Campomanes, fiscal of the Council of Castile, whose inquiry into the riots produced a long and detailed indictment of the Jesuits and provided the theoretical justification for the expulsion.[21]

In his *Dictamen* Campomanes maintained that the Jesuits were a threat to the regalist power of the crown: 'The Jesuit does not regard himself as a vassal, nor does the Society; he is the enemy of royal sovereignty, and obeys a despotic government resident abroad; to it he remits his wealth, from it he receives his instructions.'[22] These charges focused on Spain and it was in the metropolis that the Jesuits came under the direct scrutiny of the crown. But America added its own fuel to the attack on the Jesuits. The Spanish government published the data supplied by an ex-Jesuit, Bernardo Ibáñez de Echavarri, twice expelled from the order in the Río de la Plata for policy disagreements, who was present in Buenos Aires and Paraguay during the crucial years 1755–61 and compiled a malicious and mendacious work of propaganda. This was then used by the Spanish government, especially Campomanes, to justify first the expulsion and then the extinction of the order.[23]

The main thesis of Ibáñez was that the Guaraní mission was established and ruled as a sovereign state, a veritable kingdom, with the general its king and the provincials as his viceroys; and this king exercised all the legislative, fiscal, and military powers of a sovereign.[24] The fact of its independence and absolute sovereignty was proved by the existence of an Indian army, created, armed, and trained by the Jesuits. He cited a letter from the Paraguayan provincial, Ignacio de Arteaga (6 August 1727): 'if the Indians are not well trained in arms, then these missions are not well defended against the heathen, the Spaniards, and the Portuguese.'[25] And to keep the Indians under control the Jesuits 'allowed them only enough education to be useful to the Jesuits themselves'. A further line of defence was provided by the presence of more foreign priests than Spanish, and a closed-door policy towards Spanish settlers.[26] From all this the crown concluded: 'Their own documents prove that in their Paraguay missions they have established an absolute monarchy; or to speak more precisely, an incredible despotism contrary to all human and divine laws.'[27]

Ibáñez alleged that the Jesuits appropriated an 'enormous surplus' from Paraguay (by no means the richest of their American provinces) for use by the general of the Society for its common expenses. Campomanes too referred to the Jesuits' accumulation of wealth in the Indies. The religious orders had claimed papal exemption from payment of tithes on their own agricultural production. The Jesuits owned vast properties in the Indies, estates, ranches, and plantations, which they themselves managed as commercial enterprises to fund their various activities. This wealth was a sore point with royal officials:

> In the Mexican province the Society was owner of 80 haciendas of cattle, farms, and sugar mills, producing each year 400,000 pesos, on which it owed 40,000 in tithes to the king and the archbishop, while in the previous year, 1734, it had only paid some 7,000 pesos. Out of the 400,000 the province maintained 155 religious in their Colleges and still had a surplus to buy more haciendas . . . Yet the royal treasury paid an annual subsidy of 39,705 pesos for the 120 Jesuit missionaries whom they had in the province of Nueva Vizcaya.[28]

The Jesuits stubbornly resisted payment of tithes, and opposed all attempts by the authorities to force them to do so, thus depriving crown and bishops of susbstantial revenue. The dispute dragged on throughout the seventeenth and early eighteenth centuries. In 1750 the crown accepted a compromise, according to which the Jesuits had to pay a tithe of one-thirtieth of production. But the dispute continued, until a royal order of 4 December 1766, three months before the order of expulsion, obliged the Jesuits in America to pay the whole tithe.

Paraguay was the most dramatic scene of Jesuit enterprise and the focus of greatest controversy. The Jesuits had not always been opponents of the crown. Indeed the two had a mutual interest in confronting Portuguese invaders and regional creole rebels. The Jesuits had already been targets of white hostility during the revolt of the *comuneros* in 1721–35. Their powerful presence, their superior resources, their Indian militia, and their control of labour aroused the anger of the Spanish settlers, and there was competition for resources between settlers and Jesuits. In 1721 Governor José de Antequera identified with settler interests, and his cavalry defeated the forces of the viceroy and the Jesuit Indian army. This was a victory of settlers over Jesuits, of whites over Indians, of the creole rebel junta over outside authority. Gradually, however, the forces of imperial order closed in, once again backed by the Jesuit Indian militia, while the growing social extremism of the *comuneros* characteristically drove many property owners out of the revolt to make common cause with legitimate authority.[29]

At a time of Jesuit influence in Madrid the order had obtained from the Council of the Indies a royal *cédula* (decree) confirming the various privileges and immunities of its Guaraní missions. First, the Indians had to pay a low rate of tribute, in exchange for constituting a permanent militia at the orders of the royal authorities. Second, the Jesuits were allowed to retain the particular economic and social system characteristic of their Guaraní communities. And finally the moderate form of the Patronato Real (royal control in return for material support of the Church) prevailing in their mission district was confirmed. The *Cédula Grande* of 1743 was not easily obtained and cost the Jesuits considerable sums of money paid in bribes to the officials who prepared the *cédula*, transferring funds illegally from the Río de la Plata via Lisbon and London.

The victories won in 1743 and their apparently invincible position in Spain and in Rome misled the Jesuits. In 1750 the Treaty of Madrid between Spain and Portugal rearranged the boundaries of the Río de la Plata: in exchange for Portuguese Colônia Spain ceded territory which contained seven of the thirty Guaraní missions of the Jesuits.[30] The missionaries were ordered to leave immediately and resettle their Indians in Spanish territory; in an instant 30,000 Indians found themselves displaced, ruined, and homeless. Amidst a storm of protests from Jesuits and other critics in America the Jesuit general ordered obedience and the order took steps to comply. The Paraguayan province, however, was outraged and in a series of compelling arguments pressed Madrid for a change of the boundary line. What was the moral authority of the treaty? Was it right to displace 30,000 innocent people, deprive them of their property, banish them hundreds of miles to a wilderness, their only compensation one peso each? Which had primary claim to obedience, Spanish law or moral law? There were many answers from the missionaries, some of whom were passionately critical of the treaty, others openly hostile to Spanish orders and their general's advice. In the end they had to comply, partly to avoid the scandal of rebellion, partly to preserve their charges from worse harm. But they could not prevent resistance by the Indians, already alienated from the Portuguese by bitter experience of slave hunters from Brazil. Hundreds of Indian lives were lost and great suffering was inflicted upon the mission communities before the colonial authorities crushed the rebellion. The Jesuits too were victims. The Guaraní war gave the Spanish authorities the opportunity to distort or fabricate evidence against the missionaries and eventually to incriminate the whole Jesuit order.

When Spanish and Portuguese forces occupied the seven rebel missions in 1756 they found a number of foreigners among the Jesuits, a consequence of previous concessions allowing them to recruit up to one-third of their American personnel outside Spain. This was a privilege granted to no other order and was an exception to one of Spain's strictest colonial laws. In 1760 the crown revoked the concession and Campomanes subsequently explained why: 'National loyalty does not exist in such missionaries; the interest of the order is their only motivation.'[31] The expulsion was a means to exert total control over the Church in America, removing the one possibility of dissent; and to control the Church was to control society.

The response to the expulsion of the Jesuits in Spanish America, except in Mexico, was apathetic; when it came to the test the order was isolated. True, there were expressions of regret and resentment among former pupils and other friends, and the despotic nature of the measure left a memory which would later be invoked against Bourbon rule. But there was no action. Bishops were either pro-expulsion, complacent, or indifferent. The Jesuits had always fought for their exemptions from episcopal control and had few friends among bishops. From the secular clergy they could expect little solidarity; even less from other religious orders. Their disputes with Dominicans and Augustinians over theology, education, and missionary methods were notorious. Franciscans, too, had historic resentments; moreover, they had bishops in America. The attitude of laypeople was ambiguous. Some officials were well disposed. In Buenos Aires Governor Pedro de Cevallos was known as a friend of the Jesuits: when he returned to Spain in 1766 they hoped he would receive a ministerial appointment, but this did not materialize. Merchants, perhaps, saw Jesuits as entrepreneurial rivals, landowners as an obstacle to extending their holdings. Creoles valued them as educators of their children, but this was not enough to inspire a movement in their favour. Mission Indians, especially in Paraguay, had the means of creating trouble, if they had been given a lead, but in fact the Jesuits acted to calm their neophytes, conscious of their ultimate weakness.

The departure of the Jesuits was not the last gasp of a dying institution. The order was at its peak, vocations were numerous, priests models of their kind. Although the Spanish government would never admit it, the expulsion of the Jesuits from America left a gap which was not easily filled. The Church suffered from the loss of dynamic pastors and teachers, and the missions never recovered their former prosperity; these facts were frankly admitted by viceroys in New Granada and elsewhere. The expulsion was a particular blow to secondary education, which the state and ecclesiastical authorities failed to make good, in spite of some success in expanding primary education.[32] The colonial government sought to ensure that the property of the Jesuits was used for establishing new teaching centres. But in Mexico the colony's leading colleges were closed; Michoacán alone lost seven. In Bogotá hopes of establishing a public university to replace that left by the Jesuits were not fulfilled. In Buenos Aires an attempt was made to use Jesuit property to establish a university, but this failed for lack of teachers, books, equipment, and will, and Buenos Aires had to be satisfied with the Colegio de San Carlos, established in 1783, whose curriculum and teaching made few concessions to modernity or enlightenment. Royal decrees, here and throughout Spanish America, prohibited the continuation of Jesuit teaching, or alleged Jesuit teaching. This did not signify the advent of new learning, but a reversion to older orthodoxies, to Aquinas instead of Suárez, to moral certainty instead of probabilism, and to the proscription of any ultramontane doctrines opposed to the regalian rights of the crown. In the Río de la Plata there emerged a growing gap between teachers, wed to scholasticism, and students who reacted against traditional methods and doctrine taught in the University of Córdoba and the Colegio de San Carlos, preferring the exact sciences to the subjects of the past.

As missionaries they left a large number of neophytes, some 478,000 in Spanish America and the Philippines; of these 26 per cent were in New Spain, 24 per cent in the Río de la Plata. Other orders, the Dominicans and Franciscans, were still active, educating and evangelizing. In California, where the missions were wrongly reputed to be wealthy and contain silver mines but in fact were underfunded, the work of evangelization was continued with some success by the Franciscans. In other regions alternatives were sometimes found, but often a vacuum was left. In Mexico Viceroy Revillagigedo did not doubt that the missions deteriorated after the expulsion: 'When the Jesuits were expelled they were not promptly replaced by other religious, and their property was committed to incompetent and greedy individuals who totally squandered it'. In Guatemala peons on Jesuit estates were left without religious ministration of any kind and no one thought to fill the gap.[33]

In the Guaraní reductions, home of some 300,000 Indians and almost 500 missionaries, the Jesuits, however paternal, had successfully solved the problem of the material subsistence of the Indians. Now, however, it was argued that this had been done at the expense of their liberty. The reaction of the Spanish authorities against the community system established by the Jesuits thus had a theoretical as well as a practical side. Arguments were used in favour of individual liberty and private property, ironically out of tune with the leaders of the age of Enlightenment. Even opponents of the Jesuit order such as Voltaire, Montesquieu, and the ex-Jesuit Raynal commended the 'Jesuit state' as a rationalistic sociological experiment.[34] At first the unaccustomed role of Spanish authorities as advocates of freedom was more theoretical than real. In default of any alternative plan the Jesuit system of government had to be left in place and the community system maintained, substituting secular priests and administrators for the Jesuits. The result was disastrous. The new officials were not only less efficient than the Jesuits but also less disinterested, and regarded their task as a means of personal profit, while the Indians were robbed of their property by gangs of Spanish and Portuguese rustlers. They began to desert the missions and many made their way to neighbouring regions and also to Buenos Aires and Montevideo, where in spite of the alleged demoralizing effects of the Jesuit regime they were able to earn a living and work for wages as labourers and artisans.[35]

Along with the Pragmatic of 2 April 1767 ordering the expulsion, the authorities in America also received a detailed *Instruction* for the confiscation and disposal of Jesuit property and estates. Inventories were drawn up listing the possessions of the order and its members. Claims were immediately made to take over colleges; in Mexico some went to state offices, one to a hospital, others to religious orders. Franciscans and Dominicans usually claimed the churches. The rest of Jesuit property was sold and the profits supposedly applied to social programmes, especially to hospitals. In accordance with the royal *cédula* of 27 March 1769, provincial and municipal *juntas de temporalidades* were created to take charge of the administration of Jesuit property, which was sold at public auction. But it was a slow process, badly not to say fraudulently administered by treasury officials, and in Mexico much of the considerable profits went in defraying treasury losses and debts. In 1808–9 the total Jesuit real estate in America still unsold amounted to 532,524 pesos; previous purchasers still owed ten times more than this, paying in instalments or by mortgage. In general landowners and businessmen were the buyers. The principal beneficiaries of the sale of Jesuit property, therefore, were the colonial state and the creole elite; social programmes came a poor third.

The expulsion of the Jesuits from Spanish America had been preceded by their expulsion from Brazil. The two events were not dissimilar in their origins and motivation, and although the Brazilian case had distinctive features, in many ways it was almost like a rehearsal for the Spanish event. The order had grown to be a power in Brazil. In their holdings of land, plantations, slaves, and commercial networks they were without equal, and their economic resources produced the wealth to maintain churches, schools, and seminaries on a scale unrivalled by any other religious body.[36] Intellectual and spiritual qualities matched their resources and gave them a confidence that perhaps blinded them to the resentment and sheer envy their success bred among rulers and competitors, and made them complacent to the contradictions in their own position, protectors of the Indians yet defenders of the slave trade, worthy evangelists yet wise in the ways of the world. The peak of their power in Brazil coincided with the rise of a rival in political influence, the marquis of Pombal, whose modernizing project for Portugal and its empire, backed by his domination over king and government, placed him in a position to challenge and then destroy an enemy whom he hated to a degree verging on paranoia. A campaign of mendacious propaganda in Portugal and relentless pressure in Rome gave Pombal the prize he sought, the elimination of an alleged rival to the state. In the course of 1759 José I ordered first the arrest of the Jesuits, then the expulsion of the order from Portugal and its dominions, a process observed with interest in government circles in Spain.

Priests and People

The Jesuits in 1767 faced the hostility of crown, bishops, and other priests, sectors which also disputed among themselves. These were not the only divisions in the American Church. The distinction between the regular and secular clergy had existed from the beginning of evangelization and responded to a practical division of labour. But it did not satisfy all ecclesiastical interests and some worked to change it. Since the sixteenth century bishops and seculars had resented their exclusion from regular *doctrinas*, the bishops wishing to exercise total jurisdiction in their dioceses without enclaves of privilege, the seculars seeking wider opportunities of preferment. Transfer to secular clergy and parishes was sporadic in the seventeenth century, more insistent in the eighteenth.

Secularization was an ambiguous victory for the hierarchy. In effect it stripped away a whole layer of religious life and altered the spiritual landscape long familiar to Americans. As historic priories fell into ruin, their former occupants crowded into the urban houses of their order, still priests but no longer parish priests; and in some cases no longer priests, for a number applied to Rome for laicization. Meanwhile, loss of functions and of revenue from their parishes meant a fall in recruitment, as the orders had to reduce their intake. The cure of souls diminished. According to the Capuchin Ajofrin, who travelled in Mexico in the 1760s collecting for his order's missions elsewhere, parishes could hardly support one *cura* where previously they had supported six. Some parishes were left without mass, others were attended by two or three priests where previously there had been thirteen or fourteen friars. Ajofrin had once been a supporter of secularization; now he was a sceptic:

> I admit that before I came to America I thought it was a good idea to remove *doctrinas* and parishes from the regulars and assign them to seculars; but having travelled in these parts and seen for myself, I can honestly say that they have made the greatest possible mistake and the same people who sought this change now lament it. As for the poor Indians, their spiritual welfare has badly deteriorated.[37]

The transfer to secular priests was not a smooth operation. The regulars accepted the decision, though they loathed it and were often supported by their Indian parishioners, who recognized that the friars were more experienced and more aware of local conditions than their successors. Secular priests aroused mixed feelings among their parishioners and they were thought to despise Indians. Evangelization suffered. Many Indian parishes bore the marks of mendicant spirituality for generations to come, but the Church itself admitted that under the new dispensation Indians were often confused about the faith and ignorant of the catechism. Viceroy Croix confirmed that this was so, 'because the Indians are not properly instructed and the priests are not adequately maintained, while they are usually more exigent than the religious who were content with a modest subsistence . . . The priests tyrannize the parishioners more than did the religious, who had a different style.' Many of the new parish priests remained absent in Mexico City, leaving their parishioners in the hands of curates or Indian teachers, neglecting their duties but not neglecting to collect parochial dues.

Mexico had about 5,000 priests in 1650. A century and a half later, in a population which had quadrupled, there were about 6,000. The Indian population tripled in this period, but not the number of priests. But the clergy were difficult to count, and the evidence varied between an excessive number of priests and a severe shortage. In leading cities wealthy and popular parishes drew a surplus of priests, while rural and highland areas were neglected. This was the classic structure of the Latin American Church: a clerical elite of well-beneficed priests, forming some 10 per cent of the diocesan clergy, and a horde of unbeneficed clergy scraping a living as vicars, chaplains, or chantry priests.[38] Most of the clerical elite – cathedral chapters or secular parish priests – reached their positions through academic achievement, holding licentiates or doctorates in the sacred sciences. This meant that they came from wealthy families, who alone could afford to maintain their sons through years at university. Then, having taught perhaps in the diocesan seminary or practised law in the Church courts, they were in a position to compete for the best parishes. At the lower end there was a clerical working class, less educated, poorly paid, for ever vicars, often consigned to parishes in the less salubrious parts of the country or, if they had an Indian language, in remote highlands. The Church was not a place to look for equality: candidates for the priesthood did not find their vocation through diocesan recruitment, responsible bishops, or hope of a tenured appointment. The Church mirrored secular society.

As intermediaries between the Indians and God, the teacher of the Gospel and dispenser of sacraments, the rural priest had an inherent authority, which he enhanced or diminished by his own conduct, being loved, trusted, or merely respected and perhaps feared. Punishments administered by the clergy varied from excommunication to, at least in the case of Indians, severe beating. But clerical sanctions were not confined to penitential demands. Many sins, especially sexual, were treated as public offences and punished as such. In Mexico it was not unknown for poor couples found living together to be arrested by the parish priest, sentenced by the diocesan court to public humiliation, and ordered to stand at the altar dressed 'penitentially'.[39] To apply canon and moral law to a recalcitrant population, and even enforce the performance of Easter duties, a priest needed the cooperation of local officials and caciques and the support of public, that is creole, opinion. The system worked both ways. Clergy were not only clients but often agents of the Bourbon state, at a time when the state expected them to collaborate in regulating the political and fiscal life of indigenous communities at higher levels than previously. Often they were the only representatives of authority with whom these communities came into contact, for secular officials were absentees, preferring urban to rural life; this gave the *cura* considerable independence of action, strengthened by his knowledge of colonial law.[40] The humanitarian tradition of the sixteenth century was not so much in evidence in the eighteenth. But in Mexico some Indian communities spoke up for their priests and praised their exemplary character. Seculars as well as regulars were active supporters of indigenous causes in litigation and in efforts to win relief from the effects of epidemics, droughts, or other natural disasters; some of this was self-interest, for the clergy wanted Indian resources and labour for their own purposes, but Indians also learnt to manipulate the clergy into supporting Indian causes.

In Upper Peru *curas* competed with caciques and *corregidores* – the three pillars of Spanish rule in the Andes – for the resources of Indian communities; and in spite of admonitions to priests not to take excessive parochial fees contemporaries did not doubt that their income was high.[41] Appropriation of communal land and livestock by priests and the taking of Indian labour in place of unpaid fees were much resented by the Indians and provoked protest of an anti-clerical rather than a violent kind, such as litigation or abstention from mass and the sacraments.[42] The removal of one burden opened the way for another: so priests' earnings from parochial dues actually increased when *repartos*, or forced sale of goods to the Indians, were abolished in December 1780. Many priests attempted to exceed the diocesan tariff of fees, whipping and imprisoning recalcitrants and building up resentment in Indian communities.

Yet it would be a mistake to regard the rural priest as an isolated figure, remote from the concerns and interests of his largely Indian parishioners. Indian resistance to the tax demands of the Bourbons and the heavy hand of local officials was often strengthened by the parish priests who could help them in their litigation and defend them against abuses. In Upper Peru some priests supported the great rebellion of Túpac Amaru and showed solidarity with the movement, to the outrage of Spanish officials. The priest who acted as protector of the Indians was not defunct and he was still capable of inspiring greater loyalty than local officials.

The life of the rural priest, if not isolated, was solitary. Many avoided a lone existence by surrounding themselves with widowed mothers and sisters. But some supported families of another kind. The vow of celibacy was taken seriously by the higher clergy in America, less so by many secular priests. In the eighteenth century it was still regarded as a moral absolute by the Church, a rule sufficiently important to be remarked upon when it was broken. But broken it was. In Mexico, Guatemala, New Granada, and Peru it was a common occurrence for secular clergy to have children, and to provide for them: careers for sons, dowries for daughters. In New Granada Fray Juan de Santa Gertrudis, a Franciscan missionary

priest, chronicled clerical life with an unerring eye for concubines, referring casually to many cases of 'a priest who had a daughter', or a young
woman 'daughter of a priest', or on one occasion a priest hiding inside a
house while his companion directs Padre Juan to another lodging.
'Housekeepers' were often described as sisters or nieces. In one encounter
on the road to Pasto the friar congratulated an Indian parishioner on his
caring parish priest, to be told, ' "Yes, he's good, but he has given nothing
to the sick." I replied, you should ask the lady, his sister. "Father", he told
me, "that lady is not his sister but his mistress and for that reason no one
in the village can approach her; she is more of a tyrant towards the sick
than the priest, for she only collects for herself and to send money to her
mother in Quito" '.[43]

Ordination of Indians to the priesthood was not encouraged, and ironically one of the reasons traditionally given was their probable difficulty with
celibacy. There were a few cases of Indian priests, at least in Mexico, although
they tended to be assigned to distant rural parishes among their own people.
One unexpected result of secularization was an increase in the number of
Indians and mestizos ordained as priests. As early as 1697 the Spanish crown
issued a rescript calling for the admission of mestizos and Indian caciques to
the priesthood. This policy was reaffirmed in August 1769 when the crown
insisted not merely that seminaries be established in all dioceses but also that
one-third or a quarter of all students be Indians or mestizos. The prime
motive seems to have been that native speakers were needed to supply the
language deficiencies of secular priests, but like many Bourbon rules it was
not strictly applied and the colonial Church missed another opportunity to
create a native priesthood. In the course of his diocesan visitation of
Guatemala in 1768–70 Archbishop Cortés y Larraz, who was otherwise a
complete Spaniard in his outlook, attempted to recruit young Indians for the
clergy and approached Indian leaders in San Antonio Suchitepéquez:

> I earnestly requested that they give me some boys to be educated, but they
> invented all manner of excuses, and when I further insisted they were reduced
> to tears. I told them that of course I would not force them, I simply wanted it
> for the good of the boys, to ordain them and make them priests. But they
> replied, 'Father, this cannot be, for we are Indians.' 'What does being Indians
> matter?' I replied. 'Father,' they insisted, 'we are Indians, and we have never
> seen such a thing'.

He tried the same in other parts, offering monthly grants to parents for
each child, to compensate for loss of labour, but he was only able to recruit
one candidate in the whole of the archdiocese.[44] And without native priests
the cultural divide in the Church was self-perpetuating.

Blacks and mulattos were specifically barred from the priesthood, in custom if not in canon law or the views of theologians. The reason was their slave ancestry. If any applied to enter, hoping that they might pass for whites, witnesses would invariably step forward and denounce their ancestry, thus initiating an invidious and sometimes malicious process of family investigation.[45] Thus was race prejudice endorsed by the Church.

Enlightenment and the Indian World

Bourbon policy had a place for the Indians, but it was not the place envisaged by earlier Spanish evangelists and humanitarians. The new bureaucracy of intendants, sub-delegates, and other officials, and even some Bourbon prelates, insisted on redirecting the life of the Indians, and it has been argued that 'under the combined effect of Bourbon despotism and the influence of the Enlightenment, the imperatives of civilization progressively replaced those of Christianization'.[46] The pressure to hispanicize the Indians also came from the Church. Here too the concept prevailed of the Indian not as an *etnia* (ethnic group) but as a lower social group. The archbishop of Mexico, Pérez de Lanziego (1711–28), writing to the king of Spain observed that if the Indians continued to be treated as they were then 'the Indians will always be Indians': a negative view even when it was well meaning. It was a view echoed in 1768–70 by Pedro Cortés y Larraz, who remarked that even when .the Indians were Christianized 'they do not cease to be Indians'.[47] In the course of his diocesan visitation he met an old Indian who spoke Spanish and asked him why he went barefoot: 'He replied, because he was Indian. I told him that Indians were Spaniards like us. He replied that he was not Spanish but Indian. I asked him if he would like to be Spanish. He replied, no, and continued to insist that he had no wish to be Spanish. A clear example of the perception which these wretches have of the Spaniards.' It did not occur to the archbishop that the Indians' prime perception was of themselves.

Cortés y Larraz observed a Guatemala full of Indians, occupying many positions on the religious spectrum. The priests reported widespread idolatry. The cult of animals was still popular, as well as a belief in *naguales* (sorcerers). The archbishop reissued an order of one of his predecessors suppressing images in churches of Santiago on horseback, St Michael defeating the devil, St John with the lamb, and other figures of devils and animals worshipped by the Indians. On the other hand in Atitlán the young and sympathetic *cura*, Miguel Medina, reported no evidence of idolatry or lapsing from the Christian religion; the main sins were 'drunkenness and lust', and the Indian faithful responded well to encouragement to attend mass and receive communion. The archbishop was still sceptical:

'As the *cura* is so partial to the Indians it is to be expected that he can manage them satisfactorily.' He preferred to believe other reports of sins and vices, including Indians' reluctance to attend mass and school or to receive the sacraments: 'All these vices are incurable in the Indians, as the priests explain, because they are intractable and obstinate.' No doubt they are badly used by the Spaniards, but equally they hate the Spaniards, whom they consider to be foreigners and usurpers: 'therefore they regard them with implacable hatred, and in so far as they obey them it is from the most abject fear. They want nothing from the Spaniards, neither religion, nor instruction, nor culture.' And the worst misery they suffer is at the hands of their own Indian officials and leaders, who work them like slaves and punish them without mercy. 'Unhappy the *mazahuales*, that is the common people, if the Indians were lords of America and they were dominated by the Indians.'[48]

The Spanish language was regarded as a key instrument for civilizing and hispanicizing the Indian. Various attempts at diffusion of Spanish among the Indians had been made from the sixteenth century onwards, but the missionaries won the argument to instruct in native languages. Attempts to make the Indians literate were renewed in the eighteenth century. In 1754 the archbishopric of Mexico already had 84 schools of Spanish, 262 in 1756. Archbishop Rubio y Salinas declared his belief that 'thanks to business and the communication they have with us, they will manage to forget their languages and with the creation of the schools they will acquire a taste for reading and writing, motivated by the wish to accede to the sciences and liberal arts, to ennoble their spirits and to escape from the poverty, nudity and wretchedness in which they live.'[49] The object was nothing less than 'systematically abolishing the use of indigenous languages' to reduce the Indians to 'civic life', to promote 'unity and mixing with the Spanish'. One agency would be schools where teachers paid from communal funds and from any tribute surplus would teach catechism, and reading and writing Spanish.

Archbishop Lorenzana stepped up the campaign, insisting on the need to bring the Indian populations out of their isolation and integrate them in the economic and social life of the country. 'Regulations so that the natives of these kingdoms are happy in the spiritual realm as in the temporal domain', published by Archbishop Lorenzana among his *Cartas pastorales* in 1768, placed perhaps as much emphasis on housing, hygiene, clothing, and marriage as on spiritual duties proper. After the salvation of the Indians came their material well-being. Lorenzana accepted that the Indians had souls like Europeans, but he had reservations about their culture and questioned their intellectual and moral maturity; he was not in favour of their ordination to the priesthood. Lorenzana insisted on Spanish as the language of evangelization, as it was of adminstration, for it was superior to native languages and was rightly imposed on conquered Indians. For him the hero of Mexican history was Hernán Cortés, whose letters he edited and published.[50] Fabián y Fuero, bishop of Puebla, decreed that all Indian children should learn Spanish in a year, and all Indians recite doctrine in four years. Secularization was at one with hispaniciza-tion, for the new priests did not normally speak the Indian languages; for their part, many Indians went to the friars for their confessions, not to their parish priests. And hispanicization was a secular as well as a religious policy: the Bourbon state wanted to address its American subjects in one language, apply one law, and administer one people. This was a rational policy which appealed to the bureaucrats of the time and departed from the tradition of the friars. It was an expression of absolutism. Whether it was 'enlightened' in any sense, eighteenth century or otherwise, is open to question.

American attitudes were mixed. The policy was an irritant to some creole opinion, as it was regarded as an insult to the American languages. Indian leaders wanted and demanded schools for their communities. But many Indians resented having to learn and speak Spanish and they used only enough to defend themselves. They prayed in Indian and insisted that they had a right to their own language in religion.[51] In Puebla the Indian cacique Juan de la Cruz, fervent believer, demanded a confessor in Indian on his deathbed, and in default of one preferred to die without confession. Indians had their own defence mechanisms. They continued to speak, eat, and dress in their own ways, impervious to Spanish demands to conform to their civilization, speak Spanish, wear Spanish dress, abandon drunken-ness and concubinage, and become at last subjects of Church and state.

The Bourbon language programme was part of a wider policy of state control in religion, accompanied by secularization, closer scrutiny of Indian communities, and new efforts to administer their funds. But the campaign failed: there were too many obstacles to 'civilizing' the Indians, too few resources, too little appreciation of local realities. Even the Church's own attack on Indian religious practices had limited success. Spanish prelates viewed the cultural divide with deep suspicion and they too sought to hispanicize the Indian and remove the excesses of indigenous religion. They warned against the practices of popular piety, and sought to curtail the Indian theatre of religion, where extravagant processions were followed by drinking, sexual harassment of women, and often violence. In a pastoral letter of 1769 Archbishop Lorenzana condemned recourse to magic, super-stitious cures, and the use of peyote. He prescribed twenty-five strokes of the lash for 'all live representations of the Passion of Christ our Redeemer, the Volador pole, the dances of Santiago . . . representations of Shepherds and Kings'.[52] Like many of his contemporaries and successors, Lorenzana failed to distinguish clearly between culture and religion, between folk practices of Indians and their religious beliefs, and he did not understand that ritual needed to appeal to the senses and emotions of the Indians rather than the mind.

In Guatemala Archbishop Cortés y Larraz was contemptuous of popular religion in the Dominican parishes of Vera Paz:

> The solemn festivals celebrated in Guatemala and elsewhere are nothing more than occasions of drunkenness, indecency, gambling, brawling, and killing. The fear shown in not correcting them, although there is a mandate from the diocese to do so, in order to avoid losing face – is not this evidence of a people addicted to debauchery and subject to no law? As for the people outside the pueblos, they are a mixture of Spaniards, Indians, and Ladinos of mixed race, so in a single plantation you have all these kinds living side by side, the Spaniards insolent, the Indians frightened, the Ladinos deceitful and cunning, and all of them naked and thrust together at all hours of the day and night, without God, without Church, without King, without shame, and without honour.[53]

Elitist contempt for popular piety, characteristic of Bourbon Spain itself, also affected America, in a way which anticipated the policy of the anti-clerical liberals of the nineteenth century. A combination of Bourbon absolutism, imperial 'reform', and Jansenist influences among the clergy produced a kind of modernity which attacked popular cultures, especially Indian cultures, and introduced a vain campaign against processions and pilgrimages.[54] Indian confraternities were a particular target of attack, and reformers were agreed that the time had come to curtail the numbers, expenditure, and autonomy of these groups.

All confraternities fell under the scrutiny of Bourbon government, Hispanic as well as Indian, which automatically suspected any institution independent of the state. These lay organizations sustained religious cults in churches and chapels, funded many parish priests and chaplains, and paid for public and private ritual. Their functions combined those of devotional groups, mutual assistance, and burial societies, and many of them helped to define social status and corporate identity. They tended to reinforce horizontal social divisions and reflect class distinctions between Spaniards, mestizos, and Indians. Indian confraternities identified strongly with their communities and their barrios and were 'popular' in a social sense as well as in their sense of theatre. In 1776 the government in Madrid, which regarded confraternities as temporal rather than spiritual in character and their property as subject to royal rather than clerical jurisdiction,

ruled that they all required a royal licence and their conformity to royal
policy would be investigated. In 1791 a further order prohibited any
confraternity to meet without a royal official present.

In Mexico the Indian confraternities were the subject of particular intervention by the Church and then of harassment by the state. Archbishop
Lorenzana was the first to propose the systematic 'extinction' of all the
indigenous brotherhoods, proposing to reassign their property and revenues to the trusteeship of an 'educated *mayordomo*', in other words a
Spaniard. This was an attack on an Indian institution for no other reason
than that it did not conform to contemporary Spanish preferences. In 1794
the archbishop of Mexico reported to the crown that of the 951 confraternities in his diocese he had abolished 500. Elsewhere the hierarchy
proceeded with greater prudence but no less prejudice. Confraternities
now had to reapply for royal permission simply to exist, and to place their
property in the hands of a Spaniard who might confiscate their images and
curtail their collections. Indian leaders might protest that their people
needed more than an intellectual expression of the faith and better understood living representations, but neither Church nor state paid any attention to them. Thus the gulf between Indian religion and elite opinion,
between popular Catholicism and modernizing clergy, was opened.[55]

Archbishop Cortés y Larraz believed that the Indians of Guatemala were
irredeemable, lost to God and to the Church. For the adults there was no
remedy. The only solution was to take away their children at the age of five
and shut them in colleges where they could be indoctrinated anew.[56]

Indian Resistance

Spaniards held two inconsistent ideas about American Indians. They were
often seen as humble and innocent people, victims of culture and environment. Alternatively they were deceitful, malicious, and disobedient subjects.
The Jesuit father Bernardo Recio thought they lived innocent lives and
were the happiest of all classes in Quito. A Franciscan pastor from
Cuernavaca, on the other hand, spoke of Indians in 1752 as having 'a
natural aversion to all that is good', and a natural propensity to lie and
deceive.[57] The mainstream view, however, expressed by bishops, religious
manuals, and other colonial authorities, was that Indians were neither
noble innocents nor cunning brutes by nature; they had redeeming qualities that could make them faithful Christians and loyal, productive subjects
of the king, and they could be improved by education. An example of
moderate opinion was that of Bishop de la Peña y Montenegro, whose
guide to best practice towards Indians insisted that it was more sinful to
wrong an Indian than a Spaniard, for if an Indian were weak in faith this

could destroy it, and it was worse to rob an Indian because he had less to start with.[58] Because of their poverty and malnutrition Indians were exempt from the full laws of fasting and abstinence; equally, chewing coca, which churchmen agreed was necessary to give them strength to work, was not regarded as breaking the fast.

Stereotypes abounded, often revealing more of Spanish observers than of Indian people. The Spanish friar Francisco de Ajofrín attributed the heavy drinking and other excesses of the Indians to lack of education and the bad example of Spaniards. 'These wretches are most humble and submissive to everyone, even to the lower sectors of society, subordinating themselves to the blacks, mulattos, and slaves, living as captives in their own land. In the final analysis, as the proverb says, the Indians are *pobres que a muchos enriquecen, hambrientes que hartan, desnudos que visten* (the poor who enrich many, the hungry who feed many, the naked who clothe many).'[59] Father Recio, who was intrigued by what he called the beautiful colour of the Indians of Quito, 'hardly different from that of Spaniards', discounted their sullen expression which hid 'an interior peace and real happiness gained through the goodness of their life'.[60] The Indians gained little from sympathy of this kind which could easily become complacency about conditions. Poverty as religious virtue was unconvincing when the poverty was involuntary and degrading.

Most of the Indians under Spanish rule probably acquiesced in their fate, even as they found ways of quietly evading its excesses. But a series of indigenous movements in eighteenth-century Mexico, six among the Mayas of Yucatán and Chiapas, one in Oaxaca, and two in northern Mexico, expressed Indian resentment against the abuses of colonial power, pressure on land, and excessive demands for labour and taxes. Stagnating economic conditions caused the civil and ecclesiastical bureaucracies to increase their demands for taxes and tribute and sought to tighten the administration. In the Church's case this involved renewed campaigns against idolatry. So the already precarious subsistence base of the Maya was further eroded by periodic visitations of alcaldes and bishops, demanding extra labour and funds. The enemies targeted were officials and missionaries; the solution was to end rule by Spaniards, appropriate the world of the exploiters, overturn the social order, and replace it by Indian domination. No doubt the Indians were manipulated by the Mayan elites acting in defence of the material interests of their communities and of their own rank and privileges. But the unrest had more than material causes. Why did the movement begin as a religious cult?

Spanish authorities denounced the protests as expressions of 'paganism and heresy'. Amidst economic and political resentment, the protests all expressed a religious vision, a mixture of Mayan and Christian symbols, speaking of mythical heroes who returned to their homeland, saviours who came to redeem the people, worlds which were destroyed and revived, a cyclical movement of calamity and well-being, dearth and abundance. Most of the movements were impelled by millenarian visions, and inspired by apparitions, miraculous images, divine messages and prophecies. Those who came forward as messiahs were people who knew both worlds – Indian by birth, 'white' by education, their religion acquired from the friars. Thus they were able to appropriate the religion of the dominators and transform it into an agency of resistance.[61] The result was a synthesis of Maya destiny and the Christian millennium: Maya prophecies of the end of the world because of the faults of men converged with belief in the saving powers of the Virgin, who would return and restore happiness. But happiness eluded these unfortunates. The messiahs were usually taken and deported, their shrines shattered, their idols destroyed. Yet hope never died in the breasts of the millenarians: one movement defied the outside world beyond the expectations of its enemies.

The great rebellion of Cancuc in 1712 began as a cult around the Virgin who appeared to a young Indian woman and promised to help the Indians. New images were discovered and venerated in chapels constructed without clerical approval, while native prophets, men and women, spoke in the name of the Virgin. When the Spanish religious authorities rejected the miracle and punished its adherents, they were denounced as Jews and avaricious enemies of Christ. The Indians began to take their own decisions, to form an indigenous state, install a theocratic elite, and establish native Churches. On 10 August 1712 a large gathering of Indians from the Altos of Chiapas assembled in Cancuc to celebrate the feast of the Virgin and receive a further message: 'Now there is no more God or King, only the Virgin is to be obeyed, she who will descend from heaven to Cancuc to protect and govern the Indians, and at the same time they ought to obey and respect the ministers, captains, and officials, whom she would place in the villages, ordering them expressly to kill all the friars and priests, as well as Spaniards, mestizos, blacks and mulattos, so that only the Indians would remain in the land.'[62] From that point the messianic movement became openly aggressive towards whites, placing Indians in control of religious institutions and doctrine. They killed five Dominican friars and several Spanish and mestizo settlers. Ladino women were taken and forced to 'marry' rebel Indians. Captured whites had to dress as Indians, and Spaniards were called 'judíos' or 'indios'. Troops sent from Guatemala were fiercely fought by 4–5,000 'soldiers of the Virgin', armed with machetes and lances.[63]

Although the rebels of Cancuc were influenced by Maya traditions of the supernatural, they did not adopt Mayan religion or abandon the Catholic faith; their strategy was to replace the Spanish clergy with an Indian priest-hood; to manage their own religious life, create their own saints and cults.[64] They celebrated mass, using confiscated vestments and chalices, in effect taking over the ritual of the Spaniards and substituting an Indian ortho-doxy. The rebellion was violent; loyal Maya were killed and their children massacred. The Spanish response was also cruel: priests and religious repossessed their churches behind royal troops while local officials restored their tyrannies. It was 1716 before peace returned, on Spanish terms.

The rebellion of Jacinto Canek, an Indian educated by the Franciscans in Yucatán, was a further menace to Church and state. Disturbances began in the village of Quisteil during the mass of 19 December 1761, causing the priest to flee for his life. Jacinto preached the end of priests and officials, and proclaimed himself 'King of Yucatán'; his wife too occupied a special place in the movement and was designated the blue Virgin of the Conception. His followers began to organize an independent government, drawing support from a wide range of villages. They were armed and capable of resisting the Spaniards and defending their gains, until they were finally defeated by the colonial power. Bloody reprisals followed.

Among the various Indian *curanderos* who appeared in Mexico in the late eighteenth century, waiting for the end of the world and the descent of God to mankind, the most notorious was Antonio Pérez, an Indian folk doctor of Yautepec, an alcoholic and former shepherd, who made himself known in the late 1750s. The first supernatural sign was a vision of the Virgin Mary at the foot of the volcano Popocatepetl, which led to the discovery of an image of an Indianized Virgin of the Volcano. Soon Pérez's house at Tetizicayac became a sanctuary which attracted hundreds of Indians from the region, drawn by cures or curiosity or the powers of Pérez's miraculous images of Christ. This was more than a rebellion against the colonial order. Antonio imagined a new world where he and his disci-ples would rule Church and state and rid Mexico of its exploiters.

Assimilating fragments of Catholic ritual and Indian folklore, Pérez assumed the functions of priest and healer, baptizing his disciples and hearing confessions. Later he proclaimed himself a god and was worshipped. On the strength of his popular appeal he began to attack the official Church and described it as Hell; he denied the real presence and rejected traditional saints. Pérez's message contained a trace of social radicalism, as was usual in millenarian movements. Drunkenness was a sin, but not fornication, which he himself practised with young girls. He prophesied earthquake, fire, and epidemic, events which would announce the destruc-tion of Spanish rule, especially of its three agents – tribute, viceroy, and archbishop. The colonial order would make way for another world where he would be king and pontiff. 'Everything should belong to the *naturales* [the Indians] ... They alone should remain, and the Spaniards and *gente de razón* [elites] should be burned ... All the wealth should stay with the *naturales* ... The world is a cake which should be shared among everyone'.[65] Church and state in the eighteenth century distrusted popular piety of this kind as being out of harmony even with the diluted version of the Enlightenment which reached the Hispanic world; these were ignorant people, guilty of idolatry. Yet it was not a question of Indians versus whites. The local priest Domingo José de la Mota, who arrested Pérez, confiscated his image, and eventually brought charges against him, was himself an Indian, a cacique, with two brothers who were priests. With the help of the secular authorities the movement was attacked and dismantled, and its adherents were arrested or fled to the mountains.

Missionary Expansion

During the age of Enlightenment, when other European empires lapsed into defeatism and decline, the Spanish empire underwent a new phase of expansion, mainly political in inspiration, but with religious implications. New frontiers of the empire, or its weaker edges, were usually fortified not only by garrisons but also by a priestly presence: the gun and the Gospel moved together, and missionary expeditions into Indian territory received military escort 'for better security'. Charles III claimed: 'my first obligation and that of all my successors is to protect the Catholic religion in all the dominions of this vast monarchy'. Even so the prospects for missions were not entirely favourable and the Bourbons were by no means crusaders for the faith.

The American mission had three spiritual arms, Franciscans, Capuchins, and Jesuits. In 1767 it lost the Jesuits, a great setback for mission expansion, and one which caused a major replanning of existing missions. The territories hitherto evangelized by the Jesuits had to be assigned either to the secular clergy or to other orders, and many missions simply transferred into *doctrinas* or parishes, which meant an end to expansion and in some cases to serious religious instruction. This happened in north-east Mexico, the Colombian llanos of Meta and Casanare, Amazonia, and Moxos and Chiquitos. As some of these missions had already reached their limits, they were in effect frozen by the subsequent regime and remained so for the rest of the colonial period. At the same time the assignment of former Jesuit territory to new missionaries in some cases gave an impulse to renewed expansion, as happened in California, the Upper Orinoco, and the archipelago of Chiloé.

One of the most vigorous areas of mission activity in the eighteenth century was the southern extremity of New Granada around Popayán, specifically Caquetá and Putumayo, a mission field assigned to the Spanish Franciscans and chronicled by one of the great, yet forgotten, chroniclers of the colonial period, Fray Juan de Santa Gertrudis, a Mallorcan who went to America in 1756 with a group of fourteen missionaries assigned to Popayán in the Province of Quito.[66] After disembarking at Cartagena they travelled by mule and canoe along the Magdalena, restoring religion to abandoned Christians on the way. From Popayán onwards they were in mission territory and changed into their tropical habits of local cotton. As they dropped off priests and picked up Indian guides at various stations on their route, they sang the *Te Deum* with Christianized Indians, and tried to avoid their offerings of roast monkeys. Finally, only Fray Juan remained, at the end of the line, his last stage a journey by canoe to the Putumayo river to meet his Indians and bring them in from the jungle.

At first missionaries were given an interpreter, often a mestizo who knew the local language; gradually they learnt the native languages by practice and experience and taught their converts a kind of mission-speak. Fray Juan also taught them to wear clothes, a particular obsession of his, especially when two naked young girls joined his household as servants. Not all the missionaries agreed. Passing through the mission station of Santa Cruz with its tribe of Mamos Indians he asked the creole priest, Father Rosales, if decency was not offended by the presence of naked natives in the church and at mass. 'He explained to me that the climate was hot and clothes irritated them; scruples were all very well in college but here it was essential to forget them or to forget any chance of conversions. What he said was true, but I was still determined to clothe the Indians when I got the opportunity.'[67]

Nine months later, following a prolonged drinking session, the Mamos Indians killed Father Rosales when he tried to destroy their store of liquor, splitting his head with an axe and burning his body. Fray Juan thus learnt that clothing his Indians was not the only priority: it was important also to have a shotgun ready and loaded all the time. He discovered that it was useful to fire a shot in the air when approaching and leaving the village, partly as a warning, partly as a reassurance that this was the priest and he would do them no harm. And he never said mass without a gun at the ready: 'I instructed my assistant that whenever I said mass he was to stand at the side of the altar, shotgun in hand, because many of the murders of missionary priests at the hands of Indians had been committed during mass.'[68] These missions carried security risks, from men as well as from nature, and the Putumayo mission, unlike some, had no military escort for their protection.

Fray Juan was at the end of the line, nine days' journey from the last station on the Putumayo, surrounded by *bárbaros* and mosquitoes. In his first year, 1758, it was his job to found a new mission by bringing in Indians (some 280) dispersed throughout the surrounding jungle, a proud and fierce people called *encabellados*, hitherto unconquered. He called his village Agustinillo. There he not only had to build a church and call the people to mass and instruction, an awesome task in itself as they had no awareness of a personal God, but also to develop the area, by clearing, ploughing, and planting, and he himself had to take up the machete alongside the Indians, otherwise they did not work. 'Each morning I took the sacred host with one hand, the machete with the other, and I never went out without it, or else the shotgun.'[69] Missionaries led by example. Surrounded by naked women they were not immune to desire and Fray Juan was aware of it. He explains that two circumstances came to his assistance. The Indians observed and discussed everything the priest did, and he would certainly lose face among them if he took a woman. And the knowledge that 'these barbarians would take his life whenever they felt like it' made him shrink from mortal sin and dying without a confessor at hand.

The greatest fear of the missionary was that he might never break through, at least to the older Indians, and they would remain hostile to the last. It took years to teach them the Our Father, Hail Mary, and the Creed and some of them never understood. As for the mass, they would attend with their alcohol ready and their weapons to hand: 'I had a lot to overcome, but I never beat them as some missionaries did'. He offered them gifts, tobacco, and beyond this tools and equipment, and worked to provide the whole community with economic subsistence and agricultural development. 'They do not embrace the faith through knowledge of the truth or the light of natural reason, but only because that is what the missionary priest states and teaches, and because he interests them through gifts of axes, machetes, and other hardware.'[70] He also sought to attract them by appointing their own leaders as alcaldes and other officials, in the hope that if these converted, others would follow. And he created an illusion of elections, placing names in a hat and drawing them out as in a lottery. 'As they did not know the characters, I myself made the elections for these offices of the six Indians who seemed to me most suitable.'[71]

One of the greatest problems of evangelization was polygamy. Fray Juan attempted to convince his converts through rational discussion that it was natural for a man to take only one wife. He used the argument that many creatures of the surrounding jungle and mountains – parrots, macaws, lions, tigers, bears – only had one female, and men must be the same; all Christians observed this and took only one woman. But his Indians turned the same argument back on him: cocks used many hens, they said, pigs many sows. The priest concluded from this dialogue that the devil himself dictated these replies and he fell back on arguments from faith and religion, and also from persuasion, trying to enforce a choice: the material resources and advantages of village life came with baptism, but baptism depended on having only one wife. At the same time he solemnly undertook to find new husbands for the abandoned wives and in the meantime guarded them against rape and provided food and clothing for them.

Fray Juan's greatest problems in America came not from the Indians, a burden willingly undertaken, but from his own order in Popayán and the regional headquarters of the mission. From the outset Agustinillo was starved of resources for its material development by the mission superior, who appropriated as much of the mission funds as possible for his own project, a new college in Popayán, to the detriment of the missions in the field. When Fray Juan tried to generate resources by producing a surplus (mainly cacao) and selling outside, he was bitterly opposed by rival friars who denied him Indian guides and sought to get him lost in the jungle; he was opposed at every turn by his own Franciscan commissary who strove to monopolize mission resources. The discovery of gold in the mission territory sparked a fierce dispute between the commissary, who in collusion with the colonial administration wanted to invest in the mines to earn a surplus for his own agenda, and Fray Juan, who saw them as a potential danger to the missions, causing a flight of his neophytes from slave labour in the mines. In a noisy confrontation he accused the commissary, Father Barrutieta, of lying, malversation, and tyranny.[72] Fray Juan wanted to take the case before the viceroy in Santa Fe, and to make the issue one of missions versus mines, but he was stopped by his own Franciscan provincial, an appeaser, who told him that the commissary had already won over the viceroy and Fray Juan had arrived too late. If he persisted he risked being expelled from the colony and sent back to Spain.

Fray Juan accepted defeat and decided to rely on his own efforts to raise money for his mission; he travelled the length and breadth of the Pasto region preaching, arguing, and begging, and recorded his adventures in a classic of picaresque writing. He remained convinced, apparently correctly, that Barrutieta had received public revenues for the missions far in excess of what he had disbursed to the mission stations.[73]

The balance sheet of Fray Juan's mission, after ten years, showed a total population of 1,472, among whom 311 adults were baptized and married, and over 200 children baptized. There were 512 head of cattle, 623 sheep, over 200 cocks and hens, 300 quintals of cotton, 220 of wool, and six looms, various crops, numerous tools and items of hardware, 170 houses, a priest's house, and a church.[74] Starting from nothing, he had created not only a Christian community but also a rural economy.

The Church in the Eighteenth Century

At the end of the colonial period Spanish America had seven archdioceses and thirty-six suffragan dioceses, some of them eighteenth-century creations. Many dioceses were so large in size that the bishop was a remote figure pastorally. In the last fifty years of Spanish rule ten new dioceses were created and two new archdioceses. But any attempt by the crown to subdivide dioceses or create new bishoprics was fiercely resisted, for existing bishops and chaplains stoutly defended their resources and revenues, which were often far in excess of pastoral needs. For the majority of the faithful, membership of the Church meant membership of a parish. In the mid-eighteenth century Mexico had 844 parishes for a population of 5 million, Peru 527 for a population of 1.3 million, Venezuela 178 for a population of 345,000. The leading cities of the Americas were swarming with priests, friars, and nuns. In the years around 1780–90, Lima had an ecclesiastical population of over 1,300, Mexico City 1,100, and Quito, considering its smaller size, an even greater concentration of clerics, over 1,000.[75] These figures signify a close social relationship between clergy and people, for many families had sons and daughters among the clergy; at the same time numerous religious institutions held liens and mortgages on lay properties which kept their parishioners in a position of economic dependence.

Many places had no parishes, and the distances between parishes and beyond parishes could be immense. Theoretically, in the case of Indians, there should have been 300–500 to a parish, but this figure was rarely met. Many Latin Americans, therefore, nominally Catholics, did not attend mass. Yet the Church provided oases of civilization in unlikely places. Writing in the early eighteenth century, the chronicler Oviedo y Baños described Trujillo, a small town of 300 residents in a backward province of Venezuela, but with religious institutions active and intact: 'It maintains a parochial church served by two rector-curates and two monasteries, one of the Order of Santo Domingo and the other of San Francisco. It has a temple of ornate and elegant architecture; a hermitage of Nuestra Señora de Chiquinquirá, site of a hospital; and a convent for Dominican nuns who make beautiful items, especially their pita products and other needlework.'[76]

The clergy of these dioceses and parishes were members of a controlled colonial Church, though one which was still concerned with standards of appointment. Most of the candidates for bishoprics had doctorates in theology and rose from cathedral chapters or university professorships. In the second half of the eighteenth century, of the 168 bishops at the head of American dioceses all but one had been appointed in response to specific needs and circumstances. A few were promoted from important positions, but most had begun in modest cathedrals, and some even as parish priests, a sign of some mobility in promotions; by now fewer were selected from religious orders. Fifteen returned to Spain, the rest died in America. The charge is often made that this was a Church dominated by Spanish-born bishops. In the second half of the eighteenth century 56.8 per cent of the American hierarchy were *peninsulares*, 43.1 per cent creoles, a sign of increasing creolization which was accentuated by the reluctance of qualified Spanish candidates to go to American sees.[77] At certain times, two-thirds of cathedral deans were American. As for prebends, the majority were American and the government actually sought to redress the balance by offering Americans posts in Spain, in order to reserve one-third of canons and prebends for 'natives of those kingdoms'.

Nevertheless, the number of Spanish-born prelates occupying American sees, especially major sees, was still high. In the eighteenth century creole clerics were excluded from the best posts in New Spain to such an extent that between 1713 and 1800 only one American – a Cuban, not a Mexican – was named to any of the three wealthiest dioceses of New Spain, Mexico, Puebla, and Michoacán; the few Americans who were appointed were named to the poorest dioceses. In the whole period 1700–1815 the diocese of Michoacán was ruled entirely by peninsular Spaniards.[78] Bishops were served by their cathedral chapter, men of considerable talent, learning, and wealth. In the appointment of parish priests the bishop relied upon a subcommittee of the chapter, which examined candidates and made three nominations. The bishop chose one, but this had to be ratified by the viceroy, the representative of the ultimate patron, the crown.

Consciousness of rival identity between Spaniards and Americans was as strong among the clergy as among the rest of the population. In 1794 the chapter of Valladolid in Mexico (its full complement was twenty-one but there were six vacancies) contained ten peninsular Spaniards. European dominance of this kind could be established simply through the bishop exercising his considerable patronage in favour of his countrymen, all conscious of their Spanish identity and its importance in maintaining the stability of the colonial state and the character of the colonial Church. Among the ordinary clergy consciousness of identity among creoles and resentment of favour shown to Spaniards always lurked below the surface and was made explicit on occasions of particular grievance over appointments. Among the religious orders loss of status and role in the eighteenth century aggravated identity crises and reactivated the confrontation between creoles and Spaniards. This was noticeable too in the missionary orders. Conflict within the Franciscan mission in southern New Granada was provoked when it was thought that new Spaniards were gaining promotion over experienced locals. A creole missionary on the Putumayo resented being superseded by a Spaniard, for as 'a native creole he had no desire to give way to a *chapetón* Father recently arrived from Spain'.[79]

The clergy of Spanish America in the eighteenth century contained saints and sinners in unknown proportions. In Quito it was alleged that many parish priests were absentees, sometimes appointing a vicar, sometimes not; in 1790 Bishop José Pérez Calama alleged that many parishes had not seen a priest for fifty years. The bishops were not always the best judges, and their visitations were regarded as mixed blessings. Bartolomé Arzáns de Orzúa y Vela, chronicler of Potosí (1676–1736), deplored the visitation of Archbishop Luis Francisco Romero in 1727 for its harsh financial exactions and its indiscriminate attack on the clergy, when many good and honourable priests were victims of malicious gossip too readily believed by the visitor.[80] Arzáns himself could spot a lax cleric when he saw one and those who failed to set an example formed a veritable rogues' gallery in his chronicle, especially those who took advantage of their position to seduce young women or lived openly with concubines. While hordes of poor clergy were under-provided and highly taxed, the well-connected could accumulate offices and benefices effortlessly. Such was Fernando de Arango y Queipo, parish priest of the mother church of Potosí, rector of the cathedral of La Plata, vice-chancellor of the University of La Plata, professor of canon law there, provisor, visitor, and vicar general of the archbishopric of La Plata, an archdiocesan tax official, and owner of considerable wealth of his own.[81] No one looked for a Las Casas among clergy of this kind: in the eighteenth century, in so far as there was any criticism of the mines, *mita*, and treatment of the Indians in Potosi, it did not come from the Church.

The clergy of Venezuela, a less well-endowed colony than Mexico, had less chance of preferment. According to Bishop Mariano Martí few of them deserved it. In the course of his pastoral visitation he became totally disillusioned by the state of his clergy, many of them local creoles, hardly distinguishable from their parishioners in moral behaviour. The records of his visitation enumerate case after case of lax behaviour, ignorance, and incompetence among local parish priests, their lack of education, and their isolation from the Church hierarchy and current ideas.[82] Martí himself was an interesting example of a Bourbon bishop. An agent of both Church and state, his work an amalgam of functions, he was inspired by the conviction that priests should be warned against subversion as well as sin and that his visitation should yield a total view of Venezuela – its administration, geography, and resources, in addition to religion.[83] A Spaniard by birth, he was a religious reformer, determined to improve the Christian and moral level of America. After heading a diocese in Puerto Rico he became bishop of Venezuela in 1770 at the age of 41.

Martí saw his episcopacy as an almost constant *visita*, lasting from 1771 to 1784, covering the Venezuelan coast, Andes, and llanos, and including Indians, Africans, slaves, Spaniards, and mixed races, rural and urban society, priests and people. As he travelled the mountains, valleys, and plains of Venezuela he invited the populace of each town he visited to tell him in confidence the details of their 'sinful' behaviour and that of their neighbours, which he then proceeded to record and judge. His method was effective enough to earn him the enmity of regional elites and of some local clerics. In his records (seven volumes in their modern edition) he gave details of over 1,500 individuals singled out for accusation, primarily regarding sexual misdeeds. Transgressions included adultery, fornication, concubinage, incest, rape, bigamy, prostitution, lust, homosexuality, bestiality, abortion, and infanticide. The bishop's list was lengthened by drunkenness, gambling, witchcraft, murder, theft, and idolatry. He took a wide view of sin and his reprobates included *hacendados* who were cruel to their slaves, village priests who were harsh to mission Indians, and merchants and shopkeepers who levied usurious charges on their customers. Nearly 10 per cent of clerics in the province came under criticism, and even the governor of Maracaibo was denounced.

Martí was not impressed by the reluctance of the upper classes to marry their children to racial inferiors, and he insisted that unions be solemnized according to Christian morality, not left informal. But in practice he could not defeat social prejudice and widespread concubinage, which discouraged interracial marriages. In any case Martí did not challenge prevailing standards and he usually imposed punishments on female slaves rather than the slave-owners who seduced them. There was an ingrained bias in religious culture which regarded women as occasions of sin and blamed their seductiveness, behaviour, and dress for all sexual temptations, rather than men and conditions.

This mentality was characteristic of the Church throughout the Americas. Fray José Antonio de San Alberto had strong views on most subjects, not least on sex. While bishop of Tarija in the mid-eighteenth century he began a vigorous campaign, supported by the governor, to improve public morality, allegedly in serious decline. One of the worst occasions of sin was 'the provocative and scandalous dresses of women of all classes and colours, the leading ladies being the worst examples of this hellish abuse'. He sent a 73-page report to the crown illustrated with various drawings of the dresses.[84] In New Granada Fray Juan de Santa Gertrudis concluded that only a quarter of women living with men were married. He recorded a one-man morality compaign waged by a religious in Barbacoa, near Pasto, nicknamed Father 'Get Married'. 'Any man who confessed to sinning against the sixth commandment he seized by the hair and beat quite

severely, shouting "Get married! Get married!" But he was also known
never to refuse absolution, so all the wild young men about town queued
up to confess to him, watching the comic scene in which he repeated
the beatings and admonitions, thus enforcing the penance before the
absolution.'[85]

It was easier to describe America's sinful ways than to reform them. In
Venezuela Bishop Martí tried to impose a moral code and to encourage
proper Christian behaviour in social and sexual relations. He issued proc-
lamations prohibiting dancing, and he condemned improper dress for
women. On his visitation he exhorted priests to preach and apply the
commandments. But it was a losing battle to apply the rules of the Church
at every level of colonial society, or to narrow the gap between morals and
behaviour. In one village drunkenness would be 'the main sin', in another
robbery. For the majority of Venezuelans, especially the popular classes,
marriage was not an indispensable institution, nor was virginity sacro-
sanct, illegitimacy an infamy, or a casual union unacceptable.[86] For those
with little or nothing to lose, marriage and legitimacy were not a particular
advantage. They were, it is true, assets to the upper classes, but for reasons
of inheritance and public office rather than moral repute, and in Hispanic
society infidelity was rarely a serious threat to marriage.

Martí's visitation points to an enduring truth about colonial Venezuela,
and equally to the whole of Spanish America. Faith was not in doubt. The
Church preached its doctrine and performed its liturgy in a society which
easily accepted both. During his visitation the bishop saw many signs of
religious fervour. Of the white, mestizo, mulatto, and black population of
Tinaquillo he wrote that they are 'a devout people, many of them daily
mass goers; they frequent the sacraments and come to say the rosary at
3 o'clock'. Of Ocumare he reported: 'The parish priest tells me the nature of
these people is such that if they are invited to a dance they all go; equally,
if they are invited to a church service they all go. There is no particular vice
among them.' In the small village of Parapara the people were 'docile, of
good disposition, and frequent the sacraments'.[87] There was evidently
much popular piety in Venezuela. Morals, however, were a different matter,
accepted by most in theory but ignored by many in practice.

Another episcopal visitation, almost contemporary with that in
Venezuela, gave a more pessimistic impression of religious practice.
Archbishop Cortés y Larraz was pure Spaniard by birth, education, and
career, a native of Zaragoza and product of the classical clerical track, from
university to parish, canonry, and episcopacy. Archbishop of Guatemala
from 1768 to 1786, a diocese which was heavily Indianized and comprised
El Salvador, Chiapas, and Nicaragua as well as Guatemala itself, he stood
out as an efficient and well-meaning prelate and was the author of a vivid

account of his pastoral visitation of 1768–70. He himself was totally immune to Indian, or even creole, culture and gained only a faint understanding of American life. He recognized that the Indians were 'most worthy of compassion, being absolutely miserable in body and soul' and were badly exploited by the *alcaldes mayores*, but he believed that the source of all their disorder and crimes was their incurable drunkenness. And even apparently Christianized and well-ordered Indians 'are still Indians'.[88] Favourable evidence he tended to discount. When the Dominican *cura* of a parish in Vera Paz reported that drunkenness was 'extinguished', Cortés y Larraz preferred to believe that it was 'suspended' for the visitation; as for the claim that these parishioners attended mass and doctrine lessons and fulfilled their Easter duty of confession and communion, he remarked that this was 'nothing less than pure suppression of the truth'. His own attitude to religious practice in Guatemala was one of disillusion: he found little interest in religion or the fulfilment of Christian duties, and many people failed to attend mass, receive the sacraments or learn doctrine. As for the Indians, he learnt from Father Rosel, the parish priest of Huehuetenango, who knew the local language, that they were indifferent to the sacraments, and valued extreme unction but not confession.

The state of the clergy worried him. While he recorded numerous good priests, quietly going about their duties, there were many others unfit for office, and he met one 'with thirteen children by two concubines'; yet he said mass and administered the sacraments and made no attempt to hide his ways.[89] True, there were some of exceptional merit, such as Francisco Xavier Villar y Prego, parish priest of Samayac, a zealous and intelligent young Basque with a good library, a pastor who got a response from the Indians through kindness and firmness. Yet the archbishop regarded him as basically naïve: he ignored all the Indians living outside the village practising idolatry, and, like most of the Spanish clergy, had come to America totally ignorant of conditions. However, compared to the many incompetent and scandalous clerics he was a model priest. In the parish of San Sebastian in Guatemala City the parish priest accumulated wealth amidst surrounding poverty, and the parish accounts were 'unacceptably fraudulent'. The *cura* of San Jacinto in the province of San Salvador, José Dias del Castillo, was 'a vain and aggressive man, proud of his descent from the conquerors . . . a great friend of the Ladinos but very hostile to the wretched Indians'. When these reacted fiercely to ill-treatment, he had to be withdrawn.[90] While these were extreme cases, reported the archbishop, many priests were ordained who had no vocation and little education and were sent to parishes which were full of sin: concubinage, robbery, killing, and incest prevailed, with no sign of Christianity. Yet 'they do not regard these sins as exceptional; rather they excuse them, as can be seen in their letters'.

Synods, bishops, and Church leaders, of course, were naturally alarmist, and a parish priest learnt to understand his parishioners better than a visiting bishop. But there is no doubt that sin was abundant in these Catholic societies, and that drunkenness, gambling, adultery, and concubinage were common behaviour. Priests believed that Indians simply followed the example of Spaniards and became infected by sin as well as by disease. In the eyes of its Spanish archbishop, Guatemala was a country 'without God, without king, and without law'. Bishop Manuel de la Torre of Buenos Aires described morals there as so bad that they should start again from scratch with the sign of the cross. Cartagena, Mexico, and other places were all denounced by Church leaders as dens of iniquity. In Quito, a city where almost every street contained its church, monastery, or convent, the majority of people apparently did not fulfil their Easter duties: Church censuses of the 1790s record that an average of only 38 per cent of the eligible population received annual communion.[91]

No doubt many more of the faithful attended the popular fiestas which formed an integral part of the Catholic calendar. Saints' days and other feasts were a microcosm of Latin American morality: masses, processions, veneration of the saints, followed by bullfights, drink, dancing, and sex. Fray Juan de Santa Gertrudis describes a fiesta in Barbacoa, near Pasto, in honour of St Francis of Paola, the patron saint of the Negroes, mulattos, and zambos. This was an elaborate and costly ceremony beginning with a long procession to the church, punctuated by the firing of guns in the air and followed by gargantuan eating and drinking. 'By dawn it was rare for anyone not to be drunk.' His own sacristan took a whole day to sober up.[92]

These were the main targets of ecclesiastical horror and denunciation, especially among Bourbon bishops, who regarded popular religion as a hotbed of ignorance, superstition, and magic. There were periodic campaigns against iniquity in which sermons were preached and excommunications brandished, but without effect. Although many of these charges were obviously slanted against the popular classes, the Indians, mestizos, and mulattos, some were levelled at Spaniards and officials for setting a bad example. In Guatemala the Dominicans of Vera Paz took a more relaxed and charitable view of their Indian parishioners, tolerating their sinful ways because they were faithful and pious. Archbishop Cortés y Larraz on his visitation of the region had his reservations:

The fiestas reflect the character of the Indians, who spend heavily on them. The Indians taking part have statues (many of them crude and badly dressed) at the entrance of their houses, to form an altar with candles. On the day of the fiesta the statues are carried to the church accompanied by drums and bugles. After the service they return them to their houses, and the rest of the day is a holiday given over to dances and drinking. The fiesta is so natural to the Indians that they have no more secure rights than this.

A Dominican *cura* told the archbishop that 'if, after confessing his sins with the greatest sorrow and the firmest purpose of amendment, the Indian penitent were to find a bottle of brandy within reach he would get drunk immediately'.[93]

Sin, ignorance, and indifference were traditional concerns of the Church and in their periodic campaigns to raise moral standards bishops were doing no more than their duty. While admonishing the lower orders for iniquity, they also kept their eyes on the elites for faithlessness. Attempts by believers to reconcile their faith with reason, to seek secular as well as religious truth, to cultivate science as well as theology, were viewed with great suspicion by bishops in the Old World and the New, and Catholic reformers were regarded as no better than deists and agnostics. The Church in America did not engage in face-to-face confrontation with the Enlightenment, as it did in Europe. Yet it was marked by it for generations to come. The failure to come to terms with ideas of liberty and equality, to accept new knowledge and disavow obscurantism, to search the Enlightenment for good as well as for ill, meant that the Church lost the opportunity to modernize itself and thereby lost the allegiance of many exponents of Catholic reform. Many of the elites would find in utilitarianism and liberalism, two deposits of the Enlightenment, the philosophical high ground abandoned by the Church.

Meanwhile, in the years after 1750 the Church had taken or invited measures that weakened its own structure. The expulsion of the Jesuits, the marginalization of the remaining orders, the attack on clerical immunity, all served to alienate some of the clergy and alert many more. Only the bishops and higher clergy were comfortable with the Bourbons. But the commanding position gained by secular officials, the retreat of churchmen from many areas of jurisdiction, the close association of the altar and the throne, had brought the Church dangerously close to the colonial state. When this collapsed the Church would find that it did not have an independent support.

CHAPTER 4

Independence: A Sinful Revolution

The Crisis of the Colonial Church

T HE INDEPENDENCE OF Spanish America was precipitated in 1808 by Napoleon's invasion of Spain, a blow which severed the metropolis from its colonies and created a crisis of authority among its subjects. Who now ruled in America? Who should be obeyed? Demands were made for autonomy in government and a free economy, and as these were rejected, Spanish Americans took to arms. The collapse of the Bourbon state, however, was the occasion rather than the cause of these events. Independence had a long prehistory, during which colonial economies underwent growth, societies developed identity, and creoles became convinced that they were Americans, not Spaniards. The Church was not isolated from this process. The collapse of the Bourbon state and the onset of colonial rebellion in Spanish America were observed by the Church not simply as secular events but as a conflict of ideologies and a struggle for power that vitally affected its own interests. As an ally and vital arm of the Bourbon state it was now called upon to fulfil its duties. And in the war of ideas the Church saw allegiance to Spain, obedience to monarchy, and repudiation of dissent as moral imperatives. Revolution was a sin.

Along the road to these developments a number of colonial rebellions had already tested the loyalty of the clergy. In Peru creole protest against Bourbon fiscal and administrative policy was overtaken by a great Indian rebellion led by Túpac Amaru. The violent scenes in the southern highlands were the culmination of endemic grievances over tribute and *reparto* (forced sale of goods at exorbitant prices), and now aggravated by new *alcabalas* (sales taxes). The events of 1780–82 represented a basic defiance of the colonial state, whose officials closely scrutinized the reaction of the clergy. The credentials of the Church in Indian Peru were ambiguous. On the one hand, it was a common Indian complaint that priests exacted labour services without paying a just wage, charged excessive fees for the sacraments, and demanded taxes under pain of corporal punishment. On the other hand, no one denied that the clergy, most of them creoles, had great power over the Indians, a power used by some in support of royal officials but by many others in defence of Indian rights.

At the beginning of the rebellion, while Túpac Amaru was declaring his respect for the Church and 'our sacred Catholic religion', many priests were openly sympathetic to the Indian cause. When the conflict became more violent and then moved against the rebels the clergy tended to step back. Meanwhile the colonial authorities turned their anger on José Manuel Moscoso, creole bishop of Cuzco, who was slow to report the initial outbreak and was suspected of collusion with the rebels. The fact that Moscoso excommunicated Túpac Amaru and his followers, helped to organize the defence of Cuzco, and subsidized the war effort did not impress the colonial authorities; following the defeat of the rebellion and the cruel execution of its leaders, he was detained for two years in Lima and a further three in Spain before he established his loyalty. Priests in the Peruvian highlands continued to be regarded as suspect by a state which allowed not the slightest deviance by its clerical arm, least of all in an area where they were regarded as vital agents of social control. No one doubted that they had power over their Indian parishioners and could make life difficult for officials seeking to impose yet harsher royal exactions.[1]

In New Granada the rebellion of the *comuneros* in 1781 was a creole-dominated protest against tax innovation and bias in appointments. The rebellion also incorporated grievances of mestizos and Indians, and these sectors were useful to the movement in adding to its numbers and frightening the authorities. But they also frightened the creoles, who eventually lost their nerve and abandoned the struggle. A few clergy excepted, the Church stood solid with the colonial power in resisting the rebel claims, conscious perhaps that its own demands for tithes often made it a target for criticism. In rebellions of this kind the colonial clergy were expected to appear before the mob in ceremonial vestments, raise the monstrance bearing the blessed sacrament, and appeal for calm. In 1781 the rebels paid more attention to Archbishop Antonio Caballero y Góngora, who led the negotiations on the king's side and secured an agreed settlement. The crown capitalized on his moral authority by appointing him viceroy of New Granada, in which capacity he undertook to effect reconciliation of absolute monarchy and colonial subjects on the basis of economic development, applied science, and educational reform. Thus Caballero y Góngora sought to justify Bourbon policy – strong government and high taxes in a reformed economy – without, however, considering whether moderate reform merely whetted the appetite for greater change. He dealt primarily

with the elites without forgetting the poor, spending most of his considerable income, in his own words, 'on acts of charity and for political purposes',
that is buying support from interest groups.[2] He remained, however, a
convinced colonialist with no thought of regional economic development.
To those interests who appealed for industrial protection, he maintained
that agriculture and mining were 'the appropriate function of colonies',
while manufactures 'ought to be imported from the metropolis'.[3]

During the late colonial rebellions the Church played out its allotted
role. But was its loyalty misplaced? The religious mission of the Church in
the Americas was supported by two material assets, its *fueros* and its
wealth. The *fuero eclesiástico* gave clerics immunity from civil jurisdiction
and, as has been seen, was a closely guarded privilege. The wealth of the
Church was measured not only in tithes, real estate, and liens on property,
but also by its enormous capital, amassed throughout the centuries by
donations of the faithful.[4] This complex of ecclesiastical interests was one
of the principal targets of Bourbon reformers. They sought to bring the
clergy under the jurisdiction of the secular courts and to divert their
resources into the hands of the state.[5] The expulsion of the Jesuits, the
appointment of compliant bishops, the use of the Inquisition to investigate
creole clergy, the attack on Church resources, and the erosion of clerical
fueros, all these policies helped to alienate the Church and to remind it of
the liabilities of its dependence. And Bourbon policy both destabilized the
Church in general and divided it into interest groups, each with its own
grievance.

The fate of the American Church was determined by events in Spain.
Inadequate revenue combined with extravagant expenditure on court and
defence caused the Spanish government from 1798 to lay its hands on
Church property, and to initiate a policy of confiscation and sale in return
for interest payments. In December 1804 the policy of consolidation of
ecclesiastical property was extended to America. There Church wealth lay
not so much in real estate as in capital lent in mortgage-type loans. The
Consolidation of 1804 forced the Church to move its money to the royal
treasury and thence to Spain, and to accept a reduced return of 3 per cent.
Everything suffered: estates, mines, businesses, households, all suddenly
had to redeem the capital value of their loans and liens, or sell up, or have
their property seized. The clergy were embittered, especially the lower
clergy who often lived on the interest of loans and annuities. The Spanish
government was deaf to protest. From 1804 to 1809 about 15 million pesos
were raised; Mexico alone contributed the enormous sum of 10.3 million
pesos.[6] After the costs of administration and corruption had been met,
about 14 million pesos were remitted to Spain, where the money was
promptly used to cover fiscal deficits, the costs of war, and as a subsidy to

Napoleonic France. These measures, like the attack on immunity, spelt danger to the state as well as the Church, as clerical leaders pointed out, for the colonial system depended on the loyalty of the clergy: he who controlled the priests controlled the people, and the priests nearest to the people were the creoles.

In Mexico almost all the bishops and the majority of the canons and higher regulars were peninsula-born Spaniards, while the majority of the lower clergy were creoles and mestizos. In the late eighteenth century there was an excessive increase in the number of clergy, many of them unsuitable for the priesthood and drawn by the hope of a comfortable career rather than a religious vocation. In a population of 6.1 million there were 9,439 ecclesiastics (men and woman), or two clergy to 1,000 inhabitants, a much lower ratio than in Spain but probably higher than Mexico could afford. In fact there were more clergy than there were benefices and *capellanías* to support them. While the wealthiest bishops had an annual income of 100,000 pesos and upwards, and the incumbents of rich urban parishes could expect salaries of 3,000 to 5,000 pesos, their impecunious assistants (*vicarios*) had to be content with 500 pesos or less, and formed a kind of clerical proletariat with little hope of advancement.[7] Yet in spite of the structural defects of the Mexican Church there was little decline in popular religion: the Indians clung tenaciously to their feasts, pilgrimages, and processions, while the urban confraternities were still vigorous and self-supporting. And if there was a drop in recruitment to the mendicant orders there was no shortage of nuns for convents.

In the viceroyalty of Peru in 1792 there were 1,818 secular priests and 1,891 religious for a population of about a million.[8] This was not entirely a 'colonial' Church, for the majority of the secular clergy were creoles and some of these became bishops: Sebastian Goyeneche in Arequipa, Juan Manuel Moscoso and José Pérez y Armendariz in Cuzco. Though *peninsulares* dominated higher ecclesiastical offices and competed with creoles for the best benefices and for promotion in religious orders, careers were open to creoles in sufficient numbers to satisfy demand. The Peruvian Church was not as rich as the Mexican, but it still had substantial resources. The skyline of colonial Lima was crowded with churches, monasteries, and other ecclesiastical institutions – almost one-third of all buildings – and many of the religious orders owned extensive rural properties. The archbishop's income rivalled that of the viceroy himself, and the higher clergy in general enjoyed a favourable standard of living. Beneath the surface, however, in Peru no less than in Mexico, the Church was weakened by flaws and divisions. The Church mirrored the social structure of the colony and was divided between elites and masses, rich and poor, peninsular and creole, whites and Indians. Many bishops remained isolated in their palaces and contact with the Indian people of the sierra was left to the *cura doctrinero*, who was frequently absent. The *curas*, moreover, were one of the various interest groups – intendants, caciques, *hacendados*, mine owners – competing for the labour and resources of the Indian communities and imposing ever increasing financial exactions on subjects who already had to pay tribute, *alcabala*, and other dues. While some exercised their authority through pastoral care, others resorted to beatings and imprisonments, and all appeared to be part of the colonial state.

The structural weaknesses of the Church were accompanied by a religious complacency or inertia which left it vulnerable to sudden change. The lack of real political challenge or intellectual stimulus in the colonial period left the American Church unprepared for the shock of events from 1810 onwards. There was little sense of identity among the faithful. Social divisions between creoles, mestizos, Indians, and blacks were accurately reflected in the Church and these were not diminished by common religious values. They were all Catholics, of course, some more fervent than others. But to be a Catholic was not to express a strong conviction of loyalty to the Church; liberals and anti-clericals were nominally Catholics and usually attacked policies and practices rather than religion as such. Consequently, when in the course of independence the Church was subject to challenge and threat, it reacted not by calling on the faithful, much less by mobilizing the popular sectors, the forgotten souls of independence, but by looking to the state, royalist or republican, to protect it as of right. Surrounded by warring armies, the Church was concerned to guide its members, preach the Gospel, and administer the sacraments, and it invoked these religious obligations to justify whatever political position it took. But in the colony bishops and superiors often looked like bureaucrats, whose first obligation was to the crown. This attitude did not entirely change during independence. The priesthood was still seen more as a career than a vocation, and a priest was seen as one of the professionals who rendered services in return for fees. It was often difficult to distinguish between a true vocation and one motivated by interest and status, values which many priests openly avowed. But these interests existed and were perceived as threatened first by the Bourbon state and then by the various regimes which followed. To defend its doctrine and its interests, did the Church give any indication of its political thinking? To what extent did Catholic ideas influence the generation of 1810?

The Ideological Roots of Independence

In Spanish American independence three lines of political ideology converge: scholasticism, the Enlightenment, and creole nationalism. The relative influence of these ideas has been much debated. One school of thought assigns primacy to scholastic philosophy and Spanish tradition. According to this interpretation, the *doctrinas populistas* of Francisco Suárez and the Spanish neo-scholastics provided the ideological basis of the Spanish American revolutions, with the corollary that Spain not only conquered America but also supplied the argument for its liberation. Spanish 'constitutionalism', it is argued, formerly expressed in regional rights and the power of the *cabildos*, was a living tradition that could still be invoked, while the theories of popular sovereignty held by sixteenth- and seventeenth-century Spanish theologians were preserved in the colonial universities and subsequently used to justify resistance. The writings of the Jesuit Francisco Suárez contain perhaps the clearest statement of the popular origin and contractual nature of sovereignty. He argues that power is conferred by God with the consent of the people through the social contract. Once authority has been conferred on the ruler it cannot be recovered, unless there is sufficient reason, such as the absence of the ruler or his failure to observe the common good. In short, the popular origin of sovereignty, resistance to tyranny, limitations to royal power, all were present in the thought of Suárez and in Spanish traditions. A variant of this approach suggests that neo-Thomism was a vital component of Hispanic culture, the basis of the patrimonial state and an ideological accompaniment of independence.[9]

These influences were seen first in opposition to Bourbon reforms. In this interpretation, the *comuneros* of New Granada in 1781 were inspired by known and accepted ideas concerning the common good of the community, its rights to express legitimate interests by representation to the crown and negotiation with the colonial bureaucracy, and to defend these rights by force if necessary. In *comunero* rhetoric echoes of the political ideas and conventions of Spanish scholasticism and government have been detected, conventions which had been transmitted to Spanish America through the teachings of theologians and the practices of Habsburg government. The *comunero* movement, therefore, was a reaction to the violation of these customary arrangements by royal officials, and it was animated by a shared belief in 'a *corpus mysticum politicum*, with its own traditions, whose end was to achieve the common good of the whole community'.[10]

Seen first in opposition to Bourbon absolutism, these ideas were made more specific in 1810. Now it was argued that the right of the people to exercise civil authority after the enforced abdication of the king was not limited to the juntas and regency in Spain but was an inherent right of every province in Spanish territories overseas. This was the justification of the junta movement in Spanish America and ultimately of independence. The link with the crown was broken, and with it the social contract; power reverted to the people, who were free to establish a new government, as Spanish tradition and scholastic philosophy had always maintained.

Not all historians agree. Do books in libraries prove ideological influence? Were the political ideas of the neo-scholastics preserved as a continuous tradition in Spanish America, or were they rediscovered in 1810 and used as a convenient justification for revolution? What is the precise link between the contractual theories used by the revolutionaries and the political thought of Suárez? And did the revolutionaries perceive themelves as *suarecistas*? In the *cabildo abierto* of 22 May 1810 in Buenos Aires Juan José Castelli argued that the absence of a legitimate government in Spain caused 'a reversion of sovereignty to the people of Buenos Aires', who could now install a new government, which they did. This is the doctrine of 'popular sovereignty', and admittedly the idea that, in the absence of the sovereign, power reverts to the people was similar to the doctrine of Suárez. But it was not exclusive to any one school of political thought; it was divorced from all reference to the divine origin of power, which was the basis of Suárez's theory; and a more recent source of inspiration for it was at hand – the Enlightenment.

Elsewhere in Spanish America the evidence is also contradictory. About the same time as Castelli in Buenos Aires, in New Granada Camilo Torres was arguing that as the monarchy was dissolved 'the sovereignty which resides in the mass of the nation has been recovered and the nation can deposit it where it wills and administer it according to its best interests'.[11] Is this necessarily a derivation from Suárez and the Spanish school? Events moved on. The constitution of the republic of Cundinamarca (17 April 1812) spoke of the 'imprescriptible rights of man and the citizen', using language of the eighteenth century rather than of the age of scholasticism. In Mexico the priest insurgent José María Morelos asserted that sovereignty resided 'essentially in the peoples' and because of present circumstances the people had recovered its usurped sovereignty; therefore, dependence on the Spanish throne was dissolved for ever. Morelos quoted Suárez, but his policy went far beyond Suárez and responded to American interests rather than Hispanic tradition. The Enlightenment and creole nationalism: these ideological influences probably superseded those of scholasticism in the years after 1810.

The literature of the Enlightenment circulated with relative freedom in Spanish America. In Mexico, Peru, and New Granada there was a public for Newton, Locke, and Adam Smith, for Descartes, Montesquieu, Voltaire, Diderot, Rousseau, and D'Alembert. Most of the major cities had their groups of intellectuals who supported new periodicals and economic societies and survived the attentions of the Inquisition. Some were unlucky. In 1794 in Bogotá Antonio Nariño, a wealthy creole, was arrested and tried for translating and printing the French *Declaration of the Rights of Man*. In his defence before the *audiencia* he presented his ideas as Catholic and traditional and derived from various sources, though in fact some of them echoed Rousseau. The Enlightenment was a moderate influence for change, but it did not de-Catholicize America. The balance between tradition and innovation can be seen in the decision of Mariano Moreno in Buenos Aires to suppress from his translation of Rousseau's *Social Contract* the chapter on religion, while ordering 200 copies to be printed for use as a textbook to teach students 'the inalienable rights of man'.

The actions of the liberators were based on many imperatives, political, military, and financial, as well as intellectual. The basic objectives were liberation and independence, but liberty did not mean simply freedom from the absolutist state of the eighteenth century, as it did for the Enlightenment, but freedom from a colonial power. Liberty could be an end in itself and stop short of liberation. With the exception of Thomas Paine and the abbé Raynal, European intellectuals and statesmen of the eighteenth century seem to have been totally unaware of the need to apply ideas of freedom and equality to relations between peoples, or of any right to colonial independence. It needed the makers of North American and Spanish American independence to develop a concept of colonial liberation, as Bolívar did in the years after 1810. If it was not a 'cause' of independence, however, the Enlightenment was an indispensable source on which leaders drew to justify, defend, and legitimize their actions, in the course of the revolution.

Creole nationalism, rather than scholasticism or even the Enlightenment, corresponds more closely to the origins and course of the Spanish American revolutions. The demands for liberty and equality expressed a deeper awareness, a developing sense of identity, a conviction among creoles that they were Americans, not Spaniards. In the course of the eighteenth century Spanish Americans began to rediscover their own land in a uniquely American literature. Their patriotism was American, not Spanish, as creole intellectuals in Mexico, Peru, and Chile began to express and nurture a new awareness of *patria*. Among the first to give cultural expression to 'Americanism' were the creole Jesuits expelled from their homelands in 1767, who became in exile literary precursors of American nationalism. They wrote to dispel European ignorance of their countries, and in particular to destroy the myth of the inferiority and degeneracy of man, animal, and vegetable in the New World, a myth propagated by some of the writings of the Enlightenment. Juan Ignacio Molina, Francisco Javier Clavijero, Andrés Cavo, these and other Jesuit exiles reflected the thinking of many less articulate Americans. The Peruvian Jesuit Juan Pablo Viscardo was an ardent advocate of independence, to the cause of which he bequeathed his *Lettre aux espagnols – américains*, published in 1799. 'The New World', wrote Viscardo, 'is our homeland, and its history is ours, and it is in this history that we ought to seek the causes of our present situation.'[12]

In Mexico search for an American identity, a compound of exaltation of the Indian past, resentment of peninsular privileges, and the cult of Our Lady of Guadalupe, was a powerful force in the alienation of Mexicans from Spanish rule. All the ethnic groups could march under these banners – creoles, Indians, mestizos, and mulattos – and all could identify with 'Our Holy Mother of Guadalupe', who had shown a special predilection for Mexico. Morelos declared, 'All the inhabitants except Europeans will no longer be designated as Indians, mulattos or other castes, but all will be known as Americans'. This statement of racial equality sprang not from scholastic thought, nor from any declaration of the rights of man, but from awareness of a common identity as Mexicans. Creole patriotism was strongly marked by religion. Morelos asserted to the bishop of Puebla, 'We are more religious than the Europeans', and claimed to be fighting for 'Religion and our native land', and that this was 'our holy revolution'.[13]

The few creole prelates in Spanish America, hitherto firmly royalist, finally rediscovered their roots in 1820 when Spain imposed a liberal constitution on America and began to attack the Church. As Rafael Lasso de la Vega, bishop of Mérida, explained to Bolívar, 'I have always been proud to have been born in America, and wherever I have lived I have actively shown my gratitude, clear proof of my love of my native land'.[14] The majority of his episcopal colleagues had also identified with their native land – but that land was Spain.

The Church Responds to Independence

The immediate reaction of the Church to the onset of independence was determined not by scholasticism, the Enlightenment, or creole nationalism, but by a natural instinct of defence. Whatever individual priests might think, as an institution the Church was implacably hostile. If Spanish power was broken, could the Catholic religion survive? If the Spanish crown collapsed, could the Church escape? Independence exposed the colonial roots of the Church and revealed its foreign origins. It also divided the Church.

The majority of the bishops rejected the revolution and remained loyal to Spain, recognizing the threat posed by independence and liberalism to the established position of the Church. They themselves owed their appointments to the crown, they had sworn allegiance to the king, and regalism was one of their qualifications for office; so they were under immediate pressure to conform and to deliver to the king a docile people. They denounced the rebellion against legitimate authority as a sin as well as a crime, heretical as well as illegal. In Mexico Manuel Abad y Queipo, an otherwise moderate ecclesiastic, deplored rebellion as the greatest sin and crime that a man could commit, and he called his former friend, the priest insurgent, Miguel Hidalgo, an atheist and 'a mini Muhammad'; he and his allies were 'true heresiarchs'.[15] For the Mexican hierarchy this was a war of religion; they totally identified the cause of religion with royalism, and warned that revolution in Mexico would cause the same destruction to the Church as the revolution in France. Archbishop Francisco Javier de Lizana y Beaumont advised the faithful that if they followed the 'revolutionaries' they would go 'infallibly to hell'. Ignacio González del Campillo, bishop of Puebla, a creole but more Spanish than the Spaniards, ordered parish priests to withhold the sacraments from the insurgents and declared excommunicate anyone who wrote or read insurgent literature. In Oaxaca Bishop Antonio Bergosa y Jordán declared in a pastoral letter that 'God is with Fernando and the Spaniards'; he organized a militia of clergy and laity to defend 'our holy and just cause' against the insurgent invaders, though when these approached he fled by night to the safety of Mexico City, leaving his clergy with orders to confront the enemy.[16]

The hierarchy of New Granada was fanatically royalist. Gregorio José Rodríguez, installed as bishop of Cartagena during the counter-revolution of 1817, ordered the faithful to shout 'Viva el Rey!' on entering and leaving the cathedral, and in a pastoral letter denounced the patriots as 'enemies of God and the king'. In due course he had to flee Cartagena, as had his colleague Jiménez Enciso of Popayán, who forced many of those who followed him to join the royalist forces in their retreat. While they might justify their position in religious terms, the hierarchy could not disguise the fact that they were Spaniards, identified with Spain, and in effect denied the possibility of an American Church. In the *cabildo* of Buenos Aires, 22 May 1810, Bishop Benito de la Lué voted for the continuation of viceregal government, arguing that 'while there remains in Spain one piece of territory ruled by Spaniards, that piece of territory ought to rule Americans'.[17]

A bishop could not afford to be neutral: both sides demanded absolute commitment. Those whose loyalty to the crown was suspect were brought to account. The action of Bishop José Cuero y Caicedo on behalf of the revolution in Quito astonished his colleagues. Cuero y Caicedo was a creole and a somewhat reluctant participant in the early manoeuvres of the creole elite. Drawn further into the conflict in the interests of peace and resistance to Spanish aggression, he accepted the presidency of the second junta and in 1812 mobilized ecclesiastical resources in defence of the revolution. He exhorted his parish priests to encourage their parishioners in support of the patriot government, whose legitimacy rested on 'the freedom enjoyed by the people to elect their representatives'.[18] With the victory of the royalist forces he had to leave Quito: in 1815 he was expelled to Lima, where he died in 1816.

In the Cuzco rebellion of 1814, a creole movement mobilizing Indian support, the clergy played a leading role as preachers, chaplains, and soldiers, and José Pérez Armendáriz, an enlightened creole and pro-Indian bishop, blessed the rebellion with the words, 'If God places a hand on earthly matters, on the revolution of Cuzco he has placed two.'[19] Among the Peruvian hierarchy Pérez Armendáriz was a solitary voice and he was effectively deprived of his diocese.

Narciso Coll y Prat, a Catalan by birth, arrived in the archdiocese of Caracas in July 1810 to find that the revolutionaries had already deposed the colonial administration. He took the view that 'he had not come to Venezuela to be captain-general but to be an archbishop guiding his flock'. He decided to stay. His interests were primarily those of Church and king, or as he himself put it, 'of sustaining the cause of Your Majesty and keeping the diocese in peace'.[20] But in the next six years he dealt with all governments, royalist and republican, and was criticized by each for partiality to the other. Aware that the lower clergy were divided, he was prepared to recognize a republican government and in 1811 he declared, 'If Venezuela is proud to have entered the family of nations, my Venezuelan Church can also take pride in occupying its place among the national Catholic Churches.'[21] He was not naïve. As he said, there were some who wanted 'to de-Catholicize Venezuela', but he remained convinced that Catholics could support independence, on the grounds that 'the Church adjusts to all forms of government as long as its doctrine is respected'.[22] In 1816 he was recalled to Spain to give an account of his conduct and to answer charges of collaboration with the rebels. He defended himself vigorously and was vindicated, to come down in history as a royalist archbishop whose policy was tolerant and tactical.

Between the restoration of Ferdinand VII in 1814 and the liberal revolution in Spain in 1820 the king authorized the appointment of twenty-eight bishops to vacant sees in America, not all of them *peninsulares* but all of unquestioned loyalty. They were urged 'to cooperate by their example and their doctrine in preserving the rights of legitimate sovereignty which belongs to the king our lord'. This changed the composition of the hierarchy and distorted its character, giving royalism a built-in majority. During these years bishops helped to finance, arm, and activate anti-insurgency forces, and they launched weapons as well as anathemas against their enemies.

The majority of the clergy, on the other hand, supported the cause of independence. The lower clergy, especially the secular clergy, were predominantly creole. Like the creole elite in general, they were divided, but many were inclined to support the junta movement and eventually independence. Attitudes reflected the deep divide, economic and social, between the ecclesiastical hierarchy and the mass of the clergy. Some priests played outstanding roles as leaders of the struggle, many more were activists in the lower ranks, and numerous volunteers served as chaplains in the armies of liberation.

In Mexico the early insurgency was dominated by priests, two in particular, Miguel Hidalgo, a country priest of progressive views, and José María Morelos, a natural guerrilla leader. Alongside them a host of minor clerical warriors aroused the populace, Indian and mestizo, across a wide area of west-central Mexico in a war to defend religion. Was this a reaction against a colonial Church dominated by Spaniards, of whom Hidalgo said 'they are not Catholics, except politically: their God is money'?[23] Was it a protest against the Bourbon attack on clerical privilege? Whatever the reason, priests led the way. In all, 401 individual clerics were recorded as aligned with insurgency in Mexico, not to mention those who remained undetected. But these relatively modest numbers masked the clergy's real contribution: they were the leaders, both military and political, and their choice of allegiance was often decisive in determining that of large sections of the population. Creole clerics helped to direct the course of the rebellion, to lead the ideological warfare against royalists in the insurgent press, and to define political aims in manifestos and constitutions. And some led troops into battle. Under Hidalgo and Morelos there were other soldier-priests such as Mariano Matamoros, José Navarrete, Pablo Delgado, José Izquierdo, and Fray Luis Herrera. In reply to insurgent priests, on 25 June 1812 the viceroy abolished the ecclesiastical *fuero* and authorized royalist commanders to judge and execute the clerical rebels. From the beginning of the rebellion until the end of 1815, 125 priests were executed by royalists in Mexico. But the policy backfired. It was censured by the Madrid government and increased the support for insurgency among the clergy. Creole priests began to fight for clerical immunity. Mariano Matamoros raised a special squadron of dragoons to which he gave as banner a black flag bearing a crimson cross, the arms of the Church, and the legend 'Morir por la Inmunidad Eclesiástica' ('Die for clerical immunity').[24]

The careers of Hidalgo and Morelos enable the historian to judge the social policy of the Church in the age of revolution. Hidalgo led a mass movement and stood for radical, if not revolutionary, change. He retained the allegiance of his supporters by constantly enlarging the social content of his programme. He abolished the Indian tribute, the badge of a conquered people. He abolished slavery under pain of death. But the real test of his intentions was agrarian reform. This problem too he grasped. In Guadalajara he published a decree ordering the return of lands rightfully belonging to Indian communities, 'to be used only for the natives in their respective villages'. The intention was to restore lands to Indians and prevent their alienation; this could not be accomplished by decree alone, and Hidalgo never in fact had the opportunity to establish the machinery for implementing his policy. But he forced the bishops to show their hand: they opposed his policy and condemned him as a heretic; even Bishop Abad y Queipo regarded his agrarian measures as an incitement to plunder and anarchy, and his policy as 'sacrilegious and heretical'.[25] Morelos too decreed the abolition of slavery and Indian tribute and proposed absolute social equality through abolition of race and caste distinctions. He also proclaimed that the lands should be owned by those who worked them and the peasants should receive the income from those lands. Hidalgo and Morelos received short shrift from Church and state: within five years both had been taken and shot and their movements extinguished.

Hidalgo and Morelos were not only executed by royal authority, they were condemned by the Church. Hidalgo was excommunicated by the Inquisition as 'a heretic, apostate, and schismatic' who with his insurgents had fought 'to overthrow the throne and the altar', and by three bishops, whose jurisdiction over him was debatable in each case.[26] Morelos was subjected to a military trial and also to trial, excommunication, and degradation by the Inquisition, which pronounced him 'a formal heretic and instigator of heresies ... traitor to God, to the king, and to the pope'.[27] These gratuitous acts of intolerance were humiliating to the victims and damaging to the Church, whose actions were seen by many as blatantly political.

Elsewhere in Spanish America the clergy played a similar, if less dramatic, role in the movements of independence, first providing leaders and fighters, and finally reacting as an interest group opposing the Spanish liberal attack on their privileges in 1820. In Argentina a number of creole priests supported independence and took a leading role in establishing the new order. In Peru twenty-six out of fifty-seven deputies in the Congress of 1822 were priests. In Upper Peru, if the higher clergy were largely peninsular and royalist, the parish clergy were favourable to independence. In Quito three priests issued the proclamation of independence in 1809, and in 1814 a royalist general listed 100 priests among the patriots, with perhaps two to one in favour in the diocese of Quito.

In New Granada, although the bishops were almost all royalists, the majority of the clergy favoured or accepted independence. Hundreds of priests, from all parts of the viceroyalty, helped the cause. Some, such as the canon Andrés Rosillo, provided political leadership; others served as chaplains; and a few were guerrilla leaders, such as the Dominican Fray Ignacio Mariño in the eastern llanos. Their participation moved one revolutionary leader to describe the events of 20 July 1810 and the overthrow of viceregal government as 'a clerical revolution'. Sixteen of the fifty-three signatories of the Act of Independence were ecclesiastics. Fernando Caycedo y Flórez, an inspirational rector of the Colegio del Rosario and in due course first archbishop of the independent republic, added his own political ideas to the early debates and affirmed his conviction that 'The only object of the American revolution is independence of Spain, of that Spain which for so long has exercised the most cruel and inhuman tyranny'. Juan Fernández de Sotomayor, parish priest of Mompós and future bishop of Cartagena, published in 1814 the *Catecismo o instrucción popular*, in which he denounced the Spanish colonial regime as unjust and the priests who supported it as enemies of religion. True religion, he argued, encouraged New Granadans not to return to colonial dependence, for Christianity could accommodate itself to various systems of government; this was 'a just and holy war', which would liberate New Granada from slavery and lead to freedom and independence.[28] The Franciscan Diego Padilla founded a periodical, *El Aviso al Público*, to give ideological support to the revolution, advocating liberty and independence and claiming that New Granadan patriots were defending true religion against impious France.[29] There were, of course, in Colombia and elsewhere, royalist clergy who attacked these views and saw obedience to the monarchy as a religious obligation; the *Catecismo* of Fernández de Sotomayor was condemned by the Inquisition for its anti-monarchical ideas. There were also divisions of opinion among the patriot clergy themselves, between conservatives and liberals, centralists and federalists. But all, whether royalists or republicans, invoked religion to justify and popularize their cause, each side accusing the other of hypocrisy.

The turning point for the Church in Spanish America was the year 1820, when a liberal revolution in Spain forced the king to renounce absolutism and accept the constitition of 1812. The new regime (1820–23) promptly exported itself to the colonies, where it had immediate implications for the Church. Spanish liberals were just as imperialist as Spanish conservatives and offered no concessions to independence. They were also aggressively anti-clerical, attacking the Church, its privileges, and its property. Finally they forced the crown to ask the pope not to recognize any Spanish American country and to appoint bishops faithful only to Madrid. The combination of radical liberalism and renewed imperialism was too much even for the royalist bishops in America, many of whom now lost confidence in the king and began to question the basis of their allegiance. While these events unfolded, the war of independence began to turn in favour of the republicans; at Boyacá in 1819 the era of the great victories opened, and with it the eyes of the prelates.

One of the first republican bishops in America was Fray Antonio Gómez Polanco, bishop of Santa Marta, who declared in favour of Bolívar and swore to the republic of Colombia on 26 November 1820. Former royalist bishops such as Rafael Lasso de la Vega (Mérida), Higinio Durán (Panama), José Orihuela (Cuzco), and José Sebastián Goyeneche (Arequipa), all joined the independence movement after 1820, together with one of the most intransigent of royalist bishops, Salvador Jiménez de Enciso of Popayán, who in 1823 recommended the cause of independence to Pope Pius VII. In Lima Archbishop Bartolomé las Heras, who had unworthily attributed the support of Bishop Pérez de Armendáriz for the Cuzco rebellion of 1814 to senile debility, now hastened to sign the Act of Independence of Peru in July 1821; of the 3,000 citizens who signed, one-third were clerics, while in the first constituent congress (1822–23) the clergy played an active and liberal role. Lasso de la Vega, a creole born in Panama, who had excommunicated rebel leaders, now disavowed the divine right of kings and based his republicanism on the rights of the people to choose their government. He explained his conversion to republicanism in a letter to the Holy See in 1821: 'Once the Catholic king swore to the Constitution, sovereignty returned to the source from which it had come, namely the consent and will of the citizens. It returned to the Spaniards. Why not to us?'[30] A long interview with Bolívar convinced him that the Catholic religion was safer in the hands of the Liberator than in those of the Spanish Cortes. He began to work for the reconstruction of the Church in an independent Colombia, becoming one of the firmest allies of Bolívar and his first link with Rome.

In Mexico too the anti-clerical decrees of the Spanish Cortes in 1820 persuaded the Church to question its belief in the imperial government and to look more favourably on independence. Whereas the prelates had previously identified their interests with those of the Spanish government and given it financial and moral support, now they were convinced that the Spanish government was the enemy of the Church and it was their duty to resist it. The prohibition of new *capellanías* and *obras pías*, the attack on convents and monastic orders, the erosion of Church property, above all another decree abolishing clerical immunity – whether the cleric was rebel or loyalist – alerted the Church and persuaded it that the danger of liberalism came not from American revolutionaries but from Spanish constitutionalists. The new liberator, Agustín de Iturbide, officer, landowner, and Catholic, exploited the Church's dilemma and with the connivance of a number of sympathetic clergy produced a formula for independence, the Plan of Iguala, which promised 'to preserve intact the holy religion we profess' and satisfied the interest groups in Mexico on the basis of three guarantees: 'union, religion, independence'. With the exception of Pedro José de Fonte, archbishop of Mexico, who retired from the scene in disgust, the hierarchy backed Iturbide in words and with funds and thereby assured him of the support of the clergy and the general public. The endorsement of the Church was decisive for Iturbide and guaranteed the success of his bid for power; for the Church delivered the Catholic masses who might reject the interests of privilege and property but did not question the message received from priests and from pulpits that Iturbide was the saviour of religion against impious Spain. This attitude explains why, after 1820, Mexico gained independence in so short a time and with so little violence. It also explains why the Church emerged from independence with its privileges intact.

Papal Hostility

During this time of crisis and division the Church in America received little help from Rome. Pope Pius VII and his secretary of state Cardinal Consalvi were aware of the modern world, familiar with political deals, and by no means reactionaries. But their experience of the papacy in Europe and its treatment at the hands of Napoleon convinced them that the greatest danger to the Church came from revolution. Ignorant of the meaning of creole nationalism, they judged the movements of independence in Spanish America as an extension of the revolutionary upheaval they observed in Europe, and they gave their support to the Spanish crown. In a hostile world Ferdinand VII was valued as a loyal and Catholic ally, a reliable opponent of liberalism. During the years 1813–15 Spanish American rebels tried in vain to gain the ear of the pope; but when Ferdinand VII requested a papal brief in his favour, it was ready in eight days. The resultant encyclical, *Etsi longissimo* (30 January 1816), exhorted the bishops and clergy of Spanish America to 'destroy completely' the revolutionary seed sown in their countries and to make clear to their people the dire consequences of rebellion against legitimate authority; it also extolled the virtues of Ferdinand VII and the exemplary loyalty of the Spanish people to their faith and their sovereign.[31]

The influence of the encyclical in Spanish America was not decisive. No doubt it confirmed the views of those bishops who were already royalists; but as for the leaders of independence and their followers, they learnt to live with it without crisis of conscience. In 1819 the president of the Congress of Angostura, Juan Germán Roscio, instructed his representatives in Europe to open negotiations with Pius VII 'as head of the Catholic Church and not as temporal lord of his legations', and to inform him that New Granada, Venezuela, and the whole of Spanish America in rebellion against colonial dependency were Catholic, and that no authority was more legitimate than that derived from the people.[32] Rome did not yet learn these necessary lessons or accept the compatibility of republicanism and Catholicism. But in the next few years the papacy took a more neutral position, partly in response to petitions from Spanish America and concern for the needs of the faithful there, and partly in reaction to the anti-clerical drift of the Spanish government after the revolution of 1820, culminating in the expulsion of the papal nuncio in January 1823. Finally, to bring some order to the religious life of the region, the pope agreed to send a mission to the Río de la Plata and Chile under a *vicario apostólico*, Monsignor Gian Muzi, and including the young canon Gian Maria Mastai Ferretti, later Pius IX.

The Muzi mission of 1824–25 made contact with local Catholicism and gathered useful information but was otherwise a failure, thwarted by the rigidity of its leader and the intransigence of politicians in Buenos Aires and Santiago. Mastai described the Argentine leader, Bernardino Rivadavia, as 'a minister from hell', as the mission experienced the full force of republican anti-clericalism and witnessed the new form of regalism.[33] The mission's own thinking revealed deeply ingrained prejudice against liberal political thought. Ideas of sovereignty of the people and the rights of man were regarded by Muzi as 'the dominant heresy of these new governments', and American independence as 'a political disease'. No lessons seemed to have been learnt by the Roman visitors: 'The tendency of all the new governments of South America is towards an irreligious liberalism, consequence of the revolutionary spirit which has travelled from Europe to America'. On the other hand a Roman diplomat would never ignore the possibility of a deal. The time was not ripe, thought Muzi, for a concordat, but in the case of Colombia and Peru 'Señor Bolívar deserves to be heard and considered; judging only by his policy, one could hope from him for advantages to the Church in those vast regions'.[34] But in Rome itself these were not the prevailing sentiments. Even before the Muzi mission had left Italy relations between the Holy See and Spanish America had suffered a reverse. Following the death of Pius VII a new pope, Leo XII, was elected on 28 September 1823. Two days later Ferdinand VII was restored to absolute power in Spain and revived hopes, however unrealistic, of the reconquest of America. The Rome–Madrid axis appeared to be alive.

Leo XII was a strong defender of legitimate sovereignty and he saw in the restoration of Ferdinand VII an opportunity to protect the rights of crown and Church in the Americas. His opposition to independence, strongly urged by Madrid, was out of line with international opinion and came at a time when the armies of liberation were about to win their final victories. This did not deter him from issuing the encyclical *Etsi iam diu* (24 September 1824), which lamented the great ills afflicting the Church in Spanish America, recommended to the Spanish American hierarchy the 'august and distinguished qualities of our much loved son Ferdinand', guardian of religion and of his subjects, and urged them, like the Spanish people, to come to the 'defence of religion and legitimate power'.[35] In the event, the encyclical satisfied neither Ferdinand VII, who had wanted a more specific order to obey the monarch, nor the American hierarchy, who regarded it as an aberration without significance for their people. Various Spanish American bishops, to avoid the danger of the faithful losing faith in either the papacy or independence, preferred to argue that the document was apocryphal. As for the governments of Latin America, they took the view that defence of religion did not depend on loyalty to Spain and that the pope had no jurisdiction in temporal government.

Papal policy towards Spanish American independence was a political error, fruit of human judgement, not of religious doctrine. But it was a costly error. The popes could not escape responsibility for perpetuating religious confusion. They made support for the Bourbon monarchy and Spanish rule a matter of conscience, a moral imperative, and disavowal of independence became a test of loyalty to the Church. These positions were impossible to maintain and in due course the popes had to see reason. Gregory XVI recognized the independent states of New Granada in 1835, Mexico in 1836, Ecuador in 1838, and Chile in 1840. Recognition of Peru, Bolivia, and Argentina was delayed for reasons of internal politics. Venezuela, unwilling to restore an exiled archbishop, also had to wait.

In the meantime the policy of the Holy See had caused a backlash of anti-clericalism, helped to demoralize the Church in America, and debased the currency of papal encyclicals. On the ground, papal procrastination left a vacuum in the government of the Church which secular governments were tempted to fill. Many vacant sees were deprived of appointments: it was 1831 before the pope appointed six bishops for Mexico. When the irrevocability of independence and the need to fill vacant sees forced the papacy, from 1835, to recognize the new governments, great damage had been done. The new regimes, for their part, were anxious to establish direct relations with the Holy See, realizing no doubt that the task of affirming their own legitimacy and governing overwhelmingly Catholic peoples would be made easier by an understanding with Rome.

The Religion of the Liberators

The leaders of independence and the elites from which they came paid lip service to religion and sought to reassure ecclesiastical and public opinion; speeches, manifestos, and acts of independence usually paid formal deference to the Catholic religion and contained promises for its preservation. Beneath the surface, however, many of the liberators were secularists rather than religionists, and were affected by the growth of scepticism in religion. In Buenos Aires Manuel Belgrano, civil and military servant of the new regime, recalled in his autobiography that when he was a student in Spain the ideas of the French Revolution took hold of him and directed his mind towards the principles of 'liberty, equality, security, and property'. The liberal politician Bernardino Rivadavia, though outwardly a Catholic, was a devotee of utilitarianism and anxious to control religion rather than conserve it. His Law of Reform of the Clergy (21 December 1822) suppressed the ecclesiastical *fuero* and the tithe; it provided for the state to support previous charges on the tithe, including the seminary; it suppressed some religious orders and confiscated their property; and it curtailed the membership and the establishments of other religious orders.[36] Politicians like Rivadavia often proved to be more regalist than the Bourbons.

Simón Bolívar seems to have been marked by some of the secular influences of the time, though whether they destroyed his belief it is impossible to say. He usually handled the subject of religion with caution, but beneath his outward observance there was an element of scepticism, and in private he sometimes ridiculed religion. According to his aide, Daniel Florencio O'Leary, an Irish Catholic, Bolívar was 'a complete atheist', who believed that religion was necessary only for government, and whose attendance at mass was purely formal. Nevertheless, affirmed O'Leary, he always believed it necessary to conform to the religion of his fellow citizens. Bolívar was too political to allow his basic objectives to be jeopardized by gratuitous anti-clericalism, much less by overt free-thinking. He did what he could to disestablish the Church, but in a deeply Catholic society he had to proceed carefully. In his speech to the constituent congress of Bolivia he explained that his Bolivian Constitution (1826) excluded religion from any public role, and he came close to saying that it was a purely private concern, a matter of conscience, not of politics. He specifically declined to provide for an established Church or a state religion, believing that the state should guarantee freedom of religion, without prescribing any particular religion. Bolívar thus defended a view of toleration in which religion exists on its own resources and merits without the support of legal sanctions. This was an exceptional view, anticipating the position of modern Catholicism, but it did not yet prevail in Spanish America.

Bolívar was a man of ideas but he was also a realist, and the final word may be left to him. A fighter for independence from Spain, he never sought independence from Rome. He sought to re-establish relations with the Holy See and eventually, in 1827, his representatives gained from Leo XII recognition of bishops for Gran Colombia and Bolivia. In welcoming the appointment of bishops to the sees of Bogotá, Caracas, Santa Marta, Antioquia, Quito, Cuenca, and Charcas, Bolívar gave a banquet in Bogotá at which he pronounced a toast to the new bishops and to the renewed unity with the Church of Rome. 'The descendants of Saint Peter have always been our fathers, but war had left us orphans ... Now [the new bishops] will be our guides, models of religion and of political virtues.'[37] During his last regime in Colombia he decreed specific measures – the imposition of Roman Catholic teaching in education and the restoration of dissolved religious houses – in favour of the traditional religion of Spanish America. On his deathbed he received the last rites and died a Catholic, in the Church 'in whose faith and belief I have lived.'[38] Yet there are few traces of that belief in his political thought.

In the absence of strong political motivation, Bolívar seems to have developed a philosophy of life based on utilitarianism. The evidence for this comes not simply from his formal contacts with James Mill and Jeremy Bentham but also from his own writings, where the greatest happiness principle emerges as the driving force of politics. This was also true of other Spanish American leaders, such as Cecilio del Valle of Central America, Bernardino Rivadavia of Argentina, and Bolívar's own colleague Francisco de Paula Santander, all of whom were strongly influenced by Bentham. In their construction of a new political system the leaders of independence sought moral legitimacy for what they were doing, and they found inspiration no longer in Catholic political thought but in the philo-sophy of the age of reason. Seeking an alternative to royal absolutism and traditional religion, liberals seized upon utilitarianism as a modern philos-ophy capable of giving them the intellectual credibility they wanted. This was a challenge to the Church, and it reacted not by reasoned debate but by appeal to the state, not by discussion but by repression.

In Colombia Santander and his liberal associates sought to incorporate Bentham's treatises into the study of law, until their efforts were overtaken by a conservative reaction. The works of Bentham came under attack from the clergy and other conservatives, and the materialism, scepticism, and anti-clericalism of the English philosopher were declared harmful to the Catholic religion. Bolívar was forced into painful decisions. Convinced by now that the constitution and laws of Colombia were excessively liberal and threatened the dissolution of state and society, and aware that the clergy were a powerful interest group capable of undermining his position, Bolívar had to take sides. In 1828 he forbade the teaching of Bentham's *Tratados de legislación civil y penal* in the universities of Colombia, and ordered that these courses be replaced by the study of the Roman Catholic religion. Thus there began in Colombia a long process of conflict between Church and state, religion and secularism, conservatism and liberalism.

The Post-Colonial Church

The Church was weakened by independence. So close had been the ties between crown and Church that the overthrow of one could not fail to affect the other. This was an opportunity as well as a reverse. The American Church, free from the suffocating grasp of the Bourbon state, could now look more directly to Rome for leadership and authority; at first it looked in vain, but in the course of time, when the papacy responded to the needs of America, the Church moved from Spain to Rome, from Iberian religion to universal religion. This avoided the emergence of national Churches, but it did not remove the threat of state control of religion. The Church was still inclined to look for state protection. The first constitutions of the new states all established the Catholic religion as the religion of the state to the exclusion of all others. The *patronato*, the royal right of presentation to ecclesiastical benefices, was now claimed by the national governments and, with the support of some clergy, placed in the hands of liberal and agnostic politicians. Church and state contested the issue for many years. In Colombia the law of patronage passed by Congress in 1824 declared that the republic 'ought to continue in the exercise of the same right of patronage which the kings of Spain had'.[39] In Mexico there was a prolonged and unyielding debate between politicians who wanted the *patronato* for the state and clerics who wanted a role for the papacy and the Church. In Argentina Rivadavia established almost complete state control over the personnel and property of the Church, a tradition which the dictator Juan Manuel de Rosas continued and bequeathed to succeeding governments. It was only gradually that the secular states came to see the *patronato* as an anachronism and closed the subject by separating Church and state.

In the years after 1820 it became clear that independence had weakened some of the basic structures of the Church. Many bishops, such as Las Heras of Lima and the bishops of Trujillo, Huamanga, and Mainas were expelled. The diocese of Cuzco was left vacant by the infirmity of its bishop. Only the creole bishop of Arequipa, José Sebastián Goyeneche, brother of the royalist general, held out and survived through the support of the faithful; between 1822 and 1834 he was the only bishop in office for the vast region of Peru, Ecuador, Bolivia, and northern Argentina and

Chile.[40] In Mexico Bishop Pérez Suárez of Oaxaca left his diocese and returned to the peninsula. Archbishop Fonte had conscientious objections to crowning Iturbide and left the capital on the pretext of making a visitation of his archdiocese; but the only place he visited was a port on the Gulf coast, from which he sailed to Spain. Harassed by the Spanish government, the Holy See declined to repeat for Mexico what it did for Colombia in 1827, when it authorized the appointment of two archbishops and five bishops. The blame for empty dioceses, therefore, was shared between Rome, which dragged its feet over recognizing independence, and liberal governments, which would accept their own nominees or none. In Argentina, Chile, and Uruguay it was 1832 before the ordinary hierarchy was reinstated, and 1834–35 in Peru. After independence Mexico had only one bishop, Pérez of Puebla, and he died in 1829. Mexico was then without bishops until 1831, when Rome at last relented and recognized six of the bishops proposed by the Mexican government. By 1836 in all the new republics there were only eight vacant sees.

Meanwhile, however, the Church had been deeply affected by lack of direction. The absence of a bishop meant the loss of teaching authority in a diocese, lack of government and discipline, and a decline in ordinations and confirmations. Shortage of bishops was inevitably accompanied by shortage of priests and religious. The Church lost perhaps 50 per cent of its secular clergy and even more of its regulars in these years. The total number of Mexican ecclesiastics fell from 9,439 in 1810 to 7,019 in 1834; in a population of 6.2 million this signified a decline from 2 per 1,000 of the population to 1.1 per 1,000. In Peru the quality and quantity of vocations declined; in Bolivia eighty parishes were vacant at independence; in Venezuela there were 200 fewer priests in 1837 than in 1810. Throughout Spanish America parishes were left unattended, mass and the sacraments no longer available, sermons and instructions discontinued. A shortage of vocations made its appearance, and Spain was no longer an automatic source of replenishment.

The economic assets of the Church were also damaged by independence. The warring armies requisitioned cash, church plate, buildings, land, and livestock. Tithes, a basic source of income for the Church, were first reduced by the upheaval of the wars and then by the action of the new governments, which removed state sanction for their collection, in Argentina in 1821, in Peru in 1846. In 1833–34 a liberal government in Mexico ended official enforcement of tithes and sought to limit the fiscal independence of ecclesiastical corporations. Throughout Spanish America the interest from ecclesiastical loans was reduced as the new governments, dominated by property owners, took steps to reduce mortgage payments and other annuities owed to the Church. The new rulers, conservatives and

liberals alike, coveted Church property and income, not necessarily to rein-
vest them in welfare or development but as a rightful revenue of the state.
Thus the secularization of Church property begun by the Bourbons with
the confiscation of Jesuit property in 1767 was now continued at a quicker
pace by the republican governments, most of which took steps not only to
attack diocesan property but also to dispossess the religious orders. These
measures inaugurated the gradual erosion of Church property in the nineteenth century and further weakened the infrastructure of the Church.
Bishops, priests, and religious organizations came to rely for their income
not on independent resources of the Church but on contributions of the
faithful or a subsidy from the state.

CHAPTER 5

❧

Creating a Latin American Church

Continuity and Change

A NEW WORLD OPENED for the Church after independence but one still pervaded by the old. The Church survived the crisis, the loss of clergy, the disputes over patronage, the curtailment of revenue, and emerged as a model of continuity, more stable, more popular, and apparently more wealthy than many of the new states. In some countries the state was weaker than the Church and could not displace it, even in those functions such as education which the state was eager to claim as its own. Governments reacted by seeking to co-opt and to control the Church, and to tip the balance in their own favour. They did not find it easy. The initial liberalism of the new governments was replaced, from 1830 to 1850, by a period of relatively conservative rule in Spanish America, when the Church was able, at least in some countries, to restore its privileges, strengthen its institutions, and increase its personnel. The survival of ecclesiastical privilege and property, however, was unacceptable to liberals and created a backlash against the Church once they returned to power. The years 1850–80, therefore, saw the Church in conflict with the liberal state in many parts of Latin America, which now experienced a more basic rupture with the past and with the Church.

The principle behind liberal policy was individualism, a belief that the new states of Latin America could only make progress if the individual was freed from the prejudice of the past, from corporate constraints and privilege, which in the case of the Church were accompanied by wealth in real estate and income from annuities. These gave the Church political power, and in liberal eyes retarded the economy and stood in the way of social change. The Church was thus seen as a rival to the state, a focus of sovereignty which should belong to the nation alone. These assertions were not necessarily true, but they were the liberal perceptions of the time. Liberals

were also aware that the Church had moral influence over a number of
social groups, over Indians in the *doctrinas* and over upper-
and middle-class children in colleges, seminaries, and universities.
Liberalism, moreover, represented interests as well as principles. In
Mexico, for example, where typical mid-century liberals were young
upwardly mobile professionals, these considered the Church as a major
obstacle not only to nation-building but to their own economic and social
ambitions.

The post-colonial Church, therefore, was targeted by opponemts with a
venom that it had never encountered before. The tone was set by Lorenzo
Zavala, governor of the state of Mexico and author of a number of anti-
clerical decrees; he regarded the Church as a remnant of the Spanish
regime and declared in 1833 that Mexico should not humiliate its national
pride before the bishop of Rome, head of 'a monstrous theocracy'.[1] In
Bolivia the Church was acutely aware of hatred: Bishop José María
Mendizábal noted in 1840 that 'if in other times the priest was regarded as
the channel of heavenly grace, today he is seen as the agent of fanaticism'.[2]
In Guatemala the liberal government expelled Archbishop Ramón Casáus
and his fellow friars, censored ecclesiastical correspondence, seized Church
funds, and confiscated monastic property. Then, from 1832, it went
further, suppressed the tithe, confiscated more Church property, abolished
many religious feast days, authorized civil marriage and legalized divorce.
Such measures were premature and invited a conservative and populist
reaction; but this only delayed the day of reckoning.

For the first time in its history, in the period 1850–80 the Latin American
Church acquired enemies who hated it with an intensity born of frustrated
conviction. It is true that not all liberals shared these convictions. Some
were simply seeking to reform the state, to constitute the rule of law for all,
and to modernize the economy. None of these objects were necessarily a
threat to religion. In Colombia the Liberal Party merely insisted that religion should not be used as a means to government and that the two powers
ought to operate independently. But more radical liberals went beyond a
determination to establish the proper function of the state: they favoured
an all-out attack on the Church's wealth, privileges, and institutions, for
they believed that without the destruction of ecclesiastical power and the
death of its accompanying dogma no real change could be made. The battle
was fought first over the *patronato*, according to which congress and the
executive had the right to nominate bishops, create dioceses, call councils,
abolish monasteries, determine clerical incomes, and preserve ecclesiastical discipline. For religion, the danger lay not only in specific claims by
politicians but in the emergence of an interventionist state and a dependent
Church. Further secularization lay ahead, as the state took from the

Church education, marriage, and other areas of ecclesiastical jurisdiction, and appropriated them to itself. Battles were fought over the right to appoint bishops, over ownership of property, over the legal and political sanctions of religion, and over education. And secularism had a social base, principally among the elite or those aspiring to the elite. The masses, it seemed, preferred their ancient beliefs.

In reaction the Church sought allies where it could. Throughout Latin America Catholic politics became more conservative in the mid-nineteenth century. Churchmen aligned themselves with civilian conservatives in the belief that religion needed a political defence. In turn the dominant ideology of conservatism was Catholicism, and a belief that the alleged irrationality of man created a need for strong government supported by the Church and the sanctions of religion. Conservative political philosophy was not essentially religious but an interest and an ideology. Conservatives believed that without the restraints of religion people would be turbulent and anarchic, a defence of religion on the grounds not of its truth but of its social utility. In Colombia conservatives frankly used religion as a political weapon, and their programme in 1881 stated: 'The Conservative Party accepts as a rule of conduct and as the essential basis of social and political order as well as of legislation and government the morality of the religion professed by virtually all the Colombian people.'[3] In Chile churchmen identified openly with the conservative position, outside which they saw only liberals, revolutionaries, Protestants, and subversives of all kinds; their hero was Manuel Montt, authoritarian president and practising Catholic, the model of a modern statesman. Following the civil war of 1851, Archbishop Joaquín Larraín Gondarillas was of the opinion that only the conservatives and the Church were capable of saving 'the two bases of social order, authority and property'. In turn conservative governments looked to the Church for support. As the intendant of Atacama stated in 1854, faced by turbulence in the mining zone, 'religion and the law, the Church and the prison, are powerful means to stem the torrent of corruption which threatens us'.[4]

The alliance of conservatives and Catholics was harmful to the Church, for it placed it among a complex of interests identified as obstacles to change by liberals and progressives, and it shared in the reverses of its associates. The danger was recognized by the Colombian prelate, Manuel José Mosquera, who saw state protection for religion as just as compromising as state intervention. 'Here, as elsewhere in the Americas, the old clergy are disappearing and not being replaced . . . I do not know what the results will be in six or seven years, especially those stemming from the *protection of religion*. I prefer the principles of *independence of the Church*, because I see *a fatal tendency towards Anglicanism*.'[5] Anglicanism was an unlikely temptation for the Latin American Church, and in practice even Mosquera preferred protection to persecution.

Gradually, in the last quarter of the nineteenth century, the Church emerged from the age of privilege and persecution, adjusted itself to the secular state, and began a process of independent development. This took the form of modernizing its institutions and resources, increasing the number and improving the training of its priests and demanding a greater commitment from the laity. The movement of internal reform can be dated from approximately 1870 and lasted to 1930 and beyond. Religious renewal was followed by greater social awareness, as mass immigration and economic growth posed new problems for the Church and forced it to come out of the sacristy and into the street, and to discover anew the social dimension of the Gospel. Social Catholicism did not synchronize exactly with the movement of internal Church reform, and there was a time lag during which traditional attitudes endured and the religious mission of the Church was closely identified with conservatism. But from about 1890 Catholic social action can be observed in a number of countries, and by 1930 the Church began to speak out more clearly on the duties of capital, the rights of labour, and the role of the state.

Priests and Prelates

The Church mirrored the structure of secular society. Bishops and higher clergy were of the elites, alongside landowners, office-holders, and entrepreneurs. Many of the clergy came from landed families and in parts of Latin America higher clergy and even parish priests were actual landowners. In Chile in the middle decades of the nineteenth century there were a number of prelates and priests who, through either inheritance or personal enterprise, were owners of large estates.[6] Many of the lower clergy, however, belonged to the poor rather than the rich. They were a patient poor; they accepted Church and society as they found them, seeking to improve rather than transform. There was no class struggle in the Church; it was a social as well as a mystical body, one which embraced various opinions and interests while remaining ultimately united around its leaders.

The clergy traditionally derived their income from *capellanías* (endowed benefices), fees from masses, baptisms, marriages, and funerals, and from tithes and first fruits. The decline and abolition of tithes reduced the Church's revenue and the clergy became more dependent on fees from masses and other services and perhaps more preoccupied with their financial prospects. But there were great inequalities of income between upper and lower clergy, between wealthy city benefices and poor parishes in the country. In rural societies priests were often younger sons who were not expected to inherit land and found an alternative career in the Church. This created a reserve of recruits for the clergy and was an asset, though it did not in itself produce good vocations or ensure that priests kept their vows.

The republican Church was often short of priests. In Venezuela thirteen years of war damaged the fabric of the Church: chapels and monasteries were destroyed or used as barracks and hospitals, sacred objects looted, and priests ousted or tempted to flee. To encourage priests to return to the fold Bishop Lasso de la Vega offered them forty days' indulgence each time they confessed.[7] But new vocations remained few: the poor status and meagre prospects of the clergy were a deterrent in a society where ambition was measured in wealth and the dominant ideals of the elites were liberal and anti-clerical. In 1837 there were 200 fewer priests than in 1810 and regions such as the llanos of Apure hardly saw a priest from one year to the next. In Venezuela it was the common people who kept the faith alive while the bishops struggled to raise clerical standards. It was not until the end of the century that the Venezuelan Church began to renew its life and the religious orders to make their presence felt. In 1890 the Capuchins, once the evangelizers of colonial Venezuela, returned to the scenes of their early labours. They were followed by the Augustinians, the Dominicans, the Salesians, and many smaller orders specializing in work of social welfare. Intellectual life was still dominated by positivists but in 1890 a daily newspaper, *La Religión*, was founded as an alternative platform and endured against all expectations.

Peru began its independence with about 3,000 priests for a population of some 2 million, a favourable ratio which steadily declined in the course of the next hundred years; in 1841 Lima had 92 secular priests for 54,628 inhabitants, or one for 600 parishioners, while the department of Arequipa, with a population of 50,000, had 109 secular priests in 1847.[8] The governing classes of Peru, as elsewhere in Latin America, were distinctly hostile to the religious orders and took steps to suppress many of the great religious houses, forcing their members into secularization or laicization, a process begun by the colonial state. Rightly or wrongly, the regular orders were closely associated in the secular mind with their former Spanish patrons and were regarded as part of the Hispanic legacy, while the ideals of the contemplative and mendicant life found little favour with the new elites. Most of the Peruvian secular clergy were of middle-class origin, coming usually from professional families and educated along with other elite groups in college or university. For theology some priests went to a seminary, Santo Toribio in Lima, reformed in mid-century after a period of decline, San Jerónimo in Arequipa, or the diocesan seminary in Trujillo, while others went to the College of San Carlos in Lima, and many others were unacquainted with any kind of higher education.

The system produced a relaxed and somewhat secular-minded clergy, probably more worldly than the colonial clergy and more conservative than the generation of independence. Many priests did not reside in their parishes and instead appointed a vicar who was paid a portion of the parish income but whose qualifications were usually untried. Celibacy, moreover, was frequently ignored. Many priests in Lima and probably more in the sierra lived with women, a practice accepted by society though not by the bishops. Yet the Peruvian Church was not unique in its condition and was probably typical of the unreformed Church of the time. This was why the Latin American bishops at the First Vatican Council (1869–70) were so active in the sessions on clerical standards. The Peruvian bishop, Manuel Teodoro del Valle, referred with scorn to those clerics who cast aside their cassock 'in order to enter the world of business or to attend more easily public spectacles and houses of prostitution'.[9] Clerical reform was overdue but it had to await the efforts of a later generation.

In Bolivia, where in 1850 the clergy were 50 per cent fewer in number than in 1800, the Church was served by priests who were as diverse in training as they were in dedication. As elsewhere in Latin America, they suffered from a poor public image, being regarded as suspect in sexual and financial matters. In 1872 the faithful of Liqi accused their parish priest, Father J.R. Ballón, of absenteeism, exacting excessive fees, even leadership of a terrorist band. Rebuffed by the bishop, they took their complaints to the apostolic delegate in Lima. In 1875 the parish priest of Sakaba, Dr A.R. Revollo, was accused of aloofness, indifference to the parish school, charging excessive fees, and neglecting his church. The bishop of Cochabamba accused some of his clergy of permitting their parishioners to indulge in 'abuses condemned by the Church, intemperance, excesses, and disorders on the occasion of religious festivals'.[10] The Bolivian clergy were divided by nationality as well as by quality; foreign priests and religious, in many ways indispensable to the Church, suffered from the xenophobia of their Bolivian colleagues.

In Mexico, in contrast to Andean countries, statistics tell a story of more vigorous survival and growth. After the losses at independence, the number of clergy remained fairly constant throughout the nineteenth century.[11] There were 3,463 in 1826, 3,232 in 1851, 3,576 in 1895, 4,015 in 1900, and 4,533 in 1910. Assuming that the number of nominal Catholics was almost coterminous with the population, this meant that in 1895 (total population 12.6 million) there were less than three priests for every 10,000 inhabitants, and in 1910 (total population 15.1 million) just over three. The number of churches grew from 9,580 in 1895, to 12,225 in 1900, to 12,413 in 1910. The training available for priests was also expanded in this period. Diocesan seminaries increased in number from nine in 1826 to ten in 1851, and twenty-nine in 1910. The Conciliar Seminary of Mexico City was raised to the status of Pontifical University in 1896, with authority to grant degrees in theology, canon law, and philosophy. In 1907 the old Palafox Seminary became the Catholic University with faculties of theology, philosophy, canon law and civil law, medicine, and engineering. These changes were characteristic of the period 1880–1910, years of growth and renewal for the Church in Mexico after a time of conflict and contraction.

Beyond the statistics, the qualitative life of the Church and the standards of the clergy were also changing. During the first decades of independence many Mexican priests, like their Peruvian counterparts, were a source of scandal rather than sanctity, and in the 1850s Pope Pius IX commissioned the bishop of Michoacán to undertake a reform of the clergy, especially the regulars. A process of improvement and renewed evangelization gathered momentum in the fifty years from 1860 to 1910. The revival was at its strongest in rural Mexico, in Michoacán, Guanajuato, and Jalisco, and it was here that the new priests found the greatest response. A typical Mexican priest was a country priest, though since the failure of the College of Tlatelolco and other pro-Indian initiatives in the colonial period he was not normally recruited from the Indian communities. Most priests came from the middle class, and many men with vocations were found among the families of prosperous ranchers and storekeepers. They were products of the local diocesan seminary, where they learnt Latin, scholastic philosophy, and theology, and were imbued with strict moral values and a deep hostility to liberalism. They embarked on pastoral work, fired by their new seminary ideals, urging their parishioners to regular attendance at mass and the sacraments, organizing catechism classes, encouraging observance of Lent, and inculcating in their people 'a deep awareness of sin, a heightened sense of shame, and avoidance of sex outside marriage'.[12] On an already firm religious base the new priests built a more fervent Catholicism and became the leaders of a spiritual and moral renewal in the Mexican countryside. The priest lived among the peasants and the rural poor. In many places he was the centre of their life, a religious leader, a source of information, and a medium of rural culture.

The religious orders in Mexico experienced the vicissitudes of the rest of the Church – post-independence recession, mid-century anti-clericalism, and eventual renewal. In 1851 there were only eight religious orders in Mexico. By 1910 the number had grown to eighteen. Of the older religious orders, the Jesuits were the most dynamic and recovered most rapidly from persecution.[13] In 1910 they had 338 members, thirteen churches, fourteen colleges for middle-class entrants, and thirty schools for poor children; in addition they worked in a number of mission fields. Women's orders also grew, from nine in 1851 to twenty-three in 1910. The increase was mainly due to the advent of the new nineteenth-century urban and teaching orders, without which the Church in Mexico could not have maintained its position in the field of education. The Jesuits, for example, had thirty primary schools in 1900, the Marist brothers thirty-five; while the development of vocational schools for working-class boys was due almost entirely to the teaching orders.

Argentina, unlike Mexico and Peru, did not inherit from the colonial Church a distinct infrastructure on which it could later build. In Argentina the Church was less developed and the crisis of the clergy correspondingly greater. Standards began to decline at independence, when diocesan sees were left vacant, in Buenos Aires from 1812 to 1834, in Córdoba from 1810 to 1831, in Salta from 1812 to 1860. Following the exodus of Spanish priests, the Church had to rely on local recruits of inferior quality at a time when seminary training was virtually unknown. This enfeebled Church was an easy victim of the state. Argentine Catholicism, though broadly supportive of independence from Spain, subsequently identified with conservative regimes and instinctively recoiled from liberalism; Catholics never forgot the anti-clerical policies of Rivadavia, who declared freedom of worship, abolished the clerical *fuero*, and confiscated monastic property.[14] Following this experience the Church collaborated closely with the dictator Juan Manuel de Rosas, trading its freedom for protection and becoming in effect a department and a propagandist of the *rosista* state.[15] But the Church recovered no privilege and little property, and although the Jesuits were recalled they were quickly repulsed.

The period 1830–60 was the low tide of Argentine Catholicism, a time when it had little place in the social and political life of the country and hardly distinguished itself as a defender of justice and peace.[16] In these vast and underpopulated lands, bishoprics remained unfilled for decades, priests were few and far between. As late as 1864 the diocese of Buenos Aires contained only thirty-five secular priests, not all of them educated or suitable to their calling. For the twelve parishes in the city of Buenos Aires and for the fifty-four in the rest of the diocese (which then included the whole of the littoral and Patagonia) there were just eighty-four priests in 1880. Disputes with Rome over appointments and jurisdiction severed normal relations for decades. The very weakness of the Church tempered rampant clericalism and left anti-clericalism without justification. But this did not deter either side of the ideological divide.

Argentina's intellectual elite posed a philosophical challenge to religionists. They projected a programme designed to bypass the Church. Basically they regarded religious belief as a thing of the past and an affront to reason.

With their liberal and modernizing ideas they saw Argentina as an essentially secular society and religion as little more than a moral code useful for civilizing the masses. Juan Bautista Alberdi, leading intellectual and political thinker, wanted to marginalize the Church, to remove it from education, and to leave the training of future generations of lawyers, statesmen, and businessmen to professional teachers. He insisted on religious toleration in order, among other things, to accommodate Protestant immigrants and their way of life.[17] Alberdi, and with him the majority of the political elite, challenged the Argentine Church on the fundamental issue of the day: whether to join or to disavow the process of national organization. Some Catholic leaders sought a place for religion in the task of nation-making. In the words of Félix Frías, former enemy and exile of the Rosas dictatorship, religion was the only bond of unity and order among Argentines: 'Let us plant the Cross in our soil. Lawyers and artisans, businessmen and farmers . . . people of Buenos Aires and people of the provinces, let us all embrace each other as brothers and be as generous with our sense of charity as previously we were with our more cruel instincts.'[18]

But Catholicism tended to be exclusive. The Church authorities would never voluntarily concede religious toleration and control of education. When in 1867 the liberal governor of Santa Fe, Nicasio Oroño, pushed through the provincial assembly a bill establishing civil marriage, the hierarchy was outraged and condemned it as 'highly prejudicial to society, to public morals, and to the integrity and stability of the family'.[19] The Church was confident that in maintaining these principles it had a more popular base of support than Alberdi and the liberals. The intellectuals preached to the elite, while the clergy still preached to the people. By the 1860s they were preaching from a stronger institution and in a more insistent voice. The Church became a beneficiary of the liberal state as well as its leading critic.

Bartolomé Mitre, statesman and historian, was primarily a secularist, but he respected religion and saw the Church as a pillar of national unity. During his presidency (1862–68) the metropolitan diocese of Buenos Aires was created and secured its own archbishop, Mariano José de Escalada (1865–70); he was succeeded by Federico Aneiros (1873–94), who directed the Church through its long conflict with the liberal state. New seminaries were established and old ones reactivated to train priests for the expanding population of town and country; by 1869 the seminary in Buenos Aires had forty-eight students. Seculars were joined by religious, and native priests by immigrant clergy. Between 1868 and 1874, as a result of the republican revolution in Spain, some 200 Spanish priests migrated to Argentina, few of them highly trained or motivated, but additional recruits to an expanding Church. The Jesuits returned and in 1868 founded the

Colegio del Salvador in Buenos Aires, which was successful enough to be burned down in 1875 by an anti-clerical mob led by an apostate Spanish priest. The last decades of the nineteenth century were a new age for religious orders in Argentina, some of them such as the Dominicans and Franciscans already well known, others entering the country from Europe and the United States for the first time. In the 1870s Don Bosco sent Salesians to Argentina, and these were followed by Redemptorists (1883), Christian Brothers (1889), Capuchins (1897), and Marists (1903). Women's orders also arrived from abroad and soon attracted native vocations: Marie Auxiliatrice (1879), the Sacred Heart Sisters (1880), Sainte Union (1883), the Sisters of the Good Shepherd (1885), and the Daughters of the Child Jesus (1893). Many of these orders were dedicated not only to the contemplative life but also to welfare and education, and they helped to fill a gap in the social provisions of the conservative republic, providing charitable agencies of a traditional kind.

As the ranks of bishops and clergy increased and improved, a new impetus was given to the advancement of Catholic faith and morals through the pulpit, the school, and the Catholic press. Religion acquired a political edge as Catholic action took the Gospel outside the church and the cloister; a vigorous clerical movement now surfaced, indigenous in its base but reinforced by inputs from Rome. In 1869–70 several Argentine bishops attended the First Vatican Council, where they witnessed and supported the definition of papal infallibility and from which they returned home ready to do battle with the enemies of religion.

Between 1880 and 1914, in an age of mass immigration and economic growth, Catholicism underwent great expansion in Argentina. Yet immigration had mixed effects on religion. Many Spanish, Italian, and French immigrants were enemies of the Church, political exiles hostile to clericalism. Many others were indifferent or would say that their work gave them no time for religion, which was best left to women and children. And some had their faith tested for the first time. A Catholic from Galicia wrote home to say, 'Paco, on arriving in Buenos Aires I have learnt on good authority that God does not exist.'[20] On the other hand practising Catholics from northern Italy, Germany, and Ireland reinforced the faith and increased the number of recruits with vocations. Demographically Argentina remained a Catholic country, and in 1910 Catholics comprised 92 per cent of the population; in Buenos Aires there were nineteen parishes in 1900 compared to seven in 1857. But numbers counted for little in the struggle to preserve religion in the schools and in the laws of marriage, a contradiction that always bewildered the hierarchy.

This was a conservative Church which still attracted people of the upper and middle classes, whose religiosity was marked by individual piety, devotions to the Sacred Heart, belief in the Immaculate Conception (defined as a doctrine in 1854), and allegiance to Rome. But the countryside too was Christianized and it was here that elements of popular religion survived in prayers, hymns, processions, and the emotions voiced by Martín Fierro: 'vengan santos milagrosos, vengan todos en mi ayuda' ('Come down all you saints with your miracles, come to my aid').[21] Rural priests were reputed to pursue private interests and live immoral lives while they neglected the duties of instructing the people and administering the sacraments. Yet the Church did not entirely abandon peons and their families and from the 1860s sought to improve the quantity and quality of the rural clergy. Each small town or settlement came to have its priest and its chapel, as much a cultural as a religious requirement. In Fraile Muerto an English observer described the priest as 'an Italian, and not a very clerical character, but pleasant and good natured, and having been educated as a doctor, did all he could for the bodies of his parishioners, and I trust also for their souls . . . During the cholera he exerted himself nobly for the people'.[22] The cult of Our Lady of Luján, patron of Argentina, united all classes in annual pilgrimages to her shrine. But there remained still a great divide in the Argentine Church. As the institutions of religion were implanted and modernized, leadership remained entirely in the hands of the clergy and under the control of the bishops. Laypeople were allowed only a passive role, deprived of their own organizations and of movements under their own leadership.

While the faithful relied on priests for mass and the sacraments, priests depended upon bishops for selection and ordination, and the Church depended on them as teachers and administrators. According to canon law and Catholic tradition a bishop had virtually absolute power in his diocese, subject only to the pope. How he used that power varied from bishop to bishop. The Latin American episcopacy was not entirely homogeneous, either in ideas or in social status. A number of Church leaders came from landed elites, as did Archbishop Rafael Valentín Valdivieso (1804–78) in Chile, whose family of landowners went back to colonial times. But the majority of the bishops came from the middle ranks of society which supplied the priests, from traditional Catholic families in Mexico and Peru, from immigrant families in modern Argentina. They made their way in the Church through their superior qualifications, moral character, and powers of Christian leadership rather than through social or political interests. Where the state retained an element of patronage, as in Argentina, episcopal appointments tended to be the result of compromise between the government and Rome and to produce a conventional episcopacy unlikely to disturb Church or state.

The Latin American episcopacy underwent significant change in the course of the nineteenth century. The regalism and complacency inherited from the colonial and early national regimes gave way to a more insistent orthodoxy, reformist and Rome-orientated. This is often characterized as 'ultramontanist'. In some contexts this refers to no more than an intellectual background, as when it is said that all five of Brazil's bishops in the mid-nineteenth century were ultramontanist, mainly because they had been educated in Europe or had travelled there. But the word has acquired a pejorative and polemical sense, to denote the opposite to liberal or national positions in religion: in England the difference between a Manning and a Newman. These dilemmas were clear in Europe, less so in Latin America. It is true that the Latin American episcopate now looked to Rome for leadership and direction, but in most cases this signified reform and independence for the Church and became the Catholic norm rather than the extreme.

In general the bishops took a cautious and middle way, more prone to defence than to initiative, to compromise than to conflict. But during times of crisis they varied between intransigents and those seeking a consensus with society and the state. The Mexican episcopacy contained men like Eulogio Gillow, archbishop of Oaxaca (1887–1922), and Ignacio Montes de Oca, bishop of San Luis Potosí (1884–1921), both from wealthy families, both educated abroad, Gillow in England, Montes de Oca in Rome, and both true princes of the Church, though no less pastoral because of that. Eduardo Sánchez Camacho, bishop of Tamaulipas, was a different type. He aroused much indignation among Mexican Catholics by his attempt to reconcile the laws of the Church and those of the liberal reform, and for his opposition to the cult of Our Lady of Guadalupe.[23] He was dismissed by Rome from his see and died without the sacraments. Pelagio Antonio de Labastida y Dávalos, archbishop of Mexico, one of the principal supporters of the French intervention in 1861 and of accommodation with the Porfiriato, was succeeded in 1892 by Próspero María Alarcón, rumoured, though incorrectly, to be a liberal.

The political thinking of the Colombian bishops was almost entirely conservative and normally alarmed their opponents. Liberal statesmen feared the Church, believing it had great influence over consciences and could divert citizens from their proper obedience to the state. In 1852 Tomás Mosquera addressed Pope Pius IX directly, arguing that liberals too were Catholics and that churchmen who intervened in political issues perverted a divine institution, 'making it dependent on the triumph of one political party, which only seeks the pretext of calling itself defender of religion to seize possession of the government and hold the bishops and priests as its instruments'.[24] In their response to liberal policy the prelates recognized their obligation to submit to secular authority, but there was a qualifying condition. In a pastoral letter of August 1852 issued on the eve of his departure for exile following opposition to liberal laws, Archbishop

Manuel José Mosquera told the faithful that religion commanded them to obey the civil laws and respect the magistrates, since the pope said in his encyclical of 9 November 1846, 'those who resist authority resist the Divine Plan and will be condemned, and therefore the principle of obeying authority cannot be violated without sinning unless something contrary to the laws of God and the Church is required'.[25] Mosquera opposed the liberal idea of separation of Church and state, preferring 'union based on a concordat'. Specifically, he maintained a right of resistance to liberal measures when they attacked the inherent God-given rights of the Church. The Colombian bishops, like many of their Mexican colleagues, argued that disamortization was contrary to the inalienable rights of the Church and its legal power to own property and income.

The dramatic conflicts with the liberal state in which many Latin American bishops were involved tended to obscure the spiritual and pastoral functions of their office, though these were essential ingredients of Church reform. Every diocesan bishop was obliged to make pastoral visits to the parishes within his jurisdiction, so that the whole of the diocese was visited at least every five years. The object was to sustain faith and morals, promote religious life, encourage the parish clergy, and inspect the organization, buildings, and accounts of the local church. The *visita pastoral* was the point of encounter between ecclesiastical authority, pastoral care, and the life of the people, and it was the high-water mark of the local religious calendar. It was then that priests reported on the spiritual state of their parishes. Some drew attention to levels of observance, fidelity to prayers, Lenten devotions, and visitation of the sick. Others emphasized the 'principal sins' of the parish, usually involving alcohol and sex. In Peru pastoral visitations uncovered the sins of priests as well as people. In 1848 the auxiliary bishop of Lima, José Manuel Pasqual, had to suspend two priests in Callejón de Huaylas for 'their incorrigible addiction to the vice of drunkenness'.[26] In general, and especially in the period of renewal from the 1870s onwards, bishops complied scrupulously with the obligation of pastoral visitation, in spite of distance, poor communications, and adverse weather. It was through these visits that bishops gained direct knowledge of religious conditions in all parts of the diocese. And the *libros de visitas pastorales*, when they are available, are a prime source for the religious history of Latin America.

Laity and Elites

Lay membership of the Church in the nineteenth century covered a multitude of saints and sinners, and ranged over a wide spectrum of religious belief and practice, from those who went to mass every Sunday and received the sacraments regularly, to those whose only contact with religion was at birth, first communion, marriage, and death, and those whose Catholicism was primarily social and political. There was, however, an ingrained Catholicism in the mass of the people which was not easily measured by external practice but was part of national and popular culture.

The religion they received from bishops and priests often tended to be mournful and prohibitive rather than joyful and expansive. It has been said of piety and liturgy in Chile that in many ways they expressed 'a religion of Lent, of fasting and penance, rather than a religion of Easter joy and gladness'.[27] Religion sometimes gave the impression that it preached alienation from society and distance from daily life, not reconciliation of different traditions. Church teaching imposed a sharp division between the sacred and the profane, and Catholics were warned to avoid the devil, the world, and the flesh. These were universal Christian values but received special emphasis in the Hispanic tradition, perpetuated by preachers who gave their congregations a stark choice between purity and sex. A devotional text published in Chile in 1850 admonished its readers to 'flee all familiarity and contact with persons of the other sex, and to avoid the slightest touch of even a thread of clothing'.[28]

The laity were part of the ecclesiastical structure, grouped as they were in parishes and dioceses, but they also had organizations of their own. The most significant of these were traditionally, in Spanish America, the *cofradías*. Confraternities, or lay brotherhoods, were inherited from Spain and were established in churches and parishes by different social groups, to organize communal religious activities such as honouring particular saints, conducting festivals, or maintaining a church in good repair. Confraternities were not only for the elite. Urban, Indian, and mestizo sectors also had their confraternities. Some comprised different social classes, uniting them in corporate activity and emphasizing the vertical bonds within society; others reinforced stratification and social hierarchy. In Brazil the *irmandades* of blacks and mulattos served as a shelter in a white-dominated society, a source of religious service and instruction, a welfare system, and a focus of corporate identity. In Spanish America, too, the confraternities had an economic role; they were often mutual aid societies, owners of capital and property, and a source of employment and income for parish priests.

The life of the parish was acted in great measure around this socio-economic system. The *mayordomo* of a confraternity was a man of minor substance and probity within a community. It was his duty to organize the fiestas and the cult of Our Lady or the saint under his care, to guard the cult's material assets such as clothes, jewels, flowers, and money, to supervise processions and to allocate the funds needed for these and the indispensable food and drink. The confraternity offices were often closely linked to municipal offices. A single hierarchy operated in communities at a political and religious level. It was also a family network. *Mayordomos* were assisted by their wives and children, and the whole kinship lived in reflected glory, especially at times of fiesta and processions.

The confraternities were essentially lay organizations, administered by the laity for the laity. They were autonomous in their structure and finance, and they did not allow bishop or priest to interfere in their affairs; when they needed the services of a priest, say for a mass, they requested them and paid for them. This independence caused tension with ecclesiastical authorities, who considered that they had ultimate jurisdiction; and the reformed Church of the later nineteenth century sought to control the confraternities on grounds of religious discipline. Criticism focused on maladministration of property, neglect of religion, and preference for entertainment. Many of the religious fiestas of the confraternities were becoming profane celebrations; processions and vigils, according to some parish priests, were idolatrous in their excesses, and often the occasion for all-night drinking and dancing. So the Church authorities sought to scrutinize the accounts, nominate the officers, and supervise the activities of the confraternities, though not with complete success. In any case, events were moving against the confraternities and reducing their significance in the life of the Church. The economic and social changes of the late nineteenth century transformed the world in which the Church had to live and made the traditional confraternities, if not an anachronism, less relevant to the social requirements of the time; the Church now needed more outward-looking organizations to confront an increasingly secular world.

The laity knew the Church as a parish, and their most immediate contact with organized religion was through their parish priest. The Church had a strong pastoral presence in the older cities and provincial towns of Latin America, where numerous churches, schools, and other institutions served the various religious needs of the urban populations. In the countryside the framework of religion was spread more widely and often more thinly, and the services provided by the Church depended very much upon individual priests. Yet the firmness of peasant commitment to the Church was never in doubt. The Mexican Indians, though in the past neglected and to some extent exploited by the Church, were more inclined to accept the legitimacy of the clergy's authority than that of civil officials and politicians. Almost all peasants regarded themselves as Catholics, but few seem to have felt any sense of identity with the new republic and even fewer had any awareness of national identity. The peasants of central Mexico, like the Church, were victims of liberal policy and they resented attacks on communal land-holding and other menaces of modernization. They were the natural allies of the Church, though it cannot be said that the Church went out of its way to cultivate their support or to provide the priests and resources for distant communities. Some of the Indian communities of central Mexico fought for religion against its liberal enemies, or provided indirect assistance throughout the years of persecution. While they did not voluntarily support all conservative causes, they would be moved to action in defence of traditional practices such as pilgrimages and processions, or by the appeal of a particular priest or caudillo.

The Catholic elite in Mexico had little contact with the popular sectors of the Church, and they were marked off from other elite groups by their religion and their politics. They were closely associated with traditional political thought, as can be seen in the writings of Alejandro Arango y Escandón, Ignacio Aguilar y Marocho, Miguel Martínez, José Jesús de Cuevas, and Manual García Aguirre. These *católicos conservadores* had been politically destroyed by the Mexican liberals during the civil wars of the Reform and French intervention, but they remained steadfast in defence of traditionalist ideals: a social order based on Christian doctrine and a political system marked by cooperation between secular authorities and the hierarchy of an established Church.[29] Their position became more entrenched during the Restored Republic when the liberals denied them political space. Leading Catholics were exiled, debarred from office, and had their property confiscated. Gradually the regime relaxed and they began to return. In 1868 a group of lay Catholics founded the Sociedad Católica de México, modelled on similar organizations in Europe and with branches throughout the country. Although it was attacked as a reactionary political party, in fact its objects were exclusively religious and its member-ship cut across social classes. The Society provided catechism classes, organized Catholic schools, including free schools for poor children, estab-lished evening classes, and published a periodical press. But as experience of persecution receded, the Society lost its momentum.

Catholic politics were not exclusively conservative. During the Restored Republic and the Porfiriato there were two tendencies, one conservative, the other liberal. The conservatives considered the *Syllabus of Errors* as infallible doctrine which no Catholic could contradict. The Catholic liberals insisted on separating political from religious principles, the state from the Church, and they declared obedience to the pope in religion but to the constitution in politics. Conservative Catholics were probably more realistic in their analysis of the liberal state as it actually developed in Mexico. As they saw it, rapid secularization was producing disaggregation of traditional social groups and was strengthening the power of the state. They forecast the growth of an absolutist state and saw their warnings fulfilled in the government of Porfirio Díaz, to be followed by the dictator-ship of the revolution. Catholic conservatives also predicted acute agrarian problems (in the event a decisive factor in the overthrow of the Porfiriato), stemming from nationalization of Church property and subsequent land concentration. They saw also that solutions to the education question were made unnecessarily difficult by the insistence of liberals on secular schools and positivist doctrine, and their contempt for Christian morals and Mexican tradition. Having stated the problem, however, the conservatives had neither the policies nor the organization to provide a political alternative. They could only accommodate themselves to the liberal and Porfirian states, develop a social policy, and plan for a Catholic restoration.

In Peru the politics of Catholics, clergy and lay, were also conformist. The Church was bitterly denounced by the intellectual elite as an obstacle to progress, and the corrupt and debauched rural priest was a stock character in the demonology of the Peruvian left. The Church establishment adopted conservative positions, typified in the life and ideas of Bartolomé Herrera (1808–64), rector of the College of San Carlos, preacher on state occasions, government minister, and president of congress. Herrera proclaimed the Spanish colonial Church as the model for the new republic: 'The work which the Spaniards accomplished ... was the greatest work which the Almighty has accomplished through the hands of men'.[30] As the Church in Peru left the rule of the king for that of the pope, Herrera was the agent of the increasing 'romanization' of Peruvian Catholicism. He preached obedience to the government as long as it obeyed the Church, whose hierarchical structure he presented as the model for civil society. It was difficult to discern where the churchman stopped and the politician took over. Was he president of congress or bishop of Arequipa? Herrera saw Peru as a society ruled by an enlightened elite who would order the country and direct the ignorant masses. The Indians should be given education, but not the vote.

Yet the Church in Peru did not remain aloof from the issues of the time and its action on the ground was more evident of its intentions than its pastorals and sermons. In the period 1800–54 the Church was an active agent in the demise of slavery, as it began to intervene decisively in the relationship between slaves and masters. To defend the integrity of slave marriage the Church opposed the break-up of slave families. Slaves were able to exploit this concession, which thus became an instrument of greater freedom. The intervention of the Church limited the legal ability of slave-owners to block slave marriages. Moreover, masters who attempted to sell married slaves outside the city of Lima, or who sexually abused their female slaves, might find themselves attacked not only by their slaves but also by the Church. This assault on the power of slaveholders helped to bring about the end of slavery in a society where family bonds were decisive for manumission.[31]

The Peruvian Indians traditionally suffered from many exploiters, including clerics, whose extortionate behaviour frequently went far beyond the just collection of fees. But the Church was not responsible for the liberal legislation which abolished Indian reductions and community lands and opened them to market forces, often cheating the Indians of their land without giving them true independence. The Church too was a loser, for the Indian structure had lent itself to easy enforcement of attendance at mass and other obligations. The *doctrina* (Indian parish), comprising a principal village and two or three outlying villages, was still the basic model, and the priests kept the census; this was important for charging parochial dues, lower for Indians than for whites. But pastorals and pronouncements, overtly indifferent to the Indians, were not the only witness of the Church's Indian policy. In Indian rebellions of the later nineteenth century in the central and southern Andes Church leaders in the diocese of Puno and elswhere defended the interests of the Indians or at least acted as mediators between the rebels and the government.[32] The Indians responded to these initiatives and reaffirmed their attachment to religion and respect for its ministers. In pacifying the Indians, of course, priests sometimes served government interests rather than those of the rebels, and it is difficult to assess the balance of Church action in the sierra. The majority of priests in the Indian areas were white or mestizo, though many spoke Quechua or Aymara. But the allegiance of the Indians to traditional Catholicism was never in doubt, even during times of revolution, and there is no evidence that religion was used as a palliative or became an inhibiting factor in the Indians' struggle against abuses.

In Chile the Church avoided risks: the political position of the hierarchy was conservative and their social policy paternal. Yet conservatives were not the only Catholics. Support for the independence movement, followed by criticism of the conservative reaction of 1829, showed that a number of priests and laypeople were open to ideas of liberty and equality. In the civil war of 1851 numerous priests, seminarists, and religious participated in opposition to the conservative presidential candidate Manuel Montt and his supporters among the conservative hierarchy. The popular sectors in towns were becoming increasingly critical of prevailing inequalities and hostile to the elites of Church and state. The Catholic intellectual Pedro Palazuelos (1800–51) criticized the Chilean clergy from a liberal and popular standpoint: 'The clergy of the country are imbued with an ultra-montane spirit, which causes them to forget the true interests of religion, to ignore the spirit of brotherly love and the voice of the people crying out for counsel and help.'[33] The Catholic liberal politician Federico Errázuriz Zañartu (1825–77), president of Chile in 1871–75, criticized the clergy as exploiters of the poor, incurring the wrath of Archbishop Valdivieso and other members of the hierarchy; they made it clear that outside the conservative alliance there was no place for a Catholic, only association with liberals and unbelievers. In 1874 the ageing archbishop excommunicated Errázuriz and all those in parliament who approved the suppression of the *fuero eclesiástico*, a privilege from another age. Errázuriz regarded this defence of the indefensible as very damaging to religion.

These were political conflicts within the Chilean elite of Church and state. But Francisco Bilbao (1823–65), disciple of the abbé Lamennais, took the message to the popular sectors, preaching concern for the oppressed alongside love of God as the duty of all Christians. Inevitably, in 1844 and 1850, he was rebuked by Archbishop Valdivieso as a heretic and subversive, but continued his mission outside the Church and created a following for his democratic and egalitarian ideas in the Sociedad de Igualdad. In effect the religion of the poor, in spite of the support of a few clergy, was lost to the conservative Church, which regarded their social demands as subversive and their religious expressions as superstitious. In turn, in the course of the nineteenth century, the popular sectors became increasingly anti-clerical.

In Argentina Catholic elites were critical of the secular state but from a traditionalist position. Catholics shared common Argentine attitudes towards national organization and the creation of an ordered and constitutional Argentina. There were perhaps some signs of a distinctive Catholic thought emerging before the end of the century, but it was not yet reformist or particularly 'social' in character. If Catholic influence could be seen at all, it was in relation to liberty under law, strong national institutions, and the balance between a unitary state and federal rights. Men of letters and of politics such as the jurist Facundo Zuviría and the journalist Félix Frías were basically representative of nineteenth-century conservatism, advocating liberal institutions within the constraints of a strong constitution. Frías was more specifically Catholic in his opposition to the secularizing movement which began around the 1860s, and in 1876 he founded the Catholic Association, a lay pressure group whose leaders included several prominent politicians and which sought to mobilize Catholic opinion in defence of religious education in schools and opposition to a civil marriage law. It proved to be a lost cause, and by the end of the nineteenth century the majority of Catholics were content to see Argentina becoming a secular state.

The Romanization of the Latin American Church

The doctrinal heritage of Latin American Catholicism was no different from that of the rest of the Church. Bishops and priests received and transmitted traditional Catholic theology and scholastic philosophy. Whatever its past service to religion in reconciling faith and reason, scholasticism had become inert and repetitive. It failed to respond to the ideas of the Enlightenment, and in the nineteenth century Latin American Catholicism did not have the intellectual tools to confront the utilitarians, liberals, and positivists, with the result that the Christian argument went by default. The Bolivian priest Martín Castro complained of the education given in the seminaries and of the dominance of scholasticism, 'which is rightly banned by modern civilization'.[34] The Latin American Church relied not on new philosophical expression of religious dogma but on dogmatic restatement of ancient beliefs; above all, it failed to respond to conditions in Latin America and merely mirrored the model of Europe. In this sense it lost its own identity.

The doctrinal inspiration of the Latin American Church in the nineteenth century came from Rome, and standards were set by Pope Pius IX (1846–78), who in December 1864 published the encyclical *Quanta cura*, with its annexe the *Syllabus of Errors*. The Syllabus condemned liberalism, secularism, freedom of thought, and toleration. It specifically condemned lay education and the idea that state schools should be freed from ecclesiastical authority. It condemned the proposition that 'in our age it is no longer expedient that the Catholic religion should be regarded as the sole religion of the State to the exclusion of all others', and it condemned too the proposition that 'the Roman Pontiff can and should reconcile and harmonize himself with progress, liberalism, and recent civilization'. The attitude of the papacy, of course, had a philosophical and historical context. The liberalism of the time was seen as an assertion of man's emancipation in relation to God and a deliberate rejection of the primacy of the supernatural. As Rome was bound to deny a rationalist and purely humanist conception of man, so it opposed the political conclusions which liberals drew from this. The papacy, moreover, was itself beleaguered by the Piedmontese government which, as it annexed the Papal States, systematically applied a secular regime and imprisoned priests and bishops who opposed it. The Syllabus was a defence reflex. Even so, it was a crude and uncompromising compendium, which tied the Latin American Church to the papal obsession with liberalism, rationalism, Protestantism, and secularism or 'laicism' as they tended to call it.

The Syllabus was a weight round religion's neck, a burden which damaged its prospects of peaceful growth in Latin America. Catholic moderates seeking a middle way were embarrassed by its intransigence. Conservative Catholics could appeal to it against moderates. And liberals could cite it as proof of the danger from the Catholic Church. As applied to Latin America, the policy of Pius IX can be seen in his reaction to the Peruvian priest Francisco de Paula González Vigil, Director of the National Library, parliamentarian, and a true heir of Spanish regalism. Vigil attacked papal power and advocated a new national and liberal organization for the Church, only loosely linked to Rome.[35] Pius IX banned his book and excommunicated the author for denying that the Roman Catholic faith was the only true belief, for proclaiming religious toleration, and for preferring clerical marriage to celibacy. Some of these views would have been regarded as heterodox in any age of the Church and were probably unrepresentative of Catholic opinion outside a small group of liberal priests. The policy of Pius IX, therefore, did not introduce a new or 'Romanized' faith and morals to Latin America but, after a period of regalism and laxity, defined more clearly doctrines and disciplines as they were and asserted the primacy of Rome. It was papal definitions which were new, not papal authority.

Rome found that there was no such thing as a Latin American Church. Nationalism affected churchmen and their policies as it did the secular governments, and divisions between churches was a fact of religious life. There was much clerical resistance to the idea of participation in a general council of Latin American churches which Rome was anxious to organize towards the end of the nineteenth century; and no single church was qualified to draw up the agenda of such a meeting because of ignorance among churchmen of their neighbours; it was more common for prelates and priests to journey to Rome than to other Latin American countries. And in the event the Plenary Council of Latin America was held in Rome in 1899. Lack of communications and consequent ignorance of each other affected all the churches of Latin America, and territorial disputes between governments usually had implications for national churches. Rome regarded them all as Latins with common origins and unity of race, language, and interests, and was astonished to observe that 'they live divided and in virtual isolation from each other, with hardly any communication or exchange of ideas and doctrines'.[36]

Republican America gave Rome more access to the national churches than the colonial state had ever allowed. Even so there were problems. Vatican envoys were not numerous and took some time to establish themselves; and many were appointed as special rather than regular missions. Nevertheless, by the end of the nineteenth century the Holy See had diplomatic relations with Chile, Colombia, Argentina, Uruguay, Paraguay, Ecuador, Bolivia, Peru, Santo Domingo, and Venezuela, while in Mexico it had expert unofficial representation. It was extremely well informed on the Church in all these countries, not least on that in Mexico. Papal nuncios and delegates had a mixed reception from ruling groups hypersensitive to any infringement of national independence. More specifically, governments guarded their rights of patronage carefully; and even ecclesiastics were suspicious of these strangers from Rome. One papal delegate reported: 'it is noticeable that the arrival of an envoy from the Holy See is greeted with obvious suspicion. Government, bishops, clergy speculate wildly and with ill-concealed curiosity concerning his instructions and the true object of the mission, all convinced that it is not what it is claimed.'[37] It took some months to reassure local opinion that the envoy's intentions were honourable, especially if a delegate had to serve more than one country.

As it looked towards Latin America, Rome had a number of concerns. There were not enough clergy, and standards were not high. Concubinage was common and was accepted by the faithful, for 'in some parishes the family of the parish priest is known and received without scandal'. Latin America, especially the River Plate countries, was served by increasing numbers of European clergy in the course of the nineteenth century. European secular clergy, as distinct from regulars, were not well received, being regarded, with some justification in the case of the Italians, as ill-educated, unworthy, and financially motived. Even Rome had its reservations, being convinced that many who went to America were unsuitable, their bishops glad to get rid of them; these types emigrated 'only to get rich'.[38] Nevertheless Rome was convinced that the only hope for reforming the clergy and modernizing the Church came from Europe, especially in the case of religious orders, whose local recruits were 'religious only in name'. It was essential to increase and improve seminaries, and to provide a model of higher education in the Church. This was the function of Colegio Pio Latinoamericano founded in 1856 by Pius IX and subsidized by an allocation from the Latin American diocesan contributions to the Holy See. The Latin American bishops were slow to send candidates and contributions, but it was from this college that the best of bishops and seminary professors eventually came, proud bearers of degrees from the Gregorian University.

Rome deplored the *patronato*, that complex of rights over ecclesiastical personnel and resources possessed by the Spanish crown and then claimed, after independence, by the successor governments. Specifically, the *patronato* involved rights of presentation to bishoprics and other high offices in the Church, the state nominating a candidate to the pope, who then conferred canonical appointment. Rome had to concede a place to governments in making clerical appointments, and also gave in to pressure to abolish the tithes and replace them by a mixture of state subsidy and contributions of the faithful. Rome conceded these rights, not as something inherent in the state, but as usurpations. Yet Rome was also opposed to the separation of Church and state, even when it was obvious that separation could lead to the independence and reform of the Church. The preferred model was always one of Catholicism recognized as the official religion and protected by a concordat, a formal agreement between the Holy See and a secular government upon subjects of vital concern to both.

Envoys, bishops, the Catholic press, seminaries, the religious orders, these were the instruments of papal influence in Latin America, fortified by the basic respect of Catholics for the successor of St Peter. The Latin American Church came into direct contact with ultramontane Catholicism at the First Vatican Council (1869–70). Latin Americans comprised 48 of the 700 prelates who participated in that gathering, convoked by Pius IX to deal with clerical discipline, plan a catechism of Christian doctrine, consider relations between faith and reason, and between Church and state, and define papal infallibility. The Latin American bishops adopted relatively conservative positions on matters of faith and morals. And almost without exception they supported the definition of papal infallibility. Although they urged local autonomy on some issues, they championed the authority of the Holy See, partly out of principle, partly as a lever against national governments.[39]

Thirty years later the Latin American episcopate had a further opportunity to affirm its allegiance to the Holy See when Pope Leo XIII convoked the first Latin American Plenary Council, a unique occasion not previously seen in the history of the Church. The Council was held in Rome in 1899 in the Colegio Pio Latinoamericano, a site free of national pressures.[40] Out of a total episcopate of 104, 13 archbishops and 41 bishops attended; Latin American theologians and non-episcopal experts were not called upon to play a part, and essentially this was a meeting of bishops organized according to canon law and the clerical criteria of the time. The Council deliberated on problems of paganism, superstition, ignorance of religion, socialism, Freemasonry, the press, and other perceived dangers to religion in the modern world. The Church in Latin America was depicted as a Church assailed by 'the monstrous errors' of liberalism, positivism, atheism, and rationalism. None of these things were imaginary and the enemies of the Church were real enough, as the Catholics of Mexico and Central America could testify; but in general a siege mentality prevailed, and the assertion of the Church's right of jurisdiction over religious education in public schools was now unrealistic. There were 998 articles for the defence and propagation of the Catholic faith and the organization of the Church in Latin America, most of them inspired by Roman theology and canon law and the papal teaching of the nineteenth century rather than by any Latin American traditions or local needs, and more designed to conserve and defend than to increase and initiate. The bishops were concerned with the education and quality of priests, less so with their numbers, and they reaffirmed the rule of celibacy; but they also showed awareness of the hard and impoverished life of many of them. The Council, while recognizing the inevitable interaction of politics and religion, advised Catholic authors to defend the rights of religion and the Church, but not to provoke their opponents or disturb public peace. The Latin American Church was not composed of revolutionaries. This was also evident in the Council's list of prevailing sins, which was conventional: gambling, drunkenness, lust, concubinage, adultery, obscenity, murder. But there was no condemnation of sins of injustice to workers, peasants, and the poor, and references to *Rerum Novarum* were brief. In the Council's final letter to the clergy and people of Latin America, signed on 9 July, it gave thanks for 'God's special favour' in having populated 'America so generously with a Latin and Catholic race'. In spite of its limitations, the Council left one enduring legacy, which has been underlined as 'the rebirth of a collegial consciousness among the Latin American episcopate, which would yield fruit in the future'.[41] This took the form of a specific instruction urging the Church to hold conferences of bishops every three years in the ecclesiastical provinces of Latin America. In the event, however, although collegiality was planted it did not become a vigorous growth. Meanwhile, Leo XIII declared that the Council was 'one of the most precious jewels of his pontificate'.

Within Latin America itself, planning for reform was undertaken by regional councils and synods. Provincial councils directed and promoted the work of the Church in each country, and it was from these that the local churches received information and instructions on faith, morals, and Catholic practice. The synods legislated on particular needs of clergy and people at a diocesan level. With the encouragement of Rome, the Mexican Church held five provincial councils between 1892 and 1897, which also served as a preparation for the Latin American Plenary Council in Rome. Seven synods were held in Mexico between 1882 and 1910.

The organization of religion was thus improved and expanded in the period 1870–1910. The Latin American churches were now integrated more closely into the universal Church, from which they received direction and many of their personnel. The papacy, it should be said, did not so much take over the Latin American Church as move into a vacuum of ecclesiastical power left by the demise of the colonial Church, a vacuum which neither the national governments nor Churches were capable of filling. In the process the Latin American hierarchy and clergy began to discard the regalism and laxity of the past, and to conform more closely to the Roman ideal of religious vocation. Orthodoxy and reform tended to go hand in hand. Diocesan seminaries began to choose candidates more carefully and to train them in moral virtues as well as orthodox doctrine; some were sent to Rome and Paris for further study, and these were often the bishops of the future. The new priests were soon to be agents of reform throughout the Latin American Church.

Yet Romanization could be a bane as well as a blessing. The Latin American Church was developing within and around itself a basic contradiction. On the one hand Romanization was a liberation, an emancipation of the Church from royal control and the legacy of the colonial state, and resistance to pressure from the new republican states. On the other hand, the Latin American Church was committing itself to another form of authority, an authority hitherto distant and restrained and exercised with discretion. But as papal control became more insistent, now exercised with the force of infallibility, Latin American Catholics would realize that there was a price to pay for the benefits it brought. The future would show that the authority of the pope and the power of the Roman Curia could be used to deny local bishops, priests, and people freedom in their faith, or any means of discussing policy or making decisions. A time would come when the development of doctrine and the reform of morals, essential conditions for a living faith, would be out of bounds to Latin American Catholics, a time when every bishop was a Roman appointee and every appointment tested for fidelity to the Roman model.

Reform and Renewal

In Argentina a Catholic revival can be observed from about 1880.[42] Under the leadership of inspiring bishops, the Church began to emerge from its state of depression and to employ modern methods of organization, evangelization, and propaganda. First, religious teaching was improved and extended. Monsignor León Federico Aneiros, auxiliary bishop of Buenos Aires from 1870, worked for improved preaching and instruction, and to the pulpit he added the press, with the foundation of Catholic newspapers and periodicals, *La Religión*, *El Orden*, *El Católico Argentino*, *La Unión*, and *La Voz de la Iglesia*. Reform could also be seen in the improvement and extension of seminaries, especially from 1858 when it was accepted that there should be one for each diocese, and the government undertook to provide financial support. In 1860 President Derquí asked Pius IX and the General of the Society of Jesus to send Jesuits to Argentina. They returned to Santa Fe in 1862 and, as has been seen, in 1868 they opened in Buenos Aires the Colegio del Salvador, in its early years an object of some controversy, culminating in 1875 when it was attacked and burned by an anti-Jesuit mob. Meanwhile, at the request of Bishop Aneiros, St John Bosco, founder of the Salesian Fathers, sent ten of his order to Argentina in 1875; they opened their first college in San Nicolás, and in

1877 founded the first School of Technical Studies, later the Pius IX College.

Education was a source of fierce controversy between Church and state in Latin America, and Catholic expansionism clashed with the determination of liberals and positivists to free education of all religious content and bring it under the control of the secular state. In the second half of the nineteenth century secularization won the day in almost the whole of Latin America, though the rate and degree of change varied from country to country, as will be seen. In Argentina the law of secular education of 1884 seemed to settle the matter and remove Catholic religion from the schools, but this was not the end of the subject. The religious issue in education reappeared periodically, in Argentina and elsewhere, and in some countries there was a return to religious teaching in state schools, though as an optional subject. In most cases, however, the Church lost the battle for influence in public education and had to fall back on providing an alternative school system of its own, often though not invariably for those who could afford to pay. The Church also attempted to compete with the state at university level, and Catholic universities were created parallel to the state system. Such creations were more characteristic of the period after 1930, but in Argentina the idea of a Catholic university was already frequently urged by the episcopacy and in Catholic congresses. At last the time seemed right, and in 1910 the Catholic University of Buenos Aires was founded; its rector was Monsignor Luis Duprat, and it offered courses in the Faculty of Law and Social Sciences. It began to seek official recognition for its courses and degrees; but the proposal was strongly opposed by the University of Buenos Aires and this was fatal, for without real degrees to offer it could not attract students and it ceased to function in 1920. As an alternative, the so-called Courses of Catholic Culture were established in 1922, designed to provide formal instruction in Catholic doctrine to university students, graduates, and other people, an indication of Catholic concern over the loss of the elite rather than a contribution to higher education.

New Evangelists

The growth of religious resources fed a new impulse to evangelization. After the closure of the colonial missions and the vacuum created by independence, it took some time to regain momentum. From the second half of the nineteenth century, however, the Latin American Church began to expand its frontiers once more, and the first stage was the gradual return of the friars. Andrés Herrero, Franciscan commissioner general of the missions in Spanish America, formed a group of twelve Franciscans in 1834 to undertake evangelical work among the Indians of Bolivia. Soon they were joined by another eighty-three friars, and colleges in Peru, Chile, and Bolivia were opened. In 1843 the Dominicans returned to Peru.

Pius IX, recalling perhaps his visit to South America as a young canon, took a particular interest in expanding the Latin American missions and it was he who negotiated the political framework which made this possible, signing a series of concordats which included provisions for missionary activity. The Church managed to obtain material help from some governments to carry out the work of Propaganda Fide (renamed Congregation for the Evangelization of Peoples in 1967). In 1848 twelve Capuchins were assigned to evangelize the Araucanians of Chile. In 1855 twenty-four Franciscans and in 1856 fourteen more went to Argentina to establish similar missions.

The military solution to the presence of Araucanian Indians in Argentina, culminating in the Desert Campaign of 1880–85, did not arouse disquiet on the part of the Church, whose leaders, echoing the debates of the sixteenth century, assumed that pacification was necessary and was a precondition of evangelization. Individual missionaries exposed injustices committed against the Indians as they were driven back. Franciscan chaplains to the expeditionary force south of Córdoba in 1878–79 reported on the methods employed by Colonel Eduardo Racedo: 'Reporting the defeat of Epumer Rosas, Colonel Racedo recounts that he made the Indians suffer for daring to resist ... From this we assume that there has been a great slaughter of Indians.'[43] Those who survived were herded into corrals and died of smallpox. The Indian rising in the Chaco in 1887 was brutally crushed and fourteen prisoners were killed at night, including women and children.[44] While Franciscans and others conscious of injustice reported events such as these, the Church raised no voice on the morality of military action against Indians. On the other hand, in the wake of soldiers, it sent missionaries, who, while ignoring the Indians' own culture, applied the traditional methods of evangelization: baptism, instruction, and the sacraments, hampered always by the unchristian behaviour of soldiers, merchants, and landowners. Elsewhere, in the Gran Chaco and southern Córdoba, the work of evangelization was carried out by Italian Franciscans of Propaganda Fide, dispatched by the pope in the 1860s. Their work was challenged by local political and economic interests, while attempts to establish reductions were frustrated by the unwillingness of nomadic Indians to settle.

Bishop Federico Aneiros predictably played a leading role in the evangelization of the Indians of southern Argentina, a purely ecclesiastical enterprise which owed little or nothing to the government. This southern frontier, starved of ecclesiastical resources, had never reproduced the mission successes characteristic of Paraguay, Mexico, and California, and most of the Pampa Indians remained enclosed within their own religious world, immune to Christian argument and example. On the frontier 'Christian' was a cultural term used to distinguish civilized whites from savage Indians. Bishop Aneiros inaugurated a new age of evangelization. He formed a commission of clergy and laity to provide backing and requested the Lazarist fathers to undertake the task. In the years 1873–78 these established mission stations in Azul, Patagonia, Bragado, and elsewhere, concentrating scattered groups into communities for easier access, though again with mixed results. Between 1878 and 1884 Monsignor Mariano Antonio Espinosa, later archbishop of Buenos Aires, travelled over a great part of the south in the company of the first Salesian missionaries. The Salesians' first mission was to the Italian immigrants of La Boca in Buenos Aires. In the years after 1879 it was these missionaries who, following a path especially indicated by their founder, were responsible for evangelizing the whole of Patagonia, the Araucanians, and the Indians of Tierra del Fuego, as well as those in the south of Chile. Salesians also accompanied General Roca's Indian expeditions, where they ministered to soldiers rather than Indians. It was in Patagonia that they expressed their true vocation.

Other churches were not so dynamic. In Rome's eyes Peru lagged behind, and Pope Leo XIII called upon the Peruvian bishops in 1895 to make a greater effort among the Indians, who comprised so great a part of the population. The first group of Augustinian missionaries arrived there in 1900. In Mexico missionary expansion took place in the early twentieth century and owed much to Jesuit efforts. Father Magallanes of Totatiche renewed contact, broken since the eighteenth century, with the Huicholes, placing a mission post at Azqueltán under Father Lorenzo Placencia, and taking the Gospel into the sierra itself.

In Colombia serious missionary effort was delayed until the last decade of the nineteenth century. The Augustinians arrived in 1890, the Montfortians in 1903, the Lazarists in 1905, the Claretians in 1908, the Carmelites and Jesuits in 1918. But it was the Capuchin missions in southern Colombia which made the most dramatic advances, working mainly among the Inga and Sibundoy Indians. National legislation of the 1890s, particularly the renewal of the 'Convention of the Missions' in 1902, conceded absolute authority to missionary orders, including the Capuchins, to govern, police, educate, and generally control the Indians of the interior; about 75 per cent of the national territory was thus placed under missionary rule. Between 1906 and 1930 a group of Catalan Capuchins under the direction of Fray Fidel de Montclar established themselves as the dominant political and economic power in the Sibundoy region and worked to win converts and influence among the Indian population. Soon the territory of the Capuchin missions underwent further expansion, backed by a programme of economic development and one of civilizing the Indians. The missions became owners of extensive landed estates and built an infrastructure of roads and services for trade and access, as well as towns where the Indians were obliged to settle. And in the process the Capuchins became a combination of priests, magistrates, and entrepreneurs.

The Capuchin missions in Colombia have been criticized as a state within a state, a theocratic dictatorship which usurped the land and freedom of the Indians in exchange for a spurious civilization.[45] These are value judgements reminiscent of the charges levelled against the Jesuits in Paraguay in the eighteenth century, and like them they fail to do justice to the religious motivation of the missionaries and their need for a protective framework. They also fail to establish whether alternative and probably inevitable forms of contact – with merchants, landowners, officials, anthropologists – would have been superior to that of the missionaries or provided better material prospects for the Indians.

Throughout Latin America the methods and the results of evangelization were probably mixed; it is clear that mistakes were made and the failure rate was high. Doubts are expressed as to the true Christianity of Indian converts and there is a tendency to see only syncretism and 'idols behind the altars' in convert communities. But these are controversial judgements. Many Indians were real Catholics. Others were not. But it was a juxtaposition of different religious systems rather than a debased syncretism.

Religion in Brazil through Monarchy and Slavery

The Portuguese monarchy led Brazil peacefully into independence, leaving it with an emperor from the royal family supported by a powerful plantation aristocracy. Brazil also had a different religious history from the rest of Latin America.[46] Its two institutions, monarchy and slavery, in both of which the clergy were involved, were inimical to the development of a modern Church. The clergy of the old regime failed to meet the needs of society. The ecclesiastical power of the state inherited from the colonial regime and closely guarded by the Brazilian monarchy from 1822 to 1889 produced a breed of 'political priests' who owed their preferment to politicians and became in effect government servants and social parasites. Priests of this kind tended to be hostile to Rome, advocates of a fashionable liberalism and Jansenism, servants of the elite, and not even faithful to their vows. During the empire there were only about 700 secular priests, almost all of whom had been educated in state-controlled seminaries, to minister to 14 million people. As for the religious orders, they were

virtually suppressed by a government hostile to the idea of the contemplative life; in 1855 a circular from the Minister of Justice, José Tomás Nabuco
de Araújo, specifically prohibiting the entry of novices into the orders,
would eventually lead to their extinction. The decline and fall of the
monarchy gave the Church the opportunity to free itself from direct political influence and to look to its own renewal. Dioceses were established,
seminaries founded, and a new and more dedicated clergy emerged,
zealous for Catholicism, loyal to the bishops and to Rome, and orthodox in
their faith and morals. Monarchy, however, had not been the only embarrassment. The stain of slavery seeped through the whole fabric of Brazilian
society and few institutions were left untouched. The Catholic Church was
no exception.

The absence of social awareness among Brazilian Catholics reflected the
society in which they lived, where the Church was a slave-owner and a
notable absentee among abolitionists. The secular clergy, convents, and
religious orders owned slaves and were among the various interest groups
in a slave society. It is true that some set an example. In 1866 the
Benedictines, owners of some 2,000 slaves, freed all children henceforth
born to female slaves in their possession, an important precedent at the
time. After the Rio Branco Law of 1871, the so-called law of free birth, the
Benedictine and Carmelite orders freed their slaves, several thousand in
all. And individual priests campaigned for abolition. But the Catholic
Church did not significantly support the abolitionist cause. Joaquim
Nabuco, distinguished leader of abolition, had an audience with Pope Leo
XIII in 1888 but without positive results, and throughout the abolitionist
campaign the Brazilian Church remained a spectator of events.[47] According
to Nabuco, the Catholic Church never raised its voice in favour of emancipation: 'Our clergy's desertion of the role which the Gospel assigned to it
was as shameful as it could possibly be.'[48] The Church's association with the
traditional institutions of the empire damaged its integrity without particularly helping the imperial cause. Reformers and positivists criticized what
they saw as a triple alliance of Church, slavery, and monarchy as the major
obstacle to national progress, and believed, however unjustly, that they
would sink or swim together.

Yet Brazil could not be totally immune to the process of reform and
renewal experienced by the rest of the Latin American Church. In spite of
the regalism of Pedro II, his opposition to Rome, and his indifference to
Catholicism, he had to acknowledge that the reformed and orthodox clergy
were those most worthy of preferment. The new bishops then had to face
the hostility first of liberal politicians and, after 1870, of republicans who
were suspicious of Rome and wanted to strip the Church of state support.
This was still a compromised Church, but by 1889 it was free of the encum-

brance of monarchy and the scandal of slavery and could at last claim parity of esteem with the other Churches of Latin America. The separation of Church and state in 1889–91 was a further blessing in disguise, for the Church now had to generate its own resources. Attention was first focused on reorganizing the structure of the Church through the creation of new dioceses. In 1891 the Brazilian Church consisted of only twelve dioceses. By 1900 there were seventeen, in 1910 thirty, in 1928 fifty-eight. The bishops chosen to occupy the new sees were selected by Rome, and they first concentrated on two tasks: the restoration of the material fabric of religion, such as churches, chapels, and shrines, and the renewal of the religious mission of the Church through the establishment of seminaries for training priests and, in an increasingly secular world, the founding and reopening of monasteries and convents. Because of the reluctance of middle-class families to offer their children to the priesthood and the religious life and the consequent shortage of vocations in Brazil, the Holy See encouraged European orders to dispatch priests, nuns, and brothers to replenish the religious houses or undertake parish work. This accounts for the large number of foreign priests in Brazil from then onwards.

The growth of the so-called bureaucratic or organizational Church in the period 1870–1930 has been characterized as the introduction of a European model largely irrelevant to Brazilian life. According to this interpretation, the establishment of Catholic schools for the middle classes, of various pious groups and associations, of a standard liturgy, and other elements of reform were more appropriate to an urban, bourgeois society than to the needs of Brazil, which remained predominantly rural and underdeveloped.[49] In the process the Brazilian Church became middle class and European, alien to the mass of the people, whose 'popular Catholicism' deriving from the colonial past was now marginalized by the 'orthodox' Catholicism of the reformed Church. The analysis is incomplete. In the first place, the reform movement did not direct itself exclusively to the middle classes but also sought out the popular sectors. The new priests from Europe did not all remain in the towns; some went into the country and helped to organize rural parishes to minister to peasants and labourers. A frontier-type network took shape: two or more priests were often grouped in a parish house from which they periodically visited a number of chapels situated throughout the rural area of a *município*. The system functioned more effectively when it was in the hands of the religious orders, whose members were accustomed to working from a community base, but secular clergy too had a presence in rural life. Primary education, often provided by nuns, also reached a wider social group than the local middle classes. These developments are not surprising, for in Europe itself – in Italy, France, Spain, and Portugal – the Church had experience of rural societies, and if it did export a 'model' to Brazil it was not exclusively an urban or developed one. Moreover, Brazil, like other parts of Latin America, was undergoing immigration and urbanization and the Church had to respond to a new environment, not necessarily elitist.

CHAPTER 6

℘

The Religion of the People

Traditions of Belief

How do you measure belief? Statistics exist but are not a reliable guide to religion. Faith in a personal God is a matter of individual conscience and this is not easily judged or quantified. The religion of a people can be tested by outward observance, by attendance at Sunday mass, reception of the sacraments, and fulfilment of Easter duties, and these can be counted, as sociologists have done for parts of Europe, though less so for Latin America. According to modern surveys of attendance at mass in Brazil, the Church can claim no more than a minority of the people, perhaps 10–15 per cent, at the most 20 per cent. These are orthodox Catholics. The majority of Brazilians are informal Catholics who may pray to the saints but do not go to mass, and many others seek salvation in new Pentecostal churches. The historical stages of this decline in Catholic observance, however, are not known, nor is the original base. For other parts of Latin America statistics are available for the 1960s. In Mexico 95 per cent of the population were baptized, and the average attendance at Easter communion was 50 per cent. In Venezuela the average attendance at Sunday mass was 13 per cent, in Colombia 15 per cent, in Peru 12 per cent. But these contemporary figures are not a sure guide to the past, or to the rate, the geography, and the sociology of decline in religious practice. At what point, for example, did Peruvian Catholicism recede from the high attendance figures at the time of independence to the low levels of the 1960s? And are not the figures for Colombia belied by the massive crowds attending religious events or welcoming a visiting pope?

Popular religion in Spanish America owed its origins to a dual heritage: from Spain and from America. The conquerors were familiar with a religion of vows, shrines, and miracles centred on local communities, and Catholic devotions of this kind were easily transplanted to America. There they met the cultural heritage of Indian societies which had their own version of local religions. In the subsequent fusion neither side won a total victory. Spaniards preserved their religion without surrendering to cultural relativism, and Indians clung to reserves of their own culture without challenging Christian beliefs. The association of old and new gave popular religion a Latin American identity – and a diversity – not easily classified and not immediately recognizable to Spanish newcomers in America.

Towards 1770 the newly arrived archbishop of Guatemala, Pedro Cortés y Larraz, a Spaniard basically out of touch with the Indian faithful and unsympathetic to American culture, recorded that one of his first impressions on arriving in America was that Catholicism as practised by the Indians had little resemblance to that familiar to him in Europe. He concluded that Christianity among the Indians lacked any foundation except love of music, fireworks, ornament, and exterior display. He blamed the early missionaries, whom he criticized for having baptized converts before properly instructing them, and he castigated clergy in his own day for being overindulgent: 'Even though some are persuaded that the Christian religion is well established among the Indians because of what they spend on churches and ornaments, this argument is very mistaken, since they use them for their own idolatry.'[1] The archbishop himself had no practical experience of evangelization and never learnt an Indian language.

The logic of his attitude would have been to deny the possibility of any Christianity among the American Indians. This was an extreme position and not typical of the missionary mentality. Some of the excessive celebrations of popular feasts and local saints, when drinking, dancing, fighting, and rioting scandalized some people, were curbed – or not curbed in many cases – by the Church authorities. If there was a campaign against religious fiestas it came from liberals rather than bishops and priests, most of whom learnt to live with religious celebrations and their excesses.

Everyday life was pervaded by religion, which appeared to the people in metaphysical truths and physical forms; it answered their questions and satisfied needs when nature itself failed them. The great religious processions – Our Lady of Chapi in Arequipa, the Lord of Solitude in Huaraz, Our Lady of Copacabana in Bolivia, Our Lady of Luján in Argentina, Our Lady of Guadalupe in Mexico – testify to the popular base of the Church and the strength of popular religiosity. The Lord of the Miracles in Lima began in the colonial period as a devotion and procession of Negro slaves and gradually extended its appeal to virtually the whole of society. Devotions often focused on individuals who had a special sanctity, San Luis Bertrán, Saint Rose of Lima, Blessed (now Saint) Martin de Porres. But people often made their own saints and venerated spiritual heroes who had not been canonized.

A religious sociology of Latin America would recognize significant variations. Among the Indian populations attendance at mass on Sundays and reception of the sacraments were important but irregular, yet for the most part they had great respect for the clergy, for saints, and for religious ceremonies and pilgrimages. Blacks were not notably Catholic, though they were religious after their own fashion, while the extensive mulatto populations in Brazil, Venezuela, and the Caribbean were largely indifferent to organized religion though not necessarily to new churches that appealed directly to their spiritual needs. The mestizo population was the real base of orthodox Catholicism and it was in zones of mestizo settlement that the full life of the Church was best observed. Among economic groups, small proprietors and tenant farmers would be more likely to be religious than ranchers and cattlemen. There also appear to have been regional differences in the map of religion, places where regular churchgoers predominated, others where seasonal Catholics were the norm. Michoacán and Jalisco, for example, were more religious than the Mexican north.

In the plateau of Michoacán in the 1860s and 1870s lack of instruction and even of public worship did not prevent the people from remaining obedient to ecclesiastical government and faithful to the practice of religion. 'Most people could recite from beginning to end the Our Father, the Creed, the Hail Mary, the Ten Commandments, the Magnificat, the Litanies, and many other prayers. No one doubted a single article of faith. For these country people, heaven, hell and purgatory were as real as day and night.'[2] The informed minority of Catholics knew the catechism by heart, believed it, and lived by it. They believed in the mystery of the Trinity and had an eschatological view of life and destiny. The great majority, no less Catholic, professed a more simple and very personal faith, spoke directly to Christ and the saints, frequently broke the commandments, especially the sixth and ninth, and, although the remnants of primitive religions had long been Christianized, still retained a few superstitions from the past.

Large numbers of Latin Americans deserted the Catholic Church in the nineteenth century and the demography of religious belief was altered for all time. The elites lapsed into free-thinking, Freemasonry, and positivism, though it was not uncommon for a nominally Catholic family to have a secularist father and a religious mother, as were the parents of the Mexican reformist, Francisco Madero. The professional and academic classes of contemporary Latin America are the recognizable heirs of these sectors. The decline of religious practice, however, was a story not only of lapsed Catholics but also of missing priests. Parishes were so large that attendance at mass was impossible for many people. While average sizes in the dioceses of Bogotá (3,732 parishioners) and Caracas (4,722) were barely manageable, parishes in the dioceses of Santiago (over 12,000) and La Paz (over 18,000) were beyond the capacity of existing clergy to administer.[3]

And the clergy were declining in numbers. The ideal proportion of 1:1,000 cited for contemporary Europe and the United States was never reached in Latin America in the period 1830–1900; by 1912 the average was 4,480 parishioners to a priest, and even in Mexico, where vocations were more abundant, the average was only 1:3,000.[4] Guatemala, bereft of seminaries and vocations alike, had just one priest for every 10,000 faithful. In Santo Domingo, according to the papal envoy (1870), the cathedral church had only two priests, while the patronal church of Santo Domingo had no priest at all, the keys being entrusted to 'a pious woman'. The archdiocese of La Plata in Bolivia had 198 priests for almost a million Catholics. Only Ecuador in the whole of Latin America approached the Catholic model of 1:1,000.[5] In these conditions the cure of souls was a vain hope, and many nominal Catholics, especially among those on the margins of society, were left without pastoral care from one year to the next. Yet the faithful were not entirely faithless, and the lapsed not entirely forgotten.

The Church never losts its links with the popular sectors or became a captive of the elites, just as the liberals never secured the allegiance of the mass of the people. In Chile a popular song extolled the piety of the non-whites:

Moreno pintan a Cristo
morena a la Magdalena
morena es el bien que adoro.
!Viva la gente morena![6]

(Dark is the colour they paint Christ, dark that of the Magdalena, dark is the beloved I adore. Hurrah for the coloured people!)

The variety and unpredictability of Latin America could be seen in the pattern of religious observance: there were places where churchgoing was regular, others where it was infrequent, others where it was once a year at Easter or thereabouts. There was also a difference between countries: on the one hand those where historically the Church was strongly implanted, on the other hand those where religion was endemically weak. So Mexico was more Catholic than Honduras, Paraguay than Uruguay. The common people of Paraguay, influenced perhaps by their Jesuit past, wanted and practised religion with a fervour which inspired a Vatican observer to report in 1878 that 'they love Catholicism almost instinctively'. Regional contrasts in the practice of religion are often indefinable. The Vatican could even mark the difference in the alms-giving of Catholics. For some reason Brazilians were more generous in their offerings than Chileans: 'The Brazilian people', it was reported, 'are one of the most charitable in the world.'[7] But outward conformity does not tell the whole story or unveil the depth of commitment either among fervent Catholics or among apparently nominal ones; nor does it indicate the influence of political and social pressures on belief, that conventional conformity known in all societies, not only in the Americas. Moreover, there is a chronology of growth and renewal among Latin American Catholics in the nineteenth century as they responded to the Church's advance from inertia to reform. And in some places this was a movement from informal to formal religiosity.

The faith was secure, behaviour lamentable: this was the consensus of Church opinion. The records of synods, councils, and visitations describe a sinful population wallowing in adultery, drunkenness, gambling, corruption, superstition, and hedonism, and commonly sinking into religious inertia. In Santiago Bishop Casanova devoted an entire pastoral to the perils of alcohol and urged the creation of temperance societies in parishes. As reported by parish priests in El Salvador, the greatest moral problems were alcoholism and concubinage. In some parishes, two-thirds of sexual unions were informal, blessed by neither Church nor state. They blamed this on growing religious indifference, especially among men, who failed to attend mass or fulfil their Easter duties. 'Yet in spite of this, the faith is preserved intact and there is much religious enthusiasm.'[8] And on special occasions such as fiestas, or during pastoral visitations, or at times of personal crisis, the church would be full of people, the confessionals packed with penitents. So the priests made a distinction between morality and piety: their people were pious but sinful, relying in the end upon confession and looking to the Church as a refuge of sinners. This gap between faith and morals drew the contempt of secularists and the disgust of those for whom religion was primarily a code of ethics at the service of society, but it was a dilemma well known to theologians from St Augustine onwards.

Moral laxity was a feature of Latin American Catholicism which impressed all the emissaries from Rome. An apostolic delegate reported from Honduras at the end of the century: 'As for morals, behaviour is so lax that it can only be attributed to an exaggerated confidence in God's mercy or to the scandalous example of their own priests. Here it is all explained in terms of human frailty. So concubinage is widespread, tolerated by parents, who allow it before their own eyes, under the same roof.'[9] These informal relationships, in fact, were treated as virtual marriages by people who did not have access to a priest or, when they did, could not afford the fees and other expenses of a formal marriage. The clergy could see that among the poor the main problem was not divorce, espoused by the liberals as a progressive cause, but the absence of marriage in the first place. The family in Latin America was evidently not always the secure institution advocated by the Church. In Costa Rica, of some 8,500 births in 1887

more than 2,000 were illegitimate. And the Church itself admitted that the
principal obstacles to marriage were not immorality but the shortage of
clergy, the distances separating communities, and the lack of money to
defray expenses.[10]

The Latin American Church underwent a process of reform and
Romanization in the second half of the nineteenth century and the faithful
became subject to closer scrutiny than ever before. There was a growth in
the number of clergy, and a change in character as they became more
ardent, more evangelist, more hungry for souls, as it was said. The parish
priests no longer passively accepted religious inertia but actively worked to
spread belief and piety. In Chile the synod of 1895 insisted that the parish
mass should be celebrated not only as an act of worship but as an occasion
when people could be instructed in the basic elements of the faith and
recite answers to the catechism.[11] The change in ecclesiastical style was
typified by the ministry of a parish priest in El Salvador. He arrived in
Arentas in 1855, when there was 'no sign of a parish', only an old church
without ornaments or missals, and one chalice. After twenty-three years'
work, he had built five new churches for the region, could claim some
success in raising faith and morals, and confessed that, 'while there are sins
and excesses still, these must be considered an inevitable consequence of
the world around us.'[12] These were signs of the renewal of parish structures
and revival of Christian communities.

Religious life further rallied in the early twentieth century, with the
spread of devotions to the Blessed Sacrament and the Sacred Heart, the
Forty Hours, First Fridays, and novenas of various kinds. Eucharistic devotions, originally designed to make reparations for insults to Jesus Christ by
liberals, Freemasons, and others, led to more frequent communions and an
effort to convert the state itself. Individuals, families, parishes, entire countries were consecrated to the Sacred Heart. President Gabriel García
Moreno consecrated Ecuador to the Sacred Heart in 1873, and in Colombia
President Carlos E. Restrepo rendered homage to the Sacred Heart on the
occasion of the Eucharist Congress in 1913. The cult was encouraged especially by the Jesuits, in recognition of the sovereignty of Jesus over society,
and June was the special month of devotion to the Sacred Heart. There was
also a renewal of the cult of Our Lady: the Legion of Mary was popularized,
Marian Congresses were organized, special months, May and October,
were devoted to Mary, and the bells of the traditional Angelus tolled every
day. With March and April came Lent and Holy Week, and so the whole
liturgical year unfolded, newer devotions joining ancient practices.

The Latin American Church valued these public manifestations of religion at a time when liberals and secularists sought to confine religion to
churches and private conscience and to keep it off the streets and out of

sight. The Church saw them as an expression of solidarity, a defiance of persecution in countries like Mexico and Guatemala, everywhere a display of belief against unbelief, a means of encouraging the faithful and recovering lapsed Catholics. The years around 1900 witnessed the beginning of a series of great Eucharist Congresses for the promotion of devotion to the Blessed Sacrament.[13] Taking their model from that organized in Lille in 1881, those in Latin America became huge workshops of religion, occasions of striking piety and fervour as crowds flocked to masses, confessions, and communions, listened to sermons, attended art exhibitions, and participated in cultural gatherings. They were also occasions for the ruling elites to show themselves, when presidents, diplomats, military, and other *altas personalidades* were eager to be seen near altars, in processions, and on platforms. Brazil, Uruguay, Paraguay, Chile, Bolivia, Peru, Ecuador, Colombia, Venezuela, Guatemala, Nicaragua, El Salvador, Costa Rica, Mexico – each had its national Eucharistic Congress in the decades after 1900, often in the wake of hard times for Church or country. In 1934 Argentina organized an international Eucharistic Congress in Buenos Aires, distinguished by the presence of the papal legate Cardinal Eugene Pacelli, attended by thirteen cardinals, 200 bishops, and thousands of priests, and interpreted by many as the reconversion of Argentina after decades of secularism.

The new religiosity directed from the diocese and preached from the pulpits was an attempt to bring the people back to Christ and the Church, and there was a response from the mass of Catholics. The people, the parish priests still said, were faithful to religion but prone to evil. This was the limit of reform. The Church could not conquer sin or convert people to good ways. The secularization of society completed what nature began, and the consequences of original sin were plain to see. From the pulpit the priests attacked the snares of the devil, the world, and the flesh and urged more frequent recourse to the sacraments. Yet they had to be satisfied with formal observance, private piety, and individual morality. This was the object of the Redemptorist missions, a kind of religious shock treatment for backsliders, which became popular throughout Latin America from the early years of the century. It was, of course, part of the Church's mission, to bring people to personal holiness and direct them towards the sacraments. Yet there was a sense in which the Church turned in upon itself and away from the modern world. There was little sign yet, from priest or people, of a public conscience or social awareness. These were later growths.

Religion did not necessarily bring people together across social barriers. As the parish priest of San Miguel in El Salvador reported in 1878, 'there exists a deep division between the top families and the common people, a division which produces hatred and resentment.'[14] Yet there was a social unity in the Church as well as a unity of belief. The Catholic religion was implanted not only on the coasts but in the highlands, not only in the towns but in the country, among peasants, miners, and artisans. It has been said of Peru: 'From Spanish cities to the most primitive Indian communities in the bleak *altiplano* the same signs and symbols of the Christian faith were recognized and revered, pointing to a unity of religious belief that cut across steep economic, social and linguistic barriers.'[15] It is a unity instantly recognized by Catholics visiting Latin America from other cultures and from other parts of the world who can share in the same faith and participate in the same ritual.

Popular Religion, Formal Religion

As the historian explores the living world of Latin American religion, the sacred as well as the political landscape comes into view, revealing the local sites of images and relics, patron saints, vows, shrines, and miracles, and all the other spiritual aids which these urban and rural communities invoked against the scourges of plague, earthquake, drought, and famine. The religion of the people was expressed in various ways: in vows to Our Lady and the saints, relics and indulgences, and above all in the shrines and sacred centres of local religious life. These were the scenes of cures, miracles, and visions, the holy places where prayers were said and heard, the objects of processions and pilgrimages, part of the immediate world of the people. The feasts of Our Lady and of Corpus Christi in particular drew great crowds to the churches and streets and occasioned lengthy and noisy processions. Latin America was prolific in Marian shrines and cults, prolific too in local fiestas, celebrated with an exuberance that scandalized some, amused others, and intrigued anthropologists.

There was a thin barrier between the popular and the profane, keeping them ever separate and ever near. In Chile friction was frequent between Church authorities and leaders of specific local celebrations and dances such as those to the Virgen de Andacollo, though this was not necessarily a Church attack on popular religiosity in general. If there was a campaign against religious fiestas it came from liberals rather than bishops, though one bishop in Peru denounced the fiestas in his diocese as roundly as any liberal would: 'All the fiestas which the Indians celebrate are the occasion of the most revolting orgies of drinking and debauchery.'[16] In Venezuela the synod of 1904 condemned the profanation of feasts and processions in some villages, where 'the image of the saint is accompanied by ridiculous songs, dances, and other irreverent displays totally alien to the spirit of religiosity which ought to prevail.'[17]

Popular religion could menace as well as entertain. During civil wars, religion often reinforced political motivation. In the 1830s the rebellion of the conservative caudillo Rafael Carrera against the Guatemalan liberals, fanatical enemies of the Church, assumed the style of a religious crusade, and chaplains mixed with the Indian and mestizo troops, evangelizing, exhorting, even fighting. The caudillo himself explained: 'To encourage the rebel masses, Carrera inspired them with religion; he constantly had church services celebrated in as many villages as he could, he greatly respected the priests, and he ordered that all the troops under his command sing the Salve every night and morning, which became an established custom, performed with the utmost enthusiasm.' A North American observer witnessed in Guatemala City a religious procession in honour of the Virgin, led by a group of masked 'devils', followed by altar boys, priests, floats, the statue of the Immaculate Conception, and the Host. After these came Carrera's troops chanting the Salve Regina.[18] Mexico too had its religious warriors, the *religioneros* who rose in 1873 against the anti-Catholic laws of reform and subsequent expulsion of the religious orders. These precursors of the twentieth-century *cristeros* represented a popular reaction to liberal ideology and were a shock to the Church as well as the state.

Manifestations of popular religion often responded to religious persecution and became a form of protest by the common people, a spontaneous defence of their religious beliefs. The people of Nicaragua had no means of resisting the dictates of their tormentor, Santos Zelaya, or the relentless pressure of his anti-clerical state. But on the night of 31 December 1900 a large crowd of Catholics gathered in Granada to inaugurate the construction of a huge cross, a symbol of unity with the whole Catholic world as it dedicated the new century to Jesus Christ. Political protest, too, was sometimes heard in the songs and verses of the people and in the compositions of popular folk singers such as the *cantores a lo divino* in Chile, for whom Christ was born into the world to raise the poor and humble the rich.[19] Of this truth they reminded the clergy as well as the politicians:

En las novenas que corren
los padres de San Francisco
el pobre paga las velas
y el milagro es para el rico

(In the novenas currently held by the Franciscan fathers, it's the poor who light the candles and the rich who get the miracles.)

Popular religiosity could be a sign not of protest but of union between state and nation. The colonial devotion to the Virgin of Luján made of this shrine the national symbol of Argentina, in which government support followed popular enthusiasm; from the Virgin's colours, blue and white, were taken those of the Argentine flag. Titles of the Virgin could also be appropriated by sectional interests. In Chile the traditional Virgen del Carmen was converted into the patron of the armed forces and crowned as queen of Chile in 1926. No one, however, could take from the poor people of southern Chile the popular San Sebastián in Yumbel, focus of prayer and pilgrimage, whose miracles restored health and saved vine and grain crops.

Religion was the currency of everyday life; it appeared to the people in forms which gave physical expression to metaphysical truths, making the sacred real. The great religious processions, especially those of Our Lady – Copacabana, Luján, Guadalupe – testify to the strength of the people's faith. Devotion to the Lord of the Miracles in Lima, whose three processions during the month of October are thronged by devotees clad in penitential purple, began in the colonial period as an image of Jesus Christ and procession of Negro slaves and became popular among virtually all classes.

Colombian Catholicism became a byword for intransigence and intolerance, but it was more than that. Catholics were active in charity hospitals and social welfare, and the Jesuits sought to change their appeal to urban workers by transforming the old confraternities into workers' mutual aid organizations, and later into Catholic trade unions. The Catholics of Colombia took their religion into the streets as well as the churches, and popular religiosity was expressed in civic as well as pious events. Medellín, branded a *República de curas* (clerical republic) by some, staged a procession in 1875 marking a civil occasion and including magistrates, lawyers, doctors, and professional associations; in front marched the Association of the Sacred Heart of Jesus. Religious fervour took other forms than pious women in black hurrying to early morning mass. Faith promoted works of charity and involved the richer families in the needs of the poor and helpless; the faith fulfilled secular as well as spiritual expectations. Seats were full not only in churches but in libraries, lecture rooms, and other cultural venues where people searched for a better life, and in doing so contributed further to social integration. The historian of these developments concludes: 'A dynamic society characterized by growing religiosity provides a picture which differs from easy and still current assumptions that in the Hispanic American context religion must be opposed to modernization in the social and cultural fields.'[20]

Latin America produced its own saints, some of them canonized by popes, such as St Rose of Lima, St Martin de Porres, and Peter Claver, as well as others venerated by popular acclaim and confidence in the communion of saints. Where the practice of religion was weak, saints were the only icons. A report of a pastoral visitation in rural Chile in 1918 recorded: 'In this parish [Huerta del Maule] there is great devotion to their patron saint, St Francis of Assisi, but the faithful rarely receive the sacraments and there are few who go to mass on Sundays.'

The concept of popular religion is rarely defined. Does it mean traditional religion appealing to the common people? Is it a devotional religion consisting primarily of processions, pilgrimages, holy shrines, and prayers to the saints rather than one relying exclusively on theology and the Ten Commandments? Does 'popular' mean a religion created by the people as distinct from a religion imposed by the Church, religion as practised compared to religion as prescribed? There are conceptual flaws in many approaches to popular religion. Cultural differences are inappropriate as an explanatory device: in Latin America the division between urban and rural, civilized and primitive, modern and traditional was often blurred. For these reasons the concept of 'local' religion is sometimes preferred to that of 'popular' religion, and local religion itself is presented as open to the influence of universal religion and the authority of the state.[21]

Yet the concept of popular religion is not lost. If there is one factor that confirms its validity, it is social structure. The religious devotions of the poor – fiestas, processions and pilgrimages, miraculous shrines and images, prayers to special saints – were often responses to real calamities in their lives, to the ravages of plague, drought, famine, and flood, sufferings to which the poor were more exposed than the rich and more likely to react with communal prayer and supplication. Popular miseries produced popular religion. And once in place, popular religion would eventually become one of the historic institutions of Latin America, a traditional landmark in the changing times of liberation theology and revolutionary Catholicism.

To what extent did religion in Latin America conform to the concepts of 'popular' religion, as outlined above, or divide into an official Church and a popular Church? Was there a religious subculture independent of the institutional Church, the expression of marginal sectors of society, existing alongside and perhaps in opposition to the orthodox religion of the priests and bishops? Popular religion was not something complete in itself. It derived its validity from membership of a larger organization, a wider community, the Catholic Church, popular or non-popular. It is true that in the eyes of Church authorities some manifestations of religion were more acceptable and more respectable than others which were regarded as anarchic and beyond official control. So, in Lima, the procession of the Sacred Heart was more representative of conservative Catholicism, while the procession of the Lord of the Miracles appealed to the populace. But the difference between the two is one of social context rather than doctrinal significance.

Popular religion transcended social class. It was urban as well as rural, artisan as well as peasant, clerical as well as lay. Most of the fiestas were organized by specific peasant, mining, or artisan groups, who sought the protection of a favourite saint or Virgin. In some cases blacks and mulattos had their own fiestas, Indians their special feast days. But the Latin American Church was far from homogeneous and appeared to comprehend a variety of people and movements. It was not so much two levels of religion, popular and official, as many expressions. And in the ultimate analysis the beliefs and practices of popular Catholicism represented no more than the people's attempts to make the abstract more concrete, to redefine the supernatural in terms of the natural environment in which they lived. Superstition no doubt played its part in the lives of many people. It was easy to slip from authorized devotions into private spirituality, and there were probably devotees who donated money to cults in expectation of benefits to come. Usually the Church was less concerned about the substance of superstition than about its independence of Church authority.

Latin America did not provide a pure model of popular religion. In the first place no one invented a new religion. The characteristic practices of popular Catholicism expressed the Church's teaching on saints, indulgences, the Holy Souls, prayers for the dead, the veneration of relics, wearing of medals, and use of holy water; all these were orthodox practices and not 'autonomous' in any discernible way. This was how the Church itself treated them, condemning elements of paganism and superstition beyond the limits of orthodoxy but accepting and blessing those practices which were regarded as part of Catholicism. In the decades around 1900 it was the bishops who in frequent visits to Rome brought back relics, medals, new devotions, and news of recent saints and miracles, thus adding to the deposit of pious practices accumulated by the Latin American Church. Moreover, the new 'official' religiosity of the late nineteenth century, especially the Marian devotions and the Rosary, fused easily with previous popular practices, which already contained a traditional cult of the Virgin Mary. These local cults in obscure shrines were doctrinally the same as the great Marian devotions in Europe and elsewhere. The Rosary, for example, which encouraged meditation on the great mysteries of religion, was a means of instruction in the universal faith. The Rosary led the mind to Christ and the Virgin, but the Virgin to whom Latin America prayed was the universal Mary, known to popes and prelates and to the faithful everywhere.

Popular religiosity and lay organizations were not inherently anti-clerical. They had developed to some degree in response to the absence of priests, not in opposition to them. The Church authorities themselves were conscious of the need to encourage self-help among the laity in regions that were often religious deserts. The Venezuelan synod of 1904 advised that in rural communities where there might be a chapel but no priest the faithful should gather 'under the direction of a respectable and devout person from among themselves in order to recite the rosary, listen to a spiritual reading, and teach a portion of the catechism to the children or even to adults where necessary'.[22] In Brazil too the bishops encouraged distant communities to form groups who would meet to hold prayers and devotions and turn their minds to 'acts of faith, hope, charity, and contrition'. It is true that the late nineteenth-century Church looked askance at the traditional confraternities and sought either to control them or to set up alternatives such as the societies of St Vincent de Paul, and other pious, charitable, or fund-raising organizations under ecclesiastical tutelage. The confraternities, which had never been exclusively 'popular', had outlived their usefulness and tended to withdraw from the centre of parish life.

In societies with large Indian communities popular religion is difficult to define. In Mexico and Guatemala, for example, practised and prescribed religion more or less merged, and the main disquiet of the Church concerned denial and superstition rather than popular practices as such. Church authorities in Peru, not unacquainted with superstition, looked with suspicion on many of the religious practices of Andean Indians. In 1912 the bishop of Puno, Valentín Ampuero, described the religion of the Indians as distorted by ignorance: 'their religious beliefs are minimal, their Christianity is adulterated and consists in having a mass said, or praying before a saint's image on occasion of illness or death in the family or loss of a llama.'[23] Yet masses and prayers were Catholic practices, legacies of past evangelization, and signs of present faith.

Was it an informed faith? In spite of Church reform and religious revival the hierarchy was far from sanguine about religious life on the ground. Rome itself was preoccupied with the ignorance of Latin American Catholics, convinced that parish structures were dangerously weak, and that 'almost 50 million faithful in whom love of the Church is providentially innate are almost completely bereft of those spiritual aids which elsewhere priests daily dispense'. As a medium of faith popular religiosity had its limitations. Shortage of priests meant absence of sacraments and lack of instruction. In Latin America, as in many parts of Europe, it was women who kept the faith alive, went to confession and communion, listened to sermons, while the men looked on condescendingly. The men were in the habit of leaving the church during the sermon and gathered outside to talk and smoke, to the fury of the bishops; according to the Latin American Plenary Council of 1899, 'nothing is more intolerable or contemptible than to scorn or disregard the words of Jesus Christ.'[24]

Ecclesiastical authorities made an effort to appropriate popular religiosity and bring it into the churches. As the end of the century approached, Pope Leo XIII urged the faithful throughout the Catholic world to focus their minds on Christ and renew their faith. The year 1900 was designated a Holy Year, a year of jubilee, when the pope granted a special indulgence to those who did penance and visited the Roman basilicas or their own local shrines. In Latin America the faithful responded: masses, ceremonies, and celebrations were organized, and people flocked to churches. In Nicaragua, at the Church of Merced, the last day of 1900 was marked by masses, exposition of the Blessed Sacrament, and a procession of the Sacred Heart. At midnight High Mass began as the congregation poured in and overflowed into the street. By four o'clock in the morning 8,000 people had received communion, and as dawn approached the parish priest 'proceeded to burn 600 prohibited books by profane authors, whose owners brought them in for burning on this special occasion'.[25] In the course of the morning thousands of communicants approached the altars and the ceremony closed with a solemn procession of the Blessed Sacrament through the streets of the capital.

The Holy Year of 1900, one in a long series of jubilees, had a particular significance for the Church in Latin America, as a thanksgiving for deliverance from a century of liberalism and an expectation of renewal to come. The occasion lacked apocalyptic messages or meanings and was an expression of orthodox Catholicism. Yet the century and the continent had witnessed a number of outbursts by millenarians, who used the signs and symbols of the Catholic religion though not the authority of the Church.

Search for the Millennium

Faith in the millennium, voiced in the distant past by monks and friars, continued in the Christian world even when the promise of Christ's second coming was not literally fulfilled. The apocalyptic tradition lived on as a belief in a second advent which would announce the establishment of the kingdom of God on earth. This belief meant different things to different people. The millennialists believed that the kingdom of God would arrive gradually through Christian-inspired human progress. The more popular millenarians on the other hand saw the Apocalypse not as a mere allegory but as a revelation of divine intervention and cataclysmic action to establish Christ's kingdom on earth.[26] A common millenarian scenario prophesied a time of trial and tribulation, after which the world would be purified; calamities in nature – floods, famines, and earthquakes – would herald a new era of peace and prosperity, terror would be followed by joy, discord by goodwill. In that great day there would be no war, no crimes, no fear. According to these beliefs, the millennium would come suddenly in the form of group salvation, destroying the old world of sin and replacing it with a new and perfect society. Divine agency, not human effort, would be the instrument of change. A prophet or messiah would appear, who would lead and instruct the faithful and would shine by acceptance rather than personal qualities. He was not a priest but stood outside the normal religious structure. His qualifications were established by healing and counselling; these were the powers which attracted and held his followers. Around him gathered an inner band of disciples and beyond these a wider circle.

In Spanish America belief in the millennium first appeared in the sixteenth century and was fostered by Franciscan missionaries, as we have seen, drawing on the prophecies of the Cistercian monk Joachim of Fiore. The Franciscan missionaries believed that they were witnessing a new age and helping to create a new society in which the Indians would be freed from their tribulations through baptism, secure in the expectation of the second coming of Christ. The millenarian tradition was still alive in the eighteenth century. The Chilean Jesuit Manuel Lacunza, writing from exile in Europe, spoke of the coming of the Messiah in glory and majesty to establish a reign of peace and justice; though he made no reference to America in his work, the message was heard in the wider world and responded to the anxieties of a revolutionary age.[27] While Lacunza was rewriting millenarian theology, hope in a second Christianity was already active in parts of America. Many popular rebellions in the colonial period expressed apocalyptic beliefs as well as social grievances and echoed the language of the friars.[28]

There was a gulf between two Indian worlds: that of indigenous culture and that acculturated into the Catholic Church and Hispanic rule. To what extent did popular millenarianism bridge this gulf and transform ancient Indian beliefs into hope of deliverance by a Christian messiah? It has been argued that millenarian ideas in Mexico prophesying the end of the world and the establishment of a new era, 'more than being inspired in the Christian apocalyptic tradition, come from the native mythic and eschatalogical tradition', and that these ideas were present not only in the colonial rebellions but also in the struggle for independence.[29] Whether religion transformed so easily into rebellion, it is impossible at present to say. There is some evidence, on the other hand, that late colonial messianic movements wanted to invert these worlds and elevate Indian culture to supremacy. In northern Mexico in the years 1800–1 an Indian messiah, José Bernardo Herrada, expressed his hatred of Spanish whites in a campaign of deranged preaching in which he foretold the coming of an Indian millennium; sovereignty would pass from the white colonial authorities to the Indians of New Spain in the person of an Indian monarch, namely his father. None of these prophecies came to pass, but they were an uncomfortable reminder to the authorities that messiahs and millenarians were not extinct. Later in the nineteenth century popular religion in Argentina, Brazil, and Mexico added further chapters to millenarian history.

Millenarian Signals: Argentina

Millenarian movements, as they developed in England and the United States in 1750–1850, occurred in response to particular social and economic conditions, often a time of crisis, when distress, anxiety, and feelings of relative deprivation caused ordinary people to look for a leader and to follow a radical social programme. In Latin America too there was a link between political and social pressures in an age of modernization and the yearning for a better world where God would rule, wrongs would be righted, and prosperity restored.

Early on New Year's Day, 1872, in the small town of Tandil, Argentina, a band of armed gauchos yelling threats against foreigners and Freemasons embarked on a trail of killing and destruction in the nearby countryside. In a single morning they killed thirty-six people, mostly immigrant Spaniards, Italians, French, and British, a massacre which caused alarm and outrage in Argentina and Europe. Some Argentines tried to explain it as a conspiracy among the local elite to frighten foreigners. Others saw it as a cry for help from oppressed gauchos, marginalized by agrarian and social change. Most agreed that it was a nativist reaction against immigrants, who took land and work that should belong to Argentines. But many people insisted that this was a millenarian outburst and in its shadows stood a messiah.

The rebellion in Tandil approximated to the millenarian model while not entirely reproducing it. The social significance of millenarian convictions was conspicuous in Tandil. This was a period of crisis and change in the southern countryside, when the large landowner clashed with the small farmer and both marginalized the landless gaucho. Anxiety and insecurity were the normal state of gauchos and peons; and rural conditions had long made them a deprived and oppressed class. The religion of millenarians and the vision of a new age can also be identified in Tandil, though the evidence is indirect and can only be glimpsed in symbols and slogans. 'Viva la Patria y la Religión', 'Death to gringos and Masons'. Kill them all, this is a 'holy war'. The cry 'Kill Masons' was a religious slogan aimed at a composite demonology of liberals, Protestants, and atheists. To kill in this cause had a redeeming quality. Cruz Gutiérrez, bloodstained from the morning's slaughter, pleaded with his captors, 'Spare my life, Captain. We have done this for the sake of religion, because we are Christians.' As a prelude to the massacre, the assassins had been given a chilling message: 'The following morning at daybreak Jacinto distributed to everyone the red badge as a sign to those who belonged to the true Religion. He said that they came to this town in order to free religion and to show people the horrors that would appear; but those who joined him would be safe from all danger.'[30]

These were not maxims issued by the clergy but rallying cries to an action outside the limits of the Church, as would be expected of a millenarian movement. Jacinto Pérez claimed to be the emissary of a *curandero*, an itinerant folk healer, Gerónimo de Solané, known in the countryside as Tata Dios (Father God), and the promoter of this fatal project. Solané looked and behaved like a prophet, and his origins and doctrine had an aura of mystery. But Pérez was known to be a folk preacher in his own right with a reputation in the Tandil countryside. He was heard to say that the end of the world was imminent and the Last Judgement near at hand, that Tata Dios had been sent by God to punish bad Christians and to give protection and prosperity to Argentines. If they wanted to be saved they had to kill gringos and Masons, the authors of the great ills suffered by the natives of the country. Rumours were circulating that 'there was going to be a revolution', that 'on 1 January there was going to be a catastrophe in Tandil and blood would flow', that 'the common people were saying that there was going to be a great flood, and deaths would follow'.[31] A serious and sombre prospect.

Jacinto Pérez, then, played upon many of the gauchos' dreads and desires. By offering salvation and fortune in a new paradise, he appealed to both spiritual and material values, linking rural conditions with millenarian deliverance and inviting the people to join a campaign against foreigners or lose everything. It was a Christian version of the millennium: by their action they would escape calamity or perish in the flames. Pérez also insisted that this was the word of Solané and that he, Pérez, was merely the messenger.

If the movement had a messianic character, it came from Tata Dios, who seemed to embody the qualities of a demigod. He preached an apocalyptic message. The time of God's punishment was approaching for heathens and sinners, the gringos and the Masons; believers must be ready to carry out the punishments. Those who did not cooperate would see their wives and children perish and they themselves would drown in a sea of blood; those who acted now would enjoy prosperity in this life and happiness in the next.[32] On this evidence, Solané was a messiah held in reserve by God and now unleashed to fulfil a mission. His sacred character had been confirmed by his extraordinary powers of prophecy, healing, and miracles. He had made journeys to places where he was invested with mandates. He was an archetypal figure of power and majesty of the type which a movement needed if it was to convince. If his personality did not tower over Tandil, this was in line with the millenarian model. He was a messiah not in his personal qualities but because he fulfilled the messianic expectations of his people. In the event, however, he disavowed the action of those who invoked his name and disapproved of the crimes committed on 1 January. And he himself was assassinated in prison before he could give evidence.

Solané bore some of the marks of a messiah, and the rising had millenarian traits. Yet doubts remain and confine interpretation within the bounds of hypothesis. In the first place, the events occurred in too short a time span, November–December 1871, to allow for the creation of a credible movement with a millenarian message. Second, what religious motivation could possibly inspire fifty country people without serious criminal records to commit crimes of this nature? Third, Solané himself lacks absolute credibility. His position in the local community suggests that he accepted the prevailing power structure. His message, moreover, contained familiar ideas concerning foreigners and religion. Solané followed a known tradition in blaming foreigners for the problems of the country; to say that foreigners were robbing Argentines of jobs and resources was not an exceptional statement. But to link foreigners with Freemasons added another dimension, for Freemasons were regarded as cultural aliens who would destroy the Christian faith and replace it by ancient paganism; moreover, Freemasons did not acknowledge any fatherland, being a cosmopolitan movement which would diminish rather than magnify national identity. Less than a messiah, Solané was more than a folk healer. His followers, moreover, were exponents not only of millenarianism but also of popular Catholicism.

Popular religion had a history in Argentina and a tradition in rural Buenos Aires. Country people might be ignorant of doctrine, but they accepted religion when it was available; they had enough faith to attend mass and the sacraments, minimally if not regularly, and only rarely the sacrament of marriage, to say prayers and to sing hymns. Solané represented not so much a specific millenarian cult as a known tradition of popular Catholicism which mixed religion and superstition in unknown quantities. His awareness of religion, deference to Jesus Christ, and devotion to Our Lady of Luján, whose image he kept in his room, placed him in the mainstream of rural life and made his camp a substitute church. His folk medicine had an element of faith healing, but this was common currency among *curanderos* and did not make him a messiah. The proliferation of *curanderos* and the survival of popular religion merging into magic and superstition filled a vacuum left by the Catholic Church and satisfied the spiritual needs of country people.

The liberal press, never slow to attack the Church, attributed responsibility for the massacre of 1872 to ecclesiastical power and religious superstition. *La Tribuna* of Buenos Aires accused the Church of unleashing a war against Masons and encouraging religious fanaticism: 'The assassins of Tandil are not men with criminal convictions, nor people who kill for booty. They are Catholic believers who believed that they were following God's will and doing good in doing so much bad.'[33] Other newspapers took a similar line and attributed the crime of Solané to his Catholicism and to the preaching of the Catholic clergy at a time when the Church was undergoing a public revival. In this interpretation the assassins became the militant arm of popular Catholicism.

Yet the impression that the Argentine countryside was swarming with priests and that the Church had a controlling grip on the population was fanciful. Superstition rather than religion was the faith of the pampas. Gauchos were not easily recruited to any cause and were normally content to leave religion to women. The Church was not so dominant nor rural people so docile as the press implied. Religion was present somewhere in the minds of the killers, but it would be difficult to establish a precise correlation between their actions and their beliefs. These men proceeded less by reason than by instinct. For some, religion was a motive, for others a justification, for yet others a tribal cry.

The assassins of Tandil occupied a position somewhere between secular rebels and religious enthusiasts. Their rhetoric seemed to echo the Book of Revelation, though the ideology and the environment of the movement were less millenarian than Catholic. This did not mean, as liberals claimed, that the Church was an agent of xenophobia; many of the clergy of the renewed Church were themselves foreigners and had growing links with Rome. But folk Catholicism tended to give simple messages, and its adherents to count on religion for instant salvation. The assassins saw themselves as fighting foreigners and liberals. This was a popular cause, not a conspiracy with landowners. No doubt the hostility of local cattlemen and officials towards foreign settlers was an advantage to the killers. But the basic war cry was 'Kill a foreigner or die in the deluge!' A heresy or a blasphemy? Either way, the massacre was a mystery.

Messiahs in Brazil

Varieties of religious experience could be seen in Brazil, where the Church was a combination of pure Catholicism, popular religion, and marginal deviants. Pure Catholicism was expressed in dogma, the mass, the sacraments, and the orthodox cults of the Virgin Mary. Popular religion expressed a partial Catholicism comprising devotions to the saints, processions, images, and prayers for the dead, practices which supplied many religious needs in the absence of priests and parishes. This religious subculture was long tolerated by the Church because it could keep religion alive without a numerous clergy and elaborate institutions, and was really a reflection of weak infrastructure rather than defective belief.

Brazil had a long tradition of millenarian outbursts, some of them crypto-political movements, others articulating local social protests, and yet others expressing purely religious expectations of a promised land.[34] In the late nineteenth century, significantly in the 1890s, millenarianism found expression in two popular religious movements in the Brazilian north-east, Canudos and Joaseiro, each of which formed around a messianic leader and looked for deliverance from catastrophe into a heavenly city. These movements were not simply aberrations of the backlands but responded to wider national and ecclesiastical trends, in which the people of the north-east were at once actors and victims. The end of the monarchy saw the penetration of the north-east by the new republican state, bringing with it secularization, civil registration of births, marriages, and deaths, census questions concerning racial origins, and new municipal taxes. The secular state was accompanied by a more active Church, comprehensively reformed since the 1860s and looking more sternly at local religious practices. Numerous Houses of Charity made their appearance; part orphanages, part schools, these were staffed by lay brothers (*beatos*) and sisters (*beatas*), newcomers to the religious landscape. Economically the north-east was in decline, losing its labour to coffee and rubber booms in other regions, while its traditional agriculture stagnated. The ability of the new messiahs to attract pilgrims to the north-east where they remained as workers gave them some political leverage, and it also meant that they were able to deliver votes. Thus, they came to be cultivated by local political elites.

The movement known as Canudos was led by the mystic Antônio Conselheiro. His 'holy city' of about 8,000 *sertanejos* flourished in the Bahian town of Canudos from 1893 until its destruction by Brazilian federal troops four years later. Conselheiro was a layman but also a *beato*, a 'wandering servant of the Church', who helped local priests in an area short of clergy, and organized the rebuilding of churches.[35] But he also preached from church pulpits, and this brought him into conflict with the bishop of Bahia, whose programme of clerical reform had no place for amateur preachers. His defenders claimed that he was an orthodox Catholic, who did not question the doctrines of the Church or pretend to be a priest; the moral values he taught were traditional and personal. Conselheiro did not claim to be a messiah, or to work miracles, though he did promise his followers a second coming in the year 1900. He was in the tradition of popular Catholicism, appealing directly to ordinary people and becoming godfather to many children. His social views, if anything, were conservative and his criticisms of the republic were made from the standpoint of Catholic tradition and were directed against a secular state which had just disestablished the Church, introduced religious toleration, and removed ecclesiastical jurisdiction over marriage and burial.[36]

The republic, however, was supported by the bishops; under political pressure themselves, they urged the priests of the north-east to abandon Conselheiro and thus deprived him of a religious base. The Church leadership turned its back on this expression of popular religion and, ironically, looked to the state to bring it to an end. But Conselheiro had some local political support because of his influence over labour. In 1893 he campaigned against the tax policies of the republic and after a skirmish with the police he and his followers retreated to the hills of Canudos. There they created a holy sanctuary, a utopian alternative rather than a focus of rebellion, and not an expression of militancy or aggression. But messianism of this kind lent itself to political manipulation by local interests, and could suffer either from their support or from their hostility. In the event federal troops were dispatched in 1897 to destroy Canudos, which they did amidst great carnage, scattering its leader's followers and destroying his church.

Messianism travelled further from its origins in the movement of Joaseiro. Cícero Romão Batista was a priest, one of the first products of the seminary at Fortaleza and, when appointed to Joaseiro in Ceará, a prototype of the new priests in the backlands: orthodox, zealous, supporter of the St Vincent de Paul Society, promoter of the rural economy, and a friend of the community of *beatos* and *beatas*. In March 1889 the communion host which he gave to a *beata* of Joaseiro was transformed into blood, thought to be the blood of Christ. A miracle was proclaimed by priests and people; soon pilgrims were making their way to Joaseiro, and a popular cult came into being comprising priests of the backlands, landowners and middle sectors, and the Catholic faithful.[37] The bishops, on the other hand, denied the miracle and suspended Padre Cícero; his superiors appealed to Rome and there too, in 1894, the miracle was condemned. Padre Cícero then sought a deal with local political bosses, the *coronéis*, requesting support in return for his neutrality. But although he wanted to keep Joaseiro a city of God, the miracle engendered wealth and growth, as miracles often do, and so he was drawn inexorably into public life. Soon he acquired a political adviser, Dr Floro Bartholomeu, a physician from Bahia, who campaigned for Joaseiro's autonomy and elevation to *município* status in 1914. And the next step for Padre Cícero was support for armed action to defend his holy city, then entry into national politics.

Popular religiosity, fringe Catholicism, messianism, these and other manifestations of religious enthusiasm took place more or less within the boundaries of the Catholic faith. There was a tendency in messianism to abandon the sacred for the profane, but in parts of the Brazilian north-east Padre Cícero is remembered as a saint. In Brazil millenarianism was a shield protecting its adherents from an invading state and an unfriendly Church. Abandoned by the two institutions they had always respected, the people of the backlands sought salvation in cataclysm and apocalypse. In Latin America they were not alone.

Millenarian Rebels in Mexico

The millenarian sequence of hard times, culminating in apocalyptic events and followed by the creation of a better world, seems to have been the experience and the vision of the Mexican movement at Tomochic, a mestizo village in Chihuahua, in 1891–92. Again the interaction of social deprivation and religious dissent, between material expectations and belief in the second coming, hovers over events.[38] State pressure in the interests of modernization, economic hardship caused by drought and grain shortage, and accusations of banditry against malcontents were potent provocations to rebellion, but beyond these the millenarians had a religious agenda, aggravated by prolonged absence of a resident parish priest. None of them doubted that a new social and moral order was in the making, one in which the Church was an absentee. To some extent the people of Tomochic were neglected by the Church, whose resources did not stretch to this northern region. So pilgrims made their way to a holy man, Carmen María López, who had arrived in the mountains and was believed to be a second Christ. Adherents also venerated a new saint, a young girl named Teresa Urrea, or Santa Teresita, who had experienced deep trances and convulsions, perhaps self-induced. She conversed with the Virgin Mary and worked miracles in the Rancho Cabora in the neighbouring state of Sonora. She claimed to have received a mission to heal the sick, not as a mere folk doctor but as an agent of God. The Church rejected her claims and quickly identified her as an opponent who threatened to sideline its own divine mission. She was totally anti-clerical, eclectic in her religious ideas, and an advocate of a simple Christianity, devoid of hierarchy and priests; in her movement no intermediaries were needed, nor the mass, nor the sacraments. The state authorities also had their doubts about Teresa and were ready to see subversion in her claims and her crowds; deciding she was a destabilizing influence they exiled her to the United States south-west.

Admonished by the local itinerant priest to avoid charlatans who posed as messengers of God, the parishioners of Tomochic, or some 150 of them, followed their leader into rebellion against Church and state, declared their allegiance 'to no one but Santa Teresa', and began to create an alternative community. The leader was Cruz Chávez, who had the regulation beard, long hair, and disconcerting stare of a local holy man and a reputation of resistance to authority. Chávez, who often took the place of the absent priest, saw himself as God's messenger, authorized to appropriate the parish church and conduct services, and to lead unauthorized processions of a kind proscribed by the Mexican *Reforma*. In one of his services he consecrated the rifles of his followers and exhorted them to fight against the forces of Satan, to defend the law of God, and to strive for a better world to come. A military detachment sent to restore order, crush bandits, and enforce obedience to the state came under fierce attack on 7 December 1891 as the rebels, shouting 'long live the power of God', 'Long live the power of the Virgin', and 'Death to bad government', threw themselves into an apocalypse of their own making, persuaded perhaps that their personal martyrdom would bring about the millennium.[39] Then, in the course of 1892, they began to construct their own utopia in Tomochic: an alternative community based on equal rights and sharing of resources came into being, and group loyalty was maintained through the messianic leadership of Cruz Chávez.

The motivation of the millenarians was no doubt a mixture of social and personal grievances, brought to a head by a local agitator, but religious enthusiasm was inherent in the movement and probably inseparable from its aims. As they prepared their defences and serviced their arms, they welcomed allies, even bandits. They engaged in lengthy ritual in the village church, where they said Catholic prayers and recited the Rosary, and prepared themselves for eventual death in the cause of justice. Their basic demand was the right to their own religion, to live according to their own moral order. But the Mexican authorities, who had already branded them as *Indios, fanáticos,* and *bandidos*, treated them as rebels against the state, sent the troops in and crushed them, though with difficulty, in October 1892.[40] The rebels were killed, the wounded were shot, and Tomochic was destroyed.

Like other millenarian movements in Latin America, Tomochic acquired a political as well as a religious significance and evoked different responses from different people. For some, it was a symbol of protest against a brutal dictatorship. For others, it was an outburst of superstition amidst necessary modernization. But for many, it had an apocalyptic character which left a message of hope as well as a trail of destruction.

The common thread running through millenarian movements in Latin America was a sense of hopelessness, the fear of people that they had been abandoned by Church and state, the two institutions on which they relied to give security to their lives. Communities under attack from a modernizing state, and unprotected by a distant Church, looked for a new order to replace the injustices of the past and defend them from the disasters to come. Doomsday was their last hope.

The quest for the millennium in Latin America did not end in 1900. As long as anxiety existed, so too did apocalyptic belief. The peoples of Latin America were to live through times of acute anxiety in the twentieth century, when war, depression, social conflict, military dictatorship, terrorism, and violence threatened the familiar order of society, destroyed hopes, and magnified fears. If the pure millenarians – those who wait from day to day for the end of the world and the advent of a new heaven and earth – no longer made the dramatic entries they had staged in the eighteenth and nineteenth centuries, this did not mean that groups, movements, communities ceased to look for release from their secular nightmares in apocalyptic belief or that individuals abandoned hope of a personal millennium, where 'death shall be no more, neither shall there be mourning nor crying nor pain any more.'[41]

CHAPTER 7

Church and State in a Liberal World

Protestantism, Positivism, and Catholic Responses

W HILE THE CATHOLIC Church sought to consolidate and to expand, it no longer exercised a religious or cultural monopoly. The nineteenth century saw the growth of another religion in Latin America, one which did not accept the jurisdiction of the Catholic Church or the primacy of the pope. The first Protestants in modern Latin America were foreign diplomats, merchants, and residents, who from the early years of independence settled in the capitals and ports of the subcontinent, protected directly or indirectly by the British trade treaties with the new nations.[1] Congregations and churches of Anglicans, Presbyterians, and Methodists appeared in this form, tolerated enclaves that did not represent missionary expansion.

The next phase was the arrival of representatives of Bible Societies, which reached beyond foreigners Protestants to preach to the Catholic population. The precursor was the Scot, James 'Diego' Thomson, who arrived in Buenos Aires in 1818 to promote the Lancastrian System of education, whereby senior students taught the juniors and the Bible was used as the preferred text. From Buenos Aires he moved to Chile, Peru, and Mexico, presenting his mission as one of education but in fact representing the project of the British and Foreign Bible Society, the forerunner of other Bible Societies. The Catholics of Latin America were not ignorant of the sacred scriptures, for they had long encountered them in the epistles and gospels of the mass. But the Bible Societies met the needs of some and led to a further phase, that of evangelization among Catholics and unconverted Indians by missionaries.

Meanwhile, Protestant numbers were expanding with the arrival of new immigrants, mainly British, who settled on the land and were putting down roots in Argentina, Uruguay, Chile, and southern Brazil. From the 1850s Waldensian immigrants, escaping rural poverty in Europe, settled in

Uruguay and Argentina, aided by land grants and tolerant liberal governments, and eventually establishing a recognizable Waldensian Church. A
further Protestant presence emerged with the arrival of German Lutherans
who settled in Brazil, Venezuela, and Argentina, while from 1848 Chile
encouraged Germans fleeing from persecution in Europe to colonize
its underpopulated south. A different Protestant tradition entered Latin
America from the United States, when African Americans, mainly
Methodists, sought refuge from racism first in Haiti and the Dominican
Republic, then in South America, taking with them not only a determination to improve their lives but an evangelical fervour to change the lives of
others. Curiously, following their defeat in the Civil War, a number of
southern whites sought to recreate in the slave society of Brazil the lifestyle
they had lost in the Confederate States. Protestant immigration in Latin
America increased in the twentieth century with the arrival of the
Mennonites from Russia and Canada, who established colonies akin to the
Amish, first in Mexico, Bolivia, and Argentina, then more substantially in
Paraguay, where they placed their Christianity at the service of economic
and social development.

The Catholic Church did not immediately respond to the Protestant
presence. In order to survive, the new Churches and sects had to rely on
liberal policies of religious toleration and separation of Church and state;
liberals usually welcomed the new input of skill and knowledge contributed by Protestant immigrants and regarded their work ethic as an example
to Catholics. This affinity between liberalism and Protestantism further
alerted the Catholic Church and caused it to rely even more on protection
and privilege, determined to keep control of registration of births,
marriages, and deaths. In Catholic eyes Protestantism became equated
with secularization and illustrated the danger of religious toleration; it also
strengthened the Church's alliance with conservatives and reliance upon
concordats between the Holy See and the national governments, in which
control of ecclesiastical patronage was often traded for a special position
for the Church in the state. Early relations between Catholics and
Protestants, therefore, were tense. Protestant preachers tended to brand
Catholics as superstitious, while Catholics saw Protestantism as another
evil of the modern age.

Mass immigration into countries like Argentina and Brazil led to further
expansion of the immigrant Churches. From the early twentieth century
and especially from 1914 United States trade and investment in Latin
America made great advances, accompanied by an increased political and
sometimes military presence. The opportunities for American Protestantism
also expanded: new groups appeared, the Quakers, Salvation Army, Seventh
Day Adventists, and new missionary movements such as the Free Church

Missions and the Evangelical Union of South America added to Protestant numbers and to Catholic indignation. There was a convenient political dimension: the United States, defended by Protestants, was regarded by Catholics as an exploiter. Yet, even after a century of growth, Protestantism was a rare and exotic phenomenon in Latin America. It did not remain so. In the later twentieth century the Protestant religions entered a new phase of expansion and presented a new challenge to Latin American Catholics. Meanwhile, in the struggle for minds, the Catholic Church had another, more potent, rival.

The main intellectual challenge to the Catholic Church came not from Protestantism but from positivism, which, following earlier waves of utilitarianism and liberalism, succeeded in dominating the thinking of the Latin American elite in the last decades of the nineteenth century.[2] The philosophy of Auguste Comte was based on 'positive' knowledge, that is knowledge derived from observation and experiment yielding facts that could be scientifically demonstrated. In place of revealed religion he established rational and empirical principles. These would create a theory of social structure and change from which a system of social planning could be developed. The political framework for this was a dictator who ruled with popular consent, ruling for life with the aid of a technocratic elite, and promoting economic progress in an ordered society. Positivism arrived relatively late in Latin America, at a time when it was already out of favour in Europe, but it took root from the 1870s and came to exert a dominant influence in a number of countries for the rest of the century and beyond. It evoked an instant response in those who were seeking to explain the political and economic backwardness of Latin America and who welcomed its promise of renewal and modernization and its challenge to the influence of the Catholic Church over the minds of the masses. To government elites and technocrats it offered legitimacy for the prevailing economic model and its authoritarian framework. To the middle sectors it was a reassuring mixture of reformism and conservatism, promising material progress without threatening the social structure. Academics, schoolteachers, the military, and other groups interested in modernization, development, and the improvement of society all absorbed in some degree the positivist philosophy and pointed an accusing finger at religion and the Church.

Positivism was presented as an alternative to religion, and its scientific methods were greeted with enthusiasm in countries such as Brazil, Chile, and Mexico and regarded as a key to unlock the door of progress. In Brazil it made its presence felt in the central government and also among state governors. In Mexico Gabino Barreda, a professor of medicine and Minister of Education, sought to reorganize higher education and give it a uniform curriculum based on Comte's hierarchy of the sciences. In Chile too, inspired by Valentín Letelier, educational reformer, positivists believed that education should be restructured and the power of Catholicism destroyed. In Venezuela José Gil Fortoul presented national history as an exercise in positivism, and the sociologist Laureano Vallenilla Lanz hailed dictatorship as the servant of democracy and the guarantor of social order. Everywhere positivism appeared to speak clearly and look confidently towards the future. As the Brazilian Catholic publicist Jackson de Figueiredo said, 'Positivism knows how to say what it wants for the general good in the midst of this enormous confusion of ideas.'[3] But positivism also generated conflict in the liberal establishment, between authoritarianism and constitutionalism, notably in Venezuela, and it introduced an element of racism into political thinking, seen in the preference for white European immigrants to dilute Latin America's mestizo societies.

Intellectual conflict was even more bitter in Peru. There the attack on religion and the Church was spearheaded by the atheist Manuel González Prada (1848–1918), who in the decades after the War of the Pacific (1879–83) waged a relentless war of words on Catholicism and everything it stood for. He condemned Catholicism as one of the worst obstacles to progress in Peru; he wanted to eliminate the Church from all public life and substitute science, 'the only God of the future'.[4] González Prada went beyond positivism. His first project was to create a totally lay state, liberal and anti-clerical. But this was just the beginning. He wanted to bring about revolutionary change in Peru through an alliance of intellectuals and workers who would overthrow the Catholic Church, Hispanic tradition, and Peruvian conservatism. His espousal of anarchism added further weapons to his armoury, which he aimed at the state as well as the Church: 'In Peru there are two great lies: the Republic and Christianity'.[5] He identified two groups, women and Indians, captives and defenders of the Church. Women were 'slaves of the Church', utterly obedient to the priests and agents of clerical control of the family. According to González Prada there was a triple alliance of priest, official, and landlord to oppress the Indian and keep him in ignorance and poverty, offering him religious processions instead of material progress. He did not want the integration of the Indian into Peruvian society but the restoration of their separate identity, aloof from Hispanic and Catholic culture, which belonged to the elite whom the Church helped to legitimize. The crude anti-clericalism of González Prada was not shared by José Carlos Mariátegui (1894–1930), who travelled a more spiritual path in his journey from the traditional Catholicism of his youth to become the founder of Marxism in Peru. Mariátegui was still a believer in 1917 when, at the age of 23, he wrote: 'I believe in God, above all things, and I do all things devoutly and zealously in his holy name', and he respected the popular manifestations of Peruvian Catholicism. But he returned from Europe a convert to Marxism, convinced that the end of organized religion was near.

The Church's response to positivism was inflexible. From pulpit and press it rejected the new philosophy, denied that religion was dead, and demanded a place for Catholicism in public education. In Mexico the positivist version of education and politics was attacked as contrary to freedom of conscience and alien to the country's religious tradition. In Chile Catholic writers rushed to the defence of the faith, inspired by Pius IX's denouncement of liberalism, rationalism, science, and progress. In Brazil Jackson de Figueiredo (1891–1928), who had abandoned the Church of his youth in favour of agnosticism and then undergone a new conversion, went on to the offensive, appalled by positivism's conquest of the educated classes and their total indifference to religion. In the pages of his review *A Ordem* he presented a Catholic position on the leading issues of the day and sought to stir the Church out of its intellectual lethargy to lead a great crusade against materialism. Catholics also fought positivism politically, in alliance with conservative groups, in order to procure governments open to their influence, to thwart legislation hostile to religion, and in general to preserve the public position of the Church. In Chile, for example, they worked through their political club, Los Amigos del País, lobbying for Catholic causes, and in particular for Catholic education, usually one of the first targets of reformers, and they succeeded in forcing the resignation of positivist Diego Barros Arana, the head of the Instituto Nacional. In short, the Church fought positivism as a political battle for relative influence in public life. Its methods were a mixture of polemical journalism and pressure group tactics, and the results were mixed: in Colombia, after setbacks, complete success; in Chile a losing battle; in Mexico almost total failure. Everywhere the reliance on public privilege and state sanctions to secure the survival of the Church against positivist attack was negative and defeatist.

The Church did not respond to the intellectual challenge of positivism and, in terms of Comte's philosophy, the debate was never joined. There was eventually an intellectual reaction against positivism in Latin America, but this was not specifically Catholic in its inspiration. It is true that a number of Catholic writers proved themselves to be effective apologists for religion and brought religious discussion out of the cloister and into the media. In Brazil Jackson de Figueiredo and Alceu Amoroso Lima widened the terms and improved the quality of politico-religious debate, but their writings impress for their polemical rather than their philosophical content. Moreover, Figueiredo and especially Amoroso Lima took Brazilian Catholic thought along the wrong road. Their search for 'order' in politics, society, and ideas was a throwback to positivism itself, adding to it a new base of Catholic morality. Other ideas they derived from reactionary Catholic thinkers such as Joseph de Maistre, Charles Maurras, and Donoso Cortés, clothed them in Brazilian nationalism, and produced a political thought which was critical not only of materialism and capitalism but also of democracy. Yet, if the Church lost the elites and some of the arguments, it would not be correct to conclude that it lost the conflict with positivism. The philosophy of Comte was received in Latin America as an action system rather than a sociological theory. The political and economic model which it helped to legitimize was in due course overtaken by criticism, change, and collapse, while positivism itself became discredited. The social consequences of positivist models remained to be resolved, and at this point social Catholicism emerged to take the argument a stage further and give religion a new dimension. The intellectual struggle had been one for the minds of the elites, not those of the masses. The Church had never lost its base in the popular sectors and it outlived positivism to speak more directly to them in the course of the twentieth century, as will be seen. Before that happened, however, the Church had to redefine its relation to the state.[6]

The Church and the Secular State

The Romanization of the Catholic Church took place at the same time as the liberalization of the secular state. A clash appeared inevitable. The Catholic Church was traditionally opposed to the separation of Church and state and demanded for itself the position of officially established religion; in the nineteenth century this was regarded as the only defence against liberalism, positivism, and other secular enemies. To preserve its privilege the Church cultivated governments and associated with conservatives, a further provocation to its opponents. The old system had its critics within the Church itself. In France around 1830 the abbé Félicité de Lamennais, seconded by the Catholic liberals Henri Lacordaire and Charles René Montalembert, struggled to secure the independence of the Church from the state in opposition to the Gallican tradition, and to persuade the Church freely to renounce the compromising protection which it received from the secular power. Pope Gregory XVI reacted (*Mirari vos*, 1832) by denouncing liberalism, liberty of the press, separation of Church and state, and in particular the notion that liberty of conscience ought to be guaranteed. These views were confirmed and enlarged by Pope Pius IX and were transmitted to the Latin American Church if not as articles of faith then as the voice of authority. This led the Church into absolutist positions and delayed its integration into the modern world. Liberalism too became intolerant, and even conservatives took material advantage of the Church's difficulties. Thus relations between the two powers deteriorated amidst bitter recriminations.

Attacked by enemies and ill-served by friends, the Church had to accept the loss of temporal power and privilege and the triumph of the secular state in the second half of the nineteenth century. The pace of change, and the degree, differed from country to country, as did relations with Rome. Concordats were signed with Ecuador (1863), Venezuela (1863), and Colombia (1887), but not with Argentina, Peru, Bolivia, Chile, or Mexico. Each country had its own response to a range of common problems, from close association of Church and state in Ecuador to stand-off in Chile. The Church wanted independence, ownership of traditional resources, preservation of privileges, control of education, and authority on moral issues. The state wanted the same powers which the Spanish crown had possessed over the Church: control of senior appointments, recovery of resources, sole authority over national policy, and marginalization of Rome. In some cases anti-clericalism was so strong that not only was the Church disestablished but limitations were even imposed on its religious functions. In other countries a compromise was reached, and the Church continued to be subsidized by the state but also dependent upon it. In yet other countries the Church remained more or less established but had to accept state control over the appointment of bishops.

How can we explain the wide variations in Church–state relations in the different countries of Latin America? One factor was the different national histories and traditions, and the contrasting experiences of state-building in the nineteenth century. Another was the character of particular governments or caudillos, and the nature of their beliefs. But perhaps the most important factor was the relative power and wealth of the Church. Where the Church was large, in clergy and resources, it was more likely to provoke anti-clericalism and envy, both political and personal; it was also in a stronger position to defend itself. The ensuing conflict would probably be bitter and even violent, and the settlement more decisive, one way or the other. Where the Church was poor and weak it did not provoke overt hostility; but nor could it defend itself, and gradually, without dramatic conflict, it would find its privileges eroded. And in some cases there was a balance of power.

Brazil

The experience of the Church in Brazil was perhaps the most traumatic of all, for in the space of a few years it passed simultaneously from monarchy to republic, from a Catholic state to a secular state, from an established

Church to a disestablished one. The political independence of Brazil brought no independence to the Church. The power of the Portuguese crown over the colonial Church was inherited intact by the empire of Brazil. Pedro II, who had a purely political attitude to religion, retained full powers of patronage and rights of intervention between Rome and the Brazilian Church. He nominated bishops, collected tithes, paid the clergy. But the problem went deeper than the personal policy of the emperor. The advent to power of a conservative ministry in 1868 signalled a growth in the power of the state and in its expenditure. Church lands and properties were now viewed by politicians with keener interest, and the Church was subject to yet greater pressure. The progress of religion thus came to depend upon the favour or fear of the monarchy rather than the inner resources of the Church. When, in the course of reform, the Church began to behave more truly as a Church and less as a department of state, then it brought swift retribution upon itself.

The Religious Question, as it became known, began in March 1872, when a priest in Rio was suspended for refusing to abjure Freemasonry. The penetration of religious institutions by Freemasonry undoubtedly compromised the Church and was a matter of legitimate concern to its leaders. In December 1872 Dom Frei Vital M. Gonçalves de Oliveira, bishop of Olinda (later joined by Dom Antonio de Macedo Costa, bishop of Pará), ordered all Catholics who were Masons to be expelled from the confraternities. These, dominated as they were by Masons, refused to comply, and when placed under an interdict they appealed to the emperor, demanding that the bishop be restrained by the imperial power of patronage. The papal encyclicals invoked by the bishops had never been approved by the government and were therefore invalid in Brazil. So this was a conflict not only between Church and monarchy but between the monarchy and Rome. Pope Pius IX retreated from his earlier position of support for the bishops after the Brazilian government intervened. But the government was not so willing to hold back and it brought the two bishops to trial in 1874, when they were found guilty of impeding the will of the executive power and sentenced to four years' imprisonment, though they were subsequently amnestied. These spectacular events have tended to overshadow the more prosaic but no less persistent pressure on the Church by the successive administrations of the time. When the Liberals came to power in 1878 they began a sustained attack on Church institutions, while the radicals in their midst were convinced that the Church, along with slavery, was a major obstacle to modernization in Brazil. Clauses in a number of budgets restricted the Church's right to hold rural and urban property; the Liberals sought also to establish a civil registry and to limit the Church's opportunity to 'promote ignorance' in education.

The Church learnt little from this experience. In spite of the Religious Question and the subsequent liberal legislation, Catholics continued to support the monarchy against republicanism, trusting in the alliance of the altar and the throne against the enemies of God and the emperor. But the monarchy fell and the republicans came to power. This was a bewildering experience for the Church, helpless without its familiar supports. It had no influence with the new political leaders, who for their part were not anxious to see a repeat of the Religious Question of 1872–74. They took prompt and decisive action. In 1890 the Church was separated from the state; the process was completed and ratified by the constitution of 1891. Freedom of worship, civil marriage, secular education, all were now instituted; there was a ban on government subsidy of religious education, and after a year government financial support for the clergy was withdrawn. There was an inevitability about secularization which the Church had to accept, though it suspected the motives of the republicans, and not without reason, for the latter were gratuitously illiberal towards religion when they decreed that members of religious orders who were bound by a vow of obedience were to be disenfranchised.

Yet 1891 was a vital date in the history of the Brazilian Church, the date of its independence. This was not exactly how the hierarchy saw it, for they did not appreciate the long-term advantages of disestablishment; convinced that liberalism and positivism had taken over Brazil, they hankered after state support and still pursued public influence through political power. But these were now denied the Church, and it had to look to Rome for leadership and to its own resources for survival. In the event the period 1889–1930 was one of institutional growth for the Church, as it slowly recovered from the shock of separation and adjusted itself to the world of the First Republic. New dioceses were founded, more clergy recruited, religious orders encouraged, and by 1930, reinforced by foreign priests and new funds, the Church had become an independent and well-organized institution, yet even now still ready to claim a legal as well as a moral pre-eminence in the nation.

The Brazilian Church in these years was personified by Sebastião Leme da Silveira Cintra (1882–1942), archbishop of Olinda, archbishop of Rio de Janeiro, cardinal and statesman of the Church. Dom Leme was inspired by two goals: to improve the religious life of priests and people, and to gain for the Church a greater place in the affairs of the nation. He could not accept that in an 'essentially Catholic country' like Brazil the Church should have so little influence, and in a resounding pastoral letter in 1916 he lamented: 'we are a majority who count for nothing'.[7] Dom Leme fought on numerous fronts, against spiritism, secularism, and positivism. He sought to make the faith of Brazilians more orthodox and better informed by introducing

European priests and pastoral methods, and by great public manifestations of religion. This was a time of jubilees, religious feasts, Eucharistic Congresses and, in 1931, the elevation of Christ the Redeemer above Rio de Janeiro.

Meanwhile Dom Leme was applying political pressure to obtain the return of religious education in state schools, to block any move to legalize divorce, and to secure the election of politicians sympathetic to the Church. Finally, he sought to rechristianize the Brazilian elite, especially the intellectuals, and then to make them the activists of the lay apostolate. There had been distinguished precursors, Julio Cesar de Morais Carneiro, who became a Redemptorist priest and ended all his sermons with the cry 'we must make Brazil Catholic', and Joaquim Nabuco, who was influenced by John Henry Newman and English Catholicism. In 1917, Jackson de Figueiredo made his peace with the Church and began to do battle with its rivals and detractors. How, he asked, could the Catholic majority allow the minority to impose its opinions on the nation? Materialism and secularism drew strength from religious ignorance, for which Catholics themselves were responsible; so he started a periodical A Ordem, and set up the Dom Vital Centre to study Catholic doctrine and mobilize Catholic intellectuals. Dom Leme regarded his new recruit as a model lay apostle and supported him in all his work until his untimely death in 1928. Meanwhile, he himself, in 1922, founded the Catholic Confederation, the prototype of the later Brazilian Catholic Action, to form militant laymen in the service of the Church. To a later generation of Brazilian Catholics Dom Leme became an exemplar of the triumphalist tradition in the Church, and it is true that rather than rethink the Church's position in the world he preferred to seek temporal power to safeguard religion. Yet he brought the Brazilian Church out of the crisis of disestablishment, strengthened its structures, and imposed it upon the attention of the nation.

Argentina and the Southern Cone

The Argentine Church had a long tradition of regalism though its experience of this differed from that of Brazil. The Constitution of 1853 obliged the state to 'support' the Roman Catholic religion without 'professing' it. The support was real enough and included protection and finance, but it could also be seen as intervention, even though in practice each side respected the other. The crucial issue was the power given to the government to control important ecclesiastical appointments. The president was given 'the rights of the national patronage in the presentation of bishops for the Cathedral Churches, selected from three names proposed by the Senate'. The papacy did not recognize these rights, but in practice resigned itself to the process and appointed the person presented by the president. So the Argentine state began and continued its history with firm control of ecclesiastical patronage and a bias towards a national Church. The Church was barred from direct communication with Rome except with the permission of the state, which could withhold the entry of papal bulls. There was another way of resolving Church–state relations, to free the Church through separation, as the Brazilian Church was freed, but in Argentina this was very much a minority view. In any case the Church enjoyed advantages under the system, even if they were short term: in effect the Church became dependent in return for compliance, a conservative system which had permanent effects on the Argentine Church.[8]

Religious toleration, up to a point, was possible in Argentina, and the 1853 Constitution embodied freedom of conscience and freedom of worship. All inhabitants had the right 'to freely profess their religion', and the Protestant Churches were made equal before the law. This toleration, however, was an expedient rather than a principle and it did not mean that the Catholic Church had been converted to true toleration. Though the assurance of toleration was given to all faiths, they were obviously not all equal. Catholicism was seen as the traditional religion of the nation, and its majority position was reinforced in these years by mass immigration from Europe. Not all immigrants were committed Catholics and many were hostile to clericalism. But demographically Argentina remained nominally a Catholic country, and in 1910 Catholics comprised 92 per cent of the population.[9] Moreover, while Catholics subscribed to the basic freedoms of thought, speech, and religion, they were favoured by the bias in the constitution and were reluctant to share their rights with non-Catholics. Yet the constitutional position was not altogether clear. Did support for the Catholic religion oblige the state to provide religious instruction in schools, or to sanction Catholic marriage laws?

These questions were debated in an increasingly secular age, when the forces of modernization and state-building joined to marginalize the Church and to activate the anti-clerical tradition latent in Argentina. In the 1880s the organization of the Catholic Association and the establishment of two periodicals gave liberals the impression that Catholics were on the offensive. In fact Catholics were weak and these were defensive measures against what was seen as an impending liberal offensive.[10] Reason triumphed over faith among the professional classes, while positivism provided an intellectual alternative to Christian doctrines. The French secularization programme of the 1880s was invoked and strengthened Argentine resolve. Meanwhile, the Masonic lodges became the means by which liberalism was transformed into a programme of action under the direction of Freemasons, who could count on the direct support of their fellows. The burning of the Colegio del Salvador in 1875 by an anti-clerical mob was preceded by the vilification of the Jesuits in the Buenos Aires press. Priests became figures of fun in the theatre and the media. The prophets and practitioners of modernization saw religion as an irrelevance and in some cases an encumbrance. In the 1860s and 1870s state schools were founded, secular in orientation but allowing Catholic education in the curriculum and in a way compensating the Church for its own lack of free parish schools.

Tribulation came to a head in 1884 when the secular trends of General Julio Roca's government, already under attack from the Catholic hierarchy, culminated in a new education law; bowing to the liberal desire for a lay state and following pressure from professional teachers, the government removed religious instruction from the regular curriculum in state schools. Roca was a cynical politician who advised a novena and a show of popery to placate Catholics, and was not over-concerned with constitutional nice-ties or the abuse of authority. But both sides were serious, and a great national debate followed. The secularists argued that religious education violated the freedom of religion guaranteed by the constitution. The government criticized Catholics for wanting to impose their own beliefs on everyone; it also took the view that bishops were officers of state and could not attack government policy. Certain bishops were threatened with legal action for opposition to the government; the Apostolic Delegate was expelled; and steps were taken to remove a bishop from his see. The lay spokesman for the Catholic position was the scholar and publicist José Manuel Estrada, who at the Catholic Congress convoked in August 1884 to mobilize opinion asked: 'To what extent did the policy of the government interpret the general will, Catholic for the most part?'[11] Now he argued that religious instruction was a traditional part of education for the overwhelm-ingly Catholic population of Argentina. Such instruction need not be imposed, but it should be available to those who wanted it. The govern-ment was not impressed: Estrada was dismissed from all his academic posts for speaking against his employer's policy, and three professors of the University of Córdoba were fired. Catholic deputies in Congress submitted a counter-proposal for subsidizing all schools of a minimum standard irre-spective of religious denomination. But this made no progress and Catholic schools now lagged behind those of the state at the primary level, while Catholic secondary education remained private and fee paying.

Catholics tried to organize themselves politically, but they had little success and failed to prevent the Civil Marriage Law of 1888. This did not prohibit a religious ceremony for marriage, but required that it be preceded by a civil ceremony and this was obligatory for all marriages. The new legislation, like that on religious education, was part of a policy of secularization applied by the Roca and Juárez Celman administrations (1880–90) in the interests of individual freedom, a policy which had much support in Argentina among the elites but was received with indifference by the majority of the population, who were nominally Catholic and who, according to Archbishop Aneiros, 'do not accept any other authorization for matrimony than that of the parish priest nor any other law of marriage than canon law'.[12] If the Church authorities were intolerant, liberals were no less so. The new idol was the state, and the state set the standard of the new morality for believers and unbelievers alike. More than this, an unmistakable anti-Catholic bias was obvious among many of the speakers in the parliamentary debate on the new law. In the Senate the ultra-liberal Minister of the Interior, Eduardo Wilde, described the Bible as 'the most immoral of books, and where it is not immoral it is absurd, and where it is not absurd it is scandalous'. As for Catholicism and ultramontanism, 'they have been disastrous for the world'. Wilde also ranted at women, usually regarded by liberals as the mainstay of the Church: 'so far there has not been a single woman who has produced a masterpiece'.[13] Catholics concluded that the liberal programme was a comprehensive attack on religion and its place in society.

The hard-line administrations of Roca and Juárez Celman were succeeded by those of Pellegrini, Sáenz Peña, and Uriburu, which could afford to be more tolerant towards Catholicism because the basic positions had now been won. Attempts to introduce divorce (1901) and separation of Church and state (1903) failed in Congress. By the end of the nineteenth century laicization was largely complete and Argentina was a secular state. This result had been achieved without violence or civil unrest, and was accepted by Catholics, who were now concerned to show that there was no incompatibility between Catholicism and a secular state, though as in Brazil there was a conservative wing which still fought for old causes. But the basic reason for accommodation between Church and state was that the Argentine Church was neither wealthy nor powerful, and in a position neither to provoke nor defend. Nominal rolls of Catholics meant little. Politicians treated the Church as an association of women, as to a large extent it was, and as a force for social order. The brief attempt to create a Catholic party, the Catholic Union, failed, as it was a party with only a policy, without a social base or a party organization. The party called for a number of reformist measures, such as universal suffrage and legality for trade unions, and it managed to get Estrada elected as a deputy.[14] But Juárez Celman and his associates were too strong for the newcomer, while alliance with the opposition simply showed the political incompatibility of Catholics and liberals and the party folded in the 1890s. So the Church came to look not to a Catholic party but to allies within the existing parties

in opposition to common enemies – anarchists, socialists, and revolutionaries.

Uruguay was not rich in religion. The Church had even less power than
it did in Argentina and the Uruguayan hierarchy even less influence in
national affairs. In 1984 only 3.8 per cent of the country's 3 million inhabitants were practising Catholics, and there was just one priest for every
4,300 persons. At what point in the modern period this de-christianization
took place it is difficult to say, but it evidently had its origins in the past. In
the course of the nineteenth and twentieth centuries Uruguay abandoned
religion and converted to secularism.

Conflict between Church and state began in 1838 when Fructuoso
Rivera suppressed Franciscan monasteries and confiscated their properties. In subsequent years the Jesuits were expelled, readmitted and expelled
again, allegedly for meddling in government affairs but basically for being
independent of the state, at a time when the latter was seeking to build its
power and authority against all rival institutions. When President Bernardo
Berro came to power in 1860 the government grew even more hostile and
took a number of secularizing measures. Berro, who was a Freemason,
maintained that Christianity was a means of domination and oppression,
and used his power to weaken the Church and reduce its place in civil life.
There was a reaction under his successor Venancio Flores who, among
other things, readmitted the Jesuits to Uruguay. In the following decades,
however, the Church came under increasing pressure, especially on education and marriage, the two issues on which it was challenged throughout
Latin America at this time. In 1885 a new law made civil marriage compulsory and the only legally binding form of marriage. And state subsidies to
the Church were gradually eroded. From 1904 José Batlle y Ordóñez
dealt the final blow to official Church–state relations. He was actively anti-
clerical, a Mason, and did not hide his contempt for religion, removing all
signs of Christianity from public life and buildings. He established the
country's first divorce laws, and was hostile to any form of religious education; in 1909 the teaching of religion in state schools was prohibited. The
government even replaced religious feasts by secular holidays, the Epiphany
by Children's Day, Holy Week by Tourist Week, the Immaculate Conception
by Beach Day, Christmas by Family Day – no doubt an extreme example of
a certain liberal mentality but one which helps to explain Catholic distrust
of liberalism in Latin America. By now there was so little opposition from
Uruguayan Catholics – and so few real Catholics – that the state had little
difficulty in completing the work of secularization in the new Constitution
of 1 March 1919, when the Church was disestablished and the separation
of Church and state became formal. This freed the Church and left it to
survive on its own resources in a largely indifferent society. Its resources

were not impressive; in the 1920s there were only 85 churches and 200 clergy.

Paraguay, former paradise of the Jesuits, began its independent history under the dictatorship of Dr José Gaspar Rodriguez de Francia, a creole lawyer and philosopher, who promptly broke off relations with Rome, confiscated Church property, and abolished religious orders as 'unnecessary and useless'. A later dictator, Francisco Solano López, republished the 'royal' catechism (1786) of Archbishop San Alberto and ordered it to be taught in parishes and schools, including the question:

Is the king [president] subject to the people?
No, because that would be to subject the head to the feet.

In 1870 the Paraguayan people emerged from their apocalypse of war, tyranny, and terror: a living proof for the modern Church that the faith can survive and souls be saved even when institutions are collapsing and the externals of religion vanishing. In the War of the Triple Alliance Paraguay lost half its population and in the next decades its Church lay prostrate and usually silent, neglected by conservatives, occasionally attacked by liberals, and largely ignored by history, though not by Rome, whose informants were impressed by the fidelity of the Paraguayan people. Paraguayans were described in the 1890s as a people eager for religion and receptive to the sacraments, instilling in their children a traditional piety in contrast to the secular world around them.[15]

Chile's Constitution of 1833 reflected a conservative victory and ascendancy which prevailed until the 1870s. From the preceding struggle the Church had emerged intact in wealth and privilege, and now these assets were written into the constitution without dissent. The Church was given the status of a state religion, the only one permitted in public, while the state was given the right of patronage and control of communications with Rome. The heavy hand of the state in exercising its rights over the clergy put some strain on Church–state relations. The Church was also under ideological pressure from El Mercurio, the leading newspaper, and from men of letters such as Francisco Bilbao and José Victorino Lastarria whose attack on the conservative order involved an attack on its clerical allies; this was accompanied by increasing demands for religious toleration. Under Manuel Montt relations between Church and state were cordial; the Church maintained its voice in public affairs and its budget was increased.

In the middle decades of the century there was a steady erosion of the Church's privileges rather than total confrontation. Freedom of religion existed in fact, if not in the constitution; given Chile's commercial interests and the influx of foreigners, it could hardly have been otherwise. In 1865 all denominations were granted legal permission to worship and establish schools. But the conditions of consensus were changing. As elsewhere in Latin America, the liberals competed more vigorously for power in the years after 1870. The Liberal–Conservative coalition collapsed in 1873 precisely over the religious question. The principal points of dispute were the *fuero*, the secularization of cemeteries, civil marriage, and separation of Church and state. The Liberal-Radical bloc won the political struggle but could achieve only part of its desired reforms: the *fuero* was abolished in 1874; and the tithes were abolished and replaced by a tax. Further secularization was left for the future, but the contest between the conservative-Catholic and the liberal-anti-clerical tendencies was now openly joined. Cemeteries were secularized in 1883, civil marriage was made compulsory and all civil records were placed in the hands of the state in 1884. Although the Church conducted a rearguard action against all these measures, there was no stopping the advance of the secular state; for the next forty years the two powers coexisted and the state continued to subsidize the Church.

Although a number of clerical leaders in Chile were landowners or from landed families, the Church as an institution was not wealthy either in land or in property, and could not be targeted by liberals as an obstacle to economic progress. But it was a Church of the oligarchy, comfortable with its friends, obdurate with its enemies. During the late nineteenth century it acquired some controversial political allies and became closely identified with the Conservative Party, its protector, exploiter, and divider. Liberals, socialists, Radicals, these enemies of the Conservatives were automatically enemies of the Church, denounced in pastorals and sermons as enemies of God. For Conservative support the Church had to pay – at elections, with funds, in words and votes – and the alliance brought divisions into the Church, between bishops and priests, priests and laity, and among the laity themselves. The strategy was short-sighted. During the years 1891 and 1920 Chile was ruled by a strong parliamentary government based on an alliance of Conservatives and traditional Liberals. The regime was impervious to the growth of new middle sectors in commerce and industry and of an industrial working class in the mining areas of the north, and it ignored demands for a change in policy and a redistribution of power and resources in society. The lesson for the Church was clear: the social base of conservatism was shrinking and the structure of politics was ready for change. But the Church had other preoccupations. In 1895 the synod of Santiago denounced 'atheism, secularization, and lay education' as the main threats to Christian society, and Archbishop Mariano Casanova warned of 'the great conspiracy against Christ, against the Church, and against the priesthood' which was then unfolding.[16] While the Church did not clearly read the signs of the times, it could not fail to see the flaws in the Conservative alliance.

The circumstances were thus right for a final understanding with the state. Arturo Alessandri, a Radical and reforming president who first came to power in 1920, wanted separation of Church and state: the policy was traditional in his party and it might also yield the political bonus of detaching the Church from the Conservatives and strengthening the middle ground. Archbishop Crescente Errázuriz also wanted a Church independent of the state and free from exploitation by the Conservative Party. Not all bishops agreed, but many people in the Church followed the archbishop and believed that disestablishment would give the Church freedom of action and make for an impartial clergy. Rome appeared to share these views. Alessandri consulted Pope Pius XI and his secretary of state, Cardinal Gasparri, and gained acceptance of his proposals subject to certain conditions. Rome had experience of Church–state conflict and had learnt that it was invariably a losing battle which could only damage the Church, as it did in Mexico. A separation peacefully negotiated, on the other hand, which would give freedom to the Chilean Church and control of patronage to Rome, would be better by far than one accepted under duress. So the Vatican instructed the Chilean hierarchy to accept.

The Constitution of 1925 disestablished the Church.[17] It provided for the free exercise of all religions, but it recognized the legal personality of the Roman Catholic Church and guaranteed it the right to own property exempt from taxation, as it did for all religions. The government's rights of ecclesiastical appointments and of veto over papal communications were abolished. The Church was allowed to establish dioceses, seminaries, and religious communities without congressional approval, and to maintain its own education system. State payment of salaries to clerics and other subsidies for the Church were ended, though the government eased the transition by paying the Church an annual sum of 2.5 million pesos for five years. The balance of clerical and lay opinion in the Church was in favour of disestablishment. No doubt there were still right-wing Catholics who supported the Conservative alliance or went even further along the road of reaction. But the days of a privileged Church were over.

Andean America

Peru provided a different model to Chile, preferring a close union of Church and state, the one legally privileged, the other officially Catholic. Liberal anti-clericalism was relatively mild and was never a popular issue: the endurance of Spanish culture and tradition among the elite and of religious enthusiasm among the masses prevented this. In terms of clerical wealth and presence Peru occupied a middle position in the league of Churches, enough to arouse interest but not to provoke conflict.

The Constitution of 1828 declared: 'The religion of the state is the Apostolic Roman Catholic; the nation protects it by all the means in keeping with the spirit of the Gospel, and will not permit the exercise of any other religion.' This did not distinguish between public and private worship. The liberals wanted complete religious toleration but had to be content with a concession, from 1839, which limited the prohibition to public worship. On the other hand Ramón Castilla and the liberals, in a decade of growing anti-clericalism, were more successful in their efforts to abolish the clerical *fuero*, which they did in the Constitution of 1856. At the same time tithes lost the sanction of the state; in their place bishops were to receive a salary, while the clergy were expected to depend on parochial fees. Relations with the papacy had their sticking points but were basically uneventful. In 1835 formal relations were established when the pope instituted the first republican archbishop of Peru, though the government was careful not to concede the right of national patronage. Until 1926 congress nominated candidates for bishoprics; after that the president did so.

The balance of political power within Peru prevented the predominance of any extreme liberal or conservative policy towards the Church. The advent of the conservatives to power produced the Constitution of 1860, designed by Castilla as a compromise between conservatism and liberalism. It declared that the state protected the Roman Catholic religion and did not permit the public exercise of any other; it safeguarded the Church's wealth and property; and it assured the Church autonomy and freedom from political control. In practice there was little interference with personal religious beliefs. The constitution again suppressed the clerical (and military) *fueros* and ended state collection of tithes, replacing them by an annual government subsidy. It also provided for a system of public education which would end the monopoly of the Church. So this constitution gave something to the Church and to the liberals, and it lasted, with the exception of a brief 'pure' liberal interlude in 1867, until 1920. The Church accepted it as a good arrangement, as it gave the Church security, authority, and wealth. From this base it improved its structures, increased the number of dioceses and improved their incumbents, and became a strong force in the life of the nation.

But it was not a solid victory. The Church lost ground, as it did elsewhere, to secularization and official concessions to non-Catholics. In 1869 the law established the right of civil burial, and in 1897 a law of civil marriage enabled people to marry outside the Church; in 1915 liberty of worship in favour of Protestant sects was proclaimed; in 1930 this was extended to all, and the right to divorce was established. The Church fought all these measures but in vain, and it was forced, objecting and protesting, into a pluralist society. Meanwhile, from the 1870s the Church lost influence among intellectuals and statesmen, as secular values began to prevail and positivism and more radical influences replaced traditional liberalism in the minds of the elites.

From 1870 the Church in Peru began to falter, at a time when the export economy and social elites were mildly flourishing. An obvious symptom of crisis was the fall in priestly vocations; most dioceses experienced a drop in ordinations, which soon had repercussions at parish level. Lima declined from one priest for 510 inhabitants at the time of independence to one for 3,841 in 1973. As Peruvian vocations decreased, the number of foreign priests increased. In 1901, 82 per cent of the Peruvian clergy were native Peruvians; in 1973 only 38 per cent were Peruvians.[18] Various explanations are possible. While Peruvian society and ideas were becoming more liberal and pluralist, the Church remained conservative and monolithic. Although bishops and senior clerics were compensated for loss of tithes by state funding, the ordinary clergy had to live on stipends drawn from fees for masses and sacraments and from the offerings of the faithful. The prospects of poverty made the lower reaches of the Church a poor career at a time when Peru's economic improvement was creating more jobs for younger sons in commerce and the professions. An educated laity saw a priesthood of a lower cultural level than themselves, as seminaries lowered their standards to attract recruits.

Surrounded by a hostile or indifferent society and weakened by internal problems, the Church reacted not by rethinking its role but by closing ranks, retreating into trenches and deploying its traditional strategies. In 1915 the bishop of Ayacucho, Fidel Olivas Escudero, declared, 'no one can be at the same time Catholic and liberal: these are mutually exclusive terms like truth and error, good and bad, light and darkness'.[19] In opposition to its ideological enemies the Church sought to create for itself an opposing model of an institution closely linked to Rome, protected by the state, and led by upper- and middle-class Catholics. A Catholic point of view was transmitted in sermons, pastoral letters, the press, and other media of communication. Foreign religious arrived to reinforce the Church in education, welfare, and health work: the Jesuits in 1871, the Redemptorists in 1884, the Salesians in 1891, and in the same decades the Sacred Heart nuns and the Sisters of Charity. The schools run by these religious became the educational establishment of the Peruvian elite; from them came the statesmen, the politicians, and the academics of modern Peru, the Haya de la Torres, the Riva Agüeros, not all of them faithful to their teachers but all beneficiaries of a superior system of private education. The Peruvian Church itself mirrored the two nations that Peru had become: on the one hand an elite of foreign religious, Spaniards, Italians, French, and Irish, managing superior educational resources and, from 1917, a Catholic university for the benefit of the ruling groups; on the other the native secular clergy, not always well educated themselves and ministering to the mass of ordinary Peruvians.

Yet the Church could not ignore Peru's poor. Bishops and priests continued to condemn abuses against Indian communities, and the Church's influence among the Indians and *cholos* of the sierra endured. But it now sought a new constituency among urban workers. Incipient industrialization and the emergence of an industrial working class introduced the issue of workers' rights into political debate and generated the first attempts at labour organization. Here too the Church sought a role. In Arequipa, for example, it played a part in early forms of trade unionism, and the most influential of the local mutual aid societies was the Círculo de Obreros Católicos formed in 1896. But the Church was not the only voice speaking for the Indians, peasants, and workers of Peru, and here too it found it was challenged. The reformist movement APRA (Alianza Popular Revolucionaria Americana) began life in the 1920s as an enemy of the Church and religion, and only later invoked the social message of the Gospels and the role of Christ as a reformer in order to pre-empt official religion and divert the religiosity of the lower classes towards its own party. APRA was also hostile to the political associates of the Church. The model of development favoured by President Augusto B. Leguía in the decade 1919–30 – unrestricted foreign investment and a primary export economy – was criticized by APRA but not by the Church, which had close and compromising connections with the regime.

The Oncenio of Leguía was a high point in the Church's relation with the state, a low point in its own reputation. Leguía was a dictator who represented the economic interests of the elites profiting from his economic model of modernization, and who cultivated the Church for its influence on those outside the privileged sectors. The Church responded favourably and no public appearance of Leguía was complete without a cluster of bishops on the platform or in the cavalcade. The leader of the alliance was the archbishop of Lima, Emilio Lissón, a good and worthy prelate but one who lost no opportunity to underwrite the regime. In a pastoral letter of 25 April 1923 he declared that he was going to consecrate Peru to the Sacred Heart of Jesus in a ceremony in the Plaza de Armas in Lima. He invited Leguía to preside over the ceremony as 'patron of the Church'. The proposal was a pious and polemical idea, embarrassing to many Catholics, outrageous to secularists, and a bonus to the dictatorship; it was denounced as an abuse of the union of Church and state and an affront to freedom of conscience; and the voices in its favour were not very convincing.

A protest movement led by future APRA leaders gained momentum, and in the face of violence on the streets the archbishop suspended the ceremony, which he claimed had been turned into a campaign 'against the legitimately established government and social institutions'.[20] The Church in Peru was not easily reformed. In February 1929 the papal nuncio bestowed on Leguía the papal honour of Knight of the Supreme Military Order of Christ in a ceremony attended by the whole hierarchy. After the fall of Leguía the archbishop, too, quietly left Peru to spend the rest of his life in Spain. He left a Church which had sought influence and lost credibility, a model of Church–state relations not uncommon in the Church's history.

The constitution which Simón Bolívar designed for Bolivia in 1826 did not proclaim a state religion, for he regarded belief as a moral, not a political, duty; in effect he argued that the state should guarantee freedom of religion without prescribing any particular religion, a view of toleration familiar to modern religionists. But national control of patronage and restrictions on papal jurisdiction were asserted, and a law added by the constituent assembly in defiance of the Liberator's views made Roman Catholicism the religion of the republic to the exclusion of all other public cults. During the first decades of independence Bolivia was not disturbed by serious religious problems, which could have been an argument for or against a concordat. In 1851 General Santa Cruz went to Rome to seek a concordat. In this the pope conceded to the president of Bolivia the privilege of presentation and some dilution of the *fuero*. But because the pope 'conceded' these powers as privileges instead of recognizing them as rights, the Bolivian congress refused to give its approval and the concordat was abandoned. In Bolivia, as in other Latin American countries where concordats were not concluded, the pope never recognized the *patronato nacional* but tolerated it in practice and reached a working compromise with the state. In 1880 the Church lost tithes and first fruits and was assigned instead a state subsidy; this was accompanied by tax exemption for Church property. Yet the clerical *fuero* survived until 1906.

The national rulers did more than nominate bishops: they behaved like bishops. A government order of 12 March 1852 prohibited the ordination of thirty seminarists, alleging they were not licentiates in theology and that the bishops already had enough priests. Later the current dictator allowed each prelate to ordain up to twelve candidates. A ministerial resolution of 15 June 1853 set the rates of parish fees for La Paz, and a government circular informed bishops that no parish priest could absent himself from his parish without government permission, under pain of loss of salary. In accordance with the regalist principles inherited from Spain, every Bolivian government treated the Church, its bishops, and priests as employees of the

state. As one such minister declared in 1872, 'the state which declares a
religion official and sets itself as protector of that religion thereby acquires
the right of *patronato*'.[21] The intervention of the state in religious affairs
was a confession of weakness rather than of strength, a recognition that the
Church was more effective than the state in administering social and
educational policies, and was an institution indispensable to the state,
especially at the departmental level.

The Church in Bolivia, however, drew strength less from government
policies and current resources than from its centuries-old presence in the
country and from the continuing, if irregular, demand for its sacramental
services from those Indians who had been Christianized. In the course of
the nineteenth century the Church received contradictory signals from the
state. If the liberals were normally hostile, conservatives were unpredictable and not automatically allies of the Church; Catholics were to be found
in both camps. In the period 1870–1930 Bolivia heard, however faintly, the
voice of positivism, Freemasonry, demands for freedom of conscience, and
like the rest of Latin America experienced the advance of the secular
state. When, in 1890, Pedro de la Llosa, archbishop of Sucre, warned of the
growing influence of positivism on 'intellectuals', no one imagined that the
souls of Bolivian Indians were in danger; but the ruling groups knew what
he meant. After two decades of conservative rule the Liberal Party returned
to power in 1898 and secularist pressure increased. A decree of 31 May
1904 suppressed religious education in state schools. Once the Church lost
the battle of the schools, only the family remained as the prime instructor
in religious doctrine, a weak line of defence; Bolivian parents had never
been known as effective vehicles of the faith. In 1906 the government
decreed liberty of worship, to the alarm of Catholics but without greatly
increasing the number of Protestants. The Church also lost its control over
cemeteries, which were secularized by decree of 26 October 1906. And in
1911 a new marriage law was enacted which recognized only civil marriage
as binding, though this could be followed by a religious ceremony.

The response of the Church was characteristic. Ideology remained traditional: in 1890 Archbishop Pedro de la Llosa instructed fathers of families
to teach their children that the so-called right of rebellion was an absurdity,
that complete liberty of thought and the press could never be a right, and
that civil marriage was 'public concubinage'.[22] Defence of the Church in
public and private life, a campaign supported by Pope Pius X, was seen as
a political battle for rights and privileges rather than an evangelical
crusade. Bishop Miguel de los Santos Taborga, scourge of the lay state,
became the hero of conservatives but an embarrassment to thoughtful
Catholics. For more positive action the Bolivian Church relied on foreign
reinforcements. Jesuits, Salesians, Redemptorists, the Sacred Heart and

Good Shepherd nuns, these were the agents of progress in education, health and welfare, and parochial work and the means by which the native Bolivian Church saved itself from its own weakness, compensated itself for inferior seminaries, and remedied the lack of Bolivian vocations.

With the fall of the liberals the Church recovered some of the positions which it had lost. In 1920, by common demand of clergy and Indians, the religious marriage of Indians was allowed, to fulfil civil requirements. Throughout the 1920s the Church underwent some institutional growth, and in 1928 it regained a place for religious instruction in state schools.

Ecuador gave more public expression of religious belief than almost any other country of Latin America. According to the Constitution of 1830 Roman Catholicism was the religion of the state to the exclusion of any other faith. President Juan José Flores was an opportunist in religious policy, not greatly engaged one way or the other, and he was prepared to support the Church if it supported him. His successor, Vicente Rocafuerte, was more liberal and would have preferred to curb clerical power, end the *fuero*, and reform the clergy. But public opinion was too conservative and Catholic to allow him to do this. In the Constitution of 1835 Roman Catholicism was declared to be the religion of the republic to the exclusion of all others, and the government was bound to protect it. The return of Flores (1839–45) brought further reaction, but not enough for the people of Ecuador. The new Constitution of 1843, which lengthened the presidential term to eight years, confirmed Catholicism as the religion of the state but in a bid for liberal support added, 'to the exclusion of the public exercise of any other cult', thus allowing freedom of private worship to non-Catholic cults. This aroused violent opposition, especially in Quito and Cuenca, where intolerance reigned. The clergy refused to take the oath to the constitution and accused Flores of being in league with the Masons of Colombia. The liberals were also hostile to Flores for his despotic ways. So the joint forces of liberals and clericals brought down Flores and forced him into exile in 1845. The history of Ecuador then entered a period of great anarchy during which the liberals managed to dilute political and religious absolutism. This was brought to an end by Gabriel García Moreno (1821–75) who from 1859 to 1875 dominated the public life of Ecuador as politician and president, and established his rule on the firm alliance of an independent Church and strong state, in conditions where the Church should advance 'together with the civil power'. At a time when many other Latin American countries were experiencing the effects of applied liberalism Ecuador renewed its confidence in religion and gave further proofs of its devotion to traditional Catholicism.

García Moreno came from an elite background of land and trade and had a conventional education in religion and law. Europe exerted a

different influence on him than it did on most Latin American intellectuals. He used a period of exile in France not only to study science at the
Sorbonne but also to deepen his religious life and to discover the traditions
of Catholic political thought.[23] From then on his innate religiosity was
reinforced by Spanish scholasticism and the ultra-conservative views of
Joseph de Maistre and Donoso Cortés. Just as De Maistre regarded the
French Revolution as due retribution for the decadence of European states,
so García Moreno explained the disorder of Ecuador as God's punishment
for sin; and from his master he drew a lifelong belief in authority as the
only true basis of society. In Paris García Moreno became not a secularist
but a confirmed religionist; it was here that his personal piety increased
through daily mass and communion and frequent fasting. He returned to
Ecuador prepared for power. Soon the passionate and angry politician
became the committed president, who in his first presidential message in
1861, echoing De Maistre, subordinated law and liberty to 'the rule of the
moral law'. The Constitution of 1861 gave an exclusive position to the
Catholic Church and granted the vote to all men on condition that they
could read and write and were Catholics. This was followed in 1863 by a
concordat with the papacy which he regarded as a model for the political
and religious direction of his country.

The concordat opens with a declaration that the Catholic religion will
continue as the only religion of the republic of Ecuador; no other cult and
no society condemned by the Church will ever be permitted. Education in
universities, colleges, and schools 'will in all things conform to the doctrine
of the Catholic religion. The bishops will have the exclusive right to desig-
nate texts for instruction in ecclesiastical sciences as well as in moral and
religious instruction'. Bishops also have the right 'to proscribe books that
are contrary to religion and the moral law', and are the ultimate inspectors
of the whole education system, in order to ensure 'that there shall be no
instruction contrary to the Catholic religion'. All bishops, clergy, and
faithful are to have free communication with the Holy See, and there is
to be no government intervention in communications with Rome. The
autonomy of ecclesiastical courts is affirmed in ecclesiastical causes and
matrimonial cases, with appeals only to Rome. The tithes are confirmed,
with the traditional one-third to the government. The papacy grants
patronage rights to the president of Ecuador: nomination of episcopal
candidates proceeds from bishops to president to pope, and of parish
priests from bishops to president. The Church is to enjoy the right to
acquire property freely and properties already in its possession are guaranteed by law.[24]

This concordat gave the Church greater privileges than the Spanish
monarchs had ever allowed. Dissatisfaction was expressed inside and

outside Ecuador. Liberals were outraged by what they regarded as an attack on freedom of thought and were determined to resist it; in congress attempts were made to modify its clauses. But García Moreno was intransigent. The concordat was signed in Rome on 26 September 1862 and promulgated in Ecuador on 22 April 1863. Between these dates the president insisted that reform of religious orders be included in the concordat and he prevailed on the pope to agree to a reform of the clergy; thus it was the civil power which intervened to restore proper observance in religious orders. Elsewhere throughout South America the concordat was denounced as an abdication of independence and a further sign of Ecuador's subservience to Rome. From Colombia President Mosquera invited Ecuadoreans to overthrow their president and in 1863 he undertook an invasion 'to liberate the brother democrats of Ecuador from the theocratic yoke of Professor Moreno'.

Outside interference, however, served to strengthen the hold of the dictator, and he further affirmed his principles in the Constitution of 1869, the religious clauses of which tended to conform to Pius IX's Syllabus of Errors and to be a logical extension of the dictator's political thought. The Roman Catholic religion was declared to be the religion of the state, to the exclusion of all others, and Catholicism was made a requisite for citizenship. Equality had no place in García Moreno's Ecuador: anyone who belonged to a sect condemned by the Church lost his civil rights. This followed from the premise that all power came from God: the people exercised power in the name of God and an election was a religious and moral act; therefore in order to vote a person had to be a Catholic. According to García Moreno, religious unity was not only right for Ecuador, it was also necessary in a country so fragmented: 'this happy unity of belief is the only bond left to us in a country divided by the interests of parties, regions, and races'.[25] And in his last message to the legislature he declared, 'all our modest advances would be useless and ephemeral, if we had not founded the social order of our republic on the ever assailed and ever victorious Catholic Church'.

A careful reading of the concordat and of other statements of García Moreno shows that the Church in Ecuador was now vulnerable to a new form of subjection, but not to Rome The president saw himself as the leader in reform of the clergy, whatever Rome or the bishops might say; the state still had a role in the taxation of ecclesiastical persons and property and in the distribution of tithes; and the president had a prominent place in the presentation of candidates to higher ecclesiastical appointments, and in the creation of new dioceses. The concordat was criticized by secularists for the independence it gave to the Church, and by bishops and canons who were hostile to the creation of new dioceses, a potential threat to their own income. In the conflict over reform of the clergy the papal nuncio reported to Rome: 'The president is certainly pious, and zealous for the Church. But his character is impetuous and he has a will of steel . . . There is no middle way with him.'[26]

The so-called 'theocracy' in Ecuador, a term first applied to the regime by the Colombian Mosquera, was in fact a scene of conflict in which the Church was hard pressed by the state to reform itself. García Moreno regarded the Ecuadorean clergy as lazy, ignorant, and immoral, not least in their conduct towards women in the confessional. The regular clergy were especially corrupt. He pressed Rome to back him, harassed the hierarchy, and brought in foreign clergy – his preference was for French Christian Brothers – to regenerate the Church and educate the people, a process which he regarded as indispensable for the 'moral reform of this country'. García Moreno's aggressive methods alienated many bishops and priests and angered the people with whom the mendicants were popular. Priests were expelled, a bishop was suspended, and the president made it clear that he was sovereign, whatever Rome might say. There was no question of the civil power being subordinate to the Church or of submitting to a theocracy. García Moreno designed his policy not to create a clerical state but to create a Church which would be an instrument of his national project, which would work under the authority of the dictator, to improve education, administration, and social relations, part of that programme of modernization which, however distorted, mirrored the structural reforms of other Latin American states.

The Indians had a minimal role in the national project of García Moreno. Apart from empty exhortations that they should be treated with Christian charity, he saw them as prone to rebellion, addicted to alcohol, and retarded by their savage nature. Yet they were part of the Christian community and had to be instructed and evangelized; then they might enter the body politic. This was the task of the Church. In 1870 the decree on the Amazonian missions granted the Church absolute power in Ecuadorean Amazonia, on the grounds that 'it is impossible to organize a civil government among savage tribes'.[27]

The policy of García Moreno towards the papacy was ultramontane. He gave his total support to the Holy See, both for its stand on faith and morals and for its temporal power in disputes over Italian unification. When Rome was occupied in 1870, Ecuador, weak and distant though it was, solemnly protested, one of the few countries to do so. The president knew that the gesture was puny. But what did it matter? Was it not a question of principle? García Moreno, a contemporary of Pius IX, sent him frequent messages of loyalty and support, as well as modest financial help. On doctrine he was at one with the pope, enthusiastic for the Syllabus and its condemnation of the 'errors' of the modern world. He regarded the Syllabus as essential for the welfare of society and sought to keep Ecuador's laws faithful to its teaching.

Enemy and victim of liberalism, García Moreno never failed to contrast the saving doctrine of the pope with the deadening ideas of the liberals, and to dedicate Ecuador to the service of the Church. When in 1874 in the cathedral of Quito authorities of Church and state united to consecrate Ecuador to the Sacred Heart of Jesus, García Moreno's ideal of a reformed Church in a Catholic state seemed to be realized. Yet in the ultimate analysis this small clerical state was no more than a temporal paradise. The Church was deluged with rights, privileges, and powers, but all this depended upon its benefactor and did not lead to autonomous development. The dictatorship was personalist, and finite. García Moreno's re-election in 1875 was a mistake, for it deprived other factions, clans, and regions of an opportunity of power. Against his enemies he appealed to Pius IX for prayers and protection. He had a presentiment of death and saw himself as a martyr for the faith. He was assassinated in a Quito square on 6 August 1875. His dying words were 'God does not die'. In his pocket was found a paper, in effect his last message: 'The divine teaching of the Catholic Church, which neither men nor nations deny without peril, is the rule for our institutions and the law of our laws.'[28]

The Church in Ecuador did not immediately suffer from the loss of its patron, and for the next twenty years, in spite of murmurings from liberals, the conservative structure remained more or less intact. Ecuador was still 'an entirely Catholic nation', and priests claimed 'not only the right but also the duty to take part in politics'.[29] When a liberal revolution in 1895–96 threatened to oust the clerical alliance and to put the *cholo* Eloy Alfaro into power, the Church raised a call to arms. Bishop Pedro Schumacher led a small army against Alfaro with the battle cry 'God or Satan'. The archbishop of Quito denounced liberalism as 'the great whore of Babylon' and urged Catholics to fight for their faith. Not all the clergy were militants, nor all liberals fanatics. The new Constitution of 1897 confirmed the Roman Catholic religion as that of the state to the exclusion of all others. But mutual antagonism raised the temper of debate and the Church paid for its intransigence in a new wave of anti-clericalism beginning in the congress of 1899. A new patronage law gave the state the right of presentation of archbishops and bishops, whereupon the Vatican broke off diplomatic relations. Civil marriage and divorce were introduced. A spate of legislation guaranteed religious toleration, discontinued the tithe, prohibited the establishment of new religious orders, and restricted the Church's use of its own income. Yet another constitution, in 1906, separated Church and state, and removed religion from state schools, though the Church was not prevented from developing an education system of its own. As for the property of the Church, its land was disentailed and nationalized in 1908. Thus the liberals propelled Ecuador into the twentieth century, secularized the state, and deprived the Church of temporal power. Such was the norm in the modern world and there was no looking back. But the modernity of the cause could not disguise the fact that this was elite politics and the mass of the people, who were undoubtedly Catholics, were not consulted. Some of the anti-clerical laws were easier to announce than to apply, and in the face of popular resistance governments on more than one occasion approached the Vatican for an agreement, which was never forthcoming.

Colombia was second only to Ecuador in the private and public profession of Catholicism. Conservatives and liberals fought behind clerical and anti-clerical slogans, and the loathing of Catholics and secularists for each other promised a century of bitter conflict. Both sides overstepped the mark, the liberals demanding that priests obtain official permission to conduct services, the Church scattering excommunications like shot. The Church had a substantial presence; ecclesiastics expected power; and the people were loyal in the faith. Colombia was the first Spanish American republic to be recognized politically by Rome (26 November 1835), and Gregory XVI praised the government for its stability, its adherence to the Catholic religion, and its respect for the Holy See.[30] The conservative governments of 1830–49 represented the main power interests: land-owners, the Church, and the army. But conservatives were not automatically pro-clerical, and they no less than liberals cast an envious eye on the power and wealth of the Church. Their claim to inherit the colonial *patronato* was not entirely disputed by the Catholic clergy and laity. Protection of religion came at a price. Catholicism was declared the religion of the republic; the public worship of no other faith was tolerated. But the state was also a winner: the government retained the right of presentation of bishops and control over entry of papal communications. The peak of patronage control was reached in 1841: the law of 18 May provided that the police should keep watch over prelates, priests, and chapters to see that they 'introduced no novelty in external discipline, or usurped the patronage or sovereign prerogatives of the republic'. Meanwhile the ecclesiastical *fuero* was eroded by the law of 16 April 1836 which established the supremacy of civil tribunals over ecclesiastical and brought the clergy under the jurisdiction of the civil law. Conservative ambivalence towards the Church was continued under President José Ignacio Márquez (1837–41), who resisted pressure to exclude the works of Bentham from college teaching, and Tomás Cipriano de Mosquera (1845–49) who began the attack on tithes and fiscal privilege.

During the liberal ascendancy of 1849–80 the Church suffered a sustained attack on its jurisdiction. Virtually every right and privilege it had inherited came under scrutiny. In 1851 the clergy had to accept fixed salaries in place of tithes and their *fuero* was also abolished. In 1852 the archdiocesan seminary lost its independence when it was incorporated into the state education system. Prelates who opposed these measures were summarily exiled. In 1853 a new constitution separated Church and state. A law of 1855 concluded that there was no religion of the state, and instituted civil marriage. These measures ended the intervention of the civil authority in presentation to ecclesiastical benefices and in all matters religious, and theoretically implied freedom and independence for the Church. In practice it produced closer supervision.

In 1860–61 Mosquera, no stranger to violence, executed an about-turn, joined the Liberals, and sought a new base by attacking the Church and embarking on radical reforms. Identifying the Church with the Conservative regime he had just overturned, he began to tighten the screw still further. He decreed in 1861 that no cleric could exercise his religious functions without authorization of the president or a state governor. A decree of disentailment confiscated Church property except that needed for direct religious use. A liberal policy in favour of fiscal reform and free circulation of property was the justification invoked for this measure, but the gesture towards redistribution was insincere, for it never took place. Monasteries and convents were suppressed. And the Jesuits, whose sequence of expulsions and readmissions was a barometer of religious policy, influenced often by Masons and even secular priests, found themselves expelled yet again. Those prelates who opposed or criticized these measures were imprisoned or exiled. Mosquera then proceeded to 'reform' the constitution and impose what was called 'tuition' on religion: 'to support national sovereignty and maintain public security and tranquillity, the national government or that of the states may exercise the right of supreme inspection over religious cults'.[31] This was not exactly religious liberty; rather it expressed a determination to establish state control over the Church.

The Constitution of Ríonegro (1863) enacted by Mosquera's Liberal Party may be regarded as the high-water mark of Liberal policy towards the Church. It declared freedom of religion, barred the clergy from federal offices, and prohibited the Church from interfering in political matters: reasonable statements in themselves but open to anti-clerical application. Moreover, in the wake of similar legislation in Mexico, it prohibited ecclesiastical corporations from acquiring and possessing real estate. In addition, the decree of 9 September 1861 disamortized corporate property and enforced its sale in public auction. The government hoped to bring property into the market and make it more accessible to individuals. In the event these measures simply concentrated property still more, and tended to replace the Church as a landowner and creditor by more acquisitive individuals. The Church itself did not cooperate. It defended its right to property, condemned those who denied it, and punished clergy who compromised it. The faithful were warned against liberalism and forbidden to take the oath to the Constitution of 1863, except in a form excluding the anti-clerical parts. And Rome supported the Colombian Church. In an encyclical addressed to the Colombian bishops in 1863 Pius IX condemned the 'sacrileges' committed by the Liberal government in opposing the doctrines and rights of the Catholic Church.

The weaker Mosquera's political position, the more anti-clerical he became; the slightest criticism was interpreted as 'inciting the masses against constitutional government'. In 1866 he dispatched another group of bishops to prison or exile, a foretaste of his own exile the following year. And the conflict continued. From 1870 relations between Church and state entered another period of crisis when the government undertook a long-overdue reform of education. In the Decree of Primary Education (1 November 1870) provision was made for free and obligatory primary education throughout Colombia; the state would not provide religious instruction but this could be given by priests within schools. Some of the hierarchy, notably the moderate archbishop of Bogotá, Vicente Arbeláez, were willing to accept the secular schools and indeed to work for general reconciliation with the state. But conservative Catholics rejected compromise. In Cauca, whose 'neo-Catholic fanaticism' was loudly denounced by liberals, clerical opposition was intransigent. In Pasto Catholics rallied to the defence of religion against atheism and liberalism. Monsignor Carlos Bermúdez, bishop of Popayán, citing the Syllabus of Errors and insisting on Catholic control of schools, forbade parents to send their children to state elementary schools under pain of excommunication. On the other side liberal fanatics drew up their battle lines and contributed their share to the political hysteria. Caught between conservatives and liberals, moderate churchmen were unable to establish a middle ground as reason gave way to reaction. Thus opposition to educational reform contributed to a conservative–Catholic revolution in 1876 and the civil war of 1876–77.

The revolution began in Cauca, and here it took on the appearance of a religious crusade as well as a political struggle. Conservatives exploited religion for political ends, and this was well known. A captured Conservative colonel was reported as saying 'If we had not taken the pretext of religion, we would not have had even half of the people in arms.'[32] Such attitudes were doubly provocative to opponents of the Church, and after the war the Liberal congress decided to end clerical interference in politics once and for all by legislating to complete the secularization of Colombia and to prevent clerical opposition to federal and state laws; and four prelates were exiled for ten years for allegedly fomenting revolution.

By 1880, after three decades of liberal reform mixed with pure anti-clericalism, Colombia was virtually a secular state. Church and state were separated, non-Catholics tolerated, the clerical *fueros* abolished; tithes lost government sanction, ecclesiastical property with the exception of actual Church buildings and houses of the clergy were expropriated, religious orders dissolved; marriage was now a civil ceremony, and the government could apply the right of 'inspection of cults' (*tuición*) to control religion. There was some truth in the liberals' claim that they never attacked religion itself. Tomás Cipriano de Mosquera had argued directly to Pius IX that liberals too were Catholics and that churchmen who intervened in politics perverted a divine institution in the interests of one political party.[33] But in practice liberal measures amounted to harassment of the majority by a minority. *Tuición* in particular caused many priests to shut up shop, to close their churches and to refuse to administer the sacraments, anticipating the action of the Mexican Church in 1927. Yet this was not the end of the traditional Church. Colombia was still Catholic, politicians still needed power bases, and parties always wanted votes. Rafael Núñez came to power in 1880 as a liberal but with the support of the conservatives as well as independents, and respectful towards the Church; on re-election in 1884 he turned more decisively towards the conservatives and began to restore the position and influence of the Church. In 1886 a centralist and authoritarian constitution was promulgated which, together with a new concordat with the Vatican signed on 31 December 1887, re-established the Catholic Church in a position of primacy and privilege.

The concordat recognized Roman Catholicism as the religion of Colombia, to be protected and respected by the government; and the Catholic Church was to enjoy complete liberty and independence of the civil power. In a reversal of classical liberal policy, the Church had the right to acquire property, to recover that which had not been actually alienated, and to receive an annual subsidy to the value of the property sold. Religious orders could be established under ecclesiastical authority. In universities, colleges, and schools, education was to be organized 'in conformity with the dogmas and morals of the Catholic religion'. Religious instruction was obligatory in such centres and the Church was to have the right of inspection and revision of textbooks to ensure conformity with Catholic faith and morals. The president was to recommend episcopal candidates to the Holy See for appointments, and the Holy See was to announce its candidates to the president, who would determine if they were acceptable. Catholics had to marry according to the religious ceremony of the Church but witnessed by the civil registration officer.

Rome regarded the Colombian concordat as 'excellent', while conservative Catholics – and these were the majority of Colombian Catholics – were
satisfied that political intervention and military action, their 'wars of religion' as they called them, had been justified by their success. In pastoral
letters issued in the course of 1900 Monsignor Ezequiel Moreno, bishop of
Pasto, encouraged his people: 'Brave soldiers of Christ, the present war is a
war of religion and you are waging the battles of the Lord.' 'As liberalism
makes war on Christ, it is the duty of every Catholic to take up the struggle
as far as he can.' The clergy too have the right to resist: 'Priests can and
should intervene in politics and support an essentially Catholic political
party against a liberal one.' And in spite of a papal prohibition against
clerical participation in civil wars (12 July 1900), Bishop Moreno insisted
that the clergy could exhort Catholics 'to take up arms in a just war, such
as that now being waged against liberal and Masonic revolutionaries'.[34]
The same bishop left instructions in his will that during his funeral a large
placard should be displayed bearing the words 'Liberalism is a sin'. The
militant prelate was subsequently beatified.

From 1886 to 1930 the Catholic Church in Colombia consolidated its
position in the state and presented an object lesson in the preservation and
exercise of power. In the first place, it gave support and political legitimacy
to the government and in return earned important privileges. Second, the
superior education and administrative expertise of clerics made them
indispensable to the functioning of local government in areas where the
state's presence was weak. Third, the Church controlled education and
therefore the career prospects of many Colombians. Finally, the power of
the Church to open – and close – newspapers gave it the means of influ-
encing the media and silencing its enemies, and allowed it a peculiar
advantage in the battle for public opinion. The Church in Colombia had
achieved this success partly through its own inherent strength, partly
through the weakness of the state.

Republican Venezuela was governed by caudillos representing an elite of
landowners, merchants, and office-holders, and it was only after 1935 that
the process of nation-building was gradually extended to the popular
sectors. The ecclesiastical policies of successive governments, therefore,
were the result not of national debate and consultation but of the decisions
of individual dictators backed by the particular coalitions of interest
groups which they assembled. Yet it would be a mistake to attribute the
decline of the Venezuelan Church primarily to the anti-clerical policies of
caudillos such as Antonio Guzmán Blanco. The logic of events appears to
have been different. The Church in Venezuela *began* from a low base in the
years after 1830, and it was the inherent weakness of the Church, in structure, personnel, and resources, which enabled the state to treat it as it

wished. Venezuela had been on the margin of the Spanish empire and Church, and while it had flourishing missions among the indigenous population much of the rest was only lightly Christianized. The wars of independence destroyed the missions and emptied the llanos of priests. Even the centre-north lacked episcopal direction, parish priests, and new vocations, while shortage of funds was a basic constraint on the Church's mission. Yet if the Church had no power, it still had a voice, and clerics expressed their political preferences for one side or another, not always the same side, and rarely from a position of independence. For the clergy were drawn into caudillo politics and the patron–client relationships which underlay public life in Venezuela. They extolled their caudillos as saviours or denounced them as the Anti-Christ. For partisanship of this kind they would be severely punished.

Venezuelan independence in 1830 was accompanied by a declaration that the right of patronage exercised by the Spanish kings now belonged to the republican state, which thereby assumed total power in the presentation of prelates and priests, the organization of dioceses and parishes, the regulation of the Indian missions, the administration of tithes, and control of papal communications. Archbishop Ignacio Méndez raised his voice against these claims, arguing that the kings of Spain had no right to bequeath the *patronato* or to nominate the republican government to inherit it; therefore it was now suspended, and instead would be exercised by the bishops. His argument was not accepted. Restrictions on Church influence thus began earlier and were carried further in Venezuela than in most other parts of Latin America. Why was this? It was hardly a reaction to excessive clericalism, for the Church was small and weak and carried little weight in public life. This possibly explains its failure to inspire a popular response in defence of an independent Church. But the major explanation lies in the mentalities of Venezuela's political leaders and elites. Liberal philosophy had the advantage of pre-empting the debate; its exponents occupied a dominant position among policy-makers, even conservatives like President José Antonio Páez. Secular values and unrestrained anti-clericalism thus resulted in legislation restricting the Church more rigidly than elsewhere. The new rulers quickly pounced on dissident clerics: when Archbishop Méndez refused to acknowledge the constitution because of its failure to recognize Catholicism as the exclusive religion of the state he was exiled to Curaçao, as were the bishops of Mérida and Guayana. Further gains by the state in 1834–39 reaffirmed the law of patronage as a right of the civil authority, suppressed tithes, and replaced them with payments from the government, decreed freedom for Protestant sects, and suppressed monasteries. The Monagas regime of 1848–58 was slightly more friendly to the Church, but Liberals and Conservatives did not differ greatly on ecclesiastical policy and both defended patronal rights.

Following the Federal War of 1858–63 Páez returned to exercise a brief dictatorship, and his final tenure of power proved to be more favourable to the Church than his first, though retaining state control. In order to secure papal recognition of the patronage rights of the state, he authorized the archbishop of Caracas, Silvestre Guevara y Lira, to negotiate a concordat with the papacy, 'without losing sight of our law of patronage'.[35] Silvestre brought back a document (signed in Rome on 26 July 1862) that many regarded as an abdication to Rome. Compromise was reached on payment of tithes and rights of presentation, but it was the role conceded to the Church in the public life of Venezuela that alerted many.

The concordat asserted that Catholicism would continue to be the religion of the republic, and that the government would recognize the duty of defending it and preserving its rights and prerogatives. Education should conform entirely to Catholic doctrine under the scrutiny of the bishops. The bishops were thus given the right to see that nothing contrary to Catholicism was taught, and therefore to censor books and writings. Critics argued that this violated the liberty of thought guaranteed by the constitution, but Páez signed the document (6 March 1863), seeking perhaps the support of clericals for his crumbling regime. Within weeks the dictator was ousted by the federalist generals and the National Assembly rejected the concordat. The new government sought a new accord 'in harmony with the national laws and the spirit and letter of the new constitution (1864), which, like earlier ones, guarantees religious liberty and freedom of the press'. But Rome stood back and the Venezuelan government too lost interest. The Venezuelan concordat bore the mark of Pius IX and his clerical supporters in Venezuela, and they paid for their temerity in the years after 1870. Anti-clericalism was the hallmark of the dictatorship of Antonio Guzmán Blanco and the Church would take many decades to recover from his ruthless attack on its resources, institutions, and jurisdiction.

Guzmán Blanco (1870–88) emerged from Venezuela's civil wars to become master of his country for twenty years. Liberal-Federal leader, dictator in the 'order and progress' mould, Mason and anti-clerical, he dominated most institutions in Venezuela including congress, which officially titled him 'ilustro americano'. He made it clear from the beginning that he would not tolerate clergy who supported conservatives in press or pulpit. Archbishop Guevara y Lira took up the challenge, refused Guzmán Blanco an inaugural *Te Deum* unless he granted a general amnesty, and resisted attempts to appoint clergy according to party-political opinion. He was promptly exiled to Trinidad and there he remained, fulminating interminably against the dictator, until at the suggestion of Pius IX he resigned and ended the impasse. Behind this apparently trivial clash of wills lay the determination of Guzmán Blanco, conscious always of his absolute power, to allow no alternative focus of allegiance, no rival source of leadership. His political entourage, moreover, was also strongly anti-clerical. Minister Diego Bautista Urbaneja resented the refusal of ecclesiastical authority to grant him an annulment of his marriage and permission to marry his stepdaughter.

The Church was now struck by a torrent of anti-clerical legislation. In 1872 the dictator suppressed seminaries on the grounds that they isolated the clergy from the institutions of the republic. By a law of 25 May 1874 the Church was deprived of registration of births, marriages, and deaths, and of jurisdiction over cemeteries; civil marriage was made the only legal form. Clerical immunity, the traditional *fuero* of the Church, had been abolished in 1811; a new law now effectively abolished the right of the Church and its authorities to exercise jurisdiction over its own ministers. Further laws of 1874 confiscated Church property, suspended the clerical subsidy, and imposed a policy of lay education; they also abolished all monasteries, convents, colleges, and other religious institutions. In practice monasteries had long been extinguished, so the new law referred mainly to women, who were peremptorily expelled from their convents.

The mentality of Guzmán Blanco could be seen not only in what he did but in what he wanted to do and failed. He sought to legalize the marriage of the clergy and, in 1876, with the agreement of a servile congress, to establish a national Church independent of Rome, in which the bishops would be elected by the priests and the priests by their parishioners. A flurry of Vatican diplomacy resulted in the resignation of the dictator's inveterate enemy, Archbishop Guevara y Lira, and the withdrawal of the threat of schism. But Guzmán allowed no one to obstruct his special project, the construction of a Masonic temple in Caracas, in effect the headquarters of radical liberalism. Guzmán Blanco, who always described himself as a Catholic, issued a decree to suppress 'the fanatical principle that only the Catholic religion can hold religious ceremonies outside Church precincts'; as this was an infringement of equality before the law he prohibited the outside celebration of any religion.[36] By the end of the regime the Church had been almost legislated out of existence and the clergy decimated by a process of death, exile, and seminary closures. In 1881 in the whole of Venezuela, with its five dioceses – Caracas, Mérida, Guayana, Barquisimeto, Calabozo – and over 2 million inhabitants, there were only 255 parish priests for 639 parishes and just 393 priests in the whole country, as compared to 547 in 1810.

The Venezuelan Church, it has been aptly said, entered the twentieth century 'in a state of coma'.[37] Subsequent caudillos did little to revive it. Cipriano Castro (1899–1908) yielded to no one in his absolutism, though he was more benevolent towards the Church than his predecessors and did not enforce all the anti-clerical legislation available. A number of religious orders began to return and from 1900 with government permission seminaries to reopen. In the Constitution of 1904 the Roman Catholic religion was declared to be the national religion and the state contributed to its support. But the legalization of divorce was a victory for secularization, one which prevailed in spite of the opposition of the Church. Juan Vicente Gómez (1908–35), merciless to his political opponents, was mildly tolerant of the ecclesiastical establishment and subsidized a number of clerical institutions and activities, though any churchman who dared to criticize the government soon felt the dictator's displeasure. In 1929 the bishop of Valencia, Salvador Montes de Oca, was expelled to Trinidad for denying the validity of civil marriage. In this and other cases the government overreacted and treated clerical criticism in the same way as it treated political resistance. And in a show of religious nationalism it prohibited, in 1929, the entry of foreign priests and ordered the bishops to appoint only a Venezuelan clergy.[38] The archbishop of Caracas during much of the Gómez regime was Felipe Ramón González, who had close and personal ties with the dictatorship and was not the man to lead a religious resistance.

Thus by the 1930s, at the pleasure of the caudillos, the Venezuelan Church had undergone some renewal at least in public, though how widely its message reached the people was open to question. Among the elite many were seduced by positivism and a sociology of dictatorship. In the rest of society the existence of the modern folk cults of María Lionza, protector and guide to the magical world of the spirit, and of the twentieth-century medical doctor José Gregorio Hernández, a saintly son of the Church, was evidence of popular revulsion against a corrupt society and a religious void in the lives of the people which the Church had not yet begun to fill.

Central America

Central America was to prove a testing ground for the Church as it confronted the liberal states of the nineteenth century and the dictatorships of the twentieth. In Guatemala the attack on the temporal power of the Church was begun in the first flush of liberal enthusiasm in 1825–38, when intemperate anti-clerical measures antagonized the Catholic masses. Liberal policy towards the Church could be explained as a desire to create a secular state rather than an attack on the Catholic religion, but

Guatemala was not a secular society and legislation could not make it so. The rural clergy were an integral part of peasant communities; priests joined the cause of the Church to that of the peasant and from pulpit and confessional denounced the Liberal government. The Conservative reaction from 1840 to 1870, therefore, was in many respects spontaneous and its leader representative. Far from being a mere tool of the priests, Rafael Carrera was a populist caudillo who led a successful Indian and mestizo rebellion against the European-style government of the Liberals. Carrera was a mestizo, though more Indian than white. He understood the Indian communities, recognized the *ejidos* (communal lands), protected their lands and reduced their taxes. It was in this context that he restored the traditional influence and privilege of the Church and maintained good relations with Rome; there is no evidence that the mass of the people wanted otherwise.

Carrera enabled the Church to recover some, though not all, of the land lost under the Liberal regime. The clergy were restored to their protected status and to their parishes, and the village *curas* continued their role as friends, ministers, and advisers of the Indians, becoming in effect not only spokesmen of the Church but also informal representatives of the state. In 1839 the assembly restored religious orders and invited the exiled Archbishop Casáus to return to his diocese. This was a particular wish of Carrera, as the archbishop acknowledged: 'It appears that God has destined you to redeem the Guatemalan people from their oppression.'[39] Education was re-established under Church auspices; and the University of San Carlos was restored, with Father Juan José Aycinena as rector. The Church regained its *fuero*, and the tithe was restored, enforced by the state. The Conservatives were more clerical than the Catholic caudillo. Carrera objected to the reinstatement of the tithe; he refused to tolerate any reduction of religious feast days, even those sanctioned by the pope; and he objected to the clergy holding political office. He was a friend of religion rather than of clerical power.

As Liberals had anticipated their prospects in the 1830s, so churchmen exceeded their vocation in the 1860s. Clerical association with Conservative attempts to regain power after 1871 brought more radical elements into prominence among the Liberals, and in 1873 these insisted on a complete anti-clerical programme. Justo Rufino Barrios became president in 1875; he suppressed religious orders, and stripped the Church of its political and economic influence. Civil marriage was declared legal, and education was secularized. The Constitution of 1879 confirmed these measures and completed the formation of a secular state with the disestablishment of the Church. While the Church thus lost its temporal power, the expulsion of many priests and prohibition of the entry of foreign clergy – though not of American Protestant pastors – reduced its actual presence in Guatemala and its activities were rarely free of malign interference from the government.

Guatemala was a model, if an extreme one, of the Church's experience in Central America, where there was a standard pattern of policy: fanatical liberalism in the wake of independence, followed by a conservative reaction until about 1870, which was succeeded by liberal regimes, imposing classical secularism, often by force. These political conflicts sucked in the Church, unwilling victim or dubious victor, and ultimately, although the mass of the people remained solidly Catholic, government action weakened the structures of the Church. Between 1805 and 1872 the total number of regular and secular priests dropped from 453 to 119, and the Church never truly recovered. In 1944 Guatemala still had only 120 priests. The Department of Huehuetenango, with 176,000 inhabitants, contained only two priests.[40]

In Honduras the Liberals were in power from 1880. In the same year Church and state were separated, Church property was taxed and reduced to actual churches and houses of the clergy. In Nicaragua the Conservative regime of 1857–93 allowed the Church to survive with its privileges intact, and it was not until 1893–1904, under José Santos Zelaya, that Church and state were separated, religious orders suppressed, and bishops and priests exiled, to the extent that years later a Masonic writer, Jorge Corredor, could boast that 'there was no longer the slightest religious influence in the social life of Nicaragua'.[41] He was wrong: popular manifestations of religion survived persecution, but the Church's institutions were severely diminished. In El Salvador the Liberal Party, which was dominant from 1871 to 1945, produced a constitution which separated Church and state, provided for civil marriage and divorce, and for lay education; and here too religious orders were proscribed. In Costa Rica freedom of worship existed from 1864, and in 1884 a Liberal government ordered the expulsion of the Jesuits and of the bishop of San José; lay education and other stock features of liberalism were introduced, without, however, seriously damaging the Church or its relations with the state.

Mexico

In Mexico, where the Church was stronger than the state and priests more privileged than politicians, relations between the two powers were resolved by war, and one war did not suffice. The Church had been saved from the worst of liberalism by the dictator Antonio López de Santa Anna, who extracted a price for his protection: in effect he said to the Church, support me or expect worse. Payment was frequent, in money and from the pulpit. He himself practised an overt religiosity, and although at times he threatened to unleash the forces of liberalism, conservatives and Catholics continued to commit their fate to Santa Anna. In recalling him from exile to lead the country again in 1853, the Conservative statesman Lucas Alamán reminded him of his duty to the Church and the Catholic religion, 'the only bond uniting all Mexicans, when all the rest have been broken'. In the short term Santa Anna delivered. The archbishop and a number of bishops were made honorary members of the Council of State, and a bishop was appointed its president; the Jesuits were re-established, and monastic life protected. But the fall of Santa Anna brought retribution, and the liberals now closed in for a final reckoning.

Classical liberalism came to Mexico in the Laws of Reform of 1856–57, which struck at the roots of what Liberals regarded as Church privilege and wealth. The Juárez law of 23 November 1855 abolished clerical immunity from the civil law. The Lerdo law, or Law of Disamortization of 25 January 1856, ordered Church corporations to dispose of their real estate, which would be sold to tenants or at public auction. On 5 February 1857 a new constitution was issued by a constituent congress dominated by professional liberals and unrepresentative of Catholic opinion. This established freedom of press and speech; the clergy were barred from election to congress; government intervention in worship was allowed; and the Juárez and Lerdo laws were confirmed.

Benito Juárez was not the worst enemy of the Church. He had no quarrel with religion; basically he wanted to end privilege, as any good liberal did, and assert the supremacy of civil power, but beyond that he did not seek confrontation. His record as governor of Oaxaca was essentially that of a moderate. However, from 1855 the extremists were gaining ground on both sides and the leaders did nothing to rein them in. The government insisted that all office-holders take an oath to the constitution. The archbishop of Mexico and other bishops condemned the constitution and forbade any Catholic to take an oath to it. In August 1859 the bishops issued a pastoral letter strongly repudiating the charges that the clergy had promoted and funded the war, had challenged the authority of the government, or had withdrawn obedience from legitimate authority. The Lerdo law did not rob the Church; it simply diverted its land and wealth into capital and mortgages. To reject this was probably an error of judgement, one which the papacy shared. In December 1856 Pius IX condemned the appropriation of Church property as 'sacrilege', and condemned the constitution for its articles opposed to the rights of 'divine religion': 'We strongly condemn everything the Mexican government has done against religion and the Church and declare its decrees null and void.'[42] The result was to plunge the country into civil war between 'Religión y Fueros' and

'Constitución y Reforma', which lasted from 1858 to 1860 and involved the Church as one of the belligerents.

The Church lost even more by war, as each side plundered its wealth for the war effort. In 1859 the Liberal government nationalized Church property, separated Church and state, and suppressed male religious orders. This was followed by laws of civil marriage and civil registry, and by a law of religious liberty (4 December 1860). It was this which opened the door to Protestantism in Mexico, reinforcing the influence of the United States and projecting the liberal model of religion as a reform movement complementing the political *Reforma*. With victory in 1861, the Liberals applied the Reform Laws and proceeded to secularize schools, hospitals, and charitable institutions of the Church. These measures were accompanied by the expulsion of nine bishops, leaving the Church leaderless and exposed to further harassment, such as the abolition, in 1863, of all remaining religious communities except the Sisters of Charity, a cultural as well as a religious blow which destroyed a number of Mexico's historic churches and monasteries. The most dramatic victory of the Liberals was over Church property. The wealth of the Church available for appropriation amounted to between $100 million and $150 million, much less than the sums existing in the imagination of politicians and public.[43] Perhaps the greatest damage to Mexico was the loss of income by schools, hospitals, and charities, which left a gap in the social services for many years to come. Yet adversity was not complete.

The Church reacted to the Liberal victory by promoting the intervention of France, hoping to regain from a Catholic monarchy what it had lost to Mexican republicans. Many Mexican Catholics had reservations about the policy of their leaders, who were incapable of making any distinction between pure religion and temporal power. The Church's search for power and property now became a classic exercise in short-sightedness. It soon became clear that the French were less Catholic than anticipated, and the Habsburg Archduke Maximilian, who had received a brief blessing from Pius IX, was more of a French puppet than a Catholic emperor. Some of his policy was hardly less liberal than that of Juárez: the nationalization and sale of Church property was recognized as valid and purchasers were left unmolested. The clerical leader Antonio Labastida returned to Mexico as archbishop, totally miscalculating the situation. He found that the Church had not one enemy but two: the Mexican government defending the nation against foreign invaders and the French administration applying liberal policy from the capital. By the end of 1863 he could only conclude, 'we are in a worse situation than before', perplexed by the paradox of a conservative-inspired intervention seeking to become a liberal reform.[44] The papal nuncio soon decided that Maximilian's policies were not Catholic, least of all his decree of religious toleration, which was derided as irrelevant in a country of total Catholicism; the papacy was particularly outraged by the loss of clerical immunity and property. But Napoleon III and Maximilian had no intention of cancelling the Reform Laws or restoring Church property; and when France withdrew in 1867 the Church was more vulnerable than ever before.

The Restored Republic was not a happy time for Catholics. The government of Juárez (1867–72) sought to take the heat out of Church–state relations and offered a cooling solution, allowing the clergy to recover political rights and to vote in elections, and granting an amnesty to Archbishop Labastida.[45] His successor, however, Sebastian Lerdo de Tejada (1873–76), was oppressively anti-clerical. Catholics had often predicted that the liberals would not be content to disestablish the Church but would then proceed to attack its religious functions. Lerdo proved them correct. The campaign against religious orders was intensified in 1873, as many of their members were forced out of their houses, often into the street during the night, and others were imprisoned; ten Jesuits, six Passionists, two secular priests, and a Pauline father, all foreigners, were expelled from Mexico; and priests were prosecuted for administering the sacraments without prior civil registration. These incidents were just the beginning of an anti-clerical drive which included an oath of allegiance to the constitution for officials, the expulsion of the Sisters of Charity, in many cases into exile, the incorporation of all the Reform Laws into the constitution (25 September 1873), and finally the Organic Law of Reform (14 December 1874) reaffirming the anti-clerical laws on property, education, clerical dress, and the holding of religious activities outside churches; it forbade religious teaching in state schools, collecting alms for sustaining Church services and clergy; and in place of the catechism of Christian doctrine it imposed a *Catechismo constitucional* to teach Mexicans the doctrines of the Reform.

How did Mexican Catholics react to repression? The bishops protested vehemently and censured those who complied with the anti-clerical legislation, but otherwise recommended that Catholics adopt an attitude of resignation to the law, at most 'passive resistance', and exhorted them to piety and prayers, to work for the Society of St Vincent de Paul and other charities, and to place their hope only in God. But conservative Catholics, stung by the intolerant policy of Lerdo's government, looked around for political alternatives, either by alliance with dissident factions of the Liberal Party or, in the course of 1874–75, by staging minor armed rebellions, the so-called *Religioneros*, in which a few local clergy and Catholic peasants took part. When all else failed, there was only one lifeline: the Porfiriato. And for his part Porfirio Díaz believed that to govern in peace he needed the support of Catholics.

Porfirio Díaz regarded himself as a Catholic 'in private and as head of family', but 'as Head of State' he professed no religion, because the law prohibited it. His regime was based on conciliation and from the beginning he made it clear that although he adhered to the constitution he offered a policy of toleration as well: 'the individual conscience ought to be respected even when it errs'.[46] This also made political sense, for he was aware that a hostile Church could destabilize the regime. So he cultivated good personal relations with the bishops and turned a blind eye when Catholics began to venture out from underground. This is not to say that anti-clericalism was dead during the Porfiriato. It was active in the press, in congress, and among some officials, and it seemed that only Díaz stood between Catholics and their enemies.

The nationalization of Church property continued to its completion; politically and practically it was not possible to reverse this or to undo the transfer of property already made. On the other hand, Díaz allowed the Church to acquire wealth again in forms not strictly prohibited by law, such as holdings in railroads, mining, telegraph systems, and manufacturing, and, it was said, even in pre-Reform types of mortgages and real estate. This was often done through the agency of trustworthy laymen and lawyers or by other means. Many of these accusations were exercises in propaganda and the truth may never be known. But the Church took advantage of the Díaz years in other ways than wealth. Processions were held outside the churches, clerical dress was worn in public, Catholic marriages were celebrated. And this was a time of reconstruction.

Religious orders such as the Passionists, the Josephines, the Claretians, and the Salesians unobtrusively re-established themselves, and a number of new Mexican orders were founded, often specializing in education, welfare, or mission work. The Jesuits returned, with Spanish and other foreign priests, and grew in numbers and prestige as they attracted Mexicans to their ranks. The Church opened schools of its own and provided various social services. A Catholic university was established in 1896. New dioceses were created, growing from fifteen in 1863 to twenty-one in 1891, while the archdioceses increased from three to six, and provincial councils took on a new lease of life. The number of Catholic churches increased from 4,893 in 1878 to 9,580 in 1895. The Catholic press expanded and improved, and now its coverage was not exclusively religious; following the success of periodical and weekly publications a notable daily, *El Tiempo* (1883–1902), informed the Catholic public and displayed religious values to the rest. Among numerous Catholic journalists, Trinidad Sánchez stood out as the founder of *El País* (1899–1914) and a leading writer on social reform. The new position of the Church in the Porfiriato was epitomized on 12 October 1895 by the Coronation of the Virgin of Guadalupe when a great gathering of bishops, priests, and laity, including twenty-eight Indians in their native dress, was organized to symbolize the unity of Mexico around the idea of the moral grandeur of the Christian people, and to witness what one preacher described as the coronation of 'the Queen of the Mexican People ... Patron of our nationality and independence'.[47]

Yet while the Church made progress, it could not recover the power and influence of the years before 1856. In 1895 there were fewer than three priests for every 10,000 inhabitants, and in 1886 140,000 children attended Catholic schools compared to 477,000 in secular schools. The Fifth Mexican Provincial Council in 1896 ordered priests to remain aloof from politics in all matters where the Church allowed freedom of opinion. As for Catholic conservatives, after a useless effort to participate in the elections of 1877, they withdrew from political activity. And Porfirian conciliation, while it did not satisfy the absolute claims of the Church, left the revolutionaries after 1910 with a pretext for attacking the Church, to confiscate its property again and to restore the work of the Reform.

Gains from Losses

After a century of republican life the Latin American Church hovered between advance and retreat. The Church's economic wealth was probably exaggerated. Rome had given in to pressure from the national governments and gradually tithes were abolished and replaced by a mixture of state subsidy and contributions of the faithful. Peru was an example where subsidy was usually late and inadequate, because the state's revenues were themselves weak. Venezuela was an example of a country where the faithful were too poor to contribute. The Chilean Church was not rich in land or property, but its revenues were well administered and distributed. In Colombia Church income was sufficient because usually the conservative state paid its dues. In Ecuador the Church depended on state subsidies and these were declining. In Mexico the Church paid its way in spite of its property losses, which accounted for rumours of hidden income. In general, therefore, the impression is that of a Church adequately but not richly funded.[48]

Rome was opposed to the separation of Church and state, even when it was obvious that separation could lead to the independence and reform of the Church. The preferred model was that of Catholicism recognized as the official religion and protected by a concordat. This was the mentality of the Pius IX regime transmitted to Latin America in the middle decades of the nineteenth century. Ecuador and Colombia were seen as the best exemplars of Church–state relations. Rome regarded Ecuadorean religious legislation as 'perfect'. Colombia had been a problem under the liberals but the restoration of conservatism was reassuring and the concordat of 1888 was one of the most satisfying obtained by Rome in the nineteenth century. The remaining republics presented difficulties of various kinds. One of these was the question of the *exequatur*, a right claimed by governments to prevent enactments of the Holy See from taking automatic effect in their territories. This was a specific obstacle to papal communications with the Churches of Latin America, and was responsible for the ignorance in Latin America of the mind of the Church on basic issues. If it was prevented from knowing the latest doctrinal statement of Pius IX, it was also deprived of full awareness of Leo XIII's social encyclicals; regulations concerning education and marriage could also be affected. In Venezuela, where the government prohibited the publication of the encyclical *Humanum Genus* on Freemasonry, the hierarchy complained in 1889 that 'the most important papal documents cannot be published . . . hence the complaints of the faithful, who find it impossible to explain why in Venezuela, a Catholic nation, the voice of our common father cannot be heard'.[49]

In the period 1870–1930 the Church in most of Latin America lost the support of the state and ceased to rely on legal and political sanctions for the promotion and protection of religion. Catholics did not at first welcome their new status or respond positively to conditions of independence, pluralism, and toleration, but continued to look backwards to a Christian state and collaborating Church as the ideals against which to judge the secular trends of the age. Yet they were not fighting innocents. Power could change Latin American liberals into monsters of illiberalism, and it was difficult for Catholics to understand decrees expelling bishops and clergy, confiscating Church property, forbidding the wearing of soutanes in the street and the carrying of the viaticum to the sick. But gradually adjustment was made and the Church exchanged external support for inner renewal. The state's appropriation of the civil registry left the Church with pure sacraments, baptism and marriage, for which Catholics now had to opt. The secularization of state education forced Catholics to improve their own schools or devise other ways of Christian instruction. This sharpened the distinction between believers and unbelievers and made religion more of a choice and less of a habit. The result was a drop in the real numbers of Catholics but a growth in the spiritual life of the Church. Moreover, withdrawal from the state was a precondition of independent social action, a new role demanded of the Church by the force of events.

CHAPTER 8

New Century, New Challenges

Social Messages

THE INDEPENDENCE AND reform of the Church took place at the same time, 1870–1930, as society itself was undergoing profound change under the impact of mass immigration, foreign investment, and international trade. There was a time lag, however, between the onset of Church reform around 1870 and the emergence of Catholic social awareness in the 1890s. It required the dramatic impact of social conditions and urgent prompting from Rome to alert the Church to the need for change. Immigration seriously tested Church institutions in a number of countries. At the same time incipient industrialization created an urban working class largely unknown to the Church. The effect of economic change and population growth on organized religion was most obvious in large cities. The populations of Buenos Aires, Rio de Janeiro, Lima, and Mexico City grew rapidly in the period 1870–1930. The influx of new immigrants and the migration of people from the countryside into expanding capitals presented the Church with unfamiliar pastoral problems at a time when it could no longer count on the economic resources of the past. How could the Church establish contact with the isolated and impoverished masses who filled the working-class suburbs and shanty towns? While city centres had well-endowed older parishes and the services of religious orders, marginal areas might not have a church within miles. Gradually the great cities of Latin America were transformed and often de-christianized.[1]

This was the society into which the new working class was born, semi-industrial and semi-pagan. The Church was not alone in failing to 'win' the working class. Socialism too had a limited impact and failed to become a mass movement. Anarcho-syndicalism had some influence among manual and skilled labour, but it was a foreign movement, persecuted by the state and handicapped by its failure to revolutionize the workers. The Church had as much chance as any movement, if it seized the opportunity. But this required a visible presence in the new society in competition with its rivals. In the early twentieth century there was a reaction in Latin America against nineteenth-century thought and in particular against positivism. Not all the reaction was Christian in inspiration, but it was more favourable to a religious view of life and it meant that Catholic thought was no longer struggling against a single orthodoxy, as the influence of Bergson, Unamuno, Kierkegaard, and Husserl joined that of neo-Thomism to replace positivism in the universities.

The restoration of Thomist philosophy in Catholic seminaries and colleges was urged in the early encyclicals of Pope Leo XIII. The teaching of St Thomas Aquinas on the origins of authority, the nature of liberty, laws, obedience, and charity was recalled to Catholics in opposition to modern philosophy and revolutionary solutions. Scholasticism had a new lease of life in Latin America in the early twentieth century and provided a link between traditional and social Catholicism. Initiatives such as the Thomist-inspired Cursos de Cultura Católica in Argentina in the 1920s, a study movement of theology, philosophy, and social doctrines, designed to create an intellectual elite and to train Catholic leaders, and later the influence of the writings of Jacques Maritain and Christopher Dawson testified to the concern of Catholics to bring the Church into the twentieth century. Not all Catholic thought was progressive. Some of it, perhaps the papal encyclicals themselves, still owed much to Spain, to Jaime Balmes and Donoso Cortés: partial to corporatist structures and vertical social organization it was more anxious to avoid revolution than to promote reform. Liberalizing tendencies in theology and biblical studies were condemned by Pius X as 'modernism', and Catholic scholars were harassed into silence or submission. But there was a further influence from Europe. The industrial revolution had stimu-lated the emergence of Catholic social movements in France and Germany, where Bishop Wilhelm Ketteler had pioneered a new approach. There was in Catholic tradition a bias towards guild organization or corporatism in industry. The Germans, however, provided a new ingredient for Catholic thought, a clear commitment to state intervention to mitigate the conse-quences of capitalism, and an argument for effective trade unionism.[2]

These influences converged in the encyclical *Rerum Novarum* issued by Pope Leo XIII in 1891. Here was a new statement of Catholic social thought, in a modern context and confronting actual problems. It was a reaction rather than an initiative, and fear of the competing claims of socialism for the support of the masses obviously underlay many of the papal preoccupations of the time. But it was new for a pope to proclaim the rights of workers and the injustices of the liberal system, and the encyclical insisted that 'in protecting the rights of private individuals special consid-eration must be given to the weak and the poor', a prophetic claim for a preferential option for the poor. *Rerum Novarum* recognized the existence of conflict between employers and workers deriving from the growth of industry, the concentration of wealth, and the impoverishment of the masses. Condemning socialism, it defended the right to private property as a natural right and urged the concept of a just wage, 'enough to support the wage earner in reasonable and frugal comfort', from which he too could profit and save; thus the gap between rich and poor would close through peace and justice. But the encyclical also advocated a degree of state intervention in favour of workers to guarantee adequate conditions of life and labour. 'If any injury has been done to or threatens either the common good or the interests of individual groups, which injury cannot in any other way be repaired or prevented, it is necessary for public authority to intervene.'[3] Leo XIII issued a call to action. He urged Catholics to take up the struggle for social justice, and in particular to organize congresses, establish newspapers, and create worker associations.

In Latin America *Rerum Novarum* had a varied reception, in some countries prompt and serious, in others slow and timid; the lower clergy responded with enthusiasm, the hierarchies with less.[4] In Mexico there was a positive reaction. In El Salvador it was thirty years before the encyclical was studied and applied. Yet the primitive capitalism the encyclical described, if it no longer prevailed in Western Europe, was precisely that which existed in Latin America. Many Catholics there instantly recognized the conditions described. The Jesuits in most countries responded actively to papal initiatives and regarded Catholic social action as an indispensable strategy to pre-empt working-class organization and establish a Catholic presence in factories and unions.

Argentine Responses

The objectives and limits of Catholic social action were on display in Argentina. *Rerum Novarum*, though reported in the specialist religious press, had little immediate circulation or impact beyond a few dedicated Catholics. The 'modernization' of the Church in Argentina had been an internal process. Politically the Church still carried little weight and indeed had lost ground to liberalism and positivism. Argentina was a sharply divided society. A wealthy ruling class of traditional landowners was joined in the late nineteenth century by middle-class beneficiaries of a booming agro-export economy to form an elite whose political mouthpiece was the Partido Autonomista Nacional (PAN). The results could be seen in the Buenos Aires of the belle époque: palatial town houses, travel to Europe, conspicuous consumption, shopping in the Calle Florida. At the other extreme the working or unemployed poor, natives and immigrants, were crowded into tenements, exploited in factories or toiling in the fields. Alongside the material fruits of liberalism – a modern state, new buildings, roads and railways, an active port, public education – lived an alienated working population of traditional poor and unintegrated immigrants, the victims of low wages, poverty, and ill-health, and increasingly discontented. The beginnings of a working-class movement could now be seen, and the first signs of mass resistance and labour organizations. In 1895–96 a great wave of strikes was accompanied by a new type of propaganda from anarchists and socialists. As the Argentine elites celebrated the anniversary of the May Revolution of 1810 in a series of exhibitions, receptions, speeches, and conferences, the working masses looked on bewildered. But even elite politics were changing, with a shift from PAN opposed to reform to UCR (the Radical Civic Union) which stood for popular democracy and benefited from an electoral reform law of 1912.

In the years around 1900 the Argentine Church faced the 'social question' without obvious resources. In a population of some 4 million, well over 90 per cent were Catholics, or identified themselves as Catholics. But at the top a liberal-Catholic consensus dominated policy, while at the bottom a new working class was unassimilated to Church or state. Both extremes weakened the Church. The population of Buenos Aires grew from 384,492 in 1885 to around 1.5 million in 1914, while parishes increased from 17 to 33, giving an average of 47,751 to a parish.[5] The existing parties, which saw religion as a private not a public concern, had no place for Catholics and the last thing they considered was to consult them on political or social policy: to liberals they were irrelevant except as a social bond, to socialists a useless adjunct to the welfare services, to street politicians allies of the bosses and landowners. Catholics themselves were politically as well as socially divided. Some wanted to conquer the upper classes and Catholicize the liberal establishment. Others preferred to move into social action among the workers. There were Catholics of conciliation and Catholics of confrontation. These were the founding groups of the Catholic movement in Argentina.

In the years around 1900 the political preoccupations of Catholic pressure groups were joined by a new kind of activists more concerned with social work than with public policy, and pragmatic rather than ideological in their approach, avoiding the use of the word 'Catholic' as a sectarian identity. In 1892 a German Redemptorist priest, Friedrich Grote, supported by a group of laypeople, founded the Círculo de Obreros in Buenos Aires, drawing on his experience of working men's clubs in his own country. He was convinced that working men, influenced by the liberal spirit of the age but above all by socialism, would not be attracted to religion by clerical calls and mission bells but needed an association seeking material and

spiritual benefits for the working class through provision of welfare services, free education, social gatherings and lectures, newspapers and periodicals.[6] As Catholic spokesmen explained, it was essential to *ganar la calle*
(win the streets): 'We have to attract workers by the same means as our
enemies use to separate them from God and make them hate the Church.'
They needed new forms of contact, offering benefits in return for allegiance. And one of the means was a mass annual pilgrimage to Luján.
Between 1892 and 1924, in spite of hostility, indifference, and lack of
support, 87 groups were founded throughout Argentina, with 28,890
members, 38 buildings of their own, and capital of 2 million pesos.[7] The
movement was funded by the contributions of prominent Catholic families
fearful of strikes and violence. Middle-class and professional Catholics
tended to dominate the leadership and the organization of the *Círculos*.
Their presence together with the message of anti-socialism reassured the
employers.

In 1898 the *Círculos* organized the first Catholic Worker Congress, and
began to send to the national congress proposals for labour legislation of a
reformist kind – working conditions of women and children, Sunday rest
day – which coincided with a number of socialist proposals and were in
fact carried into law. Father Grote was also instrumental in founding a
Catholic daily newspaper, *El Pueblo* (1900), with 'a special orientation
towards the working class', and in 1902 a weekly *Democracia Cristiana*.[8]
These initiatives, while Catholic-inspired, could not be described as typical
of the Argentine Church at the time. Although they corresponded precisely
to the social teaching of *Rerum Novarum*, they were rejected by many
conservative Catholics, including the hierarchy who impeded Grote's work
and condemned it as subversive, while others such as Alfredo Palacios
spurned it as too cautious and deserted to socialism. The eight bishops
were indifferent to Argentina's social problems, which they tended to
equate with drinking and gambling. In defence of the *Círculos* Grote
defined them as Christian by their work, with no need of Catholic in their
title.[9] Even so, they were always plagued by divisions over objectives and
tactics; some supporters wanted to distance them from the hierarchy;
others wanted more direct political action and organization. The Catholic
social movement was split between conservatives who adopted a paternalist approach and innovators who campaigned for worker rights. Above
all perhaps the greatest weakness was the failure to produce concrete
action. In Catholic social work the problem with the hierarchy was not that
they intervened too much but that they cared too little. Their prime
concern, as seen in their pastoral addresses, was the internal state of the
Church, obedience to religious authority, attendance at mass, the state of
morals, and the lack of vocations. Grote himself was forced to resign from

the movement under pressure from the diocesan authorities. His newspaper soon ceased to be the voice of social Catholicism and became that of conservative Catholics, controlled by the Church.[10] But what he had begun, others would continue.

From social pressure the Catholic movement advanced to political action as the Círculos began to expand their objectives. In 1902 Father Grote and his associates founded the Liga Democrática Cristiana (LDC), complementary to the Círculos. This was not a political party but an attempt to apply the principles of Christian democracy in opposition to liberalism and socialism, 'two forms of the same tyranny', on an alternative platform to the free market: protection of workers' families, cuts in the military budget, tax reforms, respect for civil liberties, return of religion to public schools, proportional representation and use of the referendum, and universal and female suffrage. Experiment with political movements lasted until 1919, when it was abandoned following conflict with the archbishop of Buenos Aires.[11] Meanwhile, in 1909, the Liga Social Argentina began life under the presidency of Dr Emilio Lamarca, with the participation of the priests Miguel de Andrea and Gustavo Franchesci, names for the future. This was essentially a middle-class rather than a workers' organization and was designed to project a 'Christian organization of society' by means of education and the media, including initiatives to improve the conditions of agricultural workers and small farmers. By 1914 the League had 5,743 members and 184 centres, and was publishing *Semana Social* (1911–20) and numerous pamphlets; it aimed particularly to improve the education and organization of Catholic workers, especially in rural unions. The League's *cajas rurales* from 1911 pooled the resources of small farmers, provided cheap credit, and sought to protect farm prices against large buyers. The Catholic Congresses themselves were a new development which gave a further impetus to Catholic social action, and generated even more organizations, such as Catholic Youth Congresses and Catholic Student Centres.

The proliferation of Catholic groups roused the bishops to take more positive action and also to exercise some control. The arrival of Catholic immigrants from various parts of Europe – Spaniards, Italians, Germans, and Poles – led the Catholic authorities to 'argentinize' diverse practices, devotions, and Marian affiliations in a single movement, which would at once avoid heterodoxy and create a focus of strength. This accounts for the extraordinary encouragement of the cult of the Virgin of Luján, an attempt to homogenize religion in a national devotion and at the same time bring Catholics on to the street. In 1916 the bishops brought the first Argentine Eucharistic Congress to a close with a great procession down the Avenida de Mayo, displaying the strength of Catholicism outside the sacristy.

Uniformity reached its peak when the Unión Popular Católica Argentina, sponsored and controlled by the bishops and copied from the model imposed by Pius X in Italy, united all Catholic movements in one organization and Romanized them. The UPC was a lay organization which sought to form a Catholic social conscience by appealing to employers and other ruling groups to improve conditions of the working classes; to this extent it had a distinctly paternalist message, though it also sought to encourage labour organization and to provide a house-building programme for workers. Yet basically it remained a bureaucratic model, providing publications, information, and propaganda rather than engaging in direct action and it soon lost touch with Catholic reality.[12] Later, in 1928, it gave way to Acción Católica, modelled directly on Catholic Action in Europe.

Diverse groups and tendencies existed within UPC, as they had within the Círculos obreros. On the one hand there were Catholics of the upper, agro-export sector, hitherto liberals who had taken the view that religion was a matter of private conscience and now felt marginalized by the entry of Radicalism into government; they therefore sought reconciliation with secular political groups. The leading figure of this tendency was Monsignor Miguel de Andrea, who became in effect a link between most of the conservative sectors of society. Speaking on behalf of the *patria*, tradition, and property, he was a precursor of the future Liga Patriótica in opposing what was regarded as unpatriotic subversion. Catholicism of his kind could easily become an ally of the ruling political elite of liberal conservatives and the Radical Party. This explains why congress, with the support of the Radical government of Marcelo T. de Alvear, would nominate Andrea as archbishop of Buenos Aires in 1923. They reckoned without the Vatican, whose decision also counted and who refused to appoint Andrea, as will be seen.

Other Catholics followed other routes. Most of them did not attempt to Christianize liberalism and socialism but to fight them from within the Church, from intransigent and absolutist positions. There was a tendency to denounce innovation as dangerous; the hierarchy would react against any attempt by a Catholic movement to establish autonomy, remaining fearful of change and reluctant to offend the authorities. Thus Catholic grass-roots organizations withered and dynamism vanished. In a search for a way between capitalism and socialism many Catholics such as Monsignor Andrea opted for corporatism, a conservative model over a more radical and reformist one, which in the political context of the 1930s would lend itself to exploitation by advocates of fascist solutions. This took the Argentine Church into an Erastian position, more nativist and national than European Churches of the time But its greatest weakness lay in the timidity of the bishops and the divisions in the laity.

Social conflicts, unchanged by the shift from the elitist politics of PAN to UCR, a party of state patronage to the middle classes, culminated in the violent confrontation of January 1919 in Buenos Aires, the so-called *semana trágica*. The prolonged wave of strikes in 1917–19 led employers and conservatives to demand more decisive action of the Radical government against the working classes and trade unions. But decisive action against workers in the Vassena factory provoked a mass strike when police and armed forces crushed worker demonstrations, causing heavy casualties and signalling the end of government toleration of demands for improved wages and conditions. Strikers and workers attacked the Church as well as the state and a number of churches were burned and sacked in a wave of revolutionary violence. The *semana trágica* in Buenos Aires was followed the next year by repression in Patagonia, when demands of industrial and agricultural workers in the south of the country were met with violence by combined forces of army and local police, with even heavier casualties.

The Argentine elites felt threatened by class conflict, 'red peril', and 'alien subversion', and sought to recruit the forces of law and order to their side. Now the Catholic Church, previously despised or discounted, was seen as a vital ally, while Catholics, or some of them, saw the opportunity to make themselves useful to the state and better appreciated by the ruling classes. The liberal–conservative elite, having won the battle for secularization, could now treat the Church as 'safe'. There was much at stake. The Church too saw itself as threatened. The Russian Revolution raised the spectre of international communism and its entry into Argentina. In the University of Córdoba student riots spilled over into attacks on Catholic institutions and on a Jesuit church. In Buenos Aires violence against the Catholic Church was a prime feature of the events of January 1919. In Buenos Aires, Patagonia, and Córdoba the army was called in to quell disorder and from then onwards it remained a political factor in Argentina. The army and the Church came to be seen as the two indispensable defenders of state and society, the two vital institutions of the Argentine ruling class. Thus the Church placed itself within the liberal state, making common cause with governments against the enemies from without.[13]

In 1919–20, therefore, in answer to the social violence of the time, the Church lined up the faithful in opposition to 'revolutionary' movements and influences. On 23 April 1919 the Unión Popular Católica Argentina (UPCA), made up of three sections, socio-economic groups, women, and youth, was approved by the hierarchy. The first committees, called by the bishops to lead the movement, were drawn exclusively from members of the economic and social elites, families such as the Tornquist, Martínez Zuviría, and Martínez de Hoz.

Monsignor de Andrea had for some years been striving to unite the preaching of the Church with an 'authentic patriotism'. In 1910, in a patriotic sermon to commemorate the May Revolution, he had described the Church as 'the eternal ally of the *patria*' in the crusade against destabilizing doctrines. He regarded the great pillars of civilization as 'property, family, religion, patria', and 'the union between classes' as the essential support of the social structure.[14] In August 1919, in a series of sermons to introduce the *Gran Colecta Nacional* (Great National Collection), called by cynics *El gran calote nacional* (great national swindle), de Andrea preached on the theme of social unrest and declared: 'We seek nothing for religion, nothing for the material advantage of the Church . . . but simply to free progressive workers and their associations from the tyranny of the revolutionary societies'. The intention was to establish social and educational services and to coordinate all Catholic welfare organizations through a central office. Within a week the collection had raised more than 10 million pesos, principally from businesses. This funded the institutions belonging to the UPCA, such as cheap housing for workers, technical schools, and other welfare organizations, dedicated to 'one of the essential aims of the Union, the strengthening of a sense of nationality and in particular of *argentinismo*'.[15] *Patria*, nationality, *argentinismo*, tradition: these were now an inherent part of Catholic language, seeking reconciliation with liberalism and association with Argentina's ruling classes. But there was another Catholicism, also seeking to take religion out of the sacristy but on an exclusive route which would part company with the politicians of the day and look to Rome for its leadership and to scholasticism for its ideas. These Catholics refused all possibility of conciliation with liberalism and socialism, presenting an integral Catholicism as the sole possible truth; their policy was not to ally or submit but to conquer and lead from within the Church. Groups from the Catholic movement, therefore, headed in different directions and they did not always find a home in the Argentine political system.

There was a backlash to the *semana trágica*, as threatened interests came together in a comprehensive alliance. Conservative and Radical politicians, representatives of the big companies and commercial and financial interests, the higher military, with the support of prominent Catholic leaders, formed in 1919 a new organization, the Liga Patriótica Argentina to defend creole values, law and order, and the prevailing economic model. Monsignor Andrea was prominent among those Catholics who supported the League, prolonging the liberal–clerical alliance. There was a hard line against communism and other foreign influences. And in the violence unleashed against the Russian-Jewish barrios in the centre of Buenos Aires, youths from Catholic families were prominent among the activists and terrorists.

The death of Monsignor Espinoza, archbishop of Buenos Aires, in 1923 opened a debate on his successor. For the first time Rome refused the government's nomination of an archbishop, so provoking a constitutional crisis. These difficulties showed up basic divisions within the Catholic movement. On the one hand there were those who wished to collaborate and establish a consensus with the ruling political and economic groups, in particular the Radical government of Marcelo T. de Alvear (1922–28), in defence of the existing government system, prevailing economy, and public security. Thus Church and state could work together in harmony and the Catholic Church would be recognized as an essential part of modern liberal and capitalist Argentina, just as it had once been a necessary servant of the Bourbon state. The leading churchman in this tendency was Monsignor Andrea. But the strong reaction within the Catholic movement to his nomination as archbishop of Buenos Aires revealed the existence of other Catholic groups – laymen, priests, religious – who believed themselves marginalized from public life by the Radical government and who had different ideas for Catholic social action. These Catholics repudiated 'alliances' and 'laicism' and scorned liberal Catholics, whom they regarded as more dangerous than real liberals and socialists. Their position coincided with Rome's anxiety to halt the national tendencies of the Argentine Church. The Radical government reacted to the row over nomination by insisting on Andrea, then, when Rome too proved intransigent and rejected him, the government expelled the papal nuncio and opted for a weak compromise candidate.

Decades of division left the Argentine Church ill-prepared for trials to come.

Echoes from Andean America

The Chilean Church was a conservative Church, in politics as well as religion. Poverty was seen as an occasion for charity, alms-giving, and benevolence rather than as a social challenge. The Catholic elite of landowners and nitrate magnates were not unmindful of their duty and the early provision of welfare institutions – hospitals, asylums, sanatoriums – owed much to their initiative and funding. In the late nineteenth century the Church encouraged the formation of associations of Catholic workers, primarily to protect their members from rival ideologies and instruct them in the faith rather than to strike a blow for justice in the workplace.[16] A prototype of the conservative churchman, enclosed in traditional society, was Monsignor Joaquín Larraín Gandarillas (1822–97), who insisted that artisans, such as shoemakers and carpenters, should follow the trade of their fathers.

The birth of the labour movement in Chile and its expansion in the first years of the twentieth century in Santiago, Valparaiso, and the mining areas of the north was accompanied by an outbreak of strikes and an explosion of worker militancy. These were not developments favoured by the Church. In fact the Church was a target of bitter criticism from labour leaders and militant politicians for its close identification with the conservative forces in Chilean society and its direct opposition to any movement outside the Conservative Party. As for preaching the Gospel, Church leaders almost gave up the struggle, acknowledging their losses among the peasants and workers of central and northern Chile, for whom religion was unloved or unknown. But the Church itself tended to marginalize anyone who sought to bridge the gap between the Catholic faith and progressive politics. When, in 1901, a Catholic priest, Juan José Julio, was adopted as a candidate for the senate by the Democratic Party, he was deprived of his priestly faculties by the archbishop of Santiago and promptly became a popular hero, known as 'Pope Julio' and supported by radicals, socialists, and anarchists.[17]

The intransigence of Catholic conservatives in the face of the working-class movement caused a split among Catholics between those who turned away from demands for change and those who sought to make the Church a force for a new social order. The beginning of Christian Democracy in Chile in the years after 1901 was influenced largely by European writings and example, especially those from Italy. In Chile itself intellectual leadership was provided by Monsignor Rafael Edwards Salas (1878–1938), appointed bishop by Benedict XV in 1915, suspect to some in the hierarchy but known to many Chileans as the 'bishop of the workers', who from the beginning associated Christian Democracy with social justice. A more radical influence was Father Fernando Vives Solar (1871–1935), who specialized in the formation of Christian trade unions, including two for women, and the provision of courses of social studies; his activities earned him the hostility of the Conservative Party and two periods of exile, though a small group of bishops shared his views and pushed for Christian influence in the working-class movement. The presence of Christian Democracy within the Church accentuated the division between conservatives and progressives for many years to come.

In Peru the Church reacted to social change rather than anticipated it. A Congress of Interdiocesan Social Action, held in Cuzco in May 1921, brought together the south Andean dioceses of Cuzco, Puno, Arequipa, and Ayacucho in an effort to define maladies and policies. The promoters were the new bishop of Cuzco, Pedro Pablo Farfán, and the secular clergy of the diocese, moved by the developing social conscience of the Church, the need to react to socialist ideas, working-class movements, and more immediately the frequent uprisings in the southern Andes. Here was the heart of Peru's social problems, where exploitation was met with violence.

The congress declared its determination to seek to improve the moral condition of the region, especially in favour of Indians, workers, and women. To educate the Indians it proposed the creation of 'workshop schools' and it urged the publication of catechisms in Quechua and Aymara to continue their Christianization. Workers too needed help: the establishment of Círculos Católicos de Obreros was seen as essential, together with libraries and mutual aid societies. Alcoholism rather than poverty was the favoured target, and setting up anti-alcohol leagues for Indians and workers the preferred remedy. For the most part reform projects focused on education and social assistance, as in Argentina. Specific abuses against Indians and workers were not ignored, but social policies that were considered too radical, such as socialism and 'revolutionary feminism', were rejected, and warnings against the dangers of Protestantism and other foreign influences were given prominence. A young priest, Isaías Vargas, criticized the traditional system of exploitation in the Andes, especially the usurpation of community lands by the *gamonales* (rural bosses), and proposed the creation of '*sindicatos de indios*' to defend their rights against the landed elite, though under the protection of the government.

The Congress of 1921 showed the limits of social Catholicism. There was no lack of concern for the popular classes, but no policy beyond education and social assistance. The Church lagged behind the advances of secular research, and failed to offer alternative solutions to those of socialism and other movements of the time, usually hostile to religion. Many priests had middle-class perceptions and reacted strongly against radical analysis of social structure and social change. But the greatest limitation was the absence of Indians from these discussions, though whether they would have understood the prevailing themes is doubtful. As Bishop Farfán wrote in a pastoral defending the Indians in 1921, 'our Indians neither know that the bishop is concerned for them nor are even aware of this pastoral letter'.[18] The position of the Church towards the popular classes was therefore ambiguous. Some of the clergy came out in defence of Indians, though their failure to question social and agrarian structures weakened the force of their protests. The attitude of the Church remained paternalist. To criticize government was one thing; to question the social order was another. The Church fulfilled its perceived mission in drawing attention to specific injustices but did not depart from its traditionalist view of society; if a conservative regime showed favour to the Church it received the moral support of the Church.

To some extent the Church was compromised by its own interests. As a major landowner in the Andes it relied on Indian labour and to some extent was involved directly or indirectly in the prevailing system of exploitation. The Church rented land to the Indians and was a party to disputes over rent and property rights; in this role it often appeared no different to agrarian bosses. The rural priest in the Andes was traditionally depicted as an ignorant and uncultured person, hard on Indians and exigent for fees for masses and sacraments. He often drank too much and lived with a woman. All this, or some of it, may have been true, though there was another side. The loss of tithes meant that priests had to rely more on other sources of income, including rent from Church lands, and the unattractive nature of the position made for inferior recruitment. So the Andean clergy were of mixed vocation: they were pastors, exploiters, and victims.

The Church appeared to the Indian, therefore, in various guises. As a spokesman of the government, it would persuade rebels to lay down arms and obey the law; as an honest broker between the two, it would mediate and pacify; and finally as a protester against abuse of the Indians it might be their last line of defence. The Church as defender was exemplified in the action of Juan Ambrosio Huerta, first bishop of Puno, who in 1866 saw at first hand 'the tyrannical way in which the poor Indians were treated'. He condemned in particular the forced sale of goods to Indians by merchants, the collusion of local officials and army units in defence of these practices, and their brutality in putting down the inevitable and justifiable rebellion.[19] The Church as mediator could be seen in the example of a young *cura*, Fidel Olivas Escudero, who in 1885 faced a fierce anti-tax rebellion by the Indians of Huaraz in the central Andes. Olivas Escudero won the respect of both the Indians and the army when he mediated impartially between the two, saving some though not all lives. At the same time he condemned the rebellion and had little sympathy for its leaders, preaching peace not social change.[20] Finally, the Church acted to legitimize government and defend the established order. Whenever in the late nineteenth century the Church was reported to be active in the pacification of rebel Indians in the central and southern Andes, it meant that it was doing the government's work for it. This was its most frequent role. During the dictatorship of its favourite ruler, Leguía, it was virtually its only role.

The history of the modern Bolivian Church was undistinguished, and concern for the Indian rarely exceeded routine expressions of sympathy. Some clerics recognized their responsibilities but even these tended to plead rather than act. The Fourth Synod of La Paz (1883) admitted that 'in conscience we have to admit the terrible responsibility of the clergy, before God and before history, for the pitiful condition of the Indians, moral, social, and religious'.[21] But little was achieved to improve the status of the Bolivian Indians or to renew their evangelization. As for their social conditions, churchmen simply exhorted them to be patient. In 1891 Bishop

Baldivia urged artisans to place their trust in God when things became bad: 'Avoid idleness, source of poverty and vice; flee with horror from drunkenness which degrades the individual and ruins the family; take care to fulfil your Christian and civic duties; and respect and obey your superiors.'[22]

Catholic social action in Colombia, where the Church was part of a rigidly stratified society, was not calculated to be radical, though the Church had a traditional role in charitable work and its bishops were alert to competition from rival ideologies for influence over the working and rural classes. Religious orders and other Church organizations supported hospitals, orphanages, and various works of charity, most of them directed at the effects of poverty rather than its cause but supplying a service neglected by the state. The Jesuits went further and were active among urban workers, seeing the advantage of pre-empting their organizations. At the beginning of the twentieth-century *Círculos de Obreros*, mutual societies, and savings banks were designed to offer basic welfare provisions for the poor of society in the expectation of saving their members for the Church. While religion in Colombia flourished at a popular level, the official message was less sociable. The mentality of the hierarchy was essentially paternalist and defensive. In 1913, describing 'means of Catholic social action', they declared: 'These are essentially institutions of an economic type, designed to alleviate the economic condition of the working classes, that is to provide them with the best temporal welfare compatible with their Christian duties, demanding in exchange for these services moral standards and fulfilment of their Christian duties.'[23] A similar episcopal statement in 1916 made it clear that the purpose of social reform was moral improvement.

Raising Consciences in Mexico

In Mexico the Catholic social movement began in the 1890s. *Rerum Novarum* was published there in May 1891. At first it attracted little comment, and it was not until March 1895, when the journalist Trinidad Sánchez Santos publicized the document, that Catholic leaders began to respond and to demand action to improve labour conditions, raise wages, and create Catholic trade unions. All of the bishops most committed to social Catholicism – José Mora y del Río, Ramón Ibarra González, José Othón Núñez, and Francisco Orozco Jiménez – had studied at the Colegio Pío Latinoamericano in Rome and were graduates of the Gregorian University. Of the priests three were Jesuits, Bernardo Bergöend, Alfredo Méndez Medina, and Carlos María Heredia, and one, José Castillo y Piña, studied at the Gregorian University. Méndez Medina had the most systematic training in religious sociology, having studied in Burgos, Louvain, and Paris, as well as visiting England, Holland, and Germany. But normally Mexican Catholics produced activists rather than theoreticians. *La cuestión social en México* (1913) by Father Méndez Medina was virtually the only serious and scholarly work on the Catholic side comparable to the writings of the secularists, whose tide seemed to be rising again with the resurgence of the anti-clerical Mexican Liberal Party. Catholic journalism, on the other hand, was effective and realistic. It took a critical view of the prosperity and progress claimed by the Porfiriato, especially from 1906; it drew attention to the poverty and hunger of the popular sectors, to the lag of wages behind prices, to the lack of opportunities for the middle classes, with 'railways, industries and trade in foreign hands'.[24]

In 1903 the first Mexican Catholic Congress met in Puebla. The delegates recommended the creation of worker organizations with religious and technical training programmes. A young Jalisco lawyer, Miguel Palomar y Vizcarra, who had reconverted to Catholicism after a liberal interlude, proposed the establishment of credit cooperatives and subsequently experimented with these on a regional basis. The assembly resolved that landowners should provide schools, medical and other social services for rural labourers. At a second Catholic Congress, in Morelia in 1904, demands were made for primary education for the working class, for technical schools, worker, employer, and craft guild associations, and an end to oppressive labour contracts. A third congress at Guadalajara in 1906 reaffirmed previous proposals and in addition demanded schools for workers' children, and just wages for labourers, to be paid in cash not company scrip. A fourth congress in Oaxaca in 1909 called attention to Indian conditions. These congresses were not revolutionary gatherings; they were essentially religious but with a new social awareness. Like *Rerum Novarum*, Mexican Catholic thought rejected the class struggle and deplored revolutionary change, but it did advocate state intervention to protect the most vulnerable in society. The reforms proposed for the industrial sector were fairly comprehensive. But did the Church have a policy on the all-important agrarian problem?

Three Agricultural Congresses were held, though they concentrated on practical matters, not structures, and they were attended by *hacendados* as well as rural workers. Their object was to find specific ways of improving the moral and material conditions of rural labourers. The discussion included wages but not as yet land redistribution. Even Father Méndez Medina, who sought to establish Catholic trade unions 'to defend salaries and working conditions, procure jobs, and speak for the working class', was paternalist on agrarian problems, advocating only that 'the industrious and worthy peasant be assured as far as possible the possession or most secure

use of sufficient land to maintain his family decently'.[25] And the Liga Social
Agraria formed in 1913 with the blessing of Archbishop Mora y del Río
was designed not as an instrument of agrarian reform but for the improvement and growth of agriculture, and it was dominated by landowners,
large and small. Nevertheless, this pointed the way to a Church version
of agrarian reform, based on reducing haciendas in favour of smaller
properties.

By 1910, therefore, the Catholic social movement had begun to produce
specific results, the most significant being the formation of the Círculos de
Obreros Católicos. By 1911, with more than 43 branches and a total
membership of 12,332, the movement was strengthened by the establishment of the Confederation of Catholic Workers, its first president Salvador
Moreno Arriaga and his ecclesiastical assistant Father José María Troncoso.
The Confederation's second national convention in January 1913 was
attended by delegates from 50 branches representing 15,000 members, and
presented a policy of mutual insurance, workers' schools, and regular
conferences. But it was also decided to organize an independent Catholic
labour movement. The first Mexican trade union was founded in the same
year by Father Méndez Medina in Mexico City. The Church was now ready
to challenge its rivals for influence among workers and by the early 1920s
the Confederación Nacional Católica del Trabajo (CNCT) competed with
the Confederación Regional de Obreros Mexicanos (CROM), especially
among rural workers.

The onset of the Mexican Revolution, a violent shift of power inaugurating basic social and agrarian change, also changed the situation for the
Church. Catholics were hopeful but wary of the rising politician Francisco
Madero; some suspected that his credentials were too liberal, others that he
was not a social reformer. In the circumstances it seemed logical to form a
Catholic political party. With the blessing of the archbishop and on the
model of the German Centre Party, the Partido Católico Nacional was
formed in May 1911, not to participate in the old regime nor to give
unconditional support to Madero, but to be in a position to support the
Church in the new democratic conditions, and in particular to promote
Catholic social reform in the interests of the rural and industrial poor. In
1911–13 the party gave a good account of itself, gaining seats for twenty-
nine federal deputies, four senators, and governors of four states. In Jalisco
it was responsible for significant social and labour legislation. The hierarchy congratulated the party on its early successes.

The final years of the Porfiriato and the brief regime of Madero were a
time of renaissance for Mexican Catholicism, when it regained its strength,
confidence, and purpose. Then, suddenly, disaster came and from 1913
the Church endured a great persecution far beyond anything it had

experienced under liberalism and totally unpredictable in its process and results. How can we explain this strange reversal? In the first place the very success of the Church was its undoing. It had not only begun to reform itself but had actually regained some political space and seemed poised to make even further gains. Meanwhile the state too had been growing more powerful; in the years after 1910 the revolutionaries inherited the authoritarian and secular state of the Porfiriato and began to eliminate its rivals. The revolutionary state came into collision not with an abject Church but with a reformed and militant Church, which had its own policy for labour organization and agrarian reform, and offered in effect an alternative to the Mexican Revolution, one inspired by German social Catholicism, the teaching of Leo XIII, and its own historic traditions.[26] This precursor of Christian democracy, attractive to many Mexicans, was a challenge which an all-absorbing state could not tolerate. Moreover, the revolutionaries were not the same as liberals. They were intolerant, absolutist, and determined to destroy the Church and obliterate religion. They saw their chance and seized it.

The fall of Madero brought a struggle for power between two extremes, Victoriano Huerta leading the old military and Venustiano Carranza the revolutionaries. The Church was caught in a trap. Its traditional reputation and new popular appeal made it an object of attack by Carranza and the Constitutionalists. Their onslaught on Catholic priests and property drove Catholics closer to Huerta, or so it was alleged by the *carrancistas* and Francisco Villa, though not by Emiliano Zapata, who had no problem with the Church.[27] The Church was then accused of supporting the counter-revolution. As the revolution spread in the course of 1913–14, bishops, priests, and nuns were jailed or exiled – often simply for the ransom money they generated – church property was seized, churches sacked, confessionals burned and confession prohibited, as were fasting and abstinence. Catholics were attacked by local caudillos as enemies of the revolution, and the Partido Católico Nacional virtually ceased to exist.

The Church was therefore the victim of its own success, of revolutionary ideology, and of the conjuncture of 1913–14. From then on it was the enemy of the Revolution, and the Revolution was its tormentor. In the course of prolonged religious conflict there were a number of peaks, and the first was the Constitution of 1917, a progressive document on land and labour but ominous for the Church. The constitution repeated earlier reform laws such as the prohibition of religious vows and of Church ownership of real estate. But it went further and the tone was set in the accompanying debate. Politicians in congress used defamatory language, describing priests as 'vermin', 'foul and treacherous vampires', and 'insatiable vultures', among other things. The constitution deprived the Church of legal status, banned public worship outside church buildings, and gave the state the right to decide how many churches and how many priests there should be. The clergy were denied the right to vote and the religious press was forbidden to comment on public affairs. All primary education had to be secular, and no religious organization or minister could establish or direct a primary school. The Mexican bishops protested. The government was adamant. It was a state of war. On 11 April 1920 a multitude of Catholics, headed by the bishop of León, went in procession to the hill of El Cubilete, the geographic centre of Mexico, to inaugurate a new statue to Christ the King. The statue was blown up within a few years, but a great cry was bequeathed to the Catholic resistance: *Viva Cristo Rey*.

The response of the Church, a body of 33 bishops, 4,000 priests, and an indeterminate mass of the faithful, was far from united.[28] The most advanced position was taken by young activists, often inspired by Jesuits and grouped in the Asociación Católica de la Juventud Mexicana (ACJM), who concentrated first on spiritual formation, then on Catholicizing society, and in the final stage on political or even armed action. This tendency was anti-revolutionary and to some extent anti-democratic. The middle ground was occupied by the Mexican bishops, united in opposition to the Revolution but divided into intransigents and moderates, the latter looking for an accommodation with the Revolution and hoping for peace from Carranza and later from President Alvaro Obregón. The response of Rome was perhaps least 'Catholic' of all. The Vatican sought to reduce tension and reach an understanding with Obregón, to appoint non-political bishops, to encourage an exclusively spiritual mission, and thereby perhaps abandon Mexican social and political Catholicism. But the Revolution did not respond, and in turn the ACJM and other militant organizations intensified their opposition and denounced the Mexican government as the enemy of the Church. They seemed to have proved their point when, on 1 December 1924, Plutarco Elías Calles succeeded to the presidency.

A ruthless operator from Sonora, Calles was modern Mexico's strongman, archetype of the northern anti-clerical proponent of a new nationalism, a monolithic state and a perpetual Revolution in which there would be no alternative allegiance, least of all to the Church; in fact he was determined to 'defanaticize the masses', and to exterminate religion in the interests of state power and national progress. His government inaugurated a new purge of religion, and even an abortive attempt, with the connivance of two reprobate priests, to contrive a schism and a national Church.[29] These initiatives alerted Catholic activists such as Palomar y Vizcarra and in March 1925 brought them together from various groups to form the Liga Nacional para la Defensa de las Libertades Religiosas (National League for the Defence of Religious Liberty), to win religious freedom by means which would be 'constitutional' and also 'those required by the common good'. This soon became a political movement and then an underground organization. For in the course of 1925–26 the regime deliberately escalated the conflict. In October the state of Tabasco ended Catholic worship; Chiapas, Hidalgo, Jalisco, and Colima intensified anti-religious measures. In February the government started to close churches in the capital to the accompaniment of street protests. Persecution was not uniform, harsh in some states, milder in others, and Catholic responses varied from armed resistance to passive defiance.[30] Events culminated in the 'Calles law' of July 1926 specifying strict application on a national scale of the laws on religion with severe penalties for infringements.

For Catholic militants the Calles law was the breaking point. The bishops too saw it as a crisis, for the decree requiring compulsory registration of the clergy would take appointments out of the hands of bishops and give to the government the right to appoint and dismiss priests, while the closure of Church schools threatened to oust the Church completely from education. With the approval of the Vatican, the Mexican bishops ended all public worship and withdrew the clergy from the churches, convinced that this was 'the only way' left to them in face of the laws against religion.[31] The order was dated 31 July 1926 and on Sunday 1 August no priest celebrated mass in the parish churches of Mexico. Calles was unimpressed: calling it 'the struggle of darkness against light', he determined to fight on.

There was still another option open to League militants: insurrection. After 1 August calls for action became insistent, especially when peaceful dissenters were struck down. Anacleto González Flores, a hero of peaceful resistance, was assassinated in Guadalajara. In some states local Catholics, suffering perhaps from a specific application of the Calles law and shocked by the suspension of services, moved beyond prayers and penance into armed action. Late in September the League decided to lead the incipient rebellion, and in November in response to the argument that tyranny justified rebellion the bishops gave their informal approval. The rebellion, which came to be called the *Cristiada* and its participants the *Cristeros*, was activated on 1 January 1927 with risings in various parts of the country.[32] 'Better to die than deny Christ the King.' It managed to take root in Jalisco, Guanajuato, Michoacán, Querétaro, and Colima, and in the course of the year it became an effective resistance movement, led first by General Enrique Gorostieta and then by General Jesús Degollado Guizar, and reaching a strength of 25,000 regimental troops in 1928 with a further 25,000 operating in bands of various size. By May 1929 there were 50,000 *Cristeros* under arms.[33] Michoacán alone supported 8,000 rebels.[34]

The rebellion was a severe test for Catholic principles. League support and initial episcopal acquiescence were said to be based on traditional doctrine and neo-Thomist ideas: there exists a right to resist tyranny, if all other ways have failed and there is a chance of success. These are not necessarily valid inferences from scholastic philosophy and most of the bishops had misgivings and remained aloof from the movement. Some denied that the *Cristeros* had a right to rebel, while the few who supported them, three in all, were reprimanded by Rome. In November 1927 an unsuccessful bomb attack on the former President Obregón in Chapultepec led to a round-up of the usual suspects. But these included an underground Jesuit priest, Miguel Agustín Pro, who was not implicated in the action. Father Pro was shot without trial on 23 November, one of the hundred or so martyrs of the Mexican Revolution. Obregón, the only candidate, was duly re-elected president but did not take office, for in July 1928 he was shot by a Catholic fanatic in the restaurant La Bombilla. Many Catholics defended the action of José de León Toral in killing Obregón, because they believed that it was legitimate to kill a tyrant who shot his way to power and defied the revolutionary principle of no re-election.

Martyr of the Mexican Revolution

The leaders of the Church in Mexico were divided, hesitant and then hostile to armed resistance; the mass of Catholics also differed in their responses. Wealthy Catholics trimmed their ideas to their interests and were ready to collaborate with the regime. Even in the countryside where Catholic and peasant resistance combined to form an effective front against Calles, peasants who benefited from the dubious land policy of the Revolution were forced to join the government side and fight against their fellow Catholics. Many priests also abandoned the militant cause, leaving their rural parishes for safer ground in the cities, encouraged to move by the government and even by their own bishops.[35] If they stayed they kept a low profile, warning their people against indiscretion in case they were betrayed.[36] One person stood out, embodying the whole religious cause and uniting apparently all the virtues of Mexican Catholicism: orthodoxy, tradition, perseverance, and resistance.

Miguel Agustín Pro Juárez was born on 13 January 1891 into the large Catholic family of a mining engineer in Guadalupe, Zacatecas. He joined the Jesuit order in 1911, and soon had a foretaste of the life ahead when the religious policy of the Revolution forced the novitiate to relocate to California in 1914. There he spent a year before continuing his studies in Spain in 1915–19, followed by a teaching period in Nicaragua in 1919–22. Meanwhile the Mexican Constitution of 1917 with its strongly anti-clerical laws had outlawed religious orders and Pro had to continue his theological studies with French Jesuits in Belgium. And so he was ordained in exile in

August 1925, in poor health and far from his family. After the ceremony, he recorded, 'I went to my room, laid out all the photographs of my family on the table, and then blessed them from the bottom of my heart.' His first ministry was among the miners of Charleroi, a familiar environment for a native of Zacatecas and a reminder of the life he had seen as a youth. It was a tough assignment and a good test of his equanimity and sense of humour. Within a year he returned to Mexico, stopping at Lourdes on the way, and landed at Veracruz on 8 July 1926. He was ready for the next test, his mind and character formed by the long years of Jesuit training and familiarity with the Spiritual Exercises of St Ignatius.

Father Pro entered a country difficult for Catholics and dangerous for priests.[37] Yet he began his ministry in Mexico City, moving around openly, sometimes cycling in its streets and looking out for mad motorists rather than secret police, performing normal parish work for large numbers of people: mass, the sacraments, sick calls, extreme unction, and taking his religious message to everyone who came his way – workers, lorry drivers, professional people, prostitutes, students – and, more riskily, giving lectures to angry young men of the League. Yet it was a solitary vocation, as he admitted: 'Priests are no longer ready to court danger, they have retreated out of fear or out of obedience.' Soon he himself was ordered to go into hiding by his Jesuit superiors, who feared for his life. He was aware of the risks and ready to accept them. He knew fear but mastered it. He argued that he could work with tactical discretion, 'between excessive prudence and audacity'. 'I know I can be useful to a large number of persons, both priests and lay people, if I remain among them these days, when they have so much need of help from the Church.' So he was allowed back on the streets, urged to act with prudence but always conscious of much to do. People were dying without the sacraments, and many priests were frightened: 'not all are masters of their fear.' Back in the fray he lived an underground life, treating his disguise – dark suit, cardigan, soft collar and tie – as a joke, but as he moved between safe houses he saw danger around him and became open to the challenge to die like Christ. He was watched and a warrant was issued for his arrest as 'a religious propagandist', but the police did not realize who he was. He joked in one of his reports to his superiors that they mistook Pro for Pbro; and he had to explain that it was his surname, not the abbreviation for a priest. He was released, but kept under surveillance. His detached sense of humour never left him, nor the foreboding: 'The revolution is worsening. The perils will be terrible especially in Mexico City. The first to be arrested will be those who have had a hand in religious matters, and I have had mine up to the elbow.'

The reckoning came in November 1927. The attempted assassination of Obregón gave the security authorities the pretext to arrest Father Pro, and his brothers Humberto and Roberto, on grounds that the attackers' car could be traced to their family, a false charge never put to the test; there was to be no process, no trial, no judge, simply a peremptory order by Calles on 13 November to shoot them. They were brought to the cells in the basement of the Inspección de Policía; the sights and sounds of the prison and the movement of troops alerted them to their fate On 23 November towards 10.30 in the morning Father Pro was taken from his cell to the execution yard watched by hard-faced military and officials, the guardians of the Revolution. Aged 36, he met his death with cool courage; no one could doubt his absolute faith in a life to come. He forgave his enemies, knelt briefly in prayer with crucifix and rosary in his hands, walked to the wall, refused a blindfold, stretched his arms in the form of a cross, gave a brief nod to the execution squad, and as they took aim uttered his last words, '*Viva Cristo Rey!*' A soldier approached his prostrate body, the arms still outstretched, to give a finishing shot. The following day the cortège drew masses of mourners as it processed along the Paseo de la Reforma, and thousands crowded round and shouted '*Viva Cristo Rey*', in what has been called 'something like a spontaneous canonization'.[38] Father Pro, priest and martyr, was beatified by Pope John Paul II on 25 September 1988.

The execution of Father Pro was deliberately recorded by official photographers, but as Graham Greene wrote, 'the photographs had an effect which Calles had not foreseen'. The *Cristeros* were encouraged, and Catholic Mexico was inspired, even though the death of Father Pro had no immediate impact on the course of the war.

Warriors for Christ

The *Cristero* war was a peasant insurrection but it was also proof that many Mexican Catholics were ready to lay down their lives for their faith. Strengthened by their social coherence and geographical focus, the *Cristeros* were superior to the Federal army in purely military terms and their morale was high. They endured the relentless terrorism unleashed on them by the Federal forces and in a series of big battles and smaller guerrilla actions they gave a good account of themselves and could even seize the tactical and strategic initiative. But *Cristero* resources were finite and if they could not win quickly they would not win at all. Nor could the Federals win a final victory; but they could still prevail, if only because they represented the power of the state, with superior resources and the material backing of the United States. Some of the *Cristero* groups were led by priests who acted as fighters as well as chaplains and had no doubt that armed resistance was justified. As for the *Cristeros* themselves, they were mostly young men, raised in family piety, who prayed and received the sacraments, and many were married according to canon though not civil law; they included workers as well as peasants, and women's brigades provided logistical services.[39] The *Cristeros* sincerely believed that the cause of Christ the King and the Virgin of Guadalupe was inherently just, legitimized by its nature and its aims. Rome did not share these views, convinced as it was that armed force would not succeed and would compromise the Church in future. At the end of 1927 it ordered the Mexican bishops to distance themselves from the rebellion and work for a negotiated settlement. Through the mediation of the United States the bishops reached a compromise with the Revolution in January 1929 and formally withdrew the Church from the conflict. Their action has been described as cynical and opportunist, as perhaps it was, but they were faced with a real dilemma: they had a wider Church to govern, a future to think of, and no bishop in the twentieth century, whatever his private thoughts, would openly lead a war of religion.

But the settlement was worthless to the Church. As the rebels demobilized, the government pressed harder. Catholics gained a minimal freedom to practise their religion but no other rights, and the anti-Catholic religious legislation remained in place unchanged in the slightest degree. The government presented this as the surrender of the Church, and so it was. The Revolution had apparently crushed Catholicism and driven it back inside the churches, and there it stayed, throughout the 1930s and beyond, preserved by the sheer religiosity of the Mexican people, while the government, dedicated to perpetual revolution, repeated its anti-clerical clichés and reinforced its anti-religious ideology. Religious freedom was theoretical, diminished by the numerous petty laws of various state governments. Only in enclaves such as San Luis Potosí, where General Saturnino Cedilla was sympathetic, did Catholics and their priests find any protection.[40] And in Oaxaca Catholics endured the worst, followed the advice of Rome, and fought back, not with guns but in a 'long patient struggle of civic action and a renewed religious life.'[41]

The *Cristeros* were dismayed, but they laid down their arms and accepted the amnesty for what it was worth. 'It was a tragic thing,' recalled Palomar y Vizcarra, 'completely bewildering to us, the greatest proof Mexican Catholics have given to the Holy See of their firm adherence to the Vicar of Christ, in spite of this terrible blow to their hopes.'[42] This was the voice of the political leadership. In the countryside of Michoacán, Guanajuato, Jalisco, and other areas, where the *Cristeros* were a peasant movement defending their land against the agrarian policy of the Revolution as well as a Catholic resistance, the war cost the *Cristeros* 40,000 dead against 60,000 Federals. The defenceless rebels were massacred at the end of the war, when there was a systematic manhunt and killing of all the *Cristero* leaders and many of their followers: 5,000 in all between 1929 and 1935.[43] The *Cristeros* were never condemned by the Church and in time they came to occupy an honourable place in Catholic history. But if these events had any message it was to draw for Catholics a distinction between reformism and revolution, and to demonstrate that the Church could not sanction violent ways to power.

From 1940, following the strongly socialist and anti-religious government of Lázaro Cárdenas (1934–40), conditions improved for the Church. The new president, Manuel Avila Camacho, declared himself a 'believer' and his administration reverted to a form of Church–state relations last seen in the Porfiriato. The anti-clerical laws stood but in practice their application was either discontinued or relaxed, and a more tolerant ideology prevailed. The Church took advantage of the new mood to restore papal representation in Mexico, strengthen its diocesan and parish organization, increase the number of priests and seminarists, and quietly preach the faith to the Mexican people. Thus they could reply to their detractors, 'The Church lives!' In 1942 the monument to Christ the King was rebuilt, and in October 1945, while Calles lay dying in a clinic in Mexico City, a great multitude celebrated the fiftieth anniversary of the coronation of Our Lady of Guadalupe.

The Church in 1930: Inheritance and Legacy

The years 1870–1930 were decisive for the Church in Latin America, the time when it asserted its independence of the state, established real as distinct from nominal union with Rome, and undertook its own modernization; the time indeed when it became the 'institutionalized' and 'triumphalist' Church rejected by many contemporaries and reproached by later Catholics. But the Church, like other institutions, has to be judged in the context of the age and according to its own nature and purpose. Definitions of these vary. Bishop Bossuet defined the Church as Christ extended in time and space. In their schools and parishes Latin Americans learnt that the Church was the union of all the faithful under one head. To agnostics, the Church appeared a collection of myths, privileges, and resources, which – once it had been purged of power – might still serve a useful function in society. But how can the historian establish external norms to judge the progress of the Church, assess its mission, appraise its influence? Church attendance can be measured, and changes in organization and social action described, but such indicators provide only an approximation.

Judged by these standards, the Church in Latin America suffered some decline in the years around 1900. During an audience of Latin American pilgrims with Pope Pius X in 1908 reference was made to the '60 million Catholics' of Latin America. But was this a reality? The number of priests had diminished in the course of the nineteenth century, from some 20,000 diocesan priests in 1825 to 10–12,000 at the end of the century, when the number of Catholics per priest was estimated at 4,000.[44] The number of practising Catholics had also declined, first among the elite then among the urban working class, as they drifted into secularism or indifference. Rural Catholicism was more tenacious, though perhaps less assiduously served by the Church, which was thin on the ground outside the towns. And many Latin Americans were not only indifferent to religion but positively hated it and would try to destroy it, an unnerving experience for an institution which had long been protected from its enemies. Traditional Catholics blamed such adversity on the withdrawal of state support and did not always seize the opportunities which this presented for religion, unsure whether they were victors or victims of the secular state. The Church had not yet generated the inner resources to appeal to conscience rather than power and to compete with other philosophies in a pluralist society. Catholicism may have been forced to accept religious toleration as a lesser evil or an opportunist tactic, but it did not condone it as a doctrine or a principle.

Yet the Church in Latin America had adjusted to change. At the beginning of the nineteenth century it was a colonial Church, dependent on a metropolis: Spain or Portugal. A century later it was truly independent, compatible with the nation state yet part of the universal Church. It still fulfilled the basic mission of the Church, to preach the Gospel, to bring people into communion with God, and to preserve intact Christian doctrine and religious observance for transmission to future generations. But it had to accept new rules of engagement with the world. The compromising alliance of the altar and the throne, of Church and state, was gone for ever, thanks less to Catholics than to liberals, but in any case leaving the Church free to face the challenges to come. This new independence had a number of implications. It enabled the Church to speak more clearly to the poor and oppressed. It sharpened the division between religionists and secularists, as Catholics had to choose to be Catholics and the Church to compete with other beliefs. At the same time the Church expanded materially, increasing its resources and strengthening its institutions. These institutions, or 'structures' as they came to be called, were a cause of scandal to later theologians, who condemned them as impediments to true religion, but who forgot too readily perhaps that the Church was human as well as divine and needed institutions as society itself did. By 1930 the institutions were in place, the bishops were in their dioceses, the priests at the altars, the faithful in the pews. But there were many outside the Church who would only return to die.

CHAPTER 9

The Church and the Dictators

Brazil: Hard-line Model

THE WORLD DEPRESSION of 1930 dealt a shattering blow to Latin America: it caused a dramatic drop in production and exports, led to mass unemployment, and provoked extreme nationalist reactions in most parts of the subcontinent. In Brazil the rise to power of Getulio Vargas was a turning point, initiating a period of authoritarian government and populist policies and bringing an end to the dominance of the traditional oligarchy. The Church was co-opted into what was sometimes called a 'moral concordat', each side gaining something from the support of the other. As a reward for backing the corporatist policies of Vargas and, from 1937 to 1945, his *Estado Nôvo*, the Church received support for its schools, universities, marriage laws, and finances.[1]

The Brazilian Church was not immobile and from the 1960s, responding to the mood of the time, a number of bishops began to encourage reform and to challenge the certainties of the past. The leader of the reformers was Hélder Câmara, archbishop of Olinda and Recife, who had himself travelled a new route since his days as a young priest.[2] In 1930 he had joined Brazilian Integralist Action, a movement standing for 'God, Country and Family', influential in the *Estado Nôvo* and carrying a social as well as political message and with it a hint of fascism. His spiritual journey took him to a different destination and by the 1960s he was a known reformist in the Church and active in Vatican II. Other voices were also raised. Acción Católica became more radical and a Catholic Left emerged, prominent in the Church if not in national politics. Movements such as Juventud Universitaria Católica (JUC) and Juventud Obrera Católica (JOC) increased the social profile of the Church, while base communities (grassroots Christian groups) strengthened parish organization and became an image of Brazilian religion. Catholic reformism in Brazil reflected a general impulse in the Church towards renewal, leading to Vatican II and the Medellín conference of 1968. The Brazilian Church was itself an example to Latin American Catholics and subsequently led the way in campaigning for the poor as well as the oppressed, through its priests and lay activists, encouraged by the progressive tendency in the Brazilian Episcopal Conference (CNBB), created in 1952; this was one of the first such conferences, promoting 'the preferential option for the poor', a precept officially adopted by the Latin American bishops at Puebla in 1979. The two Catholic innovations of these years, liberation theology and base communities, were welcomed and nurtured by the Brazilian Church.

These radical pressures in the Church did not go unchallenged. Traditional Catholicism held its ground. When the military overthrew the populist President João Goulart in 1964, alleging he was making Brazil communist, conservative bishops thanked them for saving Brazil from communism, and for five years, turning their eyes from accusations of state-sponsored torture, the bishops supported the regime of the generals, as did right-wing Catholic groups such as Tradition, Family, and Property, which gave the regime a predictable welcome. The bishops sought to assuage their conscience and justify the moral compromise by undertaking in a secret Bipartite Commission (1970–74) to collaborate with the generals in exchange for concessions on poverty and human rights. Both sides shared a Catholic faith, though with different perceptions. What could be expected from concordats concocted in secrecy? Perhaps something better than inaction. According to its recent historian, the Commission 'reduced tension, allowing Church and state to coexist', and achieved specific benefits in an otherwise intractable conflict between social justice and subversion. 'The Bipartite worked to tone down and explain alleged Catholic subversion, maintain Church influence, *and* to denounce human rights violations'.[3]

This was the beginning of the conservative line in the CNBB in spite of the persistence of a few radical bishops. Hélder Câmara was now posted away from Rio to the archdiocese of Olinda and Recife.[4] There he headed the bishops of the north-east who took a more critical stand. As a spokesman for the poor and oppressed Hélder Câmara became an international figure and was awarded the Nobel Peace Prize in 1974. Bishops of the north-east had already made their position clear in 1966 when they backed workers' rights and agrarian reform in a document which enraged the military; and Hélder Câmara became a target of conservatives such as the sociologist Gilberto Freyre. The Brazilian military was now impervious to criticism; its policy of modernization through forced capital accumulation, imposed by political repression, alienated not only the left but also moderate opinion including many in the Church hierarchy.[5]

On 13 December 1968 the government closed congress, and in the notorious Institutional Act 5 removed habeas corpus and other civil liberties, gagged the press, and arrested members of the opposition, politicians, students, and clergy. It was the decisive moment of the *linha dura*, and violence followed. Guerrillas mobilized, and the security forces hit back hard, infamously using torture to obtain information The regime of General Emilio Garrastazú Médici (1969–74), one of the most oppressive in modern Brazilian history, targeted Catholic bishops, priests, and youth movements, expelling a number of foreign clergy, including the Belgian priest Joseph Comblin, teacher, writer, and liberationist. Any Catholic associated with the radical left was at risk. None of this silenced the voices of criticism from the Church, but it had the effect of dividing Catholics into supporters and critics, widening the gulf between conservatives and radicals among clergy and laity. At the peak of the repression, in 1969–73, the military's 'dirty war' resulted in 184 deaths and 138 disappearances. The international media in these years presented Brazil as a country of football, bossa nova, and carnival. Historians too, or some of them, treated the military lightly, regarding them as no more than exhibits in political science. The reality for many Brazilians was a world of trial and tribulation. As the course of repression continued in the 1970s, scores of priests, nuns, bishops, and Catholic activists were targeted by the security forces and right-wing terrorists. Under successive military regimes thousands of opponents were exiled and deprived of civil rights, hundreds of university students expelled. A Church count between 1968 and 1978 'documented more than a hundred arrests of priests, seven deaths, and numerous cases of torture, expulsion of foreigners, invasion of buildings, threats, indictments, abductions. Thirty bishops were victims of the repression.'[6] By the end of dictatorship in 1985 six clergy had been killed and thousands harassed. In response the bishops began to speak out more clearly, to criticize the repression and to defend human rights.

Torture proved to be one of the most contentious issues between Church and state. The army was officially against torture. When used against its political enemies, however, 'it simply looked the other way'. Alexandre Vannucchi Leme, a young student of the University of São Paulo, was tortured to death in March 1973, an atrocity which brought out students and Catholic priests in protest. The murder of Leme prompted the Church to raise its sights in the battle for justice and to become a rallying point in defence of human rights. Archbishop Arns offered a memorable requiem mass and from that point took the lead in criticizing the government.[7]

These were dark days for Brazil, yet light shone in the Church. Vatican II showed a new way for religion and the Medellín Conference of 1968 inspired Latin American Catholics with the hope of better times. Meanwhile the very violence of the repression forced the Brazilian Church in particular to take a firmer stand against the rule of the generals. Between 1968 and 1971 the character of the hierarchy changed as older bishops were replaced by new and a progressive tendency prevailed. The episcopal conference ceased to represent conservative interests and became a voice of opposition and a defender of victims of torture and oppression. Dom Hélder Câmara, a pioneer protester, had been edged out after 1970 by threats and harassment. The leadership then passed to others, bishops who were prominent in the Bipartisan Commission and the CNBB: Paulo Evarista Arns, Aloísio Lorscheider, Ivo Lorscheiter, Luciano Mendes de Almeida, and others. Arns in São Paulo and Lorscheider as president of the CNBB made this a Church for the times, and the archdiocese of São Paulo became a leader in the ecumenical resistance to oppression and abuse of human rights. Arns, promoted to Cardinal in 1973, from a German immigrant family, was a Franciscan theologian and professor, who took the cause of justice and peace to a new level. He founded the São Paulo office of the Commission of Peace and Justice which became his agency for investigating cases of torture and disappearances, and established solidarity with Protestants and Jews in defence of human rights. Social justice too was his concern, operating through a new Commission of Pastoral Care for the Marginalized and Street Children. In 1985, with the collaboration of Jaime Wright, a Presbyterian minister, he sponsored the report *Brasil: Nunca Mais* (Brazil: Never Again) publishing the evidence of torture and other violations of human rights.[8]

The Church also took a stand in the north-east, where Indian rights were ignored and land was appropriated by powerful estate owners and influential land companies, protected by the government under the pretext of 'development'. In May 1973 the bishops of the north-east published a radical document, *I Have Heard the Cry of My People*, which exposed the ills of the region, the poverty, malnutrition, absence of education, and oppression masquerading as development. The Church questioned the whole development policy of the government in Amazonia, which usually meant giving rights and protection to landowners and companies at the expense of natives and immigrant settlers. The clergy paid a price for commitment: violent harassment and intimidation of bishops, priests, and activists, and in 1976 the murder of two concerned priests, Rodolfo Lunkenbein and João Bosco Penido Burnier.

Justice was restored to the agenda of the CNBB by Aloísio Lorscheider, secretary general in 1968 and president in 1971, who revived the determination of Hélder Câmara's regime. Archbishop of Fortaleza in 1973, cardinal in 1976 and president of CELAM (Consejo Episcopal Latinoamericano) in 1978, Lorscheider led the north-eastern bloc and the whole of the Brazilian Church towards progressive policies and maintenance of unity in the face of government violence. The same path was followed by Ivo Lorscheiter, secretary general and subsequently president of CELAM in 1979. The CNBB condemned the rule of terror and the death squads, provoking attacks on its own offices. In November 1976 it published the *Pastoral Message to the People of God*, insisting that the national security state was totalitarian, that the state was not the nation, and that human rights were not granted by the state. The message was reinforced by a further pastoral letter in March 1977, *The Obligations of a Christian in the Political Order*, equally anathema to the government, whose death squads and paramilitary groups continued to wreak violence on the Church and to kidnap university students and seminarians. During preparations for the Puebla conference Cardinal Arns requested the Ecumenical Centre of Documentation and Information to prepare a paper on the persecution of the Church in Brazil. The result showed that between 1968 and 1978, 122 members of the Church were imprisoned, including nine bishops, 84 priests, 13 seminarians, and six religious women.[9]

The pace of persecution abated in 1978–85, when the regime, accepting that state violence had reached the limit of effectiveness without silencing the opposition, inched its way towards democratization, with freedom for political parties and unions, and revocation of the hated Institutional Act. Seeking legitimization from the Church, it received a cautious response, one which did not tie the Church's hands or prevent it from expressing support for the strikes of 1978–80 organized by the union leader Lula da Silva. Brazil returned to civilian rule in 1985 after twenty-one years of military dictatorship.

Military rule and state terrorism were moral issues for the Church. What were the rights of resistance? How far was defence justified? Hélder Câmara raised the question of violent action. He insisted that Christians were on the side of non-violence, an option rooted in the Gospel: belief in a higher power than the power of war; the power of truth, justice, and love, these were the guidelines. But he went on to say,

> With respect to those who, in conscience, feel obliged to opt for violence, not the easy violence of the guerrillas of the living room, but the violence of those who have proved their sincerity by the sacrifice of their lives, it seems to me that the memory of Camilo Torres or of Che Guevara merits as much respect as that of the Reverend Martin Luther King.[10]

This uncharacteristic lapse into demagogy contrasted with the more nuanced arguments on violence developed by Archbishop Romero.[11]

Pragmatism rather than populism was the normal style of Archbishop Arns, who emerged as one of the most determined opponents of the military dictatorship and made the archdiocese of São Paulo the ecclesiastical power base of care and concern for the persecuted and defence of labour and human rights.[12] He himself identified three phases of resistance. First, a struggle against imprisonments, torture, and disappearances, not simply by statements but by active organization of committees, agencies, and publications. Second, vigorous campaigning for the restoration of civil rights in Brazil – an end to censorship which gagged the Church, and for rights of freedom from arrest, political parties, and amnesty for those accused of political crimes. São Paulo cathedral became the venue for appeals for human rights. Third, justice for the working class. On this he spoke out and encouraged the formation of Church community groups for workers, helping in a practical way to organize meetings and distribute food.

One of the ironies of Church–state relations in Brazil was that while the state returned to democracy, the Church reverted to the Roman model of authority. Pope John Paul II led the way. In Brazil he did what the Brazilian military had not been able to do: tame the Church. Aspects of Vatican II and Medellín became objects of suspicion. Liberation theology was examined for Marxist influence, and the Brazilian clergy were instructed to sever all ties with leftist political causes. Liberal theologians came under stricter scrutiny and some felt the full weight of Rome's authority. In 1984 the Congregation for the Doctrine of the Faith headed by Cardinal Joseph Ratzinger summoned one of its principal suspects, Leonardo Boff, to answer for his views in Rome, and in May 1985 he was formally silenced. In spite of an apparent accommodation between Rome and Brazilian bishops in 1986, Ratzinger and his allies in the episcopacy continued to harass the progressive groups.[13] Religious orders were warned, publications censored, and the power of the Episcopal Conference curtailed. Experimental seminaries were suppressed and another door to progressivism closed. Rome had a strategy for the Latin American Church, applied by nominating conservative bishops; while this did not silence the progressives it introduced contrary voices in episcopal conferences and reduced the social message of recent years. In Brazil new bishops suspended activist priests and restricted grass-roots initiatives. And in subdividing the diocese of São Paulo the Vatican effectively curtailed the authority and dynamism of Cardinal Arns, to his bitter regret. The policy was neatly rounded off by the election of a conservative president of the CNBB, which further weakened the voice of reform. In the struggle for the soul of the Brazilian Church neo-Romanization had won the day.

Populist Dictator: Perón and the Church

Argentina's response to the world depression was ambiguous The Revolution of 1930 which overthew Hipólito Yrigoyen, although it received some support from the victims of high inflation and unemployment, was essentially a military coup led by conservative forces. These established a dictatorship in alliance with the landowning class, thus inaugurating the *década infame*, the time of ignominy, electoral fraud, exclusion of political parties, and repression of opponents. Meanwhile a process of rapid industrialization increased the demands of workers, their ranks now broadened by the influx of impoverished migrants from the interior.

The Catholic response to the *década infame* was weak and divided. Conservatives were still fighting the battles of the past and looking for answers from José de Maestre, Ramiro de Maeztu, and Donoso Cortés, straying into authoritarian, corporatist, Hispanist, and anti-democratic positions, and obsessed with order, orthodoxy, and hierarchy. Passing for an intellectual, the Catholic priest Julio Meinvielle argued for a return to a medieval utopia when culture was closer to God, far from modern enemies such as capitalism, socialism, Protestantism, and Judaism, and including the enemy within, liberal Catholicism infected by five centuries of apostasy. 'Confronting these revolutionary forces all looking to Moscow stands the Catholic Church, moved by the spirit of of subordination, respect for necessary hierarchy, and adherence to order'.[14]

Moderate Catholics, clerics and laity, favoured a new organization, Acción Católica, established on the Italian model from 1928 and backed by the hierarchy and the papal nunciature, as well as by leading Catholic families. Designed to bring Christ's presence and teaching into society through the action of laypeople, many of them the sons and daughters of immigrants, it was essentially a middle-class movement, though with a militant edge to it, and likened by the Jesuit historian Guillermo Furlong to an army of the Church with an army's chain of command. The views and hopes of Acción Católica were represented in the journal *Criterio*, another lay enterprise though like Acción Católica itself closely monitored by the hierarchy. Although occasional contributors included Jorge Luis Borges, Jacques Maritain, and G.K. Chesterton, it was not a liberal publication, and in its early years showed a tendency to see the great enemy as the United States, governed by Protestants out to destroy Latin America with its Hispanic past and Catholic culture.

Argentine Catholicism showed many faces, some of them masks to cover political motives, conservative, liberal, and radical. In 1910 in a population of 1.2 million, 92 per cent declared themselves to be Catholics; in 1947 in a population of 15.8 million, the proportion was 93 per cent. Buenos Aires was slightly less homogeneous, with 90 per cent declared Catholics.[15] How realistic were these figures? In the 1930s there was a movement to make things clear. *Integral* Catholicism was an attempt to shed the dubious fringe and preserve orthodox and pure Catholicism in all its integrity. The desire was not to merge or reconcile Catholicism with national culture but to reform society according to Catholic doctrine, an integral religion defined by Rome.[16] The activist wing of integral Catholicism was Acción Católica. The cultural thrust was provided by *Criterio*, which was designed to 'prepare the Catholic conscience' and apply Catholic criteria to national and world problems. Established in 1928, from 1932 it was edited by Gustavo Franceschi, a leading figure in Argentine political and social thought in the 1930s and 1940s, priest and polemicist, adviser of Acción Católica and consultant of bishops and nuncios. Variously described as 'liberal priest', 'right-wing priest', and even 'communist' (a label not difficult to acquire in Argentina), he was the prototype of the *católico integral*. In a direct line from Gregory XVI to Pius IX and Pius X, he asserted 'it is not possible to be liberal and Catholic at the same time', and believed that 'the true solution to the modern crisis lies in *Católicismo Integral* and not in the adoption of ideas of heterodox origins'.[17] In the 1930s it was difficult to repudiate both liberal democracy and dictatorship without falling into another trap, and like other Catholic intellectuals of integralist persuasion Franceschi supported the Nationalist against the Republican cause in the Spanish civil war, until he became aware of the totalitarian character of Francoism.

In search of an Argentina that was truly Catholic, integral religion wanted to move on from Catholicism subordinate to the liberal state to Catholicism central to a new state, looking not for Catholic political parties but for Catholic leaders of parties. Catholic opinion at various levels, including *Criterio*, applauded the Revolution of 6 September 1930 and wanted it to go further, to promote the Church's answers to liberalism and socialism. Argentine Catholicism was growing, in numbers of adherents and in expansion of parishes and schools. Growth reached its peak in the celebration of the International Eucharistic Congress of 1934, an occasion of mass marches and devout processions, in the presence of Cardinal Eugene Pacelli, specially sent by the Vatican. The new Catholic identity was symbolized by greater devotion to the Virgin of Luján, and in October 1934 Argentina was consecrated to the Sacred Heart of Jesus. Yet Catholic political thought in the 1930s continued to be cliché-ridden and divided. There were fascists, nationalists, and liberals; and there were even devotees of *valores criollos*, convinced that '*Dios es criollo*'. But above all, *catolicismo integral* set the standard and the tone of Argentine religious thought.

Encumbered with this ideological baggage, how did Catholics react to the next great challenge, the advent of Peronism?[18] The army coup of 4 June 1943, overtly to end a decade of infamy and corruption and to place the interests of the nation first, was acceptable to those Catholics who espoused nationalism and were close to the army. The new government could be described as a civil–military–religious coalition. Opportunities were now available to Catholics in new ministries and government institutions, and members of Acción Católica were also rewarded for their support. Gustavo Martínez Zuviría (the novelist Hugo Wast), a well-known Catholic figure, with a reputation for anti-Semitism, became the Minister of Education. But there were other sources of influence. The appointment of Juan Domingo Perón, now emerging as a leading military nationalist, as Secretary of Urban and Social Welfare in November 1943 and the increasing weight of the unions would force Catholics to make a choice.

Perón offered an alternative model to Radical and right-wing military government. He proclaimed a populist state, intervening to defend the national economy against foreign pressure and to protect the more vulnerable groups in society. A strong leader, an interventionist state, a nationalist policy, and a multi-class alliance, these classic components of populist dictatorship were there from the beginning, when Perón assembled a power base consisting of a mass following combined with key sectors of the upper classes, the miltary, and the industrialists. In 1945 he led into power a coalition of labour, conservative, and nationalist groups; he then dissolved the parties and replaced them by the Peronist Party: 'I'm your leader now. I give the orders and you follow them.'[19] When Perón fought the presidential elections of 1946 the bishops did not commit themselves but simply issued the usual instructions: no Catholic could vote for candidates who supported separation of Church and state, or who favoured the suppression of laws recognizing the rights of the Church, or who stood for the secularization of education, and legal divorce. In the elections the traditional parties of the right and centre were defeated by the heterogeneous movement led by Perón's *laborista* party representing industrial workers and the the unions, and with the support of the military and Catholic sectors.

Perón maintained that his ideology was Christian and his programme conformed to 'the social doctrine of the Church' and 'the papal encyclicals'. He claimed to represent a humanist and Christian *movement* separate from old *parties*, a third position distinct from capitalist individualism and Marxist collectivism. It was an absolutist movement, excluding other political programmes and claiming a Christian inspiration, with a vision of popular Catholicism distinct from the official Church. The Jesuit priest Hernán Benítez, a well-known preacher in the Metropolitan Cathedral in the 1940s, confessor of Eva Perón and Peronist collaborator, claimed that the papal encyclicals had been preached in Argentina for fifty years without having the slightest effect on the rich; now they could be preached in the certainty of producing results. Catholicism and papal teaching were no longer the preserve of the elites but the possession too of the popular classes, especially industrial workers. 'When read by justicialists they discover in them principles of a social and economic revolution much more advanced than even those of communism.'[20]

'Justicialism' was a new concept in Argentina increasingly invoked from 1945. Perón began referring to his political ideas as *justicialismo*, social justice, which he defined as 'Christian and humanist' with the 'best attributes of collectivism and individualism, idealism and materialism'. Verbiage of this kind was pure propaganda, but it served a purpose, appealing to a coalition of social forces – industrial working class, inhabitants of the poorest barrios, *peones de campo*, tenant farmers, and small producers. The organized worker movement, especially the unions, were its principal constituency, all held together by Peronism, with its platform of social justice, economic independence, and political sovereignty. There were tensions here, but it survived with the active participation of the armed forces, the federation of small industrial and agricultural businesses, the Confederación General de Trabajo (CGT), and the Catholic Church.

The response of the Catholic Church to Peronism changed in the course of ten years, from support or at least acceptance to outright opposition and rejection. Between the rise of Perón in 1943–45 and his fall in 1955 emerged the real Peronism, which included among its leading groups men and women from the Catholic movement but also many others from different cultures and traditions, especially at labour and union level, some of them anti-clerical. The coalition lived in peace for a decade. But was conflict inherent from the beginning, or did it develop over time? The first years of Peronism began with positive progress, a new deal for labour, improvement of workers' pay and conditions, new social services and benefits, the modernization of social and economic life, redistribution of income, and votes for women. Eva Perón's foundation was promoting various social projects – hospitals, schools, child welfare – in which many Catholic clergy and laity collaborated. A Catholic priest, Virgilio Filippo, was elected deputy on the Peronist ticket in 1948. Many labour and union activists with vaguely Catholic connections entered the government as ministers, officials, or deputies in congress.

At the beginning, therefore, there was collaboration between the government and sectors of the Catholic Church. A number of sympathetic bishops, religious orders, and priests seemed to legitimize Peronism, and many laypeople previously associated with Catholic causes and organizations, such as Arturo Sampay and Ernesto Palacio, served the regime in various capacities. Perón attended the public liturgy of the Church when it was appropriate, such as at the National Eucharistic Congress in 1950. And he affirmed his Catholic faith, claiming that just as those who declared themselves democrats were not always so, those who declared themselves

Catholics were not all inspired by Christian doctrines. In 1948 he told the bishops, 'I want to say that I have always sought inspiration in the teachings of Christ. I have sought to apply many of the principles contained in the papal encyclicals. If I interpret them badly tell me where I am wrong. If I apply them well, I hope to receive your encouragement.'[21] Eva Perón professed what she called a 'humanist' Christianity. Father Hernán Benítez, like many Peronists, equated *justicialismo* with Christianity, containing as it did the message of Jesus for workers. He preached a popular Catholicism, inspired by Peronism, distinct from a Catholicism of the middle and upper classes. All this leaves the impression that each side used words to suit its own case. But traditionally the Church and the military were close, and saw themselves as the two institutions that could save Argentina. In 1945 when the bishops went to the presidential palace to swear to the new constitution, they reaffirmed that a close relationship ought to exist between the state and the Catholic Church, understood as the official religion. They also claimed a monopoly of this position, opposing Protestantism as a danger to national identity, an agent of Yankee imperialism, a friend of liberalism and socialism, and they criticized Perón's toleration of it. They were also uneasy about claims to old patronage rights of presentation and retention of papal documents by the president.

So was the Church for or against Peronism? The Argentine sources are contradictory. The decline of Acción Católica and the existence of alternative modes of Catholic action, especially the Juventud Obrera Católica (JOC) as a Catholic workers' movement, angered Peronists, who were hostile to any competition for influence and power, especially among the working class. In a speech to provincial governors and labour leaders in November 1954 Perón claimed that he had told the bishops, 'I do not understand why they are being organized, these groups of Catholic labourers, Catholic lawyers, Catholic doctors, and Catholic farmers. We are Catholics too! But to be Peronists we do not have to proclaim that we are Catholic Peronists. And within this context we can be Catholic, Jewish, Buddhist, Orthodox . . .'[22] The cloven hoof of Peronism: absolute and exclusive, it dismissed any rival allegiance. Initial collaboration between JOC and Peronism turned to bitter rivalry, alerting the Church to a dangerous friendship. Catholic nationalists of the right, such as Father Meinvielle, had their own reservations, seeing in Peronism a move towards union power, socialism, and working-class revolution, and they identified liberalism, communism, and other hate figures with the Peronist government and its officials. Catholics of more democratic tendency, such as readers of *Criterio* and those favouring Christian democracy, opposed the totalitarian bias of the Peronist movement which saw all alternative projects such as Catholic social initiatives and youth movements as a threat. As for its apparent deference to Christianity and religion, that was a mask.

Tension was increasing and surfacing. In November 1954 Perón denounced 'the infiltration' of the clergy into unions and into public life. The time had come when the incompatible claims of Peronism and Catholicism could not be disguised. The social, political, and military conflicts within Argentine society were now being expressed in religious terms. A choice was imposed by the facts – either Peronist or Catholic. Large Peronist demonstrations were carrying placards: 'Perón sí, curas no', and 'no a la enseñanza religiosa'. The government took up the challenge and raised the stakes: it legalized divorce, suppressed the obligation of religious teaching, attacked the Church, its bishops and clergy, and demanded separation of Church and state. For its part the Church used religious processions to attack the government. Such an occasion was the Corpus Christi celebration on 11 June 1955 in Buenos Aires, when 200,000 people gathered in defiance of a police ban. This was an essentially middle-class act of protest, followed by the expulsion of two higher clerics in retaliation, and the start of church-burning, preliminaries to a more violent conflict.

On 16 June a military rising against the constitutional government was heralded by an air attack on Government House and regime supporters in the Plaza de Mayo, described by *Clarín* as monstrous and inhuman. Numbers of Catholics were linked to the military action, willing to support violence and forming with other groups 'civil commandos' in support of the 'freedom revolution'. Peronist mobs burned more churches, and by now Church efforts to calm things down were too late. In September 1955 a rising of the military backed by civil and religious groups of the right ended Peronist rule. The aircraft of the rebels displayed a cross on the fuselage and the words *Cristo vence*, more aggressive than the cry of the Mexican Catholics. General Eduardo Lonardi, the new president, claimed (on 17 September 1955) that God was on his side, appealing to Christian principles and the *Virgen capitana*; and he rewarded Catholics with jobs in the new government. He lasted two months before he was replaced by General Pedro E. Aramburu, a supposedly more liberal successor. A concerted effort was made to *desperonizar* the Argentine state. Rebels were shot, the CGT was infiltrated, the Peronist Party dissolved, and the 1949 Constitution annulled. Right-wing Catholics, always potential allies of the military, now edged even closer.

The Peronist model was suitable for times of prosperity, when the state could meet wage claims and subsidize its power base. But prosperity had a short life in Argentina and from 1950 recession brought back inflation and a return to hard times. There was a tightening of government controls and Argentines felt the the iron hand of Peronism as it resorted to familiar measures: less participation, more orders, more emphasis on production, less on redistribution. Perón was now surviving by the cult of personality and his continuing appeal to working-class and union interests. Moreover he had democratic legitimacy, now proved in two free elections. But opponents in the military, middle-class business interests, and the Church were now talking of his increasing authoritarianism and the power of the CGT. Peron's leadership brought tangible benefits to urban workers and to the military, and it appealed to a wider range of interest groups than did traditional Argentine government. But there was a price to pay. Peronism did not allow for alternatives. It became impossible to obtain any job in the bureaucracy without the endorsement of a Peronist and without an identity card of the Peronist Party.[23] And while the political base of government had been apparently democratized by the extension of participation to new social groups, the tensions thereby unleashed had encouraged the leader to take dictatorial powers, to subordinate congress and the judiciary to his will, to have recourse to the methods of the police state, and finally to urge his working-class supporters to violence. At that point his enemies struck. Threatened by violence from the army and the navy, he resigned on 19 September 1955 and went into exile.

For expelling a bishop Perón had been excommunicated in accordance with canon law. In 1962, through the mediation of Cardinal Antonio Caggiano, a familiar figure in the Peronist state, he was reconciled to the Church during his exile in Madrid. He returned to Argentina in 1973 and was elected president. He died in 1974 with the rites of the Church. But the fall of Perón left a resentment among Peronists, who saw the Church as an ally of the rich and an enemy of the working class. When Pope John Paul II visited Argentina in April 1987, however, the Peronist CGT joined a mass demonstration of welcome, part political and part religious in inspiration, and one of the banners stated 'El Papa y Perón, un solo corazón [The Pope and Perón, a single heart]'.

The Argentine Church and the Military Dictators

The years after 1960 were times of trial for Argentine Catholics, united in their faith, divided in their loyalties. Three broad currents of belief and behaviour were gathering pace. Conservative Catholics were wedded to an older vision of the Church and were politically nationalist, allying with the state and the military and not averse to using the faith for ideological and political ends. Social Christians wanted to place the Church in the modern world and to maintain dialogue with secular reformism. In this approach the Church was not seen as a perfect society but as one that would recognize its errors and reform its ways, to become a viable alternative to

Marxism. Progressive Catholics sought more radical reform, abandoning traditional modes and seeking the truth in liberation theology and the option for the poor and, where necessary, alliance with Marxists. This tripartite division of Catholicism was an analysis favoured in Chile by Christians for Socialism, a left-wing movement which placed itself in the third category and aroused the suspicion of the hierarchy, as we shall see.

In post-Perón Argentina the pace was set by the progressive clergy. Worker priests, *curas obreros*, made their appearance, and some allied themselves with protest actions and occupation of factories by worker organizations. They came into conflict with the Church hierarchy and earned predictable censure. The radicalization of the clergy in the 1960s took place outside conventional Church institutions, as priests sought new ways and objectives. On 28 June 1965 eighty priests from Greater Buenos Aires, average age about 30 and joined by two bishops, met in Quilmes, and after lively discussion drew up a document which spelt out three basic problems: priestly life and vocation, the status of the clergy in the Church, and the relation of the clergy to the world. Quilmes was a turning point towards change. Political turmoil further agitated the Church and pulled it in different directions.

The government of the so-called Argentine Revolution (1966–73) headed by General Juan Carlos Onganía installed a hard-line regime of national security, corporatist in style, to promote a model of development in which growth would be financed by national and transnational capital. Political parties were prohibited, parliament was dissolved, the universities and many trade unions were subject to government control. By any standards this was a policy of repression directed against students, intellectuals, workers, and the popular sectors in general, while the rest of the public looked on impassively. Mounting resentment exploded unexpectedly in May 1969 in the city of Córdoba, when university students and automobile workers took to the streets in a violent demonstration. This became known as the *cordobazo* and signalled the beginning of a rolling protest against repressive government and conservative economics, eventually leading to armed struggle, the emergence of guerrilla bands from mid-1970, and the end of the Argentine Revolution. The accession of General Lanusse to government was intended to lead the way back to democracy in a *Gran Acuerdo Nacional*, culminating in 1973 with the victory of Peronism in the elections. Catholics could not stand apart from these extraordinary events. Conservative Catholics of the traditional wing of the Church had become committed to the Onganía regime and gave it some legitimacy. Catholics from other sectors, however, placed autonomy of the Church before compromise with the government, articulating the theology of liberation and the conscientization of Christian groups in favour of the option for the poor. These voices were heard in the episcopal reunion of San Miguel in

1969 which adapted the principles of Medellín to the Argentine situation. For some, however, this was not enough.

The Movimiento de Sacerdotes para el Tercer Mundo (MSTM) grouped together a significant number of priests who wanted to take the thinking of Medellín and San Miguel further forward. They advanced beyond clerical circles and proclaimed their support for the popular movement against the Onganía dictatorship. Soon they clashed with the hierarchy and provoked serious divisions within the Church. The process unfolding since 1964 for the Church in Mendoza, Córdoba, Avellaneda, Tucumán, and San Isidro culminated in the conflict in Rosario in 1968–69, which reflected all the problematic issues seething in the Church – the function of priests, the role of the people of God and the challenge to authority, relations with the political regime, the demands of the conciliar documents, relations with the Church authorities, and the duties of national bishops.

At the beginning of 1968, 400 priests formed an organization made up of teams in dioceses and held a series of national meetings. Their mission statement, *Documento de Colonia Caraya*, spoke of structural changes and the need to stir public opinion, to raise consciousness of exploitation, abuses, and injustices in a society subject to a capitalist system and the international imperialism of money. They defined their movement as socialism, the recovery of Peronism, and confrontation with the military government. Relations with the episcopacy until 1969 were tense but not at breaking point, and they had a significant influence on the Document of San Miguel. But the movement could not ignore the *cordobazo* and the outbreak of violence, and a political element now entered the equation. For the *terceristas* (priests for the Third World) events in Córdoba were essentially a focus for what was happening in other parts of the country and not simply the result of extremist organizations and foreign ideologies; rather they reflected a common system of oppression and injustice which justified rebellion. Catholic youth organizations participated in support of the events of May 1969, as did the National Union of Students; and, acting outside Catholic institutions, they demanded liberation and revolution, while the activities of the Agrarian Leagues in the Chaco paralleled the political turmoil in the towns of the littoral and further alerted the bishops.

The movement to the left among semi-Catholic organizations after the *cordobazo* posed problems for the hierarchy, and although theoretically they had embraced the principles of Medellín in the Document of San Miguel, they now retreated to the right. The MSTM found itself isolated and increasingly neutralized by ecclesiastical censure and its own internal division into moderates and radicals. The bishops were also alarmed by the Catholic Rural Movement (Movimiento Rural de Acción Católica) and in 1972 attacked the Agrarian League (Ligas Agrarias) as a 'secular and profane' organization, whose political activities devalued authentic Christian values. Amidst the tumults of the early 1970s, the spread of guerrilla warfare, retaliation by counterinsurgents, and the beginning of 'disappearances', the bishops had no alternative strategy for the Church beyond repeating traditional pieties. Reformist Catholics who did not identify either with the conservative hierarchy or with armed struggle were given no options. They were opposed by the bishops and harassed by the government. Yet they were a model for the future.

The return of Perón in 1973 and the restoration of justicialism opened the possibility of democratic change. But it was an illusion and the experiment sank amidst the recriminations of politicians and violence in the streets. The death of Perón in July 1974 hastened the end of populist politics, already torn by conflict between moderates and extremists. The military gradually took over, then abruptly assumed power in 1976.

Complicity

The Church was divided in its response to these events. Conservatives among the bishops were cautious and defensive, supporting pacification but no more than that. The MSTM on the other hand welcomed the return of Peronism as a progressive movement, opting for justice and welfare for the popular sectors. They rejected the way of armed struggle and the extremism on the left of Peronism. But the MSTM itself was split on these issues. The death of Perón left the problem unsolved, and the gap was now filled by the right-wing military, who assumed a preponderant role under his widow Isabel Perón in resistance to a violent challenge from the left.

Where did the Church stand? Individual bishops spoke out against the most flagrant abuses and on behalf of victims. In 1975 Bishop Alberto Devoto of Lavalle spoke in solidarity with priests detained for their links with the Ligas Agrarias, and other bishops spoke on behalf of priests detained in Formosa and Neuquén. But these isolated voices did not amount to a Church position on the post-Perón reaction; more characteristically the hierarchy moved to control the restless Catholic youth movements. Catholics were crippled by their own divisions. Laypeople reflected the bewilderment of the rest of society. As for the bishops, they too were confused but that did not stop them supporting the growing militarization of the government and then the miltary *golpe* of 1976. Where was the voice of Christian concern?[24]

The armed forces overthrew the constitutional Peronist government on 24 March 1976, and a junta led by General Jorge Rafael Videla came to power. This quickly established a policy of state terrorism, applied by its own agents and paramilitary groups, seizing, imprisoning, torturing, and disappearing thousands of people considered dangerous: workers, students, young people, and women.[25] Through monopoly of military power, used without pause and without explanations, this minority intimidated the whole population. The figures are disputed but tens of thousands of victims disappeared in a dirty war unequalled in Argentine history, with no response or opposition from any main movement. The Church had the moral authority and the strength of numbers to provide independent opposition, but it failed to do so, failed even to protect its own people. Indeed through the attitude of its hierarchy the Church helped to legitimize the dictatorship.

Opposition was not impossible. In Chile, Brazil, and other countries of the southern cone, the Church's defence of human rights and the progressive option for the poor contributed significantly to the defence of the weakest in society in the struggle for their rights. In Paraguay in 1969 when the hand of the dictator, General Alfredo Stroessner, no friend of the Church or its activists, descended upon radical priests, students, academics, and peasant leaders the Church rallied to the victims and excommunicated the Minister of the Interior and the chief of police. The archbishop of Asunción, Monsignor Ismael Rolón, publicly refused to collaborate with the government. From 1970 he spoke up loud and clear for the oppressed, denounced breaches of human rights, and visited the suffering in prison and hospital, becoming a symbol of resistance to a dictatorship that earned further infamy by a series of arrests in Holy Week 1976, the *Pascua Dolorosa*, and its persecution of the Ligas Agrarias Cristianas.[26] In Bolivia, although the witness of the hierarchy was not so consistent, Church leaders denounced 'institutionalized injustice' and defended the 'legitimate rights of workers, peasants and servants'.[27]

But not in Argentina. There were a few protests against the worst excesses of military repression, but institutionally the Church was silent and stood aside from commitment. What is the explanation? The Argentine Church had a long tradition of conservatism, public caution, and subordination to the state, whose economic support it accepted for salaries, seminaries, and education. This was a deep-rooted culture which prevented it from changing its ways or adjusting to a modern Church. The Medellín Conference of 1968, which supported base communities and liberation theology, had come as a great shock to the Argentine hierarchy, as it did to other conservative churchmen. But there were further factors too, peculiar to Argentina. The role of military chaplains created built-in support for the action of the military authorities. These had a history going back for over fifty years and reinforced in 1957 by the establishment of the military vicariate, a special diocese for military personnel and their families, ruled by its own archbishop and ministered by its own clergy whose mission was not exclusively spiritual; it became in fact a breeding ground for spokesmen for the armed forces.

So the Church continued undisturbed as bishops, priests, religious, and laypeople were sequestered, tortured, exiled, and assassinated. The few complaints, in the most scandalous cases, were purely formal and made no impact. When concerns were raised by the Episcopal Conference it was done in so prudent and private a way that many bishops were not even aware of it and the military junta was hardly disturbed. Following the failure of these approaches, the episcopacy received the military chiefs discreetly to enable them to expound their vision of the struggle against subversion, and they were always ready to accept excuses, such as the activity of terrorists, the danger of communism, the need to restore order. 'We know that the decision to turn to violence in order to impose change was not taken without the deepest premeditation.'

Some bishops can only be described as collaborators. Archbishop Adolfo Servando Tortolo of Paraná was aware of the repression, yet urged Catholics to cooperate with the new government. Bishop Victorio Bonamín, vicar for the army, justified repression, stating in September 1975, 'The army is expiating the impurity of our country. May not Christ some time want the armed forces to go beyond their normal function?'[28] Bishop Medino, appointed to the military vicariate by Pope John Paul II, accepted the procedures of repression, was critical of human rights organizations, and in April 1982 justified torture: 'Sometimes physical repression is necessary; it is obligatory, and thus licit.'[29] The worst case was that of Archbishop Antonio José Plaza of La Plata. He identified totally with the military regime, to the end and beyond, when he was the only bishop to defend the military's self-declared amnesty in September 1983.

What did the Vatican make of all this? The papal nuncio, Archbishop Pio Laghi, was not a bad person, but he was in an ambiguous position, out of his depth. He knew what was happening and he deplored it, but he did not criticize it either face to face with the regime or privately. The popes were critical, though they did not press the issue or take an absolute stand. Paul VI had stated in Septembr 1970: 'The Argentine Church should not hold on to any privilege. It should be content to serve the faithful and the civil community in an atmosphere of tranquillity and security for all.'[30] John Paul II deplored the disappearances and the violation of human rights as 'a painful drama', and urged the Argentine bishops to act. But he did no more than this, though pressed by concerned Catholics, and he never made Argentina another Poland.

How did the mass of Catholics respond to the military dictatorship? The conservatives gave it their full support; they were waging a war against leftist subversion, communism, and atheism, and Catholics of the right were hostile not only to revolution in all its forms but to the progressive sector within the Church itself. They saw this as a Christian-military war of counterinsurgency. So they attacked the enemies of the state. Included among these, according to the Minister of the Interior General Albano Harguindeguy, was the MSTM, which he accused of being a Marxist organization. This generated an argument deep inside the Church and brought out divisions in the episcopacy, between those who agreed and those who dissented, such as Bishop De Nevares of Neuquén, one of the few churchmen who defended human rights under the dictatorship. Subsequent denunciations by those arrested and imprisoned by the police testify to the presence of priests and military chaplains in the detention centres, either to reassure the oppressors or to hear the confessions of the condemned. Even among social Christians there were some who regarded the regime as a necessary evil, to be endured with resignation or in silence. They maintained a moderate opposition to the regime without threatening to subvert it.

Progressive Catholics preserved their credibility by continuing to oppose the dictatorship in their writings and through their solidarity with the oppressed. For this they were themselves persecuted and many can be regarded as martyrs for religion. Their human rights organizations were independent of the Church and received no protection or support from it. Numerous progressive Catholics – priests, religious, laymen and women, and even some bishops – were persecuted for their witness, seized, imprisoned, exiled, and in many cases disappeared. The perpetrators? The military or their paramilitary collaborators. In the years 1974–83 sixteen Catholic priests were murdered or disappeared, beginning on 11 May 1974, when Father Carlos Francisco Múgica, a young priest popular among poor people, prominent *tercerista*, and known sympathizer with the Montoneros (leftist guerrillas), was gunned down in front of his church of San Francisco Solano in Buenos Aires after celebrating his Saturday evening mass. Two bishops, Enrique Angel Angelelli in 1976 and Carlos Ponce de León in 1977, died in similar car 'accidents'. Among the victims were many lay activists. Mónica Mignone, daughter of the historian of these events, was taken from their home in the early hours of the morning and never seen again.

Inevitably, given Argentina's situation and their own ineptitude, the dictators reached a crisis, which they sought to resolve by invading the Falklands. They were taught a military and political lesson, which in effect ended the dictatorship and in due course opened the way to the restoration of democracy. The political parties then inherited a prize they had not earned, but at least they gained an end to state terrorism. As for the armed forces, they organized for themselves an orderly retreat in Argentina, if not in the Falklands. The Church emerged with little credit. Conservative Catholics stood by the military to the end, defended the law of amnesty and argued for a mantle of oblivion over the crimes of the dictatorship. And they continued to have a dominant influence in the ranks of the episcopacy.

The Episcopal Conference was the only sector apart from the military and the ultra-right to justify the so-called *Informe final* of the dictatorship (28 April 1983), which declared that all the disappeared were dead, 'muertos por decreto', and the atrocities and crimes committed were 'actos de servicio'. There was a time to speak and a time to keep silent. The bishops had missed both. The predictable compromise and complicity of the Church was noticed at the time. 'The least thing that could be said of the bishops' position is that it was weak', commented one respected observer.[31] Catholic social Christians acted as mediators between the military power and civil leaders during the last stage of the dictatorship. It was called reconciliation, but how do you reconcile the irreconcilable? In 1996, when the Episcopal Conference made its final examination of conscience over the horrific events of 1976–83, the bishops claimed to have denounced violations of human rights and to have made their concern known privately to the military authorities. And they lamented their inability to mitigate suffering. Otherwise they admitted nothing. Few of the Argentine hierarchy were left in a state of grace.

Christian Democracy, a Chilean Option

The persistence of economic depression and chronic inflation from the 1930s made Chile a difficult country to govern. After a brief experiment with the 'Socialist Republic' in 1932 and the triumph of the Popular Front government in 1938 based on alliance between the Radicals and the Marxist left, stability of a kind was restored with the return of the authoritarian Carlos Ibañez in 1952–58, followed by the conservative Arturo Alessandri. Neither the export-led growth of the nitrate era nor the state-led industrial growth from 1930 was capable of bringing the economy out of stagnation. A small wealthy elite topped the social structure while the mass of Chileans lived in poverty, in a country of large landowners and landless peasants, bound in a system which could not even feed its own people. Industry was not dynamic enough to absorb the drift from the land; there was widespread unemployment and masses of people could only find a home in shanty towns. The large copper mines, one of the few successes of production, were American-owned.

The critical state of the economy was reflected in tension and instability. The political mobilization of the Marxist left and the decline of the

Conservative Party invited new responses from Chileans, but none came from the Catholic Church. The traditional wing of Catholicism led by a deeply conservative hierarchy, typified by Horacio Campillo, archbishop of Santiago, was bewildered by the loss of Conservative strength, and further confused by warnings from Rome. In the 1930s the papal nuncio, Ettore Felici, urged Catholics to form a new party to defend Catholic social principles and appeal to middle- and working-class people. The episcopate was not supportive. Felici took his case directly to Cardinal Pacelli, secretary of state at the Vatican, advocating political pluralism for Catholics and the need to adopt social Christian positions. The letter received from Cardinal Pacelli on 1 June 1934 was a blow to the Chilean bishops, already dismayed by the weakening of their political position, and they sought to obstruct its publication. Their conservatism included doctrinal pedantry, at least as propounded in pastoral letters such as that of 1933 which praised 'the virtues of the home, especially obedience, humility, and work'.[32] Meanwhile younger Conservatives were moving towards Christian democratic answers and in 1938 adopted the Falange Nacional, a misleading term for the birth of Christian democracy in Chile.

In the 1930s, therefore, the Chilean Church was divided between conservatives clinging to traditional positions and backed by many bishops and by the Catholic University of Chile, and reformers inspired by the writings of Jacques Maritain, working for a rechristianization of their country. In the 1940s and 1950s social Christians made a number of advances at the expense of conservative Catholics. The appointment of José María Caro Rodríguez, of peasant origins and Christian democratic persuasion, as archbishop of Santiago angered conservatives, some of whom made a fruitless journey to the Vatican to protest. They were equally affronted by the activities of Father Alberto Hurtado, a priest campaigning on behalf of social justice. Both of these were regarded by right-wing Catholics as a sign that the Church was selling out to Christian democracy. The Catholic right had a nucleus in the Catholic University, where a group of professors, headed by the historian Jaime Eyzaguire, eulogized Hispanic culture and the colonial past and proclaimed the values of Hispanidad. Eduardo Frei, the future leader of the Christian Democrat Party, was alarmed for the Catholic conscience. Where was it going? he asked, sharing his thoughts with another Catholic reformist, Gabriela Mistral. 'These wealthy Catholics, conservatives who believe they have inherited a kind of ownership of the Church along with the family estate . . . are protected by a powerful clerical sector and become ever more intolerable and reactionary.'[33]

The Falange Nacional was founded by younger Conservative activists and Catholic Action campaigners, to apply the social encyclicals to political issues in Chile. They were influenced by Jesuit sociologist Father

Hurtado, a product of Louvain University and messenger of its social Catholicism. The Falange soon came into conflict with conservative bishops over its criticism of the Franco regime in Spain and its association with the Marxist-dominated Chilean labour movement. Relations worsened in 1948 when the Falange defended the Communist Party's right to compete in the elections and conservative bishops tried to have it banned from Catholic support. It needed the Vatican's intervention to rescue the Falange and the cause of social reform.[34]

In the years 1950–58 consciousness of social needs grew in the Church, stirred by an increasing number of foreign-born priests active in working-class parishes, the appointment of non-conservative bishops with social Christian sympathies, and the work of Catholic Action. Perhaps its greatest asset was the emergence of Eduardo Frei as a political heavyweight in the 1950s and his prominence in the Senate. In 1957 the Falange joined with social Christian conservatives and other social Catholics to create the Christian Democratic Party, whose leading figure and asset was Frei. Traditionalists were still supporting the right, but Frei was attracting more radical Catholics and the Church too was benefiting from the movement of Catholic opinion towards the centre and the left. In the period 1960–65 the Church included many bishops and priests identified more clearly with the Christian Democrats. Support within the Episcopal Conference was strengthened in 1961 by the appointment of Raúl Silva Henríquez, director of the Caritas relief agency, as archbishop of Santiago. There he was an ally of Manuel Larraín, bishop of Talca. There was renewed commitment among social Christians to the poor in society, drawing on the encyclicals of John XXIII, *Mater et Magister* (1961) and *Pacem in Terris* (1963). Under these clerics and the leadership of Frei, the Catholic centre was able to consolidate, and when he was elected president in 1964 his government strengthened its power base by appointing many lay activists to posts. Frei's political talents and personal integrity attracted much support, as did his position firmly in the centre, shunning both communism and laissez-faire capitalism. In the event his 'Revolution in Liberty' promised more than it fulfilled and from 1967 supporters inside and outside the Church were embroiled in disputes over its performance. Dissension within the Catholic centre and left plagued the remaining years of Christian Democrat government, and following the victory of Salvador Allende weakened the Catholic response to his Socialist government.[35] Many Christian Democrats and their foreign sympathisers underwent a crisis of conscience and began to question the identity of their movement. Who were they and what was their relevance in Latin America?

Christian Democracy had its roots in Europe and was transplanted to Latin America in the 1930s. In a mixed political culture, ranging from recurring dictatorship to intermittent democracy, Christian Democracy represented a new movement of revolution in liberty, a Christian voice on behalf of radical reform of political and social structures. It had its greatest success in Chile, Venezuela, El Salvador, and Costa Rica, and its most distinguished leaders were Eduardo Frei in Chile and Rafael Caldera in Venezuela. Its recruiting ground was essentially younger generations of middle-class voters, but it also received extensive support from the popular sectors.

In Chile the first Christian Democrat activists were inspired by the ideas and example of Fernando Vives Solar, an early reformist and social Christian, and the message of the encyclical *Rerum Novarum*. European Catholics often find it difficult to understand the survival of Leo XIII's teaching in Latin America at a time when its significance had diminished in Europe except as a narrative of past injustice. The worst excesses of nineteenth-century capitalism had already been addressed in most of Europe and conditions of labour alleviated. But this had not happened in Latin America and in many parts of the subcontinent unreconstructed capitalism and working-class helplessness were exactly as described in *Rerum Novarum*. This accounts for the enduring relevance of the encyclical among Catholic reformers. In Chile the leaders of Christian Democracy were mainly middle-class graduates who understood the message, and in the elections of 1965 it won its greatest percentage of votes in working-class constituencies, where the victims were to be found. The party had the moral support of a number of new bishops, beholden to Rome rather than to their Chilean predecessors. The pastoral letter of 18 September 1962, *El deber social y político en la hora presente* (Social and Political Duty in the Present Hour), signalled an urgent mission for the Church: the cause of the poor, of landless peasants, of workers without a living wage and without work. It was in tune with Vatican II (1962–65) and the message of Raúl Silva Henríquez, made cardinal by John XXIII in 1962, who preached that the Church had to choose between the rich who wished to preserve the old order and people demanding structural reforms. As Bernardino Piñero, bishop of Temuco, made clear in 1961: 'We have gradually to detach the Church from the upper class and to move it towards the middle class and the people. We do not realize perhaps the extent to which the people see us linked and involved with the rich, the powerful, the masters, the authorities, the governments.' And, he added, 'a Church of the rich, a Church of the masters, that is not the Church of Christ.'[36]

Acción Católica was not the answer. A minority movement, dating from a time when the hierarchy ruled all, it failed to take acount of the new thinking and made little impact on the working class. Catholic thinkers began to introduce the concept of revolutionary change, demanding a social revolution inspired by the Gospel, and some Catholic academics, probably going beyond the evidence, and certainly beyond Maritain, one of their mentors, began to see Catholicism's mission as holy revolution, seeing the role of Christianity as fundamentally revolutionary. These ideas were not reflected on the ground. The majority of priests were from the middle and upper classes, with very few vocations among workers and peasants. Few working-class people went to mass; in Santiago barely 10 per cent of congregations were working class. The Church met not only indifference but hostility. To solve these problems was not exactly the mission of Christian Democracy; it was a political, not an evangelizing movement. There was an enduring conviction among workers that the Church was not for them. Yet popular religion was not extinct. Traditional practices lived on and were seen in processions, the cult of Our Lady, belief in miracles. These and other devotions endured, many surviving from colonial times, such as the Virgen del Carmen de Quilimarí and the pilgrimage to the Virgen de las Peñas and the Virgen de Andarollo. Traces of this culture endured, and on them reformist bishops and priests could build. The clergy had a growing consciousness of the need for a new pastoral effort among the popular classes, which would pay attention to their social needs, represent the claims of landless peasants and estate workers and assert a presence in the slums and *callampas* (shanty towns). A number of priests now established new parishes where previously there had been none, and small Christian communities of working people appeared. And in Catholic circles there was now talk of agrarian reform.

Among the new breed of bishops Manuel Larraín, bishop of Talca, led the way. Scion of an elite family of conservative politicians and clerics, graduate of the Catholic University and seminary of Santiago, he was ordained in Rome in 1927. Soon he emerged as an outstanding reformist, a promoter and defender of Maritain's ideas in Chile against the attacks of conservative Catholics, and mentor of Christian Democracy, defending its leaders against conventional bishops in its early years as 'neither heretics, nor schismatics'. He advised them to seek an alternative to the capitalist system. 'To give Chile an authentic regime of Christian democracy, it is necessary to replace the existing capitalist regime by one where human needs are protected.' In his diocese of Talca he supported peasant campaigns and the cause of strikers; he inspired the creation of the Union of Christian Peasants, and activated agrarian reform in rural properties of the Church. He identified completely with the vision of John XXIII and Vatican II. 'The Second Vatican Council will be the council that reveals the Church of the poor.'[37] As President of CELAM, his words were carried beyond Chile and his actions were known and approved in Rome. In his encyclical *Populorum Progressio* Pope Paul VI encouraged everyone to help promote the development of peoples, especially those who could do most by reason of their education, office, or authority: 'They should set a good example by contributing part of their own goods, as several of our brother bishops have done. For example Emmanuel Larraín Errázuriz, Bishop of Talca, Chile, President of CELAM.'[38]

The Second Vatican Council which opened in October 1962 was an inspiration for social Christians. The keynotes of justice and peace, decentralization of Church government, and the promotion of the people of God reinforced the efforts of Chilean bishops and strengthened their call for structural reform in Chilean society. In Chile the Church identified with the Christian Democratic Party, shared and even anticipated some of its social policies, urging the need for agrarian reform and improvement of industrial conditions. The Church, moreover, assisted by financial support from abroad, developed social programmes of its own to attack the causes as well as the symptoms of poverty. Housing cooperatives, peasant training programmes, slum dweller organizations, and trade union federations were organized under Church auspices, again providing advance models for Frei's government in 1964. Specialist personnel for some of Frei's ministries were recruited from Church organizations. Tactics were not ignored. Bishops preached the dangers of Marxist alternatives to Christian action, while political activists branded Allende a Soviet tool.

In spite of the intellectual and moral resources of Christian Democracy and the stimulus of Frei's victory, all was not well. Catholic activists soon became disillusioned with Christian Democrat government, which they criticized as too timid and too slow in confronting landed and industrial interests. Catholic campaigners in the universities and in labour and peasant organizations pressed for more progressive policies, and priests, nuns, and laypeople working among the poor were convinced that reforms in housing, education, and employment were dilatory and inadequate.[39] The critics failed to give the government due credit for its actual achievements, and they would pay dearly for this. From 1967 Frei's government encountered turbulent times. As copper prices and government revenues fell and inflation rose, Frei had to impose cuts and wage restraint. Repression of workers' and squatters' demonstrations in 1967 and 1968 was violent and damaged the government's progressive image, while the revolutionary left was taking the fight into the streets and directing urban guerrilla action. Chile became a battleground of ideologies and agitators, and in the political frenzy the fortunes of the Christian Democrats declined. Harassed from the right and the left, their prospects in the next elections were not good.

In the last two years of Frei's government (1968–70) the Chilean bishops arguably got their tactics wrong and played into the hands of the far left. In taking a more critical stance towards the Christian Democrat government – urging decisive action in housing, employment, and education – they preached social reform without taking account of economic realities. And in seeking to mediate between opposing political tendencies, they conceded moral equivalence to movements on the right and on the left that failed the test of Christian and democratic criteria. Political polarization could not be halted by talking, and in criticizing Frei the bishops added to the pressures on his government without giving it credit for holding the line of moderation and for its policy of reformism as distinct from revolution, a policy which had already demonstrated that it could improve the prospects of Chile and its citizens.

As dissent grew within the Church and the claims of the Catholic left became more insistent, demanding greater commitment to social reform and criticizing the Church as well as the government, many clerics and laypeople left the cause of Christian Democracy and espoused more leftist policies. In August 1968 Iglesia Joven (Young Church), a new radical movement with a small but vociferous membership, declared its disillusion with Frei, and occupied Santiago cathedral, claiming that the Church was not democratizing rapidly enough and was not making a serious option for the poor. In denouncing the action as a profanation, Cardinal Silva signalled the limits of Christian radicalism. The bishops sought to tread a middle path even within the Church, deferring to the poor and the young yet unwilling to force 'those who are not poor or young to become alienated'.[40] At their conference in Medellín in August 1968 the Latin American bishops denounced the prevailing 'institutional violence' against the poor, committed the Church to struggle for social justice, and endorsed the formation within larger parishes of base communities (*comunidades cristianos de base*). Chilean bishops followed these lines, but fearing further polarization insisted that base communities work on behalf of social justice, not for particular political projects.

Left-wing Catholics were not impressed. In the writings of the Jesuit Gonzalo Arroyo, leading light of Christians for Socialism, Christian reformism was scorned as inadequate. 'Its principles, deeply infected with bourgeois ideology, provided moralistic criticism of certain social injustices. But it did not expose the structural problems of capitalism, and it was decidedly anti-socialist and anti-Marxist. Hence it defended the capitalist mode of production and it condemned the revolutionary efforts of the oppressed.' Catholic reformism, in this view, simply led to 'Revolution in Liberty', as promised by Christian Democracy, which was supported by most of the hierarchy and Christians in general but was fundamentally opposed to Marxist and popular forces. 'This party appealed to principles of Christian inspiration in order to propose a new system:

communitarianism. It led to concrete reforms in agriculture, education, housing, and economic planning. But it did not lead to any real structural change in the economy or in society. It merely bolstered neocapitalism and its ideology of liberty and democracy that are the weapons of the ruling class.'[41] The analysis is honest but flawed and would leave no hope for Catholic reformism. In this approach Christian Democrats cannot win. If they propose social reforms to integrate workers and peasants into Chilean society, they are merely co-opting the working class into the very structure that is oppressing them.

The Chilean bishops were about to begin a journey into unknown territory. As they prepared to face a Marxist presidency, Allende and his government were only part of the problem. Trouble was stirring within the Church itself, where the left now saw a new opportunity.

Allende: Fateful Interlude

In 1969 the Communists, Socialists, and Radicals united to form a new alliance, Popular Unity, under the leadership of Salvador Allende, a failed presidential candidate in previous elections. Allende came to power in 1970 with a 36 per cent majority vote against 27 per cent for Radomiro Tómic, the Christian Democrat candidate. The Marxist president proclaimed a 'democratic way to socialism', but could not deliver on democracy. He was thwarted by conflicting interests within Popular Unity, by the left wing of the Socialist Party, which kept the armed way in reserve, and by the Communists who never abandoned the way of revolution leading to dictatorship of the proletariat. As resistance to the government hardened and social conflict intensified, the bishops continued to stand back, preaching peace and moderation. The military had no such agenda and would intervene decisively when it pleased them.

The Chilean episcopate headed by Cardinal Silva remained aloof but not overtly hostile to the government of Allende, proclaiming human rights, pluralism, and collaboration. In the elections, having distanced themselves from Frei in recent years, and sensing perhaps some Catholic support for Allende, the Episcopal Conference had issued statements of neutrality, emphasizing the importance of democratic procedures to avoid civil war and military rule. Their failure to exclude Allende from the Catholic vote did no favours to Radomiro Tómic. They continued to preach conciliation. In their declaration of 22 April 1971 they pointed out that the socialism on offer in Chile was predominantly Marxist in inspiration, which posed obvious questions: 'To the legitimate government of Chile we reiterate the position that comes to us from Christ: that is, respect for its authority and collaboration in its efforts to serve the people . . . We greatly appreciate the repeated statements of the President of the Republic in which he has sought to respect and safeguard the rights of the religious conscience.'[42]

Cardinal Silva told an interviewer that the Popular Unity reforms were 'supported by the Church' and that socialism contained 'important Christian values'.[43] Elsewhere he explained that he thought the doctrinal orientation of Christians for Socialism appeared to be ambiguous; otherwise he remained cool about the issues they confronted:

> In line with what the bishops of Latin America have stated at Medellín and what the bishops of Chile have stated repeatedly, he feels that liberal capitalism, based on the unrestricted quest for profit, is an outdated system responsible for many of the ills that afflict our countries. He thinks that what Latin America probably desires is some type of pluralistic and democratic socialism and that if the people opt for this type of organization and government, the Church will have no difficulty in accepting it and collaborating loyally with it.[44]

In specific cases the episcopate had to oppose the government of Allende, and they could not support its totalitarian tendencies when they challenged religious values, but in general they sought dialogue. So it was a difficult balance – to defend the Church's position and policies within its proper competence, and at the same time to preserve its evangelical freedom. Could it find a middle way between the looming alternatives, a military coup or left-wing terrorism?

The problem for the bishops was that the Church itself was seriously divided on many issues. Radical Catholics sought to throw the Church's weight behind the Popular Unity parties and policies. And among poorer Catholics there was much support for Allende and a positive response from priests and nuns working among the poor. Base communities became political rather than religious entities. In April 1971 eighty priests, claiming affiliation with the working class and adopting the dialectic of the class struggle, declared that their aim was 'to destroy the prejudice and mistrust that exist between Christians and Marxists'.[45] Other priests found this objectionable and Christian Democrats were openly hostile to the radicals on the Catholic side. The economic difficulties of the regime and predictable inflation led the government to more socialist solutions and a threat of outright nationalization. Tensions increased and violence became almost normal. In 1972 the bishops warned against violence and political strife and urged compromise. But the government did not want compromise, nor did their opponents, including the Christian Democrats. In face of a prolonged drivers' strike no one listened to the bishops, least of all radical Catholics.

While the bishops spoke in generalities, they faced specific challenges from radical priests and religious belonging to Christians for Socialism, the original group of eighty now consisting of some 350 priests and nuns mostly in working-class districts. Their mission was to align the Church with socialism and the Popular Unity government, which they had supported since its inception, though there is no evidence that they exerted any real influence on the coalition or achieved any Christian goals. But they were absolutists of the left, accepting no compromise. They claimed that in the past the Church had served the dominant class and its economic interests. Now witness to Christian values meant support for Allende's government. They met Fidel Castro on his visit to Chile in November 1971, and some of them went to Cuba to see revolution at first hand. In a direct challenge to Church leaders and episcopal authority, they consistently rejected the bishops' call for compromise and dialogue and looked to the left for answers. Eventually the bishops took up the challenge and ruled that 'no priest or religious can belong to the movement known as Christians for Socialism'.[46]

Although the Allende regime did not directly harm religion, the intense divisions it provoked undermined the unity of the Church and had a demoralizing effect on religious life. The bishops' efforts to bring Allende and the Christian Democrat leadership together failed and their attitude to the Marxist president now hardened. As the revolutionary wing of the regime took to the streets, encouraging seizures of estates and factories, a floundering and divided government looked on helplessly. The armed forces struck on 11 September 1973, attacked the presidential palace (where Allende allegedly committed suicide), scattered Popular Unity, and ended democracy. Many bishops welcomed the military coup; others believed there was no alternative. Most priests and many lay leaders thought the same.

Pinochet

The military dictatorship was headed by General Augusto Pinochet, commander-in-chief, now hero of the right and terror of the left, who looked and acted the part. The episcopacy at first avoided confrontation and tacitly accepted the new regime. Some, a minority, went further and expressed their support. When it became obvious that the regime was there to stay and was growing ever more repressive, imposing a reign of terror which killed, tortured, and disappeared thousands of political detainees, the bishops became uneasy; and as the abuse of human rights mounted in 1974 their criticism became louder. From the time of their declaration of 24 April 1974 they spoke up for the victims, declaring that they would express the voice of 'those who do not have a voice', a position backed by

Pope Paul VI. Cardinal Silva did not hide his revulsion and condemned the violence and abuses. The Episcopal Conference was less outspoken. In September 1975 in the document *Evangelio y paz* there was veiled criticism of the injustice and poverty allowed by the regime but also gratitude to the military for freeing the country 'from a Marxist dictatorship'.[47] Between the terror of the night and the noonday devil where could the persecuted find refuge?

During the worst years of oppression, in 1974–78, the Church placed itself on the side of the oppressed. The Peace Committee, founded in December 1973 by Catholic, Lutheran, and Jewish leaders, began to help families of political prisoners and the disappeared, and gradually extended its work to the *comedores infantiles* (children's soup kitchens) and other forms of assistance in the working class *poblaciones*. After two years it was disbanded under protest by Cardinal Silva on the personal demand of Pinochet, whose distorted ideology regarded it as Marxist–Leninist. But the cardinal replaced it in January 1976 by the Vicaria de la Solidaridad (Vicariate of Solidarity), which became a vehicle of the Church's resistance, funded by financial aid from Europe, the United States, and Canada and awarded the human rights prize of the United Nations in 1978. The Vicariate, which Cardinal Silva made an official ministry of the Archdiocese of Santiago and therefore difficult to attack, employed a corps of carers and advisers, providing social services, employment assistance, education, legal advice, and investigation of disappearances. It monitored human rights violations and challenged the government in the worst cases. During the winter of Chile's tribulations this was the only haven for the oppressed and hope for a better future.

As the regime's security force, the Dirección de Inteligencia Nacional (DINA), tightened its grip in 1976, attacking unions and other dissidents, including Catholic leaders and Church authorities, the bishops reacted. Enrique Alvear, imbued with the spirit of Vatican II and Medellín and the quest for 'the Church of the poor', was appointed auxiliary bishop of Cardinal Silva and *vicario* of the western zone of Santiago, an area of poor working-class districts; between 1975 and 1982 he encouraged base communities, soup kitchens, housing committees, and other forms of popular action. His concern for the victims of oppression was shown when he visited concentration camps and led the denouncement of increasing disappearances.

While the episcopacy and the Catholic Church in general stood out against Pinochet and the military regime, minority groups of Catholics supported it, as did a number of individual bishops and priests, who regarded the *golpe* as a saving defence of Chile from communism and Marxist revolution, accepting the argument of Pinochet himself.[48]

Among the Catholic minorities favourable to the dictatorship were a number of academics in the Catholic University, where hostility to Vatican II and Cardinal Silva had long been latent, accompanied by denunciation of alleged Marxist infiltration of the Church. Even more vociferous were ultra-right-wing Catholic supporters of the military government, Tradición, Familia y Propiedad, a movement of a kind which was a familiar bane of liberal Catholics elsewhere in the Church. It published a book, apparently with government approval, imputing heresy to Church leaders and encouraging Catholics to repudiate the heretics and refuse to accept the sacraments from their hands. The bishops reacted sharply to these zealots and declared that they had tried to establish a rival teaching office and had placed themselves outside the Catholic Church. One conservative bishop underwent a conversion. Starting as a firm traditionalist who declared that 'the Church has no right to abandon the rich' and not hiding his support for Pinochet, Juan Francisco Fresno Larraín, archbishop of La Serena, moved towards a more radical stance with his ascent in office. Once appointed archbishop of Santiago in 1983 and cardinal in 1985, he became a leader associated with popular and democratic demands, speaking of the poor as the main challenge to the Chilean Church. Among Christians in Chile who failed to raise a voice of protest were the Evangelical Protestants, who numbered some one million believers. In December 1974, 2,500 Evangelical pastors signed a statement characterizing the military's intervention as 'the response of God to the prayers of all believers who see in Marxism satanic forces of darkness in their highest expression'.[49] A distinction should be made between traditional Protestants who were anti-Pinochet, and Pentecostals (the majority of Chilean Protestants) who supported the regime and won the favour of the dictator. The Lutheran Bishop Helmut, co-founder of the Peace Committee, was regarded as an enemy of the Pinochet regime and was refused permission to re-enter Chile from abroad.

Meanwhile, from 1975, the Church itself had been the target of a defamatory campaign in the official media, and bishops were insulted as 'useful idiots, ambitious, malicious and resentful'. The Vicariate of Solidarity was denounced as a Soviet puppet and spying agent, and Monsignor Camus, bishop of Linares, was accused of financing leftist parties. Pinochet and his wife attacked the Vicariate as 'more communist than the communists'. Pinochet himself sanctioned the use of torture: 'The members of the MIR [Movimiento de Izquierda Revolucionaria] must be tortured as they are insane and mad. Without torture they may not sing.'[50] Sheila Cassidy, a British doctor working in a clinic in El Salto where she was sickened by the evidence of poverty and repression around her, was arrested by the DINA in November 1975 for treating a wounded *mirista*. Naïve perhaps in the circumstances of the time, she nevertheless made a Christian response to suffering and for this she was arrested, tortured by electric shock, and kept in solitary confinement in the notorious Cuatro Alamos. After two months in prison she was released and deported, her case raising an international outcry against the regime.[51]

The history of this regime records that religious arguments for justice cut no ice. In spite of its pretensions as the guardian of Christian civilization against Marxism–Leninism, it treated the Catholic Church with barely disguised disdain. The Catholic universities were subject to government control, the publication of episcopal documents impeded, and requests of the Vatican for safe conduct for refugees sheltering in the papal nunciature were rejected. The Episcopal Conference was spied upon, the walls of churches, episcopal palaces, and other religious places were plastered with graffiti, bishops' cars were attacked, clerics associated with the Vicariate were imprisoned, and foreign clergy were expelled. There was worse: five priests were killed by agents of the regime, and there were frequent attacks on lay helpers. In 1985 alone 150 young Christian leaders were arrested, tortured, and threatened. In 1984–85 churches in various parts of the country were torched. Operatives and supporters of the regime attacked three bishops returning from a conference abroad and staged a menacing affray at the airport.

The bishops moved from restrained criticism to open dissent and went on to demand information on the disappeared. In April 1977 Pinochet appeared to relent and promised an eventual return to democracy. The Church's favourable response was a mistake, for he had never intended to relax his iron grip, and in 1978 his hard-line monetarist model was ruinous for workers and the poor. Unemployment was 25 per cent and getting worse, and the economy was in crisis. And now the regime focused increasingly on Cardinal Silva and other Church leaders, who received no favours for their readiness to listen. A plebiscite held in September 1980, which the bishops declared had to be free and open to be valid, was in fact manipulated to approve a new authoritarian constitution. And the worsening economic and social crisis in 1982 drove the episcopacy to proclaim its message of 17 December 1982, *El renacer de Chile*, a brief but impelling call to struggle for democracy and the rights of workers in the spirit of Christ's resurrection.[52] From democratic forces in Chile there was a response in August 1983 with the formation of Alianza Democrática, led by Christian Democrat Gabriel Valdés, which included, among others, socialists and Christian Democrat radicals. But the use of military force against demonstrators suggested that little had changed in ten years and that Pinochet would always reach for the gun when in trouble.[53] From then on the episcopacy stood solid with political democracy for the rights of the poor. In 1986 Monsignor Carlos González, bishop of Talca, denounced the

political crimes being committed, and a group of priests and religious
wrote an open letter to the military authorities of Santiago protesting
against brutalities. The majority of Catholics welcomed the defeat of
Pinochet in the presidential elections of 1989.

In the end the Church's opposition counted for little. Yet the same could
be said of the politicians, as Christian Democrats, Socialists, and
Communists failed to provide a united front. As for the international
community, politicians, diplomats, and bankers all gave Pinochet an easy
time. Yet the Church emerged with its reputation intact and its religious life
if anything invigorated, as vocations and mass attendance increased and
many lapsed Catholics, especially leftists, began to return, encouraged by
the Church's social commitment.

The second half of the twentieth century was not a heroic period for the
Latin American Church. The record was mixed. In Brazil the Church took
a firm stand against repression and violation of human rights, and in
general could be described as a progressive Church. Most bishops in
Argentina and Chile spoke the language of the universal Church, in terms
more reasonable than their critics usually allow. Ordinary Catholics
attending mass and the sacraments would see a clergy performing their
duties with care and conscience according to the timeless ritual of the
Church. But conditions were not timeless. In the mid-twentieth century
population growth, economic transformation, and social distress produced
a situation in which the rich were getting richer and the poor were ignored,
and serious questions were raised concerning protest and repression, not
only for legislators but also for Church leaders. The Churches in the
southern cone did not respond adequately to these questions and those
members of the clergy and laity who raised their voices were not encouraged. The Church's own examination of conscience was deficient. In the
hierarchical Church then prevailing, the cardinals, archbishops, and
bishops saw morality as a simple process of applying the commandments
of God and the Church to the faithful and expecting obedience. It never
occurred to them that the Church too could sin, that they too should
confess, do penance, and make a firm purpose of amendment. The Latin
American Church was not unique in this respect. But the conditions in the
southern cone – poverty, injustice, oppression – made these dilemmas
more acute and the tests for the Church more demanding. The Argentine
Church, a prisoner of its history and character, failed the tests. The Chilean
Church passed, though not completely and not without misjudgements
along the way.

CHAPTER 10

Religion and Revolution

Cuba: A Silent Church

REVOLUTION BECAME A concept which automatically legitimized any movement that bore its name, regardless of the policies or the people. In Latin America the Cuban Revolution led the way and, in spite of its diminutive size, Cuba came to be seen by many as a model ready made for export to the rest of the subcontinent.

Pre-revolutionary Cuba illustrated on a small scale many of Latin America's traditional problems. With a stagnant economy, dependent on the export of a single product, sugar, and on the custom of a single market, the United States, it was a suitable case for change. The rigid social structure offered nothing to the depressed and landless peasantry, while the incipient middle class, though not without wealth, was without political power. This was the key factor. The revolution which Fidel Castro led against the dictatorship of Fulgencio Batista was not a peasant or working-class revolution. He himself came from a family of moderately wealthy landowners in eastern Cuba which 'had accumulated resources', as he said, sufficient to send him to Catholic schools and law studies at the University of Havana.[1] He received most of his support from middle-class radicals and democrats, especially of the younger generation, and this was reflected in his original power base among guerrillas and revolutionaries and in his early programme. He had promised to restore Cuba's democratic constitution, hold general elections, and guarantee rights to political parties; his social programme consisted of little more than a commitment to land reform and a more equitable distribution of wealth. Once in power, from 1 January 1959, he began to define democracy not in terms of elections or parties, but in terms of state-imposed reforms.

The Cuban communists had collaborated with Batista and regarded Castro's movement with suspicion. But after his victory they quickly made a bid for control of a revolution they had not fought. How can we explain Castro's conversion to communism? The argument which gained much currency – that United States' hostility left him with no alternative – lacked credibility.[2] A true revolution needs more positive reasons. From as early as April 1959 he made it clear that he was not interested in aid from his powerful neighbour, and he deliberately held aloof from the United States at a time when American policy was ineffective rather than hostile. Reasons for his conversion must be sought within Cuba itself. Castro's need for an ideology and his even greater need for a disciplined and efficient political machine, neither of which his own movement could supply, induced him to allow more and more influence to the communists and eventually to adopt communism as his own political philosophy. In December 1961, in a mammoth speech delivered in the early hours of the morning, he declared: 'We have to carry out an anti-imperialist and socialist revolution . . . We believe in Marxism, the only true revolutionary theory. I say this here with complete satisfaction and confidence. I am a Marxist–Leninist, and I will be a Marxist–Leninist until the last day of my life.'[3] Not necessarily the whole truth but what he wanted people to believe.

The application of this philosophy led him to create a new united party of the revolution, which was a merger of the Cuban Communist Party and Castro's own immediate followers. The merger was not without its tensions, but the government began to deliver: land was collectivized, business nation-alized, and a Marxist system of education created. The result was not an exact reproduction of a Stalinist state, but it led to greater social equality and to some improvement in the prospects of rural workers. The price, however, was political freedom. And economically the revolution did not fulfil its promise. The problems of industrializing what was essentially an agricultural economy were not overcome. Agricultural production itself dropped, and Cuba remained dependent on sugar, still tied to a foreign paymaster, this time the Soviet Union, from which it received not only economic assistance but also weapons, including, by October 1962, medium- and long-range missiles.

As advocates of social reform and revolutionaries who reached power by violence, the Cuban leaders were convinced that it was their mission to extend the revolution throughout the whole of the subcontinent. At first Castro appeared to many Latin Americans as a new saviour, a leader who would inspire social revolution and economic emancipation. But Latin American opinion underwent growing disillusionment. By the end of 1961 it was clear that he intended to turn Cuba into a communist state. By October 1962 it looked as though he was even ready to turn it into a Soviet base. While these developments appealed to hard-core revolutionaries, they lost Castro much following among democratic opinion in Latin America which regarded him as a betrayer of the Cuban Revolution.

Left-of-centre democratic parties began to appreciate that they were the particular enemy because they were his rivals for the support of the masses. Moreover, in some countries such as Venezuela, Peru, and Chile, the programmes of democratic parties came to have a wider appeal than the Cuban call for terrorism in the towns and warfare in the hills. Within Cuba itself, however, his position was assured. The revolution he made in the political and social life of the island was there to stay.

Cuban Catholics, many of whom had been among the opponents of Batista, watched these developments with disbelief, while the Church authorities wavered between support and suspicion. Pre-revolutionary Cuba was a secular rather than a Catholic society. It could not produce its own clergy. Two-thirds of its 220 priests and most of its 441 religious were Spaniards who had come to Cuba with a pre-Vatican II mentality and a Francoist upbringing. The Church structure was weak, with only 210 parishes in the whole country, and in 1955 just 130 seminarists.[4] In 1954 the Catholic Students' Association of the University of Havana conducted a national survey of 4,000 people, and found that 96.5 per cent believed in God, while 19 per cent belonged to no organized religion.[5] Ninety-one per cent of children were baptized as Catholics, but only 50 per cent received First Communion. Seventy-two and a half per cent of all respondents, but only 52 per cent of rural respondents, said they were Catholics, and 27 per cent reported that they had never seen a priest. Castro himself spent his childhood in rural Cuba without sight of church or priest. Just 24 per cent of Catholics attended services regularly, and only 16 per cent of all marriages were solemnized in church. The revolution dealt a further blow. Official Catholic statistics show that the proportion of baptized Catholics declined from 90.4 per cent in 1961 to 50.3 per cent in 1976. Curiously, while secularism prevailed, spiritualism flourished, and syncretic Afro-Cuban religious practices enjoyed widespread popularity.

The first response of Archbishop Enrique Pérez Serantes to the Cuban Revolution welcomed it as a popular victory. But within a month enthusiasm turned to criticism, when summary death penalties were meted out to 'war criminals' and education reforms threatened Catholic schools. The suspicion of incipient communism was confirmed in the bishops' minds by some aspects of the Agrarian Reform Law of 17 May 1959, and the growing closeness of Cuba and the Soviet Union in the course of 1960. Recalling the Soviet takeover of Eastern Europe in alliance with collaborating communists in the years after 1945, they began to make communism the central issue. As the feast of Christ the King was celebrated the hierarchy were convinced that two alternatives were facing Cuba: Rome or Moscow. Archbishop Pérez Serantes declared, 'We are not tied to the North Americans by any ties of blood, language, tradition, coexistence or training.

We don't feel embarrassed to admit, and indeed it would be cowardly not to admit it, that we have no hesitation in choosing between North Americans and Soviets.'[6] The severing of diplomatic relations between the United States and Cuba in January 1961 deprived the bishops of their only realistic alliance. And the fact remained that in 1960 there were Catholic opponents of the revolution who were not connected to the United States; such was a group of Catholic students led by Alberto Müller, nephew of the bishop of Matanzas, though he was soon forced out of the university.[7]

By the end of 1960 coexistence was impossible. Although Castro was circumspect in his relations with the Soviet Union, the bishops could not ignore the communist direction of economic and social policies; they also criticized Marxist-type textbooks, the insulting of priests, the restriction of access to the media, and the interruption of religious ceremonies. Moreover, the Church was losing its power base. The migration of large numbers of middle-class Cubans to Miami deprived the Church of committed Catholics and often of priests. Clerical teachers in schools now closed or confiscated had nowhere else to go. Were priests deserting Cuba? Not entirely. A group of more than fifty Spanish Jesuits committed themselves expressly to stay, in spite of the risks. On 7 August 1960 the bishops published a collective letter in which they acknowledged some positive aspects of the revolution, including agrarian reforms, but signalled an alert: 'The Church has nothing to fear from basic social reforms, for it is always concerned for the deprived, but it will never compromise with communism.' The bishops cannot keep quiet, for 'the absolute majority of the Cuban people, who are Catholic, are opposed to materialist and atheist communism.'[8] Castro reacted promptly, calling the bishops 'traitors to Christ', while the government press denounced the Church as 'an imperialist institution, an agent of the rich, and exploiter of the poor'.

In the course of 1961, a critical year in the history of the revolution, Cuba edged closer to the Soviet political and socio-economic model, without copying it completely. The brief Bay of Pigs invasion, staged by Cuban exiles with some United States support, was a fiasco, securing no popular uprising and no military success. Claiming, among other things, to act on behalf of Cuban Catholics in the name of God, justice, and democracy, it gave the government the opportunity to move further against the Church, to place a number of bishops and priests under house arrest, and to nationalize Catholic schools, the state taking over the appointment of teachers.

A further exodus of Catholics, now encouraged by the hierarchy, added to the Church's woes. Among those who stayed, views were polarized between reformist and conservative elements. The conservative cause was led by Monsignor Eduardo Boza Masvidal, auxiliary bishop of Havana, whose parish of Our Lady of Charity, the patroness of Cuba, became known for opposition; he called on Catholics to remain strong in their faith and to constitute a Church militant to keep religion alive. In September 1961 on the feast day of Our Lady of Charity a large procession made its way from the parish church towards the presidential palace shouting anti-government and anti-Soviet slogans. Boza claimed the people were acting within their rights. The government claimed that Boza had manipulated them to convert the procession into a counter-revolutionary demonstration. Both positions were more or less true.[9] Following the disturbances the government rounded up the clerical suspects, including Boza, and on 17 September he was expelled to Spain along with 135 priests and religious; most were Spanish, though Boza was Cuban. This was decisive for the Church. Since the beginning of the revolution it had lost its schools and with them a source of income; the number of priests was down from 800 to 200; many Catholics had left; and relations with the revolutionary government were hostile: not violent persecution, perhaps, but hostile pressure. Pope John XXIII sympathized with them in their persecution, 'not bloody, but a cause of suffering'.[10]

If the Church no longer had any confidence in the government, a minority of Catholics supported the revolution in the sense that they wanted the Church to come to terms with change and to accept reforms.[11] Others sought to reconcile their religious beliefs with socialism and expressed admiration for Castro. Protestant denominations appeared to be even more conciliatory towards the revolution. Pro-revolution Catholics included laypeople, priests, and more than one bishop, convinced enough by socialism to overlook or deny the existence of a persecuted Church. Without being especially welcomed by the government, Catholic radicals were marginalized by the Church and forced to keep a low profile. The Franciscan friar, Ignacio Biaín, editor of La Quincena, a progressive 'Christian response to the problems of the day', not only sympathized with the revolution but desired it to triumph. He was pressed to desist by his superiors and virtually retired, dying in 1963.[12] Later, in 1991, the Communist Party of Cuba, having barred believers from the Party, belatedly allowed them in. The bishops reminded Catholics that they could not be both Catholics and communists.

In the course of the 1960s the Cuban Church, weakened in numbers, in clergy, and in influence, and conscious that the government had won the battle if not the argument, settled simply for self-preservation. This was the period of the Silent Church, seven years between 1962 and 1969, when the Episcopal Conference did not speak. Largely isolated from mainstream developments in the wider Church, Vatican II, Medellín and Puebla conferences, it retained a mindset from the past. It still remained alert to excessive aggression by the government, and protested when young priests were conscripted into work camps. But in general both sides moderated their words and actions. Rome encouraged the Cuban Church to participate in Medellín in 1968, which was attended by several Cuban representatives. From Rome, too, came several prestigious visitors, including Pedro Arrupe, superior general of the Jesuits, Monsignor Alfonso López Trujillo, the secretary general of CELAM, and Cardinal Bernard Gantin, of the pontifical Council for Justice and Peace. In 1971 sixteen Cubans were ordained.

The character of the episcopacy changed, older bishops giving way to a new generation, gradually creating an all-Cuban hierarchy. Nuncio Cesare Zacchi, a young Vatican diplomat, spent fourteen years in revolutionary Cuba and took most problems in his stride, whatever side they came from. He believed that the Church 'should adapt to all regimes, since its imperative is the care of souls, and as a result the flock should not be abandoned'. He saw that the revolution was there to stay and he urged Catholics to accept the facts. 'I consider the Church to be aware of the change of political system in this country; it is an incontrovertible fact which is now irreversible. As a result the Church should adapt to these changes, as it has shown in Europe.'[13]

For some Cuban Catholics Zacchi went too far, and many bishops were uncomfortable with him.[14] He praised the Cuban Revolution for its redistribution of wealth. 'The people have obtained a radical change in their material well-being. Now there is social justice, something which was not prevalent before.' He encouraged Catholics to consider political participation and to collaborate in appropriate revolutionary institutions. Compared to Eastern Europe, where he had witnessed real persecution of the Church, the Cuban regime was mild. 'Here in socialist Cuba nothing like that has happened. The Castro government has been very tolerant.' He was even prepared to ask the question: was Castro a Christian? 'From an ideological perspective he is not, since he has declared himself to be a Marxist–Leninist. However, I consider him to be "ethically" a Christian.'[15] As an exercise in political analysis, and in the eyes of Cuba's Catholic leaders, Zacchi's take on the Cuban Revolution could only be regarded as superfluous. Catholics were exhorted to adapt to suit the Communist regime. And what did they receive in return? A minimum of tolerance. Traditional Catholics were not impressed.

The silence was broken in 1969. Two pastoral letters conveyed a revised message from the bishops, leading to dialogue with the regime in the years 1979–87. The April letter condemned the blockade imposed by the United States which it said was contributing to unnecessary suffering. In the pastoral of 8 September, the feast of Our Lady of Charity, patroness of Cuba, the bishops distinguished between an ideology and the person who believes it. They called on Catholics to respect the 'honesty' of communists; and to work with them in the practical order of things. Catholics should collaborate in 'the undertaking of development', with 'all people of good will, be they atheists or believers'.[16] 'We must approach the atheist with all the respect and family-spirited charity that one deserves simply by being a human being. We should not rule out the possibility that such a person has come to that position honestly, for it may be very sincere; nor should we avoid working with the person in the practical realm of our earthly endeavours. For example in development efforts.'[17]

While the bishops seem to have absorbed some of the sermons of Zacchi, Castro continued with a crudely class interpretation of religion which yielded nothing. 'It was a religion of one single class, for the benefit of that single class.' He saw religion as an agency of social service and development, and insisted that there was more Christianity in Marxism. The Cuban Communist Party did not change: religion was based on ignorance and would disappear. This left no room for accommodation. During his visit to Chile in November 1971 Castro's attitude towards Christianity was condescending rather than accommodating. 'Although Christianity may have arisen two thousand years ago as a utopian teaching, like a mere spiritual consolation, I think that in our age it has the possibility of being not a utopian teaching but a real one.'[18]

Prospects were not good. Protestants were moving away from the Catholic position and becoming more responsive to the regime. The Confession of Faith of the Presbyterian Reformed Church stated, 'The Church lives joyfully in the midst of the socialist revolution', because the revolution had inaugurated new development, and communists could be an inspiration to them. Such idealism was not for Catholics. The Reverend Jesse Jackson visited the island, invited by the Baptist Church in Cuba on the occasion of the anniversary of the murder of Martin Luther King. He held a press conference with Castro and together they attended a memorial ceremony in the main Methodist church in Cuba.

The existence of political prisoners revealed the true nature of the Cuban Revolution. Catholics and dissidents who endured the regime regarded it not as a *modus vivendi* but a *modus moriendi*. The Constitution of 1976 guaranteed 'free profession of any religion, and free exercise of any worship'.[19] But the same constitution declared, 'The State will promote the communist formation of the new generations'. In the same year the Communist Party of Cuba proclaimed its dialectical materialism; and declared that for the Party 'religion is not a private matter', for among the duties of the Party was that of freeing the masses from religious beliefs.[20] To some extent it succeeded and managed to de-christianize a great part of society, and to challenge the faith of what remained. Various statistics show a decline in Church membership from 89.3 per cent regarded as Catholics in 1960 to 38.9 per cent in 1983, and a decline of priests from 723 in 1960 to 213 in 1980. Now there were only 100,000 to 150,000 Church members.

More promising signs appeared in the following years. In 1984 the archbishop of Havana, Jaime Ortega, stated: 'The Church is not only bishops and priests, but it encompasses the entire Catholic people. It is necessary that Catholics recall the Second Vatican Council and realize that the Church is nothing more than the Catholic part of the people of which they are a part.'[21] In February 1986 the Encuentro Nacional Eclesial Cubano, the first national conclave, was attended by Cardinal Eduardo Pironio, representing the Vatican, and several United States and Latin American bishops. It expressed support 'for the socialist objectives of the Cuban revolution, though not for the programme of the Communist Party' and praised the social advances of the Cuban system, perpetuating the illusion that this was a social revolution gone wrong. A number of requests were made, at odds with the initial premises. First, there should be respect for religious beliefs and an end to the militant atheism in Cuba's school curriculum. There should be greater access to the media for Catholic groups.[22] The Church continued to pursue dialogue and cooperation with the government. Castro authorized the entry of foreign priests, but only gradually, most of them waiting almost a year for visas.

Some Catholics responded to Castro. They were encouraged by a Brazilian Dominican known as Frei Betto, who had been persecuted for his faith in Brazil, and spoke to Castro in a long and accommodating interview. Castro spoke of his early religious experience, his Salesian and Jesuit schools, alleging that the Jesuits taught a religion of rewards and punishments. He blamed the Church for the early conflicts and described it as an instrument of domination and exploitation used in defence of the class interests of the bourgeoisie.[23] The Protestants, he claimed, were less conflictive; their schools were accessible, and they followed a practical form of religion, working among the poorer sectors of society, and reaching a better understanding with the revolution. In most respects he was politically correct, speaking with approval of Archbishop Romero, Monsignor Zacchi, liberation theology, and base communities, and showing a bias towards Christians for Socialism and the priests in the Sandinista government. He spoke of a 'strategic alliance' between religion and the revolution, but this would depend upon the Church behaving as the revolution prescribed and within the limits the revolution allowed. 'From a strictly political viewpoint, and I believe I know something about politics, I even think that one can be a Marxist without ceasing to be a Christian, that it is possible to work together with the Marxist communist in order to transform the world.'[24] An easy ride for the dictator? Another religious, the

Franciscan Miguel Angel Loredo, who had spent some years in prison for helping to hide a fugitive involved in a hijack killing, wondered why Frei Betto abased himself before Castro, a not entirely just appraisal of the interview.

In his talks with Frei Betto, Castro said, 'I am utterly convinced that a visit from the pope would be useful and positive for the church, for Cuba and, I believe, useful for the third world, and would be useful for all countries in many respects.' It was 1996 before Castro met the pope, in Rome, when he invited the pontiff to visit Cuba. John Paul II arrived in Cuba in January 1998 and appeared with Castro at several public events, where he was always treated with respect. Both leaders had an agenda. The pope wanted greater freedom for the Church. Castro wanted support against the United States trade embargo at a time of special economic difficulty following the collapse of the Soviet Union. His speech of welcome was an expert exercise in political propaganda, little of which could be actually contradicted, describing the achievements of the Cuban Revolution and giving a partial view of toleration, without a word on persecution.[25] The pope condemned the embargo but received little in return. One hundred and one political prisoners were released, the cancellation of a negative rather than affirmation of positive progress for Cubans. Like many of the papal visits around the world, the Cuban visit aroused immediate enthusiasm but brought few long-term benefits.

For the rest of the twentieth century and beyond Cuba remained trapped in its Stalinist revolution, economically stagnant, deprived of liberty, and still a menace to anyone professing Christian ideals of freedom, to Church workers, to human rights activists and journalists. In March 2003, seventy-five dissidents were convicted of treason and imprisoned for periods of between six and twenty-eight years. Cardinal Jaime Ortega and other Church leaders, who played a prominent role in negotiating changes from the Castro government, hailed the slightest concession as 'very positive', while the wives and mothers of political prisoners, the Women in White, struggled to maintain their weekly protests.[26] This was Cuba after fifty years of revolution.

Promise and Prejudice in Nicaragua

The Nicaraguan Revolution, a prize for the left, a promise for the poor, and the darling of liberal progressives across the world, was a dilemma for the Church.

Twentieth-century Nicaragua, the largest state in Central America, with a mestizo population of some 3 million, inherited an economy based on the export of coffee and cotton; the rest was subsistence agriculture. Low

living standards, a life expectancy of 53, mass illiteracy, and rural malnutrition made survival a struggle. Politics were polarized between liberals, who
were historically anti-clerical, and conservatives, dominated by the
Chamorro family, who had come to power in 1909 aided by American
marines. Both parties were examples of elite politics and they ruled without
reference to popular interests, rarely producing stability. A modicum of
order was preserved by the presence of the marines until 1933, which did
nothing for the reputation of the United States and little for permanent
stability or welfare. A hint of the future was provided by Augusto César
Sandino, the anti-American guerrilla leader, who was assassinated by the
National Guard in 1934. The head of the National Guard, Anastasio
Somoza, became president in 1936, backed by conservative and liberal
politicians, and Nicaragua became a state virtually owned by the Somoza
dynasty. Serial dictators, they clung to power through control of the army
and police, and through handouts of spurious social reform to key interest
groups, with financial assistance from the United States and the United
Nations. Anastasio Somoza amassed a fortune in land, commercial crops,
manufactures, and shipping, and boasted, 'You'd do the same thing yourself
if you were in my place.' Nicaragua was a revolution waiting to happen.

By the 1970s, the time of the third Somoza, events were turning against
the dynasty. There were guerrillas in the hills, the Frente Sandinista de
Liberación Nacional (FSLN), and the USA withdrew its support. The FSLN
had started in the 1960s as a Castro-type movement of young revolutionaries led by Tomás Borge, appropriating the name of Sandino to screen
their Marxist and Communist ideology. It also had an urban front in
Managua, where Daniel Ortega was a leading light.

The Church allowed itself to be co-opted by the Somozas in return for
benefits. Pastorals were pious exercises in Christian resignation, prayer
made a virtue of poverty and suffering. Even when responding to changing
economic conditions and the unease of younger clergy in the 1950s, the
hierarchy still preached obedience, in order to avoid revolution and
communism. In his pastoral letter of August 1959 Archbishop González y
Robledo counselled, 'we should state that our government is not an
ungodly one, rather it is a benefactor of the Church'.[27] Bishop Calderón y
Padilla of León was exceptional; consistently hostile to the Somozas for
over thirty years he spoke out for social justice: when civil authority flouts
the divine laws, 'resistance is a duty and obedience a crime'.[28]

Nicaragua was overdue for change in the Church as well as the state. It
was a conservative Church which had lost its privileged position during the
anti-clerical government of the liberal José Santos Zelaya, but preserved a
popular tradition, seen in devotion to the Lord of Esquipulas. Subsequent
support for the Somozas enabled the Church to recover, but at a price in

moral reputation. Renewal began in the 1960s as the Church changed its attitude to the world, promoted Catholic action in parishes and evangelization in town and country, and encouraged higher education. In 1965 Ernesto Cardenal, priest and poet, began to minister to poor peasants in the island of Solentiname on Lake Nicaragua and led them in reading and meditating on the Bible, which with the comments of the peasants became *The Gospel in Solentiname*. In Nicaragua the reaction to Medellín was hesitant among the hierarchy, more positive at grass roots, and in some dioceses base communities were created. The appointment of Miguel Obando y Bravo, a Salesian priest and teacher, as archbishop of Managua in 1970 gave an impulse to the Church and a more vigorous face to Catholicism, one which would respond to events in Nicaragua, if not in the wider Church.

The Nicaraguan Church responded to Vatican II and Medellín in the *Encuentro Pastoral* of 1969, when bishops and priests came together to confront the future of the Church in Nicaragua, a future troubled by the fraudulent election of another Somoza as president and a worsening of the socio-economic condition of his people. There was a poll of clergy and laity. The Jesuit priest Noel García reported, 'The hierarchy is decrepit, conservative, stationary, advanced in age, apathetic, negative, disunited, hardly accessible to the public, some of whom have no idea about nor interest in the hierarchy . . . The Church in Nicaragua is sorely lacking true spiritual leadership from its pastors.'[29] In this report diocesan clergy fared little better: 'there is very little sensitivity to the social problems of the faithful'. 'The parish priest has little to do with the faithful, and any form of community life is sorely lacking. The priest is only seen at the Sunday mass, which is attended by very few people; the spirit of Vatican II has not reached the majority of parishes – whether that influence be on the level of the liturgy, preaching or apostolate.' A new leader was needed but none was in sight. 'The Church in Nicaragua is lacking true spiritual leadership for its pastors.' Many priests agreed with Noel García, and there was some response. But reform produced reaction and the result was polarization.

A huge earthquake in 1972 virtually destroyed Managua and filled the pockets of the dictator and his henchmen with aid money. A middle-class party of opposition came into being in 1974, the Democratic Union for Freedom. The Church too was drawing away from the Somoza regime: in their pastoral letter of 1972, the bishops demanded an end to the dictatorship. Obando now had a public role as mediator. In 1978 the assassination of Pedro Joaquín Chamorro, a critic of the regime in his newspaper *La Prensa*, stirred further opposition. But a harder challenge came from the Sandinista FSLN, which cultivated not only the urban middle class but also the Church, or at least progressives in the Church. A number of priests responded, as did Church groups and students. The Christians in the Sandinista movement did not include Obando, but for the moment he was not opposed. In the 1970s Obando consistently upbraided Somoza but refused to accept the FSLN as an alternative, preferring to throw his weight behind a middle-class alliance of traditional political opponents of the dictator and to press for reform, not revolution. This was also the preference of the other bishops. But by 1977 the increasing repression and in particular the brutalities of the National Guard opened their eyes to the impossibility of reform from Somoza. Atrocities against peasants and Church workers in Zelaya could not be ignored, and in 1978 the bishops denounced 'the state of terror, the arbitrary, indefinite detentions, the inhuman methods of interrogation, the lack of respect for life, and the accumulation of wealth in the hands of the few'.[30] 'We simply cannot keep quiet.' By January 1978 the Church leaders were in the forefront of the opposition to Somoza's rule. And in September 1978 they urged President Carter to cut off all aid to Nicaragua, 'a regime that sowed death in its wake'. But this did not alter their view of the Sandinistas, whom they regarded as 'extremists' and Marxists, and they were not blind to the preference of the FSLN for the Cuban model and its ties to the Cuban government.

On 17 July 1979 Somoza fled to Miami, and two days later the FSLN entered the capital. The bishops' pastoral letter of 17 November, four months after the insurrection, expressed support for the 'present revolutionary movement', and now seemed an opportune moment to implement the Church's preferential option for the poor.[31] But soon sympathy changed to censure. The bishops called for priests to resign from the government; by October they were openly criticizing the Sandinista regime, and Church support was confined to radical priests and the Catholic left.

The revolution against Somoza did not consist of Ortega and the FSLN alone, nor were the Sandinistas a single front. They were an awkward coalition of independent factions, brought together to topple Somoza; they then formed the National Directorate, without, however, uniting the movement. Edén Pastora, Comandante Cero (Commander Zero), who had probably done more fighting than Ortega, was leader of Alianza Revolucionaria Democrática (ARDE) in the south, some 2,000 men; but he was not a member of the Sandinistas, being too independent and hostile to Marxism, with ties to democratic politicians in Latin America. Once the Sandinistas were in power they shunted him aside, keeping him always as a deputy minister. In July 1981 he left Nicaragua and in Panama announced his rejection of the Sandinista front, which he accused of being too close to Cuba and the Soviet Union, in violation of their pledge of non-alignment. He became in effect an anti-Sandinista guerrilla leader, calling them 'a bunch of frauds who had never participated in a major battle'.[32]

The coalition also included Democrats of the centre and the left, Catholic independents, and the Church itself: all these played a vital role and expected their presence or at least their views to be acknowledged. But the core group, the pure Sandinistas, tightened their control and in the aftermath of victory showed greater political skill than the others; taking a leaf from communist tactics in post-war Eastern Europe, they gradually levered out all but the hard-core Marxists.

A junta of five was announced on 16 June 1979 to serve as Nicaragua's next government: it included Violeta Chamorra, widow of the assassinated publisher, and Alfonso Robelo, a young democrat, but also militants Sergio Ramírez, a Marxist writer, who announced that the new regime 'would take the route of representative democracy', Moisés Hassan, a mathematics professor, Tomás Borge, and Daniel Ortega, guerrilla leader. Real power was in the hands of the Sandinista *comandantes*, the National Directorate, and they, not the moderates, were ready to seize power.[33] The influence of the Cuban model was conspicuous from the beginning, strengthened by supplies of relief and weapons and hundreds of Cuban advisers, some of them assuming key posts in the ministries. Weapons also came from North Korea and the Soviet Union. The Sandinista Defence Committees seemed an obvious copy from Cuba. 'The idea was to form a party along Marxist–Leninist lines ... There was never any intention of creating a pluralist project with a broad distribution of power.'[34] In the first year socialist 'reforms' were introduced, banks and mines nationalized, agrarian reform was decreed, and a Sandinista Army recruited.

The Sandinistas forced many non-Marxist ministers to resign and replaced them with senior *comandantes*. The Council of State, which had been projected as a balanced representation, was now packed with Sandinistas. At this point, in April 1980, Violeta Chamorro and Alfonso Robelo, the two Catholic and democratic members of the junta representing the Movimiento Democrático Nicaragüense (MDN), resigned alleging that the constitutional changes were undemocratic. 'The FSLN has violated its trust and broken the political unity of Nicaragua.'[35] The government ended any hope of elections and blocked Robelo's attempt to organize a political rally by the MDN. A literacy campaign, inaugurated amidst great enthusiasm and international acclaim, become an instrument of socialist propaganda on the Cuban model and was dominated by Cuban advisers.

The Sandinista Revolution, therefore, was a misnomer. The Revolution began as a coalition of anti-Somoza interests, ranging from democratic politicians to guerrilla activists; it continued as a struggle with shared participation, in which the Sandinistas were not necessarily the most effective force; and it ended with a Sandinista takeover of a revolution of which they had been only one component. There was a price to pay for Sandinista leadership: they took control of power and of all departments of government. By 1982 the nine *comandantes* of the FSLN directorate were in charge: they controlled the security forces, the Council of State and the Junta, and held the major ministries of Defence, Interior, Planning, and Agrarian Reform. Now only the Church and its leader Archbishop Obando y Bravo were independent. It was a classic scenario. The democrats were levered out; not only their leading politicians, but anyone not approved by the *comandantes* and their Cuban advisers. The case of Donald Castillo is instructive. Economist and activist of the left, with democratic credentials of anti-Somoza vintage and cooperating with the FSLN, he returned to Nicaragua in 1979 to work for the new government. But he was questioned by intelligence officers on his loyalty to the FSLN and left Nicaragua to join the ARDE in 1982. In Caracas in 1983, a time of Bolivarian congresses, Sergio Ramírez was questioned by Latin American delegates on the direction Nicaragua was taking following the marginalization of democrats and middle-class personnel. He was unrepentant about its Marxist turn.

The exclusion of the democrats, Pastora, and the Church left the Sandinista militants, the Marxists, and leftist priests to inherit the revolution. There were five priests in the government, including Ernesto Cardenal, Minister of Culture, Fernando Cardenal, Jesuit Minister of Education, and Miguel D'Escoto, in Foreign Affairs. Controversy erupted over their presence, and Archbishop Obando never agreed to it. A statement of the bishops (1 June 1981) made it clear that the priests should leave the government and return to their priestly functions. Four priests not only resisted but declared total commitment to the Sandinista regime: 'We declare our unbreakable commitment with the Sandinista revolution, faithful to our people, which is the same as being faithful to the will of God.'[36]

Ernesto Cardenal was a convinced Marxist: 'There's no incompatibility between Christianity and Marxism . . . Marxism is a scientific method for studying society and changing it . . . I have said many times that I am a Marxist for Christ.'[37] At Solentiname he drew a parallel between the kingdom of Christ and communist society, citing Cuba as evidence: 'The Communists try to achieve a perfect society where each one contributes his labour and receives according to his needs . . . in the Gospels they were already teaching that.'[38] Fernando Cardenal refused to resign his political post and the Jesuits released him from the order. He justified his position: 'Here in Nicaragua there is no need for any serious religious problem between the Church and the revolution. There is no dogma of Christian faith at stake, no Catholic doctrine or hypothesis on Christian morals. What exists here is a political confrontation. Some bishops have a political agenda.'[39]

Faced with concern over its appropriation of the revolution, the regime sought to reassert its religious credentials. An official statement by the FSLN 'On the Role of Religion in the New Nicaragua' (7 October 1980) defended the revolution against the charge of being anti-Christian and Marxist:

> Some authors have asserted that religion is a mechanism for spreading false consciousness among people, which serves to justify the exploitation of one class by another. This assertion undoubtedly has historic validity to the extent that in different historical epochs religion has served as a theoretical basis for political domination. Suffice it to recall the role the missionaries played in the process of domination and colonization of the Indians of our country. However, we Sandinistas state that our experience shows that when Christians, basing themselves on their faith, are capable of responding to the needs of the people and of history, those very beliefs lead them to revolutionary activism. Our experience shows us that one can be a believer and a consistent revolutionary at the same time, and that there is no insoluble contradiction between the two.[40]

A crude and obdurate attempt by Marxists to reinterpret religious history.

There were further conflicts in the period 1980–82. The government blocked papal communications with the Nicaraguan bishops. The Church accused the regime of exploiting religious feast days and using religious symbols to promote the aims of the government and exceeding its competence. The case of the 'naked priest' in 1982 was more sensational. Visiting a female parishioner, Father Bismarck Carballo was alleged to have been caught in bed with her and was pursued down the street. A government TV crew happened to be passing and caught the scene on film. Archbishop Obando regarded this as deliberate entrapment, which it probably was. Obando's resistance to the government was supported by the Vatican and by Cardinal Alfonso López Trujillo, president of CELAM.

The anti-Sandinista front had a military wing, made up of former *Somocistas* but also of democrats. The Contras (counter-revolutionaries), whose aim was to topple the Sandinista government, operated in Nicaragua from Honduras with the financial and material support of President Reagan, who also had United States forces in Honduras. Like their enemies the Sandinistas, they were guilty of human rights abuses and also terrorized perceived opponents, targeting Catholic activists on the government side. Catholic lay leaders Felipe and Marías Barreda were tortured and killed by Contras in 1983, an action condemned by Bishop López Ardán of Esteli. Hundreds of other Catholic activists were killed by the Contras. Both sides had their apologists, within and outside Nicaragua, and selective indignation was common. And the brunt of the fighting on both sides was borne by young Nicaraguans from the poorer classes.

The Nicaraguan Church was led by Miguel Obando y Bravo. Small and powerfully built with the mestizo features typical of Nicaraguans, he had resisted Somoza's overtures, defended human rights, and sought to create an independent and socially conscious Church. Appointed Archbishop of Managua in 1970, his anti-Somoza credentials were recognized by all. But he condemned the concept of class struggle, favoured reform not revolution, and was always wary of the FSLN, preferring a coalition of democratic opponents of the dictatorship. Obando was faced not only by a Marxist government but also by grass-roots initiatives in his own Church, among intellectuals, students, and communities of squatters and slum dwellers, many of them activated by radical and often foreign priests. Priests and people on the left gave rise to the so-called Iglesia Popular, which worked for the poor but also had the effect of polarizing the Church between those who thought that radicalization was a step too far and those committed to a religion dedicated to the cause of justice and welfare. Obando had no time for the development of an Iglesia Popular, a parallel Church which he believed would threaten Church unity. He was determined to take the whole Church along the road not of revolution but of moderate reformism.

Criticized as an arch-reactionary, Obando was in fact more like an archbishop used to be. His religion tended towards the pre-Vatican II model and the absolute authority of the hierarchy, with little time for Medellín or liberal theology. In contrast to trends in contemporary European Catholicism, Obando's ideal Church was a Church of authority, orthodoxy, and conservative politics. Seen from the other side, in the words of D'Escoto referring to his pro-Contra position, he was 'an accomplice in the assassination of our people'. But his followers saw him as a Church leader in the mould of Pope John Paul II, who made him the first cardinal for Central America. According to an experienced and informed observer of Sandinista Nicaragua,

> Archbishop Obando's principal complaints against the Sandinistas – that they were intolerant, instinctively repressive, and contemptuous of traditional religion – were essentially correct. No one who cared for human rights could fail to cheer when Obando denounced mass jailings, mistreatment of prisoners, forced relocations, and other Sandinista outrages. He had been an inspirational voice for justice during the Somoza years, and had accumulated unparalleled moral authority among Nicaraguans. But when he refused to use that authority impartially, it slowly began to weaken.[41]

Many of Obando's public positions, especially on the Contras, were controversial, even to moderate Catholics. To accept the right of fighters to use force to defend their principles and to protect the Catholic position was morally risky, but probably defensible. But to fail to condemn Contra abuses and atrocities was to lose moral credibility and to damage the Church. He denounced only the Sandinistas, and ignored Contra crimes. Clerics in the 'popular church' were equally culpable. They accepted favours from the regime and endorsed its every action; rather than condemn its abuses, they remained silent. The 'popular church' became an appendage of the Sandinista front, and never gained legitimacy in the eyes of most Nicaraguans.[42]

The Church continued to be polarized, its radicals loyal to the regime, Obando still fighting the old battles, in spite of Vatican attempts to calm him down. But the left wing of the Church was not exempt from blame. The Iglesia Popular was in many respects a phantom Church rather than a parallel Church, a construct devised by radical priests and Sandinista theorists. Nor was it popular, being in effect a limited movement without mass support. The majority of ordinary Catholics in Nicaragua were poor people, traditionalists, loyal to Archbishop Obando whom they respected, and 'popular' only in their devotion to shrines, images, saints, and other traditional practices loved by the common people. The Iglesia Popular was a minority church supported by those committed to an exclusive liberation theology, perhaps one-third of Nicaragua's priests; other supporters were foreigners, not completely attuned to local tradition. Yet there were Nicaraguans of radical, educated inspiration, who were eager for social justice. Reynaldo Tefel was one such; his conscience stirred as a young social activist in New York, he saw Catholicism and revolutionary politics as virtually the same thing. In the 1980s he was Minister of Social Welfare in the Sandinista government, a propagandist who interpreted the history of religion as a struggle between conservative and revolutionary beliefs, between the Sermon on the Mount and Christ's betrayal by Judas, between Las Casas and the counter-revolutionaries. He denounced the theology of Obando and the bishops as 'by nature counter-revolutionary, conservative and devoid of conscience'. Nicaraguan Catholics needed to 'forge a new man out of Saint Peter, Marx, and Sandino'.[43] In this alliance St Peter was in the minority.

Tensions between Church and state increased further in the years 1982–86. The papal visit in March 1983, intended to pacify contention, in fact made it worse. At the airport Ortega delivered an endless speech on the evils of American imperialism. This was followed by a scene in which the pope rebuffed Ernesto Cardenal, who is depicted on his knees asking for a blessing. The Sandinistas put on a great show of people who were bused in displaying banners and slogans, designed to present the revolution as a great achievement and one which the pope was expected to bless. 'Welcome to Free Nicaragua, Thanks to God and the Revolution.'[44] In León the pope preached on themes of religious education, the sacraments, and the message of Christ, and added, 'You have no need of ideologies that are alien to your Christian condition in order to love and defend mankind.'[45] But in Managua, probably ill-advised by López Trujillo and the Vatican bureaucracy, he spoke not of revolution but on the need for Church unity, obedience to the bishops, the need for discipline. During the kiss of peace at mass, in a disruption orchestrated by the Sandinistas, people began chanting 'We want peace'. '*Silencio!*' shouted back the pope. It was a mutual disillusionment. The pope backed Obando and two years later, in April 1985, appointed him cardinal. Provocatively he celebrated his first cardinal's mass not in Managua but in Miami, in the midst of Contra leaders.

Obando and other bishops did not hide their support for the Contras and this made dialogue impossible. When Obando in his Easter message of 1984 argued that the war stemmed from internal dissent, not external aggression, and demanded dialogue between the government and the Contras, Sergio Ramírez replied, 'Our only dialogue will be through the barrel of a gun.'[46] Ortega charged that the document was probably written in the United States embassy, and called the bishops 'anti-Christian', 'dishonest', and 'immoral'.[47] These were not the only Sandinista replies. In October 1985 they closed the offices of the Archdiocesan Commission for Social Promotion, alleging that it used its funds (some of them international aid) for financing opposition groups. In January 1986 they closed down Catholic Radio. Opposition to Obando was also expressed through Catholic allies of the government. In 1985 Father Miguel D'Escoto staged a 'gospel insurrection' with foreign sympathizers in working-class barrios. In 1986 he made a 200-mile Stations of the Cross from the Honduran border to Managua, a political statement which was not universally welcome and some churches closed their doors, though the final ceremonies in Managua were crowded. Catholics had long been divided between reformists, who wanted a democratic revolution, and socialists, who were prepared to accept a Marxist version, and between Obando and left-wing priests. In a 1983 survey to which 220 priests responded, 46 per cent supported the Sandinistas; the rest opposed them.[48] The traditional wing of the Church was not the only source of division. There were many Catholics, priests and people, who affirmed the preferential option for the poor and rejected past prejudices; these simply carried on under the Sandinista regime.

Reconciliation was now on the agenda. In 1987 a series of meetings between the government and the Church with the encouragement of the papal nuncio discussed the dividing issues – Catholic Radio and expelled priests, among others. These were inconclusive, but in a wider context the priests of Central America and government representatives including

Ortega agreed in the Esquipulas peace process to reject foreign intervention and to opt for negotiation, not war. Each nation was to create a national reconciliation committee. Obando was not entirely convinced but in Nicaragua a committee with Obando as president and including Sergio Ramírez for the government began to meet. Ortega gave further signals; he authorized the return of expelled bishops and allowed Catholic Radio to reopen. In January 1988 he visited the pope privately. The Contras continued to be the sticking point, but at least they were now on the agenda, with Obando acting as mediator rather than apologist. Some fundamental agreements were made at Sapoa, but the Reagan administration refused to recognize them and the Contras were divided on whether to accept them.

Conditions rather than agreements lowered the intensity of the war. Political and economic adversity dictated decisions. The Contras were losing strength and the government had serious economic problems. The Vatican, with an eye always on preventing worse damage, began to see that it was getting nowhere in Nicaragua; the government was still there and united; the Church was divided; and the Contra war unsustainable on moral grounds. The Sandinista government was also disposed towards dialogue. The war was a crippling economic burden and inflation was spiralling out of control. The Iran–Contra scandal weakened the American case in Nicaragua, and Reagan's refusal to accept the Esquipulas agreement led the Vatican to criticize the American government for inflexibility, a criticism seconded by the United States episcopacy. The collapse of the communist regimes in Eastern Europe and the weakening of the Soviet Union had their effects in Nicaragua. Ortega's allies and aid suppliers were deposed and the idea of world revolution was discredited. For all these reasons, Ortega's decision to hold elections in February 1990 made sense, and the bishops exhorted Catholics to participate.

The elections were fought between two main parties, the FSLN and the UNO (National Opposition Union), a union of the centre and right parties, whose candidate was Violeta Chamorro. In elections that were perfectly free both sides appealed to religion as well as to their programmes. Defying the polls and expectations inside and outside Nicaragua, the UNO won with 55 per cent against 41 per cent for the FSLN. Ortega acepted the result and stood down. Violeta Chamorro became president. The reasons for the result were much discussed: the collapse of the national economy, the failure and expense of the military option; the moral influence of the Catholic Church and the enduring respect for Obando, which the Sandinistas underestimated; the abuse of ethnic minorities, especially of the Mistika Indians, These and other issues kept the Sandinista Revolution before the world media.

Yet tension between the Contras and their enemies did not abate. The cardinal acted as mediator, and Chamorro and the Contra leaders signed an agreement, creating development zones where the Contras could re-establish themselves. Obando hoped for a new way ahead: 'The situation of our country is very difficult. I invite all our brothers to try to solve our problems through conversation, to avoid bloodshed, acts of violence.'[49] But violence between the two sides continued, both Sandinistas and the Contras engaging in acts of terrorism. In the years after 1997 Ortega made a comeback and returned to power, but he and his associates were no longer the old revolutionaries. They were politicians of the more traditional kind well known in Nicaragua, playing the old game of wheeling and dealing, with corruption raising its head as governments came to understandings with political and business interests.

The Nicaraguan Revolution, once a star in the Marxist universe, shone briefly and fell. What did it leave? Socialism? No. Agrarian change? No. Liberation? Least of all. The economy, a precondition for all these things, was little better than it had been half a century before. Yet Nicaragua was now a different country after the fall of the Sandinistas. It was free and fairly democratic, and there were no new Somozas. This was progress, though not the progress promised by the revolution. As for the Church, it had moved on, still divided perhaps but closer to the spirit of Vatican II. Cardinal Obando y Bravo still worked for reconciliation, and the bishops for justice and peace. But without economic development these were uphill tasks.

El Salvador: Sanctity in a Time of Killing

As long as anyone could remember, El Salvador had been ruled by 'the oligarchy', fourteen wealthy and powerful families, whose spokesmen came in various forms – generals, dictators, presidents, politicians – to express the will of the power behind the palace. The coffee barons controlled 60 per cent of arable land, and any protests from the peasants were brutally repressed by their allies in the military, as they were in 'the Massacre' of 1932, when 30,000 peasants were killed. In the 1960s and 1970s the conditions of landless peasants worsened as their numbers increased. Masses of peasants spilled over from overpopulated El Salvador into larger Honduras, leading to tension between the two states at a time when their national football teams were playing each other in qualifying games for the 1970 World Cup and generating their own violence between supporters. Units of the Salvadoran army invaded Honduras and the subsequent fighting in the so-called 'Football War' led to 2,000 casualties, before the Organization of American States mediated.

In 1970 the Christian Democratic Party was formed, a middle-class party whose reformist programme would prevent it from ever gaining real power and whose most prominent politician, José Napoleón Duarte, was deported by the military after contesting the elections of 1972. In 1976 a project of agrarian reform was introduced in the legislative assembly and, weak though it was, failed to survive. Expectations among *campesinos* and signs of protest among reformist and religious groups brought renewed repression against anyone demanding even modest change. The Catholic Church was a prime target, and in the 1970s its priests and laypeople were regularly murdered. The guerrilla opposition, the Frente Farabundo Marti para la Liberación Nacional (FMLN), was also pursued, but being more elusive, left its alleged support groups among the peasants and the farm cooperatives at the mercy of the army assassins. Peaceful civilian dissent and demonstrations were persecuted as subversive.

On 22 February 1977 Bishop Oscar Romero took over as archbishop of San Salvador amidst scenes of extreme violence against activists and Catholics. On 28 February security forces struck at a demonstration in the Plaza Libertad, killing many people. Violence against the Church increased. The Salvadoran Church was small, with 461 priests in 1991 and 1,225 nuns and religious women. From the 1960s, under the influence of Vatican II and Medellín and on the initiative of reformist clergy, it began a process of reappraisal. Base communities sprang up and a stronger Church presence emerged in rural areas, where priests and nuns undertook to train catechists who in turn became leaders of peasant movements. And from Managua the Jesuit Central American University offered intellectual and pastoral support. At the same time as the Church was engaging with society guerrilla movements, the Fuerzas Populares de Liberación (FPL) and the Ejército Revolucionario del Pueblo (ERP) were being formed with their own agenda. In the warped thinking of the politico-military establishment catechists and guerrillas were a common enemy, subversives deserving destruction.

In February and March 1972 violence against the Church reached a new level. A priest was arrested and tortured, another just managed to evade capture. A house of lay activists was raided, and eight priests were prevented from entering the country. The parish priest of El Paisnal to the north of the capital, Father Rutilio Grande, was training a team of seminarians and lay activists to conduct popular missions, and in 1973 the Federación Campesina Cristiana de El Salvador (FECCAS) organized a general strike among peasants with the moral support of Grande's parish. But Grande was not a political activist and never approved of the violence of the extreme left. Yet as he undertook his work for justice and peace in the spirit of renewal, he was the victim of a campaign of vilification in the media. On 12 March 1977 Father Grande and two companions were murdered on their way to celebrate mass at his parish church. His death was an early landmark in the persecution of the Church in El Salvador and one that moved many people. It had a decisive effect on the new archbishop. Oscar Romero knew Father Grande as a friend and collaborator, and celebrated the requiem mass for him.

The year 1977 was a year of persecution. Catholics were caught between the guerrillas and the security forces and became victims of right-wing reprisals for guerrilla atrocities. Father Alfonso Navarro and a young neighbour were victims of such violence. And merely to carry a photograph of Father Grande was to risk assault.[50] Repression was institutionalized with the Law of Defence and Guarantee of Public Order (25 November 1977), which gave the government virtually unlimited power to imprison, torture, silence, and in short to eliminate its opponents. The archbishop attacked the law and began to offer assistance and shelter to its victims.[51] In his homily of 30 April 1978 he praised a group of lawyers who were seeking amnesty for political prisoners and demanding legal justice in spite of corrupt security forces, venal judges, and an inert Supreme Court. Challenged to name the 'venal judges', he asserted in his homily of 14 May that in addition to venality and corruption, 'the fundamental rights of the people of El Salvador day by day are being trodden underfoot, while no [government] agency denounces the outrages or acts sincerely and effectively to improve the situation'.[52] The situation did not improve for the Church. In 1979 two more priests were assassinated: Father Rafael Palacios on 20 June and Father Alirio Napoleón Macias on 4 August. Right-wing terrorists had a free hand in town and country. And the military mounted larger operations. On 8 May they gunned down demonstrators in front of the cathedral doors, leaving 25 dead and several hundred wounded in full view of the world's television audiences. On 22 May the outrage was re-enacted on a smaller scale in front of the Venezuelan embassy.

Archbishop Romero began his ministry in a time of killing. It was not a heroic beginning. If anything he was more eagerly welcomed by conservatives in Church and state than by Catholics looking for change. He was born in Ciudad Barrios, San Miguel, in eastern El Salvador on 15 August 1917 into a modest rural family, whose income he supplemented by work in his youth, and he was conscious of his religious vocation from an early age. After studies in El Salvador he was ordained in Rome in 1942.[53] His work as priest followed conventional lines in parish and diocese, with appointments as high school chaplain, secretary of bishops' conferences in El Salvador and Central America, and auxiliary bishop in San Salvador. So far he kept to the traditionalist wing of the church, a conservative in theology, cautious towards Vatican II and Medellín; he read the Gospel as a message of peace and reconciliation rather than liberation and division. His work in the archdiocese as a newspaper editor and seminary rector confirmed this approach and he believed that existing leaders and institutions in El Salvador were basically good and protest groups dangerous. As bishop of Santiago de María in Usulután he saw at close hand violent repression of the rural poor, though he still regarded it as an aberration which should be criticized privately, while poor peasants were offered relief and shelter in church buildings. But his eyes were being opened to reality and he was beginning to speak out more boldly and clearly. In this spirit he was converted to the theology of Vatican II, Medellín and Puebla. He was not a theoretical theologian but a pastoral one, expressing his episcopal authority in faith and morals, seeing the Church as a servant of God's kingdom and taking the kingdom to the people to create a more just society.

Romero was a man of faith and prayer who sought to stop the war against the poor by appealing to the moral law, calling on people to have faith and hope in God, but also defending their right to organize for justice.[54] He eventually took a stand on human rights, driven by conditions in El Salvador. Amidst the violence of the right and the left, his Sunday sermons and radio programmes riveted the nation. He cited actual cases of massacres, tortures, and disappearances, denouncing the war against civilians. It was a non-violent stance, difficult for the authorities to counter, except by more violence, eventually against Romero himself. He was accused not only by his enemies but also, with the notable exception of Arturo Rivera y Damas, by his fellow bishops, who accused him of taking the Church into politics and complained to Rome. Even those who did not denounce him did not support him. He stood out, and became a target, not only because of his own words, but because others stood back. These were the silent bishops of El Salvador.

Archbishop Romero's thinking goes to the heart of the Christian attitude to violence. He saw the tragedy of the war in the countryside where *campesinos* were in conflict with *campesinos*, some seeking to escape from their common poverty by accepting the benefits offered by government organizations. 'In return they are employed in various repressive activities ... threatening, kidnapping, torturing, and even, in some cases, killing their fellow *campesinos*'. Others strove to find better ways, as did groups of Christian communities.[55] And yet others responded by arming themselves. Cardinal Obando supported the Contras in their use of violence not, apparently, through theological reflection but in response to political imperatives. Archbishop Romero on the other hand sought the answer in Catholic theology. He did not shrink from the problem of violence and he accepted the right of people to defend themselves. But the defence needs careful definition.

The liberation promised by the Church 'excludes violence, considering it unchristian and unscriptural, ineffective and out of keeping with the dignity of the people'. Even when victims of the security forces are kidnapped, murdered, tortured, 'we have to go on repeating "no to violence, yes to peace"'. Romero recognized 'the repressive violence of the state ... This is a real form of violence'. Against this there is a right of defence: 'Violence can be used in legitimate self-defence, when a group or an individual repels by force the unjust aggression to which they have been subjected.'[56] He sought the answer in the moral teaching of the Church, for he recognized that 'evil may not be done to promote good. But the Church allows violence in legitimate self-defence', providing its use is proportionate, has exhausted peaceful ways, and does not create greater evil than the aggression. These are traditional Catholic conditions. Yet the Church prefers non-violence, and quoting Medellín he concludes, 'The Christian is peaceful and not ashamed of it ... not simply a pacifist, for he can fight, but prefers peace to war'. Applied to El Salvador this means that 'even in legitimate cases, violence ought to be a last resort'.[57]

The archbishop returned to the problem in his Fourth Pastoral Letter, insisting that 'the Church's judgements on the violence that disturbs the peace cannot ignore the demands of justice. The Church cannot state, in a simplistic fashion, that it condemns every kind of violence.' He recalled that there was a violence of legitimate defence, which occurred 'when a person or a group repels by force an unjust aggression that they have suffered', so resort to force could be justified by 'the existence of a tyrannical regime and an unjust social order'.[58]

Romero sought to be fair, but none of the governing juntas, those mixtures of politics and militarism in which Christian Democracy tried to act and failed, fulfilled his criteria. He ended up clearly condemning the repression and in his last sermon he called upon soldiers and security forces not to obey unjust orders: 'In the name of God, and in the name of his suffering people whose cries rise daily more loudly to heaven, I plead with you, I beg you, I order you in the name of God, put an end to this repression.'[59] Given the prevailing repression and the existing agrarian structure, he was suspicious of the agrarian reform on offer, which could make the *campesinos* more dependent without really changing anything. He also came to realize that nothing could be expected of governments in El Salvador, whatever they called themselves, whether presidents, juntas, or dictators. He warned the Christian Democrats against compromising with a repressive system. To a journalist he replied, 'Even though it is true that they have the good intention of carrying through structural reforms, the

Christian Democrats run a grave risk in being part of a government that is engaged in such fearful repression. In this way the Christian Democratic Party is becoming an accomplice in the annihilation of the people.'[60] Defiant towards the military, he was shrewder than the politicians.

In 1980 the situation in El Salvador deteriorated rapidly. As popular forces and guerrilla groups increased their attacks on the property and politicians of the right, the security forces struck back indiscriminately, opening fire at the slightest provocation: 265 people were killed in January, 236 in February, 514 in March. Christian Democrats were represented in the second junta and projected some reforms – agararian reform and nationalization of the banks. But they seemed to belong to a different world from that of the security forces and guerrillas, each with its own version of violence; meanwhile the government looked on helplessly, or not so help-lessly, for it too was involved in repression. The Christian Democrats were openly divided, some resigning from the government, some remaining to give reforms a chance, but these were what Romero called 'reforms with the big stick' and were accompanied by military occupation of the countryside and the continued murder of rural and urban workers, teachers, trade unionists, and students. For all these reasons Romero, critical of Conservative politicians and disillusioned with Catholic ones, had no faith in govern-ment-inspired reforms. In his controversial *Letter to President Carter* in which he asked the president to stop all military aid to the Salvadoran government, he noted that the junta and the Christian Democrats did not in fact rule the country and were helpless observers of the real power in El Salvador, that of the military officers who only favoured the interests of the oligarchy.[61] He seemed more encouraging, if cautious, towards some of the popular and middle-class organizations and programmes outside tradi-tional politics, especially the CRM (Mass Revolutionary Coordinating Committee). But time was running out for the archbishop.

Romero did not live to see a peaceful solution or any response to his plea to disobey orders. In his last interview he said that his death would be for the liberation of his people: and his killers would be wasting their time. 'I have frequently been threatened with death. I must say that, as a Christian, I do not believe in death but in the resurrection. If they kill me I will rise again in the people of El Salvador.'[62] He was assassinated on Monday 24 March 1980 while standing at the altar celebrating mass in the chapel of the Divine Providence hospital where he lived. The authors of the crime were Roberto D'Aubuisson, who gave the order, and his military associates, who had accused Romero of being a demagogue and an advocate of terrorism. At his funeral a great crowd gathered in front of the cathedral doors as mass was said inside; ordinary people and priests of El Salvador who had always respected him, but also prelates and bishops, who had long been silent. Bombs and shootings by the security forces scarred even this sacred occasion, leaving further dead and wounded in their wake.

The year 1980 continued to be one of killings. The military, backed and in some cases trained by the United States, the security forces, and miscellaneous death squads between them were responsible for hundreds of killings, of priests, seminarists, civilians of the left and centre, Catholic progressives. Gang rapes by right-wing terrorists were reported. On 2 December a group of soldiers from the National Guard captured four American women missionaries in remote countryside as they drove home from the airport. Ursuline Sister Dorothy Kazel, lay volunteer Jean Donovan, and Maryknoll Sisters Maura Clarke and Ita Ford all worked with poor *campesinos*. This was subversion in the eyes of the Salvadoran military, and they were beaten, raped, and murdered. For once the United States reacted, suspending military aid and pressing the Salvadoran government to investigate. After a trial four accused were sent to prison, but the true authors were never arraigned. Now pilgrims go to the chapel marking the place of the atrocity.

The war intensified, both sides sourced from outside, the FMLN from Nicaragua, Cuba, and the USSR, the Salvadoran government from the United States. In December 1981 the army massacred a whole town, El Mozote, and its surrounding villages; 500 civilians, men, women, and children, were 'deliberately and systematically' killed by the Atlacatl Battalion.[63] But the military were not the only guilty people in El Salvador. During the civil war, elections were held in 1982. The Christian Democrats won a majority, but a new party, the right-wing Alianza Republicana Nacionalista (ARENA) led by D'Aubuisson dominated the political scene. Throughout the 1980s the death squads and the guerrillas continued to fight it out, reaching a peak of violence in 1989–91. In 1989 ARENA's candidate Alfredo Cristiani was elected president. In November the FMLN fought back and captured sections of the capital. But the politicians, the Duartes and the Cristianis, had no power. That was in the hands of the military and the United States. In effect President Reagan and his supporters saved the Salvadoran military and fought an undeclared war in Central America in defence of 'democracy' against 'communism'. The government of the United States, a Jesuit historian concludes, followed a 'hypocritical policy: on the one hand, it denounced violations of human rights; and on the other, it gave huge sums of money to the very groups that most violated those rights.'[64]

After Romero the Church was floundering. Leadership could not be expected from the Episcopal Conference, which was full of conservatives, or even from Archbishop Arturo Rivera y Damas, who was not a reactionary but was more prone to mediating and reconciling than to denouncing, when it was obvious that mediation to 'humanize the war' got nowhere. The Episcopal Conference, while slow to raise a voice on behalf of justice and human rights, was quick to pounce on what it regarded as Catholic deviation. In May 1980 a group of priests, nuns, and laypeople founded CONIP, the National Coordinating Committee of the Oscar Romero Popular Church, and the conservative bishops promptly condemned it. The bishops had reason to be wary. Although the FMLN was Marxist–Leninist in its ideology, it attracted recruits from left-wing Catholics and solidarity from progressives in the Church, including some professors at the University of Central America (UCA).

But Rivera y Damas did at least establish Legal Defence, an aid organization of lawyers and social workers to investigate disappearances, torture, and other injustices, and its detailed reports became a source for denunciation by the Church of human rights abuses. Predictably it was ignored by the government and criticized by the United States. Attempts from 1982 to start dialogue between the FMLN and the government were fruitless. Neither side was interested, nor was the United States, and in any case the government did not control the army or the paramilitaries. It was only when both sides had fought to a stalemate that peace would become possible. Meanwhile dialogue meetings were usually preceded and succeeded by armed action. In 1985 the FMLN murdered four American marines, unarmed and out of uniform, and seven civilians in a restaurant in San Salvador. This ended any hopes of a dialogue.

Serial killing continued. In the period up to 1990 government forces killed between 70,000 and 75,000 people – peasants, workers, students, teachers, doctors, and journalists. At the end of the war the Truth Commission found that 5 per cent of denounced killings were the responsibility of the FMLN; 85 per cent were attributed to state agents, paramilitary groups, or death squads. In the Commission's judgement violence stemmed from 'a political mindset that rendered the concepts of political opponent, subversive and enemy synonymous'.[65] Among the victims were the Jesuit priest Ignacio Ellacuría and his companions.

The killing of the Jesuits horrified opinion in El Salvador and the rest of the world. They had long received death threats from government and army sources and endured physical attacks. They had been accused of communism and supporting the FMLN, and of being the intellectual leaders of 'delinquent terrorists'. In fact they were academics who simply believed in dialogue and non-violence and in telling the truth about El Salvador, the truth about agrarian reform, poverty, human rights. They were following the example of Archbishop Romero.

The University of Central America (UCA) was a modern Jesuit foundation that quickly excelled as a centre of teaching and research; a serious university with a social conscience. An inclusive ethos inevitably bred division, between Jesuits and lay staff, between progressives and traditionalists, between the academic and the committed, between middle-class students and a smaller working-class intake. But diversity did not detract from quality. Ellacuría had once stated, 'If the university had not suffered, we would not have performed our duty. In a world where falsehood, injustice and oppression reign, a University that fights for truth, justice and freedom cannot fail to be persecuted.'[66] Academic work went hand in hand with commitment to service of the people and of the poor. But not all the Church believed in the Jesuits' approach; they had their critics, and were regarded as dangerous by many bishops. For their part, the Jesuits believed that the Church was turning in on itself, gradually trying to silence the message of Vatican II, Medellín and Puebla, and moving away from Archbishop Romero, radical reform, and base communities. So they were not universally popular in the Latin American Church. But at their funeral mass the papal nuncio called them true sons and members of the Church, and described them as martyrs.

The victims were six Jesuits, Ignacio Ellacuría, Segundo Montes, Ignacio Martín-Baró, Amando López, Juan Ramón Moreno, and Joaquín López y López, together with two women, Julia Elba, cook, and Celina, her 15-year-old daughter. Their killers were military personnel, behind them the army command, and ultimately the whole government, guilty of a mixture of compliance and weakness. Three of the Jesuits were taken from their residence into the garden, tortured, and machine-gunned there. The other three and the two women were machine-gunned in their beds. The killers were officers and soldiers from the elite Atlacatl Battalion, about thirty men in military uniform.

The army denied any part in the atrocity, but under pressure from the United States the government admitted that the military were involved, and eventually, in September 1991, two officers were sentenced to thirty years' imprisonment. It was a cover-up, and there was a further outcry against the hidden authors of the crime, the high command of the Salvadoran army. The Jesuit order secured the release of the two officers, but the real criminals were never brought to justice. It is known that the United States participated in the cover-up to save the Salvadoran army. The truth finally came out. Colonel René Emilio Ponce, the Minister of Defence, in the presence of senior officers, had given Colonel Guillermo Alfredo Benavides the order to kill Ignacio Ellacuría and leave no witnesses.[67] Benavides instructed the Atlacatl unit that had searched the UCA two days earlier to carry out the operation and further ordered that Major Camilo Hernández should organize it.

Following the killing, the cover-up, and the subsequent revelation of the truth, it became increasingly difficult to justify the war (and United States aid), and the only way ahead was a negotiated peace. The negotiations were long and difficult, and the mediation of the United Nations was needed before a peace agreement was reached or at least a peace process was begun, involving the FMLN, the Salvadoran army, and the government. A United Nations Truth Commission was created. But there were no trials in El Salvador to settle the account, and no justice. It was a melancholy time for the faithful. Institutions, politics, and violence were not fundamentally changed. The Church emerged intact but only partially renewed. It played its part in mediating the peace, but it could not change the soul of El Salvador.

Guatemala: War in the Land of Peace

In the sixteenth century Bartolomé de Las Casas and his Dominican companions evangelized warlike peoples in northern Guatemala without use of force and turned Tuzulutlán, the land of war, into Vera Paz, the land of peace. Further south the colonial capital became the home of a renowned university, some elegant architecture, and a modest place in the Latin American Enlightenment. Modern Guatemala enacts a different history.

A classic case of underdevelopment, Guatemala survived on subsistence agriculture and primary exports, profits going to an oligarchy of land-owners and the American United Fruit Company, leaving a mass of people on the poverty line, 60 per cent of them Maya Indians. In 1954 radical President Jacobo Arbenz was given short shrift by the oligarchy and their allies in the CIA, determined to stop agrarian reform and the appropriation of the United Fruit Company. Politics reverted to their normal course, military dictatorships protecting the interests of plantation owners and politicians employing their own death squads. The Guatemalan military was a power in the land, a parallel state. Its hallmarks were brutality and corruption. From 1978 the military regimes allowed death squads to roam unchallenged, targeting priests, religious, teachers, students, and demo-crats. In this mix an expanding Protestantism with links to the United States was taking shape, and two Protestant presidents, Efraín Ríos Montt (1982–83) and Jorge Serrano Elías (1991–93), added their voices to the clamour and their weapons to the killing. Amidst the horror the Church was at once a protector and a victim.

To challenge the system two parallel movements emerged, reformist and revolutionary. The Unidad Revolucionaria Nacional Guatemalteca (URNG) drew together the various guerrilla groups, reaching a strengh of 6–8,000, attracting many more sympathizers and operating in the remote jungle and altiplano.[68] In the wake of the failure of the 1950s, reformist groups, distinct from the guerrillas and including teachers, students, and workers, reorganized themselves to form a more effective movement for change; and the Comité de Unidad Campesina (CUC), which united all peasant movements, was founded in 1978. In the 1970s a minority of Catholic activists turned from preaching the option for the poor to support for violence, though the guerrilla leadership, essentially Marxist–Leninist, did not trust Catholics. Into this unstable society the earthquake of 1976 struck and claimed 25,000 victims, mainly among the poor, resulting in familiar scenes of migration by the victims and venality by the leaders.

The military dictators and military-dominated civilian governments responded to the new political activism by use of state terrorism and American military aid, to wage war against guerrilla groups and to punish the peasant population for their presence. Disappearances, massacres, murders, torture became a way of life in northern Guatemala from the beginning of the 1960s, stepping up from 1979, in a war in which 200,000 civilians would be killed. An army lieutenant reported, 'the soldiers had to wipe out the entire town because it supported the guerrillas'. Orders came from above. 'We have a lot of guerrilla villages. We already know which entire villages are going to be wiped out.'[69] Amidst daily repression the army committed two extraordinary atrocities, a massacre of Kelchis Indians defending their lands in the north in 1978, and the killing of peasant protesters at the Spanish embassy in 1980. A decade of political turmoil in the Izcán rainforest in the northern part of El Quiché culminated in the massacre of civilians in 1982, and the survivors became a population in resistance, hiding in the rainforest from the military, or fleeing to Mexico. The Catholic Church took a strong position on behalf of the refugees and their right to return to their homes, and bishops visited the refugee camps. Even though human rights violations continued, especially in Huehuetenango, this diocese, unlike El Quiché in 1980, did not close down but persisted in its mission. Ricardo Falla, Jesuit priest and anthropologist, risked his own life by going undercover to track down and document the truth about these events.

The Guatemalan Church had experienced a hybrid history since its colonial past; liberal regimes were its worst enemy, decimating its bishops, clergy, property, and schools. The Church recovered moderately in the early twentieth century, relying in part on foreign clergy and in part on Conservative politicians and governments. By 1991 there were 218 diocesan priests, 512 male religious, and 1,539 female religious.[70] In the priest-less countryside the Church survived thanks to Catholic Action, supported by local community leaders, confraternities, and the traditions of popular religion. The hierarchical Church survived but contributed little to improvement, and when revival came it was due mainly to foreign clergy, the influence of Vatican II and Medellín, and the growth of base communities. The

Guatemalan Church was divided not so much into an official and a popular Church, as into a Church of the conventional congregations of clergy and faithful on the one hand and a Church of the poor and their pastors on the other. There was a hard core of conservative bishops led by Archbishop Mario Casariego, challenged by a few who listened to Vatican II and Medellín. In March 1974 the bishops published a collective letter on violence but Casariego and two other bishops refused to sign it. Two years later he also refused to sign a document of the Episcopal Conference on poverty, injustice, and institutionalized violence. In 1978 he virtually censored a letter advising Catholics on the coming elections. Intolerant towards his own dissidents, Casariego was indulgent towards the military. Six bishops wrote to Rome asking for his removal.

The revival of the Church through more progressive priests and programmes, and the association of a few Catholics with guerrillas, left it open to the charge of collaboration with the left, and the authorities reacted with a campaign of kidnapping and murder. It was reported that 'between 1978 and 1985 five diocesan priests, eight religious priests, two religious brothers, of whom four were foreign-born and the other four Guatemalans, were murdered'.[71] Many more were forced to leave the country and many Church agencies were closed. El Quiché diocese was a special target for the state terrorists. Father Bill Woods, Maryknoll missionary, who played a key role in Izcán, was 'brought down' in a plane on his way to say mass in November 1976. A German priest was deported in December 1978 because he was a witness to what the army was doing, and a Spanish priest, Father José María Grau, was ambushed and killed by the military. The army considered religion to be a screen for the guerrillas and often chose moments when people were in church to massacre them. Liberation of the poor was regarded as an incitement to subversion. They killed catechists; they used religious symbols to punish the population, hanging and crucifying people and leaving corpses in a kneeling position. In the period 1977–83 the Church lost thirty-four of its leaders, clergy, seminarians, and catechists, killed at the hands of state terrorists.[72] The Church came out of the great tribulation but paid a price in its blood. As Ricardo Falla recorded, 'Faith was purified by persecution, like embers that the wind brings to a blaze, but the Church fell apart and religion was greatly weakened. The Church has been reconstructed both in the communities in resistance and the refugee camps.'[73]

In El Quiché a new evangelization had taken place, when a largely Maya Indian people were converted through the work of traditional Catholic Action and Indian catechists, animated by the new spirit of Medellín. In the years 1974–85 the bishop of El Quiché, Juan Gerardi, helped by the Jesuits, supported the growth of an indigenous Church. Schools for Indian rural teachers were founded; many Indian leaders, linked to the Christian Democratic Party, ran for mayor; and political awareness was strengthened by the formation of the CUC in 1978. Tragically for these peaceful developments, El Quiché was also a refuge for guerrillas fighting their own campaign against the government.

Events in El Quiché did not go unnoticed by the military, which unleashed a campaign of terror against the Catholic Church throughout the towns and villages in the northern mountains. Catechists were tortured, priests were killed, convents and other Church buildings were attacked with grenades or turned into barracks. The guerrillas were a further menace, as they moved among the civilian population promising protection they could not deliver. But the army was the greatest criminal, virtually sealing off the Mayan altiplano to impose its own solution. Although words of protest came from Pope John Paul II, Cardinal Casariego remained silent, blessing army tanks with holy water. The military had their eye on Bishop Gerardi in his Quiché diocese; a modern bishop in the mould of Vatican II and Medellín, he sought justice for the poor, the Indians, and the victims of injustice. He had written in 1973, 'Effectively we find ourselves faced with a situation of exploitation, marginalization, illiteracy, endemic illnesses, poverty, and even misery; all of which amount to a state of injustice, and reveal a state of sin.'[74] In 1980 Bishop Gerardi narrowly escaped from an ambush. Together with several murders in his diocese, this persuaded him to withdraw all Church personnel from El Quiché, a controversial decision and hotly debated, but it was an act of defiance as well as defeat. Meanwhile the persecution of the Church continued, and death squads targeted those left behind, catechists and base communities.

State terror reached a new peak in 1982, when General Efraín Ríos Montt seized power by a military coup. He came from a Catholic family and a Christian Democrat background but he converted to Protestantism of a fundamentalist kind and became leader of the neo-Pentecostalist El Verbo Church; soon he was a hero of the religious right in the United States.[75] He surrounded himself with Protestants and admirers and preached to the nation every Sunday. Once in power, presenting the struggle against subversion as a moral crusade, he waged a relentless war on the Indian population and was regarded as a loathsome menace by Catholic and reformist politicians. His war on the guerrilla strongholds took the form of blanket massacres in the highlands and a scorched earth campaign among the surrounding population. Hundreds were massacred, over 600 villages were burned to the ground and 70,000 people killed. In a policy known as *fusiles y frijoles* (rifles and beans), peasants were forced into army patrols, simultaneously to fight the guerrillas and remain under control. They were compelled to live in 'development poles' in a militarized rural Guatemala, a strategy designed to subvert Mayan life and culture. The army distinguished between Catholics and Protestants, foes and friends. One million refugees fled from their homes into mountains and over the border into Mexico. More than a campaign, this was genocide against the Indian people, men, women, and children. Searching desperately for escape routes, many peasants formed Communities of People in Resistance (CPR), refugees who supported neither side.

Protestantism had a long history in Guatemala and modern Evangelicals, or some of them, were less critical of the military than Catholics and had no qualms in collaborating with Ríos Montt's campaign.[76] In January 1983 the Guatemalan Church in Exile, a group of Catholic dissidents who had escaped to Mexico and Managua, claimed, 'The religious sects are an arm of the counterinsurgency. The religious sects have arrived to support the Army and the Government of Ríos Montt in counterinsurgency war, as indispensable as automatic weapons or Huey helicopters.'[77] The allegation was that Ríos Montt, aided by conservative foreign evangelicals associated with the Reagan administration, was conducting a holy war against Catholic peasants. This was not entirely fanciful. The military directly targeted Catholic activists in base communities. Hundreds, perhaps thousands, of catequistas involved in social work and, in some cases, associated with guerrillas were killed. Bishops condemned the violence. 'These assassinations now belong to the category of genocide.'[78]

In spite of episcopal inertia and the surge of Protestantism, Catholics rescued the Church from complete silence by alternative movements among religious and laity. The papal visit in March 1983 was a sign of hope, but Ríos Montt offered no Christian handshake to John Paul II. He ignored papal pleas for clemency for six political prisoners. The visit was an encouragement for Catholics and huge numbers attended an outdoor mass in Guatemala City. The pope condemned violations of human rights, and urged the bishops and Catholic leaders to take a more positive stance against violence and abuses by government and law enforcers.

> The faith teaches us that Man is the image and likeness of God, and when violence is committed against him, when his rights are violated, when he is submitted to torture, when violence occurs through sequestrations or he loses the right to his own life, a crime of the gravest offence has been committed; then Christ returns to again walk the road of his passion and suffer the horror of crucifixion among the devalued and oppressed.[79]

But the visit had no dramatic effect on Guatemala. Próspero Penados del Barrios suceeded Casariego as archbishop in January 1984 and with a change at the top the Episcopal Conference was unified and invigorated. Guatemala was a country of landless peasants, with a high concentration of land in the hands of a few. In 1988 the Episcopal Conference published a letter *The Cry for Land*, demanding radical reform of land tenure. From below too there was a cry for land, when Father Andrés Girón led a march of thousands of peasants to the capital demanding land. While the bishops demanded a more just distribution of land, Penados himself displayed the character of a reformer and defender of human rights. In 1989 he founded the Archdiocesan Office of Human Rights. In 1992 a pastoral *Letter on Indigenous Peoples* reaffirmed the Church's commitment to Indian rights. And as the Church positioned itself in the cause of human rights, so its seminaries began to recruit more young men to the priesthood.

Meanwhile Bishop Gerardi had reported directly to the pope on the closure of his diocese and asked for a new assignment. The pope heard him with sympathy and in a public letter to the Guatemalan Episcopal Conference he condemned the violence against the civilian population and the persecution of the Church:

> I share your sorrow over the tragic accumulation of suffering and death that weighs, and shows no sign of abating, over so many families and your ecclesiastical communities, debilitated not only by the murders of more than just a few catechists, but also of priests, in the darkest circumstances, in vile and premeditated ways. I am particularly saddened by the grave situation in the diocese of El Quiché, where, because of multiple criminal acts and death threats against ecclesiastics, the community remains without religious assistance.[80]

But he ordered Gerardi to reopen the El Quiché diocese. At Guatemala airport the bishop was met by a military unit that put him on a plane to El Salvador. Assassins were waiting there too, so he flew on to Costa Rica, where he remained in exile for three years.

Rios Montt, military though he was, proved to be too eccentric a leader for the army, who overthrew him in August 1983. In the subsequent elections the Christian Democrats won, but it was a hollow victory. Nothing changed. The army was still the most privileged institution in Guatemala and its friends among the death squads continued their crimes of assassination, kidnapping, and violation of human rights. Guatemala was a dangerous place to live in and profess dissident beliefs. Women, academics, social workers, unarmed Indians, victims from many sectors fell to the assassins' guns and knives. On the edge of the mayhem lurked the CIA, and such was the outcry that sometimes, but not always, even the United States government was constrained to cut off its aid programme.

The return of democracy in 1986 was limited. President Vinicio Cerezo's government was unstable with an unconvincing commitment to human rights; and it lacked power either to control the death squads or to defeat the guerrillas, ineffective though they were in their mountain and jungle retreats. So conditions were ready for peace negotiations. These were tortuous, moving from Madrid to Oslo to Mexico, until 1994 when Bishop Rodolfo Quesada was chosen to direct the Association of Civil Society. This produced a comprehensive set of documents on resettlement of the displaced, the rights of indigenous people, agrarian problems, the power and purpose of the army in a democratic society, and electoral reform. A general agreement was signed in Mexico in January 1994. This concluded the Church's official role in peace-seeking. From now on it worked for peace from below.

The United Nations Mission in Guatemala was created in November 1994 and established an office in Guatemala City to verify agreement on human rights. The Church too played a role and the Archdiocesan Office of Human Rights investigated all violations since the beginning of the thirty-six-year civil war. Finally in March 1996 both sides signed a truce and the final peace settlement was signed on 29 December. All these formalities meant little in Guatemala, where violence, death squads, and immunity for political criminals continued undiminished. Any Church person adopting a high profile on behalf of the poor and oppressed was at risk.

Bishop Gerardi presented to the public on 24 April 1998 a large and intensively researched report in four volumes, *Guatemala: Nunca Más (Guatemala, Never Again!)*, prepared by the Human Rights Office of the Archdiocese, with an introduction by Gerardi himself. It identified 50,000 of the war's civilian dead and documented 410 massacres, defined as destruction and murder directed against entire communities, most in the period 1981–93. It blamed the military and paramilitary death squads for 80 per cent of the killings of civilians, and the guerrillas for less than 5 per cent.[81] The terrible details were there for all to see.

The señora was pregnant. With a knife they cut open her belly to pull out her little baby boy. And they killed them both. (Case 0976, Quiché, 1980)

On the 19th of March 1981 the Army came to the village of Chel, and took from the church the 95 people praying there, and they took them down to the river at the edge of the village, and there they massacred them with knives and bullets. (Case 4761, Quiché)

I don't know if it was a captain or a lieutenant who arrived with the soldiers and said 'We're going to finish off this village because this village is with the guerrillas'. By one in the afternoon they'd finished killing everyone and only the women and children were left. And then the lieutenant said, 'We better kill the women and children so that no one will be left'. (Case 6070, Huehuetenango, 1982)[82]

Gerardi advised many of his collaborators to take precautions or leave the country, but he did nothing for his own safety. Forty-eight hours after presenting the report Bishop Gerardi was violently murdered at his home, battered to death in his garage with a paving stone. After a seven-year investigation in which the dilatory Guatemalan legal system was exposed to every kind of corruption and chicanery, a guilty verdict was pronounced and in April 2007, the ninth anniversary of the murder, the Constitutional Court upheld the convictions of army officers Colonel Byron Lima Estrada and his son Captain Byron Lima Oliva, together with an accomplice, Father Mario Orantes, assistant priest at the parish church of San Sebastián, where the murder took place.[83] It had been a close thing but the convictions held. One of the many incidental actors in the drama, Mario Vargas Llosa, a gullible ideologue, played an ignoble role in spreading misinformation covering up the guilt of the Limas in the Madrid daily, El País.[84]

No one believed that the whole story had been told, or all the guilty exposed. These things remained in the shadows. Throughout the investigation the government was intent on covering up a political murder and hiding the crime's chain of command.

The Catholic Church in Central America, much criticized in its time, was not silent on its own sins of omission, and numerous bishops, priests, and laypeople spoke out to lament failure and faint-heartedness. Religious priorities changed in the course of four centuries. In the beginning the Church prayed to save souls. Then it prayed to resist the devil, the world, and the flesh. And in modern times it prayed for justice and peace. Judged in general, if not in detail, its record stands up to critical scrutiny. It preserved a common faith and kept the faithful more or less orthodox in troubled times. In Nicaragua Archbishop Obando resisted the false gods of the Marxists and identified the possibilities and the dangers of revolution. In El Salvador Catholics from the highest to the humblest shed their blood in defence of their beliefs. In Guatemala the religion proclaimed in the twentieth century was the same as that proclaimed by Bartolomé de Las Casas and his Dominicans, passed down in spiritual continuity to the pastors of the modern Church. If the Church was basically ineffective in the Guatemalan civil war, it identified with the poor and the Indians and supported human rights, and paid the price in violence against its more humble members, clerical and lay. In his commitment to traditional religion and modern justice Bishop Gerardi, like Archbishop Romero, epitomized the work of the Church: to preach the doctrine of salvation in the example of Christ, and to reach out to the poor and oppressed.

CHAPTER 11

Difference and Diversity

The Jews in Latin America

MODERN SPANISH AMERICA acquired attitudes towards Jews from colonial Spain. In the late eighteenth century a mission friar in New Granada recorded a revealing incident at a toll bridge crossing, where the keeper, an Indian, refused to let the friar pass without paying a charge. The friar forced his way through at gunpoint, pursued by the cries of the Indian keeper, 'Hey Friar, you Spaniard, you Jew, you renegade!'[1] Indians of South America caught the virus of anti-Semitism from colonists from Spain.

It was an ominous reputation, but not one that Jewish people making their way across the Atlantic could afford to heed. From the second half of the nineteenth century waves of Jewish migrants from Russia, Poland, and other parts of Eastern and Central Europe, mainly Ashkenazi, and Sephardi from the eastern Mediterranean, sought a new life in Latin America. The capitals of Argentina, Brazil, Uruguay, Chile, Mexico, and Venezuela soon had strong Jewish communities, many immigrants moving up into a middle class of business and the professions, while others earned their living in agriculture. There were further migrations in the twentieth century, such as the small but significant Jewish migration to the eastern coast of Colombia in the 1930s and 1940s.[2] By the year 2005 the total Jewish population in Latin America was approximately 398,000, including 185,000 in Argentina, 97,000 in Brazil, and 40,000 in Mexico.[3]

In Brazil small groups of Jews from North Africa began to settle in the mid-nineteenth century, attracted by the Amazon rubber boom. These increased to tens of thousands in the first four decades of the twentieth century, many of them thwarted in their preference for the United States but ultimately reconciled when the growing wealth of Brazil offered them good careers and the urban centres of Rio de Janeiro and São Paulo opened up opportunities in commerce and finance.[4] Mexico was different: its political and cultural environment, with a history of commitment to Catholicism, did not make it an obvious place for Jewish immigration. But Jews entered Mexico as a small and unobtrusive minority, keeping their Jewish identity private in order to avoid the hostility which was never far below the surface. After the Revolution they began to emerge and to make their way in commerce and small industries and even ventured into politics. Some with a Jewish heritage, such as Frida Kahlo, proved their brilliance in the fields of art and culture. Observing the persecution of the Catholic Church by Calles and his successors, Mexican Jews kept a low religious profile, emphasizing rather their roles in commerce and banking. Growth was limited by the unwillingness of orthodox Judaism to accept converts, and their recognizing as Jews only children born of a Jewish mother. So there were few mixed marriages in Mexico. Yet the total Jewish population continued to grow, but also to become more liberal than the older orthodox Judaism.

Jewish immigration to Bolivia, hitherto insignificant, increased notably as migrants fled persecution in Germany in 1938–39. During the Holocaust period it expanded further and by the end of the 1940s Jews were numbered in tens of thousands. The Bolivian government sought to confine Jewish immigrants to agricultural work and rural areas, and imposed these restraints as a condition of granting visas. After 1945 most of the immigrants preferred to escape from these limitations and many emigrated further to other South American countries and to the United States. Eventually the Jewish community in Bolivia became 'extraordinarily small, mobile and unstable'.[5]

In the nineteenth century Jewish immigrants to Argentina were mainly Ashkenazi, fleeing from persecution in Russia and Eastern Europe, and they became known as *Rusos*. Their numbers increased from the 1860s and they eventually became the largest Jewish community in Latin America, estimated at over 200,000 at the beginning of the twenty-first century, with a solid Zionist core and a larger public profile than that of other Jewish communities in the subcontinent. They were a middle-class and urban group, opting for careers in the professions and academic life, and congregating in Buenos Aires and other cities of the littoral. Others, especially the Sephardi, were more inclined to commercial and financial activities. But Jews had also migrated to the interior, where they settled as small farmers. Many Jewish schools were established, especially in Greater Buenos Aires, and their survival against the odds attested to the tenacity of the Jewish community. However, the tendency to mixed marriages was growing, and assimilation and intermarriage combined to reduce the Jewish population from its peak of 300,000. Argentina was known for its liberal immigration policy and until 1930 Jewish immigration was encouraged by the state. But in the late 1930s a prejudice in favour of a homogeneous nation asserted itself, and from the

1940s a specifically anti-Semitic ideology was roused by Fascist, Nazi, and extreme nationalist groups; this found a response in the larger population.

The first generations of Jewish immigrants in Buenos Aires settled in the barrios of Once and Villa Crespo, and Once is still the garment district in which they worked. There they established their synagogues and other institutions affirming their identity. The oldest synagogue in Once was the Libertad Synagogue, built in 1892 and dedicated in 1932. The Gran Templo de Paso opened in 1927. In these temples they gathered on the Sabbath and High Days for ceremonies of prayers, sermons, and hymns, accompanied by readings from biblical and rabbinic writings, as directed by the Talmud. Prayers, with denominational variations, were an integral part of Jewish worship and were sung and chanted in their traditional melodies. The early synagogues in Argentina were not only places of worship and homes of prayer and study, but also community centres where Jews could feel at home.[6] Most synagogues were Orthodox (eventually some fifty in Buenos Aires) with a lesser number of Conservative and a few Reform. Gradually Jews improved their prospects, and Once and other districts preferred by the early immigrants were abandoned in favour of middle-class Palermo Chico, Barrio Norte, and Belgrano.[7] As Jews became unmistakably Argentines, so the strong religious identity asserted by first-generation immigrants was gradually diluted, and many of the later Jews were essentially secularists, without however losing their ancestral loyalties.[8] The Jewish community of Argentina made a distinguished contribution to the academic, cultural, and artistic life of the nation, and their creative talents can be seen in the pages of the historian Boleslao Lewin.

In the twenty-first century the Jews survive and more than survive in an Argentina relatively pluralist and tolerant. But it has not always been so. Already in the nineteenth century there was a hostile reaction to their presence, some of it virulent, some of it claiming to be reasonable. The newspaper *La Nación* denounced the open immigration policy of liberal governments and especially that of the positivist-inclined President Julio A. Roca: 'To bring to our land this race of men, with their eccentric racial and religious character, not to mention their customs, is to introduce a hard core of population without connection, without involvement, without relation with our national society.'[9]

The issue became more political in the twentieth century, especially after 1930 and the rise of right-wing military regimes. During the war of 1939–45, without closing its ports to Jews or denying entry to survivors of the Holocaust, the Argentine Immigration Department, directed by Santiago Peralta, did not encourage refugees from Nazi Germany, overtly in consideration of Argentina's interests, rather than as a demonstration of anti-Semitism. Then, from 1946, Peralta and his successors specifically discriminated against Jews in a flagrant anti-Semitic policy, which favoured Spaniards and Italians, in spite of occasional intervention by Perón.[10]

Argentine Jews suspected Perón, believing he was more concerned with publicity than principles. They observed his fascist and totalitarian tendencies and the support he received from nationalists, who were instinctively anti-Semitic and made their voices heard on his behalf in the presidential campaign of 1945–46. Their suspicions were heightened in 1947 when Argentina abstained in the United Nations debate on the Partition of Palestine and the establishment of a Jewish state. The government's credentials were not improved by the presence of Gustavo Martínez Zuviría, an activist in Acción Católica and well-known author writing under the pseudonym Hugo Wast, who had published two extremely anti-Semitic novels in the mid-1930s and was now Minister of Education. Perón himself denounced attacks on Jews: 'I deny that those doing these things can be among the supporters of my principles.'[11] Both he and Evita in their speeches sought to reassure Jews and always strongly rejected anti-Semitism. Eventually the rhetoric of the nationalists subsided and Jews even entered the administration. Perón's cultivation of good economic relations with the State of Israel helped to reconcile, if not to convince, Argentina's Jews.[12] As for Perón's anti-clericalism and final conflict with the Catholic Church, the Jews steered clear of the issue, though this did not prevent their opponents returning to the attack. At the end of 1954 in Córdoba Catholic demonstrators carried posters proclaiming 'Down with Perón and his Jewish friends'.[13]

In Argentina anti-Semitic stereotypes were elevated to historical truths and people so persuaded had an almost pathological hatred of Jews. The sources of anti-Semitism in Argentina emerged from particular interests.[14] Argentine nationalists, including many right-wing Catholics, were vociferous in their opposition to Jewish immigrants, whom they regarded as alien to Argentina's cultural identity. The Jews were a large community concentrated in Buenos Aires, and for some time they were accused of left-wing and even communist sympathies; it was this reputation which made them victims of a kind of pogrom during the *semana trágica* of 1919. Alternatively their wealth and ascent to middle-class status aroused envy and created the stereotype of the wealthy Jew. Yet many Argentines, probably the majority, did not share the anti-Semitism of the nationalists and were simply indifferent to the presence of Jews in their midst; and many educated Argentines respected their Jewish teachers and professors.

The kidnapping, trial, and execution of the Nazi war criminal Adolf Eichmann, who had found asylum in Argentina for ten years, had repercussions not only on Israeli–Argentine relations but also on the Jewish

community in Argentina. Nationalist and right-wing Catholic organizations began to question the loyalty of the Argentine Jews to the republic,
and embarked on an unprecedented anti-Semitic campaign.[15] This reached
its peak in June 1962 when a nationalist gang kidnapped and tortured a
young Jewish student and told her, 'This is in revenge for Eichmann.' Jews
were accused of having 'dual loyalty' in a war of intimidation that was not
only propaganda but also involved physical violence against Jews, especially in the high schools. And when Perón returned in 1973 he was no
longer the noble defender of Jewish rights and denouncer of anti-Semitism
but was now among the critics of Jews.

During the 'dirty war' and the accompanying political repression Jews
were divided on whether those from their community who were apprehended were victims of political or of racial persecution. Some sections
of the Argentine Jewish community criticized their main organization,
the DAJA (Delegation of Jewish Argentine Associations), for putting
collective community interests before individual rights by adopting a
position of political non-involvement and pretending that only terrorists
and subversives were disappeared. There was probably some truth in this,
and rather than be identified with terrorism official Jewish positions
became conformist. It was left to international Jewish organizations to
take up the issue of 'disappeared Jews', with a focus on anti-Semitism
as well as human rights.[16] The disappearance of Jacobo Timerman, the
fearless Argentine Jewish newspaper editor of La Opinión, concentrated
world attention on the nature of the military repression in Argentina and
forced the military to acknowledge his imprisonment. Timerman was
finally released, to publicize his story, but he was stripped of his property
and his Argentine citizenship.[17] Argentine Jewish refugees in London
in the years 1975–85 were convinced, and convinced their sympathizers,
that anti-Semitism as well as political repression accounted for their
persecution.

The restoration of democracy in 1983 brought a change and Argentine
governments since then have worked to reduce discrimination against
minorities, including Jews. And although anti-Semitism has not disappeared, the decline of the Jewish population, the increase of Jewish integration and the rate of mixed marriages have worked to take the heat out of
the racial issue. But not entirely. The bomb atttack on the Israeli embassy
in Buenos Aires in March 1992 and the attack on a Jewish community
building there in 1994 were alarming signs. The perpetrators were never
apprehended, and there were reports of collaboration between the attackers
and local police.

Where did the Catholic Church in Argentina stand on anti-Semitism?
A reasonable verdict would be that the Church as an institution and its

leadership in the episcopacy were not guilty. But there is no doubt that significant groups within Catholicism were openly anti-Semitic without incurring condemnation by the Church. Leading authors such as Julio Meinvielle, integralist priest and theologian Leonardo Castellani, Jesuit graduate of the Sorbonne and the Gregorian University, and Virgilio Filippo, a parish priest of humble origins and traditional views, expressed common and current anti-Semitic opinion, though sometimes justifying it as a theological or moral position. Meinvielle, whose books were published by Catholic publishers, summarized his views in *El Judío* (1936), where be based his position on theology and history, asserting that the Jews had refused redemption, denied the divinity of Christ and had not only rejected him as Messiah but had even rebelled against him. 'The duty of the Jew is to persecute the Church; that is his mission.' As for their danger to Argentina, he claimed that the Jews controlled all the economic and productive systems of Argentina, yet curiously were also the secret agents of communism. And the solution? Not annihilation, but 'ghettoization' and denial of equality of rights.[18]

Leonardi Castellani, expelled from the Jesuit order for disobedience but later reinstated as a priest, was a supporter of the post-1943 military regimes in Argentina, and identified liberalism and democracy as the principal modern enemies of the Catholic faith. Without advocating any extreme solution, and critical of Nazi policy as inhuman, he nevertheless considered Jews a threat to the Church and to Argentina, and criticized their wealth which enabled them to influence the press and exploit the workers. His solution was not annihilation but conversion.[19] In his book *Los judíos* (1939) Virgilio Filippo, while denying that he was anti-Semitic, argued that the Jews were sworn enemies of Christianity and were condemned by God to a wandering existence for having killed Jesus Christ. For Filippo, the Jewish people were criminal, perfidious, innately rebellious, and completely lacking in patriotism. In Argentina they sought to use their wealth and economic power to control the Stock Exchange, the banks, industry, and commerce. For this reason Argentina should keep its doors closed to them, and should even have done so during their flight from persecution in the 1930s. Christians should respond to the Jewish threat not with violence but with 'moral anti-Semitism'. He maintained that Jews 'infiltrated society in order to destroy it from within. They are rebellious and insubordinate . . . a lost people.' He continued to maintain that he was not anti-Semitic but simply defending Argentina politically against the Jews.[20] These priests would claim to speak for Argentine Catholicism and their books enjoyed great acclaim in Catholic circles. They were never disavowed by the Argentine Church. Their standard-bearer was the Catholic novelist Hugo Wast.

Hugo Wast came from a Catholic family long distinguished in Córdoba. He had a privileged and successful career, crowned by employment by Church and state and eulogy as a national treasure. In 1943, shortly after the coup of 4 June opened a new surge of right-wing militarism, he was appointed Minister of Justice and Public Education and soon endeared himself to the Church when he decreed obligatory teaching of Catholicism in state schools. But as a prolific author he was already eulogized by clergy and hierarchy as an influential defender of Catholic values in his numerous books, especially his novel *Kahal-Oro* published in 1935, and soon rewarded with great popularity and many editions. Inspired by the *Protocols of the Elders of Zion*, a notorious anti-Semitic forgery, the novel tells the story of a Jewish plot to dominate the Christian world by controlling the economy, the media, culture, and government, and it excels in stereotypes of Jewish appearance and behaviour. This exercise in vulgar racism and anti-Semitism was regarded as a classic by many Catholics. The editor of *Criterio*, Monsignor Gustavo Franceschi, while distancing himself from the anti-Semitism of Wast, published his writings and praised their author, remaining peculiarly ambivalent about Wast's ideology.[21]

Mindful of papal condemnation of anti-Semitism, Franceschi, like many Argentine Catholics, sought to distinguish between racial anti-Semitism (condemned) and theological anti-Semitism (approved). He himself in the pages of *Criterio* accused the Jews of anti-Christian racism, and denied that there was a Nazi presence in Argentina in the 1940s. In Córdoba the Jesuits preached hostility to Jews in their publication *El Cruzado* and equated the Jewish 'menace' with the communist threat, while in *Criterio* Franceschi expressed hostility to the immigration of Jews from Nazi Germany in order to avoid provoking anti-Semitism and to preserve the Catholic homogeneity of Argentina.[22]

Not all Argentines and not all Catholics shared these views. To the credit of Argentina's Christian Democrats, they showed a different face of the Church from the reticence of the bishops and the anti-Semitism of the Catholic right. They did not hesitate to criticize the crimes of Nazi Germany and the sin of the Holocaust, to hope for an Allied victory, and to condemn all anti-Semitism.[23] In opposing anti-Semitism Christian Democrat priests drew inspiration from Pope Pius XI and other sources in Rome and occupied countries, and also from the words of the English Cardinal Arthur Hinsley, who condemned Hitler and declared that neutrality was not an option in this war. Meanwhile the Argentine hierarchy, no friend of Christian Democracy or its organ *Orden Cristiano*, remained closer to the nationalist right than to the claims of democracy.

There came a time, however, when Argentine Catholicism could not remain immune to wider influences in the Church. The teachings of

Vatican II and later Pope Benedict XVI's reference to Jews as 'the people of the Covenant' could not be ignored, nor the truth that Christians and Jews were inherently linked in the mystery of the Passover. The declaration *Nostra Aetate* of Vatican II established the theology of Christian–Jewish relations and made a commitment to reject all anti-Semitism, and explicitly its expression by 'the rulers of the Third Reich and their attempt to crush the entire Jewish people'. As Cardinal Ratzinger, Pope Benedict XVI had endorsed the conclusions of the Pontifical Biblical Commission that a Jewish reading of the Bible has its own independent validity and that Christians can learn from Jewish interpretation of Scripture, and in speaking to the Jewish community in Rome in 2010 he referred to the solidarity of Jews and Christians based on the Jewish Bible and especially the Ten Commandments, the terms of the Covenent through Moses.[24] The Argentine Church now lived in a new world of Christian–Jewish relations.

Afro-Latin American Religions

African religious systems, brought by slaves, survived in Latin America in the face of popular hostility and official repression. A dominant theme of the Afro-Latin American religions is the search for help and protection in life's trials and personal sufferings. For these they looked to their own gods, but Jesus Christ and the Virgin Mary were often identified with African gods or ancestors who, in return for sacrifice, would protect and assist black people in their daily lives. Candomblé, descended from the religion of the Yoruba, became the Afro-Brazilian religion of Bahia and parts of urban Brazil. It is a complex religion which believes that mankind is descended from a single ancestor, some of whose descendants assume a divinity which gives them power over nature and enables them to control the oceans and skies and to overcome disease.[25] Believers attribute special miraculous powers to ancestor gods known as *orixás*, *voduns*, *inquices*, and *caboclos*, described in a vast mythology which also explains the fates of their human followers. Their spiritual energy, or *axé*, enters their living descendants during ceremonials comprising divination, healing, music, dance, animal sacrifice (cocks, guineafowl, and goats), food offerings, and spirit possession, which is fundamental to the cult. By means of blood sacrifice and elaborate ceremonies of spirit possession, the gods are persuaded to intervene benignly in the lives of their devotees and overcome their adversaries. Herbal medicine and spiritual healing are Candomblé religious practices, following the logic of purification of the body.[26]

The Candomblé 'house' is not only a religious temple but also a social centre where the daily needs and material problems of the faithful are provided for; it is the residence of the chief priest and his assistants, as well as a shelter in times of domestic crisis and poverty and a haven for fugitives from police persecution, which Candomblé people often experienced. The chief priest is one who can dominate others and becomes in effect an expression of male leadership.[27] The chosen homes with their *pai do santo*, or spiritual leader, hold religious ceremonies, often with a statue of the Virgin Mary, and a ritual consisting of the beating of congo drums and dancing, incantations, the singing of samba songs and making the sign of the cross, many worshippers falling into a trance in which they can communicate with their ancestors and deities.[28]

Historically Candomblé took easily to the hybrid veneration of Catholic divinities and saints.[29] Indeed it was a necessary strategy to hide their liturgy in a Brazil suspicious of religious innovation, where African practices were more or less repressed by the police until the 1970s and where the law expressly prohibited the practice of magic. Followers therefore hid demonstrations of witchcraft, even though magic was important to Candomblé because through it relations with clients were established.[30] So the faithful fused their divinities with Catholic saints and in this form continued to practise their African rites. Their god is often represented clothed in white garments of purity and wearing a silver crown of majesty, and is worshipped as the creator of the human race; thus they syncretized their god with Jesus Christ, whom the Portuguese worshipped as the child Jesus in his white gown and small imperial crown. Both religions believe in the possibility of divine intervention in human affairs, answering to a universal human longing for protection against adversity, poverty, and natural disasters. Candomblé and other syncretic cults are occupied with constant negotiation, to use a word favoured by the anthropologists, of their religious identity without trouble to their conscience.[31] Catholic theologians, on the other hand, are wary of the concept of syncretism, which implies a kind of equality of parts and suggests another form of Catholicism, something which the Church denies; they prefer to treat Candomblé and other expressions of African beliefs as different and indeed rival religions. The Brazilian nation state, on the other hand, embraced Candomblé and its cult as symbols of the Brazilian nation in the sphere of international opinion.[32]

Afro-Brazilian religion displays great diversity, and other cults such as Umbanda and Macumba have sprung up with distinct identities. Umbanda was born in Rio in the 1920s and has attracted many poor people from the *favelas* as well as middle-class and professional followers, lured by the role of spiritism. Efforts were made to 'whiten' the Afro-Brazilian elements most closely linked to the Candomblé tradition of initiation, such as animal sacrifice, wild dancing, and drumming, while retaining other elements of the African tradition; these were followed by later growths borrowed from Catholicism, French spiritism, and Amerindian beliefs whose doctrines involved communicating with spirits.[33] The Portuguese language took over from the African and animal sacrifice was banned.[34] Umbanda is a protective religion. According to its doctrine, spirits survive the body's death and return to the *astral*, the world of pure spirits organized in legions, before moving on in a form of reincarnation into new bodies. Pure spirits can help people on earth through mediums acting in ceremonies of hymns and drumming; in a trance a medium can communicate from a spirit to a living person and offer protection and support in overcoming life's problems.

Various spirits fulfil different functions: *Oruxás* are African deities, representing the force of nature; *Caboclos* are spirits of Brazilian Indians employing forces from the sea, the forests, and wildlife to help people in their difficulties; *Exus* are spirits deriving from sinners who can bring guile and deceit to the solution of people's problems. The popularity of Umbanda is explained by its claim to come to the aid of people in their everyday crises. By 1970 Umbanda had 10 million adherents, but since then has been losing to the Pentecostals.

Santería or *Regla de Ocha*, deriving from the religion of the Yoruba peoples of south-western Nigeria and passed on to slaves and their descendants, became the most widespread of Afro-Cuban religious systems. Its adherents venerate the Yoruba deities called *orishas*, or guardian saints. As the *orisha* in Cuba was interpreted as the Spanish word *santos*, the practice came to be named Santería, the worship of the saints.[35] Followers do not regard their beliefs as incompatible with the Catholic religion, though the African tradition also includes pharmacology, art, music, and magic as inherent parts of its religious system. Africans share with Cuban Catholics devotion to St Lazarus and observe an annual St Lazarus pilgrimage on 17 December. The Catholic Church, which does not favour the concept of syncretism, excludes Santería from orthodox faith and practice. At the summit of the Yoruba religion is the creator, named Olofi in Cuba, the supreme being embodying *aché*, or spritual power. Beneath him is a pantheon of deities, the *orishas*, which includes spirits created prior to human beings and also spirits who were once human and evolved into deities by their exceptional qualities. The *orishas*, who are identified with their corresponding Catholic saints, intervene in the daily life of the people and if venerated and propitiated can help their devotees.

From Yoruba worship the Cuban Santería derives divination practices, ritual relationships, sacrifice, and possession, and the preservation of the ritual language that transmits essential knowledge of nature and medicine, among others things. To obtain the *aché* of the gods they must be appeased by sacrifice, offerings, and spells. Offerings can be of fruit, food, or flowers, but may also include the blood sacrifice of animals. The dead too must be honoured with offerings and ancestor worship is an essential part of Santería. There are four major rituals through which the *orisha*'s world is approached: divination, sacrifice, possession (trance), and initiation. Divination is achieved through the reading of shells and coconuts and the interpretation of proverbs.[36] Music, dance, and drums bring down the *orishas* from heaven to possess their devotees in a state of trance or ecstasy. The healing system of religion, the belief that the gods can heal through divination and sacrifice and the properties derived from plants are characteristic of Santería and one of the reasons for its survival.

The Cuban Revolution, hostile to Catholicism, was tolerant of Afro-Cuban religions, which were not regarded as a threat. These in turn supported the new regime, giving it a base among the black and popular classes, who believed they had more to gain than to lose from revolutionary change.[37] This does not prevent Santería priests, or *babalawos*, from making enigmatic predictions of a political nature.[38]

The cult of Vodou, a spirit or sacred energy, has been sensationalized in works of fiction and travel, but no less than other Afro-Latin American cults it has survived through its historic appeal to the popular classes. It was brought to Haiti from the west coast of Africa, the region of modern Benin, including Aruba- and Yoruba-speaking peoples. The cult originated in the massive slave trade to the French sugar colony of Saint-Domingue in the eighteenth century and although it had a minority following it drew strength from the revolt of the slaves in 1791 and declaration of Haitian independence in 1804. The virtual withdrawal of the Catholic Church in the years 1805–60 in response to harassment by the governments of Haiti left a minimal presence of priests and in this spiritual vacuum Vodou gained new space. Popular Catholicism survived, too, and there was a convergence of Catholic and African beliefs and practices, which continues to this day, in spite of periodic attempts to counter what the Church and state regarded as sorcery, superstition, and sacrilege.

Vodou beliefs have emerged from a fusion of African and creole gods with Catholic saints. The system begins with a supreme deity but one surrounded by powerful spirits called *loa*, providing a link between human and divine. Adherents form communities around the temple under a vodou *oungan* or leader. An elaborate form of initiation ritual beginning with prayers and hymns, apparently Catholic in style, continues with music, dance, and possession, in which the initiate surrenders to the *loa*. The essence of the surrender ritual consists in feeding the *loa*: vegetable and fruit, as well as numerous chickens, goats, and pigs, are offered to the spirits. Magic and sorcery are inherent in Haitian Vodou and have helped to cause its notoriety. Sorcery consists in casting spells setting dead people against a victim, who will then wither away and die. There is a place too for zombies, corpses revived by witchcraft, which occupy some position between the living and the dead and are controlled by a sorcerer.

The slaves did not arrive in Latin America bereft of religious beliefs, their souls a *tabula rasa* ready for conversion to new religions. Some of them remembered their ancestral faiths and in the succeeding years, in fields and plantations, the seeds of religious memory were passed to their descendants. The existence of Afro-Latin American religions in Brazil and the Caribbean, in the face of initial hostility and without great proselytizing, are signs of the enduring power of religion in Latin America and its lasting relevance to the lives of the people.

Protestants and Pentecostals

Protestantism developed many forms in Latin America, ranging from the traditional Churches to modern Pentecostalism.[39] The historic religions – Anglicanism, Presbyterianism, Methodism, and Lutheranism – entered in the course of the nineteenth century and after a century of growth were a familiar part of the religious landscape. They sought salvation in the twin truths of Scripture and faith in Christ; they tended not to proselytize except among unconverted Indians, and their relations with Catholicism were not usually controversial. In Latin America they were traditionally called *evangélicos*, not exactly the same as the term Evangelicals applied to born-again Protestants, who proclaim the Bible as their fundamental message and are committed to evangelization. The most active of the Protestants were the Pentecostals, their name derived from Pentecost, a Christian festival seven weeks after Easter, which marks the day when the Holy Spirit descended upon the disciples and they received the gifts of healing, speaking in tongues, prophecy, and personal virtue. More militant and more spiritually intolerant than the traditional Protestants, the Pentecostals' relations with Catholics were less benign. From the original Pentecostals have sprung the neo-Pentecostals, who are usually from a higher social stratum and are better educated. Some Pentecostal practices can be seen in the traditional Churches, where they are referred to as charismatic. In addition to Protestants and Pentecostals Latin America accommodates the familiar sects – Mormons, Jehovah's Witnesses, and Seventh-Day Adventists – all of them American-style in belief and practice.

The number of Protestants grew from 50,000 to 11.9 million between 1890 and 1978, and from 21 million in 1980 to 46 million in 1990, with an estimated 60 million by the end of the twentieth century. Perhaps at least 10 per cent of the population of Latin America in the 1980s were

Protestants, to the dismay of Catholic authorities, disturbed by the knowledge that the percentage was even more impressive when compared to the number of practising Catholics. Andean countries have the lowest percentages of Protestants (1–8 per cent), and Mexico too has a low percentage (2–5 per cent). Argentina has a large Protestant population in absolute terms, but not as a percentage of the total population (5–7 per cent). In Brazil, at 22 million, Protestants amount to as much as 18 per cent of the population. Statistics of religion are notoriously problematic and even specialists are divided on totals. Chile's Protestants underwent a strong rate of increase in the twentieth century, but the figure of 36 per cent of the population given for the end of the century defies anecdotal evidence, which would suggest a more realistic figure of 25 per cent. In Central America 3.3 million of the 21 million people from Guatemala to Costa Rica, or 15 per cent of the population, consider themselves Protestant. In Guatemala in the late twentieth century Protestant leaders claimed to represent almost one-quarter of the country.[40] Most of the increase in Guatemala, Brazil, and Nicaragua was accounted for by Pentecostals.

In the 1920s and 1930s a kind of cultural Protestantism emanating from the United States was active in some parts of Latin America. In Lima, for example, the Colegio Americano was a Protestant outpost of relatively free and liberal democratic thought, where Haya de la Torre and others were able to teach, free from constraint.[41] There were differences in the Protestant communities. Presbyterian missionaries had targeted educated people and members of the elite. Baptists took their message to the working classes, though the next generation tended to move upwards and to include professional people. Protestants were strongly anti-communist and ready to support hard-line military regimes; and from the 1960s they became hostile to Catholic progressives. They subsequently felt threatened by the Pentecostals. In the 1960s and 1970s, fearing the influence of Cuba and the spread of communism, many Evangelicals welcomed right-wing dictatorships.

Some Protestants, it is true, joined Catholics in denouncing human rights violations, but many others defended military rule as a lesser evil which would protect their freedom to spread the Gospel. When Catholic bishops refused to bless military dictatorships, as in Chile, prominent Evangelicals were quick to provide their own brand of legitimacy. These tactics earned them some credit with authoritarian governments and gained them access to television and radio.[42] One such opportunist was Luis Palau, an Argentine trained in evangelism in the United States. He returned to Latin America where he cultivated presidents, held prayer breakfasts with the authorities, and worked the power networks to evangelize Latin America in the 1980s. Protestantism in Chile was a religion of middle-class educated people; and these provided the majority of converts to Presbyterianism. Methodists, who grew in numbers from the end of the nineteenth century, had a more popular appeal and it was in their congregations that Pentecostalism first appeared and that claims of manifestations of the Holy Spirit and miracles of healing were made.

Guatemala became a striking example of Protestant expansion. Protestantism was taken to Guatemala by North American missionaries in the late nineteenth century and was welcomed by liberal governments in conflict with the Catholic Church. Early converts were few and marginal, but by the mid-twentieth century the missions had shed their foreign character and become more Guatemalan in identity and inspiration. Now Protestants moved into the mainstream of Guatemalan society and their numbers surged between 1960 and 1990. This coincided with social crisis, insurgency and counterinsurgency, and the seizure of the state by the military. As traditional communities were shattered in the turmoil of war and revolution, and Catholics and terrorists were the principal targets of repression, Protestants moved in to provide a safer alternative for highland people.

But Protestants sought converts not only among rural and indigenous communities, but also among the urban middle classes. They were helped by the sympathetic policy of the reformist president Juan José Arévalo, with his vague ideas of 'spiritual socialism', and then by the more radical administration of Jacobo Arbenz (1950–54). The leftist tendencies of the latter, however, divided Protestant opinion, while the Arbenz administration became 'suspicious of all Protestant missions' as allies of the United States.[43] But success lay ahead. In the years around 1970 Protestantism flourished, confident now in its Pentecostal form, boosted not by the United States but by its own roots and its innate appeal – as anti-Catholic, a response to the gifts of the Holy Spirit, an emotional worship, a form of religious entertainment. Whether this was called spectacle or theology, it brought in worshippers in steadily increasing numbers into the 1980s.

The great earthquake of 4 February 1976 caused massive damage to life, limb, and homes, leaving 20,000 dead. The 'disaster effect' helped to increase the visual presence of Protestants, as agencies and individuals rushed to help and at the same time to proselytize. There was a surge in conversions in the late 1970s and 1980s.[44] Conditions in the highands also favoured Protestantism, when an explosive mix of morals and menace unleashed a campaign of extinction against Indians, guerrillas, and Catholics. The war in the highlands was a time of tribulation, when the message of salvation and promise of a second coming had a special meaning for Protestants, who took advantage of the Catholic absence from El Quiché and the shortage of priests on the ground.[45] As the military targeted priests, catechists, and churches, and Ríos Montt's terror sweep through the highlands made life dangerous for Catholics, Protestant chapels were reckoned to be safer places of refuge than Catholic churches.[46] While Catholics took cover, Protestants gained ground in the war zones, helped by government support.[47]

In 1982, the centenary of the Protestant arrival in Guatemala, thousands of the faithful from all over the country congregated to celebrate the event and to listen to sermons by President Ríos Montt and other Protestant celebrities such as Jorge Serrano Elías and Luis Palau. Protestantism continued to grow until about 1985, then slowed down, but even so it accounted for one-third of Guatemala's total population. Pentecostals still flourished, especially neo-Pentecostals, who emphasized in addition to traditional Protestant beliefs the conviction that material goods, such as personal prosperity, health and security, were tangible evidence of God's favour, a message which gained them recruits among the middle classes.[48]

Elsewhere in Central America the demography of religion was also changing. Protestant growth in Nicaragua was strong from 1978 to 1988, reaching 15 per cent of the population, while Catholicism fell from 96 to 73 per cent.[49] This drew the hostility of the Catholic Church, less towards tradtional Protestantism than towards Pentecostalism which was felt to be more threatening, with aggressive proselytizing and little interest in ecumenical approaches. Protestants themselves were divided, Evangelicals supporting the Sandinista government and Pentecostals taking a more conservative stance against it. Meanwhile, El Salvador, the home of Archbishop Romero, moved from being a totally Catholic country to one where one-third of the population had become Evangelical Protestants by the end of the twentieth century.

Protestantism at its most dynamic was seen in Pentecostalism, and its leading historians claim that by the end of the twentieth century out of a total population in Latin America of 520 million, 170 million called themselves Pentecostals or members of independent Pentecostal churches.[50] In Chile early Pentecostalism developed as a schism from the Methodist Church. Here Protestants formed 22 per cent of the population, and of these 80 per cent were Pentecostals. In Mexico, where Catholics had fought long and hard to defend their faith, the Pentecostal movement proved more difficult to resist and it spread, impeded more by divisions in its own ranks than opposition from Catholics, first in Sonora and Chihuahua, then further south. Its leading congregation, the Apostólica de la Fe en Cristo Jesús, derived from the influx of Methodist and Presbyterian Christians; it appealed to many people attracted by speaking in tongues, though this was superseded by other Pentecostal denominations, such as La Luz del Mundo, claiming to represent 13 per cent of all Mexicans. Elsewhere

Pentecostal communities proliferated as a kind of private enterprise, when individuals from the larger Churches founded their own congregations. In Peru, where Protestants were estimated to constitute 7 per cent of the population in 1992, tiny Pentecostal communities emerged in the remote countryside of Ayacucho where there were no priests and where Sendero Luminoso (Shining Path), a violent terrorist movement, identified them as a rival source of spiritual inspiration and allegiance. In the years 1982–92 they became victims of counterinsurgency as well as of terrorists, and it is estimated that 529 Protestants were killed, including 446 by Shining Path, 49 by the armed forces.[51]

It was in Brazil that the Pentecostals staged their most dramatic entry. There the Assemblies of God traced their origins to Pentecostal communities in the United States in the years around 1910 and received early recruits from existing denominations. But they soon became Brazilianized; converted to intense evangelism, their spiritual journey developed along national lines with leadership transferred to Brazilians. Thus they grew through their own momentum. By 1950, recruiting from traditional Protestants and Catholics, they spread to most of Brazil and by the year 2000 numbered in their millions.[52] These were not entirely uncontrolled individuals or those with private consciences, dreaming of a new heaven on earth. They were communities directed by pastors who claimed and exercised authority.[53] At the same time, however, they were essentially laypeople teaching laypeople, with equality of ministry.

How can we account for the Pentecostal phenomenon in Brazil? Conditions were propitious. Population growth, crumbling rural parishes, and towns without priests left gaps in the religious landscape which the Catholic Church was slow to fill. Protestants had been there in numbers since 1900.[54] But Brazilian Pentecostals, the Assemblies of God, which first appeared in the early twentieth century, soon acquired identity by their sheer size, with 7 million followers by the 1990s.[55] Services were informal. Large choirs, preachers proclaiming God's wonders, strong moralizing on sex and drink, miracle cures, shouting and singing from the crowd, this was religion in a popular idiom, emotional and spontaneous. Newcomers were called upon to accept Christ and to believe in the operation of the Holy Spirit, the third person of the Trinity, supreme expression of the power of God. In a harsh paradox, the developing social conscience of the Catholic Church in Brazil, especially in the diocese of São Paulo, was taking the Church to the left, a move not popular with all Brazilians. The Assemblies of God, which were critical of the Catholic left, supplied a more purely spiritual message with which followers could easily identify.

In the mid-twentieth century the Foursquare Gospel began to attract followers, led by two preachers from the United States. They had a relaxed attitude towards behaviour, allowing films, TV, popular music and dancing, though alcohol and tobacco were forbidden. There were other growths, and from 1977 the Universal Church of the Kingdom of God became the principal Pentecostal community. But there were many variations and offshoots, forming a diverse pattern of Pentecostalism across Brazil. The demography of religion changed. In 1950 more than 90 per cent of Brazilians were still Catholic. By 2000 only 75 per cent of Brazil's 155 million people could be called Catholic. The Protestant share of the population grew from 2 per cent in the 1930s to 4 per cent in 1960 to 13 per cent in 1992, and in 1996 15 per cent. And Protestants were moving up as well as across. Ernesto Geisel, a Lutheran, was Brazil's first Protestant president to serve a full term (1974–78) and during his tenure the military-controlled congress approved a divorce law not to the liking of the Catholic Church.

The Universal Church of the Kingdom of God had hundreds of churches in Brazil by the 1990s and its followers were numbered in the millions. They had a TV network, radio station, and newspapers, and a self-styled bishop, Edir Macedo, a leader with celebrity appeal, denounced by some as a charlatan, defended by others as a dynamic religious leader who could command mass gatherings for his sermons. The Universal Church exemplified the modern version of Pentecostalism: a mega-Church, universal in the sense that it welcomed everyone through its open door, though its expansion was more structured than that of the other Pentecostals, it was organized from the top down, emphasizing the role of ministers, their training and vocation, and insisting that they must be married. Theology was not for them: it was regarded as a distraction from the simple message of Jesus; and services were stagy and vulgar, led by a preacher who acted more like a master of ceremonies than a pastor. In Río de Janeiro the service of *descarrego*, the unloading of spiritual affliction, would open with a hymn, followed by biblical reading and discussion led by the preacher, then more hymns; cries would rise calling for evil spirits to be expelled, amidst collective prayer, becoming ever more emotional.[56] The poor and guileless were attracted by claims to cure diseases, including cancer and AIDS, and by exorcism and the promise of financial success known as 'prosperity theology', invoking God for worldly rather than eternal salvation.

Pentecostals had no inhibitions in seeking political power in Brazil and using it to their advantage. In 1986 they entered the Constituent Assembly, gaining eighteen elected members; together with other Protestants they formed a coalition, the *baseada evangélica*, totalling thirty-six representatives. Pentecostals tended towards conservative politics, cultivating officials in the administration of Fernando Henrique Cardoso and competing with the Catholic Church for resources and privileges, such as TV concessions, in return for supporting the government. They used their media outlets to politicize and to urge their followers to support conservative candidates, denouncing Lula da Silva, who was to become president of Brazil in 2003–10, as a communist.[57] Their political manoeuvres during the Cardoso administration did not escape the attention and criticism of Cardinal Arns and other Catholic leaders. There was no love lost between Catholics and Pentecostals, and the latter were not averse to attacking Catholic practices, such as devotion to the Virgin Mary.

Pentecostalism developed many forms, changing and growing. It attracted members from the middle classes, some alienated by radical Catholicism, others by traditionalist clergy. Established Pentecostalism was eventually overtaken by a kind of 'rechristianization from above' in the form of neo-Pentecostalism, where professionals and military, and even heads of state, as in Guatemala, and politicians in Brazil and Colombia converted into born-again Christians of a fundamentalist kind, moving in the opposite direction to Catholics, even to the point of supporting or tolerating dictatorships.

Yet the success of Pentecostalism derived not from elite influences but from what has been called 'rechristianization from below', targeting the popular sectors and growing among uprooted populations on the edge of big cities. In rural areas it secured a place in Indian farming communities neglected by Catholic clergy, as in Mexico, Guatemala, Ecuador, and the Cauca Valley of Colombia; or isolated, as in Guatemala when the Church left El Quiché.[58] Protestants in effect occupied vacant space and offered services, tools, and expertise as well as religion, sometimes despite the opposition of local Catholic leaders, as in Mexico. In Chimborazo, Ecuador, historians speak of a Protestant 'boom', though this was backed by foreign funds, and the pastoral efforts of the Catholic Church among the poor were not negligible. In Cauca, Colombia, Protestantism advanced among Indian communities where Catholic action had been compromised by weak evangelization, the position of the Church as a major landowner, and its reluctance to admit indigenous influence in liturgy and worship. But social explanations are not enough. Pentecostalism is an essentially religious phenomenon, another expression of popular, though not traditional, religiosity, claiming the gift of tongues, healing and other manifestations of the Holy Spirit. At the same time it has been intolerant towards other expressions of popular religiosity, towards Afro-Latin American practices of idolatry and witchcraft. And it tended to have puritanical attitudes towards alcohol, fiestas, and sex.[59]

Pentecostalism, it has been suggested, grew in the gaps left by the Catholic Church, either literally in the absence of priests and churches, as in Brazil where the expansion of urban and rural populations bypassed existing structures, or in the failure of the Church to connect with those seeking a spiritual life. Pentecostal communities helped migrants to the city to find companionship and establish connections. These were the negative reasons. More positively the movement grew from impulses received from the United States, especially in the earlier, more missionary period of Pentecostalism. But this period was overtaken by spontaneous movements in Latin America. Local Pentecostals became the most dynamic factor in implanting and evangelizing, driven by an urge to moral transformation and intense style of worship. The original liturgy, described above, developed a more dramatic expression. Typical services would begin with a band playing and the congregation singing, clapping, dancing, lifting hands towards heaven; then the pastor enters, shouts and claps compellingly, and preaches with force, urging the faithful to convert now, to repent, to reject sin; people respond and some start falling down. Ironically, many of the things that Catholics were accused of – superstition, fanaticism, belief in divine healing, irrationalism, emotionalism – are central features of Pentecostalism in more exaggerated forms. Pentecostalism has scant message for the larger community or views on social structure; it identifies primarily with the religious community. In this narrower context it seeks miracles and faith healing and mystical experience, rather than institutional development or social commitment; and while Pentecostalists see God in their daily lives, they are devoted to a form of individualism and have little interest in the collective ideal or in changing society. In spite of the massive conversions to Pentecostalism not all Latin Americans have been convinced. It has also been found that by the 1990s many Pentecostalists had become non-observant and the apostasy rate was high. And now there was a new category of 'belief', noticed by all religions: in censuses and inquiries a growing number of people stated 'no religion'.[60]

Catholics could not be expected to welcome the growth of Protestantism and Pentecostalism. Their response would no longer follow the example of the Church militant of former centuries, when Catholicism could call on allies in government and law to stem the advance of rivals. It would have to improve its own infrastructure among the clergy, religious workers, base communities, and the use of television and radio ministries. The alarm had been sounded. The Latin American Episcopal Conference (CELAM) more than once criticized 'fundamentalist' sects, whose religion was based only on faith in Scripture to the exclusion of revelation and the Church, and raised concern over their 'increasing proselytism'. By 1980 disquiet was more urgent and at Puebla warnings about Protestant growth were prominent. In 1996 Pope John Paul II called on Catholics to resist the expansion of 'religious sects' and their 'destructive work', and he described Latin American Evangelicals as 'ravenous wolves' causing 'discord and division in our communities'.[61] In Guatemala Archbishop Penados accused Evangelicals of being 'instruments of rich foreign governments', and called them 'the opiate of the people'. In Chiapas there was active hostility towards Protestants from traditional Catholics and counter-accusations of persecution. Throughout Latin America Protestant tele-evangelists caused resentment among Catholics. Conspiracy theories abounded, the trail of accusations leading to the United States. And the finger was pointed at 'disaster evangelism', when every earthquake and natural disaster would see Protestant relief workers homing in, distributing aid, and encouraging conversions.

Pentecostals represented a new growth, open access, freedom for all, with little leadership, and no theology. Virtually anyone could found a Church and admit converts without instruction in Christian doctrine. This was unlike the Catholic ethos, which valued freedom and simplicity within a structure of authority and a framework of order. These were the values which had enabled the Church to survive 500 years in Latin America. But Pentecostal growth, the aggressive tactics of the Universal Church and increasing Pentecostal political influence moved Catholic clergy to respond. One of the responses was to be found in Catholic Charismatic Renewal, emphasizing personal salvation, traditional spirituality, and conservative religion. But not all Catholics identified with movements of this kind, regarded as pre-Vatican II. And many preferred to stay with the religion and culture they knew.

Pope Benedict XVI exhorted Brazil's bishops urgently to undertake a new evangelization aimed at discouraging Catholics from abandoning their Church and joining the Evangelical and neo-Pentecostal communities. In a message on 10 September 2010 to bishops from north-eastern Brazil the pope observed that the expansion of these 'new groups that call themselves followers of Christ' was due in part to the 'superficial' way in which the Catholic Church had passed on the faith. Reminding the bishops that Catholic missionaries were the first to bring Christian faith to their country five centuries ago the pope insisted that Catholicism was still 'fundamental to the identity of the Brazilian people'. But he blamed the 'growing influence of new elements in society that were practically foreign a few decades ago' for leading Catholics to abandon the Church and join other Christian communities. He urged bishops to reach out to lapsed Catholics and to build bridges to establish contacts through ecumenical dialogue, in spite of growing moral relativism. At the same time Catholic leaders had to meet the challenge of the 'aggressive proselytism' that some of the new groups employed.[62]

Observing the wider picture, Pope Benedict was convinced that the rapid growth of the Bible-based communities was also a clear sign that there was a widespead thirst for God in Brazil: a conclusion that might also be drawn for the whole of Latin America.

CHAPTER 12

✑

Between Liberation and Tradition

Liberation Theology

A HIERARCHICAL CHURCH and an obedient people, a model in Latin America for 500 years, was challenged in the late twentieth century, as the Church began to respond to the world and people became less docile. It was now that the Latin American Church, so long the follower in faith and morals, led the way with two innovatory movements, liberation theology and base communities.

The new theology was conceived by a Peruvian Dominican priest, Gustavo Gutiérrez, who first sketched out his thoughts in 1970, when he used a combination of biblical and early Christian sources to interpret and judge social problems actually experienced in Latin America.[1] He dismissed the concept and policies of 'development', which reduced poor nations to economic and social objects and augmented the resources of the richer nations. Development failed to attack the causes of poverty, especially 'the economic, social, political and cultural dependence of some peoples on others'. 'Liberation', he argued, is a more appropriate word, indicating the search for a society free of every kind of slavery. 'To see history as a process of man's liberation places the issue of desired social change in a dynamic context . . . To speak of liberation is to hint at the biblical sources that illuminate man's presence and actions in history: the liberation from sin by Christ our Redeemer and the bringing of new life.' He spoke of three levels of meaning in the term 'liberation': 'the political liberation of oppressed peoples and social classes; man's liberation in the course of history; and liberation from sin as a condition of a life of communion of all men with the Lord'.

Gutiérrez became the leading figure of a group of theologians – Jon Sobrino, Juan Luis Segundo, Leonardo Boff, and Enrique Dussel, among others – inspired by his book *Theology of Liberation* (1971), its author formed by his reflections on the Bible, his graduate studies at Louvain, the University of Lyon, and the Gregorian University in Rome, followed by teaching in Lima's Catholic University and pastoral experience among Lima's poor. His arguments use traditional Christian concepts but give these new meaning. He argues that salvation is gained not simply by prayer, the sacraments, and personal faith but by working for the liberation of the full human person, body and soul. Sin is not confined to private moral behaviour but has a wider dimension present in the structure of an unjust society, and to liberate the poor is to reject sin and begin a process of personal and collective salvation. In this view, redemption reaches beyond the individual to the liberation of communities. In fact, if the Church is to bear true witness to the Gospel it has to join the poor in their political struggle for liberation from poverty and injustice. Gutiérrez cites the famous text from Matthew on the Last Judgement, when Jesus says to the just who have fed him, clothed him, and nursed him, 'Come, O blessed of my Father inherit the kingdom prepared for you ... Truly I say to you, as you did it to one of the least of these my brethren, you did it to me'.[2] Gutiérrez emphasizes three points: 'The stress on communion and fellowship as the ultimate meaning of human life; the insistence on a love which is manifested in concrete actions, with "doing" being favored over simple "knowing"; and the revelation of the human mediation necessary to reach the Lord'.[3]

'Poverty', says Gutiérrez, 'is a central theme both in the Old and the New Testaments.' So liberation theology focused on the poor, the basic element, disinherited and oppressed, whose misery was rooted in the very structure of society and the dependence of the underdeveloped world on the rich nations. 'The existence of poverty represents a sundering both of solidarity among persons and also of communion with God. Poverty is an expression of sin, that is, of negation of love. It is therefore incompatible with the coming of the Kingdom of God, a Kingdom of Love and Justice.'

> Only by rejecting poverty and by making itself poor in order to protest against it can the Church preach something that is uniquely its own: 'spiritual poverty', that is, the openness of humankind and history to the future promised by God. Only in this way, will the Church be able to fulfill [sic] authentically – and with any possibility of being listened to – its prophetic function of denouncing every human injustice.[4]

Evangelization, therefore, is impossible without change and this requires a new theology. Liberation theologians become the new missionaries of society whose structure they work to change. Theology has to become political and the Church has to become an instrument of action.

Gutiérrez announces a renewal of the theology of hope, so often placed below faith and charity among the virtues. But in the pages devoted to hope he allows himself to be diverted by a variety of non-Christian authors, including Marx.[5] Jon Sobrino, Spanish Jesuit and professor in El Salvador, writes eloquently that belief in the resurrection of the crucified Jesus is a means of preserving hope; not merely of survival after death but also the hope sustained by those who are suffering now. People suffering hardship and repression, as Jesus did, have hope for the resurrection. In these people the crucified Jesus is present today, and as they seek liberation from their crosses hope becomes unwavering and present historically. This approach places liberation theology at the service of all Christians in that it helps them better to understand the meaning of Christ's resurrection.[6]

At this point liberation theology appeared a serious, worthy, and orthodox intellectual movement. Its publications were scholarly and the fruit of extensive research and reflection. True, it was action-orientated, spoke of oppressive structures, and called for social and economic change, but so did other Catholic movements of the time. For example, Leonardo Boff, a Brazilian Franciscan, insisted that Christians must take an active part in liberating the oppressed, move on from a merely intellectual approach to theology in a more biblical framework which leads to a commitment to the poor.[7] An exemplary exhortation, worthy of any pulpit. So why did Rome prowl and probe?

The reason lies in Marxism. The liberationists were not responsible for the world in which they lived, the Cuban Revolution, the myth of Guevara, Allende in Chile, Nicaragua; but the environment of revolution meant that any concession to Marxism by the Christian side looked like defeatism. Within the Church many left-wing priests and religious surfaced, claiming that Christianity was compatible with Marxism. Among liberationists there were constant references to Marxism and claims that Marxist analysis was a valuable tool. The class struggle was regarded as inevitable and indeed necessary to effect structural change. Recognition of the obvious fact of social conflict led the liberationists into adopting a Marxist position on the class struggle. However, Gutiérrez was careful to avoid a purely Marxist view.

> Recognition of the fact of class struggle means taking a position, opposing certain groups of persons, rejecting certain activities, and facing hostilities, [but] our active participation on the side of justice and in defense of the weakest members of society does not mean that we are encouraging conflict; it means rather that we are trying to eliminate its deepest root, which is the absence of love.[8]

But not all his followers were so circumspect.

Leonardo Boff became an uncompromising exponent of liberation theology, champion of the poor and defender of human rights, insisting that the Church should take the side of the poorer not the richer members of Latin American societies. He argued for the reform of the institutional Church and its hierarchical structure, greater lay participation, including women, and the ordination of women priests. Base communities pointed the way to modernization. Many Catholics of the moderate centre would agree with these opinions and Boff enjoyed wide support in Brazil. His views on Marxism were controversial but he was prepared to argue them publicly. 'Liberation theology freely borrows from Marxism certain "methodological pointers" that have proved fruitful in understanding the world of the oppressed, such as: the importance of economic factors; attention to the class struggle; the mystifying power of ideologies, including religious ones.' So it is simply an instrument, not comparable to the Gospel. Marx is a companion but never the guide, because we have only one teacher, Christ.[9] The 'pointers' are naïve, not to say unnecessary, being freely available in many sources other than Marxism.

Boff was viewed with suspicion by the Church authorities and in 1985 he was summoned to Rome to answer for his views to Cardinal Ratzinger. The Congregation for the Doctrine of the Faith, the modern Holy Office, found him guilty of three errors: institutional relativism, in arguing that the Church had evolved after Christ's resurrection to accommodate Roman and feudal society; doctrinal relativism, in interpreting dogma as appropriate only for specific times and circumstances; and calling on the Church 'to be fundamentally open to everything without exception'. He was asked not so much to recant as to submit to 'obedient silence'.[10] This meant that he was forbidden to publish or speak publicly about his work for a year. He accepted the decision, declaring 'I am not a Marxist'. He was investigated again in 1992; at this point he left the priesthood but continued to teach theology at the University of Rio de Janeiro.

Boff was never too worried about Rome's reaction to liberationism, nor was he critical of the magisterium. Although he noticed that Puebla 'watered down' the conclusions reached at Medellín and that there had been criticisms of certain tendencies within liberation theology which 'have to be taken into account', he went on to maintain, with some justification, that 'the general tenor of the pronouncements of the magisterium, whether papal or coming from the Synod of Bishops, has been to recognize the positive aspects of liberation theology, especially with reference to the poor and the need for their liberation, as forming part of the universal heritage of Christian commitment to history'.[11]

Boff and a number of like-minded observers visited the Soviet Union in 1987 at the invitation of the Russian Orthodox Church and before the years of the Gorbachev presidency. He was enthusiastic at the 'clean and healthy society' he saw. 'They are interested in our effort to create a synthesis of Christian faith and Marxist social analysis, and believe that it is a very promising development.' Socialism, he reported, 'is more capable than any other system of revealing God in communion in history'. He was happy to see the possibility of a different society, 'more social and less unequal and based on a popular democracy'.[12] Useful sympathy no doubt in the eyes of the Soviets.

The Marxist interpretation of history was pervasive among liberationists. Yet Marxism was flawed by its insistence on historical inevitability *and* moral choice, a contradiction fatal to historical analysis, and unacceptable to Christians. The Marxist interpretation of historical change in terms of economic determinism and dialectical materialism was a blind alley for many theologians. To accept the existence of a class struggle is not to see the course of history dominated only by class and conflict. People are social animals; societies and economies, in Latin America no less than elsewhere, have developed as much by cooperation as by conflict. Father Pedro Arrupe, Superior General of the Society of Jesus, wrote to Jesuit Superiors in Latin America expressing serious reservations about Marxist analysis, which he declared unacceptable. It is impossible, he argued, to undertake a Marxist analysis separate from the philosophy, ideology, and political practice of Marxism. Christians must keep their distance from economic determinism and the class struggle. And he points out that the bishops at Puebla explained that theological reflection based on Marxist analysis runs the risk of leading to 'the total politicization of Christian existence, the disintegration of the language of faith into that of the social sciences and the draining away of the transcendental dimension of Christian salvation'.[13]

From the start liberation theology employed the concept of dependence. A derivative of Marxism, dependency theory was a voguish tool among left-wing analysts and in the hands of the *dependentistas* became the key to unlock the history of Latin America's underdevelopment. They argued that the superior capital, industrial, and commercial resources of the metropolitan powers enabled them to exploit their inferior trading partners and to control the local elites in the periphery; thus they were able to siphon off the surplus produced in Latin American economies and remit the profts to London or other economic centres. The growth of underdevelopment, therefore, followed inexorably from the advance of capitalism. National obstacles to change within Latin America – existing social structures, political corruption, weak internal markets for local industries – were ignored or discounted. Even moderate Church leaders played fast and loose with this theory. The liberationists did not doubt its validity and used it as a theoretical underpinning of their own views. Leonardo Boff explicitly invoked dependency theory and deferred to its authors, such as André Gunder Frank, arguing that Latin American underdevelopment was 'the by-product of a socio-economic system that favors a small minority with wealth while keeping the vast majority of humankind in a state of dependence on the margins of societal life . . . We must break the ties of dependency.'[14]

Gutiérrez was less certain and moved on from his 1970 position to that of 1984, arguing that his use of dependency theory differed from Marxism and that Marxism's atheism was unacceptable to Christians. While not denying the contribution of Marxism, he now admitted that dependency theory was very much to the fore in the early writings on liberation theology but now insisted that 'neither the social sciences generally nor the Latin American contribution to them can be reduced to the Marxist version'.[15] In the Introduction to the revised edition of A Theology of Liberation (1988), he writes that the analytical tools for gaining knowledge of social reality vary with time: 'It is clear, for example, that the theory of dependence, which was so extensively used in the early years of our encounter with the Latin American world, is now an inadequate tool, because it does not take sufficient account of the internal dynamics of each country or of the vast dimensions of the world of the poor.'[16] The irony was that liberation theology was perfectly capable of standing on its own feet in Christian sources without recourse to Marxism and its derivatives, least of all at a time when the collapse of communism was undermining its Marxist base and when dependency theory in particular was becoming a museum piece.

Criticism of liberation theology was gathering pace. In an interview with Nicaraguan Archbishop Obando an American journalist asked him why he had originally embraced liberation theology. 'I was enthusiastic at the beginning,' he said ruefully. 'I thought liberation theology could help people, and could play a role in reducing the enormous gap between rich and poor. But now, watching it in practice, I think this is very unlikely, because I see that it foments class hatred.'[17] Many critics went further. The charge was led by Alfonso López Trujillo, Colombian ultramontanist, archbishop, and cardinal. He denounced liberation theology as an essentially political reading of the word of God which presents Christ as committed to the class struggle and interprets the whole of Christian faith in a political sense derived from Marxism. He argued that Christian people cannot be forced to work in a single socio-political movement; they have a right to legitimate choice and pluralism in temporal matters where faith does not require only one solution. The Christian logic of redemption is that Christ who liberated us from the slavery of sin expects us to strive to remove economic, social, and political forms of slavery, which are derived from sin.

These views are developed in the Declaration of Los Andes (1983) where López Trujillo, supported by twenty-three signatories of his persuasion, laymen and clergy, declared: 'An adequate solution to the present problems of Latin America will not be achieved by simplistic declarations based on Marxist ideology, but rather by vigorous action based on careful analysis of the multiple causes of the poverty of so many individuals and families.'

Not all of the criticism came from the Holy Office and its allies or from known conservatives, and not all of it was justified. It was noticed that spokesmen for the movement could be just as authoritarian and absolutist as its opponents, but some of those opponents were unscrupulous, and it was a contest with no holds barred. It was alleged that the liberationists were an elite of intellectuals, a professional academic group who did not reach the mass of the faithful. And when they were actually heard, to encourage the poor to insist on their rights meant abandoning the traditional function of religion as a refuge from oppression. Defending rights, if necessary by armed resistance, left the oppressed to face the force of the state or of landlords, where intellectuals could not help them. 'It was easy to leap from a religious base into a political disaster.'[18] But these are arguments about tactics and do not necessarily invalidate principles. Religion needs its intellectual leaders as well as its activists. As liberation theology receded in Catholic expectations, its ideas were taken up by Protestant theologians and it became a kind of ecumenical meeting ground, which did not necessarily endear it to its critics.

A more serious criticism is that to single out poverty as the unique justification of the Christian faith is to ignore other truths of revelation. The message of the Gospels and the contents of creeds and commandments do not exclude the imperative of attacking poverty and injustice, but they do not make this the prime proof of the Christian faith. The liberationists, moreover, lacked theological pragmatism. Their interpretation of Christianity seemed to address itself exclusively to landless peasants, ignoring the fact that Latin America was also an urban society, in some places a predominantly urban society.[19] It demanded that the Church place itself on the side of the oppressed classes and dominated peoples 'clearly and without qualification', otherwise its theology was of little value.[20] In themselves these were worthy sentiments and they made of liberation theology a genuine religious analysis, proclaiming Christian values distinct from those of secular humanist reformers. But it was not the whole of the Christian message, which needed a wider theological framework. Latin America had undergone some degree of development and was not all peasants and poverty. It was home to substantial middle-class communities. Some of these people had struggled to lift themselves from poverty and to create a better life for their families. Had Christian theology a message for them too? Even if their need was not urgent and they were not part of the preferential option for the poor they were a sign that poverty in itself could not be the sole proof of religious truth. Nevertheless, it is worth recalling that in an age when secularism was advancing at the expense of religion, it was the liberationists who rescued theology from oblivion and restored confidence to believers. And let us leave the concluding words to Gustavo Gutiérrez: 'The theology of liberation attempts to reflect on the experience and meaning of the faith based on the commitment to abolish injustice and to build a new society; this theology must be verified by the practice of that commitment, by active, effective participation in the struggle which the exploited social classes have undertaken against their oppressors.'[21]

Base Communities

To serve and to save the poor, the prime concern of liberation theology and the sign of a missionary Church, means proclaiming by word and action that Christ has set us free. This sign must take the form of being poor, missionary, and paschal. These were the convictions of Gustavo Gutiérrez, who wrote:

> The base-level ecclesial communities, which Paul VI greeted as 'a real hope for the church' and which Puebla described as 'an important ecclesial event that is peculiarly ours', are a manifestation of the presence of the church of the poor in Latin America. These communities are a major source of vitality within the larger Christian community and have brought the Gospel closer to the poor and the poor closer to the Gospel – and not only the poor but, through them, all who are touched by the church's actions, including those outside its boundaries.[22]

The Christian Base Communities (Comunidades eclesiales de base, CEBs), born around 1963–64, did not suddenly come to life as a modern miracle. There were a number of precursors. The *cofradías* (confraternities) were traditional groupings, especially popular among ethnic groups, devoted to the service of particular saints. Ernesto Cardenal's meetings with the peasants of Solentiname for discussion of the scriptures in relation to their daily lives was an example celebrated beyond Nicaragua. But perhaps the most immediate influence were the 'cultural circles' created by Paulo Freire, the Brazilian educationist, in which small groups would learn by interaction between teacher and students in a dialogue which aimed to create a new awareness, a 'conscientization', an independent political awakening.[23] The base communities were led by priests and nuns, sometimes by lay catechists supplying the shortage of priests. They promoted a new relation between priest, or catechist, and parishioners interacting in their search for a common faith. There were various models.[24] Some met on Sundays in churches to celebrate mass, others in private homes or parish halls to say prayers, sing hymns, and discuss their lives in the light of Scripture and revelation. They expressed a community spirit in that they brought people of the same faith and locality together. Their ecclesial nature was affirmed by their integration in the Church which was their common bond. And they were ordinary people mostly from the lower sectors of society, workers and peasants, the basic level in the Church. They were not a parallel or substitute Church and they did not normally rival the parish, but rather added a social dimension to parochial institutions with greater emphasis on a pastoral role.

The movement spread rapidly throughout Latin America but especially in Brazil and Central America. By 1978 there were about 50,000 base communities in Brazil, growing to about 70,000 in the next twenty years and outstripping the number of parishes, drawing in some 2 million people. In Argentina in 1997, 1,200 delegates representing 35 of the country's 70 dioceses gathered in Formosa to discuss 'basic ecclesial communities, hope of the poor in times of jubilee'. Soon the movement was holding international congresses at regular intervals, such as that in Paraguay in August 1997, where delegates gathered to share experiences and report on their struggle to eradicate poverty in their communities by means of health-care programmes, literacy campaigns, cooperatives, and pressures for water supplies, telephones, and electricity. In Brazil the base communities developed an ecumenical dimension. At a meeting in July 1997, as well as bishops and Catholics there were representatives from Protestant Churches, Pentecostals, Afro-Brazilian religions, and indigenous groups. Was this a compliment to a Catholic invention or a dilution of the original model? Bishop Jayme Chemello, vice-president of the Brazilian Bishops' Conference, insisted that the base communities were both ecumenical and fully Catholic, 'the most genuine face of the Latin American Church . . . It's not something modern: if we go to the Acts of the Apostles, we find that its roots are in the Bible.' But there were tensions and some bishops drew back, fearing that the openness of the communities to other Christians and to non-Christian religion marred their Catholic identity. Some traditional Catholics in Brazil expressed their opposition to these developments in Charismatic Renewal, a movement which became a bitter rival of the base communities.[25]

The communities were rightly regarded as part of the liberationist agenda and a sign of its relevance to the lives of the people. There were tensions between traditional parish structures and these dramatic innovations. Popular devotions to saints and shrines and fiestas were regarded by some liberationists as colonial remnants favouring an older religion of resignation and scorned as an obstacle to modern methods of evangelization aimed at liberating the people from the past, if necessary by revolutionary action. Although the base communities were not designed as political agencies, the act of raising consciousness often developed into discussion of current issues which in some cases led to political activism. In Brazil there were accusations that they deviated from purely religious organizations to become political cells and propaganda fronts at a time when there were no other outlets under military dictatorship. Grass-roots democracy of this kind was not a divergence from liberation theology. Some among the hierarchy were quick to accuse them of creating a parallel church, and López Trujillo suspected they were vehicles of political extremism. But Archbishop Romero welcomed them as new outlets for social action and consciousness-raising. And foreign bishops lined up to applaud them.

The base communities, encouraged by the liberationists and abhorred by the old guard, were an aid, not a threat, to priests. For some they offered hope for a revival of clerical virtues. In Cuernavaca Bishop Méndez Arceo saw liberationist theology as a means of encouraging a new mentality among priests after the grief of the Mexican Revolution. The spirit of renewal was also seen by Gustavo Gutiérrez, who welcomed the desire of priests and religious to participate more actively in the pastoral decisions of the Church, but a Church freed from its past ties to an unjust social order: 'The numbers are growing of those who have found a renewed meaning for their priesthood or religious life in the commitment to the oppressed and their struggle for liberation.'[26] Some priests went further and were radicalized by the sight of the oppressed and the need for their liberation, and they became revolutionaries. But if the base communities were not enough for some priests, they were welcomed by others who saw them as part of the Catholic tradition and parish structure, and who preferred the Gospels and traditional doctrine to class analysis and quotations from Marx. Base communities, it was agreed, treated the faithful less as sinners than as sufferers; and among many in the Church there was less talk of reconciliation and more of liberation.

A further dimension of the base communities could be seen in the role of women, especially ordinary and poor women, who had been marginalized in the traditional parish. Now they became prominent participants and in some cases majority members of base communities, actively engaged in the movement or, as Boff proclaimed, liberated. 'More and more in the basic communities women are assuming functions of leadership.' Inevitably he argued for more and made a case for women priests. 'If a woman can be a principle of unity, as she is in so many communities,

then theologically there is nothing to stand in the way of her empower-
ment, through ordination, to consecrate, to tender Christ sacramentally
present at the heart of the community's worship.'[27] This was unduly opti-
mistic. In Latin America there was a limit to women's rights and to their
freedom to express their views on women's issues. 'Public discussion of
reproductive matters is stifled, not because Latin American women are so
different from European and North American women, but because of male
power in society, buttressed by periodic ecclesiastical intervention.'[28]

What was the judgement of the Church on base communities? It was
given in an *Instruction* on the validity of the theology of liberation issued
by Cardinal Ratzinger, prefect of the Congregation for the Doctrine of the
Faith:

> The new basic communities or other groups of Christians which have arisen to
> be witnesses to the evangelical love are a source of great hope for the Church.
> If they really live in unity with the local Church and the universal Church they
> will be a real expression of communion and a means for constructing a still
> deeper communion. Their fidelity to their mission will depend on how careful
> they are to educate their members in the fullness of the Christian faith through
> listening to the Word of God, fidelity to the teaching of the Magisterium, to the
> hierarchical order of the Church and to the sacramental Life. If this condition
> is fulfilled, their experience, rooted in a commitment to the complete libera-
> tion of man, becomes a treasure of the whole Church.[29]

A wary welcome, but agreeable to the liberation theologians.

Council and Conference

The innovations in theology in Latin America developed alongside ecclesiastical awakening and the two interacted with each other, the theologians
appealing to the bishops, and the bishops quoting the theologians. The way
was prepared by the Second Vatican Council (1962–65), called by John
XXIII, benign pope and prophet of change, whose two encyclicals *Mater et
Magistra* (1961) and *Pacem in Terris* (1963) were imbued with the kind of
thinking that would mark Latin American theology for decades to come.
He wanted to 'open the windows' of the Church to the modern world and
bring in a fresh wind. In his opening speech to the Council he said 'It is not
that the Gospel has changed: it is that we have begun to understand it
better . . . the moment has come to discern the signs of the times, to seize
the opportunity and to expand the view.'[30]

The Latin American Church was ready to seize the opportunity: 573 out
of the 2,600 bishops eligible to attend were from Latin America. Vatican I

(1869–70) was principally remembered for its declaration of papal infallibility. *Gaudium et Spes*, a key document of Vatican II on the Church in the
modern world, rejected the old Catholic ethos enshrined in Pius IX's
Syllabus of Errors, which condemned a wide range of 'errors' of the modern
world. Instead it looked ahead with joy and hope. 'Ours is a new age of
history, with swift and critical upheavals spreading gradually to all corners
of the earth.' This needed 'a generation of new men, the moulders of a new
humanity'. Vatican II showed the way, in concern for political and social
issues, the role of pastoral agents, laypeople, the liturgy, in a mindset which
was called *aggiornamento* (bringing up to date). Even Gustavo Gutiérrez,
who had his reservations, admitted that 'Vatican Council II has strongly
reaffirmed the idea of a Church of service and not of power', and said that
'the council led us onto a new path on which there is no turning back:
openness to the world'.[31] Latin Americans were listening.

Vatican II affirmed its commitment to change by acknowledging the
truth in other world religions, especially Judaism. The journey to this
conclusion had been long and difficult, and even now it was not an
easy ride. The Declaration on Religious Liberty (*Dignitatis Humanae*),
one of the most contentious issues of the Council, survived strong opposition from those bishops who clung to the traditional belief that error
has no rights and the state has a duty to defend the Catholic faith.[32]
The American Jesuit John Courtney Murray had long presented compelling arguments for religious toleration and his efforts now bore fruit.
Dignitatis Humanae declared that the act of faith was a free act, based
on freedom of conscience, which should be subject to no compulsion,
but equally should enjoy no privileged legal status. To understand opinions
with which they did not agree meant that Catholics subscribed not to
relativism but to a freedom that respected diversity of belief. 'While
the religious freedom which men demand ... has to do with freedom
from coercion in civil society, it leaves intact the traditional Catholic
teaching on the moral duty of individuals and societies towards the true
religion and the one Church of Christ.' Primacy of conscience was asserted
by no less a theologian than Joseph Ratzinger, a *peritus* (expert adviser) at
the Council.

> Over the Pope as expression of the binding claim of ecclesiastical authority,
> there stands one's own conscience, which must be obeyed before all else, even
> if necessary against the requirement of ecclesiastical authority. This emphasis
> on the individual, whose conscience confronts him with a supreme and ulti-
> mate tribunal and which in the last resort is beyond the claim of external social
> groups, even the official Church, also establishes a principle in opposition to
> increasing totalitarianism.[33]

The final vote on Religious Liberty showed 2,308 in favour, 70 against. It was supported by American and English bishops, but not by the Spanish group. Latin American bishops have been reported as voting against Religious Liberty, but this is not entirely true. Cardinal Agnelo Rossi of São Paulo voted in favour of the declaration in the name of eighty-two Brazilian bishops.[34] Other Latin American bishops, it is true, had reservations about the declaration and found it difficult to endorse in the years ahead. Their problem can be understood by recalling the dramatic expansion of Protestantism in Latin America and its assertion of a political presence. Even in supposed Catholic Colombia in 1989 Protestants formed a political party with two representatives in the National Assembly. In Guatemala there were two Protestant presidents in less than ten years. In Mexico Protestants were making great strides in Chiapas, Tabasco, and Campeche, and there were many in the bureaucracy. In Peru Pastor Carlos García was elected second vice-president and had the support of fourteen deputies and four senators.[35] The reservations of some of the Latin American bishops, short-sighted though they were, had their context.

Collegiality, the doctrine that the Church is governed by the 'college' of bishops with and under the pope, was a critical issue for the Latin American Church, bringing to the surface in Vatican II an enduring conflict between two positions: the primacy of the pope and the authority of the bishops as heads of local churches. The Council witnessed an attempt by reformers to moderate the centralizing tendencies of the Roman Congregations and to give the local Church a more authoritative voice.[36] It was maintained that bishops were not to be regarded as vicars of the Roman pontiff, for they exercise the power they possess in their own right. But conciliar documents were evasive on collegiality and included too many qualifications to withstand future challenges. Traditionalists held to the position that collegiality was incompatible with papal primacy and this was never resolved. So collegiality 'ended up an abstract tendency without point of entry into the social reality of the Church. It ended up an ideal, no match for the deeply entrenched system.'[37] And in years to come it left an unspoken question in the minds of Latin American bishops: what was the point of CELAM if its conclusions were downgraded in Rome?

Vatican II was a response but not a solution to the Church's problems. Its record suffered from hyperbole and in many ways it was a missed opportunity. Every age of the Church, in greater or lesser degree, sees a process of change and development. In the eyes of many of the faithful the critical mistake of the Church in the great reforming period of the 1960s was to change what did not need changing (the liturgy) and fail to change what did need changing (moral teaching). The majority of Catholics in Latin America no less than in other parts of the Church were not clamouring for a revision of the mass, but many, especially among young people, were hoping for new guidance on marital issues. Vatican II also fell into this trap set by the power groups. Pope Paul VI kept a number of subjects, including birth control, strictly off the agenda. The events that led to *Humanae Vitae* were not inevitable or cast in stone; they involved a dispute about papal power and the ability of ordinary Catholics to make their voices heard against the views of powerful prelates. Catholic women in Latin America were not given a hearing.

Yet Vatican II gave out positive signals. It took modern society in its stride and refused to judge it negatively. For Latin America it was an encouragement. It targeted the social and political responsibility of the Church, especially in the final document, *Gaudium et Spes* (The Pastoral Constitution of the Church in the Modern World), which declared that the Church had special responsibility to work for the poor and weak, and that the right to subsistence took precedence over the right of the wealthy to accumulate private property. And it spoke out for the right to political equality. These advances were not enough for the liberationists, who regarded *Gaudium et Spes* as a flawed document, too traditional in its approach to social problems. This was the view of Gustavo Gutiérrez, who wrote: '*Gaudium et Spes* in general offers a rather irenic description of the human situation; it touches up the uneven spots, smooths the rough edges, avoids the more conflictional aspects, and stays away from the sharper confrontations among social classes and countries.'[38] But Vatican II urged national bodies to follow up its message in their own particular situations. So there were further hopes for the Latin American Church and further opportunities for differences of opinion.

In response to the initiative of Vatican II the Latin American Episcopal Conference met in Medellín, Colombia, in 1968. It included priests, nuns, and pastoral agents as well as bishops, and among the latter were progressives such as Hélder Câmara, Samuel Ruiz, and Sergio Méndez Arceo. Gustavo Gutiérrez attended as a *peritus* and had some influence on the texts adopted. It was open to the views of liberation theology as well as to Vatican II, and its documents contained criticism of Latin America's ruling classes, foreign capitalism, poverty and social injustice. It made clear its commitment to purify the Church in the spirit of the Gospel and to create a new social order based on justice and human rights: 'It is necessary to end the separation between faith and life . . . This commitment requires us to live a true scriptural poverty expressed in authentic manifestations that may be clear signs for our peoples.' The bishops also declared, 'The firm denunciation of those realities in Latin America which constitute an affront to the spirit of the Gospel also forms part of our mission.' And they gave a kind of blessing to liberation theology, calling for an 'authentic liberation', neither capitalism nor Marxism: 'It is the same God who, in the fullness of time, sends his Son in the flesh so that he might come to liberate all persons from the slavery to which sin has subjected them: hunger, misery, oppression and ignorance – in a word, that injustice and hatred which have their origin in human selfishness.'[39]

'At Medellín,' wrote Gustavo Gutiérrez, 'it was made clear that poverty expresses solidarity with the oppressed and a protest against oppression.' 'A choice was made at Medellín that has been a decisive one for the church during the years since then, the preferential option for the poor.'[40] This was the first airing of the new concept that would henceforth dominate the reformist agenda. And there was more. Ecclesial base communities with the aim of *concientización* in support of 'the downtrodden of every social class so that they might come to know their rights and how to make use of them' were endorsed by the bishops. Beyond simple preaching the Church was now encouraging the organization of the poor and reordering of the economy. So the conference could not ignore the obstacles presented by military dictatorships and their allies among foreign interests. The document on 'Peace' begins by saying, 'If development is the new name for peace, Latin American underdevelopment, with its own characteristics in its different countries, is an unjust situation promoting tensions that conspire against peace.' In its drafting Gustavo Gutiérrez was reportedly influential. These realities 'constitute a sinful situation'. 'The principal guilt for the economic dependence of our countries rests with powers inspired by uncontrolled desire for gain.' In the controversial discussion on violence the conference asserted that injustice in Latin America amounted to 'institutionalized violence' which reduced people to dependence, deprived of basic necessities, in violation of fundamental rights. This required profound transformation. Yet the bishops did not recommend the way of violence. While accepting that 'the temptation to violence is surfacing in Latin America', they concluded that violence was usually less effective and more dangerous than 'the dynamism of the awakened community at the service of justice and peace'.

Medellín stirred a new wave of pastoral, social, and theological developments in the Latin American Church. Not everyone was happy, and its conclusions had been reached against the restraint and resistance of many bishops. It is true that the bishops, or some of them, under the influence perhaps of Gustavo Gutiérrez, succumbed to the snare of dependency theory, speaking of 'the consequences for our countries of their dependence on a centre of economic power around which they gravitate. The result of this is that our nations frequently are not in control of their own goods or economic decisions.'[41] But they were not unanimous in their response to the Medellín message. 'In the post-Medellín period (as in the postconciliar one) some groups would like the surprising consequences of positions they took up to be forgotten or mitigated. They cannot contradict the letter of what was said, so they try to declare it inapplicable.'[42]

Alfonso López Trujillo was not content to let matters rest. As archbishop of Medellín, secretary (1972) and then president of CELAM (1979–83), and a Latin American favourite of Pope John Paul II, he was in a position to influence the agenda and membership of the episcopal conferences, and to exercise leadership of conservative bishops and clergy. In his book *De Medellín a Puebla* he distinguished between an authentic theology of liberation which saw the struggle for justice as a route from sin to conversion, and the political interpretation favoured by the liberationists which led to confrontation and conflict.[43] The two sides were already manoeuvring for position and membership and squaring up for a fight in anticipation of the next meeting of CELAM. This took place at Puebla, Mexico, in January–February 1979. The conservatives criticized the concept of a popular Church inspired by socialism, and the liberationists challenged them on issues of justice and poverty. Pope John Paul II, who received a warm welcome from the Mexican faithful before proceeding to the conference, took a moderately critical position towards liberation theology, but did not condemn it. He argued for a Christian, not a socio-economic, concept of liberation. His opening speech criticized the politicization of the Christian message and the idea of Christ as a revolutionary, insisted on respect for the magisterium, and rejected the concept of a popular Church in opposition to the institutional Church. He also expressed concern for the condition of the poor and the unequal distribution of wealth in Latin America. These sentiments were reflected in the final document of the conference, which was critical of both Marxism and liberal capitalism and condemned the national security state which underpinned social and economic inequality. The base communities were endorsed as the Christian response to Latin America's social problems, 'an important ecclesial event that is peculiarly ours', but the document warned of the danger from political interests that attempted to take them from their Church structure. And Puebla, advancing further than Medellín, was conscious of the new presence of women, whom it described as 'doubly oppressed and marginalized' among the poor of Latin America.[44]

Puebla was at once a reward and a restraint for the liberationist campaign. Both sides claimed victory and each had its successes. But the liberationists won a striking endorsement of their cause and an enduring commitment from the Church of the poor. In the final documents the bishops see Latin America as a continent of predominantly poor people, marginalized workers and peasants, and go on to say: 'Despite the distortions and interpretations of some, who vitiate the spirit of Medellín, and despite the disregard and even hostility of others, we affirm the need for conversion on the part of the whole church to a preferential option for the poor, an option aimed at their integral liberation.'[45] As glossed by Gustavo Gutiérrez,

> Puebla asserted that simply because of God's love for them as manifested in Christ 'the poor merit preferential attention, whatever may be the moral or personal situation in which they find themselves'. In other words, the poor deserve preference not because they are morally or religiously better than others, but because God is God, in whose eyes 'the last are first.'[46]

So the concept of liberation was not lost but came out strong and clear from Puebla. 'Continuing in the line of Medellín and Puebla, Pope John Paul II addressed these strong and sensitive words to the bishops of Brazil: "The poor of this country, whose pastors you are, and the poor of this continent are the first to feel the urgent need of this *gospel of* radical and integral *liberation*. To conceal it would be to cheat them and let them down".'[47] Medellín and Puebla did not bring about lasting change in the Latin American Church. The progressive wing moved forward but the conservatives did not retreat and so the pace of change differed from country to country, diocese to diocese, according to the relative strength of each.

The Voice of Rome

In the age of liberation theology the Church could be seen in action at the three levels where it had acted since it first arrived in Latin America. First, the level of doctrine and its development. This was the area occupied by the theologians of liberation and their critics. Second, the level of the episcopacy, occupied by the bishops and their associates in the Latin American Episcopal Conference. The last level was that of the papacy, traditionally resident in Rome but now frequently appearing in Latin America itself.

Intimations of modernity could be seen in the pontificate of Pius XII and his successors John XXIII and Paul VI. In 1955 Pius XII, convinced of the possibilities and advantages of collaboration between the hierarchies of Latin America, called upon the Church there to organize local episcopal conferences, and in the same year created CELAM, thus encouraging the movement towards regional ties and identities among bishops and religious.[48] In 1958 Pius XII created the Pontifical Commission for Latin America to link the Holy See, CELAM, and local episcopal conferences. Paul VI carried forward these initiatives. Implementing Vatican II, CELAM met in Medellín in 1968. Paul VI not only approved of the meeting but also attended, having first presided over the Eucharistic Congress which preceded it. On the eve of the Medellín Conference he sought to draw the Catholic position away from extremism. Referring to the advocacy and use of violence in the cause of development and social change, he said, 'While recognizing that initiatives of this kind frequently arise from noble impulses of justice and solidarity, we have to say and reaffirm that violence is neither evangelical nor Christian.'[49]

John Paul II visited Latin America seventeen times, and took a close interest in developments there and their impact on the Church, to the satisfaction and occasional dismay of both sides of the liberal–conservative divide. Opening Puebla he said, 'The Conference should take as its point of departure the conclusions of Medellín, in all their positive aspects, without however ignoring the misinterpretations which are sometimes made and which require calm judgement and critical clarification.'[50] He always deplored the concept of an *iglesia popular* contrasted with the traditional Church, an idea which surfaced from time to time in Latin America; and he made it clear that a popular Church was not the same as popular religiosity. Puebla had favoured *la religiosidad popular* as a treasure of Latin American Catholicism and an instrument of evangelization, though admitting its negative aspects of distortion and ignorance. John Paul II frequently referred to popular religiosity, aware perhaps that the liberation theologians had mixed feelings on the subject. He regarded it as one of the ways in which religion had been preserved in Latin America. During a visit to Brazil he said, 'If it were not for this distinctive popular piety, which is eminently Eucharistic and Marian in character, the shortage of priests and the great distances involved would have been sufficient to cause the disappearance of the faith planted in the first evangelization.'[51] His regard for popular piety became even clearer. 'In America popular piety is an expression of the enculturation of the Catholic faith, and many of its manifestations have assumed autochthonous religious forms. So it is opportune to draw attention to the possibilities of drawing from them, with discerning prudence, valid indications for a greater enculturation of the Gospel.'[52]

These frank approaches to Latin American religion were accompanied by more critical policies. John Paul II, unlike his immediate predecessors, was a conservative influence on the Church in Latin America. By comparison, Pius XII, John XXIII, and Paul VI were modernizing popes. This was seen in their choice of bishops. They nominated candidates who sought a positive relation with the modern world. The new wave of bishops who faced up to the dictators in Brazil were named by these popes. From 1978, however, John Paul II took a more conservative route. Papal nuncios also tended to be conservative, and the Latin Americans appointed to Rome, with the possible exception of the Argentine Eduardo Pironio, were not known for their progressive ideas. Alfonso López Trujillo, archbishop of Medellín and president of CELAM, who led the drive against liberation theology, was later appointed president of the Pontifical Commission on the Family, where his pronouncements on moral issues, and especially contraception, did not win the hearts of progressive Catholics. Dario Castrillón Hoyos, secretary of CELAM and another Colombian conservative, also made a career in the Curia and became known for his support of the Tridentine Rite, criticism of liberation theology, and controversial views on the treatment of paedophile priests.[53]

John Paul II's programme was one of 'restoration' of discipline and unity, doctrinal and moral, allegedly lost in the aftermath of Vatican II. His neo-Romanization policy of appointing new bishops who were safe, orthodox, and in some cases extremely conservative to fill vacant dioceses was a key feature of his strategy. Although the appointments were made in secret, the policy was no secret to Latin American churchmen. It caused tension between the Holy See and the Brazilian hierarchy, whose candidates were often deemed 'not suitable to requirements', while non-Brazilians were appointed to dioceses where they had little knowledge of local usages and customs. Cardinal Paulo Evaristo Arns, archbishop of São Paulo, made his displeasure clear as he approached retirement in 1996. If his successor was a traditionalist bishop, he said in an interview, 'I shall only stay on here as long as is needed to settle him in and then move away. I would suffer greatly to see the destruction of everything I had worked for.' The Curia was governing the Church now, he said, but 'with Paul VI it was different. He actually governed through the Curia. He had his ear to the ground, was constantly briefed by his staff and was truly in control of events ... The present Pope is much more interested in travelling, preaching, being a missionary, than watching over the Curia. He leaves everything to them, with the result that they now enjoy an incomparably greater autonomy than they had under Paul VI.'[54]

Pope or Curia, it made little difference. Progressive bishops such as Helder Cámara and Sergio Méndez were succeeded by conservatives. This made it less likely that the College of Bishops as a whole or in a particular region such as Latin America would have the will to exercise their rightful leadership and decide appropriate responses to the social, spiritual, moral, and pastoral needs of their particular people, much less to disagree with decisions taken in Rome or to seek alternatives likely to threaten papal insistence on strengthening authority and unity.[55] One of the special Vatican II principles, collegiality in decision-making, was also reined in by Rome, and it was the curial authorities with the pope who came to make decisions and not the Episcopal College. Thus papal authority was further strengthened and total acceptance of papal policies was required from bishops, priests, and people, policies which in many cases represented a central authority exercised by pope and Curia rather than a shared authority with local bishops.

Vatican II was celebrated not only for its reforming agenda but also for the near unanimity of its decisions, as bishops searched for consensus. But consensus ended in the years that followed, with a series of papal judgements, among them *Humanae Vitae* (1968) prohibiting artificial birth control, and *Ordinatio Sacerdotalis* (1994) ruling out ordination of women. The Vatican then ruled that only priests who were prepared explicitly to endorse these judgements could be appointed bishops. In due course this would leave an episcopacy consisting only of those who conformed to papal rulings. This was the revised magisterium, which amounted to a virtual lock on the Church's institutions.[56]

With the accession of John Paul II, a pope from the communist world, liberation theology, the product of a different and perhaps less intelligible world, became an obvious candidate for scrutiny. Gustavo Gutiérrez, who always sought to avoid confrontation with Church authorities and was ready to recognize 'ambiguities', aroused different opinions in the Church. In Peru, his homeland, Catholic opinion was divided, with conservative bishops wanting his writings condemned as heretical. Pope Paul VI was not persuaded, nor did John Paul II or Cardinal Ratzinger rush to judge liberation theology. The Congregation for the Doctrine of the Faith, however, accused liberationists of 'immanentism' (believing in the possibility of a perfect world here and now) and being insufficiently critical of Marxist analysis. From 1977 the Vatican wanted the agenda for the forthcoming CELAM conference at Puebla to tone down the Medellín declarations; it did not get all its own way and the opening speech of John Paul II was marked by caution rather than confrontation.

It was 1984 before Cardinal Ratzinger, prefect of the Congregation for the Doctrine of the Faith, issued *Libertatis Nuntius*, an *Instruction 'On Certain Aspects of "Liberation Theology" '*, which amounted to a critique of errors and excesses, including its emphasis on social rather than individual sin, and its deference to Marxism.[57] It warned priests and people of 'the deviation and risks of deviation, damaging to the faith and to Christian living, that are brought about by certain forms of liberation theology which use, in an insufficiently critical manner, concepts borrowed from various currents of Marxist thought'. Marxist ideas such as the class struggle, atheism, denial of human rights, and a partisan conception of the truth were not compatible with the Christian concept of society. Marxist analysis, a favourite device of the liberationists, could not be separated from Marxist ideology; Marxism itself did not separate them. The *Instruction* was a serious document, replete with scholarship and learned references, and it was not simply a denunciation. It also attacked the inequalities among people and between nations and the domination of Latin America by oligarchs, military, and foreign interests. But it insisted that the answer did not lie with Marxism or the class struggle.

In 1986 the Congregation for the Doctrine of the Faith issued a second *Instruction*, 'On Christian Freedom and Liberation', that praised the positive features of 'properly conceived' liberation theologies but warned against 'extreme' and 'insufficiently careful' versions.[58] It maintained the traditional view that sin was the cause of oppression but did not exclude structural explanations of poverty and exploitation, advising that one must work simultaneously to convert sinners and to change structures. While it was right to press for reform on behalf of justice and to suppress privilege, this should not be done by the destructive power of revolution. Armed struggle to end tyranny and preserve the rights of the individual and the common good was possible, but only as a last resort. These were hard dilemmas for religion. Violence or peaceful protest? Revolution or reform? The Church was always wary of the risk. Events in Mexico provided an example and a warning and tested the tactics of Rome and its critics in these counter-liberation years.

Bishop Samuel Ruiz of San Cristóbal de las Casas aroused the hostility of conservatives in Mexico and their allies in Rome by his innovative evangelization methods in appointing indigenous deacons and catechists in Chiapas who had been chosen by their own communities. Ruiz and his deacons advocated rights and justice as well as religious renewal, and they became targets for vituperation from local landowners and traditional Catholics. From 1994 some of his catechists and deacons became supporters of the Zapatista Army of National Liberation, the EZLN, and its mysterious leader Subcomandante Marcos. The clerical critics of Bishop Ruiz in Mexico and Rome voiced distinctly conservative values, out of tune with the progressive movement in the Latin American Church, and they had little scruple in besmirching Ruiz with subversion by association. Rome and its agents, far from supporting the bishop's efforts to pacify Chiapas, became part of his problems. Bishop Ruiz eventually resigned from the commission appointed to bring peace to Chiapas, his hopes of a positive role for the Church frustrated. In due course Rome halted the bishop's policy of creating an Indian diaconate and in 2006 suspended the whole training programme for deacons.[59]

Meanwhile what had become of the option for the poor? Ratzinger's *Instructions* faced up to the question.[60] 'Those who are oppressed by poverty are the object of a love of preference on the part of the Church, which since her origin and in spite of the failings of many of her members has not ceased to work for their relief, defence, and liberation.' How was this to be done? Not only through works of charity, which are indispensable, but also by seeking to promote 'structural changes in society'. 'The special option for the poor, far from being a sign of particularism or a sectarianism, manifests the universality of the Church's being and vision.' The document makes it clear that the option for the poor cannot be appropriated by Marxist arguments. The option excludes no one. 'This is the reason why the Church cannot express this option by means of reductive sociological and ideological categories which would make this preference a partisan choice and a source of conflict.'

The shadow of Rome hovered long over liberation theology. In 2009, twenty-five years after *Libertatis Nuntius*, Pope Benedict XVI, in a voice which seemed to have hardened since his election to the papacy, charged that Marxist traces in the movement continued to harm the Church in Brazil. In an address in Rome to bishops from southern Brazil he said, 'Its consequences, more or less visible, in the form of rebellion, division, dissent, offence [and] anarchy, are still being felt'. Liberation theology was 'creating great suffering and a serious loss of vital force in [their diocesan] communities'. He recalled the message of his 1984 document: 'It underlined the danger inherent in an acritical acceptance by some theologians of theses and methodologies coming from Marxism. I implore all those who in some way feel attracted, involved or intimately touched by certain deceptive principles of liberation theology to look again at the instruction and accept the benign light it offers with outstretched hands.' He was concerned that Brazil's Catholic universities, which were not laws unto themselves but expressions of the faith of the Church, were teaching 'deceptive principles' of liberation theology.[61] The message, and its language, raise questions about the information the papacy received from Brazil, where the Church hierarchy remained wrapped in the blanket of orthodoxy imposed by Pope Benedict's predecessor but was not insensitive to signs of the times.

Papal pessimism over Latin America contrasted harshly with the hopes raised in the decade of Medellín and Puebla, the springtime of the modern Latin American Church. Since then differences between traditionalists and progressives lived on, with influence tilting first to one side then to the other, until finally an equilibrium prevailed, each side believing more or less the same creeds and commandments, though differing in their interpretation. Liberationist theologians used to speak of the traditional Church as a Church in the dark ages, and traditionalists referred to progressives as beyond the limit. Yet the faith survived in a peaceful coexistence. Neither side pushed the limits too far and polarization was never absolute. Progressives did not usually accept the whole liberal package – married

clergy, women priests, contraception, communion for divorcees, homosexuality, collegiality – but preferred to pick and choose; and traditionalists, or most of them, wanted to restore a pre-Vatican II religion rather than
re-enact the Council of Trent.

In studying the long duration can a historian of Latin America find a
theme to give coherence to the whole? The values of justice and peace run
through the history of religion like a thread from the conquest to modern
times, revealing the mind of the Church and sometimes its limits. The
campaign of Las Casas for peaceful evangelization and justice for the
Indians is an early trace. In the seventeenth century professional persecu-
tors of heresy disturbed the peace between Indians and evangelists, but
these were a breed apart, abhorred by many in the Church and eventually
bypassed. In the eighteenth century the Jesuit enclave of peace and protection for the Guaranís was dismantled and the Jesuits themselves sacrificed
for reasons of state with the acquiescence of a dormant Church in a development which stretched the thread of continuity to breaking point. In the
twentieth century a wider concern for justice and peace was extended to
the poor and dispossessed across the whole of society. Defence of the
victims of injustice became a touchstone of faith and the preferential
option for the poor a new evangelism. At this stage the values of justice and
peace merged with those of progress and liberty to become a kind of
Catholic zeitgeist. During five centuries the Church had responded to
the world in which it lived. As society changed, so particular expressions of
religion changed, in liturgy, language, and laws. The Church's capacity
to respond to society's problems and to absorb its own inner conflicts
survived the stress of time, more successfully in some ages than in others.

The age of Christendom passed and Latin America became part of a
secular world where religionists had to keep their nerve and their faith.
The liberationists arrived at the ebb tide of religion, a time of agnosticism
and denial. Yet they found deeper waters beyond and from these they
replenished the deposit of faith and restored it to modern life. While tradition confronts modernity, authority and liberty in the Church have
remained indivisible, each a restraint on excess in the other.

Notes

1 Religion and Empire

1. Quoted by Miguel Angel Ladero Quesada, *La España de los Reyes Católicos* (Madrid, 1999), 245.
2. *The Life of Saint Teresa of Avila by Herself*, trans. J.M. Cohen (London, 1957), 41.
3. For an answer to this question see James Casey, *Early Modern Spain: A Social History* (London, 1999), 222–53.
* As used in this book 'religiosity' means a sense rather than an excess of religion.
4. Ricardo García Cárcel, *Orígenes de la Inquisición española: El tribunal de Valencia, 1478–1530* (Barcelona, 1976), 37–46; Elie Kedourie, ed., *Spain and the Jews: The Sephardic Experience 1492 and After* (London, 1992), 74–91, 140–61.
5. Bartolomé de Las Casas, *Apologética historia sumaria* (Seville, 1990), 153, 154.
6. Diego Durán, *Book of the Gods and Rites and the Ancient Calendar*, trans. and ed. Fernando Horcasitas and Doris Heyden (Norman, OK, 1971), 59, 184–85.
7. Chilam Balam, *The Ancient Future of the Itza: The Book of Chilam Balam of Tizimin*, trans. and annotated by Munro S. Edmunson (Austin, TX, 1982), [1175–82], p. 55.
8. *Popol Vuh: The Mayan Book of the Dawn of Life*, trans. Dennis Tedlick (New York, 1996).
9. Durán, *Book of the Gods*, 242–44.
10. Bernardino de Sahagún, *Florentine Codex: General History of the Things of New Spain*, trans. Arthur J.O. Anderson and Charles E. Dibble, 13 parts, 2nd edn (Santa Fe, NM, 1970–82), book 12, part 13, p. 55.
11. Durán, *Book of the Gods*, 396.
12. Ibid., 101–2, 267.
13. Ibid., 94–95.
14. Ibid., 195–96, 287–88, 289.
15. Garcilaso de la Vega, El Inca, *Comentarios reales de los Incas (Obras completas*, ed. Carmelo Sáenz de Santa María, BEA, 4 vols, Madrid, 1960), book II, chap. 2.
16. Lino Gómez Canedo, *Evangelización y conquista: experiencia franciscana en Hispanoamérica* (Mexico City, 1977), 6–17.
17. José de Oviedo y Baños, *Historia de la conquista y población de Venezuela*, trans. and ed. Jeanette Johnson Varner as *The Conquest and Settlement of Venezuela* (Berkeley, CA, 1987), 226.
18. Bernal Díaz del Castillo, *Historia verdadera de la conquista de la Nueva España* (Mexico, 1964), 416.
19. Toribio de Benavente [Motolinia], *Historia de los indios de la Nueva España* (Madrid, 1985), 80–81.

20. J. Jorge Klor de Alva, 'Spiritual Conflict and Accommodation in New Spain. Toward a Typology of Aztec Responses to Christianity', in George A. Collier, Renato I. Rosaldo and John D. Wirth, eds, *The Inca and Aztec States 1400–1800* (New York, 1982), 345–66.
21. Benavente, *Historia de los indios*, 104, 117–19, 120.
22. Louise M. Burkhart, *The Slippery Earth: Nahua–Christian Moral Dialogue in Sixteenth-century Mexico* (Tucson, AZ, 1989), 128.
23. Quoted ibid., 136; see also 131–32, 142–45, 150–59.
24. Durán, *Book of the Gods*, 102, 170–71.
25. Nancy M. Farriss, *Maya Society under Colonial Rule: The Collective Enterprise of Survival* (Princeton, NJ, 1984), 286–352.
26. Chilam Balam, *Ancient Future of the Itza*, [1333–1340, 3928–3934], pp. 60, 142.
27. See Victoria Reifler Bricker, *The Indian Christ, the Indian King. The Historical Substrata of Maya Myth and Ritual* (Austin, TX, 1981), 22–24.
28. Cristóbal de Mena, *La conquista del Perú*, in *Biblioteca peruana*, Primera Serie, Tomo I, pp. 133–69 (Lima, 1968), 134–35; John Hemming, *The Conquest of the Incas* (London, 1983), 40–41, 555.
29. Pedro de Cieza de León, *Crónica del Perú. Tercera parte*, ed. Francesca Cantú (2nd edn, Lima, 1989), 134.
30. Ibid., 168.
31. Ibid., 284.
32. Martel de Santoyo, 1542, in Emilio Lissón Chavez, *La Iglesia de España en el Perú* (Seville, 1943), doc. 86, pp. 99–100.
33. Manuel Marzal, *La transformación religiosa peruana* (Lima, 1983), 212–13.
34. Sabine MacCormack, *Religion in the Andes: Vision and Imagination in Early Colonial Peru* (Princeton, NJ, 1991), 367–68.
35. Ibid., 372–74.
36. Ibid., 141–59.
37. Rafael Varón, 'El Taki Oncoy: las raíces andinas', in Luis Millones, ed., *El retorno de las Huacas: Estudios y documentos sobre el Taki Onqoy, Siglo XVI* (Lima, 1990), 331–405, particularly 403.
38. Cristóbal de Albornoz, *Información*, Luis Millones, *El retorno de las Huacas*, 205.
39. Durán, *Book of the Gods*, 277–79.
40. Farriss, *Maya Society under Colonial Rule*, 389–95; and the same author's 'Sacred Power in Colonial Mexico: The Case of Sixteenth-Century Yucatán', in Warwick Bray, ed., *The Meeting of Two Worlds: Europe and the Americas 1492–1650* (Oxford, 1993), 145–62.
41. Durán, *Book of the Gods*, 228, 409.
42. J. Jorge Klor de Alva, 'Colonizing Souls: The Failure of the Indian Inquisition and the Rise of Penitential Discipline', in M.E. Perry and A.J. Cruz, eds, *Cultural Encounters: The Impact of the Inquisition in Spain and the New World* (Berkeley, CA, 1991), 3–22.
43. Durán, *Book of the Gods*, 150–53.
44. William B. Taylor, *Magistrates of the Sacred: Priests and Parishioners in Eighteenth-Century Mexico* (Stanford, CA, 1996), 66–7; Serge Guzinski, *The Conquest of Mexico: The Incorporation of Indian Societies into the Western World, 16th–18th Centuries* (Oxford, 1993), 151.
45. Adriaan C. van Oss, *Catholic Colonialism: A Parish History of Guatemala 1524–1821* (Cambridge, 1986), 22.
46. Arthur G. Miller and Nancy M. Farriss, 'Religious Syncretism in Colonial Yucatán: The Archaeological and Ethnohistorical Evidence from Tancah, Quintana Roo', in Norman Hammond and Gordon R. Willey, eds, *Maya Archaeology and Ethnohistory* (Austin, TX, 1979), 223–40.
47. Pierre Duviols, *La destrucción de las regiones andinas (conquista y colonia)* (Mexico, 1977), 280–93.
48. Benavente, *Historia de los indios*, 116–17.

49. Klor de Alva, 'Colonizing Souls', 8.
50. Richard E. Greenleaf, *The Mexican Inquisition of the Sixteenth Century* (Albuquerque, NM, 1969), 74.
51. Henry Roup Wagner [and] Helen Rand Parish, *The Life and Writings of Bartolomé de Las Casas* (Albuquerque, NM, 1967), 4–66, for the early activities and statements of Las Casas.
52. Paulino Castañeda, *Don Vasco de Quiroga y su 'Información en derecho'* (Madrid, 1974), 131, 138–39.
53. C.R. Boxer, *The Portuguese Seaborne Empire* (London, 1969).
54. James Hemming, *Red Gold: The Conquest of the Brazilian Indians* (Cambridge, MA, 1978).
55. Nicholas P. Cushner, *Why Have You Come Here? The Jesuits and the First Evangelization of Native America* (Oxford, 2006), 107.

2 Christianity in a New World

1. Diego de Rosales, *Historia general del reino de Chile* (Santiago, 1989), 230.
2. Quoted in Lewis Hanke, *Aristotle and the American Indians* (London, 1959), 15.
3. Durán, *Book of the Gods*, 75.
4. Bartolomé de Las Casas, *Historia de las Indias* (3 vols, Mexico, 1951), I, 151–54, 472–73.
5. Bartolomé de Las Casas, *De unico vocationis modo*, ed. Paulino Castañeda Delgado and Antonio García del Moral (*Obras completas* II, Madrid, 1990), 16–17.
6. André Saint-Lu, *La Vera Paz: Esprit évangélique et colonisation* (Paris, 1968), 117–22.
7. Ibid., 41–54.
8. Antonio de Remesal, *Historia general de las Indias occidentales y particular de la gobernación de Chiapa y Guatemala*, ed. Carmelo Sáenz de Santa María, 2 vols (BAE 175, 189, Madrid, 1964), II, 401.
9. Saint-Lu, *La Vera Paz*, 275–76.
10. Remesal, *Historia general de las Indias*, II, 417–18.
11. Ibid., II, 108.
12. Wagner, *The Life and Writings of Bartolomé de Las Casas*, 137–38.
13. Hanke, *Aristotle and the American Indians*, 41, 44–73; Anthony Pagden, *The Fall of Natural Man: the American Indian and the Origins of Comparative Ethnology* (Cambridge, 1982), 109–19.
14. Gómez Canedo, *Evangelización y conquista*, 81.
15. Hanke, *Aristotle and the American Indians*, 54–55.
16. Lewis Hanke, *La lucha española por la justicia en la conquista de América* (Madrid, 1959), 275–76.
17. D.A. Brading, *Mexican Phoenix. Our Lady of Guadalupe: Image and Tradition across Five Centuries* (Cambridge, 2001), 55–57.
18. Hernando Ruiz de Alarcón, *Treatise on the Heathen Superstitions that Today Live among the Indians Native to this New Spain*, trans. and ed. J. Richard Andrews and Ross Hassig (Norman, OK, 1984).
19. Inga Clendinnen, *Ambivalent Conquests: Maya and Spaniard in Yucatan* (Cambridge, 1987), 190.
20. Ibid., 77.
21. Quoted ibid., 114–15.
22. Ralph L. Roys, *The Book of Chilam Balam of Chumayel* (Norman, OK, 1967), 132–63.
23. Pedro Sánchez de Aguilar, *Informe contra idolorum cultores del Obispado de Yucatán, año de 1639* (Mexico, 1953), 281, 294, 301, 318.
24. Clendinnen, *Ambivalent Conquests*, 88–91.
25. Xiu chiefs to crown, 12 April 1567, *Cartas de Indias* (Mexico, 2008), 407–10.
26. Clendinnen, *Ambivalent Conquests*, 161–62.

27. Felipe Guaman Poma de Ayala, *El primer nueva crónica y buen gobierno*, ed. John V. Murra, Rolena Adorno, and Jorge L. Urioste (3 vols, Mexico, 1980), [52, 95, 694] I, 43, 75, II, 656.
28. Juan de Matienzo, *Gobierno del Perú (1567)* (Paris, Lima, 1967), 120.
29. MacCormack, *Religion in the Andes*, 186–87, 432–33.
30. Nicholas Griffiths, *The Cross and the Serpent: Religious Repression and Resurgence in Colonial Peru* (Norman, OK, 1996), 28–38.
31. Guaman Poma, *Nueva Crónica*, [1111], III, 1017.
32. Griffiths, *The Cross and the Serpent*, 147–48.
33. Kenneth Mills, *Idolatry and its Enemies: Colonial Andean Religion and Extirpation, 1640–1750* (Princeton, NJ, 1997), 246.
34. José Toribio Medina, *Historia del tribunal de la Inquisición de Lima, 1569–1822* (2 vols, Santiago de Chile, 1956), I, 63–124.
35. Richard E. Greenleaf, 'Historiography of the Mexican Inquisition', in Mary Elizabeth and Anne J. Cruz, eds, *Cultural Encounters: The Impact of the Inquisition in Spain and the New World* (Berkeley, CA, 1991), 262–64, 269–70.
36. See Fernando Cervantes, *The Devil in the New World: The Impact of Diabolism in New Spain* (New Haven, CT, 1994).
37. Rubén Vargas Ugarte, *Historia de la Companía de Jesús en el Perú*, 4 vols (Burgos, 1963–65), I, 112, 168.
38. David Block, *Mission Culture in the Upper Amazon: Native Tradition, Jesuit Enterprise, and Secular Policy 1660–1880* (Lincoln, NB, 1994), 37–46.
39. John Lockman, ed., *Travels of the Jesuits into Various Parts of the World; Compiled from their Letters by Mr. Lockman*, 2 vols (London, 1743), 93.
40. Stanislas Arlet to General of Society, 1 September 1698, Lockman, *Travels of the Jesuits*, 99–100.
41. Francisco Javier Eder, *Breve descripción de las reducciones de Mojos*, trans. and ed. Josep M. Barnadas (Cochabamba, 1985), 140.
42. Cushner, *Why Have You Come Here?*, 101–27.
43. Magnus Mörner, *The Political and Economic Activities of the Jesuits in the La Plata Region. The Hapsburg Era* (Stockholm, 1953), 36, 199–201.
44. Cushner, *Why Have You Come Here?*, 109.
45. Quoted ibid., 113.
46. Mörner, *The Political and Economic Activities of the Jesuits*, 204.
47. John Lynch, *Spanish Colonial Administration 1782–1810: The Intendant System in the Viceroyalty of the Río de la Plata* (London, 1958), 186, n.1.
48. Block, *Mission Culture in the Upper Amazon*, 103–6.
49. Ibid., 115.
50. José de Acosta, *De procuranda indorum salute* (Madrid, 1982).
51. Eder, *Breve descripción de las reducciones*, 362.
52. Ibid., 88, 98.
53. Block, *Mission Culture in the Upper Amazon*, 1–8.
54. Cushner, *Why Have You Come Here?*, 112.
55. Quoted by Anna L. Peterson and Manuel A. Vasquez, *Latin American Religions: Histories and Documents in Context* (New York, 2008), 101–2.
56. Eduardo Hoornaert, 'The Catholic Church in Colonial Brazil', in Leslie Bethell, ed., *The Cambridge History of Latin America. Volume I, Colonial Latin Amrica* (Cambridge, 1984), 541–56, and the same author's 'The Church in Brazil', in Enrique Dussel, ed., *The Church in Latin America 1492–1992* (Tunbridge Wells, 1992), 192.
57. A.J.R. Russell-Wood, *The Black Man in Slavery and Freedom in Colonial Brazil* (London, 1982), 98–99.
58. Stephen Gudeman and Stuart B. Schwartz, 'Baptismal Godparents in Slavery: Cleansing Original Sin in Eighteenth-Century Bahia', in Raymond T. Smith, ed., *Interpreting Kinship Ideology and Practice in Latin America*, (Chapel Hill, NC, 1984), 35–58.

59. Alonso de Sandoval, *Un tratado sobre la esclavitud*, ed. Enriqueta Vila Vilar (Madrid, 1987), 98–99.
60. Pedro Borges, *Historia de la Iglesia en Hispanoamérica y Filipinas [HIHF]* (2 vols, Madrid, 1992), I, 322–37, and references there.
61. Ibid., I, 322–23.
62. Ibid., 324–5.
63. Margaret M. Olsen, *Slavery and Salvation in Colonial Cartagena de Indias* (Gainesville, FL, 2004), 104–21.
64. Sandoval, *Un tratado sobre la esclavitud*, 25–36, 101–9.
65. Nicholas P. Cushner, *Lords of the Land: Sugar, Wine and Jesuit Estates of Coastal Peru, 1600–1767* (Albany, NY, 1980), 89, 93–96.
66. Arnold J. Bauer, 'Christian Servitude: Slave Management in Colonial Spanish America', in Mats Lundahl and Thommy Svensson, eds, *Agrarian Society in History: Essays in Honour of Magnus Mörner* (London, 1990), 94–97, 100.
67. Miguel Anxo Pena González, *Francisco José de Jaca: La primera propuesta abolicionista de la esclavitud en el pensamiento hispano* (Salamanca, 2003).
68. Francisco José de Jaca, *Resolución sobre la libertad de los negros*, ed. Miguel Anxo Pena González (Madrid, 2002), 1–70.
69. Epifanio de Moirans, *Siervos libres: una propuesta antiesclavista a finales del siglo XVII*, ed. Miguel Anxo Pena (Madrid, 2007).
70. Jaca, *Resolución sobre la libertad de los negros*, 340–41.
71. Pagden, *The Fall of Natural Man*, 33.
72. Ramón A. Gutiérrez, *When Jesus Came, the Corn Mothers Went Away: Marriage, Sexuality, and Power in New Mexico, 1500–1846* (Stanford, CA, 1991), 180, 185.
73. Alonso de la Peña Montenegro, *Itinerario para Parochos de Indios, en que se tratan las materias tocantes a ellos, para su buena administración* (Leon de Francia, 1678), ii, 555.
74. See below, Chapter 3.

3 Religion in the Age of Enlightenment

1. Antonio Mestre, 'La actitud religiosa de los católicos ilustrados', in Agustín Guimera, ed., *El reformismo borbónico: Una vision interdisciplinar* (Madrid, 1996), 147–63.
2. M.L. Pérez-Marchand, *Dos etapas ideológicas del siglo XVIII en México a través de los papeles de la Inquisición* (Mexico, 1945), 71–72, 90–91, 106–11, 123–24, 131–32.
3. Quoted by John Lynch, *Spanish Colonial Administration 1782–1810: The Intendant System in the Viceroyalty of the Río de la Plata* (London, 1958), 89.
4. N.M. Farriss, *Crown and Clergy in Colonial Mexico 1759–1821: The Crisis of Ecclesiastical Privilege* (London, 1968), 87, 93–94.
5. Patricia Seed, *To Love, Honor, and Obey in Colonial Mexico: Conflicts over Marriage Choice, 1574–1821* (Stanford, CA, 1988), 162–66, 167, 169.
6. Quoted by Farriss, *Crown and Clergy in Colonial Mexico*, 17–18.
7. Quoted ibid., 34.
8. Quoted by D.A. Brading, *Church and State in Bourbon Mexico: The Diocese of Michoacán 1749–1810* (Cambridge, 1994), 129–30.
9. José Miguel Guridi y Alcocer, *Apuntes de la vida de D. José Miguel Guridi y Alcocer, formados por él mismo en fines de 1801 y principios del siguiente de 1802* (Mexico City, 1906), 98.
10. Seed, *To Love, Honor, and Obey in Colonial Mexico*, 167–68, 174, 188–89, 196.
11. Richard Konetzke, ed., *Colección de documentos para la formación social de Hispanoamérica 1493–1810. Vol. III* (Madrid, 1962), 406–13.
12. Seed, *To Love, Honor, and Obey in Colonial Mexico*, 205–25.
13. Teófanes Egido, 'La expulsión de los jesuitas de España', in Ricardo García-Villoslada, ed., *Historia de la Iglesia en España*, IV (Madrid, 1979), 746–95.

14. Magnus Mörner, 'La expulsión de la Compañia de Jesús', *HIHF* (2 vols, Madrid, 1992), I, 245–60.

15. Guillermo Furlong, *José M. Peramás y su Diario del destierro (1768)* (Buenos Aires, 1952), 92–99.

16. Pastoral letter, 28 Oct. 1767, quoted by Farriss, *Crown and Clergy in Colonial Mexico*, 52.

17. Luis Sierra Nava-Lasa, *El Cardenal Lorenzana y la ilustración, I* (Madrid, 1975), 121–23; Farriss, *Crown and Clergy in Colonial Mexico*, 131–32.

18. Tadeo Xavier Henis, *Diario histórico de la rebelión y guerra de los pueblos guaraníes situados en la costa oriental del río Uruguay del año de 1754*, in *Colección general de documentos tocantes a la tercera época de las conmociones de los Regulares de la Compañia en el Paraguay. Tomo quarto* (Madrid, 1770), 103.

19. José Luis Mora Mérida, *Iglesia y sociedad en el Paraguay en el siglo XVIII* (Seville, 1976), 79.

20. John Lynch, *Bourbon Spain 1700–1808* (London, 1989), 281–83.

21. Pedro Rodríguez de Campomanes, *Dictamen fiscal de expulsión de los jesuitas de España (1766-1767)* (Madrid, 1977), 53, 64–65, 71–72, 78, 183–84.

22. Ibid., 84.

23. M.F. Bacigalupo, 'Bernardo Ibáñez de Echévarri and the Image of the Jesuit Missions of Paraguay', *The Americas*, 35 (1979), 475–94.

24. Bernardo Ibáñez de Echavarri, *El reyno jesuitico del Paraguay* (Madrid, 1770), 20–36.

25. Ibid., 32–33.

26. Ibid., 45–46, 58, 72.

27. Real consulta, 21 March 1767, in Manuel Danvila y Collado, *El reinado de Carlos III* (6 vols, Madrid, 1890–96), III, 666.

28. Letter of Audiencia of Mexico, 16 May 1735, in Ismael Sánchez Bella, *Iglesia y estado en la América Española* (Pamplona, 1990), 110–60.

29. Adalberto López, *The Revolt of the Comuneros, 1721-1735: A Study in the Colonial History of Paraguay* (Cambridge, MA, 1976), 47–63, 91–92.

30. On the Treaty of Madrid and its consequences see Guillermo Kratz, *El Tratado hispano-portugués de límites de 1750 y sus consecuencias* (Rome, 1954), 23–24, 26–27, 61; Lynch, *Bourbon Spain*, 179–82.

31. Campomanes, *Dictamen fiscal*, 130.

32. Jaime González Rodríguez, 'La Iglesia y la ilustración', in Borges, *HIHF*, I, 802–4.

33. Revillagigedo quoted by Sierra, *El Cardenal Lorenzana*, 193; on Guatemala see Pedro Cortés y Larraz, *Descripción geográfica-moral de la diócesis de Goathemala* (2 vols, Guatemala City, 1958), II, 214.

34. Mörner, *The Political and Economic Activities of the Jesuits in the La Plata Region*, 194–95.

35. Pablo Hernández, *El extrañamiento de los jesuítas del Río de la Plata y de las misiones del Paraguay por decreto de Carlos III* (Madrid, 1908), 270–78; Lynch, *Spanish Colonial Administration*, 186–95.

36. Dauril Alden, 'The Expulsion of the Jesuits', Leslie Bethell, ed. *The Cambridge History of Latin America, Volume II* (Cambridge, 1984), 612–19.

37. Quoted in Sierra, *El Cardenal Lorenzana*, 192, 193.

38. Brading, *Church and State in Bourbon Mexico*, 106–9, 112, 120–23, 154.

39. Ibid., 154.

40. Guridi y Alcocer, *Apuntes de la vida de D. José Miguel Guridi y Alcocer*.

41. David Cahill, '*Curas* and Social Conflict in the *Doctrinas* of Cuzco, 1780–1814', *Journal of Latin American Studies*, 16, 2 (1984), 241–76, esp. 243.

42. Scarlett O'Phelan Godoy, *Rebellions and Revolts in Eighteenth Century Peru and Upper Peru* (Cologne, 1985), 144–45.

43. Juan de Santa Gertrudis, *Maravillas de la naturaleza* (*MN*) (3 vols, Bogotá, 1994), II, 271, 283, 293–94; III, 66.

44. Cortés y Larraz, *Descripción de la diócesis de Goathemala*, II, 277–78.
45. Brading, *Church and State in Bourbon Mexico*, 117–20.
46. Serge Gruzinski, *The Conquest of Mexico: The Incorporation of Indian Societies into the Western World, 16th–18th Centuries* (Oxford, 1993), 271.
47. Cortés y Larraz, *Descripción de la diócesis de Goathemala*, II, 267.
48. Ibid., I, 139–40, II, 280–81.
49. Quoted by Gruzinski, *The Conquest of Mexico*, 271–72.
50. D.A. Brading, *The First America: The Spanish Monarchy, Creole Patriots, and the Liberal State 1492–1867* (Cambridge, 1991), 495–96.
51. Gruzinski, *The Conquest of Mexico*, 273–74.
52. Brading, *Church and State in Bourbon Mexico*, 163.
53. Cortés y Larraz, *Descripción de la diócesis de Goathemala*, II, 34–35.
54. Serge Gruzinski, *Man-Gods in the Mexican Highlands: Indian Power and Colonial Society, 1520–1800* (Stanford, CA, 1989), 158–59; *The Conquest of Mexico*, 268–69.
55. On the social structure of confraternities see Martin Minchom, *The People of Quito, 1690–1810: Change and Unrest in the Underclass* (Boulder, CO, 1994), 82–83.
56. Cortés y Larraz, *Descripción de la diócesis de Goathemala*, I, 141.
57. Bernardo Recio, *Compendiosa relación de la cristianidad de Quito* (Madrid, 1947), 438; Taylor, *Magistrates of the Sacred*, 175.
58. Peña y Montenegro, *Itinerario para parochos de indios*, I, 222–23, II, 681–85.
59. Francisco de Ajofrín, *Diario del viaje que hizo a la América septentrional en el siglo XVIII*, ed. Vicente Castañeda y Alcocer (2 vols, Madrid, 1958), II, 179.
60. Recio, *Compendioso relación*, 409.
61. Alicia Barabas, *Utopias indias. Movimientos sociorreligiosos en México* (Mexico, 1989), 168–69.
62. Quoted ibid., 178.
63. Kevin Gosner, *Soldiers of the Virgin. The Moral Economy of a Colonial Maya Rebellion* (Tucson, AZ, 1992), 10.
64. Bricker, *The Indian Christ, the Indian King*, 55–69, 119–25; Gosner, *Soldiers of the Virgin*, 137–55.
65. Serge Gruzinski, *Man-Gods in the Mexican Highlands*, 162–63, 208–9.
66. John Lynch, *Fray Juan de Santa Gertrudis and the Marvels of New Granada* (Institute of Latin American Studies, London, 1999).
67. Juan de Santa Gertrudis, *MN*, I, 259–60, 264, 304, 308–10.
68. *MN*, I, 261–63, 273, III, 91–92.
69. *MN*, I, 290, 307.
70. *MN*, I, 333.
71. *MN*, III, 99, 145–51.
72. *MN*, I, 353–55, 363–67, 369–70.
73. *MN*, II, 91–94, 103–9, 155–58. On Fray Juan's adventures in Pasto see *MN*, II, 199–234.
74. *MN*, III, 169.
75. Cárdenas, 'Panorama de la Iglesia diocesana', in Borges, *HIHF*, I, 342; Minchom, *The People of Quito*, 76.
76. Oviedo y Baños, *The Conquest and Settlement of Venezuela*, 110.
77. Paulino Castañeda Delgado, 'La Hiérarchie ecclésiastique dans l'Amérique des Lumières', *L'Amérique espagnole à l'époque des Lumières* (Paris, 1987), 79–100.
78. José Bravo Ugarte, *Diócesis y obispos de la Iglesia mexicana (1519–1965)* (Mexico City, 1965), 70–72; Brading, *Church and State in Bourbon Mexico*, 176, 204–8.
79. Juan de Santa Gertrudis, *MN*, I, 349.
80. On Quito see Minchom, *The People of Quito*, 78; on Upper Peru, Bartolomé Arzans de Orsúa y Vela, *Historia de la Villa Imperial de Potosí*, ed. Lewis Hanke and Gunnar Mendoza (3 vols, Providence, RI, 1965), III, 59.
81. Arzans, *Historia de la Villa Imperial de Potosí*, III, 466, entry for 1709.

82. Kathy Waldron, 'The Sinners and the Bishop in Colonial Venezuela: The *Visita* of Bishop Mariano Martí, 1771–1784', in Asunción Lavrin, ed., *Sexuality and Marriage in Colonial Latin America* (Lincoln, NB, 1989), 165–66, 170–71.
83. See biography and bibliography in *Diccionario de historia de Venezuela* (3 vols, Caracas, 1988), E–O, 839–41, and Pablo Vila, *El obispo Martí* (2 vols, Caracas, 1980).
84. Guillermo Furlong, *Historia social y cultural del Río de la Plata 1536–1810. El trasplante cultural: Ciencia* (Buenos Aires, 1969), 295.
85. Juan de Santa Gertrudis, *MN*, II, 183, 338.
86. Mariano Martí, *Documentos relativos a su visita pastoral de la diócesis de Caracas, 1771–1784* (ANH, 7 vols, Caracas, 1969), II, 276, 289; Waldron, 'The Sinners and the Bishop', 172.
87. Martí, *Documentos relativos a su visita pastoral*, II, 188, 215, 581.
88. Cortés y Larraz, *Descripción de la diócesis de Goathemala*, II, 102, 267.
89. Ibid., II, 22–23, 118, 276.
90. Ibid., I, 30–32, 112, II, 27.
91. Minchom, *The People of Quito*, 80–81
92. Juan de Santa Gertrudis, *MN*, III, 10–11.
93. Cortés y Larraz, *Descripción de la diócesis de Goathemala*, II, 16–18.

4 Independence: A Sinful Revolution

1. Scarlett O'Phelan Godoy, *Rebellions and Revolts in Eighteenth Century Peru and Upper Peru* (Cologne, 1985), 144–48; David Cahill, '*Curas* and Social Conflict in the *Doctrinas* of Cuzco, 1780–1814', *Journal of Latin American Studies*, 16, 2 (1984), 241–76.
2. John Leddy Phelan, *The People and the King: The Comunero Revolution in Colombia, 1781* (Madison, WI, 1978), 232–33, 237; Anthony McFarlane, *Colombia before Independence: Economy, Society, and Politics under Bourbon Rule* (Cambridge, 1993), 263–64, 275–78.
3. For Caballero y Góngora's reference to what he called the 'Instituto de las Colonias' see *Relación del Estado del Nuevo Reino de Granada* (1789), in José Manuel Pérez Ayala, *Antonio Caballero y Góngora, virrey y arzobispo de Santa Fe 1723–1796* (Bogotá, 1951), 361.
4. Paulino Castañeda Delgado, 'La Hiérarchie ecclésiastique dans l'Amérique des Lumières', *L'Amérique espagnole à l'époque des Lumières* (Paris, 1987), 79–100; José Bravo Ugarte, *Diócesis y obispos de la Iglesia mexicana (1519–1965)* (Mexico City, 1965), 70–72; Brading, *Church and State in Bourbon Mexico*, 176, 109–11, 204–8.
5. Manuel Abad y Queipo, 'Representación sobre la inmunidad personal del clero', in José María Luis Mora, *Obras sueltas* (Mexico, 1963), 204–12. On clerical numbers and income see Taylor, *Magistrates of the Sacred*, 78–79, 126–43.
6. Reinhard Liehr, 'Endeudamiento estatal y crédito privado: la consolidación de vales reales en Hispanoamérica', *Anuario de estudios americanos*, 41 (1984), 552–78.
7. Antonine Tibesar, 'The Peruvian Church at the Time of Independence in the Light of Vatican II', *The Americas*, 26 (April 1970), 349–75.
8. O. Carlos Stoetzer, *The Scholastic Roots of the Spanish American Revolution* (New York, 1979), 24–26, 121–23, 195–96, 201–4; Richard M. Morse, 'Claims of Political Tradition', *New World Soundings: Culture and Ideology in the Americas* (Baltimore, MD, 1989), 95–130.
9. Phelan, *The People and the King*, 87.
10. Rafael Gómez Hoyos, *La revolución granadina de 1810: Ideario de una generación y de una época, 1781–1821* (2 vols, Bogotá, 1962), II, 30, 415, 420.
11. Juan Pablo Viscardo, *Lettre aux espagnols américains*, in Merle E. Simmons, *Los escritos de Juan Pablo Viscardo y Guzmán, precursor de la independencia hispanoamericana* (Caracas, 1983), 363.

12. Morelos, Bando 17 November 1810, 8 February, 24 November 1811, in Ernesto Lemoine Villacaña, *Morelos, su vida revolucionaria a través de sus escritos y de otros testimonios de la época* (Mexico, 1965), 162, 184–85, 190.
13. Gómez Hoyos, *La revolución granadina de 1810*, II, 349.
14. Fernando Pérez Memen, *El episcopado y la independencia de México (1810–1836)* (Mexico, 1977), 83; Brading, *Church and State in Bourbon Mexico*, 238–43.
15. Pérez Memen, *El episcopado y la independencia de México*, 80–81, 85, 117, 121.
16. Josep M. Barnadas, 'La Iglesia ante la emancipación en Bolivia', *HGIAL*, VIII, *Perú, Bolivia y Ecuador*, 185–86, 191; Rubén Vargas Ugarte, *El episcopado en los tiempos de la emancipación sudamericana* (3rd edn, Lima, 1962), 293, 303–4. The creole bishop of Salta, Nicolás Videla del Pino, was also a royalist, as were many of his clergy, seeing the *porteños* as foreigners as well as rebels.
17. Quoted by J.M. Vargas, 'La Iglesia ante la emancipación en Ecuador', *HGIAL*, VIII, 200; see also L. López-Ocón, 'El protagonismo del clero de la insurgencia quiteña (1809–1812)', *Revista de Indias*, 46 (1986), 107–67.
18. Jeffrey Klaiber, 'La Iglesia ante la emancipación en el Perú', *HGIAL*, VIII, 167–68, 174–76.
19. Ibid., *HGIAL*, VII, 176.
20. Quoted by Narciso Coll y Prat, 'Exposición de 1818', *Memoriales sobre la independencia de Venezuela* (ANH, Caracas, 1960), 315.
21. Pedro de Leturia, *Relaciones entre la Santa Sede e Hispanoamérica* (3 vols, Rome, Caracas, 1959–60), II, 90, III, 179–80.
22. Quoted in Carlos María Bustamante, *Cuadro histórico de la revolución mexicana* (3 vols, Mexico, 1961), I, 331, II, 512.
23. Taylor, *Magistrates of the Sacred*, 453–55; Farriss, *Crown and Clergy in Colonial Mexico*, 231, 254–65.
24. Pérez Memen, *El episcopado y la independencia de México*, 89; Brading, *Church and State in Bourbon Mexico*, 240–41.
25. Pérez Memen, *El episcopado y la independencia de México*, 84.
26. Farriss, *Crown and Clergy in Colonial Mexico*, 203. For a discussion of the sources of Morelos's political thought and its simultaneous affirmation of 'hierarchy, religious intolerance, popular sovereignty, and equality before the law', see Taylor, *Magistrates of the Sacred*, 463–73, 521–23.
27. Fernán González, 'La Iglesia ante la emancipación en Colombia', *HGIAL*, VII, *Colombia y Venezuela*, 259. For Buenos Aires see Héctor José Tanzi, 'El clero patriota y la Revolución de Mayo', *Revista de Indias*, 37 (1977), 141–58, and for Peru Pilar García Jordán, 'Notas sobre la participación del clero en la independencia del Perú. Aportación documental', *Boletín Americanista*, 24 (1982), 139–48.
28. Goméz Hoyos, *La revolución granadina de 1810*, II, 321, 323–27; González, 'La Iglesia ante la emancipación en Colombia', *HGIAL*, VII, 262–63; 265–66.
29. Leturia, *Relaciones entre la Santa Sede e Hispanoamérica*, II, 175; Felice Cardot, 'La Iglesia ante la emancipación en Venezuela', *HGIAL*, VII, 293.
30. Leturia, *Relaciones entre la Santa Sede e Hispanoamérica*, II, 110–13.
31. Ibid., III, 432.
32. Ibid., II, 215.
33. Avelino Ignacio Gómez Ferreyra, ed., *Viajeros pontificios al Río de la Plata y Chile (1823–1825): La primera misión pontificia a Hispano-América, relatada por sus protagonistas* (Córdoba, Argentina, 1970), 502, 543–44, 573.
34. Leturia, *Relaciones entre la Santa Sede e Hispanoamérica*, II, 265–71.
35. Guillermo Gallardo, *La política religiosa de Rivadavia* (Buenos Aires, 1962), 67–78, 105–34, 277–80.
36. Leturia, *Relaciones entre la Santa Sede e Hispanoamérica*, II, 314.
37. John Lynch, *Simón Bolívar: A Life* (London, 2006), 277.

38. Quoted by Felice Cardot, 'La Iglesia ante la emancipación en Venezuela', *HGIAL*, VII, 295.
39. Klaiber, 'La Iglesia ante la emancipación en el Perú', 212.
40. Leturia, *Relaciones entre la Santa Sede e Hispanoamérica*, II, 378–85.

5 Creating a Latin American Church

1. Quoted by Luis Medina Ascensio, 'La Iglesia en la formación del estado mexicano', *HGIAL*, V, *Mexico*, 201.
2. Quoted by Josep M. Barnadas, 'La Iglesia en la formación del nuevo estado boliviano', *HGIAL*, VIII, *Peru, Bolivia y Ecuador*, 240.
3. Quoted by Fernán González, 'La reorganización de la Iglesia ante el estado liberal colombiano (1850–1886)', *HGIAL*, VII, *Colombia y Venezuela*, 353.
4. Maximiliano Salinas, 'La Iglesia chilena ante el surgimiento del orden colonial', *HGIAL*, IX, *Cono Sur (Argentina, Chile, Uruguay y Paraguay)*, 306.
5. Archbishop Mosquero to Dr Santiago Arroyo, 1836, in Fernán González, 'La Iglesia en la formación del estado colombiano (1830–1850)', *HGIAL*, VII, 307.
6. Salinas, 'La Iglesia chilena ante el surgimiento del orden colonial', *HGIAL*, IX, 303–5.
7. Gustavo Ocando Yamarte, 'La Iglesia ante el naciente estado de Venezuela 1830–1847', *HGIAL*, VII, 310; Carlos Felice Cardot, 'La renovación eclesial a partir de la administración Rojas Paúl (1888)', *HGIAL*, VII, 491–93.
8. Rubén Vargas Ugarte, *Historia de la Iglesia en el Perú* (5 vols, Burgos, 1962), V, 3; Antonine Tibesar, 'The Peruvian Church at the Time of Independence in the Light of Vatican II', *The Americas*, 26, 2 (1968), 349–75; Jeffrey Klaiber, *La Iglesia en el Perú: Su historia social desde la independencia* (Lima, 1988), 59–61.
9. Quoted by C.J. Beirne, 'Latin American Bishops of the First Vatican Council, 1869–1870', *The Americas*, 25, 1 (1968), 273.
10. Quoted by Barnadas, 'La Iglesia en la formación del nuevo estado boliviano', *HGIAL*, VIII, 237.
11. José Gutiérrez Casillas, SJ, *Historia de la Iglesia en México* (Mexico, 1974).
12. Luis González, *Pueblo en vilo. Microhistoria de San José de Gracia* (Mexico, 1968), 164.
13. José Gutiérrez Casillas, SJ, *Jesuítas en México durante el siglo XIX* (Madrid, 1972), 169.
14. Austen Ivereigh, *Catholicism and Politics in Argentina, 1810–1960* (London, 1995), 44–49.
15. John Lynch, *Argentine Dictator: Juan Manuel de Rosas 1829–1852* (Oxford, 1981), 183–86.
16. Guillermo Furlong, SJ, 'El catolicismo argentino entre 1860 y 1930', Academia Nacional de la Historia, *Historia argentina contemporánea 1862–1930* (Buenos Aires, 1964–66), II, part 1, pp. 251–54.
17. Juan Bautista Alberdi, *Las 'Bases' de Alberdi*, ed. Jorge M. Mayer (Buenos Aires, 1969), 234–35, 258–59.
18. Félix Frías, 12 Oct. 1853, in Tulio Halperín Donghi, *Proyecto y construcción de una nación (Argentina 1846–1880)* (Caracas, 1980), 43.
19. Quoted by Furlong, 'El catolicismo argentina', 261, see also pp. 254–59.
20. E. Mignone, 'La Iglesia argentina en la organización nacional', *HGIAL*, IX, 342.
21. José Hernández, *Martín Fierro* (Buenos Aires, EUDEBA, 1962), 7.
22. Richard Arthur Seymour, *Pioneering in the Pampas; or, The First Four Years of a Settler's Experience in the La Plata Camps* (London, 1869), 80–81.
23. Brading, *Mexican Phoenix. Our Lady of Guadalupe*, 307–8; Alfonso Alcalá Alvarado, 'La Iglesia camina por nuevos senderos (1873–1900)', *HGIAL*, V, 264–85.
24. Tomás Mosquera to Pius IX, 15 Jan. 1852, in González, 'La reorganización de la Iglesia ante el estado liberal colombiano', *HGIAL*, VII, 368.
25. Quoted in Robert J. Knowlton, 'Expropriation of Church Property in Nineteenth-century Mexico and Colombia: A Comparison', *The Americas*, 25, 1 (1968), 395.

26. Jeffrey Klaiber, 'La Iglesia en la formación del nuevo estado del Perú', *HGIAL*, VIII, 226.
27. Salinas, 'La Iglesia chilena ante el surgimiento del orden colonial', *HGIAL*, IX, 308.
28. Quoted by Salinas, ibid., IX, 309.
29. Jorge Adame Goddard, *El pensamiento político y social de los católicos mexicanos, 1867–1914* (Mexico, 1981), 37–45.
30. Quoted by Fredrick B. Pike, *The Modern History of Peru* (London, 1967), 15.
31. Christine Hünefeldt, *Paying the Price of Freedom. Family and Labour among Lima's Slaves, 1800–1854* (Berkeley, CA, 1994), 149–61.
32. Klaiber, *La Iglesia en . . . el Perú*, 268–79.
33. Salinas, 'La Iglesia chilena ante el surgimiento del orden colonial', *HGIAL*, IX, 311–12, 313–16.
34. Josep M. Barnadas, 'Martín Castro. Un clérigo boliviano combatiente combatido', *Estudios bolivianos en homenaje a Gunnar Mendoza L.* (La Paz, 1978), 189.
35. Fredrick B. Pike, 'Heresy, Real and Alleged in Peru: An Aspect of the Conservative–Liberal Struggle, 1830–1875', *Hispanic American Historical Review*, 47, 1 (1967), 50–74.
36. Quoted by Antón Pazos, *La Iglesia en la América del IV Centenario* (Madrid, 1992), 41.
37. Quoted ibid., 24–25.
38. Ibid., 55.
39. Beirne, 'Latin American Bishops of the First Vatican Council', 265–80.
40. On the proceedings of the Council see Pazos, *La Iglesia en la América del IV Centenario*, 389–98; Eduardo Cárdenas, *La Iglesia hispanoamericano en el siglo XX (1890–1990)* (Madrid, 1992), 86–93.
41. Enrique D. Dussel, *Historia de la Iglesia en América Latina. Coloniaje y liberación (1492–1973)* (3rd edn, Barcelona, 1974), 175–76.
42. Furlong, 'El catolicismo argentino', 251–92.
43. Quoted by Emilio Mignone, 'La Iglesia argentina en la organización nacional', *HGIAL*, IX, 351.
44. Ibid., 352.
45. Victor Daniel Bonilla, *Servants of God or Masters of Men? The Story of a Capuchin Mission in Amazonia* (London, 1972), is an example of polemical criticism.
46. Eduardo Hoornaert, 'The Church in Brazil', in Enrique Dussel, ed., *The Church in Latin America 1492–1992* (London, 1992), 195–96; O. de F. Lustosa, *Reformistas na Igreja do Brasil Império* (São Paulo, 1977); George C.A. Boehrer, 'The Church in the Second Reign 1840–1889', in Henry H. Keith and S.F. Edwards, eds, *Conflict and Continuity in Brazilian Society* (Columbia, SC, 1969), 113–40; Roque Spencer M. de Barros, 'A questão religiosa', *História Geral da Civilização Brasileira* VI (São Paulo, 1971), 317–65.
47. Robert Brent Toplin, *The Abolition of Slavery in Brazil* (New York, 1975), 85–95.
48. Joaquim Nabuco, *Abolitionism: The Brazilian Antislavery Struggle*, trans. and ed. Robert Conrad (Chicago, 1977), 19; see also Robert Conrad, *The Destruction of Brazilian Slavery 1850–1888* (Berkeley and Los Angeles, 1972), 75–76, 112–13, 151.
49. Thomas C. Bruneau, *The Church in Brazil. The Politics of Religion* (Austin, TX, 1982), 18, 31.

6 The Religion of the People

1. Cortés y Larraz, *Descripción geográfico-moral de la diócesis de Goathemala*, I, 122, II, 185–227.
2. Luis González, *Pueblo en vilo. Microhistoria de San José de Gracia* (Mexico, 1968), 110.
3. Cárdenas, *La Iglesia hispanoamericana en el siglo XX*, 76–77. Figures for the early twentieth century.
4. G. Pérez-Ramírez and Yvan Labelle, *El problema sacerdotal en América Latina* (Cidoc, Freiburg, Bogotá, 1964), 17.
5. Antón Pazos, *La Iglesia en la América del IV Centenario* (Madrid, 1992), 231–32. Figures refer to end of nineteenth century.

6. Quoted in Maximiliano Salinas, 'La Iglesia chilena ante el surgimiento del orden colonial', *HGIAL*, IX, *Cono Sur (Argentina, Chile, Uruguay y Paraguay)* (CEHILA, Salamanca, 1994), 321.

7. Pazos, *La Iglesia en la América del IV Centenario*, 222, 274, 277–78.

8. Quoted by Rodolfo Cardenal, SJ, *El poder eclesiástico en El Salvador* (San Salvador, 1980), 163.

9. Quoted by Pazos, *La iglesia en la América del IV Centenario*, 223.

10. Ibid., 225–26, 228.

11. Ibid., 243–44.

12. Quoted by Cardenal, *El poder eclesiástico en El Salvador*, 167.

13. Patricia Londoño-Vega, *Religion, Culture and Society in Colombia: Medellín and Antioquia, 1850–1930* (Oxford, 2002), 153, 160; Cárdenas, *La Iglesia hispanoamericana en el siglo XX*, 185–90.

14. Cardenal, *El poder eclesiástico en El Salvador*.

15. Jeffrey Klaiber, *Religion and Revolution in Peru, 1824–1976* (Notre Dame, IN, 1977), 2.

16. Quoted by Jeffrey Klaiber, 'La reorganización de la Iglesia ante el estado liberal en el Perú (1860–1930)', *HGIAL*, VIII, *Perú, Bolivia y Ecuador* (CEHILA, Salamanca, 1987), 301, 303–4.

17. Quoted by Pazos, *La Iglesia en la América del IV Centenario*, 292.

18. John Lynch, *Caudillos in Spanish America 1800–1850* (Oxford, 1992), 374, 382.

19. Maximiliano Salinas, 'Cristianismo popular en Chile, 1880–1920', *Nueva Historia*, 3, 12 (1984), 275–302.

20. Londoño-Vega, *Religion, Culture and Society in Colombia*, 8, 55, 163, 299–305; on Maule see Salinas, 'La Iglesia chilena y la madurez del orden neocolonial', *HGIAL*, IX, 402.

21. William A. Christian, Jr, *Local Religion in Sixteenth-Century Spain* (Princeton, NJ, 1981), 8, 178; Taylor, *Magistrates of the Sacred*, 48, 549 n. 2. On the adoption of the concept in the late twentieth century see above, Chapter 10.

22. Quoted by Pazos, *La Iglesia en la América del IV Centenario*, 244.

23. Klaiber, 'La reorganización de la Iglesia ante el Estado liberal en el Perú', *HGIAL*, VIII, 301.

24. Quotations from Pazos, *La Iglesia en la América del IV Centenario*, 256–57, 292.

25. J.E. Arellano, 'Nicaragua', *HGIAL*, VI, *América Central* (Salamanca, 1985), 324–31.

26. J.F.C. Harrison, *The Second Coming: Popular Millenarianism 1780–1850* (London, 1979), 3–10, 11–12; Damian Thompson, *The End of Time: Faith and Fear in the Shadow of the Millennium* (London, 1996), 20–28, 57–60. See also Norman Cohn, *The Pursuit of the Millennium: Revolutionary Millenarians and Mystical Anarchists of the Middle Ages* (London, 1993).

27. John Leddy Phelan, *The Millennial Kingdom of the Franciscans in the New World* (Berkeley, CA, 1970), 45–48; W. Hanisch, 'Manuel Lacunza S.I. y el milenarismo', *Archivum Historicum Societatis Jesu*, 40 (1971), 496–511.

28. Barabas, *Utopías indias*, 168–69.

29. Enrique Florescano, *Memory, Myth, and Time in Mexico: From the Aztecs to Independence* (Austin, TX, 1994), 172, 215–17; Eric van Young, 'Millennium in the Northern Marches: The Mad Messiah of Durango and Popular Rebellion in Mexico, 1800–1805', *Comparative Studies in Society and History*, 28 (1986), 385–413. On millenarianism and popular insurrection see the comments of Taylor, *Magistrates of the Sacred*, 782 n. 64.

30. Statements by Cruz Gutiérrez and Juan Villalba in Hugo Nario, *Los crímenes del Tandil* (Buenos Aires, 1983), 56, 58–59; see also Juan Carlos Torre, 'Los crímenes de Tata Dios, el mesías gaucho', *Todo es Historia*, 4 (Aug. 1967), 40–45; Hugo Nario, *Tata Dios: El Mesías de la última montonera* (Buenos Aires, 1976), 124.

31. Statements by various witnesses in Hugo Nario, *Mesías y bandoleros pampeanos* (Buenos Aires, 1993), 33–35; *Los crímenes del Tandil*, 62–63; and *Tata Dios*, 91–92.

32. Juan Fugl, *Memorias de Juan Fugl: Vida de un pionero danés durante 30 años en Tandil, Argentina, 1844–1875*, trans. Alice Larsen de Rabal (Buenos Aires, 1986), 409–13.

33. 'Los asesinatos del Tandil', *La Tribuna*, Buenos Aires, 9 Jan. 1872.

34. Robert M. Levine, *Vale of Tears: Revisiting the Canudos Massacre in Northeastern Brazil, 1893–1897* (Berkeley, CA, 1992), 217–26, who identifies eight millenarian movements in addition to Canudos.

35. Ralph Della Cava, 'Brazilian Messianism and National Institutions: A Reappraisal of Canudos and Joaseiro', *Hispanic American Historical Review*, 48, 3 (1968), 402–20.

36. Levine, *Vale of Tears*, 230–31.

37. Ralph Della Cava, *Miracle at Joaseiro* (New York, 1970), 76–78.

38. Paul J. Vanderwood, *The Power of God against the Guns of Government: Religious Upheaval in Mexico at the Turn of the Nineteenth Century* (Stanford, CA, 1998), 32–44; for reflections on these events see the same author's ' "None but the Justice of God": Tomochic, 1891–92', in Jaime E. Rodríguez O., *Patterns of Contention in Mexican History* (Wilmington, DE, 1992), 227–41.

39. Vanderwood, *The Power of God*, 206, 210–11.

40. Ibid., 135–41, 258–59.

41. Apocalypse [Revelation] 21: 4.

7 Church and State in a Liberal World

1. Ondina E. González and Justo L. González, *Christianity in Latin America, A History* (Cambridge, 2008), 184–239, an authoritative account of Protestant immigration and settlement. For further examples of the available bibliography see Jean-Pierre Bastian, 'Protestantism in Latin America', in Dussel, ed., *The Church in Latin America*, 313–50; Robert Leonard McIntire, *Portrait of Half a Century: Fifty Years of Presbyterianism in Brazil (1859–1910)* (Cuernavaca, 1969); Emilio Willems, *Followers of the New Faith: Culture Change and the Rise of Protestantism in Brazil and Chile* (Nashville, TN, 1967); Arnoldo Canclini, *Jorge A. Humble. Médico y misionero patagónico* (Buenos Aires, 1980); see also entries in *HGIAL*, VII, 501–13, 639–46, VIII, 260–73, IX, 593–636.

2. Positivism in Latin America is best studied in Charles A. Hale, 'Political and Social Ideas in Latin America', in Bethell, ed., *The Cambridge History of Latin America*, IV (Cambridge, 1986), 382–414.

3. Quoted in Robert G. Nachman, 'Positivism, Modernization, and the Middle Class in Brazil', *HAHR*, 57, 1 (1977), 22.

4. Klaiber, *Religion and Revolution in Peru*, 34.

5. Ibid., 40.

6. For a shorter account of these themes see John Lynch, 'The Catholic Church in Latin America, 1830–1930', Bethell, ed., *The Cambridge History of Latin America*, IV, 527–95.

7. Irma Maria Regina do Santo Rosário, *O Cardeal Leme (1882–1942)* (Rio de Janeiro, 1961), 66, 68.

8. Ivereigh, *Catholicism and Politics in Argentina*, 53.

9. Ibid., 213.

10. Néstor Tomás Auza, *Católicos y liberales en la generación del ochenta* (Buenos Aires, 1975), 145–70, 229, 307–8.

11. Quoted in Furlong, 'El catolicismo argentino', II, Part 1, 273.

12. Néstor Tomás Auza, *Aciertos y fracasos sociales del catolicismo argentino* (3 vols, Buenos Aires, 1987–88), III, 504.

13. Auza, *Católicos y liberales*, 516–17.

14. Ivereigh, *Catholicism and Politics in Argentina*, 61.

15. Pazos, *La Iglesia en la América del IV Centenario*, 274–5. On the history of the Paraguayan Church in the nineteenth century see the chapters by Margarita Durán in *HGIAL* IX, 286–89, 326–32, 421–26.

16. Cárdenas, *La Iglesia hispanoamericana en el siglo XX*, 83.

17. Brian H. Smith, *The Church and Politics in Chile. Challenges to Modern Catholicism* (Princeton, NJ, 1982), analyses Church–state relations in the Constitution of 1925.

18. Jeffrey Klaiber, 'La reorganización de la Iglesia ante el estado liberal en el Perú (1860–1930)', *HGIAL*, VIII, 284–85.
19. Quoted ibid., 294.
20. Quoted by Klaiber, *Religion and Revolution in Peru*, 133.
21. Barnadas, 'La Iglesia en la formación del Nuevo Estado boliviano', *HGIAL*, VIII, 245.
22. Ibid., 315.
23. Marie-Danielle Demélas and Yves Saint-Geours, *Jerusalen y Babilonia: Religión y política en el Ecuador 1780–1880* (Quito, 1988), 135–39.
24. William Martin King, 'Ecuadorian Church and State Relations under García Moreno, 1859–1863', Austin, University of Texas Ph.D. thesis, 1974, University Microfilms, Ann Arbor, MI, 1986, 144–75, 244. See also Peter V.N. Henderson, *Gabriel García Moreno and Conservative State Formation in the Andes* (Austin, TX, 2009).
25. Mensaje a la Convención Nacional, 16 May 1869, in Demélas and Saint-Geours, *Jerusalen y Babilonia*, 153.
26. Ibid., 166.
27. Ibid., 166–68, 171–72.
28. Quoted ibid., 139.
29. On the Church after García Moreno see José María Vargas, 'La reorganización de la Iglesia ante el estado liberal en Ecuador', *HGIAL*, VIII, 334–48.
30. Leturia, *Relaciones entre la Santa Sede e Hispanoamérica*, II, 399–403, III, 315, 318.
31. Fernán González, 'La reorganización de la Iglesia ante el estado liberal colombiano (1850–1886)', *HGIAL*, VII, 366–69.
32. Jane Meyer Loy, 'Primary Education during the Colombian Federation: The School Reform of 1870', *HAHR*, 51, 2 (1971), 275–94.
33. González, 'La reorganización de la Iglesia', 367–68.
34. Fernán E. and G. González, *Partidos políticos y poder eclesiástico* (Bogotá, 1977), 161–62.
35. Gustavo Ocando Yamarte, 'La Iglesia en Venezuela ante el nuevo estado', *HGIAL*, VII, 445–49.
36. Jesús Leopoldo Sánchez, 'La Iglesia en Venezuela ante el nuevo estado', *HGIAL* VII, 471.
37. Cárdenas, *La Iglesia hispanoamericana en el siglo XX*, 127.
38. C. Felice Cardot, *La libertad de culto en Venezuela* (Madrid, 1959), 169.
39. On the religious policy of Carrera see Lynch, *Caudillos in Spanish America*, 373, 384, and Ralph Lee Woodward, *Rafael Carrera and the Emergence of the Republic of Guatemala, 1821–1871* (Athens, GA, 1993).
40. Bruce Johnson Calder, *Crecimiento y cambio de la Iglesia católica guatemalteca, 1944–1946* (Guatemala City, 1970), 19.
41. Cárdenas, *La Iglesia hispanoamericana en el siglo XX*, 85
42. Quoted Luis Medina Ascensio, *HGIAL*, V, 219; see also Brian Hamnett, *Juárez* (London, 1993), 96–100.
43. Robert J. Knowlton, *Church Property and the Mexican Reform, 1856–1910* (De Kalb, IL, 1976), 121.
44. Alfonso Alcalá Alvarado, *HGIAL*, V, 241, 249–51, 262.
45. Hamnett, *Juárez*, 205–6.
46. Quoted by Adame Goddard, *El pensamiento político y social de los católicos mexicanos*, 101.
47. Brading, *Mexican Phoenix. Our Lady of Guadalupe*, 302.
48. Pazos, *La Iglesia en la América del IV Centenario*, 32–40.
49. Quoted ibid., 87.

8 New Century, New Challenges

1. On the Catholic Church in the twentieth century and its response to changing conditions see Christopher Abel, 'Latin America, c.1914–c.1950', in *World Christianities*

c.1914–c.2000, ed. Hugh McLleod, *The Cambridge History of Christianity*, IX (Cambridge, 2006), 179–96.

2. Roger Charles with Drostan MacLaren, *The Social Teaching of Vatican II* (Oxford, San Francisco, 1982), 250–51.

3. *Rerum Novarum*, Encyclical of Pope Leo XIII, *On the Condition of the Working Classes*, 15 May 1891, arts 49–52.

4. Pazos, *La Iglesia de la América del IV Centenario*, 62, 161–62.

5. Néstor T. Auza, *Iglesia y la migración en la Argentina* (4 vols, Buenos Aires, 1991–2000), I, 50.

6. Auza, *Aciertos y fracasos*, I, 33.

7. Fortunato Mallimaci, 'La Iglesia argentina ante el liberalismo', *HGIAL*, IX, 365–66.

8. Auza, *Aciertos y fracasos*, I, 50.

9. Ibid., I, 116.

10. Ibid., I, 62.

11. Ibid., I, 155–228.

12. Ibid., III, 36.

13. Ivereagh, *Catholicism and Politics in Argentina*, 66–69.

14. Mallimaci, 'La Iglesia argentina', 387.

15. Auza, *Aciertos y fracasos*, III, 26–28.

16. Maximiliano Salinas, *HGIAL*, IX, 306–8, 400–1, 404–6.

17. Maximiliano Salinas, 'La Iglesia y los orígenes del movimiento obrero en Chile, 1880–1920', *Revista Mexicana de Sociología*, 49, 3 (1987), 171–84.

18. Quoted Klaiber, *HGIAL*, VIII, 296.

19. Ibid., VIII, 298–99.

20. Klaiber, *Religion and Revolution in Peru*, 55–68.

21. Quoted Barnadas, *HGIAL*, VIII, 321.

22. Quoted ibid., VIII, 323.

23. Rodolfo Ramón de Roux, 'La Iglesia colombiana en el período 1930–1962', *HGIAL*, VII, 539.

24. *La Voz de México*, 10 Nov. 1906, in Goddard, *Pensamiento político y social de los católicos mexicanos*, 205.

25. Goddard, *Pensamiento político y social de los católicos mexicanos*, 244.

26. In matters of religion the Mexican Revolution and its leaders long had an easy ride from historians, mainly through omission, until the French historian Jean Meyer arrived on the scene to contribute an element of realism and understanding to the Catholic position. See Jean E. Meyer, *La Cristiada* (3 vols, Mexico City, 1973–74), II, 230.

27. Ibid., I, 95–99.

28. Evaristo Olmos, *La jerarquía eclesiástica y el conflicto religioso en México 1926–1929* (Rome, 1984).

29. Dudley Ankerson, *Agrarian Warlord: Saturnino Cedillo and the Mexican Revolution in San Luis Potosí* (De Kalb, IL, 1984), 121–22; Meyer, *La Cristiada*, I, 71–88, 115–17.

30. Adrian A. Bantjes, 'The Regional Dynamics of Anticlericalism and Defanaticization in Revolutionary Mexcio', in Matthew Butler, ed., *Faith and Impiety in Revolutionary Mexico* (London, 2007), 111–30.

31. Cárdenas, *La Iglesia hispanoamericana en el siglo XX*, 241.

32. Meyer, *La Cristiada*, I, 130–37, 199–200.

33. Jean A. Meyer, *The Cristero Rebellion; The Mexican People between Church and State 1926–1929* (Cambridge, 1976), 52.

34. Matthew Butler, *Popular Piety and Political Identity in Mexico's Cristero Rebellion: Michoacán, 1927–29* (Oxford, 2004), 197.

35. Meyer, *The Cristero Rebellion*, 69–75, 203–4, 21–11.

36. Butler, *Popular Piety and Political Identity in Mexico's Cristero Rebellion*, 166–68.

37. The sources for Father Pro's last ministry in Mexico City and the quotations from his letters are taken from Paolo Molinari, SJ, 'Il Beato Michele Agostino Pro, Martire della Fede', *La Civiltà Cattolica*, IV (1988), 128–40.

38. Matthew Butler, 'Trouble Afoot? Pilgrimage in *Cristero* Mexico City', in Butler, *Faith and Impiety in Revolutionary Mexico*, 149–66.

39. Butler, *Popular Piety and Political Identity in Mexico's Cristero Rebellion*, 183–84, 208–9.

40. Ankerson, *Agrarian Warlord*, 132–33, 152–53.

41. Jean Meyer, 'Religious Conflict and Catholic Resistance in 1930s Oaxaca', in Butler, *Faith and Impiety in Revolutionary Mexico*, 185–202.

42. Miguel Palomar y Vizcarra, in James W. Wilkie and Edna Monzón de Wilkie, *México visto en el siglo veinte: Entrevistas de historia oral* (Mexico, 1969), 447.

43. On the slaughter of disarmed *Cristeros*, see Meyer, *The Cristero Rebellion*, 204.

44. Cárdenas, *La Iglesia hispanoamericana en el siglo XX*, 49, 57.

9 The Church and the Dictators

1. Scott Mainwaring, *The Catholic Church and Politics in Brazil, 1916–1985* (Stanford, CA, 1986), 40–45.

2. Kenneth P. Serbin, 'Dom Hélder Câmara, The Father of the Church of the Poor', in Peter M. Beattie, ed., *The Human Tradition in Brazil* (Wilmington, DE, 2004), 249–66.

3. Kenneth P. Serbin, *Secret Dialogues: Church–State Relations, Torture and Social Justice in Authoritarian Brazil* (Pittsburgh, PA, 2000), 2, 234.

4. On the Church in Brazil in 1964–85 see Jeffrey Klaiber, *The Church, Dictatorships and Democracy in Latin America* (Eugene, OR, 1998), 20–41.

5. Kenneth P. Serbin, 'Brazil', in Paul E. Sigmund, ed., *Religious Freedom and Evangelization in Latin America: The Challenge of Religious Pluralism* (Maryknoll, NY, 1999), 209–13.

6. Serbin, *Secret Dialogues*, 39.

7. Ibid., 199, 200, 216–18, and the same author's 'The Anatomy of a Death: Repression, Human Rights and the Case of Alexandre Vannucchi Leme in Authoritarian Brazil', *JLAS*, 30 (1998), 1–33.

8. Arquidiocese de São Paulo, *Brasil: Nunca mais* (São Paulo, 1985).

9. Arquidiocese de São Paulo, *Repressão na Igreja no Brasil, 1968–1978*, p. 11; Klaiber, *The Church. Dictatorships, and Democracy in Latin America*, 35.

10. Quoted in Lee M. Penyak and Walter J. Petry, *Religion in Latin America: A Documentary History* (Maryknoll, NY, 2006), 272.

11. See below, pp. 309–11.

12. See Penyak and Petry, *Religion in Latin America*, 268–70.

13. Kenneth P. Serbin, *Needs of the Heart: A Social and Cultural History of Brazil Clergy and Seminaries* (Notre Dame, IN, 2006), 143, 260, 285.

14. Quoted by F. Mallimaci, 'La Iglesia argentina desde la década del 30', *HGIAL*, IX, 436–37.

15. Ivereigh, *Catholicism and Politics in Argentina*, 83, 213–17.

16. Ibid., 84–86.

17. Quoted by Mallimaci, *HGIAL*, IX, 443.

18. On the onset and growth of Peronism see David Rock, *Argentina 1516–1982: From Spanish Colonization to the Falklands War* (Berkeley, CA, 1985), 262–319.

19. Quoted by Joseph A. Page, *Perón: A Biography* (New York, 1983), 139, 161.

20. Mallimaci, *HGIAL*, IX, 471–72.

21. Quoted ibid., 486.

22. Quoted in Frederick B. Pike, ed., *The Conflict between Church and State in Latin America* (New York, 1964), 184–85.

23. Félix Luna, *Perón y su tiempo* (3 vols, Buenos Aires, 1984–86), II, 17.

24. Leonardo Pérez Esquivel, 'La Iglesia argentina durante la dictadura militar', *HGIAL*, IX, 541–61.

25. Rock, *Argentina 1516–1982*, 366–78.
26. Margarita Durán, 'La Iglesia en Paraguay desde el Concilio Vaticano II', *HGIAL*, IX, 581–92.
27. Josep M. Barnadas, 'La Iglesia boliviana (1962–1975)', *HGIAL*, VIII, 457.
28. Emilio Mignone, *Iglesia y dictadura: El papel de la Iglesia a la luz de sus relaciones con el régimen militar* (Buenos Aires, 1986), 22.
29. Ibid., 30.
30. Ibid., 102.
31. Ernesto Sábato, quoted ibid., 81.
32. Quoted Salinas, *HGIAL*, IX, 497.
33. Quoted ibid., IX, 499.
34. Michael Fleet and Brian H. Smith, *The Catholic Church and Democracy in Chile and Peru* (Notre Dame, IN, 1997), 44–46.
35. Ibid., 46–49.
36. Quoted Salinas, *HGIAL*, IX, 503–4.
37. Quoted ibid., 507.
38. *Populorum Progressio*, 26 March 1967, art. 32–33, n. 33.
39. Fleet and Smith, *The Catholic Church and Democracy in Chile and Peru*, 52–53.
40. Quoted ibid., 54.
41. John Eagleson, *Christians for Socialism: Documentation of the Christians for Socialism Movement in Latin America* (Maryknoll, NY, 1975), 85–87.
42. Ibid., 12–15.
43. Quoted by Fleet and Smith, *The Catholic Church and Democracy in Chile and Peru*, 55.
44. Authorized summary of Cardinal Silva's views, 22 April 1972, in Eagleson, *Christians for Socialism*, 64–66.
45. Declaration of the eighty, 16 April 1971, ibid., 220–28.
46. 10 April 1973, confirmed 16 Oct. 1973, ibid., 179–228.
47. Quoted Fleet and Smith, *The Catholic Church and Democracy in Chile and Peru*, 61.
48. See M. Salinas, 'La Iglesia en Chile del Vaticano II a la opresión militar', *HGIAL*, IX, 572–75.
49. Quoted in Fleet and Smith, *The Catholic Church and Democracy in Chile and Peru*, 305.
50. Quoted by Sheila Cassidy, *Audacity to Believe* (London, 1988), 158.
51. Ibid., 170–81.
52. Ibid., 66–67.
53. Frederick M. Nunn, *One Year in the Life of Augusto Pinochet: Gulag of the Mind* (Portland State University, OR, 1984).

10 Religion and Revolution

1. Fidel Castro, *Fidel Castro y la religión, conversaciones con Frei Betto* (Santiago, 1986), 96.
2. See, for example, the view of John M. Kirk, *Between God and the Party: Religion and Politics in Revolutionary Cuba* (Tempa, FL, 1989), 76, that in the course of 1960 'Cuba, under increasing pressure from Washington, turned towards Moscow for economic assistance, and a market for her sugar'.
3. Andrés Suárez, *Cuba: Castroism and Communism 1959–1960* (Cambridge, MA, 1969), 140–42.
4. Raúl Gómez Treto, *The Church and Socialism in Cuba* (Maryknoll, NY, 1988), 1–11.
5. Jorge I. Domínguez, *Cuba, Order and Revolution* (Cambridge, MA, 1978), 471–2.
6. Pastoral letter, 10 Sept. 1960, quoted by Kirk, *Between God and the Party*, 85.
7. Hugh Thomas, *The Cuban Revolution* (London, 1986), 498.
8. Cárdenas, *La Iglesia hispanoamericana en el siglo XX*, 170.
9. Gómez Treto, *The Church and Socialism in Cuba*, 43–45.
10. Cárdenas, *La Iglesia hispanoamericana en el siglo XX*, 172.

11. Margaret E. Crahan, 'Cuba', in Sigmund, ed., *Religious Freedom and Evangelization in Latin America*, 87–112.
12. Gómez Treto, *The Church and Socialism in Cuba*, 23–24.
13. Quoted by Kirk, *Between God and the Party*, 118–19.
14. Gómez Treto, *The Church and Socialism in Cuba*, 84–86.
15. Quotations in Kirk, *Between God and the Party*, 119–21.
16. Quoted by Domínguez, *Cuba, Order and Revolution*, 410–12.
17. Quoted by Gómez Treto, *The Church and Socialism in Cuba*, 70.
18. Quoted ibid., 79.
19. Ibid., 89.
20. Cárdenas, *La Iglesia hispanoamericana en el siglo XX*, 239.
21. Quoted by Kirk, *Between God and the Party*, 154.
22. Ibid., 146–47.
23. Castro, *Fidel Castro y la religión*, 33–34, 209, 214, 277, 331–32.
24. Ibid., 333.
25. Penyak and Petry, *Religion in Latin America*, 326–28.
26. *The Tablet*, 12, 19, 26 June, 17 July 2010; *The Times*, 9 July 2010. By 2010 all dissidents were apparently free, though appearances could deceive.
27. Quoted in John M. Kirk, *Politics and the Catholic Church in Nicaragua* (Gainesville, FL, 1992), 51.
28. Philip Williams, *The Catholic Church and Politics in Nicaragua and Costa Rica* (London, 1989), 22.
29. Report in Kirk, *Politics and the Catholic Church in Nicaragua*, 53–57.
30. Quoted ibid., 93.
31. Andrew Bradstock, *Saints and Sandinistas: The Catholic Church in Nicaragua and its Response to the Revolution* (London, 1987), 30.
32. Stephen Kinza, *Blood of Brothers: Life and War in Nicaragua* (Cambridge, MA, 2007), 173–74.
33. Ibid., 72–73.
34. Junta member, quoted ibid., 78.
35. Ibid., 79.
36. Quoted by Kirk, *Politics and the Catholic Church in Nicaragua*, 124.
37. Quoted ibid., 232.
38. Quoted by Bradstock, *Saints and Sandinistas*, 14.
39. Quoted by Kirk, *Politics and the Catholic Church in Nicaragua*, 170–71.
40. Reproduced in Penyak and Petry, *Religion in Latin America*, 286.
41. Kinza, *Blood of Brothers*, 207.
42. Ibid.
43. Ibid., 200, 420–21.
44. Klaiber, *The Church, Dictatorships, and Democracy in Latin America*, 206.
45. Quoted by Kirk, *Politics and the Catholic Church in Nicaragua*, 148.
46. Quoted by Kinza, *Blood of Brothers*, 207.
47. Kirk, *Politics and the Catholic Church in Nicaragua*, 160.
48. Joseph E. Mulligan, *The Nicaraguan Church and the Revolution* (Kansas City, 1991), 203.
49. 16 May 1990, in Kirk, *Politics and the Catholic Church in Nicaragua*, 210.
50. Ignacio Martín-Baró, 'Oscar Romero: Voice of the Downtrodden', in Archbishop Oscar Romero, *Voice of the Voiceless: The Four Pastoral Letters and Other Statements* (Maryknoll, NY, 1985), 7–8.
51. Ibid., 9.
52. Quoted ibid., 11.
53. On the life and thought of Romero see Marie Dennis, Kenny Golden, and Scott Wright, *Oscar Romero: Reflections on his Life and Writings* (Maryknoll, NY, 2000), and Scott Wright, *Oscar Romero and the Communion of Saints* (London, 2010).

54. Jon Sobrino, *Archbishop Romero: Memories and Reflections* (Maryknoll, NY, 1990), 11–17.
55. Third Pastoral Letter, 6 August 1978, Romero, *The Four Pastoral Letters*, 91–92.
56. Ibid., 107.
57. Ibid., 109–10.
58. Fourth Pastoral Letter, 6 August 1979, ibid., 143–45.
59. 23 March 1980, in Romero, *The Four Pastoral Letters*, 42–43.
60. Quoted by Jon Sobrino, 'A Theologian's View of Romero', in Romero, *The Four Pastoral Letters*, 43.
61. *Letter to President Carter*, 17 February 1980, Romero, *The Four Pastoral Letters*, 188–90.
62. Interview with *Excelsior*, Mexico, quoted by Sobrino, 'A Theologian's View of Romero', 50–51.
63. Truth Commission, quoted by Teresa Whitfield, *Paying the Price: Ignacio Ellacuría and the Murdered Jesuits of El Salvador* (Philadelphia, PA, 1994), 386.
64. Klaiber, *The Church, Dictatorships, and Democracy in Latin America*, 171.
65. Quoted by Whitfield, *Paying the Price*, 386.
66. Speech on receiving Honorary Doctorate, Santa Clara University, California, 1982, ibid., 257.
67. Truth Commission, established in July 1992, ibid., 7–14, 72–74, 386. See also Jon Sobrino, *Companions of Jesus. The Murder and Martyrdom of the Salvadoran Jesuits* (London, 1990).
68. Ricardo Falla, *Massacres in the Jungle: Ixcán, Guatemala, 1975–1982* (Boulder, CO, 1994), 8.
69. Quoted ibid., 89.
70. Klaiber, *The Church, Dictatorships, and Democracy in Latin America*, 223.
71. Quoted ibid., 226.
72. Virginia Garrard-Burnett, *Terror in the Land of the Holy Spirit: Guatemala under General Efraín Ríos Montt, 1982–83* (Oxford, 2010), 127.
73. Falla, *Massacres in the Jungle*, 188.
74. Quoted by Francisco Goldman, *The Art of Political Murder. Who Killed Bishop Gerardi?* (London, 2008), 12.
75. Virginia Garrard-Burnett, *Protestantism in Guatemala: Living in the New Jerusalem* (Austin, TX, 1998), 143–48.
76. Tim Steigenga, 'Guatemala', in Sigmund, *Religious Freedom and Evangelization in Latin America*, 150–74.
77. Quoted by Garrard-Burnett, *Terror in the Land of the Holy Spirit*, 113. ·
78. Garrard-Burnett, *Protestantism in Guatemala*, 148–49.
79. 7 March 1983, quoted by Garrard-Burnett, *Terror in the Land of the Holy Spirit*, 131.
80. Quoted by Goldman, *The Art of Political Murder*, 19.
81. Ibid., 22.
82. Ibid., 23–24.
83. Ibid., 356–57.
84. Ibid., 267–68, 288, 301.

11 Difference and Diversity

1. Santa Gertrudis, *Maravillas de la naturaleza*, II, 111–12.
2. Louise Fawcett and Eduardo Posada Carbo, 'Arabs and Jews in the Development of the Colombian Caribbean 1850–1950', in Ignacio Klich and Jeffrey Lesser, eds, *Arab and Jewish Immigration in Latin America: Images and Realities* (London, 1998), 57–79.
3. *American Jewish Yearbook 2006* (New York, 2006).
4. Jeffrey Lesser, 'Elite Images of Arabs and Jews in Brazil', in Klich and Lesser, *Arab and Jewish Immigration in Latin America*, 38–56.

5. Marc J. Osterweil, 'The Economic and Social Condition of Jewish and Arab Immigrants in Bolivia, 1890–1980', ibid., 58.
6. Ricardo Feierstein, *Historia de los judíos argentinos* (3rd edn, Buenos Aires, 2006), 55. See also Judith Laikin Elkin and Gilbert W. Merks, *The Jews in Latin America* (New York, 1998).
7. Feierstein, *Historia de los judíos argentinos*, 371.
8. Ibid., 362–63.
9. *La Nación*, Buenos Aires, 20 Aug. 1881, quoted by Feierstein, *Historia de los judíos argentinos*, 56.
10. Raanan Rein, *Argentina, Israel, and the Jews: Perón, the Eichmann Capture and After* (Bethesda, MD, 2006), 52–59.
11. Quoted ibid., 39.
12. Ibid., 73–105.
13. Quoted ibid., 139.
14. See ibid., 35–36, 215–16.
15. Ibid., xviii, 196–228.
16. Michael Humphrey, 'Ethnic History, Nationalism and Transnationalism in Argentine Arab and Jewish Cultures', in Klich and Lesser, *Arab and Jewish Immigration in Latin America*, 167–88.
17. Jacobo Timerman, *Prisoner without a Name, Cell without a Number* (London, 1981).
18. Graciela Ben-Dror, *Católicos, nazis y judíos: La Iglesia argentina en los tiempos del Tercer Reich* (Buenos Aires, 2003), 57–70.
19. Ibid., 70–79.
20. Ibid., 79–88.
21. Ibid., 112–13.
22. Ibid., 179–223.
23. Ibid., 264–71.
24. See John Borelli, 'Of a Different Order', *The Tablet*, 21 Aug. 2010.
25. See J. Lorand Matory, *Black Atlantic Religion. Tradition, Transnationalism, and Matriarchy in the Afro-Brazilian Candomblé* (Princeton, NJ, 2005), 5–8, for a general outline; and Stephania Capone, *Searching for Africa in Brazil: Power and Tradition in Candomblé* (Durham, NC, 2010), 27.
26. Matory, *Black Atlantic Religion*, 32.
27. Ibid., 215.
28. Account by Kathleen de Azevedo, in Penyak and Petry, *Religion in Latin America*, 342–45.
29. Matory, *Black Atlantic Religion*, 120.
30. Capone, *Searching for Africa in Brazil*, 10.
31. Ibid., 256.
32. Matory, *Black Atlantic Religion*, 149–87.
33. Lindsay Hale, 'Umbanda', in Lee M. Penyak and Walter J. Petry, eds, *Religion and Society in Latin America* (Maryknoll, NY, 2009), 225–42.
34. Capone, *Searching for Africa in Brazil*, 69–91; see also Diana Brown, *Umbanda: Religion and Politics in Urban Brazil* (New York, 1994).
35. Margarite Fernández Olmos and Lizabeth Paravisini-Gebert, *Creole Religions of the Caribbean: An Introduction from Vodou and Santería to Obeah and Espiritismo* (New York, 2003), 29–30.
36. Ibid., 62–69.
37. Ibid., 73–74, 104.
38. *The Tablet*, 9 Jan. 2010.
39. See Edward L. Cleary, 'The Transformation of Latin American Christianity, c.1950–c.2000', in *World Christianities c.1914–2000, The Cambridge History of Christianity*, IX, 366–84. See also David Martin, *Tongues of Fire: The Explosion of Protestantism in Latin America* (Cambridge, MA, 1990), and Philip Berryman, 'Is Latin

America Turning Pluralist? Recent Writings on Religion', *Latin American Research Review*, 30, 3 (1995).

40. For these figures see Cárdenas, *La Iglesia hispanoamericana en el siglo XX*, 228–29, and David Stoll, *Is Latin America Turning Protestant? The Politics of Evangelical Growth* (Berkeley, CA, 1990), 7–9, 333–38, which for Chile seem more realistic than the estimate of González and González, *Christianity in Latin America*, 280, who give a total of 36 per cent by 2000.

41. See Jean-Pierre Bastian, *Le Protestantisme en Amérique Latine: Une approche sociohistorique* (Geneva, 1994).

42. Stoll, *Is Latin America Turning Protestant?*, 121–24.

43. Garrard-Burnett, *Protestantism in Guatemala*, 98.

44. Ibid., 120–23.

45. Ibid., 130–36.

46. Virginia Garrard-Burnett, ' "Like a Mighty Rushing Wind": The Growth of Protestantism in Latin America', in Penyak and Petry, *Religion and Society in Contemporary Latin America*, 190–206.

47. Garrard-Burnett, *Protestantism in Guatemala*, 150–51, 167.

48. Ibid., 164.

49. Stein, 'Nicaragua', in Sigmund, *Religious Freedom and Evangelization in Latin America*, 182.

50. González and González, *Christianity in Latin America*, 270–96, for a scholarly and accessible account of Pentecostalism.

51. Klaiber, *The Church, Dictatorships, and Democracy in Latin America*, 148–50.

52. The estimate of 47 per cent of all Brazilians cited by González and González, *Christianity in Latin America*, 283, seems excessive.

53. Stoll, *Is Latin America Turning Protestant?*, 109–11.

54. Serbin, 'Brazil', in Sigmund, *Religious Freedom and Evangelization in Latin America*, 213–18.

55. Philip Berryman, *Religion in the Megacity: Catholic and Protestant Portraits from Latin America* (New York, 1996), 21–25.

56. Eric W. Kramer, 'Descarrego', in Peterson and Vásquez, *Latin American Religions*, 255–59.

57. Serbin, 'Brazil', in Sigmund, *Religious Freedom and Evangelization in Latin America*, 216.

58. See Christian Gros, 'Evangelical Protestantism and Indigenous Populations', *Bulletin of Latin American Research*, 18, 2 (1999), 175–97.

59. See Yvon L. Bot, 'Churches, Sects and Communities: Social Cohesion Recovered?', *Bulletin of Latin American Research*, 18, 2 (1999), 165–74.

60. Cleary, 'The Transformation of Latin American Chrstianity', 382.

61. Quoted by Moreno in Sigmund, *Religious Freedom and Evangelization in Latin America*, 57.

62. *The Tablet*, 18 Sept. 2010.

12 Between Liberation and Tradition

1. Gustavo Gutiérrez, 'Notes for a Theology of Liberation', *Theological Studies*, 31, 2 (1970), 242–50.

2. Matthew 25: 34–40.

3. Gustavo Gutiérrez, *A Theology of Liberation: History, Politics, and Salvation* (revised edn, London, 2001), 187.

4. Ibid., 257, 261, 268.

5. Ibid., 200–5.

6. Jon Sobrino, *Jesus in Latin America* (Maryknoll, NY, 1987), 158.

7. Leonardo and Clodovis Boff, *Introducing Liberation Theology* (Maryknoll, NY, 1987), 9.

8. Gutiérrez, *A Theology of Liberation*, 249.
9. Boff and Boff, *Introducing Liberation Theology*, 28.
10. Paul E. Sigmund, *Liberation Theology at the Crossroads: Democracy or Revolution?* (New York, 1990), 159–61.
11. Boff and Boff, *Introducing Liberation Theology*, 9, 77.
12. Quoted by Sigmund, *Liberation Theology at the Crossroads*, 173.
13. Pedro Arrupe, 8 Dec. 1980, *La Civiltà Cattolica*, 4 April 1981.
14. Quoted by Sigmund, *Liberation Theology at the Crossroads*, 82.
15. Quoted ibid., 216.
16. Gutiérrez, *A Theology of Liberation*, 14.
17. Kinza, *Blood of Brothers*, 197–98; Declaration of Los Andes, July 1985, in *Liberation Theology: A Documentary History*, ed. Aldred T. Hennelly (Maryknoll, NY, 1990), 444–50.
18. Stoll, *Is Latin America Turning Protestant?*, 313–14.
19. Berryman, *Religion in the Megacity*, 159–60.
20. Gutiérrez, *A Theology of Liberation*, 269.
21. Ibid.
22. Ibid., 38.
23. Ibid., 113–14.
24. Outlined by Frei Betto, in Peterson and Vásquez, *Latin American Religions*, 221–26.
25. *The Tablet*, 2 Aug., 17 Aug., 25 Oct. 1997.
26. Gutiérrez, *A Theology of Liberation*, 119–20.
27. Leonardo Boff, *Ecclesiogenesis: The Base Communities Reinvent the Church* (London, 1986), 76–95.
28. Berryman, *Religion in the Megacity*, 158–60.
29. Cardinal Ratzinger, *Instruction on Christian Freedom and Liberation*, 22 March 1986.
30. Quoted by Gutiérrez, *A Theology of Liberation*, 44.
31. Ibid., 145.
32. John W. O'Malley, *What Happened at Vatican II* (Cambridge, MA, 2008), 212.
33. Father Joseph Ratzinger, *peritus* (expert theologian), Vatican II, quoted by Archbishop Kevin Dowling of Rustenburg, South Africa, in *The Tablet*, 17 July 2020.
34. O'Malley, *What Happened at Vatican II*, 256.
35. Cárdenas, *La Iglesia hispanoamericana en el siglo XX*, 233–34.
36. O'Malley, *What Happened at Vatican II*, 303–5.
37. Ibid., 311.
38. Gutiérrez, *A Theology of Liberation*, 73.
39. Quoted ibid., 124.
40. Ibid., 131, 245.
41. Quoted by Sigmund, *Liberation Theology at the Crossroads*, 243.
42. Gutiérrez, *A Theology of Liberation*, 136.
43. Sigmund, *Liberation Theology at the Crossroads*, 93–107.
44. Gutiérrez, *A Theology of Liberation*, 10, 12.
45. Quoted Sigmund, *Liberation Theology at the Crossroads*, 105.
46. Gutiérrez, *A Theology of Liberation*, 19.
47. Ibid., quoting letter of April 1986, emphasis added.
48. Josep Ignaci Saranyana and Carmen José Alejos Grau, *El siglo de las teologías latinoamericanistas: 1899–2001. Teología en América Latina*, III (Madrid, 2002), 104–5.
49. Ibid., 120–21.
50. Ibid., 128–29.
51. Ibid., 432.
52. Ibid., 434.
53. See Elena Curti, 'Study in Scarlet', *The Tablet*, 8 May 2010.
54. *The Tablet*, 21 Sept. 1996, 7 June 1997.
55. See Kevin Dowling, Bishop of Rustenburg, South Africa, *The Tablet*, 17 July 2010.

56. *The Tablet*, 21 Aug. 2010. The lock did not seem to be entirely secure in the case of the Brazilian episcopacy.

57. Congregation for the Doctrine of the Faith, *Instruction on Certain Aspects of the 'Theology of Liberation'*, 6 Aug. 1984. For a summary see Sigmund, *Liberation Theology at the Crossroads*, 161–63.

58. Congregation for the Doctrine of the Faith, *Instruction on Christian Freedom and Liberation*, 22 March 1986. See Sigmund, *Liberation Theology at the Crossroads*, 167–69.

59. On the conflict in Chiapas see Klaiber, *The Church, Dictatorships, and Democracy in Latin America*, 252–62. See also Hugh O'Shaughnessy, 'The Key in Don Sam's Hand', *The Tablet*, 31 Jan. 1998.

60. Sigmund, *Liberation Theology at the Crossroads*, 161–62, 167–68.

61. *The Tablet*, 12 Dec. 2009.

Bibliography

Sources

The historiography of religion in Latin America has been variable in coverage and quality and in general has lagged behind that of other areas of Latin American history. One of the objects of the Comisión de Historia de la Iglesia en América Latina (CEHILA) has been to remedy this situation, and the results of its work can be seen in the multi-volume *Historia general de la Iglesia en América Latina* (*HGIAL*), under the general editorship of Enrique Dussel, individual volumes of which began to appear from 1981. The standard is uneven, but it remains an indispensable source. The fifth centenary of the discovery occasioned numerous studies with a religious dimension. The most authoritative history of religion in Latin America in its formative stage, in the work of evangelization, and in the changing world of the eighteenth century is Pedro Borges, ed., *Historia de la Iglesia en Hispanoamérica y Filipinas (siglos XV–XIX)* (2 vols, Madrid, 1992), a further source for the present work. The writings and experience of modern theologians, historians, evangelists, and catechists have enriched the subject in the last thirty years. Moreover, there are numerous monographs on particular aspects and periods of religion indispensable for constructing a general history.

Yet general histories of the Church in Latin America are few in number. A one-volume composite history edited by Dussel is the leading example in English, *The Church in Latin America 1492–1992* (Tunbridge Wells, 1992). 'The Catholic Church in Latin America, 1830–1930' by the present author in *The Cambridge History of Latin America. Volume IV*, edited by Leslie Bethell (Cambridge, 1986), provides a chronological and conceptual structure of the subject as well as a narrative of developments. A valuable combination of research and interpretation is provided by Antón Pazos, *La Iglesia en la América del IV Centenario* (Madrid, 1992). For the age of dictatorship and revolution, Jeffrey Klaiber, *The Church, Dictatorships and Democracy in Latin America* (Eugene, OR, 2009), is a model of research and judgement. The most recent general history is by Justo González and Ondina González, *Christianity in Latin America: A History* (Cambridge, 2008). The author is a Methodist theologian and historian who has written extensively on the history of Christianity; the co-author is his niece, an independent researcher.

Individual countries have their church histories, often traditional in character and mainly useful as sources of information. Exceptional examples are Jean A. Meyer, *La Cristiada* (3 vols, Mexico, 1973–74), Jeffrey L. Klaiber, *Religion and Revolution in Peru, 1824–1976* (Notre Dame, IN, 1977), and Patricia Londoño-Vega, *Religion, Culture, and Society in Colombia: Medellín and Antioquia 1850–1930* (Oxford, 2002). In recent years, a large number of social science studies of modern Latin American religion have appeared few of which have a historical dimension.

Two useful aids to study have appeared in recent years, collecting key texts with commentaries: *Religion in Latin America, A Documentary History*, edited by Lee M. Penyak and Walter J. Petry (Maryknoll, NY, 2006); and *Latin American Religions: Histories and Documents in Context*, edited with introductions by Anna L. Peterson and Manuel A. Vásquez (New York, 2008).

General

Bethell, Leslie, ed., *The Cambridge History of Latin America* (12 vols, Cambridge, 1984–2008).

Dussel, Enrique D., *Historia de la Iglesia en América Latina. Coloniaje y liberación (1492–1973)* (3rd edn, Barcelona, 1974).

—— ed., *The Church in Latin America 1492–1992* (Tunbridge Wells, 1992).

González, Ondina E. and Justo L. González, *Christianity in Latin America, A History* (Cambridge, 2008).

Historia general de la Iglesia en América Latina (HGIAL) (CEHILA, Salamanca, 1981–).

—— eds, *Religion in Latin America: A Documentary History* (Maryknoll, NY, 2006).

Penyak, Lee M. and Walter J. Petry, eds, *Religion and Society in Latin America* (Maryknoll, NY, 2009).

Peterson, Anna L. and Manuel A. Vásquez, *Latin American Religions: Histories and Documents in Context* (New York, 2008).

Colonial

Acosta, José de, *De procuranda indorum salute* (Madrid, 1982).

Barabas, Alicia, *Utopias indias. Movimientos sociorreligiosos en México* (Mexico, 1989).

Benavente, Toribio de [Motolinia], *Historia de los indios de la Nueva España* (Madrid, 1985).

Block, David, *Mission Culture in the Upper Amazon: Native Tradition, Jesuit Enterprise, and Secular Policy 1660–1880* (Lincoln, NB, 1994).

Borges, Pedro, *Historia de la Iglesia en Hispanoamérica y Filipinas [HIHF]* (2 vols, Madrid, 1992).

Brading, D.A., *Church and State in Bourbon Mexico: The Diocese of Michoacán 1749–1810* (Cambridge, 1994).

—— *The First America: The Spanish Monarchy, Creole Patriots, and the Liberal State 1492–1867* (Cambridge, 1991).

—— *Mexican Phoenix. Our Lady of Guadalupe: Image and Tradition across Five Centuries* (Cambridge, 2001).

Bricker, Victoria Reifler, *The Indian Christ, the Indian King. The Historical Substrata of Maya Myth and Ritual* (Austin, TX, 1981).

Casey, James, *Early Modern Spain: A Social History* (London, 1999).

Castañeda, Paulino, *Don Vasco de Quiroga y su 'Información en derecho'* (Madrid, 1974).

Cervantes, Fernando, *The Devil in the New World: The Impact of Diabolism in New Spain* (New Haven, CT, 1994).

Chilam Balam, *The Ancient Future of the Itza. The Book of Chilam Balam of Tizimin*, trans. and annotated by Munro S. Edmunson (Austin, TX, 1982).

Cieza de León, Pedro de, *Crónica del Perú. Tercera Parte*, ed. Francesca Cantú (2nd edn, Lima, 1989).

Clendinnen, Inga, *Ambivalent Conquests: Maya and Spaniard in Yucatán* (Cambridge, 1987).

Cortés y Larraz, Pedro, *Descripción geográfica-moral de la diócesis de Goathemala* (2 vols, Guatemala City, 1958).

Cushner, Nicholas P., *Lords of the Land: Sugar, Wine and Jesuit Estates of Coastal Peru, 1600–1767* (Albany, NY, 1980).

—— *Why Have You Come Here? The Jesuits and the First Evangelization of Native America* (Oxford, 2006).

Díaz del Castillo, Bernal, *Historia verdadera de la conquista de la Nueva España* (Mexico, 1964).

Durán, Diego, *Book of the Gods and Rites and the Ancient Calendar*, trans. and ed. Fernando Horcasitas and Doris Heyden (Norman, OK, 1971).

Eder, Francisco Javier, *Breve descripción de las reducciones de Mojos*, trans. and ed. Josep M. Barnadas (Cochabamba, 1985).

Egido, Teófanes, 'La expulsión de los jesuitas de España', in Ricardo García-Villoslada, ed., *Historia de la Iglesia en España*, IV (Madrid, 1979).

Farriss, N.M., *Crown and Clergy in Colonial Mexico 1759–1821: The Crisis of Ecclesiastical Privilege* (London, 1968).

—— *Maya Society under Colonial Rule: The Collective Enterprise of Survival* (Princeton, NJ, 1984).

Garcilaso de la Vega, El Inca, *Comentarios reales de los Incas (Obras completas*, ed. Carmelo Sáenz de Santa María, BAE, 4 vols, Madrid, 1960).

Gómez Canedo, Lino, *Evangelización y conquista: experiencia franciscana en Hispanoamérica* (Mexico, 1977).

Gosner, Kevin, *Soldiers of the Virgin. The Moral Economy of a Colonial Maya Rebellion* (Tucson, AZ, 1992).

Griffiths, Nicholas, *The Cross and the Serpent: Religious Repression and Resurgence in Colonial Peru* (Norman, OK, 1996).

Guaman Poma de Ayala, Felipe, *El Primer Nueva Crónica y Buen Gobierno*, ed. John V. Murra, Rolena Adorno, and Jorge L. Urioste (3 vols, Mexico, 1980).

Guridi y Alcocer, José Miguel, *Apuntes de la vida de D. José Miguel Guridi y Alcocer, formados por él mismo en fines de 1801 y principios del siguiente de 1802* (Mexico City, 1906).

Hanke, Lewis, *Aristotle and the American Indians* (London, 1959).

—— *La lucha española por la justicia en la conquista de América* (Madrid, 1959).

Ibáñez de Echavarri, Bernardo, *El reyno jesuitico del Paraguay* (Madrid, 1770).

Jaca, Francisco José de, *Resolución sobre la libertad de los negros*, ed. Miguel Anxo Pena González (Madrid, 2002).

Klor de Alva, J. Jorge, 'Spiritual Conflict and Accommodation in New Spain. Toward a Typology of Aztec Responses to Christianity', in George A. Collier, Renato I. Rosaldo and John D. Wirth, eds, *The Inca and Aztec States 1400–1800* (New York, 1982), 145–66.

Kratz, Guillermo, *El Tratado hispano–portugués de límites de 1750 y sus consecuencias* (Rome, 1954).

Ladero Quesada, Miguel Angel, *La España de los Reyes Católicos* (Madrid, 1999).

Las Casas, Bartolomé de, *Apologética historia sumaria* (Seville, 1990).

—— *De unico vocationis modo*, ed. Paulino Castañeda Delgado and Antonio García del Moral (*Obras completas* II, Madrid, 1990).

—— *Historia de las Indias* (3 vols, Mexico, 1951).

Lockman, John, ed., *Travels of the Jesuits into Various Parts of the World; compiled from their letters by Mr. Lockman* (2 vols, London, 1743).

Lynch, John, *Bourbon Spain 1700–1808* (London, 1989).

—— *Fray Juan de Santa Gertrudis and the Marvels of New Granada* (Institute of Latin American Studies, London, 1999).

MacCormack, Sabine, *Religion in the Andes: Vision and Imagination in Early Colonial Peru* (Princeton, NJ, 1991).

Martí, Mariano, *Documentos relativos a su visita pastoral de la diócesis de Caracas, 1771–1784* (ANH, 7 vols, Caracas, 1969).

Miller, Arthur G. and Nancy M. Farriss, 'Religious Syncretism in Colonial Yucatán: The Archaeological and Ethnohistorical Evidence from Tancah, Quintana Roo', in Norman

Hammond and Gordon R. Willey, eds, *Maya Archaeology and Ethnohistory* (Austin, TX, 1979).

Mills, Kenneth, *Idolatry and its Enemies: Colonial Andean Religion and Extirpation, 1640–1750* (Princeton, NJ, 1997).

Moirans, Epifanio de, *Siervos libres: una propuesta antiesclavista a finales del siglo XVII*, ed. Miguel Anxo Pena (Madrid, 2007).

Mora Mérida, José Luis, *Iglesia y sociedad en el Paraguay en el siglo XVIII* (Seville, 1976).

Mörner, Magnus, 'La expulsión de la Compañía de Jesús', *HIHF* (2 vols, Madrid, 1992), I, 245–60.

—— *The Political and Economic Activities of the Jesuits in the La Plata Region. The Hapsburg Era* (Stockholm, 1953).

Olsen, Margaret M., *Slavery and Salvation in Colonial Cartagena de Indias* (Gainesville, FL, 2004).

O'Phelan Godoy, Scarlett, *Rebellions and Revolts in Eighteenth Century Peru and Upper Peru* (Cologne, 1985).

Oss, Adriaan C. van, *Catholic Colonialism: A Parish History of Guatemala 1524–1821* (Cambridge, 1986).

Oviedo y Baños, José de, *Historia de la conquista y población de Venezuela*, trans. and ed. Jeanette Johnson Varner as *The Conquest and Settlement of Venezuela* (Berkeley, CA, 1987).

Pagden, Anthony, *The Fall of Natural Man: The American Indian and the Origins of Comparative Ethnology* (Cambridge, 1982).

Pena González, Miguel Anxo, *Francisco José de Jaca: la primera propuesta abolicionista de la esclavitud en el pensamiento hispano* (Salamanca, 2003).

Peña y Montenegro, Alonso de la, *Itinerario para Parochos de Indios, en que se tratan las materias tocantes a ellos, para su buena administración* (2 vols, Leon de Francia, 1678).

Pérez Ayala, José Manuel, *Antonio Caballero y Góngora, virrey y arzobispo de Santa Fe 1723–1796* (Bogotá, 1951).

Pérez-Marchand, M.L., *Dos etapas ideológicas del siglo XVIII en México a través de los papeles de la Inquisición* (Mexico, 1945).

Phelan, John Leddy, *The Millennial Kingdom of the Franciscans in the New World* (Berkeley, CA, 1970).

—— *The People and the King: The Comunero Revolution in Colombia, 1781* (Madison, WI, 1978).

Popol Vuh: The Mayan Book of the Dawn of Life, trans. Dennis Tedlick (New York, 1996).

Remesal, Antonio de, *Historia general de las Indias occidentales y particular de la gobernación de Chiapa y Guatemala*, ed. Carmelo Sáenz de Santa María (2 vols, Madrid, 1964–)

Rodríguez de Campomanes, Pedro, *Dictamen fiscal de expulsión de los Jesuitas de España (1766–1767)* (Madrid, 1977).

Sahagún, Bernardino de, *Florentine Codex: General History of the Things of New Spain*, trans. Arthur J.O. Anderson and Charles E. Dibble, 13 parts (2nd edn, Santa Fe, NM, 1970–82).

Saint-Lu, André, *La Vera Paz: Esprit évangélique et colonisation* (Paris, 1968).

Sánchez Bella, Ismael, *Iglesia y estado en la América Española* (Pamplona, 1990).

Sandoval, Alonso de, *Un tratado sobre la esclavitud*, ed. Enriqueta Vila Vilar (Madrid, 1987).

Santa Gertrudis, Juan de, *Maravillas de la naturaleza* (3 vols, Bogotá, 1994).

Seed, Patricia, *To Love, Honor, and Obey in Colonial Mexico: Conflicts over Marriage Choice, 1574–1821* (Stanford, CA, 1988).

Sierra Nava-Lasa, Luis, *El Cardenal Lorenzana y la Ilustración, I* (Madrid, 1975).

Taylor, William B., *Magistrates of the Sacred: Priests and Parishioners in Eighteenth-Century Mexico* (Stanford, CA, 1996).

Thomas, Hugh, *The Slave Trade. The History of the Atlantic Slave Trade, 1440–1870* (London, 1997).

Vargas Ugarte, Rubén, *Historia de la Compañía de Jesús en el Perú* (4 vols, Burgos, 1963–65).

Varón, Rafael, 'El Taki Oncoy: Las raíces andinas', in Luis Millones, ed., *El retorno de las Huacas: Estudios y documentos sobre el Taki Onqoy, Siglo XVI* (Lima, 1990).

Wagner, Henry Roup [and] Helen Rand Parish, *The Life and Writings of Bartolomé de Las Casas* (Albuquerque, NM, 1967).

Waldron, Kathy, 'The Sinners and the Bishop in Colonial Venezuela: The *Visita* of Bishop Mariano Martí, 1771–1784', in Asunción Lavrin, ed., *Sexuality and Marriage in Colonial Latin America* (Lincoln, NB, 1989).

Independence and Early Modern

Barnadas, Josep M., 'La Iglesia ante la emancipación en Bolivia', *HGIAL*, VIII, *Perú, Bolivia y Ecuador*.

Boehrer, George C.A., 'The Church in the Second Reign 1840–1889', in Henry H. Keith and S.F. Edwards, eds, *Conflict and Continuity in Brazilian Society* (Columbia, SC, 1969), 113–40.

Bruneau, Thomas C., *The Church in Brazil. The Politics of Religion* (Austin, TX, 1982).

Demélas, Marie-Danielle and Yves Saint-Geours, *Jerusalen y Babilonia: Religión y política en el Ecuador 1780–1880* (Quito, 1988).

Furlong, Guillermo, 'El catolicismo argentino entre 1860 y 1930', Academia Nacional de la Historia, *Historia argentina contemporánea 1862–1930* (Buenos Aires, 1964–66), II, part 1, pp. 251–54.

Gallardo, Guillermo, *La política religiosa de Rivadavia* (Buenos Aires, 1962).

Goddard, Jorge Adame, *El pensamiento político y social de los católicos mexicanos, 1867–1914* (Mexico, 1981).

Gómez Ferreyra, Avelino Ignacio, ed., *Viajeros pontificios al Río de la Plata y Chile (1823–1825): La primera misión pontificia a Hispano-América, relatada por sus protagonistas* (Córdoba, Argentina, 1970).

Gómez Hoyos, Rafael, *La revolución granadina de 1810: Ideario de una generación y de una época, 1781–1821* (2 vols, Bogotá, 1962).

González, Luis, *Pueblo en vilo. Microhistoria de San José de Gracia* (Mexico, 1968).

Gutiérrez Casillas, José, *Historia de la Iglesia en México* (Mexico, 1974).

―― *Jesuítas en México durante el siglo XIX* (Madrid, 1972).

Hanisch, W., 'Manuel Lacunza S.I. y el milenarismo', *Archivum Historicum Societatis Jesu*, 40 (1971), 496–511.

Henderson, Peter V.N., *Gabriel García Moreno and Conservative State Formation in the Andes* (Austin, TX, 2009).

Hünefeldt, Christine, *Paying the Price of Freedom. Family and Labour among Lima's Slaves, 1800–1854* (Berkeley, CA, 1994).

Ivereigh, Austen, *Catholicism and Politics in Argentina, 1810–1960* (London, 1995).

King, William Martin, 'Ecuadorian Church and State Relations under García Moreno, 1859–1863', Austin, University of Texas Ph.D. thesis, 1974, University Microfilms, Ann Arbor, MI, 1986.

Klaiber, Jeffrey, 'La Iglesia ante la emancipación en el Perú', *HGIAL*, VIII.

―― *La Iglesia en el Perú: Su historia social desde la Independencia* (Lima, 1988).

Lemoine Villacaña, Ernesto, *Morelos, su vida revolucionaria a través de sus escritos y de otros testimonios de la época* (Mexico, 1965).

Leturia, Pedro de, *Relaciones entre la Santa Sede e Hispanoamérica* (3 vols, Rome, Caracas, 1959–60).

Lynch, John, 'The Catholic Church in Latin America, 1830–1930', in Bethell, ed., *The Cambridge History of Latin America*, IV, 527–95.

Memoriales sobre la independencia de Venezuela (ANH, Caracas, 1960).

Nario, Hugo, *Tata Dios: El Mesías de la última montonera* (Buenos Aires, 1976).

Pérez Memen, Fernando, *El episcopado y la independencia de México (1810-1836)* (Mexico, 1977).

Stoetzer, Carlos, *The Scholastic Roots of the Spanish American Revolution* (New York, 1979).

Tibesar, Antonine, 'The Peruvian Church at the Time of Independence in the Light of Vatican II', *The Americas*, 26 (April 1970).

Vargas Ugarte, Rubén, *El episcopado en los tiempos de la emancipación sudamericana* (3rd edn, Lima, 1962).

—— *Historia de la Iglesia en el Perú* (5 vols, Burgos, 1962).

Viscardo, Juan Pablo, *Lettre aux Espagnols Américains*, in Merle E. Simmons, *Los escritos de Juan Pablo Viscardo y Guzmán, Precursor de la independencia hispanoamericana* (Caracas, 1983).

Modern and Contemporary

Abel, Christopher, 'Latin America, *c.*1914–*c.*1950', in *World Christianities c.1914–c.2000*, ed. Hugh McLeod, *The Cambridge History of Christianity*, IX (Cambridge, 2006), 179–96.

Ankerson, Dudley, Agrarian Warlord: Saturnino Cedillo and the Mexican Revolution in San Luis Potosí (DeKalb, IL, 1985).

Arquidiocese de São Paulo, *Brasil: Nunca mais* (São Paulo, 1985).

Auza, Néstor Tomás, *Aciertos y fracasos sociales del catolicismo argentino* (3 vols, Buenos Aires, 1987–88).

—— *Católicos y liberales en la generación del ochenta* (Buenos Aires, 1975).

—— *Iglesia y la migración en la Argentina*, 4 vols (Buenos Aires, 1991–2000).

Bastian, Jean-Pierre, *Le Protestantisme en Amérique Latine: une approche socio-historique* (Geneva, 1994).

Ben-Dror, Graciela, *Católicos, nazis y judíos: La Iglesia argentina en los tiempos del Tercer Reich* (Buenos Aires, 2003).

Berryman, Philip, *Religion in the Megacity: Catholic and Protestant Portraits from Latin America* (New York, 1996).

Boff, Leonardo, *Ecclesiogenesis: The Base Communities Reinvent the Church* (London, 1986).

Boff, Leonardo and Clodovis, *Introducing Liberation Theology* (Maryknoll, NY, 1987).

Bradstock, Andrew, *Saints and Sandinistas: The Catholic Church in Nicaragua and its Response to the Revolution* (London, 1987).

Brown, Diana, *Umbanda: Religion and Politics in Urban Brazil* (New York, 1994).

Butler, Matthew, ed., *Faith and Impiety in Revolutionary Mexico* (London, 2007).

—— *Popular Piety and Political Identity in Mexico's Cristero Rebellion: Michoacán, 1927–29* (Oxford, 2004).

Capone, Stephania, *Searching for Africa in Brazil: Power and Tradition in Candomblé* (Durham, NC, 2010).

Cardenal, Rodolfo, *El poder eclesiástico en El Salvador* (San Salvador, 1980).

Cárdenas, Eduardo, *La Iglesia hispanoamericana en el siglo XX (1890–1990)* (Madrid, 1992).

Castro, Fidel, *Fidel Castro y la religión, conversaciones con Frei Betto* (Santiago, 1986).

Cleary, Edward L., 'The Transformation of Latin American Christianity, *c.*1950–*c.*2000', in *World Christianities c.1914–2000, The Cambridge History of Christianity*, IX, 366–84.

Della Cava, Ralph, *Miracle at Joaseiro* (New York, 1970).

Dennis, Marie, Kenny Golden and Scott Wright, *Oscar Romero: Reflections on his Life and Writings* (Maryknoll, NY, 2000).

Eagleson, John, *Christians for Socialism: Documentation of the Christians for Socialism Movement in Latin America* (Maryknoll, NY, 1975).

Elkin, Judith Laikin and Gilbert W. Merks, *The Jews in Latin America* (New York, 1998).

Falla, Ricardo, *Massacres in the Jungle: Ixcán, Guatemala, 1975–1982* (Boulder, CO, 1994).

Feierstein, Ricardo, *Historia de los judíos argentinos* (3rd edn, Buenos Aires, 2006).

Fernández Olmos, Margarite and Lizabeth Paravisini-Gebert, *Creole Religions of the Caribbean: An Introduction from Vodou and Santería to Obeah and Espiritismo* (New York, 2003).

Fleet, Michael and Brian H. Smith, *The Catholic Church and Democracy in Chile and Peru* (Notre Dame, IN, 1997).

Garrard-Burnett, Virginia, *Protestantism in Guatemala: Living in the New Jerusalem* (Austin, TX, 1998).

—— *Terror in the Land of the Holy Spirit: Guatemala under General Efraín Ríos Montt, 1982–83* (Oxford, 2010).

Goldman, Francisco, *The Art of Political Murder. Who Killed Bishop Gerardi?* (London, 2008).

Gómez Treto, Raúl, *The Church and Socialism in Cuba* (Maryknoll, NY, 1988).

González G. and Fernán, E. *Partidos políticos y poder eclesiástico* (Bogotá, 1977).

Gutiérrez, Gustavo, 'Notes for a Theology of Liberation', *Theological Studies*, 31, 2 (1970), 242–50.

—— *A Theology of Liberation: History, Politics, and Salvation* (revised edn, London, 2001).

Hennelly, Aldred T., ed., *Liberation Theology: A Documentary History* (Maryknoll, NY, 1990).

Keogh, Dermot, ed., *Church and Politics in Latin America*, foreword by Graham Greene (New York, 1990).

Kinza, Stephen, *Blood of Brothers: Life and War in Nicaragua* (Cambridge, MA, 2007).

Kirk, John M., *Between God and the Party: Religion and Politics in Revolutionary Cuba* (Tempa, FL, 1989).

—— *Politics and the Catholic Church in Nicaragua* (Gainesville, FL, 1992),

Klaiber, Jeffrey, *The Church, Dictatorships and Democracy in Latin America* (Eugene, OR, 1998).

—— *Religion and Revolution in Peru, 1824–1976* (Notre Dame, IN, 1977).

Klich, Ignacio and Jeffrey Lesser, eds, *Arab and Jewish Immigration in Latin America: Images and Realities* (London, 1998).

Knowlton, Robert J., *Church Property and the Mexican Reform, 1856–1910* (De Kalb, IL, 1976).

Levine, Robert M., *Vale of Tears: Revisiting the Canudos Massacre in Northeastern Brazil, 1893–1897* (Berkeley, CA, 1992).

Londoño-Vega, Patricia, *Religion, Culture and Society in Colombia: Medellín and Antioquia, 1850–1930* (Oxford, 2002).

Mainwaring, Scott, *The Catholic Church and Politics in Brazil, 1916–1985* (Stanford, CA, 1986).

Martin, David, *Tongues of Fire: The Explosion of Protestantism in Latin America* (Cambridge, MA, 1990).

Matory, J. Lorand, *Black Atlantic Religion. Tradition, Transnationalism, and Matriarchy in the Afro-Brazilian Candomblé* (Princeton, NJ, 2005).

Meyer, Jean E., *La Cristiada* (3 vols, Mexico City 1973–74).

Mignone, Emilio, *Iglesia y dictadura: El papel de la Iglesia a la luz de sus relaciones con el régimen militar* (Buenos Aires, 1986).

Molinari, Paolo, 'Il Beato Michele Agostino Pro, Martire della Fede', *La Civiltà Cattolica*, IV (1988).

Mulligan, Joseph E., *The Nicaraguan Church and the Revolution* (Kansas City, 1991).

Olmos, Evaristo, *La jerarquía eclesiástica y el conflicto religioso en México 1926–1929* (Rome, 1984).

O'Malley, John W., *What Happened at Vatican II* (Cambridge, MA, 2008).

Pazos, Antón, *La Iglesia en la América del IV Centenario* (Madrid, 1992).

Pérez Medina, Tomás, *La Santería cubana: El camino de Osha: ceremonias, ritos y secretos* (Madrid, 1998).

Pike, Frederick B., ed., *The Conflict between Church and State in Latin America* (New York, 1964).

Rein, Raanan, *Argentina, Israel, and the Jews: Perón, the Eichmann Capture and After* (Bethesda, MD, 2006).

Romero, Archbishop Oscar, *Voice of the Voiceless: The Four Pastoral Letters and Other Statements* (Maryknoll, NY, 1985).

Salinas, Maximiliano, 'Cristianismo popular en Chile, 1880–1920', *Nueva Historia*, 3, 12 (1984), 275–302.

Santo Rosário, Irma Maria Regina do, *O Cardeal Leme (1882–1942)* (Rio de Janeiro, 1961).

Saranyana, Josep Ignaci and Carmen José Alejos Grau, *El siglo de las teologías latinoamericanistas: 1899–2001. Teología en América Latina*, III (Madrid, 2002).

Serbin, Kenneth P., 'Dom Hélder Câmara, The Father of the Church of the Poor', in Peter M. Beattie, ed., *The Human Tradition in Brazil* (Wilmington, DE, 2004).

—— *Needs of the Heart: A Social and Cultural History of Brazil Clergy and Seminaries* (Notre Dame, IN, 2006).

—— *Secret Dialogues: Church–State Relations, Torture and Social Justice in Authoritarian Brazil* (Pittsburgh, PA, 2000).

Sigmund, Paul E., *Liberation Theology at the Crossroads: Democracy or Revolution?* (New York, 1990).

—— ed., *Religious Freedom and Evangelization in Latin America: The Challenge of Religious Pluralism* (Maryknoll, NY, 1999).

Smith, Brian H., *The Church and Politics in Chile. Challenges to Modern Catholicism* (Princeton, NJ, 1982).

Sobrino, Jon, *Archbishop Romero: Memories and Reflections* (Maryknoll, NY, 1990).

—— *Companions of Jesus. The Murder and Martyrdom of the Salvadoran Jesuits* (London, 1990).

—— *Jesus in Latin America* (Maryknoll, NY, 1987).

Stoll, David, *Is Latin America Turning Protestant? The Politics of Evangelical Growth* (Berkeley, CA, 1990).

Vanderwood, Paul J., *The Power of God against the Guns of Government: Religious Upheaval in Mexico at the Turn of the Nineteenth Century* (Stanford, CA, 1998).

Whitfield, Teresa, *Paying the Price: Ignacio Ellacuría and the Murdered Jesuits of El Salvador* (Philadelphia, PA, 1994).

Williams, Philip, *The Catholic Church and Politics in Nicaragua and Costa Rica* (London, 1989).

Wright, Scott, *Oscar Romero and the Communion of Saints* (London, 2010).

Index

Abad y Queipo, Manuel 68, 115, 118
Acosta, José de 17
  on Inca religion 21, 23
  on Indian culture 51
Afro-Brazilian religion 54–55,
    331–33
Ajofrin, Francisco de 82, 91
Alberdi, Juan Bautista 137
Albornoz, Bartolomé de 56
Alcalá, University of 3
Alexander VI, pope 2
Allende, Salvador
  Catholic response to 280–82
  'Soviet tool' 278
Alvarado, Pedro de 17
Amoroso Lima, Alceu 189–90
Andrea, Miguel de 234–35
Aneiros, Federico, archbishop 137, 153–54,
    155–56
Antonil, André João 53–54
Argentina
  Church and social question
    232–36
  Church-state conflict 194–97
  integral Catholicism 260–61
  laity 147
  militarism 267–73
  modern evangelization 156
  Perón 262–66
  postcolonial Church 136–39
  progressive Catholics 272
  semana trágica 236, 237
Arns, Paulo Evaristo, cardinal 257,
    258–59, 362
Arroyo, Gonzalo 279–80
Arrupe, Pedro, S.J. 348
Arzáns de Orzúa y Vela, Bartolomé 100
Atahualpa 18–19, 26
Aztec religion 7–10

Base communities
  forms of 352–54
  growth 352
  origins 351
Batlle y Ordóñez, José 198
Benavente, Toribio de (Motolinia)
    12–13, 14
Benedict XIV, pope 57
Benedict XVI, pope 330–31
  on liberationists in Brazil 365
  see also Ratzinger, Joseph, cardinal
Bergosa y Jordán, Antonio, bishop 115
Boff, Leonardo 347–48, 353–54
Bolívar, Simón
  religion of 124–25
  religious policy of 205
Bolivia
  Church and Indians 241–42
  Church-state relations 205–7
  clergy 134
Borge, Tomás 299
Boza Masvidal, Eduardo, bishop 290–91
Brandão, Luis 55–56
Brazil
  evangelization of 29, 52–53
  messiahs in 180–82
  military hard-line 254–58
  monarchy 157–58
  secularization 193
  slavery 53–56, 158

Caballero y Góngora, Antonio de,
    archbishop viceroy 66, 107–8
California missions 79–80
Calles, Plutarco Elías 246–48, 250, 252
Câmara, Hélder, archbishop 254, 255,
    257, 258
Cancun rebellion 92–93
Candomblé 331–32

Canek, Jacinto,
  rebellion of 93
Cardenal, Ernesto 297, 300, 303
Cardenal, Fernando 300
Carillo, Alfonso, archbishop 1
Carrera, Rafael 169, 221
Carthusians, in Spain 2
Casariego, Mario 317, 318
Cassidy, Sheila 284–85
Castellani, Leonardi 329
Castillo, Donald 300
Castrillón Hoyos, Dario 362
Castro, Fidel
  communist 287–89
  hostility to Church 290, 293
  interview with Fray Betto 294–95
Catholicism
  in Colombia 170
  in Peru 239–40
  social Catholicism 132
Charles III, king 74–75
Chávez, Cruz 183
Chiapas 35–36, 364
Chilam Balam, book of 8, 18
Chile
  Christian Democracy 239, 274–80
  Church-state relations 199–201
  conservative Church 131
  early Christians 32
  laity 146–47
  quality of religion 142
Christians for Socialism 279–80, 281, 282
Church
  and Argentine military 267–73
  in Bourbon America 98–105
  in Brazil 159–60, 255–59
  Catholic morality 165–66
  clergy, ninetenth century 132–39
  clergy secularization 82
  colonial clergy 83–86, 108–9
  in colonial state 67–72
  and comunero rebellion 107
  consolidation of 1804 108–9
  and Cuban Revolution 289–94
  hierarchy 132, 139–41
  and independence 117–21
  justice for Indians 19, 32–33
  laity 141–45
  and liberalism 131, 195–97
  marriage policy 71–72
  and Peronism 263–66
  postcolonial 126–28, 129–30
  and slavery 62–63, 145
  in Spain 1–2
  and state in nineteenth century
    227–28
  and Tupac Amaru rebellion 106–7

Cieza de León, 18–19
Claver, Peter, saint 58–59
Colegio Pio Latinoamericano 150
Coll i Prat, Narciso, archbishop 116
Colombia
  Capuchin mission 156–57
  Catholicism 170, 212
  Catholic social action 242
  Church-state relations 213–16
  Concordat 215–16
  conservatives 131
  hierarchy 140–41
  Liberal Party 130
Columbus 6, 11
Comuneros revolt of
  in New Granada 107–8, 111–12
  in Río de la Plata 77
confraternities
  in Brazil 54
  in Spanish America 142–43
Consejo Episcopal Latinoamericano
  (CELAM) 356, 357–58, 360–61
Conselheiro, Antônio 180–81
Contras 301–2, 303, 304–6
Cortés, Hernán 7, 12
Cortés y Larraz, Pedro, archbishop 85,
    86–87, 89, 90
  criticism of popular religion 162
  visitation in Guatemala 102–3, 104–5
Costa Rica 222
Cristeros 247, 250–52
Cruz, Francisco de la 46–47
Cuba
  colonial conditions 287
  Cuban Revolution 288–91
  response of Catholics to 289–95
Cuero y Caicedo, José, bishop 115–16

Díaz, Porfirio 226–27
Dominicans
  in Caribbean 11
  Guatemala 35
  and Jesuits 78
  Mexico 14, 26, 33
  in Spain
Durán, Diego 7
  defends Dominicans 33
  on Mexican ritual 9–10, 22–23

Ecuador
  Church-state relations 207–10
  liberalism in 211–12
  and papacy 210–11
Eder, Francisco Javier 51
education 154, 196, 214
Ellacuría, Ignacio, S.J., victim of military
  atrocity 313, 314–15

El Salvador
  atrocity against Jesuits 313–15
  liberalism 222
  state violence against Catholics 307, 313
encomienda 25–26, 33–34, 35
Enlightenment
  in Spain 64
  in Spanish America 65–67
  and Spanish American independence
Estrada, Manuel 196, 197
Eucharistic Congresses 166–67

Fabián y Fuero, Francisco, bishop 68, 74, 88
Ferdinand II, king of Aragon 1, 2–3, 6
Ferdinand VII, king of Spain
  121–22, 123
Fernández de Sotomayor, Juan 119
Figueiredo, Jackson de 188, 189–90, 194
Filippo, Virgilio 329
Franceschi, Gustavo 261, 330
Franciscans
  in Brazil 30
  in Caribbean 11
  and Jesuits 78
  in Mexico 12–15
  new evangelization 154–55
  Putumayo mission 94–97
  in Spain 2, 3
  in Yucatán 18, 39–41
Frei Betto 294–95
Frei, Eduardo 274–75, 276, 278–79
Fresno Larraín, Juan Francisco,
  cardinal 284
Frías, Félix 137, 147
Frías, Luis de 58
fueros, clerical 70–71, 108

García Moreno, Gabriel
  Catholicism of 209–10
  concordat 208–9
  his formation 207–8
  and papacy 210–11
Garcilaso de la Vega, Inca 10–11
  on Inca religioin 20–21
Garrastazu Médici, Emilio, geneal 256
Gerardi, Juan
  assassination 322
  bishop of El Quiché 317–18, 320
  report on military terrorism 321–22
Gómez, Juan Vicente 220
González Prada, Manuel 188
Granada, Spain 6
Grande, Rutilio 307–8
Greene, Graham 250
Gregory XVI, pope 57, 123, 190, 212
Guaman Poma de Ayala, Felipe
  42–44

Guaraní
  Indians 49–50, 52
  reductions 76, 80, 366
Guatemala
  Church and state 221–22
  early conversions 17, 35, 36
  Protestantism 315, 319
  state terrorism 316–18
Guridi, José Miguel 71
Gutiérrez, Gustavo 344–45, 346, 349, 351,
  353, 355, 357, 358
Guzmán Blanco, Antonio 218–19

Hidalgo y Costilla, Miguel 115, 117–18

Ibañez de Echavarri, Bernardo 76
idolatry, extirpation of 43–44
Iglesia Popular 302–3
Inca, religion of 20–22, 42
Indians
  Araucanian evangelization 155
  Bourbon policy for 86–90
  Brazil 30
  and Inquisition 47
  and Jesuits 48–52
  Mexican converts 14–16, 17, 25–26
  Peru 19–21
  and priesthood 85–86
  Putumayo mission 95–97
  rebellion of, Mexico 91–94
  religion of, Peru 173
  and slavery 32–34, 62–63
Inquisition
  Mexico 66
  Peru 66
  Spain 5
  Spanish America 25, 45–47
Isabella I, queen of Castile 1, 2–3, 4, 6, 11
Islam 5–6
Iturbide, Agustín de 120–21

Jaca, José de 60–61
Jesus, Society of, Jesuits 3, 366
  and Americanism 113–14
  in Argentina 153–54
  in Brazil 29–30, 52–55
  expulsion from Americas 72–81
  in Moxos 48–49, 51
  in Paraguay 49–52
  and slavery 56–57, 59–60
Jews
  anti-semitism in Argentina 327–28
  Catholic Church and anti-semitism
  328–30
  immigrants in Latin America 324–26
  and Perón 327
  in Spain 4–5

Jiménez de Cisneros, Francisco, cardinal 2, 3, 4
Joaseiro, Brazil 181–82
John XXIII, pope 354, 360, 361
John Paul II, pope 259, 271, 295, 303–4, 360
  in Guatemala 319
  and Latin America 361–63
  at Puebla 359
Juan de Santa Gertrudis, fray
  on clerical concubines 84–85
  in New Granada 101–2, 104
  in Putumayo 95–97
Juan Diego 38
Juárez, Benito 223, 225
justice
  for Indians 366
  Spanish struggle for 24–28, 36–37

Lacunza, Manuel 175
Landa, Diego de, bishop 39–41
Larraín, Manuel, bishop 275, 277–78
Las Casas, Bartolomé de 7, 366
  condemns armed conquest 25–26, 34, 35, 37
  in Cumaná 11–12
  and slavery 33–34, 37, 58
  and Tuzulutlán 35–36
Lasso de la Vega, Rafael 114, 120
Leguía, Augusto B. 204–5
Leo XIII, pope 151–52, 156, 174, 230
liberalism
  in Argentina 196–97
  in Brazil 192
  and Enlightenment 67, 105
  nineteenth-century 129–30, 190–91, 227–28
Liberation Theology
  critics 349–51
  and marxism 346–49
  on poverty 344–46
Lima, Lord of the Miracles 38
Lissón, Emilio, archbishop 204–5
Lizana y Beaumont, Francisco Javier, archbishop 71, 115
López Trujillo, Alfonso, cardinal 349–50, 353, 359, 362
Lorenzana, Francisco Antonio, cardinal 68, 74, 87–89, 90
Lorscheider, Aloísio, cardinal 257
Lorscheiter, Ivo, bishop 257–58

Madero, Francisco 163, 244
Madrid, Treaty of (1750) 77–78
Mariátegui, José Carlos 188–89
Martí, Mariano, bishop 100–1, 102
Martínez Zuviría, Gustavo 262
  see also Hugo Wast

Maximilian, archduke 224–25
Maya, religion 7–8
Medellín, Conference 279, 357–58, 360, 361
Meinvielle, Julio 329
Mennonites 186
Mercado, Tomás de 56
Messía, Alonso 50–51
Mexican Revolution 244–52, 381 n.26
Mexico
  Catholic social movement 242–43
  church and state 223–27
  clergy and independence 117–18, 120–21
  colonial Church 9, 24, 27, 97
  hierarchy 140
  laity 143–45
  millenarians 182–4
  nineteenth-century clergy 134–36
  Our Lady of Guadalupe 38, 114
  Porfiriato 144–45, 226–27
  postcolonial Church 127
  religious orthodoxy, Michoacán 163
Mignone, Mónica 272
Millennium, belief in 14
  Argentina 176–79
  Brazil 179–82
  Mexico 182–83
  Spanish America 174–76
missions 94–97
Mitre, Bartolomé 137
Mogrovejo, Toribio Alfonso de, Saint 42, 43
Moirans, Epifanio de 60–61
Montesinos, Antonio de 33
Montt, Manuel 131, 146, 199
Montufar, Alonso de 56, 58
Moors 5–6
Morelos, José María
  ideas 112
  religion of 114
  revolutionary priest 117–18
Moreno, Ezequiel, bishop 216
Moreno, Mariano 113
Moscoso, José Manuel, bishop 107
Mosquera, Manuel José 131–32, 140–41
Mosquera, Tomás Cipriano de 140, 212–13, 214, 215
Múgica, Carlos Francisco 272
Muzi, Gian 122

Nabuco, Joaquim 158, 194
Nariño, Antonio 112–13
New Granada
  Comuneros 107–8, 111–12
  missions in 101–2, 104
  patriot clergy 118–19
  royalists 115

Nicaragua
    Holy Year 174
    persecution of Church 222
    Revolution 295, 299–300, 306
    Sandinistas 297–98

Obando y Bravo, Miguel, cardinal 297–98,
        300, 302–3, 304, 305–6, 349
O'Leary, Daniel Florencio 124
Ortega, Daniel 298, 299, 303, 305–6
Ortega, Jaime, archbishop 294–95
Oviedo y Baños, José de 98

Pacelli, Eugene, cardinal 167, 261
    see also Pius XII, pope
Palomar y Vizcarra, Miguel 243, 246, 251
Papacy
    and independence 121–23
    and modern Latin America 360–65
Paraguay
    Church and human rights 270
    Jesuit missions 49–50, 77–78
    religion in 199
Pastora, Edén 298, 300
patronato 126, 150
Paul III, pope 57
Paul VI, pope 277–78, 283, 360–61
Peña y Montenegro, Alonso de la, bishop
        90–91
Pentecostalism
    Brazil 339–41, 342
    Chile 338–39
    forms of 342–43
    Latin America 341–42
Pérez, Antonio, rebellion of 93–94
Pérez Serantes, Enrique, archbishop
        289–90
Perón, Eva 262–64
Perón Juan Domingo
    dictator 262–65
    fall of 266
    return and death 269
Peronism 261
    crisis of 265
    justicialismo 263
Peru
    Church-state relations 201–6
    clergy and independence 118
    Enlightenment in 65
    evangelization in 19–20, 41–42
    Indians 146
    laity 145
    nineteenth-century clergy 133–34
    postcolonial Church 127
    social Catholicism 239–40
Pinochet, Augusto, general
    Catholic response to 282–84

    opposed by Church 285–86
    sanctions torture 284
Pius II, pope 57
Pius VII, pope 57
Pius IX, pope 122, 140, 148–49, 155, 190,
        192, 214, 223, 224, 227
Pius X, pope 206, 253
Pius XI, pope 201, 330
Pius XII, pope 360, 361
    see also Pacelli, Eugene
Pizarro, Francisco 18–19, 26
Plenary Council of Latin America 149,
        151–52, 173
Polo de Ondegardo, Juan 43
Pombal, marquis of 81
Popayán 94–95, 97
Popol Vuh 8
Popular religion
    Argentina 178–79
    Chile 164, 168, 169–70
    concept of 171–73
    New Granada 104
    Spanish America 161–62, 168–70
Portugal
    and bulls of donation 28
    Portuguese and Inquisition in Spanish
        America 46
positivism 187–88, 189–90
Potosí 100
Pro, Miguel Agustín, S.J., Blessed
    priest and martyr 248–50
Propaganda Fide 155
Protestants
    arrival in Latin America 185–87
    in Brazil 336
    and dictatorship 284
    in Guatemala 315, 337
    see also Pentecostalism
Puebla, Conference 359–60
Putumayo 94–97, 99–100

Quetzalcoatl 7, 9
Quiroga, Vasco de
    influence of More's Utopia 27
    on slavery 58

Ratzinger, Joseph, cardinal 259
    on base communities 354
    on conscience 355
    and Jews 331
    and liberation theology 363–64, 364–65
Recio, Bernardo 90, 91
Remesal, Antonio de 17, 36
Rerum Novarum 152, 230–31, 233, 276
Ríos Montt, Efraín 315, 318–19, 320
Rivadavia, Bernardino 122, 124,
        125, 136

Rivera y Damas, Arturo, archbishop 312–13
Rodríguez de Campomanes, Pedro 75–76, 78
Rodríguez de Francia, José Gaspar 199
Romanization 149–53
Romão Batista, Cícero, Padre Cícero 181–82
Romero, Oscar, archbishop
 assassination 311
 on human rights 309
 on violence 309–10
Rosas, Juan Manuel de 126, 136
Rubio y Salinas, Manuel José, archbishop 87
Ruiz, Samuel 364
Ruiz de Alarcón, Hernando 38–39

Sacerdotes para el Tercer Mundo 268–69
Sacred Heart, devotion to 166, 170, 204, 211
Sahagún, Bernardino de 9, 16
Saints in Latin America 162, 170
Salamanca, University of 3–4
Salesians, in Argentina 156
San Alberto, José Antonio de, archbishop 68–69, 101, 199
Sandoval, Alonso de 55–56, 58–59
Santa Anna, Antonio López de 222–23
Santander, Francisco de Paula 125–26
Santería 333–34
Santo Tomás, Domingo de, bishop 43
scholastic philosophy 111–12, 147–48
Sepúlveda, Juan Ginés de 34, 37, 56
Silva Henríquez, Raúl, cardinal 275, 280–81, 283
Silveira Cintra, Sebastião Leme, Dom Leme, cardinal 193–94
Sixtus IV, pope 2
Slaves, slavery
 and Afro-Latin American religions 335
 and Church 56–63
 in colonial Brazil 30–31, 53–56
 in Spain 32
Sobrino, Jon, S.J. 346
Solané, Gerónimo, Tata Dios 177–79
Somoza family 296, 298
Soto, Domingo de 56
Suárez, Francisco 111–12
Syllabus of Errors 148

Taki Onqoy 21–22
Talavera, Hernando de, archbishop 1–2
Tandil, Argentina 176–79

Tenochtitlán 8
Teresa of Avila, saint 3
Tlatelolco 14, 135
Tomochic 183
Toral, Francisco de, bishop 40–41
Tuzulutlán, Guatemala 35, 315

Umbanda 332–33
University of Central America 307, 313–14
Urban VIII, pope 57
Urrea, Teresa, Santa Teresita 182
Uruguay, Church-state conflict 198
utilitarianism 67, 105

Valdivieso, Rafael Valentín, archbishop 146–47
Valverde, Vicente, friar 18–19, 26
Vatican II
 aggiornamento 355
 collegiality 356, 362–63
 influence in Chile 278
 law of missions 34
 religious liberty 356
Venezuela
 Church and state in 217–20
 colonial Church 98, 100–1, 102
 nineteenth-century clergy 133
Vera Paz, Guatemala 36, 315
vicariato 69, 70
Videla, Jorge, general 269–70
Vieira, Antônio 52–53
Virgin Mary
 devotion to 4, 172
 Immaculate Conception 139
 Our Lady of Guadalupe 38, 114, 140, 252
 Virgin of Luján, 234, 261
Viscardo y Guzmán, Juan Pablo 113–14
Vitoria, Francisco de 26, 56, 62
Vodou 334–35

Wast, Hugo 330
 see also Martínez Zuviría, Gustavo
Women
 in base communities 353–54
 missionaries killed in El Salvador 312
 religion and women's rights 354

Yucatán
 alleged idolatry 39–41
 early evangelization 18

Zacchi, Cesare 292–93
Zumarraga, Juan de, bishop 33, 45